29.95

D0117132

Building Internet Firewalls

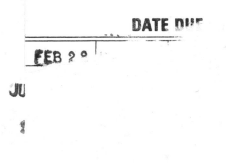

Building Internet Firewalls

D. Brent Chapman and Elizabeth D. Zwicky

O'Reilly & Associates, Inc.
103 Morris Street, Suite A
Sebastopol, CA 95472

Building Internet Firewalls
by D. Brent Chapman and Elizabeth D. Zwicky

Editor: Deborah Russell

Production Editor: Mary Anne Weeks Mayo

Printing History:

   September 1995:   First Edition.

This book is printed on acid-free paper with 85% recycled content, 15% post-consumer waste. O'Reilly & Associates is committed to using paper with the highest recycled content available consistent with high quality.

ISBN: 1-56592-124-0

Table of Contents

Foreword .... *xvii*

Preface .... *xxi*

I: Network Security *1*

1: Why Internet Firewalls? *3*

What Are You Trying to Protect? 4
What Are You Trying To Protect Against? 7
How Can You Protect Your Site? 13
What Is an Internet Firewall? 17

2: Internet Services *25*

Electronic Mail 26
File Transfer 28
Remote Terminal Access and Command Execution 30
Usenet News 31
The World Wide Web 32
Other Information Services 34
Information About People 35
Real-Time Conferencing Services 37
Name Service 38
Network Management Services 39
Time Service 40
Network File Systems 41

Window Systems 42
Printing Systems 42

3: Security Strategies 45

Least Privilege 45
Defense in Depth 47
Choke Point 48
Weakest Link 48
Fail-Safe Stance 49
Universal Participation 52
Diversity of Defense 53
Simplicity 54

II: Building Firewalls 55

4: Firewall Design 57

Some Firewall Definitions 57
Firewall Architectures 63
Variations on Firewall Architectures 71
Internal Firewalls 82
What the Future Holds 88

5: Bastion Hosts 91

General Principles 92
Special Kinds of Bastion Hosts 93
Choosing a Machine 94
Choosing a Physical Location 98
Locating the Bastion Host on the Network 99
Selecting Services Provided by the Bastion Host 100
Don't Allow User Accounts on the Bastion Host 102
Building a Bastion Host 103
Operating the Bastion Host 126
Protecting the Machine and Backups 128

6: *Packet Filtering* *131*

Why Packet Filtering? 132
Configuring a Packet Filtering Router 136
What Does a Packet Look Like? 138
What Does the Router Do with Packets? 154
Conventions for Packet Filtering Rules 158
Filtering by Address 161
Filtering by Service 164
Choosing a Packet Filtering Router 168
Where to Do Packet Filtering 180
Putting It All Together 182

7: *Proxy Systems* *189*

Why Proxying? 190
How Proxying Works 193
Proxy Server Terminology 195
Using Proxying with Internet Services 197
Proxying Without a Proxy Server 199
Using SOCKS for Proxying 200
Using the TIS Internet Firewall Toolkit for Proxying 202
What If You Can't Proxy? 204

8: *Configuring Internet Services* *207*

Electronic Mail 209
    Simple Mail Transfer Protocol (SMTP) 211
    Post Office Protocol (POP) 218
    Multimedia Internet Mail Extensions (MIME) 221
File Transfer 222
    File Transfer Protocol (FTP) 223
    Trivial File Transfer Protocol (TFTP) 234
    File Service Protocol (FSP) 235
    UNIX-to-UNIX Copy Protocol (UUCP) 236
Terminal Access (Telnet) 238
    Packet Filtering Characteristics of Telnet 239
    Proxying Characteristics of Telnet 240
    Summary of Telnet Recommendations 240
Remote Command Execution 240
    BSD 'r' Commands 240

rexec 243

rex 244

Network News Transfer Protocol (NNTP) 245

Packet Filtering Characteristics of NNTP 245

Proxying Characteristics of NNTP 246

Dangerous Ways to Set up NNTP in a Firewall Environment 247

Good Ways to Set up NNTP in a Firewall Environment 249

Using Packet Filtering with NNTP 250

Summary of NNTP Recommendations 250

World Wide Web (WWW) and HTTP 250

Packet Filtering Characteristics of HTTP 251

Proxying Characteristics of HTTP 253

HTTP Security Concerns 254

Secure HTTP 259

Summary of WWW Recommendations 259

Other Information Services 260

Gopher 260

Wide Area Information Servers (WAIS) 262

Archie 264

Information Lookup Services 266

finger 267

whois 268

Real-Time Conferencing Services 270

talk 270

Internet Relay Chat (IRC) 272

The Multicast Backbone (MBONE) 275

Domain Name System (DNS) 278

Packet Filtering Characteristics of DNS 279

Proxying Characteristics of DNS 281

DNS Data 282

DNS Security Problems 284

Setting Up DNS to Hide Information 286

Setting up DNS Without Hiding Information 294

Summary of DNS Recommendations 296

syslog 296

Packet Filtering Characteristics of syslog 297

Proxying Characteristics of syslog 297

Summary of syslog Recommendations 297

Network Management Services 297

Simple Network Management Protocol (SNMP) 297
Routing Information Protocol (RIP) 300
ping 301
traceroute 302
Other ICMP Packets 304
Summary of Network Management Recommendations 305
Network Time Protocol (NTP) 306
Packet Filtering Characteristics of NTP 306
Proxying Characteristics of NTP 307
Configuring NTP to Work with a Firewall 307
Summary of NTP Recommendations 308
Network File System (NFS) 309
Packet Filtering Characteristics of NFS 311
Proxying Characteristics of NFS 312
Summary of NFS Recommendations 312
Network Information Service/Yellow Pages (NIS/YP) 312
Packet Filtering Characteristics of NIS/YP 313
Proxying Characteristics of NIS/YP 313
Summary of NIS/YP Recommendations 313
X11 Window System 313
Packet Filtering Characteristics of X11 315
Summary of X11 Recommendations 317
Printing Protocols (lpr and lp) 317
Packet Filtering Characteristics of lpr 318
Proxying Characteristics of lpr 318
Packet Filtering and Proxying Characteristics of lp 319
Summary Recommendations for Printing Protocols 319
Analyzing Other Protocols 319

9: *Two Sample Firewalls* *321*

Screened Subnet Architecture 321
Screened Host Architecture 340

10: *Authentication and Inbound Services* *351*

Risks of Using Inbound Services 352
What Is Authentication? 356
Authentication Mechanisms 359
Complete Authentication Systems 365
Network-Level Encryption 370

Terminal Servers and Modem Pools 374

III: Keeping Your Site Secure *377*

11: Security Policies *377*

Your Security Policy 378
Putting Together a Security Policy 384
Getting Strategic and Policy Decisions Made 387
What If You Can't Get a Security Policy? 392

12: Maintaining Firewalls *393*

Housekeeping 393
Monitoring Your System 396
Keeping Up to Date 405
How Long Does It Take? 408
When Should You Start Over? 409

13: Responding to Security Incidents *411*

Responding to an Incident 411
What To Do After an Incident 419
Pursuing and Capturing the Intruder 420
Planning Your Response 423
Being Prepared 432

IV: Appendixes *441*

A: Resources *443*

WWW Pages 443
FTP Sites 444
Mailing Lists 444
Newsgroups 446
Response Teams and Other Organizations 447
Conferences 450
Papers 452
Books 454

B: Tools 457

Authentication Tools 458
Analysis Tools 459
Packet Filtering Tools 461
Proxy Systems Tools 462
Daemons 462
Utilities 463

C: TCP/IP Fundamentals 465

Introduction to TCP/IP 465
A Data Communications Model 466
TCP/IP Protocol Architecture 469
Network Access Layer 470
Internet Layer 472
Transport Layer 477
Application Layer 481
Addressing, Routing, and Multiplexing 483
The IP Address 485
Internet Routing Architecture 490
The Routing Table 493
Protocols, Ports, and Sockets 496

Index 503

Figures

1-1 A firewall usually separates an internal network from the Internet ... 18

4-1 Using a screening router to do packet filtering 59
4-2 Using proxy services with a dual-homed host 62
4-3 Dual-homed host architecture 64
4-4 Screened host architecture 65
4-5 Screened subnet architecture (using two routers) 68
4-6 Architecture using two bastion hosts 72
4-7 Architecture using a merged interior and exterior router 73
4-8 Architecture using a merged bastion host and exterior router 75
4-9 Architecture using a merged bastion host and interior router 76
4-10 Architecture using multiple interior routers 77
4-11 Multiple internal networks (separate interfaces in a ....
        single router) 78
4-12 Multiple internal networks (backbone architecture) 79
4-13 Architecture using multiple exterior routers 80
4-14 Architecture using multiple perimeter nets (multiple firewalls) 81
4-15 Firewall architecture with a laboratory network 84

5-1 The bastion host may run a variety of Internet services 100
5-2 Use a PC attached by a serial line to create catastrophe logs 107

6-1 Source address forgery 134
6-2 Data encapsulation 139
6-3 TCP header and body 141
6-4 Data fragmentation 143

6–5 ACK bits on TCP packets 146
6–6 Dynamic packet filtering at the UDP layer 148
6–7 RPC and the portmapper 150
6–8 Outbound Telnet 164
6–9 Packet filtering restrictions on different interfaces 178
6–10 Packet filtering: inbound SMTP (sample packets 1 and 2 183
6–11 Packet filtering: outbound SMTP (sample packets 3 and 4) 184
6–12 Packet filtering: inbound SMTP (sample packets 5 and 6) 185
6–13 Packet filtering: inbound SMTP (sample packets 7 and 8) 187

7–1 Proxies—reality and illusion 191
7–2 Store-and-forward services (like SMTP) naturally ....
    support proxying 200
7–3 Using SOCKS for proxying 201
7–4 Using the TIS FWTK for proxying 203

8–1 A generic direct service 208
8–2 A generic proxy service 209
8–3 Outbound SMTP 216
8–4 Inbound SMTP 217
8–5 POP via packet filtering 220
8–6 A normal-mode FTP connection 224
8–7 A passive-mode FTP connection 225
8–8 Outbound Telnet 239
8–9 NNTP via packet filtering 246
8–10 NNTP via proxy services 247
8–11 How talk works 271
8–12 IRC server tree 273
8–13 DNS name lookup 280
8–14 DNS zone transfer 282
8–15 A firewall can be used to hide DNS information 287
8–16 DNS with forwarding 291
8–17 DNS without forwarding 292
8–18 DNS without information hiding 294
8–19 NTP with packet filtering 308

9–1 Screened subnet architecture 322
9–2 Screened host architecture 341

10–1 How S/Key works 361
10–2 How the SNK-004 card works 364
10–3 How the TIS FWTK authentication server works 368

10–4 Network-level encryption 374

13–1 A network connection has many links 421
13–2 An alert tree 428
13–3 A notification message 429
13–4 Activity logs 435

C–1 The OSI Reference Model 467
C–2 Layers in the TCP/IP protocol architecture 470
C–3 Data encapsulation 471
C–4 IP datagram format 473
C–5 Routing through gateways 474
C–6 Networks, gateways, and hosts 475
C–7 UDP message format 478
C–8 TCP segment format 479
C–9 Three-way handshake 480
C–10 TCP data stream 482
C–11 TCP/IP protocols inside a sample gateway 483
C–12 Sample network 484
C–13 IP address structure 487
C–14 Gateway hierarchy 491
C–15 Routing domains 492
C–16 Table-based routing 495
C–17 Protocol and port numbers 499
C–18 Passing port numbers 500
C–19 Clients on multiple hosts connecting to the same ....
        port on a server 501
C–20 Multiple clients on a single host connecting to ....
        the same port on a server 502

Foreword

In any society, a small percentage of people are malicious. It is estimated that the Internet now has about 30 to 40 million users. Even if the percentage of malicious users is less than one percent of the overall society, the potential number of malicious users is large enough so that it should concern you.

The number of security incidents reported to the Computer Emergency Response Team Coordination Center (CERT-CC) increases every year—less than 200 in 1989, about 400 in 1991, 1400 in 1993, and 2,241 in 1994. Estimates are that we'll see more than 3000 reported incidents in 1995. Incidents occur at government and military sites, among Fortune 500 companies, at universities, and at small startups. Some incidents involve a single account on a single system. Some (for example, those involving packet sniffers) might involve as many as 100,000 systems. Of course, these numbers are only the tip of the iceberg. Many intrusions aren't reported to the CERT Coordination Center or to other computer security incident response organizations. In fact, many aren't reported at all—in some cases, because the victimized organization would rather avoid publicity or charges of carelessness, in other cases because the intrusions are not even detected.

Nobody knows the correct statistics on how many attacks are actually detected by the sites broken into, but most people in the security community agree that only a few percent are. Here's one of the few statistics I can cite: one incident response team offers a network intrusion service to its customers. With the customer's permission, they try to penetrate a system using the same tools that intruders use in their own attacks. This team found that only 4% of the sites probed detected the penetration attempts. An even more frightening estimate: Bill Cheswick of AT&T Bell Labs believes that of those attacks that do succeed, at least 40% of the attackers gain root access.[*]

---

[*] *Firewalls Digest*, March 31, 1995.

It isn't only the numbers of incidents that are growing; it's the sophistication of the methods of attack. When the CERT Coordination Center was founded in the wake of the Internet worm in the fall of 1988, the attacks we faced fell into two major categories: password guessing and the exploiting of security holes in operating systems and system programs. Although too many sites still fall victim to such attacks, we're now seeing increasing technical complexity in most of the newer incidents. To some extent, this is the result of increasing consciousness among system users and system administrators—users are choosing better passwords, and administrators are applying system patches more quickly. Unfortunately, the result of this increased security consciousness isn't to stamp out security attacks; it's simply to force the attackers to learn new tricks. Many of today's attacks are more sophisticated. They include the forging of Internet Protocol (IP) addresses (intruders are guessing the sequence numbers associated with network connections and the acknowledgments between machines), the exploiting of the source routing option on IP packets on certain types of UNIX systems, and the hijacking of open terminal or login sessions.

This is not to say that all users and administrators have learned their lessons about old-style attacks. There is still more education that needs to be done among·users and administrators, as well as among managers, who too often won't budget what's needed for security training. It's a dangerous world in cyberspace, and too few people realize it. This is one way in which the growth of the Internet may actually have hurt us. In the early days of the Internet, sites connected to the net usually had a whole staff of hardware and software gurus. Today, connecting to the Internet is so easy that sites forget it takes technical sophistication to connect safely and to stay secure.

Several years ago, I worked with a site in Europe that apparently had been broken into by someone who used a site in the United States to launch the attack. When I contacted the system administrator at the U.S. site, she assured me that they didn't even have computers at their location that were connected to the Internet. I told her the full domain name of the suspect system, and she replied, "Oh, you mean the Sun." It turned out that the Sun had been installed for use in a special application and had been running for years without anyone at the site realizing that it was connected to the Internet. The administrator assured me that they would disconnect the machine. Well, next morning, the European manager sent me another flaming email message—another break-in from the same U.S. system. I called the U.S. system administrator. Yes, she'd disconnected the modems. Yes, she'd disconnected the CRTs. But through it all, she'd managed to leave the system connected to the Internet. She didn't know it, but the attacker did, and he continued to take advantage of the fact.

I talk to system administrators all the time who are frustrated by break-ins, but who haven't done the basics that might prevent these break-ins from succeeding. One system administrator complained that he had reloaded his systems multiple times, and he was still being attacked. It turned out that, although he knew about CERT advisories and vendor security bulletins, he'd never bothered installing them. For example, CERT Advisory CA-93:16 was posted to the net in November of 1993; it advised the UNIX community about a problem with most versions of Sendmail. Vendors had cooperated by providing replacement programs, and the advisory contained a replacement for the */bin/sh* program used in the MProg line of the *sendmail.cf* file. A year and a half later, CERT still gets calls from sites that are broken into using this old Sendmail vulnerability.

Although the number of security incidents continues to increase and the types of attacks become ever more sophisticated, still there is good news for those who care about security. Overall, we've seen a huge growth in awareness of the dangers of connecting to the Internet, and there's a lot of activity in the security community. One manifestation of that is the growth of the Forum of Incident Response and Security Teams (FIRST), which brings together a variety of computer security incident response teams (more than 40 at the time I'm writing this) from government, commercial, and academic organizations. Also heartening is the existence of ever-better security tools that our community makes freely available. The Computer Operations, Audit, and Security Technology (COAST) archive at Purdue is a central point for the collection and testing of many of these tools. (Appendix A of this book tells you how to contact both organizations.) Finally, the publication of some excellent books and papers on Internet security makes the hard-won wisdom of those at the front available to others.

In these dangerous times, firewalls are the best way to keep your site secure. Although you've got to include other types of security in the mix, if you're serious about connecting to the Internet, firewalls should be at the very center of your security plans. Brent Chapman has been known as the firewalls guru since the early days of firewalls on the Internet; his Firewalls mailing list and his tutorials are witness to that. Elizabeth Zwicky, especially through her work at the System Administrators Guild (SAGE) is the voice of safe and rational system administration. Together, they have written a book that will raise consciousness of, and competence in, Internet security to a new level.

Ed DeHart
CERT Technical Advisor at the
CERT Coordination Center (CERT-CC)
Software Engineering Institute
Carnegie Mellon University
Pittsburgh, PA
June 1995

Preface

This book is a practical guide to building your own firewall. It provides step-by-step explanations of how to design and install a firewall at your site, and how to configure Internet services such as electronic mail, FTP, the World Wide Web, and others to work with a firewall. Firewalls are complex, though, and we can't boil everything down to simple rules. Too much depends on exactly what hardware, operating system, and networking you are using at your site, and what you want your users to be able to do, and not do. We've tried to give you enough rules, examples, and resources here so you'll be able to do the rest on your own.

What is a firewall, and what does it do for you? A firewall is a way to restrict access between the Internet and your internal network. You typically install a firewall at the point of maximum leverage, the point where your network connects to the Internet. The existence of a firewall at your site can greatly reduce the odds that outside attackers will penetrate your internal systems and networks. The firewall can also keep your own users from compromising your systems by sending dangerous information—unencrypted passwords and sensitive data—to the outside world.

The attacks on Internet-connected systems we are seeing today are more serious and more technically complex than those in the past. To keep these attacks from compromising our systems, we need all the help we can get. Firewalls are a highly effective way of protecting your site from these attacks. For that reason, we strongly recommend you include a firewall in your site's overall Internet security plan. However, a firewall should be only one component in that plan. It's also vital that you establish a security policy, that you implement strong host security, and that you consider the use of authentication and encryption devices that work with the firewalls you install. This book will touch on each of these topics while maintaining its focus on firewalls.

Scope of This Book

This book is divided into four parts:

Part I, *Network Security*, explores the problem of Internet security and focuses on firewalls as part of an effective strategy to solve that problem.

Chapter 1, *Why Internet Firewalls?*, introduces the major risks associated with using the Internet today; discusses what to protect, and what to protect it against; discusses various security models; and introduces firewalls in the context of what they can and can't do for your site's security.

Chapter 2, *Internet Services*, outlines the services users want and need from the Internet, and summarizes the security problems posed by those services.

Chapter 3, *Security Strategies*, outlines the basic security principles an organization needs to understand before it adopts a security policy and invests in specific security mechanisms.

Part II, *Building Firewalls*, describes how to build firewalls and configure services to run with them.

Chapter 4, *Firewall Design*, outlines the basic components and major architectures used in constructing firewalls: dual-homed hosts, screened hosts, screened subnets, and variations on these basic architectures.

Chapter 5, *Bastion Hosts*, presents step-by-step instructions on designing and building the bastion hosts used in many firewall configurations.

Chapter 6, *Packet Filtering,* describes how packet filtering systems work, and discusses what you can and can't accomplish with them in building a firewall.

Chapter 7, *Proxy Systems*, describes how proxy clients and servers work, and how to use these systems in building a firewall.

Chapter 8, *Configuring Internet Services*, describes how to configure each major Internet service to run with a firewall.

Chapter 9, *Two Sample Firewalls*, presents two sample configurations for basic firewalls.

Chapter 10, *Authentication and Inbound Services*, discusses the problem of allowing users to access your systems from the Internet, and describes a variety of authentication strategies and products.

Part III, *Keeping Your Site Secure*, describes how to establish a security policy for your site, maintain your firewall, and handle the security problems that may occur with even the most effective firewalls.

Chapter 11, *Security Policies*, discusses the importance of having a clear and well-understood security policy for your site, and what that policy should and should not contain. It also discusses ways of getting management and users to accept the policy.

Chapter 12, *Maintaining Firewalls*, describes how to maintain security at your firewall over time and how to keep yourself aware of new Internet security threats and technologies.

Chapter 13, *Responding to Security Incidents*, describes what to do when a break-in occurs, or when you suspect that your security is being breached.

Part IV, *Appendixes*, consists of the following summary appendixes:

Appendix A, *Resources*, contains a list of places you can go for further information and help with Internet security: World Wide Web pages, FTP sites, mailing lists, newsgroups, response teams, books, papers, and conferences.

Appendix B *Tools*, summarizes the best freely available firewall tools and how to get them.

Appendix C, *TCP/IP Fundamentals*, contains background information on TCP/IP that is essential for anyone building or managing a firewall.

Audience

Who should read this book? Although the book is aimed primarily at those who need to build firewalls, large parts of it are appropriate for everyone who is concerned about Internet security. This list tells you what sections are particularly applicable to you:

System administrators
> You should read the entire book. As we've mentioned, a thorough knowledge of TCP/IP is essential for understanding and building firewalls. If you are not already familiar with TCP/IP, you should read at least Appendix C right now.[*]

Managers of sites that are considering connecting to the Internet
> You should at least read Part I of the book. The chapters in Part I will introduce you to the various types of Internet threats, services, and security approaches and strategies. They will also introduce you to firewalls and describe what they can and cannot do to enforce Internet security. You should also read Chapter 4, which provides an overview of firewall design. In addition, Appendix A will tell you where to go for more information and resources.

---

[*] And we strongly recommend that you read all of Craig Hunt's excellent book, *TCP/IP System Administration* (O'Reilly & Associates, 1992), from which the appendix is adapted.

Managers and users of sites that are already connected to the Internet
> You should read all of the chapters we've cited for the managers in the previous category. In addition, you should read Part III, which explains the kinds of issues that may arise at your site over time, e.g., how to develop a security policy, keep up to date, and react if someone attacks your site.

Platforms

To a large extent, this book is platform-independent. Because most of the information provided here consists of general principles, most of it should be applicable to you, regardless of what equipment, software, and networking you are using. The most platform-specific issue is what type of system to use as a bastion host. People have successfully built bastion hosts (which we describe in Chapter 5 of this book) using all kinds of computers, including UNIX systems, Windows NT machines, Macintoshes, VMS VAXes, and others.

Having said this, we must acknowledge that there is a strong UNIX orientation to the specific examples in this book. There are several reasons for this. This is a book about building firewalls, and at the present time, the richest source of freely available tools for accomplishing this task is in the UNIX world. As a result, the vast majority of the firewalls being built today use UNIX systems as their bastion hosts (although, of course, many other types of machines may be included in the overall configurations). We expect that this situation may change in the next few years, as more commercial systems become available for many types of systems. Another reason is, of course, that our own experience is primarily in the UNIX world.

Comments and Questions

Please address comments and questions concerning this book to the publisher:

> O'Reilly & Associates
> 103 Morris Street, Suite A
> Sebastopol, CA 95472
> 1-800-998-9938 (in the U.S. or Canada)
> 1-707-829-0515 (international or local)
> 1-707-829-0104 (FAX)

You can also send us messages electronically. See the insert in the book for information about all of O'Reilly & Associates' online services.

To ask technical questions or to comment on the book, send email to:

> *firewalls-book@greatcircle.com*

Online Information

Information related to this book is available via anonymous FTP at:

    ftp://ftp.greatcircle.com/pub/firewalls-book/

and on the World Wide Web at:

    http://www.greatcircle.com/firewalls-book/

Errata are available from:

    ftp://ftp.greatcircle.com/pub/firewalls-book/Errata

Acknowledgments

When we set out to write this book, we had no idea that it would consume so much time and energy. We would never have succeeded without the help of many people.

Special thanks to Ed DeHart and Craig Hunt. Ed worked with Brent in the early stages of this book and wrote the foreword to it; we appreciate all that he has done to help. TCP/IP is essential for understanding the basics of firewall construction, and Craig Hunt, author of *TCP/IP System Administration* has kindly let us excerpt much of that book's Chapter 1 and Chapter 2 in this book's Appendix C so readers who do not already have a TCP/IP background can get a jump start.

Thanks to all those who reviewed drafts of the book before publication and made helpful suggestions: Fred Avolio, Steve Bellovin, Niels Bjergstrom, Rik Farrow, Simson Garfinkel, Eliot Lear, Evi Nemeth, Steve Simmons, Steve Romig, Gene Spafford, Phil Trubey, and Mark Verber. Thanks as well to Eric Allman for answering many Sendmail questions and Paul Traina for answering many Cisco questions.

Thanks to all the people at O'Reilly & Associates who turned this manuscript into a finished book: to Mary Anne Weeks Mayo, the wonderful and patient project manager/copyeditor for the book; Len Muellner, Ellen Siever, and Norm Walsh who converted the book from Word to SGML and contributed their tool-tweaking prowess; Chris Reilley who created the many excellent diagrams; Edie Freedman who designed the cover and Nancy Priest who designed the interior layout; John Files and Juliette Muellner who assisted with production; Seth Maislin who prepared the index; and Sheryl Avruch and Kismet McDonough-Chan who did the final quality control on the book.

Brent says: I would like to extend personal thanks to my friends and family, for keeping me going for a year and a half while I worked on the book; to my staff at Great Circle Associates, for keeping my business going; to the many hundreds of folks who've attended my Internet Security Firewalls Tutorial, for providing the impetus for this whole endeavor (and for keeping my bills paid!); and to the many thousands of subscribers to the Firewalls mailing list on the Internet, for providing a stimulating environment to develop many of the ideas found in this book. I also owe a lot of thanks to Debby Russell, our editor at O'Reilly & Associates, for all her help and guidance, and to our technical reviewers, for all their wonderful comments and suggestions. Most of all, though, I'd like to thank my very good friend and coauthor, Elizabeth Zwicky, without whose collaboration and encouragement this book probably never would have been finished, and certainly wouldn't have been as good.

Elizabeth says: My thanks go to my friends, my family, and my colleagues at Silicon Graphics, for an almost infinite patience with my tendency to alternate between obsessing about the book and refusing to discuss anything even tangentially related to it. I'd like to particularly thank Arnold Zwicky, Diana Smetters, Greg Rose, Eliot Lear, and Jeanne Dusseault for their expert moral support (often during similar crises of their own). But the most thanks for this effort have to go to Debby and Brent, for giving me a chance to be part of an unexpected but extremely rewarding project.

Network Security

Part I explores the problem of Internet security and focuses on firewalls as part of an effective strategy to solve that problem.

Chapter 1, *Why Internet Firewalls?*, introduces the major risks associated with using the Internet today; discusses what to protect, and what to protect it against; discusses various security models; and introduces firewalls in the context of what they can and can't do for your site's security.

Chapter 2, *Internet Services*, outlines the services users want and need from the Internet and summarizes the security problems posed by those services.

Chapter 3, *Security Strategies*, outlines the basic security principles an organization needs to understand before it adopts a security policy and invests in specific security mechanisms.

1

Why Internet Firewalls?

It is scarcely possible to enter a bookstore, read a magazine or a newspaper, or listen to a news broadcast without seeing or hearing something about the Internet in some guise. It's become so popular that it no longer requires explanations when mentioned in nontechnical publications, and it gets mentioned plenty, in magazines ranging from *The New Yorker* to *Bead and Button*. While nontechnical publications are obsessed with the Internet, the technical publications have moved on and are obsessed with security. It's a logical progression; once the first excitement of having a superhighway in your neighborhood wears off, you're bound to notice that not only does it let you travel, it lets a very large number of strangers show up where you are, and not all of them are people you would have invited.

Both views are true: The Internet is a marvelous technological advance that provides access to information, and the ability to publish information, in revolutionary ways. But it's also a major danger that provides the ability to pollute and destroy information in revolutionary ways. This book is about one way to balance the advantages and the risks—to take part in the Internet while still protecting yourself.

Later in this chapter, we describe different models of security people have used to protect their data and resources on the Internet. Our emphasis in this book is on the network security model and, in particular, the use of Internet firewalls. A firewall is a form of protection that allows a network to connect to the Internet while maintaining a degree of security. The section later in this chapter called "What is an Internet Firewall?" describes the basics of firewalls and summarize what they can—and cannot—do to help make your site secure. Before we discuss what you can do with a firewall, though, we want to describe briefly why you need one. What are you protecting on your systems? What types of attacks and attackers are we seeing today? What types of security can you use to protect your site?

What Are You Trying to Protect?

A firewall is basically a protective device. If you are building a firewall, the first thing you need to worry about is what you're trying to protect. When you connect to the Internet, you're putting three things at risk:

- Your data: the information you keep on the computers

- Your resources: the computers themselves

- Your reputation

Your Data

Your data has three separate characteristics that need to be protected:

- *Secrecy:* you might not want other people to know it.

- *Integrity:* you probably don't want other people to change it.

- *Availability:* you almost certainly want to be able to use it yourself.

People tend to focus on the risks associated with secrecy, and it's true that those are usually large risks. Many organizations have some of their most important secrets—the designs for their products, their financial records, or student records—on their computers. On the other hand, you may find that at your site it is relatively easy to separate the machines containing this kind of highly secret data from the machines that connect to the Internet.

Suppose that you *can* separate your data in this way, and that none of the information that is Internet accessible is secret. In that case, why should you worry about security? Because secrecy isn't the only thing you're trying to protect. You still need to worry about integrity and availability. After all, if your data isn't secret, and if you don't mind its being changed, and if you don't care whether or not anybody can get to it, why are you wasting disk space on it?

Even if your data isn't particularly secret, you'll suffer the consequences if it's destroyed or modified. Some of these consequences have readily calculable costs: if you lose data, you'll have to pay to have it reconstructed; if you were planning to sell that data in some form, you'll have lost sales regardless of whether the data is something you sell directly, the designs you use to build things from, or the code for a software product. There are also intangible costs associated with any security incident. The most serious is the loss of confidence (user confidence, customer confidence, investor confidence, staff confidence, student confidence, public confidence) in your systems and data and, consequently, a loss of confidence in your organization.

Has Your Data Been Modified?

Security incidents are different from many other types of crimes because detection is unusually difficult. Sometimes, it may take a long time to find out that someone has broken into your site. Sometimes, you'll never know. Even if somebody breaks in but doesn't actually *do* anything to your system or data, you'll probably lose time (hours or days) while you verify that they didn't do anything. In a lot of ways, a brute-force trash-everything attack is a lot easier to deal with than a break-in by somebody who doesn't appear to damage your system. If they trash everything, you bite the bullet, restore from backups, and get on with your life. But, if they don't appear to have done anything, you spend a lot of time second-guessing yourself, trying to make *sure* they haven't done anything to damage your system or data. Although this book is about preventing security incidents, Chapter 13 supplies some general guidelines for detecting, investigating, and recovering from security incidents.

Your Resources

Even if you have data you don't care about—even if you enjoy reinstalling your operating system every week because it exercises the disks, or something like that—if other people are going to use your computers, you probably would like to benefit from this use in some way. Most people want to use their own computers, or they want to charge other people for using them. Even people who give away computer time and disk space usually expect to get good publicity and thanks for it; they aren't going to get it from intruders. You spend good time and money on your computing resources, and it is your right to determine how they are used.

Intruders often argue that they are using only excess resources; as a consequence, their intrusions don't cost their victims anything. There are two problems with this argument.

First, it's impossible for an intruder to determine successfully what resources are excess and use only those. It may look as if your system has oceans of empty disk space and hours of unused computing time; in fact, though, you might be just about to start computing animation sequences that are going to use every bit and every microsecond. An intruder can't give back your resources when you want them. (Along the same lines, I don't usually use my car between midnight and 6 A.M., but that doesn't mean I'm willing to lend it to you without being asked. What if I have an early-morning flight the next day, or what if I'm called out to deal with an emergency?)

Second, it's your right to use your resources the way you want to, even if you merely feel some sort of Zen joy at the sight of empty disk space, or if you like the way the blinky lights look when nothing's happening on your computer. Computing resources are not natural resources, nor are they limited resources that are wasted or destroyed if they're not used.

Your Reputation

An intruder appears on the Internet with your identity. Anything he does appears to come from you. What are the consequences?

Most of the time, the consequences are simply that other sites—or law enforcement agencies—start calling you to ask why you're trying to break into their systems. (This isn't as rare an occurrence as it may seem. One site got serious about security when its system administration staff added a line item to their time cards for conversations with the FBI about break-in attempts originating from their site.)

Sometimes, such impostors cost you a lot more than lost time. An intruder who actively dislikes you, or simply takes pleasure in making life difficult for strangers, may send electronic mail or post news messages that purport to come from you. Generally, people who choose to do this aim for maximum hatefulness, rather than believability, but even if only a few people believe these messages, the cleanup can be long and humiliating. Anything even remotely believable can do permanent damage to your reputation.

A few years ago, an impostor posing as a Texas A&M professor sent out hate email containing racist comments to thousands of recipients. The impostor was never found, and the professor is still dealing with the repercussions of the forged messages. In another case, a student at Dartmouth sent out email over the signature of a professor late one night during exam period. Claiming a family emergency, the forged mail canceled the next day's exam, and only a few students showed up.

It's possible to forge electronic mail or news without gaining access to a site, but it's much easier to show that a message is a forgery if it's generated from outside the forged site. The messages coming from an intruder who has gained access to your site will look exactly like yours because they *are* yours. An intruder will also have access to all kinds of details that an external forger won't. For example, an intruder has all of your mailing lists available and knows exactly who you send mail to.

Even if an intruder doesn't use your identity, a break-in at your site isn't good for your reputation. It shakes people's confidence in your organization. In addition, most intruders will attempt to go from your machines to others, which is going to make their next victims think of your site as a platform for computer criminals. Many intruders will also use compromised sites as distribution sites for pirated software and/or pornography, which is not going to endear you to many folks either. Whether or not it's your fault, having your name linked to other intrusions, software piracy, and pornography is hard to recover from.

What Are You Trying To Protect Against?

What's out there to worry about? What types of attacks are you likely to face on the Internet, and what types of attackers are likely to be carrying them out? And what about simple accidents or stupidity? In the sections below, we touch on these topics but we don't go into any technical detail; later chapters describe different kinds of attacks in some detail and explain how firewalls can help protect against them.

Types of Attacks

There are many types of attacks on systems, and many ways of categorizing these attacks. In this section, we break attacks down into three basic categories: intrusion, denial of service, and information theft.

Intrusion

The most common attacks on your systems are *intrusions*; with intrusions, people are actually able to use your computers. Most attackers want to use your computers as if they were legitimate users.

Attackers have dozens of ways to get access. They range from social engineering attacks (you figure out the name of somebody high up in the company; you call a system administrator, claiming to be that person and claiming to need your password changed *right now*, so that you can get important work done), to simple guesswork (you try account name and password combinations until one works), to intricate ways to get in without needing to know an account name and password.

As we describe in this book, firewalls help prevent intrusions in a number of ways. Ideally, they block all ways to get into a system without knowing an account name and password. Properly configured, they reduce the number of accounts accessible from the outside that are therefore vulnerable to guesswork or social engineering. Most people configure their firewalls to use one-time passwords that prevent guessing attacks. Even if you don't use these passwords, which we describe in Chapter 10, a firewall will give you a controlled place to log attempts to get into your system, and, in this way, they help you detect guessing attacks.

Denial of Service

A *denial of service* attack is one that's aimed entirely at preventing you from using your own computers.

In late 1994, writers Josh Quittner and Michelle Slatalla were the target of an "electronic mail bomb." Apparently in retaliation for an article on the cracker community they'd published in *Wired* magazine, someone broke into IBM, Sprint, and the writers' network provider, and modified programs so their email and telephone service was disrupted. A flood of email messages so overwhelmed their network service that other messages couldn't get through; eventually, their Internet connection was shut down entirely. Their phone service also fell victim to the intruders, who reprogrammed the service so that callers were routed to an out-of state number where they heard an obscene recording.

Although some cases of electronic sabotage involve the actual destruction or shutting down of equipment or data, more often they follow the pattern of flooding seen in the Quittner-Slatalla case or in the case of the Internet worm. An intruder so floods a system or network—with messages, processes, or network requests—that no real work can be done. The system or network spends all its time responding to messages and requests, and can't satisfy any of them.

While flooding is the simplest and most common way to carry out a denial of service attack, a cleverer attacker can also disable services, reroute them, or replace them. For example, the phone attack in the Quittner-Slatalla case denied phone service by rerouting their phone calls elsewhere; it's possible to mount the same kind of attack against Internet services.

It's close to impossible to avoid all denial of service attacks. Sometimes it's a "heads, I win; tails, you lose" situation for attackers. For example, many sites set accounts up to become unusable after a certain number of failed login attempts. This prevents attackers from simply trying passwords until they find the right one. On the other hand, it gives the attackers an easy way to mount a denial of service attack: they lock any user's account simply by trying to log in a few times.

Most often, the risk of denial of service attacks is unavoidable. If you accept things from the external universe—electronic mail, telephone calls, or packages—it's possible to get flooded. The notorious college prank of ordering a pizza or two from every pizzeria in town to be delivered to your least favorite person is a form of denial of service; it's hard to do much else while arguing with 42 pizza deliverers. In the electronic world, denial of service is as likely to happen by accident as on purpose (have you ever had a persistent fax machine try to fax something to your voice line?). The most important thing is to set up services so that if one of them is flooded, the rest of your site keeps functioning while you find and fix the problem.

Fortunately, deliberate denial of service attacks are not terribly popular. They're so easy that they're considered "unsporting" by many attackers; they tend to be simple to trace back and are therefore risky to the attacker; and they don't provide the attacker with the information or the ability to use your computers (the payoff for most other attacks). Intentional denial of service attacks are the work of people who are angry at your site in particular, and at most sites such people are quite rare.

You are far more likely to encounter unintentional denial of service problems, as we discuss in the section on "Stupidity and Accidents" later in this chapter.

Information Theft

Some types of attacks allow an attacker to get data without ever having to directly use your computers. Usually these attacks exploit Internet services that are intended to give out information, inducing the services to give out more information than was intended, or to give it out to the wrong people. Many Internet services are designed for use on local area networks, and don't have the type or degree of security that would allow them to be used safely across the Internet.

Information theft doesn't need to be active or particularly technical. People who want to find out personal information could simply call you and ask (perhaps pretending to be somebody who had a right to know): this is an active information theft. Or they could tap your telephone: a passive information theft. Similarly, people who want to gather electronic information could actively query for it (perhaps pretending to be a machine or a user with valid access) or could passively tap the network and wait for it to flow by.

Most people who steal information try to get access to your computers; they're looking for usernames and passwords. Fortunately for them, and unfortunately for everybody else, that's the easiest kind of information to get when tapping a network. Username and password information occurs quite predictably at the beginning of many network interactions, and such information can be reused in the same form.

How would you proceed if you want to find out how somebody answers her telephone? Installing a tap would be an easy and reliable way to get that information, and a tap at a central point in the telephone system would yield you the telephone greetings of hundreds or thousands of people in a short period of time.

On the other hand, what if you want to know how somebody spells his last name, or what the names and ages of his children are? In this case, a telephone tap is a slow and unreliable way to get that information. A telephone tap at a central point in the system will probably yield that information about some people, and it will certainly yield some secret information you could use in interesting ways, but the information is going to be buried among the conversations of hundreds of people setting up lunch dates and chatting about the weather.

Similarly, network taps, which are usually called *sniffers*, are very effective at finding password information, but are rarely used to gather other kinds of information. Getting more specific information about a site requires either extreme dedication and patience, or the knowledge that the information you want will reliably pass through a given place at a given time. For example, if you know that somebody calls his bank to transfer money between his checking and savings accounts at 2

P.M. every other Friday, it's worth tapping that phone call to find out the person's access codes and account numbers. However, it's probably not worth tapping somebody else's phone, on the off chance that they too will do such a transfer, because most people don't transfer money over the phone at all.

Network sniffing is much easier than tapping a telephone line. Traditionally, the connectors used to hook a computer up to a network are known as *network taps* (that's why the term *tapping* isn't used for spying on a network), and the connectors behave like taps too. In most common network technologies, such as Ethernet and token ring, any computer on a local area network is capable of seeing all the traffic that passes across that local area network. Traffic that crosses the Internet may cross any number of local area networks, any one of which can be a point of compromise. Network service providers and public-access systems are very popular targets for intrusions; sniffers placed there can be extremely successful because so much traffic passes through these networks.

There are several types of protection against information theft. A properly configured firewall will protect you against people who are trying to get more information than you intended to give. Once you've decided to give information out across the Internet, however, it's very difficult to protect against that information reaching an unintended audience, either through misauthentication (somebody claiming to be authorized, when they're not) or through sniffing (somebody simply reading information as it crosses a correctly authorized channel). Although these risks are outside of the protection a firewall can give (because they occur once information has intentionally been allowed to go outside your network), we do discuss them, and the methods used to reduce them, as appropriate in this book.

Types of Attackers

This section very briefly describes the types of attackers who are out there on the Internet. There are many ways to categorize these attackers; we can't really do justice to the many variants of attackers we've seen over the years, and any quick summary of this kind necessarily presents a rather stereotyped view. Nevertheless, this summary may be useful in distinguishing the main categories of attackers.

All attackers share certain characteristics. They don't want to be caught, so they try to conceal themselves. If they gain access to your system, they will certainly attempt to preserve that access, if possible, by building in extra ways to get access (and they hope you won't notice these access routes even if you find the attackers themselves). Most of them have some contact with other people who have the same kinds of interests ("the underground" is not hard to find), and most will share the information they get from attacking your system.

Joyriders

Joyriders are bored people looking for amusement. They break in because they think you might have interesting data, or because it would be amusing to use your computers, or because they have nothing better to do. They might be out to learn about the kind of computer you have or about the data you have. They're curious, but not actively malicious; however, they often damage the system through ignorance or in trying to cover their tracks. Joyriders are particularly attracted to well-known sites and uncommon computers.

Vandals

Vandals are out to do damage, either because they get their kicks from destroying things, or because they don't like you. When one gets to you, you'll know it.

Vandals are a big problem if you're somebody that the Internet underground might think of as The Enemy (for example, the phone company or the government) or if you tend to annoy people who have computers and time (for example, you're a university with failing students, or a computer company with annoyed customers, or you have an aggressively commercial presence on the Internet). You can also become a target simply by being large and visible; if you put a big white wall up in certain neighborhoods, people will put graffiti on it no matter how they feel about you.

Fortunately, vandals are fairly rare. People don't like them, even people in the underground who have nothing against breaking into computers in general. Vandals also tend to inspire people to go to great lengths to find them and stop them. Unlike more mundane intruders, vandals have short but splashy careers. Most of them also go for straightforward destruction, which is unpleasant but is relatively easily detected and repaired. In most circumstances, deleting your data, or even ruining your computer equipment, is not the worst thing somebody could do to you, but it is what vandals do. (Actually, introducing subtle but significant changes in programs or financial data would be much harder to detect and fix.)

Unfortunately, it's close to impossible to stop a determined vandal; somebody with a true vendetta against your site is going to get you, sooner or later. Certain attacks are attractive to vandals but not to other types of attackers. For example, denial of service attacks are not attractive to joyriders; while joyriders are around in your system, they are just as interested as you are in having your computers up, running, and available to the Internet.

Score Keepers

Many intruders are engaging in an updated version of an ancient tradition. They're gaining bragging rights, based on the number and types of systems they've broken into.

Like joyriders and vandals, *score keepers* may prefer sites of particular interest. Breaking into something well-known, well-defended, or otherwise especially neat is usually worth more points to them. However, they'll also attack anything they can get at; they're going for quantity as well as quality. They don't have to want anything you've got, or care in the least about the characteristics of your site. They may or may not do damage on the way through. They'll certainly gather information and keep it for later use (perhaps using it to barter with other attackers). They'll probably try to leave themselves ways to get back in later. And, if at all possible, they'll use your machines as a platform to attack others.

These people are the ones you discover long after they've broken in to your system. You may find out slowly, because something's odd about your machine. Or you'll find out when another site or a law enforcement agency calls up because your system is being used to attack other places. Or you'll find out when somebody sends you a copy of your own private data, which they've found on a cracked system on the other side of the world.

Spies (Industrial and Otherwise)

Most people who break into computers do so for the same reason people climb mountains—because they're there. While these people are not above theft, they usually steal things that are directly convertible into money or further access (e.g., credit card, telephone, or network access information). If they find secrets they think they can sell, they may try to do so, but that's not their main business.

As far as anybody knows, serious computer-based espionage is much rarer, outside of traditional espionage circles. (That is, if you're a professional spy, there are probably other professional spies watching you and your computers). Espionage is much more difficult to detect than run-of-the-mill break-ins, however. Information theft need not leave any traces at all, and even intrusions are relatively rarely detected immediately. Somebody who breaks in, copies data, and leaves without disturbing anything is quite likely get away with it at most sites.

In practical terms, most organizations can't prevent spies from succeeding. The precautions that governments take to protect sensitive information on computers are complex, expensive, and cumbersome; therefore they are used on only the most critical resources. These precautions include electromagnetic shielding, careful access controls, and absolutely no connections to unsecured networks.

What can you do to protect against attackers of this kind? You can ensure that your Internet connection isn't the easiest way for a spy to gather information. You don't want some kid to break into your computers and find something that immediately appears to be worth trying to sell to spies; you don't want your competitors to be trivially able to get to your data; and you do want to make it expensive and risky to spy on you. Some people say it's unreasonable to protect data from network access when somebody could get it easily by coming to your site physically. We don't agree; physical access is generally more expensive and more risky for an attacker than network access.

Stupidity and Accidents

Most disasters are not caused through ill will; they're accidents or stupid mistakes. One recent study estimates that 55% of all security incidents actually result from naive or untrained users doing things they shouldn't.[*]

Denial of service incidents, for example, frequently aren't attacks at all. Apple's corporate electronic mail was rendered nonfunctional for several days (and their network provider was severely inconvenienced) by an accident involving a single mail message sent from a buggy mail server to a large mailing list. The mail resulted in a cascade of hundreds of thousands of error messages. The only hostile person involved was the system administrator, who wasn't hostile until he had to clean up the resulting mess.

Similarly, it's not uncommon for companies to destroy their own data, or release it to the world, by accident. Firewalls aren't designed to deal with this kind of problem. In fact there is no known way to protect yourself from either accidents or stupidity. Unfortunately, whether people are attacking you on purpose, or are simply making mistakes, the results are quite similar. (Hence the saying, "Never ascribe to malice that which can adequately be explained by stupidity.") When you protect yourself against evil-doers, you also help protect yourself against the more common, but equally devastating, unintentional or well-intentioned error.

How Can You Protect Your Site?

What approaches can you take to protect against the kinds of attacks we've outlined in this chapter? People choose a variety of security models, or approaches, ranging from no security at all, through what's called "security through obscurity" and host security, to network security.

No Security

The simplest possible approach is to put no effort at all into security, and run with whatever minimal security your vendor provides you by default. If you're reading this book, you've probably already rejected this model.

Security Through Obscurity

Another possible security model is the one commonly referred to as "security through obscurity." With this model, a system is presumed to be secure simply because (supposedly) nobody knows about it—its existence, contents, security measures, or anything else. This approach seldom works for long; there are just too many ways to find an attractive target.

---

[*] Richard Power, *Current and Future Danger: A CSI Primer on Computer Crime and Information Warfare*, San Francisco, CA: Computer Security Institute, 1995.

Many people assume that even though attackers can find them, they won't bother to. They figure that a small company or a home machine just isn't going to be of interest to intruders. In fact, many intruders aren't aiming at particular targets; they just want to break into as many machines as possible. To them, small companies and home machines simply look like easy targets. They probably won't stay long, but they will attempt to break in, and they may do considerable damage if they do get in while they try to cover their tracks.

To function on any network, the Internet included, a site has to do at least a minimal amount of registration, and much of this registration information is available to anyone, just for the asking. Every time a site uses services on the network, someone—at the very least, whoever is providing the service—will know they're there. Intruders watch for new connections, in the hope that these sites won't yet have security measures in place. Some sites have reported automated probes apparently based on new site registrations.

You'd probably be amazed at how many different ways someone can determine security-sensitive information about your site. For example, knowing what hardware and software you have and what version of the operating system you're running gives intruders important clues about what security holes they might try. They can often get this information from your host registration, or by trying to connect to your computer. Many computers disclose their type of operating system in the greeting you get before you log in, so an intruder doesn't need access to get it.

Intruders have a lot of time on their hands, and can often avoid having to figure out obscure facts by simply trying all the possibilities. In the long run, relying on obscurity is not a smart security choice.

Host Security

Probably the most common model for computer security is host security. With this model, you enforce the security of each host machine separately, and you make every effort to avoid or alleviate all the known security problems that might affect that particular host. What's wrong with host security? It's not that it doesn't work on individual machines; it's that it doesn't scale to large numbers of machines.

The major impediment to effective host security in modern computing environments is the complexity and diversity of those environments. Most modern environments include machines from multiple vendors, each with its own operating system, and each with its own set of security problems. Even if the site has machines from only one vendor, different releases of the same operating system often have significantly different security problems. Even if all these machines are from a single vendor and run a single release of the operating system, different configurations (different services enabled, and so on) can bring different subsystems into play (and into conflict) and lead to different sets of security problems.

And, even if the machines are all absolutely identical, the sheer number of them at some sites can make securing them all difficult. It takes a significant amount of up-front and ongoing work to effectively implement and maintain host security. Even with all that work done correctly, host security still often fails due to bugs in vendor software, or due to a lack of suitably secure software for some required functions.

Host security also relies on the good intentions and the skill of everyone who has privileged access to any machine. As the number of machines increases, the number of privileged users generally increases as well. Securing a machine is much more difficult than attaching it to a network, so insecure machines may appear on your network as unexpected surprises. The mere fact that it is not supposed to be possible to buy or connect machines without consulting you is immaterial; people develop truly innovative purchasing and network-connection schemes if they feel the need.

A host security model may be highly appropriate for small sites, or sites with extreme security requirements. Indeed, all sites should include some level of host security in their overall security plans. Even if you adopt a network security model, as we describe in the next section, certain systems in your configuration will benefit from the strongest host security. For example, even if you have built a firewall around your internal network and systems, there will be certain systems exposed to the outside world that need host security. (We discuss this in detail in Chapter 5.) The problem is, the host security model alone just isn't cost-effective for any but small or simple sites; making it work requires too many restrictions and too many people.

Network Security

As environments grow larger and more diverse, and as securing them on a host-by-host basis grows more difficult, more sites are turning to a network security model. With a network security model, you concentrate on controlling network access to your various hosts and the services they offer, rather than on securing them one by one. Network security approaches include building firewalls to protect your internal systems and networks, using strong authentication approaches (such as one-time passwords), and using encryption to protect particularly sensitive data as it transits the network.

A site can get tremendous leverage from its security efforts by using a network security model. For example, a single network firewall of the type we discuss in this book can protect hundreds, thousands, or even tens of thousands of machines against attack from networks beyond the firewall, regardless of the level of host security of the individual machines.

NOTE

Although this book concentrates on network security, please note that
we aren't suggesting you ignore host security. As mentioned above, you
should apply the strongest possible host security measures to your most
important machines, especially to those machines that are directly connected to the Internet. You'll also want to consider using host security
on your internal machines in general, to address security problems other
than attacks from the Internet.

No Security Model Can Do It All

No security model can solve all your problems. No security model—short of
"maximum security prison"—can prevent a hostile person with legitimate access
from purposefully damaging your site or taking confidential information out of it.
To get around powerful host and network security measures, a legitimate user can
simply use physical methods. These may range from pouring soda into your computers to carrying sensitive memos home. You can protect yourself from accidents
and ignorance internally, and from malicious external acts, but you cannot protect
yourself from your legitimate users without severely damaging their ability to use
their computers. Spies succeed in breaching government security with depressing
regularity despite regulations and precautions well beyond the resources and toler-
ance of civilians.

No security model can take care of management problems; computer security will
not keep your people from wasting time, annoying each other, or embarrassing
you. Sites often get sucked into trying to make security protect against these
things. When people are wasting time reading Usenet news, annoying each other
by playing tricks with window systems, and embarrassing the company with horrible email, computer security looks like a promising technological solution that
avoids difficult issues. Unfortunately, a security model won't work here. It is
expensive and difficult to even try to solve these problems with computer security,
and you are once again in the impossible situation of trying to protect yourself
from legitimate users.

No security model provides perfect protection. You can expect to make break-ins
rare, brief, and inexpensive, but you can't expect to avoid them altogether. Even
the most secure and dedicated sites expect to have a security incident every few
years.[*]

Why bother, then? Security may not prevent every single incident, but it can keep
an incident from seriously damaging or even shutting down your business. At one
high-profile company with multiple computer facilities, a manager complained that

---

[*] You can impress a security expert by saying you've only been broken into once in the last
five years; if you say you've never been broken into, they stop being impressed and decide
that either you can't detect break-ins, or you haven't been around long enough for anyone
to try seriously!

his computer facility was supposed to be the most secure, but it got broken into along with several others. The difference was that the break-in was the first one that year for his facility; the intruder was present for only eight minutes; and the computer facility was off the Internet for only 12 hours (from 6 P.M. to 6 A.M.), after which it resumed business as usual with no visible interruption in service to the company's customers. For one of the other facilities, it was the fourth time; the intruder was present for months before being detected; recovery required taking the facility down for four days; and they had to inform customers that they had shipped them tapes containing possibly contaminated software. Proper security made the difference between an annoying occurrence and a devastating one.

What Is an Internet Firewall?

As we've mentioned, firewalls are a very effective type of network security. This section briefly describes what Internet firewalls can do for your overall site security. Chapter 4 describes the various types of firewalls in use today, and the other chapters in Part II describe the details of building those firewalls.

In building construction, a firewall is designed to keep a fire from spreading from one part of the building to another. In theory, an Internet firewall serves a similar purpose: it prevents the dangers of the Internet from spreading to your internal network. In practice, an Internet firewall is more like a moat of a medieval castle than a firewall in a modern building. It serves multiple purposes:

- It restricts people to entering at a carefully controlled point.

- It prevents attackers from getting close to your other defenses.

- It restricts people to leaving at a carefully controlled point.

An Internet firewall is most often installed at the point where your protected internal network connects to the Internet, as shown in Figure 1-1.

All traffic coming from the Internet or going out from your internal network passes through the firewall. Because it does, the firewall has the opportunity to make sure that this traffic is acceptable.

What does "acceptable" mean to the firewall? It means that whatever is being done—email, file transfers, remote logins, or any kinds of specific interactions between specific systems—conforms to the security policy of the site. Security policies are different for every site; some are highly restrictive and others fairly open, as we'll discuss in Chapter 11.

Logically, a firewall is a separator, a restricter, an analyzer. The physical implementation of the firewall varies from site to site. Most often, a firewall is a set of hardware components—a router, a host computer, or some combination of routers, computers, and networks with appropriate software. There are various ways to configure this equipment; the configuration will depend upon a site's particular security policy, budget, and overall operations.

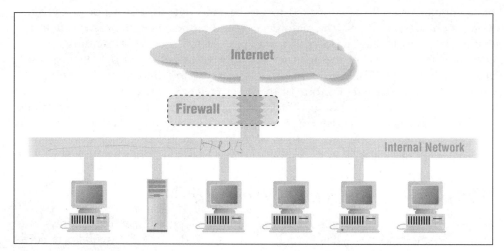

Figure 1–1: A firewall usually separates an internal network from the Internet

A firewall is very rarely a single physical object, although some of the newest commercial products attempt to put everything into the same box. Usually, a firewall has multiple parts, and some of these parts may do other tasks besides function as part of the firewall. Your Internet connection is almost always part of your firewall. Even if you have a firewall in a box, it isn't going to be neatly separable from the rest of your site; it's not something you can just drop in.

We've compared a firewall to the moat of a medieval castle, and like a moat, a firewall is not invulnerable. It doesn't protect against people who are already inside; it works best if coupled with internal defenses; and, even if you stock it with alligators, people sometimes manage to swim across. A firewall is also not without its drawbacks; building one requires significant expense and effort, and the restrictions it places on insiders can be a major annoyance.

Given the limitations and drawbacks of firewalls, why would anybody bother to install one? Because a firewall is the most effective way to connect a network to the Internet and still protect that network. The Internet presents marvelous opportunities. Millions of people are out there exchanging information. The benefits are obvious: the chances for publicity, customer service, and information gathering. The popularity of the information superhighway is increasing everybody's desire to get out there. The risks should also be obvious: any time you get millions of people together, you get crime; it's true in a city, and it's true on the Internet. Any superhighway is fun only while you're in a car. If you have to live or work by the highway, it's loud, smelly, and dangerous.

How can you benefit from the good parts of the Internet without being overwhelmed by the bad? Just as you'd like to drive on a highway without suffering the nasty effects of putting a freeway off-ramp into your living room, you need to carefully control the contact that your network has to the Internet. A firewall is a tool for doing that, and in most situations, it's the single most effective tool for doing that.

There are other uses of firewalls. For example, they can be used as firewalls in a building that divide parts of a site from each other when these parts have distinct security needs (and we'll discuss these uses in passing, as appropriate). The focus of this book, however, is on firewalls as they're used between a site and the Internet.

Firewalls offer significant benefits, but they can't solve every security problem. The following sections briefly summarize what firewalls can and cannot do to protect your systems and your data.

What Can a Firewall Do?

Firewalls can do a lot for your site's security. In fact, some advantages of using firewalls extend even beyond security, as described below.

A firewall is a focus for security decisions

Think of a firewall as a choke point. All traffic in and out must pass through this single, narrow checkpoint. A firewall gives you an enormous amount of leverage for network security because it lets you concentrate your security measures on this checkpoint: the point where your network connects to the Internet.

Focusing your security in this way is far more efficient than spreading security decisions and technologies around, trying to cover all the bases in a piecemeal fashion. Although firewalls can cost tens of thousands of dollars to implement, most sites find that concentrating the most effective security hardware and software at the firewall is less expensive and more effective than other security measures—and certainly less expensive than having inadequate security.

A firewall can enforce security policy

Many of the services that people want from the Internet are inherently insecure. The firewall is the traffic cop for these services. It enforces the site's security policy, allowing only "approved" services to pass through and those only within the rules set up for them.

For example, one site's management may decide that certain services such as Sun's Network File System (NFS) and Network Information Services (formerly known as Yellow Pages) (NIS/YP) are simply too risky to be used across the firewall. It doesn't matter what system tries to run them or what user wants them. The firewall will keep potentially dangerous services strictly inside the firewall. (There, they can still be used for insiders to attack each other, but that's outside of the firewall's control.) Another site might decide that only one internal system can communicate with the outside world. Still another site might decide to allow access from all systems of a certain type, or belonging to a certain group; the variations in site security policies are endless.

A firewall may be called upon to help enforce more complicated policies. For example, perhaps only certain systems within the firewall are allowed to transfer files to and from the Internet; by using other mechanisms to control which users have access to those systems, you can control which users have these capabilities. Depending on the technologies you choose to implement your firewall, a firewall may have a greater or lesser ability to enforce such policies.

A firewall can log Internet activity efficiently

Because all traffic passes through the firewall, the firewall provides a good place to collect information about system and network use—and misuse. As a single point of access, the firewall can record what occurs between the protected network and the external network.

A firewall limits your exposure

Although this point is most relevant to the use of internal firewalls, which we describe in Chapter 4, it's worth mentioning here. Sometimes, a firewall will be used to keep one section of your site's network separate from another section. By doing this, you keep problems that impact one section from spreading through the entire network. In some cases, you'll do this because one section of your network may be more trusted than another; in other cases, because one section is more sensitive than another. Whatever the reason, the existence of the firewall limits the damage that a network security problem can do to the overall network.

What Can't a Firewall Do?

Firewalls offer excellent protection against network threats, but they aren't a complete security solution. Certain threats are outside the control of the firewall. You need to figure out other ways to protect against these threats by incorporating physical security, host security, and user education into your overall security plan. Some of the weaknesses of firewalls are discussed below.

A firewall can't protect you against malicious insiders

A firewall might keep a system user from being able to send proprietary information out of an organization over a network connection; so would simply not having a network connection. But that same user could copy the data onto disk, tape, or paper and carry it out of the building in his or her briefcase.

If the attacker is already inside the firewall—if the fox is inside the henhouse—a firewall can do virtually nothing for you. Inside users can steal data, damage hardware and software, and subtly modify programs without ever coming near the firewall. Insider threats require internal security measures, such as host security and user education. Such topics are beyond the scope of this book.

A firewall can't protect you against connections that don't go through it

A firewall can effectively control the traffic that passes through it; however, there is nothing a firewall can do about traffic that doesn't pass through it. For example, what if the site allows dial-in access to internal systems behind the firewall? The firewall has absolutely no way of preventing an intruder from getting in through such a modem.

Sometimes, technically expert users or system administrators set up their own "back doors" into the network (such as a dial-up modem connection), either temporarily or permanently, because they chafe at the restrictions that the firewall places upon them and their systems. The firewall can do nothing about this. It's really a people-management problem, not a technical problem.

A firewall can't protect against completely new threats

A firewall is designed to protect against known threats. A well-designed one may also protect against new threats. (For example, by denying any but a few trusted services, a firewall will prevent people from setting up new and insecure services.) However, no firewall can automatically defend against every new threat that arises. Periodically people discover new ways to attack, using previously trustworthy services, or using attacks that simply hadn't occurred to anyone before. You can't set up a firewall once, and expect it to protect you forever. (See Chapter 12 for advice on keeping your firewall up to date.)

A firewall can't protect against viruses

Firewalls can't keep PC and Macintosh viruses out of a network. Although many firewalls scan all incoming traffic to determine whether it is allowed to pass through to the internal network, the scanning is mostly for source and destination addresses and port numbers, not for the details of the data. Even with sophisticated packet filtering or proxying software, virus protection in a firewall is not very practical. There are simply too many types of viruses and too many ways a virus can hide within data.

Detecting a virus in a random packet of data passing through a firewall is very difficult; it requires:

* Recognizing that the packet is part of a program

- Determining what the program should look like

- Determining that the change is because of a virus

Even the first of these is a challenge. Most firewalls are protecting machines of multiple types with different executable formats. A program may be a compiled executable or a script (e.g., a UNIX shell script, or a HyperCard stack), and many machines support multiple, compiled executable types. Furthermore, most programs are packaged for transport, and are often compressed as well. Packages being transferred via email or Usenet news will also have been encoded into ASCII in different ways.

For all of these reasons, users may end up bringing viruses behind the firewall, no matter how secure that firewall is. Even if you could do a perfect job of blocking viruses at the firewall, however, you still haven't addressed the virus problem. You've done nothing about the far more common sources of viruses: software downloaded from dial-up bulletin-board systems, software brought in on floppies from home or other sites, and even software that comes presinfected from manufacturers are more common than virus-infected software on the Internet. Whatever you do to address those threats will also address the problem of software transferred through the firewall.

The most practical way to address the virus problem is through host-based virus protection software, and user education concerning the dangers of viruses and precautions to take against them.

Buying Versus Building

Until recently, if a site wanted a firewall, they had little choice but to design and build it themselves (perhaps with their own staff, or perhaps by hiring a consultant or contractor). Over the last few years, however, more and more commercial firewall offerings have reached the market. These products continue to grow in number and functionality at an astounding rate, and many sites may find that one of these products suits their needs.

In deciding whether or not a particular commercial firewall product will meet your needs, you have to understand what your needs are. Even if you decide to buy a firewall, you still need to understand a fair bit about how they're built and how they work in order to make an informed purchasing decision. Many sites spend as much or more effort evaluating commercial firewall products as they would building their own firewall.

We're not saying that nobody should buy a firewall, or that everybody should build their own. Our point is merely that it's not necessarily any easier to buy than it is to build; it all depends on your particular situation, and what resources you have at your disposal. Sites with money to spend but little staff time or expertise available often find buying an attractive solution, while sites with expertise and time but little money often find building more attractive.

Just what expertise do you need to design and build your own firewall? Like everything else, it depends; it depends on what services you want to provide, what platforms you're using, what your security concerns are, and so on. To install most of the tools described in this book, you need basic Internet skills to obtain the tools, and basic system administration skills to configure, compile, and install them. If you don't know what those skills are, you probably don't have them; you can obtain them, but that's beyond the scope of this book.

Some people feel uncomfortable using software that's freely available on the Internet, particularly for security-critical applications. We feel that the advantages outweigh the disadvantages. You may not have the "guarantees" offered by vendors, but you have the ability to inspect the source code and to share information with the large community that helps to maintain the software. In practice, vendors come and go, but the community endures. The packages we discuss in this book are widely used; many of the largest sites on the Internet base their firewalls on them. These packages reflect years of real-life experience with the Internet and its risks.

Furthermore, while it's perfectly possible to build a firewall consisting solely of freely available software, there's no reason to feel that it's all or nothing; freely available tools provide a valuable complement to purchased solutions. Buying a firewall shouldn't make you reluctant to supplement with freely available tools, and building one shouldn't make you reluctant to supplement with purchased tools. Don't rule out a product just because it's commercial, or just because it's freely available. Truly excellent products with great support appear in both categories, as do poorly thought out products with no support.

In This Chapter:
- *Electronic Mail*
- *File Transfer*
- *Remote Terminal
  Access and
  Command Execution*
- *Usenet News*
- *The World Wide Web*
- *Other Information
  Services*
- *Information About
  People*
- *Real-Time
  Conferencing Services*
- *Name Service*
- *Network
  Management Services*
- *Time Service*
- *Network File Systems*
- *Window Systems*
- *Printing Systems*

2

Internet Services

In Chapter 1 we discussed, in general terms, what you're trying to protect when you connect to the Internet: your data, your resources, and your reputation. In designing an Internet firewall, your concerns are more specific; what you need to protect are those services you're going to use or provide over the Internet.

There are a number of standard Internet services that users want and that most sites try to support. There are important reasons to use these services; indeed, without them, there is little reason to be connected to the Internet at all. But there are also potential security problems with each of them.

What services do you want to support at your site? Which ones can you support securely? Every site is different. Every site has its own security policy and its own working environment. For example, do all your users need electronic mail? Do they all need to transfer files outside your organization? How about downloading files from sites outside the organization's own network? Who should be able to log in remotely from another location over the Internet?

This chapter briefly summarizes the major Internet services your users may be interested in using. It provides only a high-level summary (details are given in Chapter 8). None of these services are really secure; each one has its own security weaknesses, and each has been exploited in various ways by attackers. Before you decide to support a service at your site, you will have to assess how important it is to your users and whether you will be able to protect them from its dangers. There are various ways of doing this: running the services only on certain protected machines, using especially secure variants of the standard services; or, in some cases, blocking the services completely to or from some or all outside systems.

This chapter doesn't list every Internet service—it can't. Such a list would be incomplete as soon as it was finished, and would include services of interest only to a few sites in the world. Instead, we attempt to list the major services, and we hope this book will give you the background you need to make decisions about new services as you encounter them.

Managers and system administrators together need to decide which services to support at your site and to what extent. Chapter 8 describes what is necessary to support these services securely once you've decided to provide them, and the decisions you may need to make about them when building your site's firewall.

Electronic Mail

Electronic mail is one of the most popular and basic network services. It's relatively low risk, but that doesn't mean it's risk free. Forging electronic mail is trivial (just as is forging regular postal mail), and forgeries facilitate two different types of attacks: attacks against your reputation and social manipulation attacks (e.g., attacks in which users are sent mail purporting to come from an administrator and advising them to change to a specific password). Accepting electronic mail ties up computer time and disk space, opening you up for denial of service attacks, although with proper configuration, only email service will be denied. Particularly with modern multimedia mail systems, people can send electronic mail containing programs that run with insufficient supervision and may turn out to be *Trojan horses*.

Although people worry most about the last risk mentioned above, in practice the most common problems with electronic mail are inadvertent floods (including chain letters) and people who put entirely inappropriate confidence in the confidentiality of electronic mail and send proprietary data via electronic mail across the Internet. However, as long as users are educated, and the mail service is isolated from other services so that inadvertent or purposeful denial of service attacks shut down as little as possible, electronic mail is reasonably safe.

Simple Mail Transfer Protocol (SMTP) is the Internet standard protocol for sending and receiving electronic mail. SMTP itself is not usually a security problem, but SMTP servers can be. A program that delivers mail to users often needs to be able to run as any user that might receive mail. This gives it broad power and makes it a tempting target for attackers.

Getting Started with Internet Services

Are you just getting connected? Or, have you been connected for a while but are getting concerned about Internet security? Where should you start? Many system administrators try to be too ambitious. If you attempt to develop and deploy the be-all and end-all of firewall systems right from day one, you probably aren't going to succeed. The field is just too complex, and the technology is changing so fast that it will change out from under you before you get such an endeavor "finished."

Start small. At many sites, it boils down to six basic services. If you can provide these services securely, most of your users will be satisfied, at least for a while.

- Electronic mail (SMTP)

- File transfer (FTP)

- Usenet news (NNTP)

- Remote terminal access (Telnet)

- World Wide Web access (HTTP)

- Hostname/address lookup (DNS): users generally don't use this service directly, but it underlies the other five services by translating Internet hostnames to IP addresses and vice versa.

All six of these services can be safely provided in a number of different ways, including packet filtering and proxies—firewall approaches discussed in Part II of this book. Providing these services lets your users access most Internet resources, and it buys you time to figure out how to provide the rest of the services they'll be asking for soon, such as Archie, Gopher, WAIS, and other information services.

The most common SMTP server on UNIX is Sendmail. Sendmail has been exploited in a number of break-ins, including the Internet worm, which makes people nervous about using it. Many of the available replacements, however, are not clearly preferable to Sendmail; the evidence suggests they are less exploited because they are less popular, not because they are less vulnerable. There are exceptions in programs designed explicitly for security, but these don't support all the functions necessary to send and receive arbitrary mail messages; some things are still best handled by Sendmail running in a secured space.

File Transfer

Electronic mail transfers data from place to place, but it's designed for small files, in human-readable form. Electronic mail transfer protocols are allowed to make changes in a message that are acceptable to humans (for instance, inserting ">" before the word "from" at the beginning of a line, so that the mailer doesn't get it confused with a header line), but are unacceptable to programs.*

Although electronic mail systems these days include elaborate workarounds for such problems, so that a large binary file may be split into small pieces and encoded on the sending side and decoded and reassembled on the receiving side, the workarounds are cumbersome and error prone. Also, people may want to actively go out and look for files, instead of waiting for someone to send them. Therefore, even when electronic mail is available it's useful to have a method designed for transferring files on request.

File Transfer Protocol (FTP) is the Internet standard protocol for this purpose. In theory, allowing your users to bring files in is not an increase of risk over allowing electronic mail; in fact, some sites offer services allowing you to access FTP via email. In practice, however, people will do more file transfers when FTP is available, and are more likely to bring in undesirable programs and data.

What makes these programs and data undesirable? The primary worry at most sites is that users will bring in Trojan horse software. Although this can happen, actually the larger concern is that users will bring in computer games, pirated software, and pornographic pictures, which tend to take up an annoying amount of time and disk space, but don't represent a major security risk. If you make sure to do the following, then you can consider inbound FTP to be a reasonably safe service that eases access to important Internet resources:

- Educate your users to appropriately mistrust any software they bring in via FTP.

- Communicate to users your site's guidelines about sexual harassment policies and organizational resource usage.

How about the other side of the coin: allowing other people to use FTP to transfer files from your computers? This is somewhat riskier. Anonymous FTP is an extremely popular mechanism for giving remote users access to files without having to give them full access to your machine. If you run an FTP server, you can let users retrieve files you've placed in a separate, public area of your system without letting them log in and potentially get access to everything on your system. Your site's anonymous FTP area can be your organization's public archive of papers, standards, software, graphics images, and information of other kinds that people

---

* Inserting ">" before "from" is so common that some published books still contain the occasional ">from" in the text, where the ">" was inserted as authors exchanged drafts via electronic mail.

need from you or that you want to share with them. For many organizations, establishing an FTP site is the first step towards doing business on the Internet.

To get access to the files you've made available, users log into your system using FTP with the special login name "anonymous." Most sites request that users enter their own email address, in response to the password prompt, as a courtesy so that the site can track who is using the anonymous FTP server, but this requirement is rarely enforced (mostly because there is no easy way to verify the validity of an email address).

In setting up an anonymous FTP server, you'll need to ensure that people who use it can't get access to other areas or files on the system, and that they can't use FTP to get shell-level access to the system itself. Writable directories in the anonymous FTP area are a special concern, as we'll see in Chapter 8.

You'll also need to ensure that your users don't use the server inappropriately. It can be very tempting for people to put up files that they want specific people to read. Many times people don't realize that anybody on the Internet can read them, or they do realize this, but believe in security through obscurity. Unfortunately for these innocents, a number of tools attempt to index anonymous FTP servers, and they succeed in removing most of the obscurity.

You may have heard of other file transfer protocols. Trivial File Transport Protocol (TFTP) is a simplified FTP protocol that diskless machines use to transfer information. It's extremely simple so that it can be built into hardware, and therefore supports no authentication. There's no reason to provide TFTP access outside of your network; ordinary users don't transfer files with TFTP.

UUCP (UNIX to UNIX CoPy) is an older file transfer protocol used over modems, and it is sometimes still used for the transfer of Usenet news and email even over the Internet, particularly by sites with intermittent Internet connections. Such sites use UUCP-over-TCP to obtain their email from their service provider whenever they bring their network connection up. While it used to be common, few sites now provide anonymous UUCP service for file access. As a file transfer protocol, it is of interest only to people who don't have an Internet connection and use modems. Unless your entire business involves providing information for downloading, UUCP is probably not useful for your external users.

File Service Protocol (FSP) is a file transfer protocol developed for circumventing FTP restrictions. Ordinary users can't set up FTP servers, but they can set up FSP servers, and FSP transfers will go through when FTP transfers have been blocked. There are two disadvantages in setting up an FSP server:

- Security is not a particular concern to the designers and users of FSP; although it shouldn't inherently reduce the security of your machine, it's susceptible to the same kinds of bugs as FTP, and fewer attempts have been made to avoid or fix them.

- Providing FSP service is not going to make friends for you among remote system administrators, since the point of FSP is to allow people to transfer files after their sites have decided to block file transfers.

FSP does have some actual advantages over FTP—being designed for stealth makes it a very sparing user of resources—but there are almost no legitimate FSP users, and its history makes it unlikely there will be many.

Within a site, you may want to use *rcp* to transfer files between systems. *rcp* (described in Chapter 8 with the rest of the so-called "Berkeley 'r' commands") is a file transfer program that behaves like an extended version of the UNIX *cp* command. It is inappropriate for use across the Internet, because it uses a trusted host authentication model. Rather than requiring user authentication on the remote machine, it looks at the IP address of the host the request is coming from. Unfortunately, you can't know that packets are really coming from that host.

Remote Terminal Access and Command Execution

Programs that provide remote terminal access allow you to use a remote system as if it were a directly attached terminal.

Telnet is the standard for remote terminal access on the Internet. It truly imitates a terminal, not a graphics workstation; it provides access to character-based applications only. Telnet allows you to provide remote access for your users from any Internet-connected site without making special arrangements.

Telnet was once considered a fairly secure service because it requires users to authenticate themselves. Unfortunately, Telnet sends all of its information unencrypted, which makes it extremely vulnerable to sniffing and hijacking attacks. For this reason, Telnet is now considered one of the most dangerous services when used to access your site from remote systems. (Accessing remote systems from your site is *their* security problem, not yours.) Telnet is safe only if the remote machine and all networks between it and the local machine are safe. This means that Telnet is not safe across the Internet, where you can't reliably identify the intervening networks, much less trust them. On the other hand, Telnet can be extremely useful—and extremely cost-effective—as a remote access mechanism if your users frequently travel to Internet-connected sites. In places where using a modem is expensive, difficult, and slow, using an existing Internet connection via Telnet may be the best available solution. For this practical reason, you may need to provide Telnet service, but with caution.

There are various kinds of authentication schemes for doing remote logins (in particular, see the discussion of one-time passwords in Chapter 10), but although authentication protects your password, you may still find that your session can be tapped or hijacked. Chapter 8 describes in detail the dangers of Telnet and the ways you can increase the safety of this service, particularly with a packet filtering firewall.

There are programs besides Telnet that can be used for remote terminal access and remote execution of programs—most notably *rlogin*, *rsh*, and *on*. These programs are used in a trusted environment to allow users remote access without having to re-authenticate themselves. The host they're connecting to trusts the host they're coming from to have correctly authenticated the user. The trusted host model is simply inappropriate for use across the Internet, because you generally cannot trust hosts outside your network. In fact, you can't even be sure the packets are coming from the host they say they are.

rlogin and *rsh* may be appropriate for use within a network protected by a firewall, depending on your internal security policies. *on*, however, places all of its security checks in the client program, and anyone can use a modified client that bypasses these checks, so *on* is completely insecure for use even within a local area network protected by firewall (it lets any user run any command as any other user). You disable *on* by disabling the *rexd* server, as we'll describe in Chapter 5.

Usenet News

While electronic mail allows people to communicate, it's most efficient as a way for one person to send a message to another, or to a small list of people interested in a particular topic. Newsgroups are the Internet counterpart to bulletin boards, and are designed for many-to-many communication. Mailing lists also support many-to-many communication, but much less openly and efficiently, because there's no easy way to find out about all mailing lists, and every recipient has his own copy of every message. The largest discussion mailing lists (i.e., lists where discussions take place among subscribers, rather than lists used to simply distribute information or announcements to subscribers) have tens of thousands of subscribers; the most popular newsgroups have hundreds of thousands. Usenet news is rather like television: there's a lot going on; most of it has little socially redeeming value; some of it is fantastically amusing or informative; and everybody wants it.

The risks of news are much like those of electronic mail: your users might foolishly trust information received; they might release confidential information; and you might get flooded. News resembles a flood when it's functioning normally—most sites receive hundreds of megabytes a day, and the amount increases steadily, doubling in volume approximately every six months—so you must make absolutely sure to configure news so that floods don't affect other services. Because news is rarely an essential service, denial of service attacks on a single site are usually just ignored. The security risks of news are therefore quite low. You might want to avoid news because you don't have the bandwidth or the disk space to spare, but it's not a significant security problem.

Network News Transfer Protocol (NNTP) is used to transfer news across the Internet. In setting up the news server at your site, you'll need to determine the most secure way for news to flow into your internal systems so NNTP can't be used to penetrate your system. Some sites put the news server on the bastion host, others on an internal system, as we'll describe in Chapter 8. NNTP doesn't do much, and your external transfers of news will all be with specific other machines (it's not like mail, which you want to receive from everybody), so it's not particularly difficult to secure.

The biggest security issue you'll face with news is what to do with private newsgroups. Many sites create private local newsgroups to facilitate discussions among their users; these private newsgroups often contain sensitive, confidential, or proprietary information. Someone who can access your NNTP server can potentially access these private newsgroups, resulting in disclosure of this information. If you're going to create private newsgroups, be sure to configure NNTP carefully to control access to these groups. (The configuring of NNTP to work in a firewall environment is discussed more fully in Chapter 8.)

The World Wide Web

Mail, FTP, Telnet, and Usenet news have been around since the early days of the Internet; they're actually extensions of services provided well before the Internet even existed. The World Wide Web (WWW) is a new, entirely Internet-based concept, based in part on existing services, and in part on a new protocol, HyperText Transfer Protocol (HTTP).

Many people confuse the functions and origins of WWW, Mosaic, and HTTP, and the terminology used to refer to these three distinct entities has become muddy. Some of the muddiness was introduced intentionally; Web browsers attempt to provide a seamless interface to a wide variety of information through a wide variety of mechanisms, and blurring the distinctions makes it easier to use, if more difficult to comprehend. Here is a quick summary of what the individual entities are about.

The WWW is the collection of HTTP servers (see the description of HTTP below) on the Internet. The Web is responsible, in large part, for the recent explosion in Internet activity. WWW is based on concepts developed at the European Particle Physics Laboratory (CERN) in Geneva, Switzerland, by Tim Berners-Lee and others. Much of the groundbreaking work on Web clients was done at the National Center for Supercomputing Applications (NCSA) at the University of Illinois in Urbana-Champaign. There are many organizations and individuals developing Web client and server software these days, and many more using these technologies for a huge range of purposes. Nobody "controls" the Web, however, much as nobody "controls" the Internet.

The Web uses hypertext technology to link together a web of documents, which may include text, graphics images, sound files, video files, and other formats. The documents can be traversed in any way—not only hierarchically—to search for information. Hypertext provides the navigation from one document to another on the Internet. Users can move freely from one to another, regardless of where the documents are located, by simply clicking on a word or picture for which an HTTP link has been defined.

HTTP is the primary application protocol that underlies the World Wide Web: it provides users access to the files that make up the Web. As mentioned above, these files might be in many different formats (text, graphics, audio, video, etc.), but the most common format on the Web is the HyperText Markup Language (HTML). HTML is a standardized page description language for creating Web pages. It provides basic document-formatting capabilities (including the ability to include graphics), and allows you to specify hypertext links to other servers and files.

Mosaic, developed by Marc Andreessen and others at NCSA, is an HTTP client, which is used as a browser of the Web. NCSA Mosaic is free and runs on Windows, the Macintosh, and many different flavors of UNIX. There are many other web browsers available and as this book goes to press, the most popular is Netscape Navigator, a commercial product that is available free for nonprofit and educational use or for commercial evaluation. It also runs on Windows, the Macintosh, and various UNIX machines. (Other Web browsers include Lynx, ViolaWWW, perl-WWW, and MidasWWW.) HTTP is but one protocol spoken by Mosaic; Mosaic clients typically also speak at least the FTP, Gopher, and WAIS protocols. Netscape Navigator speaks all of those and also NNTP and SMTP. Thus, when users say "we want Mosaic" or "we want Netscape," what they really mean, from a protocol level, is that they want access to the HTTP servers that make up the WWW, as well as the associated Gopher, WAIS, and FTP servers (plus, for Netscape, NNTP and SMTP servers).

Web browsers are fantastically popular, and for good reason. They provide a rich, graphical interface to an immense number of Internet resources. Information and services that were unavailable or expert-only before are now easily accessible. In Silicon Valley, you can use the Web to have dinner delivered without leaving your computer except to answer the door. It's hard to get a feel for the Web without experiencing it; it covers the full range of everything you can do with a computer, from the mundane to the sublime with a major side trip into the ridiculous.

Unfortunately, Web browsers and servers are hard to secure. The usefulness of the Web is in large part based on its flexibility, but that flexibility makes control difficult. Just as it's easier to transfer and execute the right program from a Web browser than from FTP, it's easier to transfer and execute a malicious one. Web browsers depend on external programs, generically called "viewers" (even if they play sounds instead of showing pictures), to deal with data types that the browsers themselves don't understand. (The browsers generally understand basic data types such as HTML, plain text, and JPEG and GIF graphics.) You should be very careful about which viewers you configure by default; you don't want a viewer that can do dangerous things because it's going to be running on your computers, as if it were one of your users, taking commands from an external source. You also want to warn users not to add viewers, or change viewer configurations, based on advice from strangers.

Because an HTML document can easily link to documents on other servers, it's easy for people to become confused about exactly who is responsible for a given document. New users may not notice when they go from internal documents at your site to external ones. This has two unfortunate consequences. First, they may trust external documents inappropriately (because they think they're internal documents.) Second, they may blame the internal Web maintainers for the sins of the world. People who understand the Web tend to find this hard to believe, but it's a common misconception: the dark side of having a very smooth transition between sites.

Most Web servers are reasonably secure, as shipped. However, they can also call external programs. These programs are relatively easy to write, but very difficult to secure. You should treat server-side extensions with the same caution you would treat a new server of any kind.

(We discuss the security of Web clients and servers in more detail in Chapter 8.)

Other Information Services

Many users also want access to additional information services; Gopher, WAIS, and Archie are the most popular.

Gopher is a menu-oriented, text-based tool that helps users find information on the Internet. "Gopher" isn't an acronym for anything; it was developed at the University of Minnesota, whose mascot is the "Golden Gopher." Information on a Gopher server is organized as a series of hierarchical menus from which a user selects items. Each item can be a file, a form, or an additional menu, with its own items. There are a number of different Gopher clients available, including free, shareware, and commercial clients for Windows, Macintosh, and UNIX. Gopher clients and servers use an extensible data scheme, much as Web clients and servers do, and are thus subject to many of the same security concerns.

Wide Area Information Service (WAIS) was developed by a consortium of companies: Thinking Machines, Apple, Dow Jones, and KPMG Peat Marwick; the development was led by Brewster Kahle. A WAIS user submits a simple query (typically a keyword or a phrase), and the WAIS server sends back a list of the documents containing those words, along with a score for each document. This score is a composite of the number of times the keywords are mentioned and the length of the document; shorter documents get higher scores, as do documents that mention the keywords more often. The list of documents is returned sorted by score, so that with any luck the most relevant documents appear first in the list. The server maintains extensive indexes of the contents of all the documents on the server to allow it to do these searches efficiently. There are currently several hundred WAIS servers on the Internet. You can access them with WAIS-protocol clients, or by using a Web browser to access one of the sites that provides HTTP-WAIS gateways (e.g., `http://www.ai.mit.edu/the-net/wais.html`).

Archie is an Internet service that searches indexes of anonymous FTP servers for file and directory names. Archie servers typically provide service via Telnet and email in addition to dedicated Archie clients. Archie service providers generally prefer that users use dedicated Archie clients, because they impose less of a load on the server. Archie is also accessible through Web browsers via sites that provide HTTP-Archie gateways, such as the one at `http://www.nexor.co.uk/archie.html`. At this point, there are only about 20 Archie servers throughout the world, partly because of the significant resources (computing power, disk space, network bandwidth, and administrator time) required to run an Archie server, and partly because each Archie server searches much of the Internet for FTP'able files on a regular basis. If there were a large number of Archie servers, so much bandwidth would be consumed looking for resources that it would be impossible to use the resources.

WAIS and Archie are less open to mischief than HTTP and Gopher, because they don't return data of arbitrary types. If a WAIS server advises you that a document is about gardening, and it turns out to be about manufacturing jewelry in your spare time, this may be annoying, but it's not a problem for the security of your computers. Unfortunately, providing access to some of these services may open other security holes unrelated to the service itself. For example, allowing your users to access Archie directly may allow attackers to access your NFS and NIS/YP servers, as we discuss in Chapter 8.

Running servers is somewhat riskier. Unlike the clients, the servers for these protocols—including WAIS and Archie—accept arbitrary queries, and you must be sure that they aren't going to produce unexpected results. Any server that acts on requests from potentially hostile users is vulnerable to denial of service attacks and to executing unexpected commands on the server machine with the permissions of the server program.

Information About People

The Internet does not have a proper service for looking up information about people on the network as a whole, although a few attempts at registries have sprung up. Even if you know a person's real name and where they work, for example, you can't go to a central place to look up that person's user name or email address. However, there are two common services that provide some information about people, *finger* and *whois*.

The *finger* service looks up information about a user who has an account on the machine being queried, whether or not that user is currently logged in to the machine. This information may include the person's real name, login, phone number, office location, information about when and where they most recently logged in, and a brief message specified by the user.

You don't need to know the user name in order to use *finger*; it will generally give you information about anybody whose user name or real name contains the string you specify. If you don't specify a string, it will list information about everybody currently logged in to the machine being queried. *finger* can provide invaluable information to intruders, e.g., by identifying users who rarely log in, or names of gateway systems. You may wish to block *finger* requests that come from outside your internal network, or to supply only minimal information in response to these requests. *finger* is legitimately used by plenty of people who are simply trying to figure out what user name to send mail to, but those people don't need all the information that *finger* normally gives out.

It's less risky to use a *finger* client than to run a *finger* server. It's not without risk, however. The user-customizable message can contain control characters, and some *finger* clients rely on the length limitations normally built into the *finger* server to keep the returned information short. It's easy to construct a *finger* server that will be a denial of service attack. Depending on the *finger* client and the terminal, or terminal emulator, it's running on, control characters may produce effects anywhere from the annoying (it beeps maniacally and makes your screen look weird) to the disastrous (it downloads macros to your terminal, and then tells your terminal to pretend you'd typed the keys to invoke those macros, which can issue arbitrary commands as you, for example, to mail off your password file or delete all your files). You should run a *finger* client that doesn't permit control characters.

The *whois* service is similar to *finger*, but it obtains publicly available information about hosts, networks, domains, and their administrators. By default, *whois* clients query the host *rs.internic.net* at the Internet's Network Information Center (Inter-NIC), which maintains information about Internet domain and network administrators.[*]

Because *whois* is the closest thing to an Internet white pages protocol, some sites choose to write servers that use the *whois* protocol to distribute information about their users. If you decide to do this, the usual concerns apply about writing servers so they don't give out too much information, and so they don't allow queries to cause them to execute arbitrary commands.

---

[*] People who have been on the Internet a long time may remember when everybody who was anybody on the Internet was in the NIC database, but there isn't enough room for everybody anymore.

Real-Time Conferencing Services

There are a number of different real-time conferencing services available on the Internet, including *talk*, IRC, and the various services provided over the Multicast Backbone (MBONE). All of these services provide a way for people to interact with other people, as opposed to with databases or information archives. Electronic mail and Usenet news are designed to facilitate asynchronous communications; they work even if the participants aren't currently logged in. The next time they log in, the email messages or news postings will be waiting for them. Real-time conferencing services, on the other hand, are designed for interactive use by on-line participants.

talk is the oldest real-time conferencing system used on the Internet. It is available on most UNIX machines and allows two people to hold a conversation. A user initiates a *talk* session by issuing the command "talk other-user@host", specifying the other user's address in basically the same way as their email address. The other user gets a message on his screen that says "so-and-so is requesting a talk session" and explaining how to answer. When the contacted user answers (the equivalent of picking up the phone when someone calls you), *talk* finishes establishing the connection between the caller and the contacted user; both users see a split screen, where what they type appears in the top half of the screen, and what the other user types appears in the bottom half.

talk is not widely used between strangers on the Internet, although it is often used between colleagues or friends at different sites (or even different parts of the same building). Some people find it convenient, useful, or enjoyable to keep a window open with a *talk* session to a colleague (or a friend) while they work; it's less intrusive than a phone call, and allows you to convey textual information—commands to be run, output from commands cut-and-pasted for the other user to see, etc.—more conveniently than over the phone. There aren't really any network security implications for *talk* itself; the only issue is that it can be very tricky to allow across a firewall without unintentionally opening other security holes, as we describe in Chapter 8.

Internet Relay Chat (IRC) is sort of like Citizens Band (CB) radio on the Internet; it has its own little culture involving lots of people talking at each other. Users access IRC via dedicated IRC clients, or by using Telnet to access a site that provides public IRC client service. IRC servers provide hundreds (sometimes thousands) of named "channels" for users to join. These channels come and go (anyone can create a new channel, and a channel survives as long as there's anyone on it), although some popular channels are more or less permanent. Unlike *talk*, which is limited to a pair of users, any number of people can participate on an IRC channel simultaneously. Some IRC clients allow a user to participate in multiple channels simultaneously (sort of like taking part in two different conversations at once at a party).

There are a number of security problems with IRC; most of the problems aren't with the protocol itself, but with the clients, and with who uses IRC and how. Many of the clients allow servers far more access to local resources (files, processes, programs, etc.) than is wise; a malicious server can wreak havoc with a weak client. Further, many of the most frequent users of IRC are pranksters and crackers who use IRC to pass technical information among themselves, and to try to trick other IRC users. Their idea of a fine time is to tell some neophyte IRC user "Hey, give this command to your IRC client so that I can show you this neat new toy I wrote." Then, when the unsuspecting user follows the prankster's directions, the commands trash the system. Anyone using IRC needs a good client program and a healthy dose of wariness and suspicion.

The Multicast Backbone (MBONE) is the source of a new set of services on the Internet, focusing on expanding real-time conference services beyond text-based services like *talk* and IRC to include audio, video, and electronic whiteboard. The MBONE is still in its infancy, but it is already used to send real-time video of many technical conferences and programs over the Internet, e.g., Internet Engineering Task Force meetings, keynote sessions from USENIX conferences, space shuttle flight operations, and so on. At this point, the commonly used MBONE services appear to be reasonably secure. Unintentional denial of service can be a real concern with the MBONE, however, because audio and video use so much memory. The methods used to distribute MBONE across the Internet also present some interesting risks, which are discussed in Chapter 8.

Name Service

Name service is what translates between the host names that people use and the numerical IP addresses that machines use. In the early days of the Internet, it was possible for every site to maintain a host table that listed the name and number for every machine on the Internet that they might ever care about. With millions of hosts attached, it isn't practical for any single site to maintain a list of them, much less for every site to do so. Instead, the Domain Name Service (DNS) allows each site to maintain information about its own hosts, and be able to find the information for other sites. DNS isn't a user-level service, per se, but it underlies SMTP, FTP, Telnet, and virtually every other service users need, because users want to be able to type "telnet fictional.com" rather than "telnet 10.100.242.32". Furthermore, many anonymous FTP servers will not allow connections from clients unless they can use DNS to look up the client host's name, so that it can be logged.

The net result is that you must both use and provide name service in order to participate in the Internet. The main risk in providing DNS service is that you may give away more information than you intend. For example, DNS lets you include information about what hardware and software you're running, information that you don't want an attacker to have. In fact, you may not even want an attacker to know the names of all your internal machines. Chapter 8 discusses how to configure name service in order to make full information available to your internal hosts, but only partial information to external inquirers.

Using DNS internally and then relying on host names for authentication makes you vulnerable to an intruder who can install a lying DNS server. This can be handled by a combination of methods, including:

- Using IP addresses (rather than hostnames) for authentication on services that need to be more secure.

- Authenticating users instead of hosts on the most secure services, because IP addresses can also be spoofed.

Some sites use Sun's Network Information Service, formerly known as Yellow Pages (NIS/YP) to distribute hostname information internally. It is not necessary to do this: you can use DNS clients instead on any platform that supports NIS/YP; but it may be more convenient for configuring your internal machines. It is certainly neither necessary nor advisable to provide NIS/YP service to external machines. NIS/YP is designed to administer a single site, not to exchange information between sites, and it is highly insecure. For example, it would not be possible to provide your host information to external sites via NIS/YP without also providing your password file, if both are available internally.

Network Management Services

There are a variety of services that are used to manage and maintain networks; these are services that most users don't use directly—indeed, that many of them have never even heard of—but they are very important tools for network managers.

The two most common network management tools are *ping* and *traceroute*. Both are named after the UNIX programs that were the first implementations, but both are now available in some form on almost all Internet-capable platforms. They do not have their own protocols, but make use of the same underlying protocol, the Internet Control Message Protocol (ICMP). Unlike most of the programs we've discussed, they are not clients of distinguishable servers. ICMP is implemented at a low level as a required part of the TCP/IP protocols all Internet hosts use.

ping simply tests reachability; it tells you whether or not you can get a packet to and from a given host, and often additional information like how long it took the packet to make the round trip. *traceroute* tells you not only whether you can reach a given host (and whether it can answer), but also the route your packets take to get to that host; this is very useful in analyzing and debugging network trouble somewhere between you and some destination.

Because there aren't servers for *ping* and *traceroute*, you can't simply decide not to turn the servers on. It's possible to use packet filtering to prevent the packets from being transmitted from your site or received at your site, but it's usually not necessary. There are no known risks for outbound *ping* or *traceroute*, and very few for inbound *ping* and *traceroute*. They can be used for denial of service attacks, but no more so than other protocols. More threateningly, they can be used to determine which hosts at your site exist, as a preliminary step to attacking them. For this reason, many sites either prevent or limit the relevant packets inbound.

Simple Network Management Protocol (SNMP) is a protocol designed to make it easy to centrally manage network equipment (routers, bridges, concentrators, hubs, and, to a certain extent, even hosts). SNMP management stations can request information (whether a given interface is up or down, how many bytes have been moved through that interface, how many errors there have been on that interface, etc.) from network equipment via SNMP. SNMP management stations can also control certain functions of the network equipment (taking an interface up or down, setting its parameters, and so on). The network equipment can also report urgent information (for example, that a line has gone down, or that there are a significant number of errors occurring on a given line) to SNMP management stations via SNMP. The major security risk with SNMP is that someone else might be able to take over control of your network equipment and reconfigure it for their purposes (disabling packet filtering, changing routing, or simply trashing your configuration).

Time Service

Network Time Protocol (NTP) is an Internet service that sets the clocks on your system with great precision. Synchronizing time among different machines is important in many ways. From a security point of view, examining the precise times noted on the log files of different machines may help in analyzing patterns of break-ins. Having synchronized clocks is also a requirement for preventing attackers from recording an interaction and then repeating it (a playback attack); if time stamps are encoded in the interaction, they will be incorrect the second time the transaction is replayed. Kerberos authentication, for example, which we discuss in Chapter 10, depends on time synchronization. From a practical point of view, synchronized clocks are also required to successfully use NFS.

You do not have to use NTP across the Internet; it will synchronize clocks to each other within your site, if that's all you want. The reason that people use NTP from the Internet is that a number of hosts with extremely accurate clocks—radio clocks that receive the time signal from the United States master atomic clocks or from the atomic clocks in the Global Positioning System (GPS) satellites—provide NTP service to make certain that your clocks are not only synchronous with each other but also correct. Without an external time service, you might find that all your computers have exactly the same wrong time. Accepting an external service makes you vulnerable to spoofing, but because NTP won't move the clocks very far very fast, a spoofed external clock is unlikely to make you vulnerable to a playback attack, although it could succeed in annoying you by running all your clocks slow or fast. Radio clocks suitable for use as NTP time sources are not terribly expensive, however, and if you are using NTP to synchronize clocks for an authentication protocol like Kerberos, you should buy your own and provide all time service internally, instead of using an external reference.

Network File Systems

There are several protocols available for allowing computers to mount filesystems that are physically attached to other computers. This is highly desirable, because it lets people use remote files without the overhead of transferring them back and forth and trying to keep multiple versions in sync. It's also extremely dangerous, because it means that you're allowing people to read your data without separately authenticating themselves to the machine that the data is on. The Network File System (NFS) and the Andrew File System (AFS) are the two most frequently used network file systems in UNIX. NFS was designed for use in local area networks, and assumes fast response, high reliability, time synchronization, and a high degree of trust between machines. AFS was designed for use across larger networks, and better tolerates poor performance and lower degrees of trust.

There are some serious security problems with NFS. If you haven't properly configured NFS (which can be tricky), an attacker may be able to simply NFS-mount your filesystems. The way NFS works, client machines are allowed to read and change files stored on the server without having to log in to the server or enter a password. Because NFS doesn't log transactions, you might not even know that someone else has full access to your files.

NFS does provide a way for you to control which machines can access your files. A file called */etc/exports* lets you specify which filesystems can be mounted, and which machines can mount them. If you leave a filesystem out of */etc/exports,* no machine can mount it. If you put it in */etc/exports,* but don't specify what machines can mount it, you're allowing any machine to mount it.

A number of subtler attacks on NFS are also possible. For example, NFS has very weak client authentication, and an attacker may be able to convince the NFS server that a request is coming from a client that's permitted in the *exports* file. There are also situations where an attacker can hijack an existing NFS mount.

These problems are mostly due to the fact that NFS uses host authentication, which is easily spoofed. Because NFS doesn't actually work well across the Internet in any case (it assumes a much faster connection between hosts), there isn't much point in allowing it between your site and the Internet. It creates a security problem without adding functionality.

AFS uses Kerberos for authentication, and optionally encryption, and is designed to work across wide area networks, including the Internet. NFS is shipped as part of the operating system with most versions of UNIX, while AFS is a third-party product. Because of this, and because AFS and Kerberos require significant technical expertise to set up and maintain, AFS is not widely used outside of a small number of large sites. If you have a need to do secure, wide area network filesystems, it may be worth investigating AFS, but it is not covered here.

Window Systems

Most UNIX machines currently provide window systems based on the X11 window system. Network access is an important feature of X11. As more and more programs have graphical user interfaces, remote terminal access becomes less and less useful; you need graphics, not just text. X11 gives you remote graphics. Unfortunately, it does this by providing complete access to all of the capabilities it gives you when you are sitting in front of the machine.

X11 servers are tempting targets for intruders. An intruder with access to an X11 server may be able to do any of the following types of damage:

Get screen dumps
These are copies of whatever is shown on the users' screens.

Read keystrokes
These may include users' passwords.

Inject keystrokes
They'll look just as if they were typed by the user. Imagine how dangerous this could be in a window in which a user is running a root shell.

By default, X11 servers use address-based authentication if they use any authentication at all; many users disable this feature in the name of convenience. X11, therefore, isn't safe to use across the Internet. The server does provide the option of using stronger authentication, but most clients aren't capable of using it, and it is thus rarely turned on. In practice, it usually prevents anybody from authenticating.

Printing Systems

Both *lp*, the System V printing system, and *lpr*, the Berkeley Software Distribution (BSD) printing system, provide remote printing options. These allow a computer to print to a printer that is physically connected to a different computer. Obviously, in a local area network this is highly desirable; you shouldn't need as many printers as you have machines. However, the remote printing options are both insecure and inefficient as ways to transfer data across the Internet. There is no reason to allow them. If you have a need to print at a site across the Internet, or to allow another site to use your printers, it's possible to set up special mail aliases that print the mail on receipt. This is the method many companies use even across in-house wide-area networks because it's considerably more reliable.

In This Chapter:
- *Least Privilege*
- *Defense in Depth*
- *Choke Point*
- *Weakest Link*
- *Fail-Safe Stance*
- *Universal Participation*
- *Diversity of Defense*
- *Simplicity*

3

Security Strategies

Before we discuss the details of firewalls, it's important to understand some of the basic strategies employed in building firewalls and in enforcing security at your site. These are not staggering revelations; they are straightforward approaches. They're presented here so that you can keep them in mind as you put together a firewall solution for your site.

Least Privilege

Perhaps the most fundamental principle of security (any kind of security, not just computer and network security) is that of *least privilege*. Basically, the principle of least privilege means that any object (user, administrator, program, system, whatever) should have only the privileges the object needs to perform its assigned tasks—and no more. Least privilege is an important principle for limiting your exposure to attacks and for limiting the damage caused by particular attacks.

Some car manufacturers set up their locks so that one key works the doors and the ignition, and a different key works the glove compartment and the trunk; that way, you can enforce least privilege by giving a parking lot attendant the ability to park the car without the ability to get at things stored in the trunk. Many people use splittable key chains, for the same reason. You can enforce least privilege by giving someone the key to your car, but not the key to your house as well.

In the Internet context, the examples are endless. Every user probably doesn't need to access every Internet service. Every user probably doesn't need to modify (or even read) every file on your system. Every user probably doesn't need to know the machine's root password. Every system administrator probably doesn't need to know the root passwords for all systems. Every system probably doesn't need to access every other system's files.

Applying the principle of least privilege suggests that you should explore ways to reduce the privileges required for various operations. For example:

- Don't give a user the root password for a system if all she needs to do is reset the print system. Instead, write a privileged program the user can run that resets the print system.

- Don't make a program run *setuid* to root if all it needs to do is write to one protected file. Instead, make the file group-writable to some group and make the program run *setgid* to that group rather than *setuid* to root.

- Don't have your internal systems trust one of your firewall machines just so it can do backups. Instead, make the firewall machine trust the internal system, or, better yet, put a local tape drive on the firewall machine so that it can do its own backups.

Many of the common security problems on the Internet can be viewed as failures to follow the principle of least privilege. For example, there have been and continue to be any number of security problems discovered in Sendmail, which is a big, complex program; any such program is going to have bugs in it. The problem is that Sendmail runs (at least some of the time) *setuid* to root; many of the attacks against Sendmail take advantage of this. Because it runs as root, Sendmail is a high-value target that gets a lot of attention from attackers; the fact that it's a complex program just makes their jobs easier. This implies both that privileged programs should be as simple as possible and that, if a complex program requires privileges, you should look for ways to separate and isolate the pieces that need privileges from the complex parts.[*]

Many of the solutions you'll employ in protecting your site are tactics for enforcing the strategy of least privilege. For example, a packet filtering system is designed to allow in packets for the services you want. Running insecure programs in an environment where only the privileges the programs absolutely need are available to them (e.g., a machine that's been stripped down in one way or another) is another example; this is the essence of a bastion host.

There are two problems with trying to enforce least privilege. First, it can be complex to implement when it isn't already a design feature of the programs and protocols you're using. Trying to add it on may be very difficult to get right. Some of the cars that try to implement least privilege with separate keys for the trunk and the ignition have remote trunk release buttons that are accessible without the keys, or fold-down rear seats that allow you to access the trunk without opening it the traditional way at all. You need to be very careful to be sure that you've actually succeeded in implementing least privilege.

Second, you may end up implementing something less than least privilege. Some cars have the gas cap release in the glove compartment. That's intended to keep parking lot attendants from siphoning off your gas, but if you lend a friend your car, you probably want them to be able to fill it up with gas. If you give your friend only the ignition key, you're giving them less than the minimum privilege

---

* It's important to realize that Sendmail is far from the only example we could cite; you can find similar problems in almost any large, complex, privileged piece of software.

you want them to have (because they won't be able to fill up the gas tank), but adding the key to the trunk and the glove compartment may give them more privilege than you want them to have.

You may find similar effects with computer implementations of least privilege. Trying to enforce least privilege on people, rather than programs, can be particularly dangerous. You can predict fairly well what permissions Sendmail is going to need to do its job; human beings are less predictable, and more likely to become annoyed and dangerous if they can't do what they want to. Be very careful to avoid turning your users into your enemies.

Defense in Depth

Another principle of security (again, any kind of security) is *defense in depth*. Don't depend on just one security mechanism, however strong it may seem to be; instead, install multiple mechanisms that back each other up. You don't want the failure of any single security mechanism to totally compromise your security. You can see applications of this principle in other aspects of your life. For example, your front door probably has both a doorknob lock and a deadbolt; your car probably has both a door lock and an ignition lock; and so on.

Although our focus in this book is on firewalls, we don't pretend that firewalls are a complete solution to the whole range of Internet security problems. Any security—even the most seemingly impenetrable firewall—can be breached by attackers who are willing to take enough risk and bring enough power to bear. The trick is to make the attempt too risky or too expensive for the attackers you expect to face. You can do this by adopting multiple mechanisms that provide backup and redundancy for each other: network security (a firewall), host security (particularly for your bastion host), and human security (user education, careful system administration, etc.). All of these mechanisms are important and can be highly effective, but don't place absolute faith in any one of them.

Your firewall itself will probably have multiple layers. For example, one architecture has multiple packet filters; it's set up that way because the two filters need to do different things, but it's quite common to set up the second one to reject packets that the first one is supposed to have rejected already. If the first filter is working properly, those packets will never reach the second; however, if there's some problem with the first, then hopefully you'll still be protected by the second. Here's another example: if you don't want people sending mail to a machine, don't just filter out the packets, also remove the mail programs from the machine. In situations where the cost is low, you should always employ redundant defenses.

Choke Point

A *choke point* forces attackers to use a narrow channel, which you can monitor and control. There are probably many examples of choke points in your life: the toll booth on a bridge, the check-out line at the supermarket, the ticket booth at a movie theatre.

In network security, the firewall between your site and the Internet (assuming that it's the only connection between your site and the Internet) is such a choke point; anyone who's going to attack your site from the Internet is going to have to come through that channel, which should be defended against such attacks. You should be watching carefully for such attacks and be prepared to respond if you see them.

A choke point is useless if there's an effective way for an attacker to go around it. Why bother attacking the fortified front door if the kitchen door around back is wide open? Similarly, from a network security point of view, why bother attacking the firewall if there are dozens or hundreds of unsecured dial-up lines that could be attacked more easily and probably more successfully?

A second Internet connection—even an indirect one, like a connection to another company which has its own Internet connection elsewhere—is an even more threatening breach. Internet-based attackers might not have a modem available, or might not have gotten around to acquiring phone service they don't need to pay for, but they can certainly find even roundabout Internet connections to your site.

A choke point may seem to be putting all your eggs in one basket, and therefore a bad idea, but the key is that it's a basket you can guard carefully. The alternative is to split your attention among many different possible avenues of attack. If you split your attention in this way, chances are that you won't be able to do an adequate job of defending any of the avenues of attack, or that someone will slip through one while you're busy defending another (where they may even have staged a diversion specifically to draw your attention away from their real attack).

Weakest Link

A fundamental tenet of security is that a chain is only as strong as its *weakest link* and a wall is only as strong as its weakest point. Smart attackers are going to seek out that weak point and concentrate their attentions there. You need to be aware of the weak points of your defense so that you can take steps to eliminate them, and so that you can carefully monitor those you can't eliminate. You should try to pay attention evenly to all aspects of your security, so that there is no large difference in how insecure one thing is as compared to another.

There is always going to be a weakest link, however; the trick is to make that link strong enough and to keep the strength proportional to the risk. For instance, it's usually reasonable to worry more about people attacking you over the network than about people actually coming to your site to attack you physically; therefore you can usually allow your physical security to be your weakest link. It's not reasonable to neglect physical security altogether, however, because there's still some threat there. It's also not reasonable, for example, to protect Telnet connections very carefully, but not protect FTP connections, because of the similarities of the risks posed by those services.

Host security models suffer from a particularly nasty interaction between choke points and weak links; there's no choke point, which means that there are a very large number of links, and many of them may be very weak indeed.

Fail-Safe Stance

Another fundamental principle of security is that, to the extent possible, systems should *fail safe*; that is, if they're going to fail, they should fail in such a way that they deny access to an attacker, rather than letting the attacker in. The failure may also result in denying access to legitimate users as well, until repairs are made, but this is usually an acceptable tradeoff.

Safe failures are another principle with wide application in familiar places. Electrical devices are designed to go off—to stop—when they fail in almost any way. Elevators are designed to grip their cables if they're not being powered. Electric door locks generally unlock when the power fails, to avoid trapping people in buildings.

Most of the applications we discuss automatically fail safely. For example, if a packet filtering router goes down, it doesn't let any packets in. If a proxying program goes down, it provides no service. On the other hand, some host-based packet filtering systems are designed such that packets are allowed to arrive at a machine that runs a packet filtering application and separately runs applications providing services. The way some of these systems work, if the packet filtering application crashes (or is never started at boot time), the packets will be delivered to the applications providing services. This is not a fail-safe design and should be avoided.

The biggest application of this principle in network security is in choosing your site's *stance* with respect to security. Your stance is, essentially, your site's overall attitude towards security. Do you lean towards being restrictive or permissive? Are you more inclined to err in the direction of safety (some might call it paranoia) or freedom?

There are two fundamental stances that you can take with respect to security decisions and policies:

- The default deny stance: Specify only what you allow and prohibit everything else.

- The default permit stance: Specify only what you prohibit and allow everything else.

It may seem obvious to you which of these is the "right" approach to take; from a security point of view, it's the default deny stance. Probably, it will also seem obvious to your users and management; from their point of view, it's the default permit stance. It's important to make your stance clear to users and management, as well as to explain the reasons behind that stance. Otherwise, you're likely to spend a lot of unproductive time in conflict with them, wondering "How could they be so foolish as to even suggest that?" time and again, simply because they don't understand the security point of view.

Default Deny Stance: That Which Is Not Expressly Permitted Is Prohibited

The *default deny stance* makes sense from a security point of view because it is a fail-safe stance. It recognizes that what you don't know *can* hurt you. It's the obvious choice for most security people, but it's usually not at all obvious to users.

With the default deny stance, you prohibit everything by default; then, to determine what you are going to allow, you:

- Examine the services your users want.

- Consider the security implications of these services and how you can safely provide them.

- Allow only the services that you understand, can provide safely, and see a legitimate need for.

Services are enabled on a case-by-case basis. You start by analyzing the security of a specific service, and balance its security implications against the needs of your users. Based on that analysis and the availability of various remedies to improve the security of the service, you settle on an appropriate compromise.

For one service, you might determine that you should provide the service to all users and can do so safely with commonly available packet filtering or proxy systems. For another service, you might determine that the service cannot be adequately secured by any currently available means, but that only a small number of your users or systems require it. In the latter case, perhaps its use can be restricted to that small set of users (who can be made aware of the risks through special training) or systems (which you may be able to protect in other ways; e.g., through host security). The whole key is to find a compromise that is appropriate to your particular situation.

Default Permit Stance:
That Which Is Not Expressly Prohibited Is Permitted

Most users and managers prefer the *default permit stance*. They tend to assume that everything will be, by default, permitted, and that certain specific, troublesome actions and services will then be prohibited as necessary. For example:

- NFS is not permitted across the firewall.

- WWW access is restricted to users who have received awareness training about its security problems.

- Users are not allowed to set up unauthorized servers.

They want you to tell them what's dangerous; to itemize those few (they think) things that they can't do, and to let them do everything else. This is definitely not a fail-safe stance.

First, it assumes that you know ahead of time precisely what the specific dangers are, how to explain them so users will understand them, and how to guard against them. Trying to guess what dangers might be in a system or out there on the Internet is essentially an impossible task. There are simply too many possible problems, and too much information (e.g., new security holes, new exploitations of old holes, etc.) to be able to keep up to date. If you don't know that something is a problem, it won't be on your "prohibited" list. In that case, it will go right on being a problem until you notice it and you'll probably notice it because somebody takes advantage of it.

Second, the default permit stance tends to degenerate into an escalating "arms race" between the firewall maintainer and the users. The maintainer prepares defenses against user action or inaction (or, he just keeps saying, "Don't do that!"); the users come up with fascinating new and insecure ways of doing things; and the process repeats, again and again. The maintainer is forever playing catch up. Inevitably, there are going to be periods of vulnerability between the time that a system is set up, the time that a security problem is discovered, and the time that the maintainer is able to respond to the problem. No matter how vigilant and cooperative everyone may be, some things are going to fall through the cracks forever: because the maintainer has never heard about them, because he has never realized the full security consequences; or because he just plain hasn't had time to work on the problem.

About the only people who benefit from the default permit stance are potential attackers, because the firewall maintainer can't possibly close all the holes, is forever stuck in "fire fighting" mode, and is likely to be far too busy to notice an attacker's activities.

For example, consider the problem of sharing files with collaborators at another site. Your users' first idea will probably be to use the same tool that they use to share files internally—NFS. The problem is, NFS is completely unsafe to allow across a firewall (for reasons discussed in Chapter 2 and Chapter 8). Suppose that your stance is a permissive one, and you haven't specifically told your users that it's not safe to run NFS across your firewall (or even if you have told them, but don't remember or don't care). In this case, you're probably going to find yourself running NFS across your firewall because it seemed like a good idea to somebody who didn't understand (or care about) the security issues. If your stance is default deny, on the other hand, your users' attempts to set up NFS will fail. You'll need to explain why to them, suggest alternatives that are more secure (such as FTP), and look for ways to make those more secure alternatives easier to use without sacrificing security.

Universal Participation

In order to be fully effective, most security systems require the *universal participation* (or at least the absence of active opposition) of a site's personnel. If someone can simply opt out of your security mechanisms, then an attacker may be able to attack you by first attacking that exempt person's system and then attacking your site from the inside. For example, the best firewall in the world won't protect you if someone who sees it as an unreasonable burden sets up a back-door connection between your site and the Internet in order to circumvent the firewall. This can be as easy as buying a modem, obtaining free PPP or SLIP software off the Internet, and paying a few dollars a month to a local low-end Internet service provider; this is well within the price range and technical abilities of many users and managers.

Much more mundane forms of rebellion will still ruin your security. You need everybody to report strange happenings that might be security-related; you can't see everything. You need people to choose good passwords; to change them regularly; and not to give them out to their friends, relatives, and pets.

How do you get everyone to participate? Participation might be voluntary (you convince everybody that it's a good idea) or involuntary (someone with appropriate authority and power tells them to cooperate or else), or some combination of the two. Obviously, voluntary participation is strongly preferable to involuntary participation; you want folks helping you, not looking for ways to get around you. This means that you may have to work as an evangelist within your organization, selling folks on the benefits of security and convincing them that the benefits outweigh the costs.

People who are not voluntary participants will go to amazing lengths to circumvent security measures. On one voicemail system that required passwords to be changed every month, numerous people discovered that it recorded only six old passwords, and took to changing their passwords seven times in a row (in seven separate phone calls!) in order to be able to use the same password. This sort of behavior leads to an arms race (the programmers limit the number of times you can change your password), and soon numerous people are sucked into a purely internal battle. You have better things to do with your time, as do your users; it's worth spending a lot of energy to convince people to cooperate voluntarily, because you'll often spend just as much to force them, with worse side effects.

Diversity of Defense

Just as you may get additional security from using a number of different systems to provide depth of defense, you may also get additional security from using a number of different types of systems. If all of your systems are the same, somebody who knows how to break into one of them probably knows how to break into all of them.

The idea behind *diversity of defense* is that using security systems from different vendors may reduce the chances of a common bug or configuration error that compromises them all. There is a tradeoff in terms of complexity and cost, however. Procuring and installing multiple different systems is going to be more difficult, take longer, and be more expensive than procuring and installing a single system (or even several identical systems). You're going to have to buy the multiple systems (at reduced discounts from each vendor, because you're buying less from them) and multiple support contracts to cover them. It's also going to take additional time and effort for your staff to learn how to deal with these different systems.

Beware of illusionary diversity. Simply using different vendors' UNIX systems probably won't buy you diversity, because most UNIX systems are derived from either the BSD or System V source code. Further, most common UNIX networking applications (such as Sendmail, *telnet/telnetd, ftp/ftpd,* and so on), are derived from the BSD sources, regardless of whether they're on a BSD- or System V-based platform. There were any number of bugs and security problems in the original releases that were propagated into most of the various vendor-specific versions of these operating systems; many vendor-specific versions of UNIX still have bugs and security problems that were first discovered years ago in other versions from other vendors, and have not yet been fixed.

Also beware that diverse systems configured by the same person (or group of people) may share common problems if the problems stem from conceptual rather than technological roots. If the problem is a misunderstanding about how a particular protocol works, for example, your diverse systems may all be configured incorrectly in the same way according to that misunderstanding.

Although many sites acknowledge that using multiple types of systems could potentially increase their security, they often conclude that diversity of defense is more trouble than it's worth, and that the potential gains and security improvements aren't worth the costs. We don't dispute this; each site needs to make its own evaluation and decision concerning this issue.

Simplicity

Simplicity is a security strategy for two reasons. First, keeping things simple makes them easier to understand; if you don't understand something, you can't really know whether or not it's secure. Second, complexity provides nooks and crannies for all sorts of things to hide in; it's easier to secure a studio apartment than a mansion.

Complex programs have more bugs, any of which may be security problems. Even if bugs aren't in and of themselves security problems, once people start to expect a given system to behave erratically, they'll accept almost anything from it, which kills any hope of their recognizing and reporting security problems with it when these problems do arise.

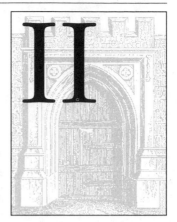

Building
Firewalls

Part II describes how to build firewalls and configure services to run with them.

Chapter 4, *Firewall Design*, outlines the basic components and major architectures used in constructing firewalls—dual-homed hosts, screened hosts, screened sub-nets, and variations on these basic architectures.

Chapter 5, *Bastion Hosts*, presents step-by-step instructions for designing and building the bastion hosts used in many firewall configurations.

Chapter 6, *Packet Filtering*, describes how packet filtering systems work and dis-cusses what you can and can't accomplish with them when building a firewall.

Chapter 7, *Proxy Systems*, describes how proxy clients and servers work and how to use these systems in building a firewall.

Chapter 8, *Configuring Internet Services*, describes how to configure each major Internet service to run with a firewall.

Chapter 9, *Two Simple Firewalls*, presents two sample configurations for basic fire-walls.

Chapter 10, *Authentication and Inbound Services*, discusses the problem of allow-ing users to access your systems from the Internet and describes a variety of authentication strategies and products.

In This Chapter:
- *Some Firewall Definitions*
- *Firewall Architectures*
- *Variations on Firewall Architectures*
- *Internal Firewalls*
- *What the Future Holds*

4

Firewall Design

In Chapter 1, we introduced Internet firewalls and summarized what they can and cannot do to improve network security. In this chapter, we present major firewalls concepts. What are the terms you will hear in discussions of Internet firewalls? What types of firewall architectures are used at sites today? What are the components that can be put together to build these common firewall architectures? In the remaining chapters of this book, we'll describe these components and architectures in detail.

Some Firewall Definitions

You may be familiar with some of the firewall terms listed below, and some may be new to you. Some may seem familiar, but they may be used in a way that is slightly different from what you're accustomed to (though we try to use terms that are as standard as possible). Unfortunately, there is no completely consistent terminology for firewall architectures and components. Different people use terms in different—or, worse still, conflicting—ways. Also, these same terms sometimes have other meanings in other networking fields; the definitions below are for a firewalls context.

These are very basic definitions; we describe these terms in greater detail elsewhere.

Firewall
> A component or set of components that restricts access between a protected network and the Internet, or between other sets of networks.

Host

    A computer system attached to a network.

Bastion host

    A computer system that must be highly secured because it is vulnerable to attack, usually because it is exposed to the Internet and is a main point of contact for users of internal networks. It gets its name from the highly fortified projections on the outer walls of medieval castles.[*]

Dual-homed host

    A general-purpose computer system that has at least two network interfaces (or homes)

Packet

    The fundamental unit of communication on the Internet.

Packet filtering

    The action a device takes to selectively control the flow of data to and from a network. Packet filters allow or block packets, usually while routing them from one network to another (most often from the Internet to an internal network, and vice versa). To accomplish packet filtering, you set up a set of rules that specify what types of packets (e.g., those to or from a particular IP address or port) are to be allowed and what types are to be blocked. Packet filtering may occur in a router, in a bridge, or on an individual host. It is sometimes known as *screening*.[†]

Perimeter network

    A network added between a protected network and an external network, in order to provide an additional layer of security. A perimeter network is sometimes called a *DMZ*, which stands for *De-Militarized Zone* (named after the zone separating North and South Korea).

Proxy server

    A program that deals with external servers on behalf of internal clients. Proxy clients talk to proxy servers, which relay approved client requests on to real servers, and relay answers back to clients.

The next few sections briefly describe packet filtering and proxy services, two major approaches used to build firewalls today.

---

[*] Marcus Ranum, who is generally held responsible for the popularity of this term in the firewalls professional community, says, "Bastions . . . overlook critical areas of defense, usually having stronger walls, room for extra troops, and the occasional useful tub of boiling hot oil for discouraging attackers."

[†] Some networking literature (in particular, the BSD UNIX release from Berkeley) uses the term "packet filtering" to refer to something else entirely (selecting certain packets off a network for analysis, as is done by the *etherfind* or *tcpdump* programs).

Packet Filtering

Packet filtering systems route packets betweeen internal and external hosts, but they do it selectively. They allow or block certain types of packets in a way that reflects a site's own security policy as shown in Figure 4-1. The type of router used in a packet filtering firewall is known as a *screening router*.

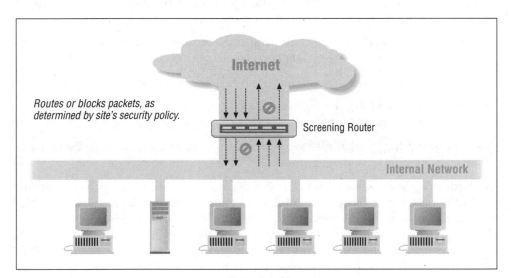

Figure 4-1: Using a screening router to do packet filtering

As we discuss in Chapter 6, every packet has a set of headers containing certain information. The main information is:

- IP source address
- IP destination address
- Protocol (whether the packet is a TCP, UDP, or ICMP packet)
- TCP or UDP source port
- TCP or UDP destination port
- ICMP message type

In addition, the router knows things about the packet that aren't reflected in the packet headers, such as:

- The interface the packet arrives on
- The interface the packet will go out on

The fact that servers for particular Internet services reside at certain port numbers lets the router block or allow certain types of connections simply by specifying the appropriate port number (e.g., TCP port 23 for Telnet connections) in the set of rules specified for packet filtering. (Chapter 6 describes in detail how you construct these rules.)

Here are some examples of ways in which you might program a screening router to selectively route packets to or from your site:

- Block all incoming connections from systems outside the internal network, except for incoming SMTP connections (so that you can receive email).

- Block all connections to or from certain systems you distrust.

- Allow email and FTP services, but block dangerous services like TFTP, the X Window System, RPC, and the "r" services (*rlogin, rsh, rcp*, etc.).

To understand how packet filtering works, let's look at the difference between an ordinary router and a screening router.

An ordinary router simply looks at the destination address of each packet and picks the best way it knows to send that packet towards that destination. The decision about how to handle the packet is based solely on its destination. There are two possibilities: the router knows how to send the packet towards its destination, and it does so; or the router does not know how to send the packet towards its destination, and it returns the packet, via an ICMP "destination unreachable" message, to its source.

A screening router, on the other hand, looks at packets more closely. In addition to determining whether or not it *can* route a packet towards its destination, a screening router also determines whether or not it *should.* "Should" or "should not" are determined by the site's security policy, which the screening router has been configured to enforce.

Although it is possible for only a screening router to sit between an internal network and the Internet, as shown in Figure 4-1, this places an enormous responsibility on the screening router. Not only does it need to perform all routing and routing decision-making, but it is the only protecting system; if its security fails (or crumbles under attack), the internal network is exposed. Furthermore, a straightforward screening router can't modify services. A screening router can permit or deny a service, but it can't protect individual operations within a service. If a desirable service has insecure operations, or if the service is normally provided with an insecure server, packet filtering alone can't protect it.

A number of other architectures have evolved to provide additional security in packet filtering firewall implementations. Later in this chapter, we show the way that additional routers, bastion hosts, and perimeter networks may be added to the firewall implementations in the screened host and screened subnet architectures.

Proxy Services

Proxy services are specialized application or server programs that run on a firewall host: either a dual-homed host with an interface on the internal network and one on the external network, or some other bastion host that has access to the Internet and is accessible from the internal machines. These programs take users' requests for Internet services (such as FTP and Telnet) and forward them, as appropriate according to the site's security policy, to the actual services. The proxies provide replacement connections and act as gateways to the services. For this reason, proxies are sometimes known as *application-level gateways.**

Proxy services sit, more or less transparently, between a user on the inside (on the internal network) and a service on the outside (on the Internet). Instead of talking to each other directly, each talks to a proxy. Proxies handle all the communication between users and Internet services behind the scenes.

Transparency is the major benefit of proxy services. It's essentially smoke and mirrors. To the user, a proxy server presents the illusion that the user is dealing directly with the real server. To the real server, the proxy server presents the illusion that the real server is dealing directly with a user on the proxy host (as opposed to the user's real host).

NOTE

> Proxy services are effective only when they're used in conjunction with a mechanism that restricts direct communications between the internal and external hosts. Dual-homed hosts and packet filtering are two such mechanisms. If internal hosts are able to communicate directly with external hosts, there's no need for users to use proxy services, and so (in general) they won't. Such a bypass probably isn't in accordance with your security policy.

How do proxy services work? Let's look at the simplest case, where we add proxy services to a dual-homed host. (We'll describe these hosts in some detail in "Dual-Homed Host Architectures" later in this chapter.)

As Figure 4-2 shows, a proxy service requires two components: a proxy server and a proxy client. In this situation, the *proxy server* runs on the dual-homed host. A *proxy client* is a special version of a normal client program (i.e., a Telnet or FTP client) that talks to the proxy server rather than to the "real" server out on the Internet; in addition, if users are taught special procedures to follow, normal client programs can often be used as proxy clients. The proxy server evaluates requests from the proxy client, and decides which to approve and which to deny. If a

---

* Firewall terminologies differ. Whereas we use the term *proxy service* to encompass the entire proxy approach, other authors refer to *application-level gateways* and *circuit-level gateways.* Although there are small differences between the meanings of these various terms, which we'll explore in Chapter 7, in general our discussion of proxies refers to the same type of technology other authors mean when they refer to these gateway systems.

request is approved, the proxy server contacts the real server on behalf of the client (thus the term "proxy"), and proceeds to relay requests from the proxy client to the real server, and responses from the real server to the proxy client.

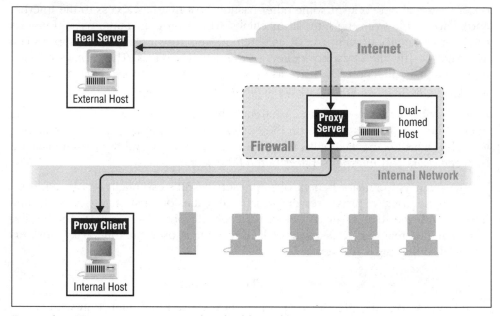

Figure 4–2: Using proxy services with a dual-homed host

In some proxy systems, instead of installing custom client proxy software, you'll use standard software, but set up custom user procedures for using it. (We'll describe how this works in Chapter 7.)

A proxy service is a software solution, not a firewall architecture per se. You can use proxy services in conjunction with any of the firewall architectures described in the section called "Firewall Architectures" below.

The proxy server doesn't always just forward users' requests on to the real Internet services. The proxy server can control what users do, because it can make decisions about the requests it processes. Depending on your site's security policy, requests might be allowed or refused. For example, the FTP proxy might refuse to let users export files, or it might allow users to import files only from certain sites. More sophisticated proxy services might allow different capabilities to different hosts, rather than enforcing the same restrictions on all hosts.

There is some excellent software available for proxying. SOCKS is a proxy construction toolkit, designed to make it easy to convert existing client/server applications into proxy versions of those same applications. The Trusted Information Systems Internet Firewall Toolkit (TIS FWTK) includes proxy servers for a number of common Internet protocols, including Telnet, FTP, HTTP, *rlogin*, X11, and others; these proxy servers are designed to be used in conjunction with custom user procedures. See the discussion of these packages in Chapter 7.

Many standard client and server programs, both commercial and freely available, now come equipped with their own proxying capabilities, or with support for generic proxy systems like SOCKS. These capabilities can be enabled at run time or compile time.

Using a Combination of Techniques and Technologies

The "right solution" to building a firewall is seldom a single technique; it's usually a carefully crafted combination of techniques to solve different problems. Which problems you need to solve depend on what services you want to provide your users and what level of risk you're willing to accept. Which techniques you use to solve those problems depend on how much time, money, and expertise you have available.

Some protocols (e.g., Telnet and SMTP) can be more effectively handled with packet filtering. Others (e.g., FTP, Archie, Gopher, and WWW) are more effectively handled with proxies. (Chapter 8 describes how to handle specific services in a firewall environment.) Most firewalls use a combination of proxying and packet filtering.

Firewall Architectures

This section describes a variety of ways to put various firewalls components together.

Dual-Homed Host Architecture

A *dual-homed host architecture* is built around the dual-homed host computer, a computer which has at least two network interfaces. Such a host could act as a router between the networks these interfaces are attached to; it is capable of routing IP packets from one network to another. However, to implement a dual-homed host type of firewalls architecture, you disable this routing function. Thus, IP packets from one network (e.g., the Internet) are not directly routed to the other network (e.g., the internal, protected network). Systems inside the firewall can communicate with the dual-homed host, and systems outside the firewall (on the Internet) can communicate with the dual-homed host, but these systems can't communicate directly with each other. IP traffic between them is completely blocked.

The network architecture for a dual-homed host firewall is pretty simple: the dual homed host sits between, and is connected to, the Internet and the internal network. Figure 4-3 shows this architecture.

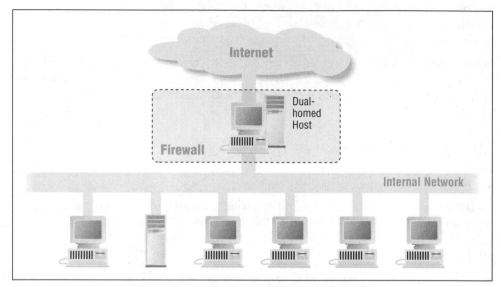

Figure 4-3: Dual-homed host architecture

Dual-homed hosts can provide a very high level of control. If you aren't allowing packets to go between external and internal networks at all, you can be sure that any packet on the internal network that has an external source is evidence of some kind of security problem. In some cases, a dual-homed host will allow you to reject connections that claim to be for a particular service but that don't actually contain the right kind of data. (A packet filtering system, on the other hand, has difficulty with this level of control.) However, it takes considerable work to consistently take advantage of the potential advantages of dual-homed hosts.

A dual-homed host can only provide services by proxying them, or by having users log into the dual-homed host directly. As we discuss in Chapter 5, user accounts present significant security problems by themselves. They present special problems on dual-homed hosts, where they may unexpectedly enable services you consider insecure. Furthermore, most users find it inconvenient to use a dual-homed host by logging into it.

Proxying is much less problematic, but may not be available for all services you're interested in. Chapter 7 discusses some workarounds for this situation, but they do not apply in every case. The screened subnet architecture we describe in the next section offers some extra options for providing new and/or untrusted services (e.g., you can add to the screened subnet a worthless machine that provides only an untrusted service).

Screened Host Architecture

Whereas a dual-homed host architecture provides services from a host that's attached to multiple networks (but has routing turned off), a *screened host architecture* provides services from a host that's attached to only the internal network, using a separate router. In this architecture, the primary security is provided by packet filtering. (For example, packet filtering is what prevents people from going around proxy servers to make direct connections.)

Figure 4-4 shows a simple version of a screened host architecture.

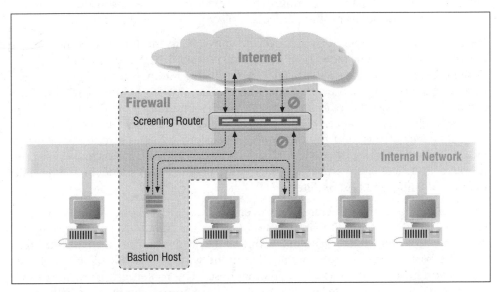

Figure 4-4: Screened host architecture

The bastion host sits on the internal network. The packet filtering on the screening router is set up in such a way that the bastion host is the only system on the internal network that hosts on the Internet can open connections to (for example, to deliver incoming email). Even then, only certain types of connections are allowed. Any external system trying to access internal systems or services will have to connect to this host. The bastion host thus needs to maintain a high level of host security.

The packet filtering also permits the bastion host to open allowable connections (what is "allowable" will be determined by your site's particular security policy) to the outside world. The section about bastion hosts in the discussion of the screened subnet architecture later in this chapter, contains more information about the functions of bastion hosts, and Chapter 5 describes in detail how to build one.

The packet filtering configuration in the screening router may do one of the following:

*   Allow other internal hosts to open connections to hosts on the Internet for certain services (allowing those services via packet filtering, as discussed in Chapter 6),

*   Disallow all connections from internal hosts (forcing those hosts to use proxy services via the bastion host, as discussed in Chapter 7).

You can mix and match these approaches for different services; some may be allowed directly via packet filtering, while others may be allowed only indirectly via proxy. It all depends on the particular policy your site is trying to enforce.

Because this architecture allows packets to move from the Internet to the internal networks, it may seem more risky than a dual-homed host architecture, which is designed so that no external packet can reach the internal network. In practice, however, the dual-homed host architecture is also prone to failures that let packets actually cross from the external network to the internal network. (Because this type of failure is completely unexpected, there are unlikely to be protections against attacks of this kind.) Furthermore, it's easier to defend a router, which provides a very limited set of services, than it is to defend a host. For most purposes, the screened host architecture provides both better security and better usability than the dual-homed host architecture.

Compared to other architectures, however, such as the screened subnet architecture discussed in the following section, there are some disadvantages to the screened host architecture. The major one is that if an attacker manages to break in to the bastion host, there is nothing left in the way of network security between the bastion host and the rest of the internal hosts. The router also presents a single point of failure; if the router is compromised, the entire network is available to an attacker. For this reason, the screened subnet architecture has become increasingly popular.

Screened Subnet Architecture

The *screened subnet architecture* adds an extra layer of security to the screened host architecture by adding a perimeter network that further isolates the internal network from the Internet.

Why do this? By their nature, bastion hosts are the most vulnerable machines on your network. Despite your best efforts to protect them, they are the machines most likely to be attacked, because they're the machines that *can be* attacked. If, as in a screened host architecture, your internal network is wide open to attack from your bastion host, then your bastion host is a very tempting target. There are no other defenses between it and your other internal machines (besides whatever host security they may have, which is usually very little). If someone successfully breaks into the bastion host in a screened host architecture, he's hit the jackpot.

By isolating the bastion host on a perimeter network, you can reduce the impact of a break-in on the bastion host. It is no longer an instantaneous jackpot; it gives an intruder some access, but not all.

With the simplest type of screened subnet architecture, there are two screening routers, each connected to the perimeter net. One sits between the perimeter net and the internal network, and the other sits between the perimeter net and the external network (usually the Internet). To break into the internal network with this type of architecture, an attacker would have to get past *both* routers. Even if the attacker somehow broke in to the bastion host, he'd still have to get past the interior router. There is no single vulnerable point that will compromise the internal network.

Some sites go so far as to create a layered series of perimeter nets between the outside world and their interior network. Less trusted and more vulnerable services are placed on the outer perimeter nets, fathest from the interior network. The idea is that an attacker who breaks into a machine on an outer perimeter net will have a harder time successfully attacking internal machines because of the additional layers of security between the outer perimeter and the internal network. This is only true if there is actually some meaning to the different layers, however; if the filtering systems between each layer allow the same things between all layers, the additional layers don't provide any additional security.

Figure 4-5 shows a possible firewall configuration that uses the screened subnet architecture. The next few sections describe the components in this type of architecture.

Perimeter network

The perimeter network is another layer of security, an additional network between the external network and your protected internal network. If an attacker successfully breaks into the outer reaches of your firewall, the perimeter net offers an additional layer of protection between that attacker and your internal systems.

Here's an example of why a perimeter network can be helpful. In many network setups, it's possible for any machine on a given network to see the traffic for every machine on that network. This is true for most Ethernet-based networks, (and Ethernet is by far the most common local area networking technology in use today); it is also true for several other popular technologies, such as token ring and FDDI. Snoopers may succeed in picking up passwords by watching for those used during Telnet, FTP, and *rlogin* sessions. Even if passwords aren't compromised, snoopers can still peek at the contents of sensitive files people may be accessing, interesting email they may be reading, and so on; the snooper can essentially "watch over the shoulder" of anyone using the network.

With a perimeter network, if someone breaks into a bastion host on the perimeter net, he'll be able to snoop only on traffic on that net. All the traffic on the perimeter net should be either to or from the bastion host, or to or from the Internet.

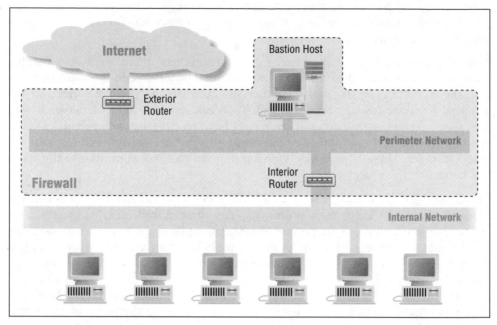

Figure 4–5: Screened subnet architecture (using two routers)

Because no strictly internal traffic (that is, traffic between two internal hosts, which is presumably sensitive or proprietary) passes over the perimeter net, internal traffic will be safe from prying eyes if the bastion host is compromised.

Obviously, traffic to and from the bastion host, or the external world, will still be visible. Part of the work in designing a firewall is ensuring that this traffic is not itself confidential enough that reading it will compromise your site as a whole. (This is discussed in Chapter 5.)

Bastion host

With the screened subnet architecture, you attach a bastion host (or hosts) to the perimeter net; this host is the main point of contact for incoming connections from the outside world; for example:

- For incoming email (SMTP) sessions to deliver electronic mail to the site

- For incoming FTP connections to the site's anonymous FTP server

- For incoming domain name service (DNS) queries about the site

and so on.

Outbound services (from internal clients to servers on the Internet) are handled in either of these ways:

- Set up packet filtering on both the exterior and interior routers to allow internal clients to access external servers directly.

- Set up proxy servers to run on the bastion host (if your firewall uses proxy software) to allow internal clients to access external servers indirectly. You would also set up packet filtering to allow the internal clients to talk to the proxy servers on the bastion host and vice versa, but to prohibit direct communications between internal clients and the outside world.

In either case, the packet filtering allows the bastion host to connect to, and accept connections from, hosts on the Internet; which hosts, and for what services, are dictated by the site's security policy.

Much of what the bastion host does is act as proxy server for various services, either by running specialized proxy server software for particular protocols (such as HTTP or FTP), or by running standard servers for self-proxying protocols (such as SMTP).

Chapter 5 describes how to secure the bastion host, and Chapter 8 describes how to configure individual services to work with the firewall.

Interior router

The *interior router* (sometimes called the *choke router* in firewalls literature) protects the internal network both from the Internet *and* from the perimeter net.

The interior router does most of the packet filtering for your firewall. It allows selected services outbound from the internal net to the Internet. These services are the services your site can safely support and safely provide using packet filtering rather than proxies. (Your site needs to establish its own definition of what "safe" means. You'll have to consider your own needs, capabilities, and constraints; there is no one answer for all sites.) The services you allow might include outgoing Telnet, FTP, WAIS, Archie, Gopher, and others, as appropriate for your own needs and concerns. (For detailed information on how you can use packet filtering to control these services, see Chapter 6.)

The services the interior router allows between your bastion host (on the perimeter net itself) and your internal net are not necessarily the same services the interior router allows between the Internet and your internal net. The reason for limiting the services between the bastion host and the internal network is to reduce the number of machines (and the number of services on those machines) that can be attacked from the bastion host, should it be compromised.

You should limit the services allowed between the bastion host and the internal net to just those that are actually needed, such as SMTP (so the bastion host can forward incoming email), DNS (so the bastion host can answer questions from internal machines, or ask them, depending on your configuration), and so on. You should further limit services, to the extent possible, by allowing them only to or from particular internal hosts; for example, SMTP might be limited only to connections between the bastion host and your internal mail server or servers. Pay careful attention to the security of those remaining internal hosts and services that can be contacted by the bastion host, because those hosts and services will be what an attacker goes after—indeed, will be all the attacker *can* go after—if the attacker manages to break in to your bastion host.

Exterior router

In theory, the *exterior router* (sometimes called the *access router* in firewalls literature) protects both the perimeter net and the internal net from the Internet. In practice, exterior routers tend to allow almost anything outbound from the perimeter net, and they generally do very little packet filtering. The packet filtering rules to protect internal machines would need to be essentially the same on both the interior router and the exterior router; if there's an error in the rules that allows access to an attacker, the error will probably be present on both routers.

Frequently, the exterior router is provided by an external group (for example, your Internet provider), and your access to it may be limited. An external group that's maintaining a router will probably be willing to put in a few general packet filtering rules, but won't want to maintain a complicated or frequently changing rule set. You also may not trust them as much as you trust your own routers. If the router breaks and they install a new one, are they going to remember to reinstall the filters? Are they even going to bother to mention that they replaced the router so that you know to check?

The only packet filtering rules that are really special on the exterior router are those that protect the machines on the perimeter net (that is, the bastion hosts and the internal router). Generally, however, not much protection is necessary, because the hosts on the perimeter net are protected primarily through host security (although redundancy never hurts).

The rest of the rules that you could put on the exterior router are duplicates of the rules on the interior router. These are the rules that prevent insecure traffic from going between internal hosts and the Internet. To support proxy services, where the interior router will let the internal hosts send some protocols as long as they are talking *to* the bastion host, the exterior router could let those protocols through as long as they are coming *from* the bastion host. These rules are desirable for an extra level of security, but they're theoretically blocking only packets that can't exist because they've already been blocked by the interior router. If they do exist, either the interior router has failed, or somebody has connected an unexpected host to the perimeter network.

So, what does the exterior router actually need to do? One of the security tasks that the exterior router *can* usefully perform—a task that usually can't easily be done anywhere else—is the blocking of any incoming packets from the Internet that have forged source addresses. Such packets claim to have come from within the internal network, but actually are coming in from the Internet.

The interior router could do this, but it can't tell if packets that claim to be from the perimeter net are forged. While the perimeter net shouldn't have anything fully trusted on it, it's still going to be more trusted than the external universe; being able to forge packets from it will give an attacker most of the benefits of compromising the bastion host. The exterior router is at a clearer boundary. The interior router also can't protect the systems on the perimeter net against forged packets. (We'll discuss forged packets in greater detail in Chapter 6.

Variations on Firewall Architectures

We've shown the most common firewall architectures in Figure 4-3 through Figure 4-5. However, there is a lot of variation in architectures. There is a good deal of flexibility in how you can configure and combine firewall components to best suit your hardware, your budget, and your security policy. This section describes some common variations, and their benefits and drawbacks.

It's OK to Use Multiple Bastion Hosts

Although we tend to talk about a single bastion host in this book, it may make sense to use multiple bastion hosts in your firewall configuration, as we show in Figure 4-6. Reasons you might want to do this include performance, redundancy, and the need to separate data or servers.

You might decide to have one bastion host handle the services that are important to your own users (such as SMTP servers, proxy servers, and so on), while another host handles the services that you provide to the Internet, but which your users don't care about (for example, an anonymous FTP server). In this way, performance for your own users won't be dragged down by the activities of outside users.

You may have performance reasons to create multiple bastion hosts even if you don't provide services to the Internet. Some services, like Usenet news, are resource-intensive and easily separated from others. It's also possible to provide multiple bastion hosts with the same services for performance reasons, but it can be difficult to do load balancing. Most services need to be configured for particular servers, so creating multiple hosts for individual services works best if you can predict usage in advance.

How about redundancy? If your firewall configuration includes multiple bastion hosts, you might configure them for redundancy, so that if one fails, the services can be provided by another, but beware that only some services support this

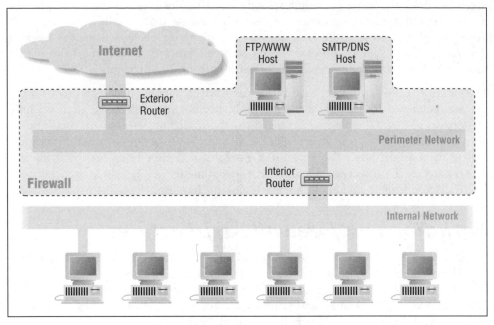

Figure 4–6: Architecture using two bastion hosts

approach. For example, you might configure and designate multiple bastion hosts as DNS servers for your domain (via DNS NS [Name Server] records, which specify the name servers for a domain), or as SMTP servers (via DNS MX [Mail Exchange] records, which specify what servers will accept mail for a given host or domain), or both. Then, if one of the bastion hosts is unavailable or overloaded, the DNS and SMTP activity will use the other as a fallback system.

You might also use multiple bastion hosts to keep the data sets of services from interfering with each other. In addition to the performance issues discussed earlier, there may be security reasons for this separation. For example, you might decide to provide one HTTP server for use by your customers over the Internet, and another for use by the general public. By providing two servers, you can offer different data to customers and possibly better performance, by using a less loaded or more powerful machine.

You could also run your HTTP server and your anonymous FTP server on separate machines, to eliminate the possibility that one server could be used to compromise the other. (For a discussion of of how this might be done, see the description of HTTP server vulnerabilities in Chapter 8.)

It's OK to Merge the Interior Router and the Exterior Router

You can merge the interior and exterior routers into a single router, but only if you have a router sufficiently capable and flexible. In general, you need a router that allows you to specify both inbound and outbound filters on each interface. In Chapter 6, we discuss what this means, and we describe the packet filtering problems that may arise with routers that have more than two interfaces and don't have this capability.

If you merge the interior and exterior routers, as we show in Figure 4-7, you'll still have a perimeter net (on one interface of the router) and a connection to your internal net (on another interface of the router). Some traffic would flow directly between the internal net and the Internet (the traffic that is permitted by the packet filtering rules set up for the router), and other traffic would flow between the perimeter net and the Internet, or the perimeter net and the internal net (the traffic that is handled by proxies).

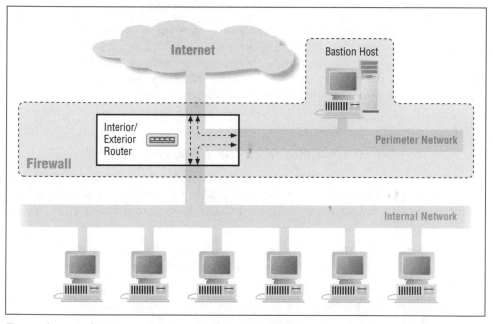

Figure 4-7: Architecture using a merged interior and exterior router

This architecture, like the screened host architecture, makes the site vulnerable to the compromise of a single router. In general, routers are easier to protect than hosts, but they are not impenetrable.

It's OK to Merge the Bastion Host and the Exterior Router

There might be cases in which you use a single dual-homed machine as both your bastion host and your exterior router. Here's an example: suppose you only have a dial-up SLIP or PPP connection to the Internet. In this case, you might run something like the Morning Star PPP package on your bastion host, and let it act as both bastion host and exterior router. This is functionally equivalent to the three-machine configuration (bastion host, interior router, exterior router) described for the screened subnet architecture shown earlier in this chapter.

Using a dual-homed host to route traffic won't give you the performance or the flexibility of a dedicated router, but you don't need much of either for a single low-bandwidth connection. Depending on the operating system and software you're using, you may or may not have the ability to do packet filtering. Several of the available interface software packages, such as the Morning Star PPP package mentioned earlier, have quite good packet filtering capabilities. However, because the exterior router doesn't have to do much packet filtering anyway, using an interface package that doesn't have good packet filtering capabilities is not that big a problem.

Unlike merging the interior and exterior routers, merging the bastion host with the exterior router, as shown in Figure 4-8, does not open significant new vulnerabilities. It does expose the bastion host further. In this architecture, the bastion host is more exposed to the Internet, protected only by whatever filtering (if any) its own interface package does, and you will need to take extra care to protect it.

It's Dangerous to Merge the Bastion Host and the Interior Router

While it is acceptable to merge the bastion host and the exterior router, as we discussed in the previous section, it's not a good idea to merge the bastion host and the interior router, as we show in Figure 4-9. Doing so compromises your overall security.

The bastion host and the exterior router each perform distinct protective tasks; they complement each other but don't back each other up. The interior router functions in part as a backup to the two of them.

If you merge the bastion host and the interior router, you've changed the firewall configuration in a fundamental way. In the first case (with a separate bastion host and interior router), you have a screened subnet firewall architecture. With this type of configuration, the perimeter net for the bastion host doesn't carry any strictly internal traffic, so this traffic is protected from snooping even if the bastion host is successfully penetrated; to get at the internal network, the attacker still must get past the interior router. In the second case (with a merged bastion host and interior router), you have a screened host firewall architecture. With this type

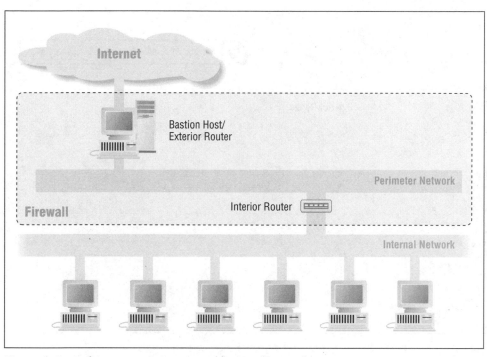

Figure 4–8: Architecture using a merged bastion host and exterior router

of configuration, if the bastion host is broken into, there's nothing left in the way of security between the bastion host and the internal network.

One of the main purposes of the perimeter network is to prevent the bastion host from being able to snoop on internal traffic. Moving the bastion host to the interior router makes all of your internal traffic visible to it.

It's Dangerous to Use Multiple Interior Routers

Using multiple interior routers to connect your perimeter net to multiple parts of your internal net can cause a lot of problems, and is generally a bad idea.

The basic problem is that the routing software on an internal system could decide that the fastest way to another internal system is via the perimeter net. If you're lucky, this approach simply won't work, because it will be blocked by the packet filtering on one of the routers. If you're unlucky, it will work, and you'll have sensitive, strictly internal traffic flowing across your perimeter net, where it can be snooped on if somebody has managed to break in to the bastion host.

It's also difficult to keep multiple interior routers correctly configured. The interior router is the one with the most important and the most complex set of packet filters and having two of them doubles your chances of getting the rule sets wrong.

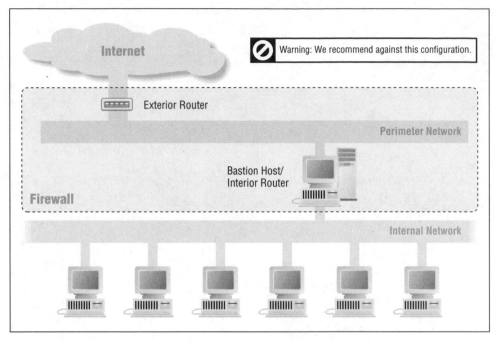

Figure 4-9: Architecture using a merged bastion host and interior router

Nevertheless, you may still end up wanting to do this. On a large internal network, having a single interior router may be both a performance problem and a reliability problem. If you're trying to provide redundancy, that single point of failure is a major annoyance. In that case, the safest (and most redundant) thing to do is to set up each interior router to a separate perimeter net and exterior router; this configuration is discussed later in this chapter. This configuration is more complex and more expensive, but it increases both redundancy and performance, as well as making it highly unlikely that traffic will try to go between the interior routers (if the Internet is the shortest route between two parts of your internal network, you have much worse problems than most sites) and extraordinarily unlikely that it will succeed (four sets of packet filters are trying to keep it out).

If performance problems alone are motivating you to look at multiple interior routers, it's hard to justify the expense of separate perimeter networks and exterior routers. In most cases, however, the interior router is not the performance bottleneck. If it is, then one of the following cases is occurring:

- There is a lot of traffic going to the perimeter net that is not then going to the external network.

- Your exterior gateway is much faster than your interior gateway.

In the first case, you have misconfigured something; the perimeter net may take occasional traffic that isn't destined for the external world in some configurations (for example, DNS queries about external hosts when the information is cached), but that traffic should never be significant. In the second case, you should seriously consider upgrading the interior router to match the exterior router, instead of adding a second one.

Figure 4-10 shows the basic architecture using multiple interior routers.

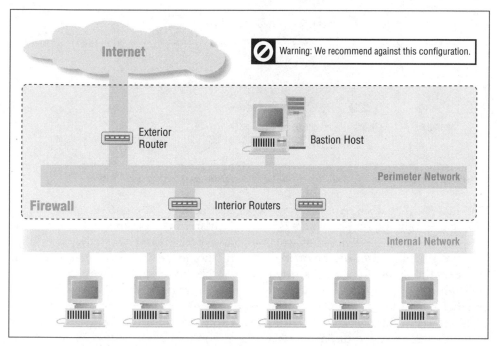

Figure 4-10: Architecture using multiple interior routers

Another reason for having multiple interior routers is that you have multiple internal networks, which have technical, organizational, or political reasons not to share a single router. The simplest way to accommodate these networks would be to give them separate interfaces on a single router, as shown in Figure 4-11. This complicates the router configuration considerably (how considerably depends a great deal on the router in question, as discussed in Chapter 6), but doesn't produce the risks of a multiple interior router configuration. If there are too many networks for a single router, or if sharing a router is unpalatable for other reasons, consider making an internal backbone and connecting it to the perimeter network with a single router, as shown in Figure 4-12.

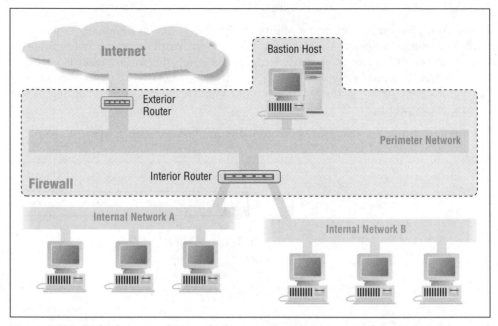

Figure 4-11: Multiple internal networks (separate interfaces in a single router)

You may find that an effective way to accommodate different security policies among different internal networks is to attach them to the perimeter through separate routers, (e.g., one network wants to allow connections that others consider insecure.) In this case, the perimeter network should be the *only* interconnection between the internal networks; there should be no confidential traffic passing between them; and each internal network should treat the other as an untrusted, external network. This is likely to be extremely inconvenient for some users on each network, but anything else will either compromise the security of the site as a whole or remove the distinction that caused you to set up the two routers in the first place.

If you decide that you are willing to accept the risks of having multiple interior routers, you can minimize those risks by having all the interior routers managed by the same group (so conflicting security policies aren't being enforced). You should also keep a careful watch for internal traffic crossing the perimeter network and act promptly to cure the sources of it.

It's OK to Use Multiple Exterior Routers

There are some cases in which it makes sense to connect multiple exterior routers to the same perimeter net, as we show in Figure 4-13.

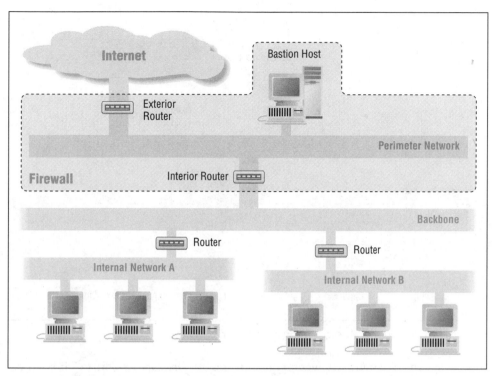

Figure 4–12: Multiple internal networks (backbone architecture)

Examples are:

- You have multiple connections to the Internet (for example, through different service providers, for redundancy).

- You have a connection to the Internet plus other connections to other sites.

In these cases, you might instead have one exterior router with multiple exterior network interfaces.

Attaching multiple exterior routers which go to the same external network (e.g., two different Internet providers) is not a significant security problem. They may have different filter sets, but that's not critical in exterior routers. There is twice the chance that one will be compromisable, but a compromise of an exterior router is not particularly threatening.

Things are more complex if the connections are to different places (for example, one is to the Internet and one is to a site you're collaborating with and need more bandwidth to). To figure out whether such an architecture makes sense in these cases, ask yourself this question: what traffic could someone see if they broke into a bastion host on this perimeter net? For example, if an attacker broke in, could he

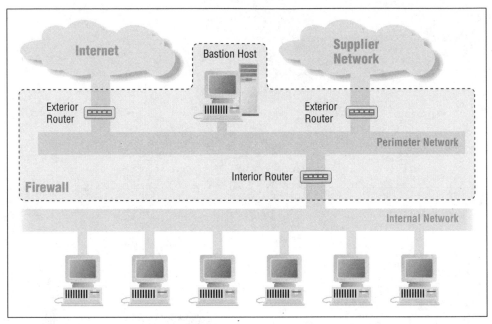

Figure 4-13: Architecture using multiple exterior routers

snoop on sensitive traffic between your site and a subsidiary or affiliate? If so, then you may want to think about installing multiple perimeter nets instead of multiple exterior routers on a single perimeter net. (This case is shown in the next section.)

There are other significant problems involved in setting up connections to external networks with which you have special relationships, which are discussed later in this chapter, in the section called "Internal Firewalls."

It's OK to Have Multiple Perimeter Networks

As we've mentioned above, you'll find in certain situations that it makes sense for your configuration to include multiple perimeter networks. Figure 4-14 shows this configuration.

You might put in multiple perimeter nets to provide redundancy. It doesn't make much sense to pay for two connections to the Internet, and then run them both through the same router or routers. Putting in two exterior routers, two perimeter nets, and two interior routers ensures that there is no single point of failure between you and the Internet.[*]

---

[*] Providing, of course, that your two Internet providers are actually running on different pieces of cable, in different conduits. Never underestimate the destructive power of a backhoe.

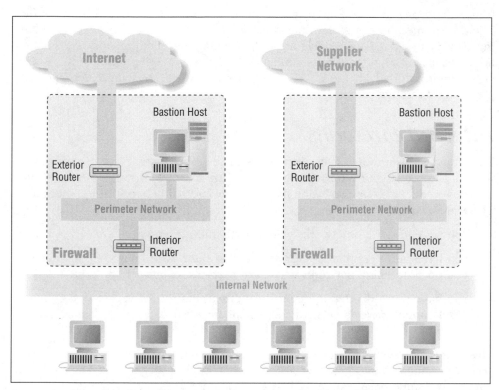

Figure 4-14: Architecture using multiple perimeter nets (multiple firewalls)

You might also put in multiple perimeter nets for privacy, so that you can run moderately confidential data across one, and an Internet connection across the other. In that case, you might even attach both perimeter nets to the same interior router.

Having multiple perimeter nets is less risky than having multiple interior routers sharing the same internal net, but it's still a maintenance headache. You will probably have multiple interior routers, presenting multiple possible points of compromise. Those routers must be watched very carefully to keep them enforcing appropriate security policies; if they both connect to the Internet, they need to enforce the same policy.

It's OK to Use Dual-Homed Hosts and Screened Subnets

You can get significant increases in security by combining a dual-homed host architecture with a screened subnet architecture. To do this, split the perimeter network and insert a dual-homed host. The routers provide protection from forgery, and protect from failures where the dual-homed host starts to route traffic. The dual-homed host provides finer controls on the connections than packet filtering. This is a belt-and-suspenders firewall, providing excellent multilayered protection, although it requires careful configuration on the dual-homed host to be sure you're taking full advantage of the possibilities. (There's no point in running simple, straight-through proxies.)

Internal Firewalls

The assumption in most of the discussions in this book is that you are building a firewall to protect your internal network from the Internet. However, in some situations, you may also be protecting parts of your internal network from other parts. There are a number of reasons why you might want to do this:

- You have test or lab networks with strange things going on there.

- You have networks that are less secure than the rest of your site, e.g., demonstration or teaching networks where outsiders are commonly present.

- You have networks that are more secure than the rest of your site, e.g., secret development projects or networks where financial data or grades are passed around.

This is another situation where firewalls are a useful technology. In some cases, you will want to build *internal firewalls*; that is, firewalls that sit between two parts of the same organization, or between two separate organizations that share a network, rather than between a single organization and the Internet.

It often makes sense to keep one part of your organization separate from another. Not everyone in an organization needs the same services or information, and security is frequently more important in some parts of an organization (the accounting department, for example) than in others.

Many of the same tools and techniques you use to build Internet firewalls are also useful for building these internal firewalls. However, there are some special considerations that you will need to keep in mind if you are building an internal firewall.

Laboratory Networks

Laboratory and test networks are often the first networks that people consider separating from the rest of an organization via a firewall (usually as the result of some horrible experience where something escapes the laboratory and runs amok). Unless people are working on routers, this type of firewall can be quite simple. Neither a perimeter net nor a bastion host is needed, because there is no worry about snooping (all users are internal anyway), and you don't need to provide many services (the machines are not people's home machines). In most cases, you'll want a packet filtering router that allows any connection inbound to the test network, but only known safe connections from it. (What's safe will depend on what the test network is playing with, rather than on the normal security considerations.)

In a few cases (for example, if you are testing bandwidth on the network), you may want to protect the test network from outside traffic that would invalidate tests, in which case you'll deny inbound connections and allow outbound connections.

If you are testing routers, it's probably wisest to use an entirely disconnected network; if you don't do this, then at least prevent the firewall router from listening to routing updates from the test network. You can do this a number of ways, depending on your network setup, what you're testing, and what routers you have available. You might do any of the following:

- Use a different routing protocol from the one under test and entirely disable the protocol under test.

- Tell the router not to accept any routing updates from the interface under test and to filter out packets in the routing protocol.

- Specify which hosts the router will accept updates from.

If you have a number of test networks, you may find it best to set up a perimeter net for them and give each one a separate router onto the perimeter net, putting most of the packet filtering in the router between the perimeter and the main network. That way, if one test network crashes its router, the rest still have their normal connectivity. Figure 4-15 shows this architecture.

If your testing involves external connections, the test network has to be treated as an external network itself; see "Joint Venture Firewalls" below.

Insecure Networks

Test networks are dangerous, but not necessarily less secure than other networks. Many organizations also have some networks that are intrinsically less secure than most. For example, a university may consider networks that run through student dormitories to be particularly insecure; a company may consider demonstration networks, porting labs, and customer training networks to be particularly insecure. Nevertheless, these insecure networks need more interaction with the rest of the organization than does a purely external network.

Networks like dormitory networks and porting labs, where external people have prolonged access and the ability to bring in their own tools, are really as insecure as completely external networks and should be treated that way. Either position them as a second external connection (a new connection on your exterior router or a new exterior router) or set up a separate perimeter network for them. The

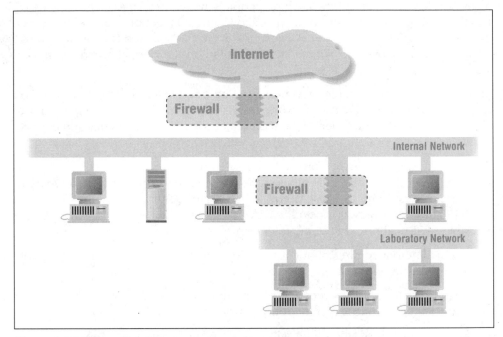

Figure 4–15: Firewall architecture with a laboratory network

only advantage these networks offer over purely external networks is that you can specify particular software to be run on them, which means you can make use of encryption effectively. (See Chapter 10 for a discussion of how to provide services to external, untrusted networks.)

Demonstration and training labs, where external people have relatively brief, supervised access and cannot bring in tools, can be more trusted (as long as you are sure that people really do have relatively brief, supervised access and cannot bring in tools!). You still need to use a packet filtering router or a dual-horned host to prevent confidential traffic from flowing across those networks. You will also want to limit those networks to connections to servers you consider secure. However, you may be willing to provide NFS service from particular servers, for example, which you wouldn't do to a purely untrusted network. One of your main concerns should be preventing your trusted users from doing unsafe things while working on those networks (for example, logging in to the machines on their desks and forgetting to log out again, or reading confidential electronic mail). This should be done with a combination of training and force (ensuring that the most insecure uses fail).

This is a place where a dual-homed host can be quite useful, even with no proxies on it; the number of people who need to use the host is probably small, and having to log into it will ensure that they see warning messages. The host will also be unable to provide some tempting but highly insecure services; for example, you won't be able to run NFS except from the dual-homed host, and people won't be able to mount their home machine's filesystems.

Extra-Secure Networks

Just as most organizations have points where they're particularly insecure, most of them have points where they're particularly security-conscious. At universities, these may be particular research projects, or the registrar's office; at commercial companies, these may be new products under development; at almost any place, the accounting and finance machines need extra protection. Some unclassified government work also requires extra protections.

Networks for doing classified work—at any level of classification—not only need to be more secure, but also need to meet all relevant government regulations. Generally speaking, they will have to be separated from unclassified networks. In any case, they are outside of the scope of this book. If you need to set one up, consult your security officer; traditional firewalls will not meet the requirements.[*]

You can choose to meet your requirements for extra security either by encrypting traffic that passes over your regular internal networks, or by setting up separate networks for the secure traffic. Separate networks are technically easier as long as there are separate machines on them. That is, if you have a secure research project that owns particular computers, and if people log into them to work on that project, it's reasonably simple to set up a straightforward single-machine firewall (a packet filtering router, most likely). That firewall will treat your normal network as the insecure external universe. Because the lab machines probably don't need many services, a bastion host is unnecessary, and a perimeter net is needed only for the most secret ventures.

If you are dealing with people whose day-to-day work is secure, and who don't have separate machines for that work, a separate network becomes harder to implement. If you put their machines onto a more secure network, they can't work easily with everybody else at the site, and they need a number of services. In this case, you'll need a full bastion host, and therefore probably a perimeter net to put it on. It's tempting to connect their machines to *two* networks, the secure net and the insecure net, so they can transmit confidential data over one and participate with the rest of the site on the other, but this is a configuration nightmare. If they're attached to both at once, each host is basically a dual-homed host firewall, with all the attendant maintenance problems. If they can only be attached to one at a time, things are more secure. However, configuring the machines is unpleasant for you, and moving back and forth is unpleasant for the user.

At a university, which tends not to have a single coherent network to start with, putting the registrar's office and the financial people on secure networks,

---

[*] If you don't have a security officer, you're not going to have a classified network, either.

firewalled from the rest of the university, will probably work. At a company or government office, where most people work in the same environment, look into using encryption in your applications instead.

Joint Venture Firewalls

Sometimes, organizations come together for certain limited reasons, such as a joint project; they need to be able to share machines, data, and other resources for the duration of the project. For example, look at the decision of IBM and Apple to collaborate on the PowerPC, a personal computer that runs a common operating system; undertaking one joint project doesn't mean that IBM and Apple have decided to merge their organizations or to open up all their operations to each other.

Although the two parties have decided to trust each other for the purposes of this project, they are still competitors. They want to protect most of their systems and information from each other. It isn't just that they may distrust each other; it's also that they can't be sure how good the other's security is. They don't want to risk that an intruder into their partner's system might, through this joint venture, find a route into their system as well. This security problem occurs even if the collaborators aren't also competitors.

You may also want to connect to an external company because it is an outside vendor to you. A number of services depend on information transfer, from shipping (you tell them what you want to ship; they tell you what happened to your shipment) to architecture (you give them specifications; they give you designs) to chip fabrication (you send them the chip design, they give you status on the fabrication process). These outside vendors are not competitors in any sense, but they frequently also work for competitors of yours. They are probably aware of confidentiality issues and try to protect the information they are supposed to have, to the best of their ability. On the other hand, if there are routing slip-ups, and data you're not explicitly sending to them crosses their networks, they are probably going to be completely unconscious of it, and the data will be at risk.

This may seem far-fetched, but it turns out to be a fairly routine occurrence. One company was mystified to discover routes on its network for a competitor's internal network, and still more baffled to discover traffic using these routes. It turned out that the shortest route between them and their competitor was through a common outside vendor. The traffic was not confidential, because it was all traffic that would have gone through the Internet. On the other hand, the connection to the outside vendor was not treated as if it were an Internet connection (the outside vendor itself was not Internet-connected, and nobody had considered the possibility of it cross-connecting Internet-connected clients). Both companies had sudden, unexpected, and unprotected vulnerabilities.

An internal firewall limits exposure in such a situation. It provides a mechanism for sharing some resources, while protecting most of them. Before you set out to build an internal firewall, be sure you're clear on what you want to share, protect, and accomplish. Ask these questions:

- What exactly do you want to accomplish by linking your network with some other organization's network? The answer to this question will determine what services you need to provide (and, by implication, what services should be blocked).

- Are you just looking to exchange email or files with the other organization privately, without having to communicate over the Internet? If that's all you want, then maybe a dial-up UUCP connection is all you need, not an IP-level connection between your nets.

- Are you trying to create a full work environment for a joint project in which team members from both organizations can work together and yet still have access to their own "home" systems (which need to be protected from the other organization)? In such a case, you might actually need two firewalls: one between the joint project net and each of the home organizations.

- Are you looking for something in between? Exactly what you're trying to accomplish, and what your security concerns are, will determine what firewall technologies are going to be useful to you.

A Shared Perimeter Network Allows an 'Arms-length' Relationship

Shared perimeter networks are a good way to approach joint networks. Each party can install its own router, under its own control, onto a perimeter net between the two organizations. In some configurations, these two routers might be the only machines on the perimeter net, with no bastion host. If this is the case, then the "net" might simply be a high-speed serial line (e.g., a 56 Kb/s or T1/E1 line) between the two routers, rather than an Ethernet or another type of local area network.

This is highly desirable with an outside vendor. Most of them are not networking wizards, and they may attempt to economize by connecting multiple clients to the same perimeter network. If the perimeter net is an Ethernet or something similar, any client that can get to its router on that perimeter network can see the traffic for all the clients on that perimeter network—which, with some providers, is almost guaranteed to be confidential information belonging to a competitor. Using a point-to-point connection as the "perimeter net" between the outside vendor and each client, rather than a shared multiclient perimeter net, will prevent them from doing this, even accidentally.

An Internal Firewall May or May Not Need Bastion Hosts

You might not actually need to place a bastion host on the perimeter network between two organizations. The decision about whether you need a bastion host depends on what services are required for your firewall and how much each organization trusts the other. Bastion hosts on the perimeter net are rarely required for relationships with outside vendors; usually you are sending data over one particular protocol and can adequately protect that as a screened host.

If the organizations have a reasonable amount of trust in each other (and, by extension, in each other's security), it may be reasonable to establish the packet filters so that clients on the other side can connect to internal servers (such as SMTP and DNS servers) directly.

On the other hand, if the organizations distrust each other, they might each want to place their own bastion host, under their own control and management, on the perimeter net. Traffic would flow from one party's internal systems, to their bastion host, to the other party's bastion host, and finally to the other party's internal systems.

What the Future Holds

Systems that might be called "third generation firewalls"—firewalls that combine the features and capabilities of packet filtering and proxy systems into something more than both—are just starting to become available.

More and more client and server applications are coming with native support for proxied environments. For example, many WWW clients include proxy capabilities, and lots of systems are coming with run-time or compile-time support for generic proxy systems such as the SOCKS package.

Packet filtering systems continue to grow more flexible and gain new capabilities, such as dynamic packet filtering. With dynamic packet filtering, such as that provided by the CheckPoint Firewall-1 product, the Morning Star Secure Connect router, and the KarlBridge/KarlBrouter, the packet filtering rules are modified "on the fly" by the router in response to certain triggers. For example, an outgoing UDP packet might cause the creation of a temporary rule to allow a corresponding, answering UDP packet back in.

The first systems that might be called "third generation" are just starting to appear on the market. For example, the Borderware product from Border Network Technologies and the Gauntlet 3.0 product from Trusted Information Systems[*] look like proxy systems from the external side (all requests appear to come from a single host), but look like packet filtering systems from the inside (internal hosts and users think they're talking directly to the external systems). They accomplish this magic through a generous amount of internal bookkeeping on currently active

---

[*] The same folks who produce the free TIS FWTK discussed throughout this book.

connections and through wholesale packet rewriting to preserve the relevant illusions to both sides. The KarlBridge/KarlBrouter product extends packet filtering in other directions, providing extensions for authentication and filtering at the application level. (This is much more precise than the filtering possible with traditional packet filtering routers.)

While firewall technologies are changing, so are the underlying technologies of the Internet, and these changes will require corresponding changes in firewalls.

The underlying protocol of the Internet, IP, is currently undergoing major revisions, partly to address the limitations imposed by the use of four-byte host addresses in the current version of the protocol (which is version 4; the existing IP is sometimes called IPv4), and the blocks in which they're given out. Basically, the Internet has been so successful and become so popular that four bytes simply isn't a big enough number to assign a unique address to every host that will join the Internet over the next few years, particularly because addresses must be given out to organizations in relatively large blocks.

Attempts to solve the address size limitations by giving out smaller blocks of addresses (so that a greater percentage of them are actually used) raise problems with routing protocols. Stop-gap solutions to both problems are being applied but won't last forever. Estimates for when the Internet will run out of new addresses to assign vary, but the consensus is that either address space or routing table space (if not both) will be exhausted sometime within a few years after the turn of the century.

While they're working "under the hood" to solve the address size limitations, the people designing the new IP protocol (which is often referred to as "IPng" for "IP next generation"—officially, it will be IP version 6, or IPv6, when the standards are formally adopted and ratified) are taking advantage of the opportunity to make other improvements in the protocol. Some of these improvements have the potential to cause profound changes in how firewalls are constructed and operated; however, it's far too soon to say exactly what the impact will be. It will probably be at least 1997, if not later, before IPng becomes a significant factor for any but the most "bleeding edge" organizations on the Internet. (Chapter 6 describes IPv6 in somewhat more detail.)

The underlying network technologies are also changing. Currently, most networks involving more than two machines (i.e., almost anything other than dial-up or leased lines) are susceptible to snooping; any node on the network can see at least some traffic that it's not supposed to be a party to. Newer network technologies, such as frame relay and Asynchronous Transfer Mode (ATM), pass packets directly from source to destination, without exposing them to snooping by other nodes in the network.

Private IP Addresses

In general, sites should obtain and use IP addresses that have been assigned specifically to them by either their service provider or their country's Network Information Center (NIC). This coordinated assignment of addresses will prevent sites from having difficulties reaching other sites because they've inadvertently chosen conflicting IP addresses. Coordinated assignment of addresses also makes life easier (and therefore more efficient) for service providers and other members of the Internet routing core.

Unfortunately, some organizations have simply picked IP addresses out of thin air, because they didn't want to go to the trouble of getting assigned IP addresses, because they couldn't get as many addresses as they thought they needed for their purposes (Class A nets are *extremely* difficult to come by because there are only 126 possible Class A network numbers in the world), or because they thought their network would never be connected to the Internet. The problem is, if such organizations ever *do* want to communicate with whoever really owns those addresses (via a direct connection, or through the Internet), they'll be unable to because of addressing conflicts.

RFC1597[*] recognizes this long-standing practice and sets aside certain IP addresses (Class A net 10, Class B nets 172.16 through 172.31, and Class C nets 192.168.0 through 192.168.255) for private use by any organization. These addresses will never be officially assigned to anyone and should never be used outside an organization's own network.

As RFC1627 (a followup to RFC1597) points out, RFC1597 doesn't really address the problem; it merely codifies the problem so that it can be more easily recognized in the future. If a site chooses to use these private addresses, they're going to have problems if they ever want to link their site to the Internet (all their connections will have to be proxied, because the private addresses must never leak onto the Internet), or if they ever want to link their site to another site that's also using private addresses (for example, because they've bought or been bought by such a site).

Our recommendation is to obtain and use registered IP addresses if at all possible. If you *must* use private IP addresses, then use the ones specified by RFC1597, but beware that you're setting yourself up for later problem. We use the RFC1597 addresses throughout this book as sample IP addresses, because we know they won't conflict with any site's actual Internet-visible IP addresses.

---

* RFCs (Requests for Comments) are Internet standards documents.

In This Chapter:
- *General Principles*
- *Special Kinds of Bastion Hosts*
- *Choosing a Machine*
- *Choosing a Physical Location*
- *Locating the Bastion Host on the Network*
- *Selecting Services Provided by the Bastion Host*
- *Don't Allow User Accounts on the Bastion Host*
- *Building a Bastion Host*
- *Operating the Bastion Host*
- *Protecting the Machine and Backups*

5

Bastion Hosts

A bastion host is your public presence on the Internet. Think of it as the lobby of a building. Outsiders may not be able to go up the stairs and may not be able to get into the elevators, but they can walk freely into the lobby and ask for what they want. (Whether or not they will get what they ask for depends upon the building's security policy.) Like the lobby in your building, a bastion host is exposed to potentially hostile elements. The bastion host is the system that any outsiders—friends or possible foes—must ordinarily connect with to access a system or a service that's inside your firewall.

By design, a bastion host is highly exposed, because its existence is known to the Internet. For this reason, firewall builders and managers need to concentrate security efforts on the bastion host. You should pay special attention to the host's security during initial construction and ongoing operation. Because the bastion host is the most exposed host, it also needs to be the most fortified host.

Although we talk about a single bastion host in this chapter and elsewhere in this book, remember there may be multiple bastion hosts in a firewall configuration. The number depends on a site's particular requirements and resources, as discussed in Chapter 4. Each is set up according to the same general principles, using the same general techniques.

Bastion hosts are used with many different firewall approaches and architectures; most of the information in this chapter should be relevant regardless of whether you're building a bastion host to use with a firewall based on packet filtering, proxying, or a hybrid approach. The principles and procedures for building a bastion host are extensions of those for securing any host. You want to use them, or variations of them, for any other host that's security critical, and possibly for hosts that are critical in other ways (e.g., major servers on your internal network).

General Principles

There are two basic principles for designing and building a bastion host: Keep it simple, and be prepared for the bastion host to be compromised.

Keep it simple
> The simpler your bastion host is, the easier it is to secure.
>
> Any service the bastion host offers could have software bugs or configuration errors in it, and any bugs or errors may lead to security problems. Therefore, you want the bastion host to do as little as possible. It should provide the smallest set of services with the least privileges it possibly can, while still fulfilling its role.

Be prepared for the bastion host to be compromised
> Despite your best efforts to ensure the security of the bastion host, break-ins can occur. Don't be naive about it. Only by anticipating the worst, and planning for it, will you be most likely to avert it. Always keep the question, "What if the bastion host is compromised?" in the back of your mind as you go through the steps of securing the machine and the rest of the network.
>
> Why do we emphasize this point? The reason is simple: the bastion host is the machine most likely to be attacked because it's the machine most accessible to the outside world. It's also the machine from which attacks against your internal systems are most likely to come because the outside world probably can't talk to your internal systems directly. Do your best to ensure that the bastion host *won't* get broken into, but keep in mind the question, "What if it does?"
>
> In case the bastion host is broken into, you don't want that break-in to lead to a compromise of the entire firewall. You can prevent this by not letting internal machines trust the bastion host any more than is absolutely necessary for the bastion host to function. You will need to look carefully at each service the bastion host provides to internal machines, and determine, on a service-by-service basis, how much trust and privilege each service really needs to have.
>
> Once you've made these decisions, you can use a number of mechanisms to enforce them. For example, you might install standard access control

mechanisms (passwords, authentication devices, etc.) on the internal hosts, or you might set up packet filtering between the bastion host and the internal hosts.

Special Kinds of Bastion Hosts

Most of this chapter discusses bastion hosts that are screened hosts or service-providing hosts on a screened network. There are several kinds of bastion hosts, however, that are configured similarly but have special requirements.

Nonrouting Dual-homed Hosts

A nonrouting dual-homed host has multiple network connections, but doesn't pass traffic between them. Such a host might be a firewall all by itself, or might be part of a more complex firewall. For the most part, nonrouting dual-homed hosts are configured like other bastion hosts, but need extra precautions, discussed below, to make certain they truly are nonrouting. If a nonrouting dual-homed host is your entire firewall, you need to be particularly paranoid in its configuration and follow the normal bastion host instructions with extreme care.

Victim Machines

You may want to run services that are difficult to provide safely with either proxying or packet filtering, or services that are so new that you don't know what their security implications are. For that purpose, a victim machine (or sacrificial goat) may be useful. This is a machine that has nothing on it you care about, and that has no access to machines that an intruder could make use of. It provides only the absolute minimum necessary to use it for the services you need it for. If possible, it provides only one unsafe or untested service, to avoid unexpected interactions.

Victim machines are configured much as normal bastion hosts are, except that they almost always have to allow users to log in. The users will almost always want you to have more services and programs than you would configure on a normal bastion host; resist the pressure as much as possible. You do not want users to be comfortable on a victim host: they will come to rely on it, and it will no longer work as designed. The key factor for a victim machine is that it is disposable, and if it is compromised, nobody cares. Fight tooth and nail to preserve this.

Internal Bastion Hosts

In most configurations, the main bastion host has special interactions with certain internal hosts. For example, it may be passing electronic mail to an internal mail server, coordinating with an internal name server, or passing Usenet news to an internal news server. These machines are effectively secondary bastion hosts, and they should be configured and protected more like the bastion host than like normal internal hosts. You may need to leave more services enabled on them, but you should go through the same configuration process.

Choosing a Machine

The first step in building a bastion host is to decide what kind of machine to use. You want reliability (if the bastion host goes down, you lose most of the benefit of your Internet connection), supportability, and configurability. This section looks at which operating system you should run, how fast the bastion host needs to be, and what hardware configuration should be supported.

What Operating System?

The bastion host should be something you're familiar with. You're going to end up customizing the machine and the operating system extensively; this is not the time to learn your way around a completely new system. Because a fully configured bastion host is a very restricted environment, you'll want to be able to do development for it on another machine, and it helps a great deal to be able to exchange its peripherals with other machines you own. (This is partly a hardware issue, but it doesn't do you any good to be able to plug your UNIX-formatted SCSI disk into a Macintosh SCSI chain: the hardware interoperates, but the data isn't readable.)

You need a machine that reliably offers the range of Internet services you wish to provide your users, with multiple connections simultaneously active. If your site is completely made up of MS-DOS, Windows, or Macintosh systems, you may find yourself needing some other platform (perhaps UNIX, perhaps Windows NT, perhaps something else) to use as your bastion host. You may not be able to provide or access all the services you desire through your native platform, because the relevant tools (proxy servers, packet filtering systems, or even regular servers for basic services such as SMTP and DNS) may not be available for that platform.

UNIX is the operating system that has been most popular in offering Internet services, and tools are widely available to make bastion hosts on UNIX systems. If you already have UNIX machines, you should seriously consider UNIX for your bastion host. If you have no suitable platforms for a bastion host and need to learn a new operating system anyway, we recommend you try UNIX, because that's where you'll find the largest and most extensive set of tools for building bastion hosts.

If all of your existing multiuser, IP-capable machines are something other than UNIX machines (such as VMS systems, for example), you have a hard decision to make. You can probably use a machine you are familiar with as a bastion host and get the advantages of familiarity and interchangeability. On the other hand, solid and extensive tools for building bastion hosts are not likely to be available to you, and you're going to have to improvise. You might gain some security through obscurity (don't count on it; your operating system probably isn't as obscure as you think), but you may lose as much or more if you don't have the history that UNIX-based bastion hosts offer. With UNIX, you have the advantage of learning through other people's mistakes as well as your own.

Most of this chapter assumes that you will be using some kind of UNIX machine as your bastion host; this chapter is more UNIX-centric than any other part of this book. This is because most bastion hosts *are* UNIX machines, and some of the details are extremely operating system dependent. The principles will be the same if you choose to use another operating system, but the details will vary considerably.

If you have a UNIX machine, which version of UNIX should you choose? Again, you want to balance what you're familiar with against which tools are available for which versions. If your site already uses one version of UNIX, you will most likely use that version. If your site has some familiarity with several versions of UNIX, and the relevant tools (discussed throughout this chapter) are available for all of them, use the *least* popular one that you still like. Doing so maximizes your happiness and minimizes the likelihood that attackers have precompiled ways of attacking your bastion host. If you have no UNIX familiarity, choose any version you like, provided that it is in reasonably widespread use (you don't want "Joe's UNIX, special today $9.95"). As a rule of thumb, if your chosen version of UNIX has a user's group associated with it, it's probably well-known enough to rely on.

Although UNIX vendors differ vastly in their openness about security issues, the difference in the actual security between different versions of UNIX is much smaller. Don't assume that the publicity given to security holes reflects the number of security holes; it's a more accurate reflection of the popularity of the operating system and the willingness of a vendor to admit and fix security problems. Ironically, the operating systems with the most worrisome tales may be the most secure ones, because they're the ones getting fixed.

How Fast a Machine?

The bastion host doesn't have to be a fast machine; in fact, it's better not being especially powerful. There are several good reasons, besides cost, to make your bastion host as powerful as it needs to be to do its job, but no more so. It doesn't take much horsepower to provide the services required of the bastion host.

Many people use machines in the 2- to 5-MIPS range (for example, Sun-3, MicroVAX II, or 80386-based UNIX platforms) as their bastion hosts. This is plenty of power for an average site. The bastion host really doesn't have much work to do. What it needs to do is mostly limited by the speed of your connection to the outside world, not by the CPU speed of the bastion host itself. It just doesn't take

Useful UNIX Capabilities

Every operating system has certain special capabilities or features that can be useful in building a bastion host. We can't describe all these capabilities for all systems, but we'll tell you about a few special features of UNIX because it's a common bastion host platform.

setuid/setgid

Every UNIX user has a numeric user identification (*uid*) in addition to his or her login name, and belongs to one or more groups of users, also identified by numbers (*gids*). The UNIX kernel uses the *uid* and the various *gids* of a particular user to determine what files that user has access to. Normally, UNIX programs run with the file access permissions of the user who executes the program. The *setuid* capability allows a program to be installed so that it always runs with the permissions of the owner of the program, regardless of which user is running the program. The *setgid* capability is similar; it allows the program to temporarily (while running the program) grant membership in a group to users who are not normally members of that group.

chroot

The *chroot* mechanism allows a program to irreversibly change its view of the filesystem by changing the program's idea of where the root of the filesystem is. Once a program *chroot*s to a particular piece of the filesystem, that piece becomes the whole filesystem as far as the program is concerned; the rest of the filesystem ceases to exist, from the program's point of view.

Environmental modifications, such as those made by *setuid/setgid* and *chroot,* are inherited by any subsidiary processes a program starts. A common way of restricting what the programs on a bastion host can do is to run the programs under "wrapper" programs; the wrapper programs do whatever *setuid/setgid, chroot,* or other environmental change work is necessary, and then start the real program. *chrootuid* is a wrapper program for this purpose; Appendix B gives information on how to get it.

that much of a processor to handle mail, DNS, FTP, and proxy services for a 56 Kb/s or even a T-1 (1.544 Mb/s) line. You may need more power if you are running programs that do compression/decompression (e.g., NNTP servers) or searches (e.g., full-featured WWW servers), or if you're providing proxy services for dozens of users simultaneously.

You may also need more power to support requests from the Internet if your site becomes wildly popular (e.g., if you create something that everybody and their mothers want to access, like The Great American Web Page or a popular and well-stocked anonymous FTP site).* At that point, you might also want to start using multiple bastion hosts, as we describe in Chapter 4. A large company with multiple Internet connections and popular services may need to use multiple bastion hosts *and* large, powerful machines. (Fortunately, most companies in that position are also computer manufacturers and buy computers wholesale.)

There are several reasons not to oversize the bastion host:

- A slower machine is a less inviting target. There's no prestige for somebody who brags, "Hey, I broke into a Sun 3/60!" or some other slow (to an attacker, at least) machine. There is far more prestige involved in breaking into the latest, greatest hardware. Don't make your bastion host something with high prestige value (a Cray, for example, would be a poor choice of a bastion host . . .).

- If compromised, a slower machine is less useful for attacking internal systems or other sites. It takes longer to compile code; it's not very helpful for running dictionary or brute-force password attacks against other machines; and so on. All of these factors make the machine less appealing to potential attackers, and that's your goal.

- A slower machine is less attractive for insiders to compromise. A fast machine that's spending most of its time waiting for a slow network connection is effectively wasted, and the pressure from your own users to use the extra power for other things (for example, as a compilation server, rendering server, or database server) can be considerable. You can't maintain the security of a bastion host while using it for other purposes. Extra capacity on the bastion host is an accident waiting to happen.

What Hardware Configuration?

You want a reliable hardware configuration, so you should select a base machine and peripherals that aren't the newest thing on the market. (There's a reason people call it the "bleeding edge" as well as the "leading edge.") You also want the configuration to be supportable, so don't choose something so old you can't find replacement parts for it. The middle range from your favorite manufacturer is probably about right.

While you don't need sheer CPU power, you do need a machine that keeps track of a number of connections simultaneously. This is memory-intensive, so you'll want a large amount of memory and probably a large amount of swap space as

---

* If you find yourself (or want to find yourself) in such a position, see *Managing Internet Information Services* by Cricket Liu, et al (O'Reilly & Associates, 1994). This book contains lots of helpful information and advice.

well. Caching proxies also need a large amount of free disk space to use for the caches.

Here are some suggestions about tape and disk needs:

- The bastion host can't reasonably use another host's tape drive for backups, as we'll discuss later in this chapter, so it needs its own tape drive of a size suitable to back itself up.

- A CD-ROM drive also comes in handy for operating system installation and possibly for keeping checksums on (or for comparing your current files to the original files on the CD-ROM). You may only need the CD-ROM drive initially when you first install and configure the machine, so an external drive that you "borrow" from another machine temporarily may be sufficient.

- You should be able to easily add another disk temporarily to the configuration for maintenance work.

- The boot disk should remove easily and attach to another machine—again, for maintenance work.

Both of the disk considerations mentioned suggest the bastion host should use the same type of disks as your other machines. For example, it should not be the only machine at your site running IPI disks.

The bastion host doesn't need interesting graphics, and shouldn't have them. This is a network services host; nobody needs to see it. Attach a dumb terminal (the dumber the better) to be the console. Having graphics will only encourage people to use the machine for other purposes and might encourage you to install support programs (like the X Window System and its derivatives) that are insecure.

Choosing a Physical Location

The bastion host needs to be in a location that is physically secure.[*] There are two reason for this:

- It is impossible to adequately secure a machine against an attacker who has physical access to it; there are too many ways the attacker can compromise it.

- The bastion host provides much of the actual functionality of your Internet connection, and if it is lost, damaged, or stolen, your site may effectively be disconnected. You will certainly lose access to at least some services.

Never underestimate the power of human stupidity. Even if you don't believe that it's worth anyone's time and trouble to get physical access to the machine in order to break into it, secure it to prevent well-meaning people within your organization from inadvertently making it insecure or nonfunctional.

---

[*] *Practical UNIX Security* by Simson Garfinkel and Gene Spafford (O'Reilly & Associates, second edition, 1995) contains an excellent and extensive discussion of physical security.

Your bastion host should be in a locked room, with adequate air conditioning and ventilation. If you provide uninterruptible power for your Internet connection, be sure to provide it for the bastion host as well.

Locating the Bastion Host on the Network

The bastion host should be located on a network that does not carry confidential traffic, preferably a special network of its own.

Most Ethernet and token ring interfaces can operate in "promiscuous mode" In this mode, they are able to capture *all* packets on the network the interfaces are connected to, rather than just those packets addressed to the particular machine the interface is a part of. Other types of network interfaces, such as FDDI, may not be able to capture all packets, but depending on the network architecture, they can usually capture at least some packets not specifically addressed to them.

This capability has a useful purpose: for network analysis, testing, and debugging, e.g., by programs like *etherfind* and *tcpdump*. Unfortunately, it can also be used by an intruder to snoop on all traffic on a network segment. This traffic might include Telnet, FTP, or *rlogin* sessions (from which logins and passwords can be captured), confidential email, NFS accesses of sensitive files, and so on. You need to assume the worst: the bastion host can be compromised. If it is compromised, you don't want the bastion host to snoop on this traffic.

One way to approach the problem is to not put the bastion host on an internal network; instead, put it on a perimeter network. As we've discussed in earlier chapters, a perimeter network is an additional layer of security between your internal network and the Internet. The perimeter network is separated from the internal network by a router or bridge. Internal traffic stays on the internal net and is not visible on the perimeter net. All the bastion host on a perimeter network can see are packets that are either to or from itself, or to or from the Internet. Although this traffic might still be somewhat sensitive, it's likely to be a lot less sensitive than your typical internal network traffic, and there are other places (for instance, your Internet service provider) that can already see much of it.

Using a perimeter net with a packet filtering router between it and the internal network gives you some additional advantages. It further limits your exposure, if the bastion host is compromised, by reducing the number of hosts and services the bastion host can access.

If you can't put the bastion host on a perimeter network, you might consider putting it on a network that's not susceptible to snooping. For example, you might put it on an intelligent 10baseT hub, an Ethernet switch, or an ATM network. If you do only this, you need to take additional care to make sure that nothing trusts the bastion host, because there's no further layer of protection between it and the internal network. Using such a network technology for your perimeter network is the best of both worlds: the bastion host is isolated from internal systems (as with a traditional perimeter network) but can't snoop on traffic on the perimeter network.

Selecting Services Provided by the Bastion Host

The bastion host provides any services your site needs to access the Internet, or wants to offer to the Internet—services you don't feel secure providing directly via packet filtering. (Figure 5-1 shows a typical set.) You should not put any services on the bastion host not intended to be used to or from the Internet. For example, it shouldn't provide booting services for internal hosts (unless, for some reason, you intend to provide booting services for hosts on the Internet). You have to assume that the bastion host will be compromised, and that all services on it will be available to the Internet.

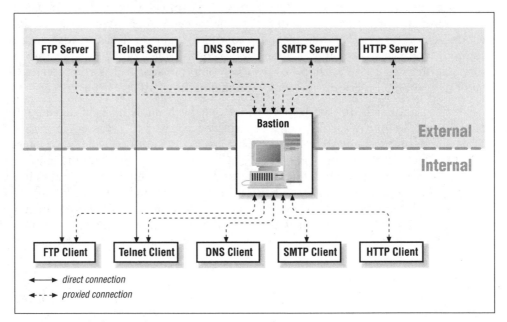

Figure 5-1: The bastion host may run a variety of Internet services

You can divide services into four classes:

Services that are secure
> Services in this category can be provided via packet filtering, if you're using this approach. (In a pure-proxy firewall, *everything* must be provided on the bastion host or not provided at all.)

Services that are insecure as normally provided but can be secured
    Services in this category can be provided on the bastion host.

Services that are insecure as normally provided and can't be secured
    These will have to be disabled and provided on a victim host (discussed above) if you absolutely need them.

Services that you don't use, or that you don't use in conjunction with the Internet
    You must disable services in this category.

We'll discuss individual services in detail in Chapter 8, but here we cover the most commonly provided and denied services for bastion hosts.

Electronic mail (SMTP) is the most basic of the services bastion hosts normally provide. You may also want to access or provide information services such as:

- FTP—file transfer

- Gopher—menu-based information retrieval

- WAIS—keyword-search information retrieval

- HTTP—hypertext-driven information retrieval (the World Wide Web)

- NNTP—Usenet news

In order to support any of these services (including SMTP), you must access and provide domain name service (DNS). DNS is seldom used directly, but it underlies all the other protocols by providing the means to translate hostnames to IP addresses and vice versa, as well as providing other distributed information about sites and hosts.

You may also want to provide some version of the *finger* service, to provide information about your site and the people at it. However, you should decide what information you want people to have, and use a modified *finger* daemon that provides only that. It is generally not desirable to tell the world which accounts are available on the bastion host and which are in use. Not only is this information useful to attackers, it's useless to genuine inquirers, who want to know information about your site as a whole, not about the bastion host in particular. The section on *finger* in Chapter 8 discusses some possible modified *finger* daemons.

The book *Managing Internet Information Services*, referenced above, has a good chapter on providing information services through *finger*, *inetd*, and Telnet. One particular technique described, that of creating "captured" or "no-break" shells, creates site-specific modified-procedure proxy services fairly easily. These services are a way for users within your network to be able to run *ping* or *traceroute* against external hosts, from a captured shell on the bastion host.

Many LAN-oriented services include vulnerabilities that attackers can exploit from outside, and all of them are opportunities for an attacker who has succeeded in compromising the bastion host. Basically, you should disable anything that you aren't going to use, and you should choose what to use very carefully.

Don't Allow User Accounts on the Bastion Host

If at all possible, don't allow any user accounts on the bastion host. Keeping such accounts off the bastion host will give you the best security. There are several reasons why, including:

- Vulnerabilities of the accounts themselves

- Vulnerabilities of the services required to support the accounts

- Reduced stability and reliability of the machine

- Inadvertent subversion of the bastion host's security by users

- Increased difficulty in detecting attacks

User accounts provide relatively easy avenues of attack for someone who is intent on breaking into the bastion host. Each account usually has a reusable password[*] that can be attacked through a variety of means, including dictionary searches, brute force searches, or capture by network eavesdropping. Multiply this by many users, and you have a disaster in the making.

Supporting user accounts in any useful fashion requires the bastion host to enable services (for example, printing and local mail delivery services) that could otherwise be disabled on the bastion host. Every service that is available on the bastion host provides another avenue of attack, through software bugs or configuration errors.

Having to support user accounts also can reduce the stability and reliability of the machine itself. Machines that do not support user accounts tend to run predictably and are stable. Many sites have found that machines without users tend to run pretty much indefinitely (or at least until the power fails) without crashing.

Users themselves can contribute to security problems on the bastion host. They don't (usually) do it deliberately, but they can subvert the system in a variety of ways. These range from trivial (e.g., choosing a poor password) to complex (e.g., setting up an unauthorized information server that has unknown security implications). Users are seldom trying to be malicious; they're normally just trying to get their own jobs done more efficiently and effectively.

It's usually easier to tell if everything is "running normally" on a machine that doesn't have user accounts muddying the waters. Users behave in unpredictable ways, but you want a bastion host to have a predictable usage pattern, in order to detect intrusions by watching for interruptions in the pattern.

---

[*] We discuss ways to support nonreusable passwords in Chapter 10.

If you need to allow user accounts on the bastion host, keep them to a minimum. Add accounts individually, monitor them carefully, and regularly verify that they're still needed.

Building a Bastion Host

Now that you've figured out what you want your bastion host to do, you need to actually build the bastion host. In order to do that, follow these steps:

1. Secure the machine.

2. Disable all nonrequired services.

3. Install or modify the services you want to provide.

4. Reconfigure the machine from a configuration suitable for development into its final running state.

5. Run a security audit to establish a baseline.

6. Connect the machine to the network it will be used on.

You should be very careful to make sure the machine is not accessible from the Internet until the last step. If your site isn't yet connected to the Internet, you can simply avoid turning on the Internet connection until the bastion host is fully configured. If you are adding a firewall to a site that's already connected to the Internet, you need to configure the bastion host as a standalone machine, unconnected to your network.

If the bastion host is vulnerable to the Internet while it is being built, it may become an attack mechanism instead of a defense mechanism. An intruder who gets in before you've run the baseline audit will be difficult to detect and will be well-positioned to read all of your traffic to and from the Internet. Cases have been reported where machines have been broken into within minutes of first being connected to the Internet; while rare, it can happen.

The following sections describe each of the main steps involved in building a bastion host. They also touch briefly on ongoing maintenance and protection of the bastion host; note, though, that maintenance issues are discussed primarily in Chapter 12.

Securing the Machine

To start with, build a machine with a standard operating system, secured as much as possible. Start with a clean operating system and follow the procedures we describe in this section.

Start with a minimal clean operating system installation

Start with a clean operating system installation, straight from vendor distribution media. If you do this, you will know exactly what you're working with. You won't need to retrofit something that may already have problems. Using such a system will also make later work easier. Most vendor security patches you later obtain, as well as the vendor configuration instructions and other documentation, assume you're starting from an unmodified installation.

While you're installing the operating system, install as little as you can get away with. It's much easier to avoid installing items than it is to delete them completely later on. For that matter, once your operating system is minimally functional, it's not hard to add components if you discover you need them. Don't install any optional subsystems unless you know you will need them.

Fix all known system bugs

Get a list of known security patches and advisories for your operating system; work through them to determine which are relevant for your own particular system, and correct all of the problems described in the patches and advisories. You get this information from your vendor sales or technical support contacts, or from the user groups, newsgroups, or electronic mailing lists devoted to your particular platform.

A helpful list of contacts is available via anonymous FTP at the Firewalls mailing list archive:

```
ftp://ftp.greatcircle.com/pub/firewalls/vendor_security_contacts
```

In addition, be sure to get from the Computer Emergency Response Team Coordination Center (CERT-CC) any advisories relevant to your platform, and work through them. (For information on how to contact CERT-CC and retrieve its information, see the list of resources in Appendix A.)

Use a checklist

To be sure you don't overlook anything in securing your bastion host, use a security checklist. There are several excellent checklists around. Be sure to use one that corresponds to your own platform and operating system version.

Appendix A of *Practical UNIX Security*, referenced earlier, contains an extensive checklist that covers most UNIX platforms. More specific checklists for particular operating system releases are often available through the formal or informal support channels for those platforms; check with your vendor support contacts, or the user groups, newsgroups, or mailing lists that are devoted to the platform.

Safeguard the system logs

As a security-critical host, the bastion host requires considerable logging. The next step in building the bastion host is to make sure that you have a way of safeguarding the system logs for the bastion host. The system logs on the bastion host are important for two reasons:

- They're one of the best methods of determining if your bastion host is performing as it should be. If everything the bastion host does is logged (and it should be), you should be able to examine the logs to determine exactly what it's doing and decide if that's what it's supposed to be doing. Chapter 12 describes the use of system logs in maintaining your firewall.

- When (not if!) someday someone does successfully break in to the bastion host, the system logs are one of the primary mechanisms that determine exactly what happened. By examining the logs and figuring out what went wrong, you should be able to keep such a break-in from happening again.

Where should you put the system logs? On the one hand, you want the system logs to be somewhere convenient; you want them to be where they can be easily examined to determine what the bastion host is doing. On the other hand, you want the system logs to be somewhere safe; this will keep them from any possible tampering in case you need to use them to reconstruct an incident.

The solution to these seemingly contradictory requirements is to keep two copies of the system logs—one for convenience, the other for catastrophes.

System logs for convenience The first copy of the system logs is the one you'll use on a regular basis to monitor the ongoing activity of the machine. These are the logs against which you run your daily and weekly automated analysis reports. You can keep these logs either on the bastion host itself or on some internal host.

The advantage of keeping them on the bastion host is simplicity: you don't have to set up logging to go to some other system, nor do you have to configure the packet filters to allow this. The advantage to keeping them on an internal host is ease of access: you don't have to go to the bastion host, which doesn't have any tools anyway, to examine the logs. Avoid logging in to the bastion host, in any case.

System logs for catastrophes The second copy of the system logs is the one you'll use after a catastrophe. You can't use your convenience logs at a time like this. Either the convenience logs won't be available, or you won't be sure of their integrity any longer.

One of the simplest ways to create catastrophe logs is to attach a line printer to one of the bastion host's serial ports, and simply log a copy of everything to that port. There are some problems with this approach, though. First, you have to keep the printer full of paper, unjammed, and with a fresh ribbon. Second, once the logs are printed, there's not much you can do with them except look at them. Because they aren't in electronic form, you have no way to search or analyze them in an automated fashion.

A more effective way to create catastrophe logs is to connect a dedicated personal computer to a serial port on the bastion host, as a *dropsafe* logging device. Configure the PC in such a way that it boots up into a terminal program in "record" mode, and that every so often (every 100,000 bytes, for example), the log files are rotated and pruned so the system never runs out of disk space. In this way, anything the bastion host spits out to that serial port will be recorded on the personal computer's disk. Unless someone has physical access to the PC (the PC should *not* be connected to a network), the logs will remain safely out of reach. The advantage of this approach over the first method is that the data remains in electronic form. If you have to do searches and analyses on the data (after an incident, for example), you can retrieve it from the dropsafe machine.

If you have a write-once device available to you, use that device; doing so is probably technically easier, especially if your write-once device can emulate a filesystem. Be sure you can trust the write-once feature. Some magneto-optical drives are capable of both multiple-write and write-once operations, and keep track of the mode they're in via software. If the system is compromised, it may be possible to rewrite supposedly write-once media.

Some operating systems (notably BSD 4.4-Lite and systems derived from it, such as current releases of BSDI, FreeBSD, and NetBSD) support append-only files. These are not an advisable alternative to write-once media or a dropsafe machine. Even if you can trust the implementation of append-only files, the disk that they're on is itself writable, and there may be ways to access it outside of the filesystem, particularly for an intruder who wants to destroy the logs.

Figure 5-2 shows how you can connect a personal computer to your system to do logging.

Setting up system logs   On a UNIX system, logging is handled through *syslog*. The *syslog* daemon records log messages from various local and remote clients (programs with messages they want logged). Each message is tagged with facility and priority codes: the facility code tells *syslog* what general subsystem this message is from (for example, the mail system, the kernel, the printing system, the Usenet news system, etc.), and the priority code tells *syslog* how important the message is (ranging from debugging information and routine informational messages through several levels up to emergency information). The */etc/syslog.conf* file controls what *syslog* does with messages, based on their facility and priority. A given message might be ignored, logged to one or more files, forwarded to the *syslog* daemon on another system, flashed onto the screens of certain or all users who are currently logged in, or any combination.

When you configure *syslog* to record messages to files, you could configure it to send all messages to a single file, or to split messages up to multiple files by

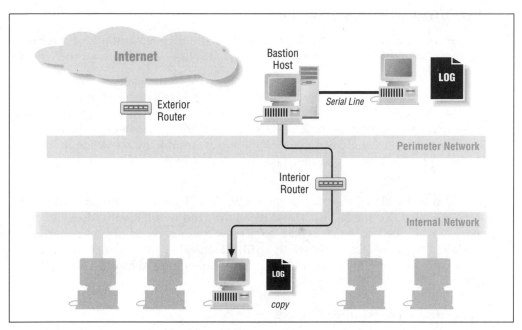

Figure 5–2: Use a PC attached by a serial line to create catastrophe logs

facility and priority codes. If you split messages by facility and priority codes, each log file will be more coherent, but you'll have to monitor multiple files; you may have an easier time finding messages from a particular service. If you direct everything to a single file, on the other hand, you'll only have a single file to check for all messages, but that file will be much larger.

Many non-UNIX systems, particularly network devices such as routers, can be configured to log messages via *syslog*. If your systems have that capability, configuring them to so they all log to your bastion host provides a convenient way to collect all their messages in a single place.

Be aware that remote logging via *syslog* (e.g., from a router to your bastion host, or from your bastion host to some internal host) is not 100% reliable. For one thing, *syslog* is a UDP-based service, and the sender of a UDP packet has no way of knowing whether or not the receiver got the packet unless the receiver tells the sender (*syslog* daemons don't confirm receipt to their senders). For another thing, even if *syslog* were TCP-based, you still couldn't absolutely depend on it not to lose messages; what if the receiving system was down or otherwise unavailable? This is one reason that it's important to have a locally attached dropsafe machine to reliably capture all *syslog* messages.

Despite its weaknesses, though, *syslog* is a useful service; you should make extensive use of it.

Disabling Nonrequired Services

Once you've completed the basic process of securing your bastion host, go on to the next step: disabling any services that aren't absolutely necessary for the bastion host to provide.

Any service provided by the bastion host might have bugs or configuration problems that could lead to security problems. Obviously, you'll have to provide some services that users need, as long as your site's security policy allows them. But, if the service isn't absolutely necessary, don't borrow trouble by providing it. If a service isn't provided by the bastion host, you won't have to worry about possible bugs or configuration problems.

If you can live without a service, it should be turned off. It's worth suffering some inconvenience. This means that you're going to need to think very carefully about services. You'll be disabling not just services you never heard of and never used, but also services you've purposefully enabled on other machines. Look at every service and ask yourself "How could I avoid enabling this? What do I lose if I turn it off?"

How are services managed?

On UNIX machines, most services are managed in one of two ways:

- By controlling when they start and who can use them

- By service-specific configuration files

There are two ways services get started on UNIX systems:

- At boot time from a machine's */etc/rc* files

- On demand by the *inetd* daemon (which is itself started at boot time)

A few services—for example, Sendmail—can be configured to run under either or both mechanisms.

Services started by /etc/rc files   Services in the first category are designed to run indefinitely. They are started once (when the machine boots), and they are never supposed to exit. (Of course, sometimes they do exit, either because they're killed by a system administrator, or because they trip over a bug or some other error.) Servers are written in this way if they need to handle small transactions quickly, or if they need to "remember" information. Writing them in this way avoids the delays associated with starting a new copy of the server to handle each request made to it.

Servers of this kind are started from a UNIX system's */etc/rc* files, which are shell scripts executed when the machine boots. Examples of servers typically started from */etc/rc* files are those that handle NFS, SMTP, and DNS. In BSD-based versions of UNIX, there are customarily a few files in */etc* with names that start with "rc." (for example */etc/rc.boot*). In System V-based versions of UNIX, there are customarily directories in */etc* instead of files (for instance, */etc/rc.0.d*); the directories contain the various startup commands, each in its own little file.

In either case, you need to be careful to look at all of the startup scripts and all of the scripts they call, recursively. Usually more than one script is run in the process of bringing a system all the way up. On modern UNIX systems, those scripts often call others, sometimes through multiple levels of indirection. For example, you may find that a startup script calls another script to start up networking, and that one calls yet another script to start up file service. You may also find that startup scripts use mystical options to familiar commands (e.g., they often run *ifconfig* with little-used options that cause *ifconfig* to pick up configuration information from obscure places). Be sure you understand these options and that you replace any that tell the machine to pick up information about itself from the network (or from services it normally provides but that you are going to turn off).

Some versions of UNIX also have an additional process started from these files that is designed to restart other servers if they fail. If such a program exists on a system, it will try to start the other servers if they are removed from the startup files but not from its configuration file. Either turn off this program or be sure to remove from the program's configuration file any servers removed from the startup files. You'll notice the program when you work through the startup files.

Services started by inetd Some servers are designed to be started "on demand," and to exit after they provide the requested service. Such servers are typically used for services that are requested infrequently; for services that aren't sensitive to delays in starting a new server from scratch; and for services that require a new server process to deal with each request (for example, Telnet or FTP sessions, where a separate server is used for each active session).

Servers of this kind are usually run from the *inetd* server. (The *inetd* server itself, because it runs indefinitely, is started from the */etc/rc* files, as described in the previous section.) The *inetd* server listens for requests for services specified in the */etc/inetd.conf* configuration file. When it hears such a request, it starts the right server to process the request.

How to disable services

If you disable a critical service, you must first make certain you have a way to boot the machine. This could be a second hard disk with a full root partition on it or a CD-ROM drive with the operating system install disk. You need to be ruthless; if you delete the wrong thing and can't reboot, at best you're going to be overcautious about deleting things, and at worst you're going to end up with an unusable computer.

Second, you must save a clean copy of every file before you modify it. Even when you're just commenting things out, every so often your fingers slip, and you delete something you didn't mean to, or you change a critical character.

Once you've taken these precautions, walk through the startup files for your system, line by line, making sure you know exactly what each line does—including the command line options—and commenting out or deleting the lines that start services you don't need. In a perfect world, you would comment out every line, and then uncomment or rewrite the ones you need. Unfortunately, if you do this and the machine crashes in the middle, it will not reboot. It's rather a lot of trouble for a small increase in security over merely commenting out with a very free hand.

You will frequently see services that are started after a check for some configuration file. If you don't want the service to run, comment out the entire code block. Don't leave the code active simply because the configuration file doesn't *currently* exist and the service won't *currently* be started. Someone or something might create the configuration file some time in the future. Commenting out the entire thing is more secure and less risky.

Commenting out lines is preferable to removing them, because it leaves evidence of your intent. When you comment something out, add a comment about why you have commented it out. If you delete something, replace it with a comment about why you have deleted it. Make sure that the next person to look at the files knows that you got rid of things on purpose and doesn't helpfully "fix" it for you. If you comment out a call to another script, add a comment in that script indicating that it's not supposed to be started, and why. Renaming it or commenting out its contents are also good ways to help ensure that it won't accidentally reappear.

For every service that you leave enabled, apply the same line-by-line procedure to the service's configuration files. Obviously, you want to pay particular attention to *inetd*'s configuration file. On most systems, this file is called */etc/inetd.conf.* (On other systems, this file might be called */etc/servers* or something else; check your manual pages for *inetd*). If you have a daemon-watcher and have decided to leave it on, its configuration files are also particularly important.

In general, you'll need to reboot your machine after you have changed the configuration files. The changes won't take effect until you do so.

After you have rebooted and tested the machine, and you are comfortable that the machine works without the disabled services, you may want to remove the executables for those services. If the executables are lying around, they may be started by somebody—if not you, some other system administrator, or an intruder. A few services may even be executable by nonroot users if they use nonstandard ports.

If you feel uncertain about removing executables, consider encrypting them instead. Do not use the standard UNIX *crypt* program; the encryption algorithm it uses is little more than a toy and can be trivially broken. Instead, use a more secure encryption program like *snuffle* or something that uses the DES or IDEA algorithm. Choose a secure key; if you forget the key, you're no worse off than if you'd deleted the files, but if an intruder gets the key, you're considerably worse off.

Which services should you leave enabled?

Certain services are essential to the operation of the machine, and you'll probably need to leave these enabled, no matter what else the machine is configured to do. On a UNIX system, these processes include:

init, swap, and *page*
> The three kernel pseudo-processes used to manage all other processes

cron
> Runs other jobs at fixed times, for housekeeping and so on

syslogd
> Collects and records log messages from the kernel and other daemons

inetd
> Starts network servers (such as *telnetd* and *ftpd*) when such services are requested by other machines

In addition, you'll obviously need server processes for the services that you've decided to provide on your bastion host, e.g., real or proxy Telnet, FTP, SMTP, and DNS servers.

Which services should you disable?

You will want to disable all services except the ones you have decided to provide, and the supporting services necessary for those to run, as described above. You may not always know which services are the required support services, particularly because UNIX names tend to be cryptic and uninformative.

How do you know which services to disable?

There are three simple rules to apply:

- If you don't need it, turn it off.

- If you don't know what it does, turn it off (you probably didn't need it anyway).

- If turning it off causes problems, you now know what it does, and you can either turn it back on again (if it's really necessary) or figure out how to do without it.

NFS and related services   Start with NFS and related network services. You aren't going to need these. No internal machine should trust your bastion host enough to let the bastion host mount the internal machine's disks via NFS. Besides that, there probably won't be anything on the bastion host that you'll want to export via NFS. NFS is very convenient, but it's incredibly insecure.

NFS services are provided by a whole set of servers; the specific set of servers, and the names of the individual servers, varies slightly from one version of UNIX to the next. Look for these names or names like them:

- *nfsd*

- *biod*

- *mountd*

- *statd*

- *lockd*

- *automount*

- *keyserv*

- *rquotad*

- *amd*

Most of these services are started at boot time from the */etc/rc* files, although some are started on demand by *inetd*. *mountd* is somewhat peculiar in that it is often started at boot time *and* is listed in the *inetd* configuration file, apparently so that it will be restarted if for some reason the copy that was started at boot time crashes.

Other RPC services   You should also disable other services based on the Remote Procedure Call (RPC) system. The most critical of these is NIS/YP, a service which is provided by the following servers:

- *ypserv*

- *ypbind*

- *ypupdated*

These servers are generally started at boot time from the */etc/rc* files.

Also disable these RPC-based services:

- *rexd* (the remote execution service, started by *inetd*)

- *walld* (the "write all", or *wall* daemon, started by *inetd*)

All RPC-based services depend on a single service usually called *portmap* (on some machines it is known as *rpcbind*). If you've disabled all of the RPC-based services, you can (and should) also disable the *portmap* service. How can you tell if you've disabled all the RPC-based services? Before disabling *portmap*, but after disabling what you think are the rest of the RPC-based services, reboot the machine and then issue a *rpcinfo -p* command. If the output of that command shows only entries for *portmap* itself, this means that no other RPC services are running. On the other hand, if the output shows that other RPC services are still running, you will need to investigate further to determine what and why. If you decide to provide any RPC-based services, you must also provide the *portmap* service. In that case, consider using Wietse Venema's replacement *portmap*, which is more secure than the versions shipped with most UNIX systems (see Appendix B for information on where to find it).

Booting services Your bastion host should probably not provide booting services; nothing should trust the host enough to be willing to boot from it. This means that, in most cases, you should disable these services:

- *tftpd*

- *bootd*

- *bootpd*

BSD 'r' command services These should all be disabled. The servers for these services are typically named *rshd, rlogind,* and *rexecd,* and are typically started by *inetd*. The remaining "r" services are based on these and will not run without them.

routed Another server that your bastion host probably doesn't need is *routed*. This server is started at boot time from the */etc/rc* files, listens to routing information broadcasts, and updates the kernel routing table based on what it hears.

You probably don't need *routed* on your bastion host, because your bastion host is probably located on the perimeter of your network, where routing should be fairly simple. A more secure approach is to create static routes pointing to your internal networks and a default route pointing to your Internet gateway router. You do this at boot time by adding appropriate "route add" commands to the */etc/rc* files.

If you must do dynamic routing on your bastion host, obtain and use *gated* (see Appendix B for information on how to get it) rather than *routed*. *gated* understands the same routing protocols as *routed* (plus several more), but *gated* can be specifically told who to accept routing information from, while *routed* will accept information from anyone. Be sure that you set up the configuration files for *gated* to limit which hosts it listens to.

fingerd   The *finger* server supplies information about existing accounts and accounts on UNIX systems. This server is started on demand by *inetd*. The information provided by *fingerd* can be valuable to crackers; it tells them information about potential targets, such as:

- Which accounts exist. This tells them which accounts they should try to guess passwords for.

- Personal information about the people with accounts. This tells them what passwords to start guessing with.

- Which accounts are in use. This tells them which accounts should be avoided, at least until they're not in use.

- Which accounts haven't been used lately. This tells them which accounts are good targets for attack, because the owners probably won't notice that the accounts are being used.

On the other hand, Internet users often use *finger* (the program that talks to your *fingerd* daemon) quite legitimately. *finger* is helpful in locating email addresses and telephone numbers. Instead of simply disabling *fingerd*, you might want to replace it with a program that obtains information from a more basic source of contact information for your site; the information might include:

- Your main phone number

- Who to contact if they have questions about your site's products or services

- Sample email addresses if standardized aliases such as *Firstname_Lastname* are maintained for users at your site

- Who to contact in case of network or security problems involving your site

You can provide this kind of generic information to anybody who uses *finger* to check on your site, regardless of what specific information they've requested. The easiest way to accomplish this is to put the information in a file (for example, */etc/finger_info*) and then replace the part of the */etc/inetd.conf* entry for *fingerd* that specifies the program to run with something like */bin/cat/etc/finger_info*. Doing this causes the contents of the */etc/finger_info* file to be returned to anyone contacting your *fingerd* server.

For example, here is the old */etc/inetd.conf* line from Great Circle Associate's system:

```
finger stream tcp nowait nobody /usr/libexec/fingerd fingerd
```

and here is the new */etc/inetd.conf* line:

```
finger stream tcp nowait nobody /bin/cat cat /etc/finger_info
```

and here are the contents of the */etc/finger_info* file:

```
Great Circle Associates
Phone: +1 415 962 0841
Email: Info@GreatCircle.COM

For more information, or to report system problems, please
send email or call.
```

ftpd   If you're going to provide anonymous FTP service on your bastion host, you need to reconfigure the FTP server appropriately. You should replace the *ftpd* program with one more suited to providing anonymous FTP service than the standard *ftpd* programs shipped by most UNIX vendors. (See Chapter 8 for information about providing anonymous FTP service.)

If you're *not* going to provide anonymous FTP, you can probably disable your FTP server entirely; it's started on demand by *inetd*.

Even if you've disabled the FTP server on your bastion host, you can still use the FTP client program (typically called simply *ftp*) on the bastion host to transfer files to and from other systems. You'll just have to do the work from the bastion host, instead of from the other systems.

Other services   There are lots of other services you probably don't need and should disable. Although the specific list depends on your own site's security policy and needs, and on the platform you're using, it should probably include the following:

* *uucpd* (UUCP over TCP/IP)

* *rwhod* (sort of like *fingerd*, in that it tells you who's currently logged in on the system)

* *lpd* (the printer daemon)

Turning off routing

If you have a dual-homed host that is not supposed to be a router, you will need to specifically disable routing. In order to act as an IP router, a dual-homed host needs to accept packets that are addressed to its network interface, but another machine's IP address, and to send them on appropriately. This is known as *IP forwarding*, and it's usually implemented at a low level in the operating system kernel. An IP-capable host with multiple interfaces normally does this automatically, without any special configuration.

Other machines have to know that the dual-homed host is a router in order to use it as such. Sometimes this is done simply by configuring those machines to always route packets for certain networks to the dual-homed host (this is called *static routing*). More often, however, the dual-homed host is configured to broadcast its routing capabilities via a routing protocol such as Routing Information Protocol (RIP). Other machines hear these routing broadcasts and adjust their own routing tables accordingly (this is called *dynamic routing*). This broadcast of routing information by the dual-homed host is usually done by an additional program (for example, *routed* or *gated* on a UNIX system), which often has to be turned on explicitly.

To use a dual-homed host as a firewall, you need to convert it to a nonrouting dual-homed host; you take a machine that has two network interfaces, and you configure it so it *can't* act as a router between those two interfaces. This is a two-step process:

1. Turn off any program that might be advertising it as a router; this is usually relatively straightforward.

2. Disable IP forwarding; this is considerably more difficult, and may require modifying the operating system kernel.

Fortunately, these days a number of UNIX vendors provide supported parameters for turning off IP forwarding. Even for vendors that don't, it's about as easy as kernel patches get on most machines: turning off IP forwarding necessitates only a change in the value of a single kernel variable. You need to consult your vendor to find out how to turn off IP forwarding on your machines.

Unfortunately, it's not always that easy to turn off all routing, particularly on BSD-based systems, such as SunOS and Ultrix. On such systems, you can patch the kernel to turn off IP forwarding, but the IP source-routing option usually remains a security hole.

What is *source routing?* Normal IP packets have only source and destination addresses in their headers, with no information about the route the packet should take from the source to the destination. It's the job of the routers in between the source and the destination to determine the most efficient route. However, source-routed IP packets contain additional information in the IP header that specifies the route the packet should take. This additional routing information is specified by the source host; thus the term source-routed.

When a router receives a source-routed packet, it follows the route specified in the packet, instead of determining the most efficient route from source to destination. The source-routing specification overrides the ordinary routing. Because of the way the routing code is implemented in most UNIX kernels, turning off IP forwarding does *not* disable forwarding of source-routed packets. It's implemented completely separately. Unlike IP forwarding, source routing is not generally an easily patchable option. It is possible to disable it (you can disable anything with persistence and/or source code), but it's much more difficult.

Source-routed packets can easily be generated by modern applications like the Telnet client that's freely available on the Internet as part of the BSD 4.4 release. Unless you block source-routed packets somewhere else, such as in a router between the dual-homed host and the Internet, source-routed packets can blow right past your dual-homed host and into your internal network.

Worse still, source routing goes both ways. Once source-routed packets make their way to an internal system, the system is supposed to reply with source-routed packets that use the inverse of the original route. The reply from your internal system back to the attacker will also blow right through your dual-homed host, allowing two-way connection through a firewall that was supposed to block all communications across it.

If you are not going to screen your dual-homed host, you will need to patch your operating system so that it rejects source-routed packets. Consult your vendor, and/or appropriate security mailing lists (discussed in Appendix A) for information on how to do this on your platform. This is not the sort of thing most vendors' customer support structures deal with rapidly and painlessly; expect to have to dig to find what you need to know.

Installing and Modifying Services

Some of the services you want to provide may not be provided with your operating system (for example, WWW generally is not). Others may be provided but are inappropriate for use in a secure environment or are missing features you probably want (for example, stock *fingerd* and *ftpd*). Even those few remaining services that are provided, secure, and up-to-date in your vendor's operating system release should be protected with the TCP Wrapper package or the *netacl* program from the TIS FWTK to improve security and provide logging. (Although TCP Wrapper and *netacl* will increase security, they're not perfect; they rely on the source IP address to identify hosts, and IP addresses can be forged.)

For detailed information about individual services, including advice on selecting WWW, NNTP, and FTP servers, see Chapter 8.

Whatever services you do leave enabled should also be protected to the extent possible by the TCP Wrapper package or the *netacl* program, as we describe in the following sections. For example, you might want to set up your bastion host so that it only accepts Telnet connections from one specific machine, such as the workstation you normally use.

Using the TCP Wrapper package to protect services

The TCP Wrapper package, written by Wietse Venema, monitors incoming network traffic and controls network activity. It is a simple but very effective piece of publicly available software set up to run whenever certain ports (corresponding to certain services) are connected. TCP Wrapper provides simple access control list protection, as well as improved logging, for services that are started by *inetd*.

Using the TCP Wrapper package is easy. Here's what you do:

1. Install the package and set up a pair of simple access control files that define which hosts and networks are allowed to access which services.

2. Reconfigure your *inetd* to run the main TCP Wrapper program (called *tcpd*) instead of the "real" server.

3. When a request for a service comes in, *inetd* starts *tcpd*, which evaluates the request against the TCP Wrapper configuration files. This program decides whether or not to log the request, and whether or not to carry out the request.

4. If *tcpd* decides that the request is acceptable, it starts the "real" server to process the request.

For example, if you want to allow Telnet connections from a specific host (172.16.1.2) to your machine, but deny Telnet connections from all other hosts, you would change the line for *telnetd* in your */etc/inetd.conf* file to say something like:

```
telnet stream tcp nowait root /usr/local/libexec/tcpd telnetd
```

You would also need to create an */etc/hosts.allow* file that tells the TCP Wrapper package (the *tcpd* program) which host to allow connections from:

```
telnetd : 172.16.1.2
```

And finally, you'd need to create an */etc/hosts.deny* file to tell the TCP Wrapper package to deny all connections from all hosts by default, and to send email to root about each probe:

```
ALL : ALL : (/usr/local/etc/safe_finger -l @%h | \
    /usr/ucb/Mail -s "PROBE %d from %c" root)&
```

Note that the */etc/hosts.deny* file only applies to services protected by the TCP Wrapper package (that is, services for which you've configured *inetd* to run *tcpd* instead of the real server). If you don't tell *inetd* to run the TCP Wrapper package (the *tcpd* program) for a given service, then the TCP Wrapper package won't do anything regarding that service.

Despite its name, the TCP Wrapper package supports UDP-based services in addition to TCP-based services. Beware, however, that the TCP Wrapper package can only control when to *start* UDP-based servers; it cannot control access to those servers once they're started, and many UDP-based servers will hang around and continue to process requests for some period of time beyond the initial start-up request. Many eventually time out and exit, but once they've been started through a legitimate request, they're vulnerable to illegitimate requests.

Using netacl to protect services

The *netacl* component of the TIS FWTK (described in some detail in Chapter 7) provides much the same capability as the TCP Wrapper package. To implement the same example as above (except for the ability to trace probes from unauthorized systems) using *netacl*, you would change the line for *telnetd* in your */etc/inetd.conf* file to:

```
telnet stream tcp nowait root /usr/local/lib/netacl telnetd
```

Then, you would add the following lines to your FWTK *netperm* configuration file (wherever that is on your system):

```
netacl-telnetd: permit-hosts 172.16.1.2 -exec /usr/libexec/telnetd
```

Reconfiguring for Production

Now it's time to move the machine from the configuration that was useful to you when you were building it to the best configuration for running it. You'll need to do several things:

- Reconfigure and rebuild the kernel.

- Remove all unnecessary programs.

- Mount as many filesystems as possible to read-only.

Once you've deleted all the services that aren't used on a day-to-day basis, you'll find that it is very difficult to work on the bastion host, e.g., when you need to install new software packages or upgrade existing ones. Here are some suggestions for what to do when you find it necessary to do extensive work on the bastion host:

- Write all the tools to a tape before deleting them, and then restore them from tape when needed. Don't forget to delete them each time after you're done.

- Set up a small, external, alternate boot disk with all the tools on it. Then, plug the disk in and boot from it when you need the tools. Don't leave the disk connected during routine operations, however; you don't want an attacker to be able to mount the disk and use the tools against you.

You don't want an intruder to attack the machine while you're working on it. To keep that from happening, follow these steps:

1. Either disconnect the bastion host from the network or disconnect your network from the Internet before you begin.

2. Give the bastion host back the tools you'll need to use (as we've described above).

3. After you've finished your work on the machine, return it to its normal (stripped down) operating condition.

4. Reconnect the bastion host to the network or your network to the Internet.

You may find it easier to simply remove the bastion host's disk and attach it to an internal host as a nonsystem disk; you can then use the internal host's tools without fear of having them remain available when the bastion host is returned to service. This procedure also guarantees that the bastion host is not vulnerable to compromise from the outside while you are doing the work, since it is entirely nonfunctional while its disk is removed and not susceptible to accidental reconnection.

Reconfigure and rebuild the kernel

The first step in this phase of building your bastion host is to rebuild the operating system kernel to remove kernel capabilities you don't need. This may sound intimidating, but it's generally a relatively straightforward operation; it needs to be, because you'll be using the same capabilities you'd use to install a new type of device on your system. Every UNIX system, as shipped, contains some form of configuration support (they range considerably in how kernel reconfiguration is supported and in what you can do). Besides reducing the size of your kernel (and thereby making more memory available for other purposes), rebuilding the kernel denies to attackers the chance to exploit these capabilities.

Some capabilities are particularly dangerous. In particular, you should probably remove the following capabilities or device drivers:

- NFS and related capabilities

- Anything that enables network sniffing, e.g., Network Interface Tap (NIT) or Berkeley Packet Filter (BPF)

Although NIT and BPF are provided for testing and debugging purposes, they are frequently used by attackers. NIT and BPF are dangerous because they let the machine grab all packets off the Ethernet it's attached to, instead of only the packets addressed to it. Disabling these capabilities may prevent you from using the machine as a packet filtering system, so you may not be able to delete them in all architectures.

If your bastion host is a dual-homed host, this is the time to disable IP forwarding.

You have to be more careful when you disable kernel capabilities than when you disable services started by *inetd* or at boot time from the */etc/rc* files (as described earlier). There are a lot of interdependencies between kernel capabilities. For this reason, it's sometimes hard to determine exactly what a given capability is used for. The consequences of disabling a capability that is actually needed can be severe, e.g., the new kernel might not boot.

Make sure you follow your vendor's instructions for building and installing new kernels. Always keep a backup copy of your old kernel. If you have a backup, you can boot from it if you find out that something is wrong with the new kernel. Be sure you know how to boot a backup kernel and look up the procedure before you try to boot onto the new kernel. Be sure the backup kernel is in the root partition; you can't boot from a kernel that isn't on the root partition.

When you can reboot the machine, go through the kernel configuration files the same way you went through the startup files, checking every single line to make certain that it's something you want. Again, watch for places where one configuration file contains another, and check your documentation to be sure that you've looked at all the configuration files that are consulted. Often there is one file for including device drivers and one or more for parameters; IP forwarding will be in the latter.

Once you've got a working kernel, you'll probably want to delete or encrypt your old "full function" kernel. Replace it with a backup copy of the working minimal kernel. Doing so will keep a cracker who somehow manages to break into your machine from simply using that old kernel to reboot, and thereby restore all of the services you so carefully disabled. For similar reasons, you'll probably also want to delete the files and programs needed to build a new kernel.

If your kernel uses loadable modules, it may be difficult to determine when they're used. You will want to delete or encrypt all the ones that you don't want used, but because they're not always explicitly loaded, you may not know which those are. Keeping an alternate boot medium handy, try moving them out of the directory for loadable modules. Run the machine through its paces before you finally remove or encrypt them.

Beware! Your vendor may have provided copies of "generic" kernels (which typically have every possible capability enabled) in unexpected locations for use during the installation of the machine and its (nonexistent) client machines. SunOS 4.x, for example, has such kernels in the */usr/stand* directory. Poke around in all the directories where installation files are kept and all the directories for clients. The documentation generally tells you where client kernels are, but rarely tells you about the internals of the install process. Check the documentation for disaster recovery advice, which may helpfully tell you where to locate spare kernel images.

Remove nonessential programs

The next step is to remove all of the programs that aren't essential for day-to-day operation. If a program isn't there, an attacker can't exploit any bugs that it might contain. This is especially true for *setuid/setgid* programs, which are a very tempting target for an attacker. You should remove programs you normally think of as being essential. Remember that the bastion host is purely providing Internet services; it does not need to be a comfortable environment to work in.

Window systems and compilers are examples of major programs you can get rid of. Attackers find these programs very useful: window systems are fertile ground for security problems, and compilers can be used to build the attacker's own tools.

Before deleting programs like compilers, make sure you've finished using them yourself; make sure you've built, installed, and tested everything you're going to need on this machine, such as the tools for auditing the system (discussed later in this chapter).

Instead of simply deleting key tools you'd expect an attacker to use, such as the compiler, you might want to replace them with programs that raise an alarm (for example, sending email or tripping your pager) when someone tries to run them. You might even want to have the programs halt the system after raising the alarm, if you believe it's better for the machine to be down than under attack. This is a prime way to humiliate yourself, however; you yourself are probably the one person most likely to forget where you are to try to run a forbidden command. It's also a good way to set yourself up for denial of service attacks.

You'll want to do two scans looking for things to delete:

1. Walk through all the standard directories for binaries on your system (everything that's in root's path or in the default user path). If you're unsure whether a program is needed, turn off execute permission on it for a while (a few days) before you remove or encrypt it and see what happens. You may also want to run the machine for a while before you do the scan and check the access times on files to see if they've been used.

2. Use *find* to look for every file on the system that has the *setuid* or *setgid* bit turned on. The arguments to *find* differ radically from system to system, but you will probably want something like this:

   ```
   find / -type f \( -perm -04000 -o -perm -02000 \) -ls
   ```

3. Some versions of *find* provide special primitives for identifying *setuid* and *setgid* files.

Mount filesystems as read-only

Once you've got the bastion host configured, you don't want anybody (particularly an attacker) to be able to change the configuration. To guard against this happening, mount the filesystems on the bastion host as read-only if possible (particularly the filesystems that contain program binaries) to protect against tampering.

It's much better if you can use hardware write-protect; an attacker may be able to remount disks with write permission without getting physical access to the machine, but it's not going to do any good if the hardware write-protect on the disk is on. Most IPI and SMD disks have switches for this on their front panels. Many SCSI disks have a "write-disable" jumper you can set. If you find powering the disk down and removing it from the case unacceptable as a way to get write access, you could wire this jumper to an external switch on the drive enclosure.

You can't write-protect everything, of course. You have to provide a certain amount of writable filesystem space for things like scratch space, system logs, and the mail spool. You might be able to use a RAM disk for this; however, you'll have to be sure that your operating system supports this, that you have enough RAM, and that you think you can afford to lose the contents of the RAM disk (for example, electronic mail in transit between internal hosts and the Internet) whenever your machine reboots.

With most versions of UNIX, you'll also have to either provide writable disk space for memory swapping or turn off swapping. Many versions of UNIX do not allow you to turn off swapping; however, they will usually allow you to use a separate disk for swap space, and that disk can safely be left writable. Using a RAM disk will increase your memory usage to the point where you will probably need swap space.

Systems based on BSD 4.4-Lite (for instance, current releases of NetBSD, FreeBSD, and the BSDI product) have a new immutable attribute that can be set on a per-file basis. If a file is marked "immutable," the file cannot be changed, not even by root, unless the system is running in single-user mode. If your operating system provides this capability, use it to protect your programs and configuration files from tampering by an attacker. (We recommend that approach only if you cannot use hardware write protection, or an additional layer of security to use with hardware write protection. Because it's implemented in software, it is more likely to be compromisable.)

Running a Security Audit

Once you've got the bastion host reconfigured, the next step is to run a security audit. There are two reasons for doing this. First, it gives you a way to ensure you haven't overlooked anything during system setup. Second, it establishes a "baseline," or a basis for comparison, against which you can compare future audits. In this way, you'll be able to detect any tampering with the machine.

Auditing packages

Most auditing packages have two basic purposes:

- Checking for well-known security holes. These are holes that have been uncovered by system administrators, exploited by attackers in system break-ins, or documented in computer security books and papers.

- Establishing a database of checksums of all files on a system; doing this allows a system administrator to recognize future changes to files—particularly unauthorized changes.

There are several very good automated auditing packages freely available on the Internet. The three most commonly used are these:

- *COPS*—The Computer Oracle and Password System, developed by Dan Farmer and Gene Spafford

- *Tiger*—Developed as part of the TAMU package by Texas A&M University

- *Tripwire*—Developed by Gene H. Kim and Gene Spafford

COPS and Tiger both check for well-known security holes. There is significant overlap in what COPS and Tiger check; however, they're both free, so it's a good idea to obtain and run both of them to get the best possible coverage. Tripwire is a filesystem integrity checker. It is strictly a tool for dealing with checksum databases; it is much better at this than either COPS or Tiger (which both have basic checksum database capabilities), but has no ability to check for well-known security holes. These packages are independent of each other; there's nothing to prevent you from using all three of them in combination on your bastion host, and that would probably be a good idea. Appendix B gives you information on how to get all three packages.

Because the well-known security holes tend to be somewhat operating system-specific, the effectiveness of the packages that check for these security holes is very dependent on which operating system you have, and which version of the operating system it is. If it's an operating system and version the package knows about, that's great. If it isn't, then the package has to grope around blindly, trying to guess what holes might exist. (Fortunately, attackers will usually have the same problem, if not to the same extent.)

Commercial packages that perform similar functions are starting to become available, but none yet have the complete capabilities and widespread acceptance of COPS, Tiger, and Tripwire.

Use the auditing packages

How do you use the various auditing packages to audit your system? The details of what you do depend upon which package you're using. (See the documentation provided with the packages for detailed instructions.) This section provides some general tips.

You will need to do some configuration. Don't just install the program, run it, and expect you'll get reasonable results. Expect to go through several iterations of running the auditing package, getting warnings, and reconfiguring your machine or the auditing package to get rid of warnings. When you get warnings, you have to decide whether the auditing package is wrong, or you are. There will be some cases where the right thing to do is to turn off checks, but it shouldn't be your automatic response.

Once you've used the tools described in the previous section to create your initial baseline, store a copy of the tools and these initial audit results somewhere safe.

Under no circumstances should you store the only copy of the baseline or the tools on the bastion host. Prepare for the worst: if someone were to break into the bastion host and tamper with the only copy of the baseline audit, this would compromise your ability to use the audit later on to detect illicit changes on the system. If intruders can change the auditing software, it doesn't matter whether they can change the baseline; they could simply set up the auditing software to reproduce the baseline. Keeping a copy of the baseline audit on a floppy disk or magnetic tape that's locked up someplace safe is a good way to protect against such a compromise. Preferably, you don't want an intruder to even read the audit results; why tell them what you expect the system to look like and what files you aren't watching?

Periodically, e.g., daily or weekly, depending on your own site's needs and capabilities, audit the machine once again and compare the new audit to the baseline. Make sure you can account for any differences you find. Ideally, you should automate this periodic re-audit so it happens regularly and reliably. Unfortunately, this is easier said than done. Arranging for automatic audits that can't be defeated by "replay" attacks can be a neat trick. In a replay attack, an attacker who has compromised your auditing system simply sends you a recording of a prior good audit whenever your system invokes the automatic auditing capability. The most practical defense against this is to run your automated auditing system often enough that it's unlikely an attacker could break in, discover the auditing system, and subvert it (covering his tracks) before the next audit runs. This suggests that you should run an audit at least daily.

About checksums for auditing

Checksums are very helpful in auditing. An intruder who changes a program or configuration file will almost certainly correct the modification dates afterwards, so you can't use these dates as a reliable index. Comparing every file to a baseline copy avoids that problem, but takes a lot of time and requires that you store a copy of every single file, effectively doubling your storage requirements. Checksums are probably your best bet.

A checksum is a number calculated from the contents of the file that will change if the file is changed. Checksum calculation is time-consuming, but not as time-consuming as reading everything twice to do a bit-by-bit compare. In addition, storing the checksums takes up much less space than storing the entire file. Checksums are not full representations of the file, however, and every checksum algorithm has cases where it will give the same checksum for two different files. The better the checksum algorithm, the less likely it is that files with the same checksum resemble each other in any other way.

For example, the common UNIX *spell* command uses a hashing algorithm that shares this property with checksums. *spell* will relatively reliably detect misspelled

English words, but will often happily accept complete garbage, because random character strings may happen to have the same hashes as good words. This represents a problem only if you are likely to type "qzx" when you meant to type "the". Similarly, a good checksum algorithm may come up with the same number for */bin/login* and a document containing the text of "Jabberwocky," but it won't come up with the same number for */bin/login* and any other executable capable of logging people in (especially a modified copy of */bin/login*).

However, the standard UNIX checksum programs (*/bin/sum*, for example) don't have this property. Those checksum programs use simple cyclic redundancy counter (CRC) algorithms designed to catch bit errors during data transfers. They can't keep up with the latest tools crackers use to subvert traditional checksum programs. Crackers now have programs that manipulate the unused bytes in a file (particularly an executable binary file) to make the checksum for that file come out to whatever they want it to be. They can make a modified copy of */bin/login* that produces the same checksum, and *sum* will not be able to detect any difference

For real security, you need to use a "cryptographic" checksum algorithm like MD5 or Snefru; these algorithms produce larger and less predictable checksums that are much more difficult to spoof. The COPS, Tiger, and Tripwire auditing packages described above all include and use such algorithms in place of the normal UNIX checksum programs.

Connecting the Machine

Now that you have the machine fully secured, you can finally connect it to its destination network and run it. You want to do this when you're going to be around to see what happens; don't make it the last thing you do before that long overdue vacation.

Operating the Bastion Host

Once you put the bastion host into production, your job has only just begun. You'll need to keep a close watch on the operations of the bastion host. Chapter 12 provides more information on how to do this; this section discusses specific concerns for bastion hosts.

Learn What the Normal Usage Profile Is

If you're going to monitor the bastion host, looking for abnormalities that might indicate break-ins or other types of system compromise, you will need to first develop an understanding of what the "normal" usage profile of the bastion host is. Ask these questions, and others like them:

- How many jobs tend to be running at any one time?

- How much CPU time do these jobs consume relative to each other?

- What is the typical load at different times throughout the day?

Your goal is to develop an almost intuitive grasp of what your system normally runs like, so you'll be able to recognize—and investigate—anomalous activity very quickly.

Consider Writing Software to Automate Monitoring

Doing a thorough job of system monitoring is tough. Although the logs produced by your system provide lots of useful information, it's easy to get overwhelmed by the sheer volume of logging data. The important information may often be buried. Too often, the logs end up being used only *after* a break-in, when, in fact, they could be used to detect—and thus perhaps stop—a break-in while it is occurring.

Because each operating system and site is different, each bastion host is configured differently, and each site has different ideas about what the response of a monitoring system should be. For example, some want email; some want the output fed to an existing SNMP-based management system, some want the systems to trip the pagers of the system administrators, and so on. Monitoring tends to be very site- and host-specific in the details. However, there are some useful tools out there that you should be able to configure and adapt for your own use. The SWATCH (Simple WATCHer) package is a good example.

SWATCH, developed by Stephen E. Hansen and E. Todd Atkins, automates the monitoring of UNIX systems. SWATCH enhances the standard *syslog* facility in various ways. (See the discussion of *syslog* in "Setting Up System Logs" earlier in this chapter.) It sifts through the logs as they're created by *syslog*, and takes certain actions when certain types of log messages are found, e.g., sounding an alert when repeated unsuccessful login attempts are made to the same account, or a "file system full" message is encountered. SWATCH also includes modifications for a number of daemons to make their logging more useful; these include *fingerd, ftpd, ruserok, rshd,* and *login.* For example, *login* has been modified so that it allows only three login atempts; it reports to syslog on any "Incomplete Login Attempt", "Repeated Login Attempt", and "Root Login Refused" events; and it includes the account names attempted and the originating host. SWATCH can also watch files other than ones generated by *syslog.* Appendix B gives you information on where to get SWATCH.[*]

SWATCH is written in Perl, which is an unfortunately powerful tool to have sitting on a bastion host; it provides almost everything an intruder could get through

---

[*] The 1993 and 1994 USENIX/SAGE LISA conferences (see Appendix A for information about USENIX, SAGE, and the LISA conferences) have produced a number of papers on other automated monitoring tools that were originally intended for system administration use, but that might be adapted to use in monitoring system security.

having a compiler except the ability to build new kernels. You will probably want to run SWATCH on the machine that the bastion host is logging to, rather than on the bastion host itself.

Protecting the Machine and Backups

Once the bastion host has been fully configured and is in operation, protect the physical machine and make sure that its backups are protected from theft or other compromise.

Watch Reboots Carefully

How will you know if someone has breached security? Sometimes, it's painfully obvious. But sometimes, you'll have to draw conclusions from the behavior of the system. Unexplained reboots or downtime on the system may be a clue. Many attacks, e.g., modifying a kernel, can't succeed unless the system is rebooted.

On the bastion host, crashes and reboots should be rare occurrences. Once the bastion host has been fully configured and is in production, it should be a very stable system, often running for weeks or months at a stretch without a crash or a reboot. If a crash or a reboot does occur, investigate it immediately to determine whether it was caused by some legitimate problem or might have been the result of some kind of attack.

You might want to consider configuring the bastion host so that it doesn't bring itself up automatically after an attempted reboot. That way, if someone does manage to crash or force a reboot of the machine, you'll know about it: the machine will sit there waiting for you to reboot it. The machine won't be able to come back up until you decide to do so. Even if your machine does not appear to allow you to disable autobooting, you can usually cause autoboots to fail by configuring the machine to autoboot from a nonexistent disk.

Do Secure Backups

Backups on a bastion host are tricky because of trust issues. Who can you trust?

You definitely don't want internal machines to trust the bastion host enough for it to dump to their tape drives. If the bastion host has somehow been compromised, this could be disastrous. You also don't want the bastion host to trust the internal machines; this could lead to subversion of the bastion host by (well-intentioned) internal users, or to attack from some host pretending to be an internal system.

Common remote dump mechanisms (for example, those used by the BSD *dump* and *rdump* programs) will probably be blocked by packet filtering between the bastion host and the internal systems anyway (we discuss this issue in Chapter 6).

Therefore, you will normally want to do backups to a tape device attached directly to the bastion host. Under no circumstances should you rely on backing up the bastion host to disks that remain attached to the bastion host. You must do backups that are removed from the bastion host so they cannot be accessed by an attacker who compromises it.

Fortunately, because the bastion host is an infrequently changing machine, you won't have to do frequent backups. Once the bastion host is fully configured and in production, it should be very stable. A weekly or even monthly manual backup will probably be sufficient.

Backups of the bastion host aren't done just to guard against normal system catastrophes like disk crashes. They're also a tool that you can use later to investigate a break-in or some other security incident. They give you a way to compare what's currently on the bastion host's disk with what was there before the incident.

If you're only doing weekly or monthly backups, how you handle logging becomes an issue. If the bastion host is not being backed up daily, you *must* do your logging to some system other than the bastion host itself. If an incident does occur, the logs are going to be critical in reconstructing what happened. If it turns out that your only copy of the logs was on the (compromised) bastion host, and backups of the logs haven't been done for three weeks, you're going to be severely hampered in your investigative efforts.

As with all backups on all systems, you need to guard your bastion host backups as carefully as you guard the machine itself. The bastion host backups contain all the configuration information for the bastion host. An attacker who gets access to these backups would be able to analyze the security of your bastion host without ever touching it. With the information these backups provide, he may possibly find a way to break in without setting off any of the alarms on the bastion host.

In This Chapter:
- *Why Packet Filtering?*
- *Configuring a Packet Filtering Router*
- *What Does a Packet Look Like?*
- *What Does the Router Do with Packets?*
- *Conventions for Packet Filtering Rules*
- *Filtering by Address*
- *Filtering by Service*
- *Choosing a Packet Filtering Router*
- *Where to Do Packet Filtering*
- *Putting It All Together*

6

Packet Filtering

Packet filtering is a network security mechanism that works by controlling what data can flow to and from a network. We provide a very brief introduction to high-level IP networking concepts (a necessity for understanding packet filtering) here, but if you're not already familiar with the topic, then before continuing, you should refer to Appendix C for a more detailed discussion.

To transfer information across a network, the information has to be broken up into small pieces, each of which is sent separately. Breaking the information into pieces allows many systems to share the network, each sending pieces in turn. In IP networking, those small pieces of data are called *packets*. All data transfer across IP networks happens in the form of packets.

The basic device that interconnects IP networks is called a *router*. A router may be a dedicated piece of hardware that has no other purpose, or it may be a piece of software that runs on a general-purpose UNIX or PC (MS-DOS, Windows, Macintosh, or other) system. Packets traversing an internetwork (a network of networks) travel from router to router until they reach their destination. The Internet itself is sort of the granddaddy of internetworks—the ultimate "network of networks."

A router has to make a routing decision about each packet it receives; it has to decide how to send that packet on towards its ultimate destination. In general, a packet carries no information to help the router in this decision, other than the IP address of the packet's ultimate destination. The packet tells the router where it wants to go, but not how to get there. Routers communicate with each other using "routing protocols" such as the Routing Information Protocol (RIP) and Open Shortest Path First (OSPF) to build *routing tables* in memory to determine how to get the packets to their destinations. When routing a packet, a router compares the packet's destination address to entries in the routing table and sends the packet onward as directed by the routing table. Often, there won't be a specific route for a particular destination, and the router will use a "default route;" generally, such a route directs the packet towards smarter or better-connected routers. (The default routes at most sites point towards the Internet.)

In determining how to forward a packet towards its destination, a normal router looks only at a normal packet's destination address and asks only "*How* can I forward this packet?" A packet filtering router also considers the question "*Should* I forward this packet?" The packet filtering router answers that question according to the security policy programmed into the router via the packet filtering rules.

NOTE

> Some unusual packets do contain routing information about how they are to reach their destination, using the "source route" IP option. These packets, called *source-routed packets*, are discussed in the section called "IP Options" below.

Why Packet Filtering?

Packet filtering lets you control (allow or disallow) data transfer based on:

- The address the data is (supposedly) coming from

- The address the data is going to

- The session and application protocols being used to transfer the data

Most packet filtering systems don't do anything based on the data itself; they don't make content-based decisions.* Packet filtering will let you say:

> Don't let anybody use Telnet (an application protocol) to log in from the outside.

or:

> Let everybody send us email via SMTP (another application protocol).

or even:

> That machine can send us news via NNTP (yet another application protocol), but no other machines can do so.

---

* Some packages, like CheckPoint's FireWall-1 product, are limited exceptions to this rule.

However, it won't let you say:

This user can Telnet in from outside, but no other users can do so.

because "user" isn't something a packet filtering system can identify. And, it won't let you say:

You can transfer these files but not those files.

because "file" also isn't something the packet filtering system can identify.

The main advantage of packet filtering is leverage: it allows you to provide, in a single place, particular protections for an entire network. Consider the Telnet service as an example. If you disallow Telnet by turning off the Telnet server on all your hosts, you still have to worry about someone in your organization installing a new machine (or reinstalling an old one) with the Telnet server turned on. On the other hand, if Telnet is not allowed by your filtering router, such a new machine would be protected right from the start, regardless of whether or not its Telnet server was actually running. This is an example of the kind of "fail safe" stance we discussed in Chapter 3.

Routers also present a useful choke point (also discussed in Chapter 3) for all of the traffic entering or leaving a network. Even if you have multiple routers for redundancy, you probably have far fewer routers, under much tighter control, than you have host machines.

Certain protections can be provided *only* by filtering routers, and then only if they are deployed in particular locations in your network. For example, it's a good idea to reject all packets that have internal source addresses—that is, packets that claim to be coming from internal machines but that are actually coming in from the outside—because such packets are usually part of address-spoofing attacks. In such attacks, an attacker is pretending to be coming from an internal machine. Decision-making of this kind can be done only in a filtering router at the perimeter of your network. Only a filtering router in that location (which is, by definition, the boundary between "inside" and "outside") is able to recognize such a packet, by looking at the source address and whether the packet came from the inside (the internal network connection) or the outside (the external network connection). Figure 6-1 illustrates this type of source address forgery.

Advantages of Packet Filtering

Packet filtering has a number of advantages.

One screening router can help protect an entire network

One of the key advantages of packet filtering is that a single, strategically placed packet filtering router can help protect an entire network. If there is only one

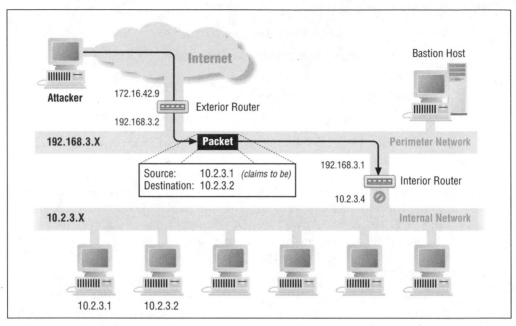

Figure 6-1: Source address forgery

router that connects your site to the Internet, you gain tremendous leverage on network security, regardless of the size of your site, by doing packet filtering on that router.

Packet filtering doesn't require user knowledge or cooperation

Unlike proxying, described in Chapter 7, packet filtering doesn't require any custom software or configuration of client machines, nor does it require any special training or procedures for users. When a packet filtering router decides to let a packet through, the router is indistinguishable from a normal router. Ideally, users won't even realize it's there, unless they try to do something that is prohibited (presumably because it is a security problem) by the packet filtering router's filtering policy.

This "transparency" means that packet filtering can be done without the cooperation, and often without the knowledge, of users. The point is not that you can do this subversively, behind your users' backs (while actions like that are sometimes necessary—it all depends on the circumstances—they can be highly political). The point is that you can do packet filtering without their having to learn anything new to make it work, and without your having to depend on them to do (or not do) anything to make it work.

Packet filtering is widely available in many routers

Packet filtering capabilities are available in many hardware and software routing products, both commercial and freely available over the Internet. Most sites already have packet filtering capabilities available in the routers they use.

Most commercial router products, such as the routers from Livingston Enterprises and Cisco Systems, include packet filtering capabilities. Packet filtering capabilities are also available in a number of packages, such as Drawbridge, KarlBridge, and *screend*, that are freely distributed on the Internet; these are discussed in Appendix B.

NOTE

In this book, it's impossible to give a complete list of commercial and publicly available packages, because new products are constantly being introduced and packet filtering capabilities are constantly being added to existing products. Instead, in this chapter we concentrate on discussing generic packet filtering features and capabilities, and the consequences of having—or not having—particular capabilities, so that you can make your own evaluation of the products currently available to you.

Disadvantages of Packet Filtering

Although packet filtering provides many advantages, there are some disadvantages to using packet filtering as well:

Current filtering tools are not perfect

Despite the widespread availability of packet filtering in various hardware and software packages, packet filtering is still not a perfect tool. The packet filtering capabilities of many of these products share, to a greater or lesser degree, common limitations:

- The packet filtering rules tend to be hard to configure. Although there is a range of difficulty, it mostly runs from slightly mind-twisting to brain-numbingly impossible.

- Once configured, the packet filtering rules tend to be hard to test.

- The packet filtering capabilities of many of the products are incomplete, making implementation of certain types of highly desirable filters difficult or impossible.

- Like anything else, packet filtering packages may have bugs in them; these bugs are more likely than proxying bugs to result in security problems. Usually, a proxy that fails simply stops passing data, while a failed packet filtering implementation may allow packets it should have denied.

Some protocols are not well suited to packet filtering

Even with perfect packet filtering implementations, you will find that some protocols just aren't well suited to security via packet filtering, for reasons we'll discuss later in this book. Such protocols include the Berkeley "r" commands (*rcp, rlogin, rdist, rsh*, etc.) and RPC-based protocols such as NFS and NIS/YP. (The problems of using packet filtering to deal with these protocols are discussed in Chapter 8.)

Some policies can't readily be enforced by normal packet filtering routers

The information that a packet filtering router has available to it doesn't allow you to specify some rules you might like to have. For example, packets say what host they come from, but generally not what user. Therefore, you can't enforce restrictions on particular users. Similarly, packets say what port they're going to, but not what application; when you enforce restrictions on higher-level protocols, you do it by port number, hoping that nothing else is running on the port assigned to that protocol. Malicious insiders can easily subvert this kind of control.

Configuring a Packet Filtering Router

To configure a packet filtering router, you first need to decide what services you want to allow or deny, and then you need to translate your decisions into rules about packets. In reality, you probably don't care about the details of packets at all. What you want is to get your work done. For example, you want to receive mail from the Internet, and whether that's managed by packets or by Murphy's ghost is irrelevant to you. The router, on the other hand, cares only about packets, and only about very limited parts of them. In constructing the rules for your routers, you have to translate the general statement "Receive mail from the Internet" into a description of the particular kinds of packets you want the router to allow to pass.

The following sections outline the general concepts you need to keep in mind when translating decisions about services into rules about packets. The specific details for each service are described in Chapter 8.

Protocols Are Usually Bidirectional

Protocols are usually bidirectional; they almost always involve one side sending an inquiry or a command, and the other side sending a response of some kind. When you're planning your packet filtering rules, you need to remember that packets go both ways. For example, it doesn't do any good to allow outbound Telnet packets that carry your keystrokes to a remote host, if you don't also allow the incoming packets for that connection that carry the screen display back to you.

Conversely, it also won't do you any good to block only half a connection. Many attacks can be carried out if attackers can get packets into your network, even if the attackers can't get any responses back. This is possible because the responses may be predictable enough to allow attackers to carry on their side of the conversation without having to actually see the responses at all. If the responses are predictable, an attacker doesn't need to see them. They won't be able to extract any information directly if they don't see the responses, but they may be able to do something that gives them the data indirectly. For example, even if they can't see your */etc/passwd* file directly, they can probably issue a command to mail themselves a copy.

Be Careful of 'Inbound' Versus 'Outbound' Semantics

When you're planning your packet filtering strategy, you need to be careful in your discussions of "inbound" versus "outbound." You need to carefully distinguish between inbound and outbound *packets,* and inbound and outbound *services.* An outbound service (e.g., the Telnet service mentioned above) involves both outbound packets (your keystrokes) and inbound packets (the responses to be displayed on your screen). Although most people habitually think in terms of *services*, you need to make sure you think in terms of *packets* when you're dealing with packet filtering. When you talk to others about filtering, be sure to communicate clearly whether you're talking about inbound versus outbound packets, or inbound versus outbound services.

Default Permit Versus Default Deny

In Chapter 3, we distingushed between the two stances you can choose in putting together your security policy: the default deny stance (that which is not expressly permitted is prohibited) and the default permit stance (that which is not explicitly prohibited is permitted). From a security point of view, it is far safer to take the attitude that things should be denied by default. Your packet filtering rules should reflect this stance. As we discussed earlier, start from a position of denying everything and then set rules that allow only protocols that you need, that you understand the security implications of, and that you feel that you can provide safely enough (according to your own particular definition of "safely enough") for your purposes

The default deny stance is much safer and more effective than the default permit stance, which involves permitting everything by default and trying to block those things that you know are problems. The reality is that with such an approach, you'll never know about all the problems, and thus you'll never be able to do a complete job.

In practical terms, the default deny stance means that your filtering rules should be a small list of specific things that you allow, perhaps with a few very specific things you deny scattered throughout to make the logic come out right, followed by a default deny that covers everything else. We'll explain in detail how these rules work later in this chapter.

What Does a Packet Look Like?

To understand packet filtering, you first have to understand packets and how they are handled at each layer of the TCP/IP protocol stack:

- Application layer (e.g., FTP, Telnet, HTTP)

- Transport layer (TCP or UDP)

- Internet layer (IP)

- Network access layer (e.g., Ethernet, FDDI, ATM)

Packets are constructed in such a way that layers for each protocol used for a particular connection are wrapped around the packets, like the layers of skin on an onion.

At each layer, a packet has two parts: the header and the body. The header contains protocol information relevant to that layer, while the body contains the data for that layer which often consists of a whole packet from the next layer in the stack. Each layer treats the information it gets from the layer above it as data, and applies its own header to this data. At each layer, the packet contains all of the information passed from the higher layer; nothing is lost. This process of preserving the data while attaching a new header is known as *encapsulation*.

At the application layer, the packet consists simply of the data to be transferred (for example, part of a file being transferred during an FTP session). As it moves to the transport layer, the Transmission Control Protocol (TCP) or the User Datagram Protocol (UDP) preserves the data from the previous layer and attaches a header to it. At the next layer, IP considers the entire packet (consisting now of the TCP or UDP header and the data) to be data, and now attaches its own IP header. Finally, at the network access layer, Ethernet or another network protocol considers the entire IP packet passed to it to be data, and attaches its own header. Figure 6-2 shows how this works.

At the other side of the connection, this process is reversed. As the data is passed up from one layer to the next higher layer, each header (each skin of the onion) is stripped off by its respective layer. For example, the Internet layer removes the IP header before passing the encapsulated data up to the transport layer (TCP or UDP).

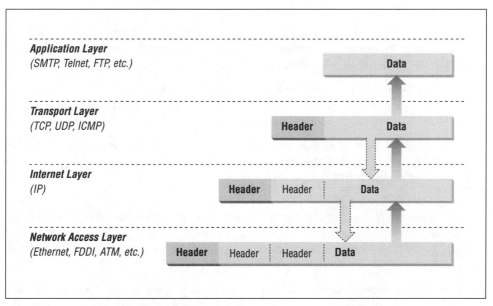

Figure 6–2: Data encapsulation

In trying to understand packet filtering, the most important information from our point of view is in the headers of the various layers. The sections below look at several examples of different types of packets and show the contents of each of the headers that packet filtering routers will be examining. We assume a certain knowledge of TCP/IP fundamentals, and concentrate on discussing the particular issues related to packet filtering. For a detailed introduction to TCP/IP, see Appendix C.

In the discussion below, we start with a simple example demonstrating TCP/IP over Ethernet. From there, we go on to discuss IP's packet filtering characteristics, then protocols above IP (such as TCP, UDP, ICMP, and RPC), protocols below IP (such as Ethernet), and finally non-IP protocols (such as AppleTalk or IPX).

TCP/IP/Ethernet Example

Let's consider an example of a TCP/IP packet (for example, one that is part of a Telnet connection) on an Ethernet. There are four layers that we're interested in here: the Ethernet layer, the IP layer, the TCP layer, and the data layer. In this section, we'll consider them from bottom to top and look at the contents of the headers that the packet filtering routers will be examining.

Ethernet layer

At the Ethernet layer, the packet consists of two parts: the Ethernet header and the Ethernet body. In general, you won't be able to do packet filtering based on information in the Ethernet header. Basically, the header tells you:

- *What kind of packet this is*—we'll assume in this example that it is an IP packet, as opposed to an AppleTalk packet, a Novell packet, a DECNET packet, or some other kind of packet.

- *The Ethernet address of the machine that put the packet onto this particular Ethernet network segment*—the original source machine, if it's attached to this segment; otherwise, the last router in the path from the source machine to here.

- *The Ethernet address of the packet's destination on this particular Ethernet network segment*—perhaps the destination machine, if it's attached to this segment; otherwise, the next router in the path from here to the destination machine.

Because we are considering IP packets in this example, we know that the Ethernet body contains an IP packet.

IP layer

At the IP layer, the IP packet is made up of two parts: the IP header and the IP body. From a packet filtering point of view, the IP header contains four interesting pieces of information:

- *The IP source address*—four bytes long, and typically written as something like 172.16.244.34.

- *The IP destination address*—just like the IP source address.

- *The IP protocol type*—identifies the IP body as a TCP packet, as opposed to a UDP packet, an Internet Control Message Protocol (ICMP) packet, or some other type of packet.

- *The IP options field*—which is almost always empty, but which is where options like the IP source route and the IP security options would be specified if they were used for a given packet. (See the discussion in "IP options" below.)

IP may divide up a packet that is too large to cross a given network into a series of smaller packets called *fragments*. Fragmenting a packet doesn't change its structure at the IP layer (the IP headers are duplicated into each fragment), but it may mean that the body contains only a part of a packet at the next layer. (See the discussion in "IP fragmentation" below.)

The IP body in this example contains an unfragmented TCP packet, although it could just as well contain the first fragment of a fragmented TCP packet.

TCP layer

At the TCP layer, the packet again contains two parts: the TCP header and the TCP body, shown in Figure 6-3.

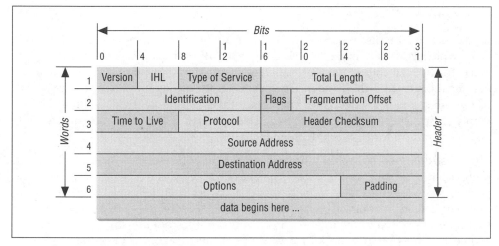

Figure 6-3: TCP header and body

From a packet filtering point of view, the TCP header contains three interesting pieces of information:

- *The TCP source port*—a two-byte number, which specifies what client or server process the packet is coming from on the source machine

- *The TCP destination port*—just like the TCP source port

- *The TCP flags field*

The TCP flags field contains one bit of interest for packet filtering: the ACK bit. By examining the ACK bit, a packet filtering router can determine whether a given packet is the first packet initiating a TCP connection (if the ACK bit is not set) or is a subsequent packet (if the ACK bit is set). The ACK bit is part of the TCP mechanism that guarantees delivery of the data. The ACK bit is set whenever one side of a connection has received data from the other side (it acknowledges the received data). Therefore, the ACK bit is set on all packets going in either direction except the very first packet from the client to the server.

The TCP body contains the actual "data" being transmitted—e.g., for Telnet the keystrokes or screen displays that are part of a Telnet session, or for FTP the data being transferred or commands being issued as part of an FTP session.

IP

IP serves as a common middle ground for the Internet. It can have many different layers below it, such as Ethernet, token ring, FDDI, PPP, or carrier pigeon.* IP can have many other protocols layered on top of it, with TCP, UDP, and ICMP being by far the most common, at least outside of research environments. In this section, we discuss the special characteristics of IP relevant to packet filtering.

IP options

As we saw in the discussion of the IP layer above, IP headers include an options field, which is usually empty. In its design, the IP options field was intended as a place for special information or handling instructions that didn't have a specific field of their own in the header. However, TCP/IP's designers did such a good job of providing fields for everything necessary that the options field is almost always empty. In practice, IP options are very seldom used except for break-in attempts and (very rarely) for network debugging.

The most common IP option a firewall would be confronted with is the IP source route option. Source routing lets the source of a packet specify the route the packet is supposed to take to its destination, rather than letting each router along the way use its routing tables to decide where to send the packet next. Source routing is supposed to override the instructions in the routing tables. In theory, the source routing option is useful for working around routers with broken or incorrect routing tables; if you know the route that the packet should take, but the routing tables are broken, you can override the bad information in the routing tables by specifying appropriate IP source route options on all your packets. In practice though, source routing is commonly used only by attackers who are attempting to circumvent security measures by causing packets to follow unexpected paths.

Many packet filtering systems take the approach of dropping any packet that has any IP option set, without even trying to figure out what the option is or what it means; in general, this seems to work well, without causing any special problems.

IP fragmentation

Another IP-level consideration for packet filtering is fragmentation. One of the features of IP is its ability to divide a large packet that otherwise couldn't traverse some network link (because of limitations on packet size along that link) into smaller packets, called *fragments*, which can traverse that link. The fragments are then reassembled into the full packet by the destination machine (not by the machine at the other end of the limited link; once a packet is fragmented, it stays fragmented until it reaches its destination).

---

* See RFC1149, dated 1 April 1990, which defines the Avian Transport Protocol; RFCs dated 1 April are usually worth reading.

IP fragmentation is illustrated in Figure 6-4.

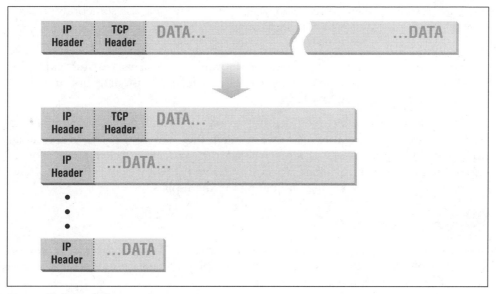

Figure 6–4: Data fragmentation

From a packet filtering point of view, the problem with fragmentation is that only the first fragment will contain the header information from higher-level protocols, like TCP, that the packet filtering system needs in order to decide whether or not to allow the full packet. The common packet filtering approach to dealing with fragmentation is to allow any nonfirst fragments through, and to do packet filtering only on the first fragment of a packet. This is safe because, if the packet filtering decides to drop the first fragment, the destination system will not be able to reassemble the rest of the fragments into the original packet, regardless of how many of the rest of the fragments it receives. If it can't reconstruct the original packet, the partially reassembled packet will not be accepted.

The destination host will hold the fragments in memory for a while, waiting to see if it gets the missing piece; this makes it possible for attackers to use fragmented packets in a denial of service attack. When the destination host gives up on reassembling the packet, it will send an ICMP "packet reassembly time expired" message back to the source host, which will tell an attacker that the host exists, and why the connection didn't succeed. There is nothing to be done about such denial of service attacks, but you can filter out the ICMP messages.

Outbound fragments could conceivably contain data you don't want to release to the world. For example, an outbound NFS packet would almost certainly be fragmented, and if the file was confidential, that information would be released. If this happens by accident, it's unlikely to be a problem; people do not generally hang around looking at the data in random packets going by just in case there's something interesting in them. You could wait a very long time for somebody to accidentally send a fragment out with interesting data in it.

If somebody inside intentionally uses fragmentation to transmit data, you have hostile users within the firewall, and no firewall can deal successfully with this problem. (They probably aren't very clever hostile users, though, because there are easier ways to get data out.)

The only situation in which you need to worry about outbound fragments is the one in which you allow a request in but block the outbound reply. In this situation, nonfirst fragments of the reply will get out, and the attacker has reason to expect them and look for them. You can deal with this by being careful to filter out requests and by not relying on filtering out the replies.

Protocols Above IP

IP serves as the base for a number of different protocols; by far the most common are TCP, UDP, and ICMP. These are, in fact, the only IP-based protocols that you're likely to see outside a research environment.

We discuss Remote Procedure Calls (RPCs) as well in this section, although RPC is, strictly speaking, based on either TCP or UDP, not on IP itself. It makes sense to discuss it here, however, because, like TCP and UDP, RPC is intended to operate as a general-purpose session protocol on which application protocols can be layered.

In addition, we briefly discuss IP over IP (i.e., an IP packet encapsulated within another IP packet), which is used primarily for tunneling multicast IP packets over nonmulticast IP networks.

TCP

TCP is the protocol most commonly used for services on the Internet. For example, Telnet, FTP, SMTP, NNTP, and HTTP are all TCP-based services. TCP provides a reliable, bidirectional connection between two endpoints. Opening a TCP connection is like making a phone call: you dial the number, and after a short setup period, a fairly reliable connection is established between you and whomever you're calling.

TCP is *reliable* in that it makes three guarantees to the application layer:

- The destination will receive the application data in the order it was sent.

- The destination will receive all the application data.

- The destination will not receive duplicates of any of the application data.

TCP will kill a connection rather than violate one of these guarantees. For example, if TCP packets from the middle of a session are lost in transit to the destination, the TCP layer will arrange for those packets to be retransmitted before handing the data up to the application layer. It won't hand up the data following the missing data until it has the missing data. If some of the data cannot be recovered, despite repeated attempts, the TCP layer will kill the connection and report this to the application layer, rather than hand up the data to the application layer with a gap in it.

These guarantees incur certain costs in both setup time (the two sides of a connection have to exchange startup information before they can actually begin moving data) and ongoing performance (the two sides of a connection have to keep track of the status of the connection, to determine what data needs to be resent to the other side to fill in gaps in the conversation).

TCP is bidirectional in that once a connection is established, a server can reply to a client over the same connection. You don't have to establish one connection from a client to a server for queries or commands and another from the server back to the client for answers.

If you're trying to block a TCP connection, it is sufficient to simply block the first packet of the connection. Without that first packet (and, more importantly, the connection startup information it contains), any further packets in that connection won't be reassembled into a data stream by the receiver, and the connection will never be made. That first packet is recognizable because the ACK bit in its TCP header is not set; every other packet in the connection, regardless of which direction it's going, will have the ACK bit set.

Recognizing these "start-of-connection" TCP packets allows you to enforce a policy that allows internal clients to connect to external servers, but prevents external clients from connecting to internal servers. You do this by allowing start-of-connection TCP packets (those without the ACK bit set) only outbound and not inbound. Start of connection packets would be allowed out from internal clients to external servers, but would not be allowed in from external clients to internal servers. Attackers cannot subvert this approach simply by turning on the ACK bit in their start-of-connection packets, because the absence of the ACK bit is what identifies these packets as start of connection packets.

Packet filtering implementations vary in how they treat and let you handle the ACK bit. Some packet filtering implementations give direct access to the ACK bit—for example, by letting you include "ack" as a keyword in a packet filtering rule. Some other implementations give indirect access to the ACK bit. For example, the Cisco "established" keyword works by examining this bit (established is "true" if the ACK bit is set, and "false" if the ACK bit is not set). Finally, some implementations don't let you examine the ACK bit at all.

Figure 6-5 shows what ACK is set to on packets that are part of a TCP connection.

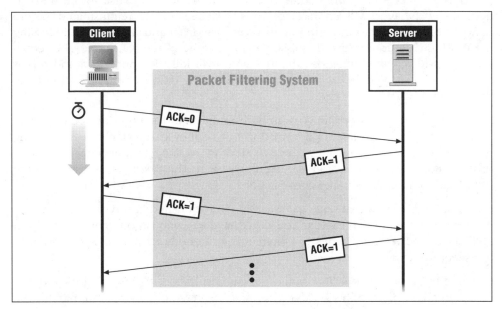

Figure 6–5: ACK bits on TCP packets

UDP

The body of an IP packet might contain a UDP packet instead of a TCP packet. UDP is a low-overhead alternative to TCP.

UDP is *low overhead* in that it doesn't make any of the reliability guarantees (delivery, ordering, and nonduplication) that TCP does, and, therefore, it doesn't need the mechanism to make those guarantees. Every UDP packet is independent; UDP packets aren't part of a "virtual circuit" as TCP packets are. Sending UDP packets is like dropping postcards in the mail: if you drop 100 postcards in the mail, even if they're all addressed to the same place, you can't be absolutely sure that they're all going to get there, and those that do get there probably won't be in exactly the same order they were in when you sent them.

Unlike postcards, UDP packets can actually arrive more than once (without being ripped to shreds, which is normally the only way the same postcard gets delivered multiple times). Multiple copies are possible because the packet might be duplicated by the underlying network. For example, on an Ethernet, a packet would be duplicated if a router thought that it might have been the victim of an Ethernet collision. If the router was wrong, and the original packet had not been the victim of a collision, both the original and the duplicate would eventually arrive at the destination. (A confused application may also decide to send the same data twice, perhaps because it didn't get an expected response to the first one.)

All of these things can happens to TCP packets, too, but they will be corrected for before the data is passed to the application. With UDP, the application is responsible for dealing with the packets, not corrected data.

UDP packets are very similar to TCP packets in structure. A UDP header contains UDP source and destination port numbers, just like the TCP source and destination port numbers. However, a UDP header does not contain anything resembling an ACK bit. The ACK bit is part of TCP's mechanism for guaranteeing reliable delivery of data. Because UDP makes no such guarantees, it has no need for an ACK bit. There is no way for a packet filtering router to determine, simply by examining the header of an incoming UDP packet, whether that packet is a first packet from an external client to an internal server, or a response from an external server back to an internal client.

Some packet filtering implementations, such as CheckPoint's FireWall-1 product, Janus; Morning Star's SecureConnect Router; and the KarlBridge/KarlBrouter, have the capability of "remembering" outgoing UDP packets that they've seen. They can then allow only the corresponding response packets back in through the filtering mechanism. In order to be counted as a response, the incoming packet has to be from the host and port that the outbound packet was sent to, and has to be directed to the host and port that sent the outbound packet. This capability is often referred to as *dynamic packet filtering*, because the router is essentially modifying the filtering rules on the fly to accommodate these returning packets. The rules created to allow the responses are time-limited; they time out after a few seconds or minutes. Dynamic packet filtering may also be used for any situation in which the packet filtering rules change without somebody explictly changing the configuration; different products support different capabilities.

Figure 6-6 illustrates dynamic packet filtering at the UDP layer.

ICMP

ICMP is used for IP status and control messages. ICMP packets are carried in the body of IP packets, just as TCP and UDP packets are. Examples of ICMP messages include:

- *Echo request*—what a host sends when you run *ping*.

- *Echo response*—what a host responds to an "echo request" with.

- *Time exceeded*—what a router returns when it determines that a packet appears to be looping; a more intuitive name might be *maximum hopcount exceeded*.

- *Destination unreachable*—what a router returns when the destination of a packet can't be reached for some reason (e.g., because a network link is down).

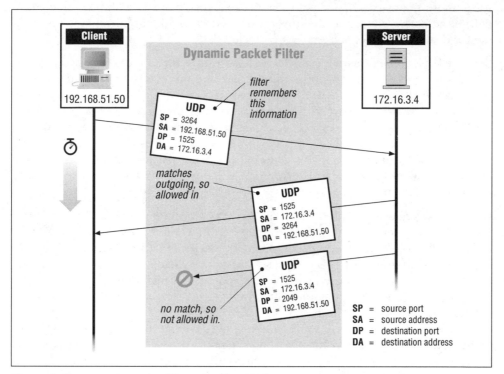

Figure 6–6: Dynamic packet filtering at the UDP layer

- *Redirect*—what a router sends a host in response to a packet the host should have sent to a different router; the router handles the original packet anyway (forwarding it to the router it should have gone to in the first place), and the redirect tells the host about the more efficient path for next time.

Unlike TCP or UDP, ICMP has no source or destination ports, and no other protocols layered on top of it. Instead, there is a set of defined ICMP message type codes; the particular code used dictates the interpretation of the rest of the ICMP packet.

Many packet filtering systems let you filter ICMP packets based on the ICMP message type field, much as they allow you to filter TCP or UDP packets based on the TCP or UDP source and destination port fields.

RPC

There are multiple remote procedure call protocols known as RPCs. The most popular is sometimes called "Sun RPC" because it was originally developed at Sun Microsystems. This is the protocol we'll be discussing, and it is the protocol most frequently referred to as simply "RPC". Other remote procedure call mechanisms are specific to particular UNIX implementations or implementation families. (For example, OSF DCE has its own remote procedure call protocol.) These mechanisms differ in detail from RPC, but tend to have similar problems.

Strictly speaking, the RPC mechanism is not built on top of IP, but rather on top of UDP and TCP. However, like TCP and UDP, RPC is used as a general-purpose transport protocol by a variety of application protocols (such as NFS and NIS/YP, as we discuss in Chapter 8), so it makes sense to describe it here. NFS and NIS/YP are vulnerable services from a network security point of view. An attacker with access to your NFS server can probably read any file on your system. An attacker with access to your NIS/YP server can probably obtain your password file, on which he can run a password-cracking attack against your system.

In the TCP and UDP protocols, port numbers are two-byte fields. This means that there are only 65,536 possible port numbers for TCP and UDP services. There aren't enough ports to be able to assign a unique well-known port number to every possible service and application that might want one. Among other things, RPC addresses this limitation. Each RPC-based service is assigned a unique four-byte "RPC service number." This allows for 4,294,967,296 different services, each with a unique number. That's more than enough to assign a unique number to every possible service and application you'd need.

RPC is built on top of TCP and UDP so there needs to be some way of mapping the RPC service numbers of the RPC-based servers in use on a machine to the particular TCP or UDP ports those servers are using. This is where the *portmapper* server comes in.

The *portmapper* is the only RPC-related server that is guaranteed to run on a particular TCP or UDP port number (it is at port number 111 on both). When an RPC-based server such as an NFS or NIS/YP server starts, it allocates a random TCP and/or UDP (some use one, some the other, some both) port for itself.[*] Then, it contacts the *portmapper* server on the same machine to "register" its unique RPC service number and the particular port(s) it is using at the moment.

An RPC-based client program that wishes to contact a particular RPC-based server on a machine first contacts the *portmapper* server on that machine (which, remember, always runs on both TCP and UDP port 111). The client tells *portmapper* the unique RPC service number for the server it wishes to access, and *portmapper* responds with a message saying, in effect, either "I'm sorry, but that service isn't available on this machine at the moment," or "That service is currently running on TCP (or UDP) port N on this machine at the moment." At that point, the client contacts the server on the port number it got from the *portmapper*, and continues its

---

[*] Actually, most NFS implementations that we've seen always use port 2049; however, we're not willing to assume that NFS always will use that port, in every implementation. In fact, RFC 1094, the NFS protocol specification, says "The NFS protocol currently uses the UDP port number 2049. This is not an officially assigned port, so later versions of the protocol use the 'Portmapping' facility of RPC."

conversation directly with the server, without further involvement from the *portmapper*. (Figure 6-7 shows this process.)

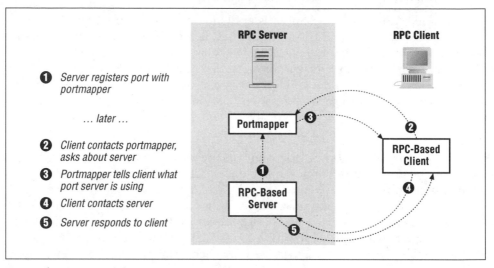

Figure 6–7: RPC and the portmapper

It's very difficult to use packet filtering to control RPC-based services, because you don't know what port the service will be using on a particular machine—and chances are that the port used will change every time the machine is rebooted. Blocking access to the *portmapper* isn't sufficient. An attacker can bypass the step of talking to the *portmapper*, and simply try all TCP and/or UDP ports (the 65,536 possible ports can all be checked on a particular machine in a matter of minutes), looking for the response expected from a particular RPC-based server like NFS or NIS/YP.

Some newer packet filtering products can talk to *portmapper* to determine what services are where and filter on that basis. Note that this has to be verified on a per-packet basis for UDP-based services. The packet filter will have to contact *portmapper* every time it receives a packet, because if the machine has rebooted, the service may have moved. Because TCP is connection-oriented, the port number only has to be verified on a per-connection basis. Using this mechanism to allow UDP-based services is going to result in high overhead and is probably not wise for data-intense applications like NFS.

NOTE

Even though it is not sufficient, you should still block access to the *portmapper*, because some versions of *portmapper* are capable of being used as proxies for an attacker's clients.

So, what do you do to guard RPC-based services? A couple of observations: First, it turns out that most of the "dangerous" RPC-based services (particularly NIS/YP and NFS) are offered only over UDP. Second, most services you'd want to access through a packet filter are TCP-based, *not* UDP-based; the notable exceptions are DNS, NTP, *syslog*, and Archie. These twin observations lead to the common approach many sites take in dealing with RPC using packet filtering: block UDP altogether, except for specific and tightly controlled "peepholes" for DNS, NTP, syslog and Archie. (See the discussion of these services in Chapter 8.)

With this approach, if you wish to allow any TCP-based RPC service, you'll need to allow them all. TCP-based NFS servers, while available, are not yet widely used; if you're using them, however, you'll need to modify this approach accordingly.

IP over IP

In some circumstances, IP packets are encapsulated within other IP packets for transmission, yielding so-called "IP over IP." The most common use of IP over IP is to carry multicast IP packets (that is, packets with multicast destination addresses) between networks that do support multicasting over intermediate networks that don't. To cross these intermediate networks, a special multicast router (or *mrouter*) on each multicast network encapsulates the multicast IP packets that it wants to send into nonmulticast (i.e., normal) IP packets addressed to other *mrouter*s. The other *mrouter*s, upon receiving these encapsulated multicast packets, strip off the outer (nonmulticast) packet and then handle the inner (multicast) packet.

Multicast IP is becoming more and more popular on the Internet, primarily because of the conferencing and other services offered through the MBONE. We discuss the MBONE, and multicast services in general, in more detail in Chapter 2 and Chapter 8.

Protocols Below IP

It's theoretically possible to filter on information from below the IP level—for example, the Ethernet hardware address. However, doing so is very rarely useful because in most cases, all packets from the outside are coming from the same hardware address (the address of the router that handles your Internet connection). Furthermore, many routers have multiple connections with different lower-level protocols. As a result, doing filtering at lower levels would require configuring different interfaces with different kinds of rules for the different lower-level protocols. You couldn't write one rule to apply to all interfaces on a router that had two Ethernet connections and an FDDI connection, because the headers of Ethernet and FDDI packets, while similar, are not identical. In practice, IP is the lowest level protocol at which people choose to do packet filtering.

Application Layer Protocols

In most cases, there is a further protocol on top of TCP or UDP, specific to the application. These protocols differ widely in their specificity, and there are hundreds, if not thousands, of them (almost as many as there are network-based applications). Some newer packet filtering applications provide the ability to filter on application-layer protocols for particular well-known applications. For example, they may be able to recognize particular information in an FTP transaction in order to set up dynamic filters, or they may be able to compare the information in a packet to the application that it's supposed to be going to, to be sure that packets addressed to a DNS port are actually DNS packets.

IP Version 6

The current version of IP (at the time this book was written) is officially known as IP Version 4; throughout this book, whenever we talk about IP with no further qualification, that's what we're talking about. There is, however, a new version of IP in the works right now, known as IP Version 6 (IPv6 for short). Why do we need a new version of IP, and how will IPv6 affect you?

As we mentioned in the section called "What the Future Holds" in Chapter 4, the impetus to create IPv6 was one simple problem: the Internet is running out of IP addresses. The Internet has become so popular that there just won't be enough IP network numbers (particularly Class B network numbers, which have proven to be what most sites need) to go around; by some estimates, if nothing had been done, the Internet would have run out of addresses in 1995 or 1996. Fortunately, the problem was recognized, and something was done. Two things, actually—first, the implementation of a set of temporary measures and guidelines to make best possible use of the remaining unassigned addresses, and second, the design and implementation of a new version of IP that would permanently deal with the address-exhaustion issue.

If you're going to create a new version of IP in order to deal with address-space exhaustion, you might as well take advantage of the opportunity to deal with a whole raft of other problems or limitations in IP as well, such as encryption, authentication, source routing, and dynamic configuration. According to Steve Bellovin of AT&T Bell Laboratories, a well-known firewalls expert on the Internet and a participant in the IPv6 design process:[*]

> IPv6 is based on the concept of nested headers. That's how encryption and authentication are done; the "next protocol" field after the IPv6 header specifies an encryption or an authentication header. In turn, their next protocol fields would generally indicate either IPv6 or one of the usual transport protocols, such as TCP or UDP.

---

[*] Steve Bellovin, posting to the Firewalls mailing list, December 31, 1994.

Nested IP over IP can be done even without encryption or authentication; that can be used as a form of source routing. A more efficient way is to use the source routing header—which is more useful than the corresponding IPv4 option, and is likely to be used much more, especially for mobile IP.

Some of the implications for firewalls are already apparent. A packet filter must follow down the full chain of headers, understanding and processing each one in turn. (And yes, this can make looking at port numbers more expensive.) A suitably cautious stance dictates that a packet with an unknown header be bounced, whether inbound or outbound. Also, the ease and prevalence of source routing means that cryptographic authentication is absolutely necessary. On the other hand, it is intended that such authentication be a standard, mandatory feature. Encrypted packets are opaque, and hence can't be examined; this is true today, of course, but there aren't very many encryptors in use now. That will change. Also note that encryption can be done host-to-host, host-to-gateway, or gateway-to-gateway, complicating the analysis still more.

Address-based filtering will also be affected, to some extent, by the new autoconfiguration mechanisms. It's vital that any host whose address is mentioned in a filter receive the same address each time. While this is the intent of the standard mechanisms, one needs to be careful about proprietary schemes, dial-up servers, etc. Also, high-order address bits can change, to accommodate the combination of provider-based addressing and easy switching among carriers.

Finally, IPv6 incorporates "flows." Flows are essentially virtual circuits at the IP level; they're intended to be used for things like video, intermediate-hop ATM circuit selection, etc. But they can also be used for firewalls, given appropriate authentication: the UDP reply problem might go away if the query had a flow id that was referenced by the response. This, by the way, is a vague idea of mine; there are no standards for how this should be done. The regular flow setup protocol won't work; it's too expensive. But a firewall traversal header might do the job.

As you can see, IPv6 could have a major impact on firewalls, especially with respect to packet filtering. As this book is being written, though, it's still too soon to tell just what those effects will be, and when we'll start to feel them.

Keep in mind that IPv6 won't be deployed overnight. IPv4 will be around for a long time, and many sites will continue to run it through the foreseeable future. The IPv6 designers are very sensitive to the transition issues, and a lot of attention is being paid to that area, and to various migration strategies sites might employ.

Non-IP Protocols

Other protocols at the same level as IP, e.g., AppleTalk and IPX, provide similar kinds of information as IP, although the headers and operations for these protocols, and, therefore their packet filtering characteristics, vary radically. Most packet filtering implementations support IP filtering only, and simply drop non-IP packets. Some packages provide limited packet filtering support for non-IP protocols, but this support is usually far less flexible and capable than the router's IP filtering capability.

At this time, packet filtering as a tool isn't as popular and well developed for non-IP protocols, presumably because these protocols are rarely used to communicate outside a single organization over the Internet. (The Internet is, by definition, a network of IP networks). Non-IP protocols are more of an issue for firewalls that are internal to an organization, and for this application, you would want to choose one of the packages that supports non-IP filtering.

Across the Internet, non-IP protocols are handled by encapsulating them within IP protocols. In most cases, you will be limited to permitting or denying encapsulated protocols in their entirety; you can accept all Appletalk-in-UDP connections, or reject them at all. A few packages that support non-IP protocols can recognize these connections when encapsulated and filter on fields in them.

What Does the Router Do with Packets?

Once a packet filtering router has finished examining a specific packet, what can it do with that packet? There are two choices:

- Pass the packet on. Normally, if the packet passes the criteria in the packet filtering configuration, the router will forward the packet on towards its destination, just as a normal router (not a packet filtering router) would do.

- Drop the packet. The other obvious action to take is to drop the packet if it fails the criteria in the packet filtering configuration.

Logging Actions

Regardless of whether the packet is forwarded or dropped ("permitted" or "deniedx" in some packet filtering implementations), you might want the router to log the action that has been taken. This is especially true if you drop the packet because it runs afoul of your packet filtering rules. In this case, you'd like to know what's being tried that isn't allowed.

You probably aren't going to log every packet that is allowed, but you might want to log some of these packets. For example, you might want to log start-of-connection TCP packets, so that you can keep track of incoming and outgoing TCP connections. Not all packet filters will log allowed packets.

Different packet filtering implementations support different forms of logging. Some will log only specific information about a packet, and others will forward or log an entire dropped packet. Generally, your packet filter will need to be configured to log to a host somewhere via the *syslog* service. You don't want the only copy of the logs to be on the packet filter if it is compromised. Most packet filtering also occurs on dedicated routers, which rarely have large amounts of disk space to dedicate to logging. See the discussion of setting up logging in Chapter 5 and Chapter 12.

Filtering by Interface

There is one key piece of information that would be useful when you are making a packet filtering decision, that can't be found in the headers of the packet; this is the interface on which the packet came into the router or is going out of the router. This is important information because it allows the router to detect forged packets.

If the sole router between your internal net and the external world receives a packet with an internal source address from the internal interface, there is no problem; all packets coming from the inside will have internal source addresses. If, however, the router receives a packet with an internal source address from the external interface, it means either that someone is forging the packet (probably in an attempt to circumvent security), or that there is something seriously wrong with your network configuration.

You can get these packets without forgery. For example, someone might have set up a second connection between your net and the outside world, such as a dial-up PPP link from a user's desk, probably with little or no thought to security. As a result, the traffic that should be staying internal to your net is "leaking" out through this second connection, going across the Internet, and trying to come back in through your "front door"). There's little you can do to detect such illicit "back door" connections except by detecting internal packets arriving from the outside; about the best you can do is have a strong and well-publicized policy against them, and provide as many as possible of the services your users desire through the front door (the firewall), so that they don't feel a compelling need to create their own back door.

These packets should be logged and treated as urgent issues. If someone is forging them, that person is attacking you with some seriousness. If the packets are leaked from a back door, you have a security problem because of the extra Internet connection. You may also have a routing problem: a host that claims to be internal and advertises routes for itself is in danger of getting all of your internal network's traffic. This is bad if it's a PPP link, which is probably not going to handle the load. It's much worse if it's not connected to your network at all, because some or all of your network's traffic is going to disappear.

Returning ICMP Error Codes

If a packet is to be dropped, the router may or may not send back an ICMP error code indicating what happened. Sending back an ICMP error code has the effect of warning the sending machine not to retry sending the packet; thereby saving some network traffic and some time for the user on the remote side. (If you send back an ICMP error code, the user's connection attempt will fail immediately; otherwise it will time out, which may take several minutes.)

There are two sets of relevant ICMP codes to choose from:

- The generic "destination unreachable" codes—in particular, the "host unreachable" and "network unreachable" codes.

- The "destination administratively unreachable" codes—in particular, the "host administratively unreachable" and "network administratively unreachable" codes.

ICMP's designers intended the first pair of ICMP error codes that the router might return, "host unreachable" or "network unreachable", to indicate serious network problems: the destination host is down or something in the only path to the host is down. These error codes predate firewalls and packet filtering. The problem with returning one of these error codes is that some hosts (particularly if they're running older versions of UNIX) take them quite literally. If these machines get back a "host unreachable" for a given host, they will assume that the host is totally unreachable and will close all currently open connections to it, even if the other connections were permitted by the packet filtering.

The second set of ICMP error codes the router might return, "host administratively unreachable" and "network administratively unreachable", were added to the official list of ICMP message types a few years ago, specifically to give packet filtering systems something to return when they dropped a packet. Many systems do not yet recognize these codes, although that should not cause your system problems. Systems are supposed to simply ignore ICMP error codes they don't understand, so this should be equivalent to returning no error code to such systems. On the other hand, many devices comply poorly with standards, and this is the kind of boundary condition some of them may not handle gracefully. The fact that the standard requires a system to ignore unknown error codes does not ensure that a system will not, in fact, react fatally to such an error code. It simply ensures that you will be able to argue persuasively that it is not your fault if they do so!

There are several issues to consider when you are deciding whether or not your packet filtering system should return ICMP error codes.

- Which message should you send?

- Can you afford the overhead of generating and returning error codes?

- Will returning these codes enable attackers to get too much information about your packet filtering?

Which set of error codes makes sense for your site?

Returning the old "host unreachable" and "network unreachable" codes is technically incorrect (remember that the host may or may not be unreachable, according to the packet filtering policy, depending on what host is attempting to access what service). Also, these error codes can cause many systems to react excessively (shutting down all connections to that host or network).

Returning the new "host administratively unreachable" or "network administratively unreachable" codes advertises the fact that there is a packet filtering system at your site, which you may or may not want to do. These codes may also cause excessive reactions in faulty IP implementations.

There is another consideration as well. Generating and returning ICMP error codes takes a certain small amount of effort on the part of the packet filtering router. An attacker could conceivably mount a denial of service attack by flooding the router with packets the router would reject, and for which it would try to generate ICMP error packets. The issue isn't network bandwidth; it's CPU load on the router. (While it's busy generating ICMP packets, it's not able to do other things as quickly, like make filtering decisions.) On the other hand, not returning ICMP error codes will cause a small amount of excess network traffic, as the sending system tries and retries to send the packet being dropped. This traffic shouldn't amount to much, because the number of packets blocked by a packet filtering system should be a fraction of the total number of packets processed. (If it's not a small fraction, you've got more serious problems, because people are apparently trying lots of things that "aren't allowed.")

If your router returns an ICMP error code for every packet that violates your filtering policy, you're also giving an attacker a way to probe your filtering system. By observing which packets evoke an ICMP error response, attackers can discover what types of packets do and don't violate your policy (and thus what types of packets are and are not allowed into your network). You should not give this information away, because it greatly simplifies the attacker's job. The attacker knows that packets that don't get the ICMP error are going somewhere, and can concentrate on those protocols, where you actually have vulnerabilities. You'd rather that the attacker spent plenty of time sending you packets that you happily throw away. Returning ICMP error codes speeds up attack programs; if they get back an ICMP error for something they try, they don't have to wait for a timeout.

All in all, the safest thing to do seems to be to drop packets without returning any ICMP error codes. If your router offers enough flexibility, it might make sense to configure it to return ICMP error codes to internal systems (which would like to know immediately that something is going to fail, rather than wait for a timeout), but not to external systems (where the information would give an attacker a means to probe the filtering configuration of the firewall). Even if your router doesn't seem to offer such flexibility, you may be able to accomplish the same result by specifying packet filtering rules to allow the relevant inbound ICMP packets and disallow the relevant outbound ICMP packets.

Conventions for Packet Filtering Rules

The rest of this chapter and Chapter 8 show the kinds of rules you can specify for your packet filtering router in order to control what packets can and cannot flow to and from your network. There are a few things you need to know about these rules.

To avoid confusion, the example rules are specified with abstract descriptions, rather than with real addresses, as much as possible. Instead of using real source and destination addresses (e.g., 172.16.51.50), we use "Internal" or "External" to identify which networks we're talking about. Actual packet filtering systems usually require you to specify address ranges explicitly; the syntax varies from router to router.

In all of our packet filtering examples, the assumption is that, for each packet, the router goes through the rules in order until it finds one that matches, and then it takes the action specified by that rule. We assume an implicit default "deny" if no rules apply, although it's a good idea to specify an explicit default (and we generally do).

The syntax used in our filtering examples specifies the number of bits significant for comparison to other address after a slash character (/). Thus, 10.0.0.0/8 matches any address that starts with 10; it's equivalent to 10.0.0.0 with a UNIX netmask of 255.0.0.0, or 10.0.0.0 with a Cisco wildcard mask of 0.255.255.255, or (if it were a filename) 10.*.*.*.

Although we try to be as specific as possible in these examples, it's impossible to tell you precisely what you have to specify for your particular packet filtering product. The exact mechanism for specifying packet filtering rules varies widely from product to product. Some products (such as the *screend* package) allow you to specify a single set of rules that are applied to all packets routed by the system. Others (such as the Telebit NetBlazer) allow you to specify rules for particular interfaces. Still others (such as the Livingston and Cisco products) allow you to specify sets of rules and then apply sets by name to particular interfaces (so that you might define one set of rules that is shared by a number of different interfaces, for example, and put the rules that are unique to a given interface into a different set).

Packet Filtering Tips and Tricks

Here are a couple of tips and tricks that can help you deal with packet filtering rules more effectively and make them more secure.

Edit your filtering rules offline

The filter editing tools on most systems are usually pretty minimal. Also, it's not always clear how new rules will interact with existing rule sets. In particular, it's often difficult to delete rules, or to add new rules in the middle of an existing rule set.

You might find it more convenient to keep your filters in a text file on one of your UNIX or PC systems, so that you can edit them there with the tools you're familiar with, and then load the file on the filtering system as if it contained commands you were typing at the console. Different systems support various ways of doing this. For example, on Cisco products, you can use TFTP to obtain command files from a server. (Be careful of where you enable a TFTP server, though. See the discussion of TFTP in Chapter 8 and think about using something like TCP Wrapper to control what hosts can activate that TFTP server). On Livingston products, there is a program available from Livingston called *pmcommand* that downloads commands to the box. On other products, there are other mechanisms.

An added advantage of keeping the filters elsewhere as a file is that you can keep comments in the file (stripping them out of the copy sent to the router, if necessary). Most filtering systems discard any comments in the commands they're given; if you later go look at the active filters on the system, you'll find that the comments aren't retained.

Reload rule sets from scratch each time

The first thing the file should do is clear all the old rules, so that each time you load the file you're rebuilding the rule set from scratch; that way, you don't have to worry about how the new rules will interact with the old. Next, specify the rules you want to establish, followed by whatever commands are necessary to apply those rules to the appropriate interfaces.

Always use IP addresses, never hostnames

Always specify hosts and networks in filtering rules by IP address, never by hostname or by network name (if your filtering product even supports that). If you specify filtering rules by hostname, your filtering could be subverted if someone accidentally or intentionally corrupts the name-to-address translation (e.g., by feeding false data to your DNS server).

Here's a simple example to illustrate the differences. We chose these three systems because they represent somewhat different ways of specifying filters, not because of any particular preference for them; in general, other systems are similar to these. For example, Cisco's products are similar to Livingston's products in that you create sets of rules, then apply those rules to packets going in a particular direction through a particular interface. They are different in details of their syntax, such as in how you specify host addresses and bitmasks.

Let's say that you want to allow all IP traffic between a trusted external host (host 172.16.51.50) and hosts on your internal network (Class C net 192.168.10.0). In our examples, we would show this case as follows:

Rule	Direction	Source Address	Destination Address	ACK Set	Action
A	Inbound	Trusted external host	Internal	Any	Permit
B	Outbound	Internal	Trusted external host	Any	Permit
C	Either	Any	Any	Any	Deny

With *screend*, you would specify:

```
between host 172.16.51.50 and net 192.168.10 accept ;
between host any and host any reject ;
```

With a Telebit NetBlazer, you also have to specify which interface the rule is to be applied to, and whether the rule applies to incoming or outgoing packets on that interface. For an external interface named "syn0", your rules would be:

```
permit 172.16.51.50/32 192.168.10/24 syn0 in
deny 0.0.0.0/0 0.0.0.0/0 syn0 in

permit 192.168.10/24 172.16.51.50/32 syn0 out
deny 0.0.0.0/0 0.0.0.0/0 syn0 out
```

On a Livingston PortMaster or IRX, you would specify rules as a set and then apply the relevant set to the right direction on the right interface. If your external interface is named "s1", your rules would look something like this:

```
add filter s1.in
set filter s1.in 1 permit 172.16.51.50/32 192.168.10.0/24
set filter s1.in 2 deny 0.0.0.0/0 0.0.0.0/0
set s1 ifilter s1.in

add filter s1.out
set filter s1.out 1 permit 192.168.10.0/24 172.16.51.50/32
set filter s1.out 2 deny 0.0.0.0/0 0.0.0.0/0
set s1 ofilter s1.out
```

On a Cisco router, you also specify rules as sets, and apply the relevant sets to the right direction on the right interface. If your external interface is named "serial1", your rules would look like this:

```
access-list 101 permit ip 172.16.51.50 0.0.0.0 192.168.10.0 0.0.0.255
access-list 101 deny ip 0.0.0.0 255.255.255.255 0.0.0.0 255.255.255.255
interface serial 0
access-group 101 in

access-list 102 permit ip 192.168.10.0 0.0.0.255 172.16.51.50 0.0.0.0
access-list 102 deny ip 0.0.0.0 255.255.255.255 0.0.0.0 255.255.255.255
interface serial 0
access-group 102 out
```

For detailed information on the syntax of a particular package or product, consult the documentation for that package or product. Once you understand the syntax for the particular system you are using, you shouldn't have too much difficulty translating from our tables to that system's syntax.

NOTE

Watch out for implicit defaults. Different filtering systems have different default actions they take if a packet doesn't match any of the filtering rules specified. Some systems deny all such packets. Other systems make the default the opposite of the last rule; that is, if the last rule was a "permit," the system default is to "deny," and if the last rule was a "deny," the default is to "permit." In any case, it's a good idea to put an explicit default rule at the end of your list of packet filtering rules, so you don't have to worry about (or even remember) which implicit default your system is going to use.

Filtering by Address

The simplest, although not the most common, form of packet filtering is filtering by address. Filtering in this way lets you restrict the flow of packets based on the source and/or destination addresses of the packets, without having to consider what protocols are involved. Such filtering can be used to allow certain external hosts to talk to certain internal hosts, for example, or to prevent an attacker from injecting forged packets (packets handcrafted so they appear to come from somewhere other than their true source) into your network.

For example, let's say that you want to block incoming packets with forged source addresses; you would specify this rule:

Rule	Direction	Source Address	Destination Address	Action
A	Inbound	Internal	Any	Deny

Note that Direction is relative to your internal network. In the router between your internal network and the Internet, you could apply an inbound rule either to incoming packets on the Internet interface or to outgoing packets on the internal interface; either way, you will achieve the same results for the protected hosts. The difference is in what the router itself sees. If you filter outgoing packets, the router is not protecting itself.

Risks of Filtering by Source Address

It's not necessarily safe to trust source addresses because source addresses can be forged. Unless you use some kind of cryptographic authentication between you and the host you want to talk to, you won't know if you're really talking to that host, or to some other machine that is pretending to be that host. The filters we've discussed above will help you if an external host is claiming to be an internal host, but they won't do anything about an external host claiming to be a different external host.

There are two kinds of attacks that rely on forgery: *source address* and *man in the middle*.

In a basic *source address* forgery attack (shown in Figure 6-1), an attacker sends you packets that claim to be from someone you trust in some way, hoping to get you to take some action based on that trust, without expecting to get any packets back from you. If the attacker doesn't care about getting packets back from you, he doesn't need to be on the path between you and whoever he is pretending to be; he can be anywhere.

In fact, your responses will go to whomever the attacker is pretending to be, not to the attacker. However, if the attacker can predict your responses, he doesn't need to see them. Many (if not most) protocols are predictable enough for a skilled attacker to be successful at this. There are plenty of attacks that can be carried out without the attacker needing to see the results directly. For example, suppose an attacker issues a command to your system that causes it to email your password file to him; if your system is going to send the attacker the password file in the mail, there is no need for him to see it during the attack itself.

In many circumstances—particularly those involving TCP connections—the real machine (that the attacker is pretending to be) will react to your packets (packets that are attempting to carry on a conversation it knows nothing about) by trying to reset the bogus connection. Obviously, the attacker doesn't want this to happen. He has to ensure the attack completes before the real machine gets the packets you're sending, or before you get the reset packets from the real machine. There are a number of ways to ensure this—for example:

- Carrying out the attack while the real machine is down

- Crashing the real machine so the attack can be carried out

- Flooding the real machine while the attack is carried out

- Confusing the routing between the real machine and the target

- Using an attack where only the first response packet is required, so that the reset doesn't matter

Attacks of this kind used to be considered a theoretical problem with little real-world effect, but they are now common enough to be considered a serious threat. (In general, it's not a good idea to dismiss theoretical attacks completely, because they eventually become actual attacks. This kind of attack was known as a theoretical possibility for many years before it actually occurred, and yet many people didn't bother to protect against it.)

The *man in the middle* forgery attack depends on being able to carry out a complete conversation while claiming to be the trusted host. In order to do this, the attacking machine needs to be able to not only send you packets, but also intercept the packets you reply with. To do this, the attacker needs to do one of the following:

- Insinuate his attacking machine into the path between you and the real machine. This is easiest to do near the ends of the path, and most difficult to do somewhere in the middle, because given the nature of modern IP networks, the path through "the middle" can change at any second.

- Alter the path between the machines so it leads through his attacking machine. This may be very easy or very difficult, depending on the network topology and routing system used by your network, the remote network, and the Internet service providers between those networks.

Although this kind of attack is called "man in the middle," it's relatively rare for it to actually be carried out in the middle, external to the sites at each end, because nobody but a network provider is in a position to carry it out in that way, and network providers are rarely compromised to that extent. (People who compromise network providers tend to be working on quantity. Packet sniffing will give them many hosts rapidly, but man in the middle attacks give them only one site at a time.) These attacks tend to be problems only if one of the involved sites has hostile users who have physical access to the network (for example, this might be the case if one site is a university.)

So, who *can* you trust? At the extreme, nobody, unless you trust the machines involved at both ends and the path between them. If you trust the machines but not the path, you can use encryption to give you a secure connection over an insecure path. Unfortunately, as we discuss in Chapter 10, there are no widespread and commonly available tools to do that yet, but a number of sites are experimenting with ad hoc solutions, and commercial solutions are beginning to appear.

Filtering by Service

Blocking incoming forged packets, as discussed previously, is just about the only common use of filtering solely by address. Most other uses of packet filtering involve filtering by service, which is somewhat more complicated.

From a packet filtering point of view, what do the packets associated with particular services look like? As an example, we're going to take a detailed look at Telnet. Telnet allows a user to log in to another system, as if the user had a terminal directly connected to that system. We use Telnet as an example because it is fairly common, fairly simple, and from a packet filtering point of view representative of several other protocols such as SMTP and NNTP. We need to look at both outbound and inbound Telnet service.

For detailed discussions of the packet filtering characteristics of other protocols, see Chapter 8.

Outbound Telnet Service

Let's look first at outbound Telnet service, in which a local client (a user) is talking to a remote server. We need to handle both outgoing and incoming packets. (Figure 6-8 shows a simplified view of outbound Telnet.)

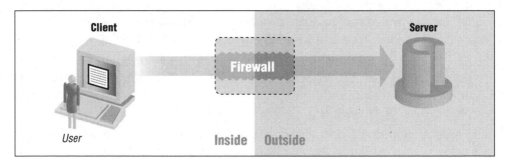

Figure 6–8: Outbound Telnet

The outgoing packets for this outbound service contain the user's keystrokes and have the following characteristics:

- The IP source address of the outgoing packets is the local host's IP address.

- The IP destination address is the remote host's IP address.

- Telnet is a TCP-based service, so the IP packet type is TCP.

- The TCP destination port is 23; that's the well-known port number Telnet servers use.

- The TCP source port number (which we'll call "Y" in this example) is some seemingly random number greater than 1023.

- The first outgoing packet, establishing the connection, will not have the ACK bit set; the rest of the outgoing packets will.

The incoming packets for this outbound service contain the data to be displayed on the user's screen (for example, the "login:" prompt) and have the following characteristics:

- The IP source address of the incoming packets is the remote host's IP address.

- The IP destination address is the local host's IP address.

- The IP packet type is TCP.

- The TCP source port is 23; that's the port the server uses.

- The TCP destination port is the same "Y" we used as the source port for the outgoing packets.

- All incoming packets will have the ACK bit set (again, only the first packet, establishing a connection, does not have the ACK bit set; in this example, that first packet was an outgoing packet, not an incoming packet).

Note the similarities between the header fields of the outgoing and incoming packets for Telnet. The same addresses and port numbers are used; they're just exchanged between source and destination. If you compare an outgoing packet to an incoming packet, the source and destination addresses are exchanged, and the source and destination port numbers are exchanged.

Why is the client port—the source port for the outgoing packets, and the destination port for the incoming packets—restricted to being greater than 1023? This is a legacy of the BSD versions of UNIX, to which almost all UNIX networking code can trace its origins. BSD UNIX reserved ports from 0 to 1023 for local use only by root. These ports are normally used only by servers, not clients. (The major exceptions are the BSD "r commands" like *rcp* and *rlogin*, as we'll discuss in Chapter 8.) Other operating systems, even those that have no concept analogous to a privileged root user, e.g., Macintosh and MS-DOS systems, have followed this convention. When client programs need a port number for their own use, and any old port number will do, the programs are assigned a port above 1023.

Inbound Telnet Service

Next, let's look at inbound Telnet service, in which a remote client (a remote user) communicates with a local Telnet server. Again, we need to handle both incoming and outgoing packets.

The incoming packets for the inbound Telnet service contain the user's keystrokes and have the following characteristics:

- The IP source address of these packets is the remote host's address.

- The IP destination address is the local host's address.

- The IP packet type is TCP.

- The TCP source port is some random port number greater than 1023 (which we'll call "Z" in this example).

- The TCP destination port is 23.

- The TCP ACK bit will not be set on the very first inbound packet, establishing the connection, but it will be set on all other inbound packets.

The outgoing packets for this inbound Telnet service contain the server responses (the data to be displayed for the user) and have the following characteristics:

- The IP source address is the local host's address.

- The IP destination address is the remote host's address.

- The IP packet type is TCP.

- The TCP source port is 23 (these packets are from the Telnet server).

- The TCP destination port is the same random port "Z" that was used as the source port for the inbound packets.

- The TCP ACK bit will be set on all outgoing packets.

Again, note the similarities between the relevant headers of the incoming and the outgoing packets: the source and destination addresses are exchanged and that the source and destination ports are exchanged.

Telnet Summary

The following table illustrates the various types of packets involved in inbound and outbound Telnet services.

Service Direction	Packet Direction	Source Address	Dest. Address	Packet Type	Source Port	Dest. Port	ACK Set
Outbound	Outgoing	Internal	External	TCP	Y	23	[a]
Outbound	Incoming	External	Internal	TCP	23	Y	Yes
Inbound	Incoming	External	Internal	TCP	Z	23	[a]
Inbound	Outgoing	Internal	External	TCP	23	Z	Yes

[a] The TCP ACK bit will be set on all but the first of these packets, which establishes the connection.

Note that Y and Z are both random (from the packet filtering system's point of view) port numbers above 1023.

If you want to allow outgoing Telnet, but nothing else, you would set up your packet filtering like this:

Rule	Direction	Source Address	Dest. Address	Protocol	Source Port	Dest. Port	ACK Set	Action
A	Out	Internal	Any	TCP	>1023	23	Either	Permit
B	In	Any	Internal	TCP	23	>1023	Yes	Permit
C	Either	Any	Any	Any	Any	Any	Either	Deny

- Rule A allows packets out to remote Telnet servers.

- Rule B allows the returning packets to come back in. Because it verifies that the ACK bit is set, rule B can't be abused by an attacker to allow incoming TCP connections from port 23 on the attacker's end to ports above 1023 on your end, e.g., an X11 server on port 6000.

- Rule C is the default rule. If none of the preceding rules apply, the packet is blocked. Remember from our discussion above that any blocked packet should be logged, and that it may or may not cause an ICMP message to be returned to the originator.

Risks of Filtering by Source Port

Making filtering decisions based on source port is not without its risks. There is one fundamental problem with this type of filtering: you can trust the source port only as much as you trust the source machine.

Suppose you mistakenly assume the source port is associated with a particular service. Someone who is in control of the source machine, e.g., someone with root access on a UNIX system (or anyone at all with a networked PC), could run whatever client or server they wanted on a "source port" that you're allowing through your carefully configured packet filtering system. Furthermore, as we've discussed above, you can't necessarily trust the source address to tell you for certain what the source machine is; you can't tell for sure if you're talking to the real machine with that address, or to an attacker who is pretending to be that machine.

What can you do about this situation? You want to restrict the local port numbers as much as possible, regardless of how few remote ports you allow to access them. If you only allow inbound connections to port 23, and if port 23 has a Telnet server on it that is trustworthy (a server that will only do things that a Telnet client should be able to tell it to do), it doesn't actually matter whether the program that is talking to it is a genuine Telnet client or not. Your concern is to limit inbound connections to only ports where you are running trustworthy servers, and to be sure that your servers are genuinely trustworthy. Chapter 8 discusses how you can achieve these ends for various services.

Because many services use random ports above 1023 for clients, and because some services use ports above 1023 for servers, you will often need to accept inbound packets for ports that might have untrustworthy servers on them. In TCP, you can accept inbound packets without accepting inbound connections by requiring the ACK bit to be set. With UDP, you have no such option, because there is no equivalent to the ACK bit. Fortunately, very few protocols used across the Internet are UDP-based.

Choosing a Packet Filtering Router

A number of packet filtering routers are available, some good and some not so good. Almost every dedicated router supports packet filtering in some form. In addition, packet filtering packages are available for many general-purpose UNIX and PC platforms you might want to use as routers.

How do you choose the best packet filtering router for your site? This section outlines the most important capabilities a filtering router should have. You should determine which of these capabilities are important to you and select a filtering system that offers at least those capabilities.

It Should Have Good Enough Packet Filtering Performance for Your Needs

Many people worry unnecessarily about packet filtering performance. In most Internet firewalls, in fact, the limiting factor on performance is the speed of your connection to the Internet, not the speed of the packet filtering system. The right question to ask about a packet filtering system is not "How fast is it?" The right question is "Is it fast enough for my needs?"

Internet connections are commonly either 56-Kb/s or 1.544-Mb/s (T1) lines. Packet filtering is a per-packet operation. Therefore, the smaller the packets, the more packets will be handled every second, and the more filtering decisions a packet filtering system will have to make every second. The smallest possible IP packet—a bare packet containing only an IP header and no data whatsoever—is 20 bytes (160 bits) long. Thus, a line capable of 56 Kb/s can carry at most 350 packets per second, and a line capable of 1.544 Mb/s (a T-1 line, for example) can carry at most 9,650 packets per second, as shown in the following table.

Connection Type	Bits/Second (approximate)	Packets/Second (20-byte packets)	Packets/Second (40-byte packets)
v.32bis modem	14,400	90	45
56-Kb/s leased line	56,000	350	175
T-1 leased line	1,544,000	9,650	4,825
Ethernet (practical)	3,000,000	18,750	9,375

Connection Type	Bits/Second (approximate)	Packets/Second (20-byte packets)	Packets/Second (40-byte packets)
Ethernet (theoretical)	10,000,000	62,500	31,250
T-3 leased line	45,000,000	281,250	140,625
FDDI	100,000,000	625,000	312,500

In fact, though, you will rarely see bare IP packets; there is always something in the data segment (e.g., a TCP, UDP, or ICMP packet). A typical packet crossing a firewall would be a TCP/IP packet because most Internet services are TCP-based. The minimum possible TCP/IP packet size, for a packet containing only the IP header and TCP header and no actual data, is 40 bytes, which cuts the maximum packet rates in half, to 175 packets per second for a 56-Kb/s line and 4825 packets per second for a 1.544-Mb/s line. Real packets containing real data are going to be larger still, reducing the packet-per-second rates still further.

These per-second packet rates are well within the capabilities of many of the packet filtering systems, both commercial and freely available off the Internet, that are available today. Some can go much faster.

Speed is likely to be more of an issue in a firewall that is internal to an organization's network. Such a firewall will need to run at LAN speeds, which are usually theoretically at least 10 Mb/s, and may be much higher. (Firewalls are not practical within a gigabit-per-second network at this point. Fortunately, from a firewalls perspective, such networks are rare at present.)

A firewall with more than two connections may also have higher speed requirements. With two connections, the maximum required speed is that of the slowest connection. With three connections, the required speed can rise. For example, if you put a second Internet connection onto an external router, it now needs to drive both at full speed if it's not going to be a limiting factor. If you put two internal networks onto it, it's going to need to achieve the higher LAN speed to route between the two internal networks.

It Can Be a Single-Purpose Router or a General-Purpose Computer

Don't expect a single device to serve as your packet-filtering router and also to do something that's not part of your firewall. (You may have a device that's doing packet filtering and proxying, or packet filtering and selected bastion host services, or even all three.) In a practical sense, you should expect to be using a dedicated packet-filtering router. This doesn't mean you have to buy a single-purpose router, however. You might choose to use either a traditional, single-purpose router, or a general-purpose computer dedicated to routing. What are the pros and cons of each choice?

If you have a large number of networks or multiple protocols, you will probably need a single-purpose router. Routing packages for general-purpose computers usually do not have the speed or flexibility of single-purpose routers, and you may find you will need an inconveniently large machine to accommodate the necessary interface boards.

On the other hand, if you are filtering a single Internet link, you may not need to do any more than route IP packets between two Ethernets. This is well within the capabilities of a reasonable 486-based (or comparable) computer, and such a machine may well be cheaper than a single-purpose router. (It may even be free, if you already have one available within your organization.) Routing and filtering packages are available for MS-DOS and most variants of UNIX. (See Appendix B for information about available packages.)

Whatever device you use for your filtering router, firewalling should be all the router does. For example, if possible, don't use one device as both your filtering router and the backbone router that ties together multiple separate internal networks. Instead, use one device to tie together your internal networks and a separate (much smaller) device as your filtering router. The more complex the filtering router and its configuration, the more likely it is that you'll make a mistake in its configuration, which could have serious security implications. Filtering also has a significant speed impact on a router and may slow the router down to the point where it has difficulty achieving acceptable performance for the internal networks.

Some commercial firewall packages combine packet filtering with proxying on a machine that behaves like a single-purpose router. Others combine packet filtering with proxying or bastion host services on a high-powered general-purpose computer. This is fine, although it will increase your speed requirements. Don't expect to use a small machine to do this. Depending on what machines you have available, this may either be a good bargain (you buy a single large machine instead of multiple medium-sized ones) or a bad one (you buy a single large machine instead of adding a small machine to an existing configuration). As we've said in Chapter 4, combining the bastion host with the external packet filter is a reasonable thing to do from a security perspective.

It Should Allow Simple Specification of Rules

You want to be able to specify the rules for your packet filtering as simply as possible. Look for this feature in any device you select. From a conceptual point of view, packet filtering is complicated to begin with, and it's further complicated by the details and quirks of the various protocols. You don't want your packet filtering system to add any more complexity to the complications you already have to deal with.

In particular, you want to be able to specify rules at a fairly high level of abstraction. Avoid any packet filtering implementations that treat packets as simply unstructured arrays of bits and require you to state rules in terms of the offset and state of particular bits in the packet headers.

As we discussed before, you'll also probably want to be able to download the rules from another machine if you're using a single-purpose router. Nevertheless, you need a user interface that allows you to create and edit the rules without extreme pain, because you may periodically have to do so.

It Should Allow Rules Based on Any Header or Meta-packet Criteria

You want to be able to specify rules based on any of the header information or meta-packet information available for your packets. Header information includes the following:

- IP source and destination address

- IP options

- Protocol, such as TCP, UDP, or ICMP

- TCP or UDP source and destination port

- ICMP message type

- Start-of-connection (ACK bit) information for TCP packets

and similar information for any other protocols you're filtering on. Meta-packet information includes any information about the packet that the router knows, but that isn't in the headers themselves, e.g., which router interface the packet came in or is going out on. You want to be able to specify rules based on combinations of these header and meta-packet criteria.

For various reasons, many filtering products don't let you look at the TCP or UDP source port in making packet filtering decisions; they let you look only at the TCP or UDP destination port. This makes it impossible to specify certain kinds of filters. Some manufacturers who omit TCP/UDP source ports from packet filtering criteria maintain that such filtering isn't useful anyway, or that its proper use is "too dangerous" for customers to understand (because, as we've pointed out above, source port information is not reliable). We believe that this is a fallacy, and that such decisions are better left to well-informed customers.

Let's consider an example in which filters based on source port might be useful—access to Archie servers. As we discuss in Chapter 8, Archie access presents some troublesome problems. The biggest is that the native Archie protocol is UDP-based, and at Internet firewalls UDP is generally blocked altogether (except for small "peepholes" for services such as DNS, NTP, and Archie). The reason for this blocking is usually to prevent outsiders from attacking RPC-based services like NIS/YP and NFS. Because RPC-based services don't run on fixed port numbers, you can't simply block access to the ports the RPC-based services run on (because you don't know what they are). Unlike TCP, UDP doesn't have ACK bits; thus, you can't do start-of-connection filtering. The packet filtering system can't tell, just by examining an incoming packet, whether that packet is a response from an external server to an internal client, or a command from an external client (possibly an attack program) to an internal server (such as NIS/YP or NFS). With all of these obstacles, how, then, do you construct a rule set to allow Archie?

One of the characteristics of Archie is that there are only 20 or so Archie servers in the world. For performance reasons, your users will generally only want to talk to the handful of those servers that are "near" your site in the network topology (for example, there are only five servers in the United States). If you're willing to make certain assumptions about the security of the Archie servers (we discuss these in Chapter 8), you could enable Archie access for your users by allowing packets out to the Archie servers, and by allowing packets back in from the Archie servers (using source port filtering to determine this).

This is somewhat risky. If someone forges packets from port 1525 at an Archie server to an internal NFS server, they will succeed in getting responses from you. In order to do that, they need to guess that you might allow such packets, figure out an internal host address and the port that its NFS server is on, forge the packets, and intercept the answers. None of this is impossibly difficult for an attacker to do, although it's arguably more trouble than most attackers are willing to go to to attack most sites. Note that NFS packets normally fragment, and fragments are normally passed through packet filters, so they will probably succeed in getting some data (all but the first fragment of each NFS packet) even if your packet filter is smart enough to block outbound NFS by examining application-level protocol information. If you are facing determined attackers, this type of filtering is not sufficiently secure.

The following table shows a simple rule set that allows internal clients to interact with a known Archie server, and that disallows everything else. We assume that, for each packet, rules are evaluated in the order listed until a match is found; in that case, "Action" specifies what to do):

Rule	Direction	Source Address	Dest. Address	Protocol	Source Port	Dest. Port	Action
A	Out	Internal	Archie Server	UDP	>1023	1525	Permit
B	In	Archie Server	Internal	UDP	1525	>1023	Permit
C	Either	Any	Any	Any	Any	Any	Deny

- Rule A lets the clients talk to the Archie server.

- Rule B allows the Archie server to talk back to the clients.

- Rule C is the default rule that blocks everything else.

You can only do this if your filtering system allows you to filter based on source port.

It Should Apply Rules in the Order Specified

You want your packet filter to apply, in a predictable order, the rules you specify for it. By far the simplest order is the order in which you, the person configuring the router, specify the rules. Unfortunately, some products, instead of applying rules in the order you specify, try to reorder and merge rules to achieve greater efficiency in applying the rules. This causes several problems:

- Reordering rules makes it difficult for you to figure out what's going on, and what the router is going to do with a particular set of filtering instructions. Configuring a packet filtering system is already complicated enough, without having a vendor add additional complications by merging and reordering rule sets.

- If there are any quirks or bugs in the merging or reordering of rule sets (and there often are, because it's something that's very difficult for the vendors to test), it becomes impossible to figure out what the system is going to do with a given set of filters.

- Most importantly, reordering rules can break a rule set that would work just fine if it had not been reordered.

Let's consider an example. Imagine that you're in a corporation, working on a special project with a local university. Your corporate Class B network is 172.16 (i.e., your IP addresses are 172.16.0.0 through 172.16.255.255). The university owns Class A net 10 (i.e., their IP addresses are 10.0.0.0 through 10.255.255.255).[*]

For the purposes of this project, you're linking your network directly to the university's, using a packet filtering router. You want to disallow all Internet access over this link (Internet access should go through your Internet firewall). Your special project with the university uses the 172.16.6 subnet of your Class B network (i.e., IP address 172.16.6.0 through 172.16.6.255). You want all subnets at the university to be able to access this project subnet. There is one eight-bit subnet at the university, the 10.1.99 subnet, that you know has a lot of hostile activity on it; you want to ensure that this subnet can only reaches your project subnet.

---

[*] 172.16 and 10 are both reserved network numbers, which no company or university could have. They're used for example purposes only. Not all the IP addresses in a network's range are valid host addresses; addresses where the host portion is all ones or all zeros are reserved and cannot be allocated to hosts, making the range of host addresses on 172.16 actually 172.16.0.1 though 172.16.255.254.

How can you meet all these requirements? Specify the three packet filtering rules listed below. (In this example, we are considering only the rules for traffic incoming to your site; you'd need to set up corresponding rules for outgoing traffic.)

Rule	Source Address	Dest. Address	Action
A	10.0.0.0/8	172.16.6.0/24	Permit
B	10.1.99.0/24	172.16.0.0/16	Deny
C	Any	Any	Deny

- Rule A permits the university to reach your project subnet.

- Rule B locks the hostile subnet at the university out of everything else on your network.

- Rule C disallows Internet access to your network.

Now let's look at what happens in several different cases, depending on exactly how these rules are applied.

If rules are applied in the order ABC

If the rules are applied in the order ABC—the same order specified by the user—the following table shows what happens with a variety of sample packets.

Packet	Source Address	Dest. Address	Desired Action	Actual Action (by Rule)
1	10.1.99.1	172.16.1.1	Deny	Deny (B)
2	10.1.99.1	172.16.6.1	Permit	Permit (A)
3	10.1.1.1	172.16.6.1	Permit	Permit (A)
4	10.1.1.1	172.16.6.1	Deny	Deny (C)
5	192.168.3.4	172.16.1.1	Deny	Deny (C)
6	192.168.3.4	172.16.6.1	Deny	Deny (C)

- Packet 1 is from a machine at the university on the hostile subnet to a random machine on your network (not on the project subnet); you want it to be denied; it is, by rule B.

- Packet 2 is from a machine at the university on the hostile subnet to a machine on your project subnet; you want it to be permitted; it is, by rule A.

- Packet 3 is from a random machine at the university to a machine on your project subnet; you want it to be permitted; it is, by rule A.

- Packet 4 is from a random machine at the university to a random machine on your project subnet; you want it to be denied; it is, by rule C.

- Packet 5 is from a random machine on the Internet to one of your nonproject machines; you want it to be denied; it is, by rule C.

- Packet 6 is from a random machine on the Internet to one of your project machines; you want it to be denied; it is, by rule C.

Thus, if the rules are applied in the order ABC, they accomplish what you want.

If the rules are applied in the order BAC

What would happen if the router reordered the rules by the number of significant bits in the source address, so that more specific rules are applied first? In other words, rules applying to more specific IP source addresses (i.e., rules that apply to a smaller range of source addresses) would be applied before rules applying to less specific IP source addresses? In this case, the rules would be applied in the order BAC.

Rule	Source Address	Dest. Address	Action
B	10.1.99.0/24	172.16.0.0/16	Deny
A	10.0.0.0/8	172.16.6.0/24	Permit
C	Any	Any	Deny

Here are the same six sample packets, with the new outcomes if the rules are applied in the order BAC; in bold face, we show how the actions differ from the previous case (in which rules are applied in the order specified by the user):

Packet	Source Address	Dest. Address	Desired Action	Actual Action (by Rule)
1	10.1.99.1	172.16.1.1	Deny	Deny (B)
2	10.1.99.1	172.16.6.1	Permit	**Deny (B)**
3	10.1.1.1	172.16.6.1	Permit	Permit (A)
4	10.1.1.1	172.16.1.1	Deny	Deny (C)
5	192.168.3.4	172.16.1.1	Deny	Deny (C)
6	192.168.3.4	172.16.6.1	Deny	Deny (C)

If the rules are applied in the order BAC, then packet 2, which should be permitted, is improperly denied by rule B. Now, denying something that should be permitted is safer than permitting something that should be denied, but it would be better if the filtering system simply did what you wanted it to do.

You can construct a similar example for systems that reorder rules based on the number of significant bits in the destination address, which is the most popular other reordering criteria.

Rule B is actually not necessary

If you consider this example carefully, you can see that the discussion about the hostile subnet, which is the reason for rule B, is redundant, and isn't necessary to achieve the desired results. Rule B is intended to limit the hostile subnet to accessing only your project subnet. Rule A, however, already restricts the entire university—including the hostile subnet—to accessing only your project subnet. If you omit rule B, then the rules will be applied in order AC regardless of whether or not the system reorders based on the number of significant bits in the IP source address. The tables below shows what happens in either case:

Rule	Source Address	Dest. Address	Action
A	10.0.0.0/8	172.16.6.0/24	Permit
C	Any	Any	Deny

Packet	Source Address	Dest. Address	Desired Action	Actual Action (by Rule)
1	10.1.99.1	172.16.1.1	Deny	Deny (C)
2	10.1.99.1	172.16.6.1	Permit	Permit (A)
3	10.1.1.1	172.16.6.1	Permit	Permit (A)
4	10.1.1.1	172.16.1.1	Deny	Deny (C)
5	192.168.3.4	172.16.1.1	Deny	Deny (C)
6	192.168.3.4	172.16.6.1	Deny	Deny (C)

Packet filtering rules are tricky

The point here is that getting filtering rules right is tricky. In this example, we are considering a relatively simple situation, and we've still managed to come up with a rule set that had a subtle error in it. Real-life rule sets are significantly more complex than these, and often include tens or hundreds of rules. Considering the implications and interactions of all those rules is nearly impossible, unless they are simply applied in the order specified. So-called "help" from a router, in the form of reordering rule sets, can easily turn an over-specified but working rule set into a nonworking rule set. You should make sure the packet filtering router you select doesn't reorder rule sets.

It's OK if the router does optimization, as long as the optimization doesn't change the effect of the rules. Pay close attention to what kind of optimizations your packet filtering implementation tries to do.

It Should Apply Rules Separately to Incoming and Outgoing Packets, on a Per-Interface Basis

For maximum flexibility, capability, and performance, you want to be able to specify a separate rule set for incoming and outgoing packets on each interface. In this section, we'll show an example that demonstrates the problems you can run into with routers that aren't that flexible.

A limitation unfortunately shared by many packet filtering systems is that they let you examine packets only as they are leaving the system. This limitation leads to three problems:

- The system is always "outside" its own filters.

- Detecting forged packets is difficult or impossible.

- Configuring such systems is extremely difficult if they have more than two interfaces.

Let's look at the first problem. If a router lets you look only at outgoing packets, then packets directed to the router itself are never subjected to packet filtering. The result is that the filtering doesn't protect the router itself. This is usually not too serious a problem, because there are typically few services on the router that could be attacked, and there are other ways to protect those services. Telnet is an example of a service that can be attacked in this way, but you can usually get around the routing problem by disabling the Telnet server, or by controlling from where it will accept incoming connections. SNMP is another commonly available and vulnerable service.

Now consider the second problem. If a router can only filter outgoing packets, it's difficult or impossible to detect forged packets being injected from the outside (that is, packets coming in from the outside, but which claim to have internal source addresses), as is illustrated in Figure 6-1. Forgery detection is most easily done when the packet enters the router, on the inbound interface. Detecting forgeries on the outbound interface is complicated by packets generated by the router itself (which will have internal source addresses if the router itself has an internal address) and by legitimate internal packets mistakenly directed to the router (packets that should have been sent directly from their internal source to their internal destinations, but were instead sent to the filtering router, for instance by systems following a default route that leads to the filtering router).

The third problem with outbound-only filtering is that it can be difficult to configure packet filtering on such a router when it has more than two interfaces. If it has only two interfaces, then being able to do only outbound filtering on each interface is no big deal. There are only two paths through the router (from the first interface to the second, and vice versa). Packets going one way can be filtered as outgoing packets on one interface, while packets going the other way can be filtered as outgoing packets on the other interface. Consider, on the other hand, a router with four interfaces: one for the site's Internet connection, one for a finance network, and two for engineering networks. In such an environment, it wouldn't be unreasonable to want to impose the following policy:

- The two engineering networks can communicate with each other without restrictions.

- The two engineering networks and the Internet can communicate with each other with certain restrictions.

- The two engineering networks and the finance network can communicate with each other with certain restrictions—restrictions that are different from those between the engineering nets and the Internet.

- The finance network cannot communicate with the Internet under any circumstances.

Figure 6-9 illustrates this environment.

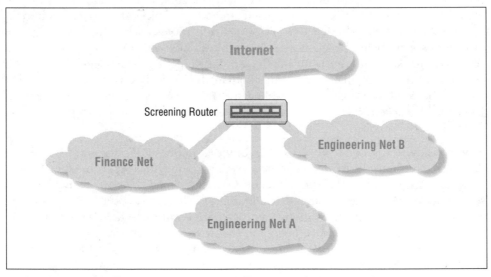

Figure 6–9: Packet filtering restrictions on different interfaces

There are 12 paths through this router, from each of four interfaces to each of three other interfaces (in general, there are N * N-1 paths through an N-interface router). With an outbound-only filtering system, you would have to establish the following filtering on each interface:

- Engineering A—Internet filters, finance filters, engineering B filters

- Engineering B—Internet filters, finance filters, engineering A filters

- Finance—Internet filters, engineering A filters, engineering B filters

- Internet—engineering A filters, engineering B filters, finance filters

Merging multiple filtering requirements in a single interface like this can be very tricky. Depending on the complexity of the filters and the flexibility of the filtering system, it may actually be impossible in some situations.

A more subtle problem with such a setup is that it imposes packet filtering overhead between the two engineering networks (which may result in a significant performance problem). With this setup, the router has to examine all the packets flowing between the two engineering nets, even though it will never decide to drop any of those packets.

Now look at the same scenario, assuming that the packet filtering system has both inbound and outbound filters. In this case, you could put:

- All the filters related to the Internet (regardless of whether they apply to the engineering nets or the finance net) on the Internet interface.

- All the filters related to the finance net (regardless of whether they apply to the engineering nets or the Internet) on the finance interface.

- No filters at all on the engineering interfaces (thus allowing maximum performance for traffic between the engineering nets, because it wouldn't pass through any filters).

What if a packet filtering system had inbound-only filters, rather than outbound-only filters? A system of this kind would address the first problem we described in this section: a router with inbound-only filters *can* be protected by its own filters. However, such a system would not address the second and more serious problem; you still have problems merging filtering rules on routers with more than two interfaces.

It Should Be Able to Log
Accepted and Dropped Packets

Make sure the packet filtering router gives you the option of logging all of the packets it drops. You want to know about any packets that are blocked by your packet filtering rules. These rules reflect your security policy and you want to know when somebody attempts to violate that policy. The simplest way to learn about these attempted violations is through such a log.

You'd also like to be able to log selected packets that were accepted. For example, you might want to log the start of each TCP connection. Logging all accepted packets is going to be too much data in normal operation, but may be worth it occasionally for debugging and for dealing with attacks in progress. Although you will probably be doing some logging at the packet destination, that logging won't work if the destination host has been compromised, and won't show packets that make it through the packet filter but don't have a valid destination. Those packets are interesting, because they may be probes from an attacker. Without information from the router, you won't have the complete picture of what the attacker is doing.

The logging should be flexible; the packet filter should give you the ability to log via *syslog* and to a console or a local file. It would also be helpful if the logging included the ability to generate SNMP traps on certain events.

It Should Have Good Testing and Validation Capabilities

An important part of establishing a firewall is convincing yourself (and others within your organization) that you've done the job right, and haven't overlooked anything. To do that, you need to be able to test and validate your configuration. Most of the packet filtering packages currently available have little or nothing in the way of testing and validation capabilities.

Testing and validation comes down to two related questions:

- Have you properly told the router to do what you want?

- Is the router doing what you've told it to?

Unfortunately, with many products available today, both of these questions tend to be difficult to answer. In the few products that provide any kinds of testing capabilities, what the test says it will do with a given packet and what it actually does with such a packet are sometimes different, often because of subtle caching and optimization bugs. Some sites (and, we hope, some vendors!) have constructed filtering test beds, where they can generate test packets on one side of a filtering router and watch to see what comes through to the other side, but that's beyond the capabilities and resources of most sites. About the best you can do is pick something with a good reputation for not having many problems and good support for when it inevitably does have problems.

Where to Do Packet Filtering

If you look at the various firewall architectures outlined in Chapter 4, you see that there are a variety of places you might perform packet filtering. Where should you do it? The answer is simple: anywhere you can.

Many of the architectures (e.g., the screened host architecture or the single-router screened subnet architecture) involve only one router. In those cases, that one router is the only place where you could do packet filtering, so there's not much of a decision to be made.

However, other architectures, such as the two-router screened subnet architecture, and some of the architectural variations, involve multiple routers. You might do packet filtering on any or all of these routers.

Our recommendation is to do whatever packet filtering you can wherever you can. This is an application of the principle of least privilege (described in Chapter 3). For each router that is part of your firewall, figure out what types of packets should legitimately be flowing through it, and set up filters to allow only those packets and no more. You may also want to put packet filters on destination hosts, using *screend, ipfilterd*, or TCP Wrapper. This is highly advisable for bastion hosts.

This may lead to duplication of some filters on multiple routers; in other words, you may filter out the same thing in more than one place. That's good; it's redundancy, and it may save you some day if you ever have a problem with one of your routers—for example, if something was supposed to be done, but wasn't (because of improper configuration, bugs, enemy action, or whatever). It provides defense in depth, and gives you the opportunity to fail safely—other strategies we outlined in Chapter 3.

If filtering is such a good idea, why not filter on all routers, not just those that are part of the firewall? Basically, because of performance and maintenance issues. We discuss above what "fast enough" means for a packet filtering system on the perimeter of your network. However, what's fast enough at the edge of your network (where the real bottleneck is probably the speed of the line connecting you to the Internet) is probably not fast enough within your network (where you've probably got many busy LANs of Ethernet, FDDI, or perhaps something even faster). Further, if you put filters on all your routers, you're going to have to maintain all those filter lists. Maintaining filter lists is a manageable problem if you're talking about one or a handful of routers that are part of a firewall, but it gets out of hand in a hurry as the number of routers increases. This problem is worsened if some of the routers are purely internal. Why? Because you probably want to allow more services within your network than you allow between your network and the Internet. This is either going to make your filter sets longer (and thus harder to maintain), or make you switch from a "default deny" stance to a "default permit" stance on those internal filters (which is going to seriously undermine the security they provide anyway). You often reach a point of diminishing returns fairly quickly when you try to apply filtering widely within a LAN, rather than just at its perimeter.

You may still have internal packet filtering routers at boundaries within the LAN (between networks with different security policies, or networks that belong to different organizations). As long as they're at clearly defined boundaries, and they're up to the performance requirements, that's not a problem. Whether or not you duplicate the external rules on these internal packet filters is going to depend on how much you trust the external packet filters, and how much complexity and overhead the external rules are going to add.

Putting It All Together

This section works through a few more examples to show how many of the concepts we've talked about in this chapter come together in the real world. For detailed discussions of the packet filtering characteristics of particular protocols, see Chapter 8.

This section is designed to demonstrate the process of developing a filter set; filters are elaborated as we go on, rather than being produced in final form. We aren't attempting to show a complete filter set for any site. Every site is different, and you can get burned by packet filtering if you don't understand all the details and implications of its use in your particular environment. We want people to carefully consider and understand what they're doing—not blindly copy something out of a book (even ours!) without a careful consideration of how relevant and appropriate it is for their own situation. In any case, a full solution for a site requires considering packet filtering, proxying, and configuration issues. That process is illustrated in Chapter 9.

Let's start with a simple example: allowing inbound and outbound SMTP (so that you can send and receive electronic mail) and nothing else. You might start with the following rule set.

NOTE

We assume in this example that, for each packet, your filtering system looks at the rules in order. It starts at the top until it finds a rule that matches the packet, and then it takes the action specified.

Rule	Direction	Source Address	Dest. Address	Protocol	Dest. Port	Action
A	In	External	Internal	TCP	25	Permit
B	Out	Internal	External	TCP	>1023	Permit
C	Out	Internal	External	TCP	25	Permit
D	In	External	Internal	TCP	>1023	Permit
E	Either	Any	Any	Any	Any	Deny

- Rules A and B allow inbound SMTP connections (incoming email).

- Rules C and D allow outbound SMTP connections (outgoing email).

- Rule E is the default rule that applies if all else fails.

Now, let's consider some sample packets to see what happens. Let's say that your host has IP address 172.16.1.1, and that someone is trying to send you mail from the remote host with IP address 192.168.3.4. Further, let's say the sender's SMTP client uses port 1234 to talk to your SMTP server, which is on port 25. (SMTP servers are always assumed to be on port 25; see the discussion of SMTP in Chapter 8):

Packet	Direc-tion	Source Address	Dest. Address	Pro-XStocol	Dest. Port	Action (Rule)
1	In	192.168.3.4	172.16.1.1	TCP	25	Permit (A)
2	Out	172.16.1.1	192.168.3.4	TCP	1234	Permit (B)

Figure 6-10 shows this case.

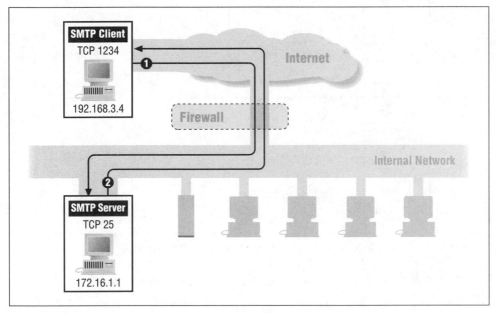

Figure 6–10: Packet filtering: inbound SMTP (sample packets 1 and 2

In this case, the packet filtering rules permit your incoming email:

- Rule A permits incoming packets from the sender's SMTP client to your SMTP server (represented by packet number 1 above).

- Rule B permits the responses from your server back to the sender's client (represented by packet number 2 above).

What about outgoing email from you to them? Let's say that your SMTP client uses port 1357 to talk to their SMTP server:

Packet	Direc-tion	Source Address	Dest. Address	Pro-tocol	Dest. Port	Action (Rule)
3	Out	172.16.1.1	192.168.3.4	TCP	25	Permit (C)
4	In	192.168.3.4	172.16.1.1	TCP	1357	Permit (D)

Figure 6-11 shows this case.

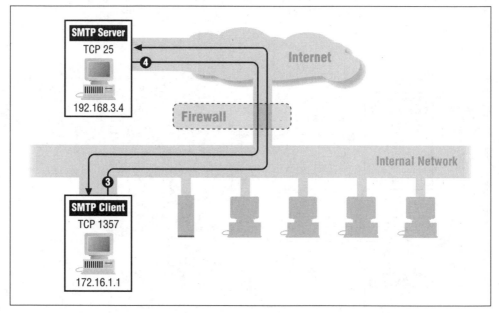

Figure 6–11: Packet filtering: outbound SMTP (sample packets 3 and 4)

Again, in this case, the packet filtering rules permit your outgoing email:

- Rule C permits outgoing packets from your SMTP client to their SMTP server (represented by packet number 3 above).

- Rule D permits the responses from their server back to your client (represented by packet number 4 above).

Now, let's stir things up. What happens if someone in the outside world (for example, someone on on host 10.1.2.3) attempts to open a connection from port 5150 on his end to the X11 server on port 6000 on one of your internal systems (for example, 172.16.3.4) in order to carry out an attack? (See Chapter 8 for a discussion of X11 and some of its vulnerabilities.)

Packet	Direc- tion	Source Address	Dest. Address	Pro- -tocol	Dest. Port	Action (Rule)
5	In	10.1.2.3	172.16.3.4	TCP	6000	Permit (D)
6	Out	172.16.3.4	10.1.2.3	TCP	5150	Permit (B)

Figure 6-12 shows this case.

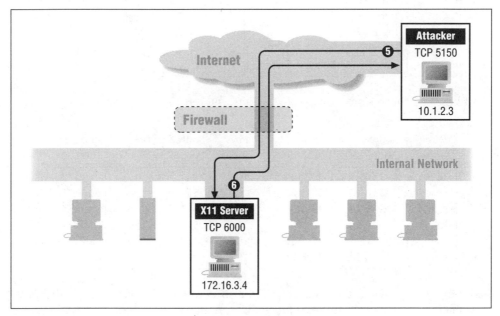

Figure 6–12: Packet filtering: inbound SMTP (sample packets 5 and 6)

The rule set shown above allows this connection to take place! In fact, the rule set shown above allows any connection to take place as long as both ends of the connection are using ports above 1023. Why?

- Rules A and B together do what you want to allow inbound SMTP connections.

- Rules C and D together do what you want to allow outbound SMTP connections.

- But Rules B and D together end up allowing *all* connections where both ends are using ports above 1023, and this is certainly not what you intended.

There are probably lots of vulnerable servers listening on ports above 1023 at your site. Examples are X11 (port 6000), OpenWindows (port 2000), databases (Sybase, Oracle, Informix, and other databases commonly use site-chosen ports above 1023), and so on. This is why you need to consider a rule set as a whole, instead of assuming that if each rule or group of rules is OK, the whole set is also OK.

What can you do about this? Well, what if you also looked at the source port in making your filtering decisions? Here are those same five basic rules with the source port added as a criterion:

Rule	Direction	Source Address	Dest. Address	Protocol	Source Port	Dest. Port	Action
A	In	External	Internal	TCP	>1023	25	Permit
B	Out	Internal	External	TCP	25	>1023	Permit
C	Out	Internal	External	TCP	>1023	25	Permit
D	In	External	Internal	TCP	25	>1023	Permit
E	Either	Any	Any	Any	Any	Any	Deny

And here are those same six sample packets, filtered by the new rules:

Rule	Direction	Source Address	Dest. Address	Protocol	Source Port	Dest. Port	Action (Rule)
1	In	192.168.3.4	172.16.1.1	TCP	1234	25	Permit (A)
2	Out	172.16.1.1	192.168.3.4	TCP	25	1234	Permit (B)
3	Out	172.16.1.1	192.168.3.4	TCP	1357	25	Permit (C)
4	In	192.168.3.4	172.16.1.1	TCP	25	1357	Permit (D)
5	In	10.1.2.3	172.16.3.4	TCP	5150	6000	Deny (E)
6	Out	172.16.3.4	10.1.2.3	TCP	6000	5150	Deny (E)

As you can see, when the source port is also considered as a criterion, the problem packets (numbers 5 and 6, representing an attack on one of your X11 servers) no longer meet any of the rules for packets to be permitted (rules A through D). The problem packets end up being denied by the default rule.

OK, now what if you're dealing with a slightly smarter attacker? What if the attacker uses port 25 as the client port on his end (he might do this by killing off the SMTP server on a machine he controls and using its port, or by carrying out the attack from a machine that never had an SMTP server in the first place, like a PC), and then attempts to open a connection to your X11 server? Here are the packets you'd see:

Rule	Direction	Source Address	Dest. Address	Protocol	Source Port	Dest. Port	Action (Rule)
7	In	10.1.2.3	172.16.3.4	TCP	25	6000	**Permit (D)**
8	Out	172.16.3.4	10.1.2.3	TCP	6000	25	**Permit (C)**

Figure 6-13 shows this case.

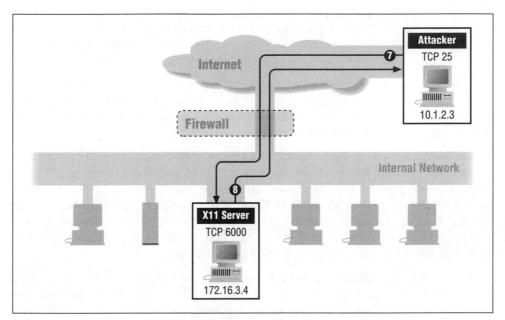

Figure 6–13: Packet filtering: inbound SMTP (sample packets 7 and 8)

As you can see, the packets would be permitted, and the attack would likely succeed (X11 security being as weak as it is).

So what can you do? The solution is to also consider the ACK bit as a filtering criterion. Again, here are those same six rules with the ACK bit also added as a criterion:

Rule	Direc- tion	Source Address	Dest. Address	Pro- tocol	Source Port	Dest. Port	ACK Set	Action
A	In	External	Internal	TCP	>1023	25	Any	Permit
B	Out	Internal	External	TCP	25	>1023	Yes	Permit
C	Out	Internal	External	TCP	>1023	25	Any	Permit
D	In	External	Internal	TCP	25	>1023	Yes	Permit
E	Either	Any	Any	Any	Any	Any	Any	Deny

Now, packet 7 (the attacker attempting to open a connection to your X11 client) will fail:

Rule	Direc- tion	Source Address	Dest. Address	Pro- tocol	Source Port	Dest. Port	ACK Set	Action
7	In	10.1.2.3	172.16.3.4	TCP	25	6000	No	Deny (E)

The only difference in this rule set are in rules B and D. Of these, rule D is the most important, because it controls incoming connections to your site. Rule B applies to connections outgoing from your site, and sites are generally more interested in controlling incoming connections than outgoing connections.

Rule D now says to accept incoming packets from things that are supposedly SMTP servers (because the packets are coming from port 25) only if the packets have the ACK bit set; that is, only if the packets are part of a connection started from the inside (from your client to his server).

If someone attempts to open a TCP connection from the outside, the very first packet that he sends will not have the ACK bit set; that's what's involved in "opening a TCP connection." (See the discussion of the ACK bit in the "TCP" section of "Protocols above IP" earlier in this chapter.) If you block that very first packet (packet 7 in the example above), you block the whole TCP connection. Without certain information in the headers of the first packet—in particular, the TCP sequence numbers—the connection can't be established.

Why can't an attacker get around this by simply setting the ACK bit on the first packet? If he does, the packet will get past the filters, but the destination will believe the packet belongs to an existing connection (instead of the one with which the packet is trying to establish a new connection). When the destination tries to match the packet up with the supposed existing connection, it will fail because there isn't one, and the packet will be ignored.

NOTE

As a basic rule of thumb, any filtering rule that permits incoming TCP packets for outgoing connections (that is, connections initiated by internal clients) should require that the ACK bit be set.

In This Chapter:
- *Why Proxying?*
- *How Proxying Works*
- *Proxy Server Terminology*
- *Using Proxying with Internet Services*
- *Proxying Without a Proxy Server*
- *Using SOCKS for Proxying*
- *Using the TIS Internet Firewall Toolkit for Proxying*
- *What If You Can't Proxy?*

7

Proxy Systems

Proxying provides Internet access to a single host, or a very small number of hosts, while appearing to provide access to all of your hosts. The hosts that have access act as proxies for the machines that don't, doing what these machines want done.

A proxy server for a particular protocol or set of protocols runs on a dual-homed host or a bastion host: some host that the user can talk to, which can, in turn, talk to the outside world. The user's client program talks to this proxy server instead of directly to the "real" server out on the Internet. The proxy server evaluates requests from the client and decides which to pass on and which to disreguard. If a request is approved, the proxy server talks to the real server on behalf of the client (thus the term "proxy"), and proceeds to relay requests from the client to the real server, and to relay the real server's answers back to the client.

As far as the user is concerned, talking to the proxy server is just like talking directly to the real server. As far as the real server is concerned, it's talking to a user on the host that is running the proxy server; it doesn't know that the user is really somewhere else.

Proxying doesn't require any special hardware, although it does require special software for most services.

NOTE

Proxy systems are effective only when they are used in conjunction with some method of restricting IP-level traffic between the clients and the real servers, such as a screening router or a dual-homed host that doesn't route packets. If there is IP-level connectivity between the clients and the real servers, the clients can bypass the proxy system (and presumably so can someone from the outside).

Why Proxying?

There's no point in connecting to the Internet if your users can't access it. On the other hand, there's no safety in connecting to the Internet if there's free access between it and every host at your site. Some compromise has to be applied.

The most obvious compromise is to provide a single host with Internet access for all your users. However, this isn't a satisfactory solution because these hosts aren't transparent to users. Users who want to access network services can't do so directly. They have to log in to the dual-homed host, do all their work from there, and then somehow transfer the results of their work back to their own workstations. At best, this multiple-step process annoys users by forcing them to do multiple transfers and work without the customizations they're accustomed to.

The problem is worse at sites with multiple operating systems; if your native system is a Macintosh, and the dual-homed host is a UNIX system, the UNIX system will probably be completely foreign to you. You'll be limited to using whatever tools are available on the dual-homed host, and these tools may be completely unlike (and may seem inferior to) the tools you use on your own system.

Dual-homed hosts configured without proxies therefore tend to annoy their users and significantly reduce the benefit people get from the Internet connection. Worse, they usually don't provide adequate security; it's almost impossible to adequately secure a machine with many users, particularly when those users are explicitly trying to get to the external universe. You can't effectively limit the available tools, because your users can always transfer tools from internal machines that are the same type. For example, on a dual-homed host you can't guarantee that all file transfers will be logged because people can use their own file transfer agents that don't do logging.

Proxy systems avoid user frustration and the insecurities of a dual-homed host. They deal with user frustration by automating the interaction with the dual-homed host. Instead of requiring users to deal directly with the dual-homed host, proxy systems allow all interaction to take place behind the scenes. The user has the illusion he is dealing directly (or almost directly) with the server on the Internet that he really wants to access, with a minimum of direct interaction with the dual-homed host. Figure 7-1 illustrates the difference between reality and illusion with proxy systems.

Proxy systems deal with the insecurity problems by avoiding user logins on the dual-homed host and by forcing connections through controlled software. Because the proxy software works without requiring user logins, the host it runs on is safe from the randomness of having multiple logins. It's also impossible for anybody to

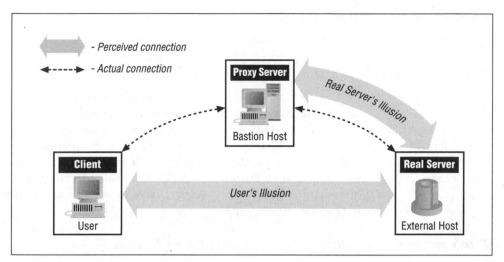

Figure 7–1: Proxies—reality and illusion

install uncontrolled software to reach the Internet; the proxy acts as a control point.

Advantages of Proxying

There are a number of advantages to using proxy services.

Proxy services allow users to access Internet services 'directly'

With the dual-homed host approach, a user needs to log into the host before using any Internet services. This is often inconvenient, and some users become so frustrated that they look for ways around the firewall. With proxy services, users think they're interacting directly with Internet services.

Of course, there's more going on behind the scenes but it's usually transparent to users. While proxy services allow users to access Internet services from their own systems, they do so without allowing packets to pass directly between the user's system and the Internet. The path is indirect, either through a dual-homed host, or through a bastion host and screening router combination.

Proxy services are good at logging

Because proxy servers understand the underlying protocol, they allow logging to be performed in a particularly effective way. For example, instead of logging all of the data transferred, an FTP proxy server logs only the commands issued and the server responses received; this results in a much smaller and more useful log.

Disadvantages of Proxying

There are also some disadvantages to using proxy services.

Proxy services lag behind nonproxied services

Although proxy software is widely available for the older and simpler services like FTP and Telnet, proven software for newer or less widely used services is harder to find. There's usually a distinct lag between the introduction of a service and the availability of proxying servers for it; the length of the lag depends primarily on how well the service is designed for proxying. This makes it difficult for a site to offer new services immediately as they become available. Until suitable proxy software is available, a system that needs new services may have to be placed outside the firewall, opening up potential security holes.

Proxy services may require different servers for each service

You may need a different proxy server for each protocol, because the proxy server has to understand the protocol in order to determine what to allow and disallow, and in order to masquerade as a client to the real server and as the real server to the proxy client. Collecting, installing, and configuring all these various servers can be a lot of work.

Products and packages differ greatly in the ease with which they can be configured, but making things easier in one place can make it harder in others. For example, servers that are particularly easy to configure are usually limited in flexibility; they're easy to configure because they make certain assumptions about how they're going to be used, which may or may not be correct or appropriate for your site.

Proxy services usually require modifications to clients, procedures, or both

Except for a few services designed for proxying, proxy servers require modifications to clients and/or procedures. Either kind of modification has drawbacks; people can't always use the readily available tools with their normal instructions.

Because of these modifications, proxied applications don't work as well as nonproxied applications. They tend to bend protocol specifications, and some clients and servers are less flexible than others.

Proxy services aren't workable for some services

Proxying relies on the ability to insert the proxy server between the client and the real server; that requires relatively straightforward interaction between the two. A service like *talk* that has complicated and messy interactions may never be possible to proxy (see the discussion of *talk* in Chapter 8).

Proxy services don't protect you from all protocol weaknesses

As a security solution, proxying relies on the ability to determine which operations in a protocol are safe. Not all protocols provide easy ways to do this. The X Window System protocol, for example, provides a large number of unsafe operations, and it's difficult to make it work while removing the unsafe operations. HTTP is designed to operate effectively with proxy servers, but it's also designed to be readily extensible, and it achieves that goal by passing data that's going to be executed. It's impossible for a proxy server to protect you from the data; it would have to understand the data being passed and determine whether it was dangerous or not.

How Proxying Works

The details of how proxying works differ from service to service. Some services provide proxying easily or automatically; for those services, you set up proxying by making configuration changes to normal servers. For most services, however, proxying requires appropriate proxy server software on the server side. On the client side, it needs one of the following:

Custom client software
> With this approach, the software must know how to contact the proxy server instead of the real server when a user makes a request (for example, for FTP or Telnet), and how to tell the proxy server what real server to connect.

Custom user procedures
> With this approach, the user uses standard client software to talk to the proxy server and tells it to connect to the real server, instead of to the real server directly.

Using Custom Client Software for Proxying

The first approach is to use custom client software for proxying. There are a few problems associated with this approach.

Appropriate custom client software is often available only for certain platforms. If it's not available for one of your platforms, your users are pretty much out of luck. For example, the *Igateway* package from Sun is a proxy package for FTP and Telnet, but you can only use it on Sun machines because it provides only precompiled Sun binaries. If you're going to use proxy software, you obviously need to choose software that's available for the needed platforms.

Even if software is available for your platforms, it may not be software your users want. For example, on the Macintosh, there are dozens of FTP client programs. Some of them have really impressive graphical user interfaces. Others have other useful features; for example, *anarchie* is a program that combines an Archie client and an FTP client into a single program, so that you can search for a file with Archie and then retrieve it with FTP, all with a single consistent user interface. You're out of luck if the particular client you want to use, for whatever reason, doesn't support your particular proxy server mechanism. In some cases, you may be able to modify clients to support your proxy server, but doing so requires that you have the source code for the client, as well as the tools and the ability to recompile it. Few client programs come with support for any form of proxying.

The happy exception to this rule is WWW client programs, like Mosaic. Many of these programs support proxies of various sorts (typically SOCKS and the CERN HTTP daemon). Most of these programs are fairly new, and were thus written after firewalls and proxy systems had become common on the Internet; recognizing the environment they would be working in, their authors chose to support proxying by design, right from the start.

Using client changes for proxying does not make proxying completely transparent to users. Most sites will use the unchanged clients for internal connections and the modified ones only to make external connections; users need to remember to use the modified program in order to make external connections. Following procedures they've become accustomed to using elsewhere, or procedures that are written in books, may leave them mystified at apparently intermittent results as internal connections succeed and external ones fail. (Using the modified clients internally will work, but it introduces unneccessary dependencies on the proxy server, which is why most sites avoid it.)

In addition to having to choose the right program, users may find themselves doing extra configuration, because the proxy client needs to know how to contact the proxy server. This shouldn't represent a major burden, but it provides an extra place for things to go wrong.

Using Custom User Procedures for Proxying

With the custom procedure approach, the proxy servers are designed to work with standard client software; however, they require the users of the software to follow custom procedures. The user tells the client to connect to the proxy server and then tells the proxy server which host to connect to. Because few protocols are designed to pass this kind of information, the user needs to remember not only what the name of the proxy server is, but also what special means are used to pass the name of the other host.

How does this work? You need to teach your users specific procedures to follow for each protocol. Let's look at FTP. Suppose a user wants to retrieve a file from an anonymous FTP server (e.g., *ftp.greatcircle.com*). Here's what the user does:

1. Using any FTP client, the user connects to your proxy server (which is probably running on the bastion host—the gateway to the Internet) instead of directly to the anonymous FTP server.

2. At the user name prompt, in addition to specifying the name he wants to use, the user also specifies the name of the real server he wants to connect to. If he wants to access the anonymous FTP server on *ftp.greatcircle.com*, for example, then instead of simply typing "anonymous" at the prompt generated by the proxy server, he'll type "anonymous@ftp.greatcircle.com".

For a more complete example, see the discussion of the TIS Internet Firewall Toolkit later in this section.

Just as using custom software requires some modification of user procedures, using custom procedures places limitations on which clients you can use. Some clients try to do anonymous FTP automatically; they won't know how to go through the proxy server. Some clients may interfere in simpler ways, e.g., by providing a graphical user interface that doesn't allow you type a user name long enough to hold the username and the hostname.

The main problem with using custom procedures, however, is that you have to teach them to your users. If you have a small user base and one that is technically adept, this may not be a problem. However, if you have 10,000 users spread across four continents, it's going to be a problem. On the one side, you have arrayed hundreds of books, thousands of magazine articles, and tens of thousands of Usenet news postings, not to mention whatever previous training or experience the users might have had, all of which attempt to teach users the standard way to use basic Internet services like FTP. On the other side is your tiny voice, telling them how to use a procedure that is at odds with all the other information they're getting. On top of that, your users will have to remember the name of your gateway and the details of how to use it. In any organization of a reasonable size, this approach can't be relied upon.

Proxy Server Terminology

This section describes a number of specific types of proxy servers.

Application-Level Versus Circuit-Level Proxies

An *application-level proxy* is one that knows about the particular application it is providing proxy services for; it understands and interprets the commands in the application protocol. A *circuit-level proxy* is one that creates a circuit between the client and the server without interpreting the application protocol. The most extreme version of an application-level proxy is an application like *Sendmail*, which implements a store-and-forward protocol. The most extreme version of a circuit-level proxy is one of the modern hybrid proxy gateways that looks like a proxy to the outside but like a filtering router to the inside.

In general, application-level proxies use modified procedures, and circuit-level proxies use modified clients. This has to do with the practicalities of proxying. In order to make a proxy connection, you have to know where the connection is supposed to go. A hybrid gateway can simply intercept connections, but a proxying host can only receive connections that are bound for it; something else has to tell it where to make the onward connection. An application-level proxy can get that information in the application protocol (either by using design features, or by reinterpreting user-supplied data). A circuit-level proxy can't interpret the application protocol and needs to have the information supplied to it through other means (e.g., by using a modified client that gives the server the destination address). Because the ability to use unmodified clients is a useful feature, application-level proxies generally are designed to take advantage of their application protocol knowledge (so they use modified procedures). Circuit-level proxies usually have no way to use modified procedures, so they use modified clients.

Although there are no known modified-client application-level proxies, there are modified-procedure circuit-level proxies. *plug-gw*, for example, described in "Generic Proxying with TIS FWTK" later in this chapter, uses modified procedures (the connection is made to the proxy server, instead of the destination host) and is a circuit-level proxy. It bases destination decisions purely on the source address, and the source and destination ports of the connection.

The advantage of a circuit-level proxy is that it provides service for a wide variety of different protocols. Most circuit-level proxy servers are also generic proxy servers; they can be adapted to serve almost any protocol. Not every protocol can easily be handled by a circuit-level proxy, however. Protocols like FTP, which communicate port data from the client to the server, require some protocol-level intervention, and thus some application-level knowledge. The disadvantage of a circuit-level proxy server is that it provides very little control over what happens through the proxy. Like a packet filter, it controls connections on the basis of their source and destination and can't easily determine whether the commands going through it are safe or even in the expected protocol. Circuit-level proxies are easily fooled by servers set up at the port numbers assigned to other servers.

Generic Versus Dedicated Proxies

Although "application-level" and "circuit-level" are frequently used terms, we more often distinguish between "dedicated" and "generic" proxy servers. A *dedicated proxy server* is one that serves a single protocol; a *generic proxy server* is one that serves multiple protocols. In practice, dedicated proxy servers are application-level, and generic proxy servers are circuit-level. Depending on how you argue about shades of meaning, it might be possible to produce a generic application-level proxy server (one that understands a wide range of protocols) or a dedicated circuit-level proxy server (one that provides only one service, but doesn't understand the protocol for it). Neither of these ever occur, however, so we use "dedicated" and "generic" merely because we find them somewhat more intuitive terms than "application-level" and "circuit-level."

Intelligent Proxy Servers

A proxy server can do a great deal more than simply relay requests; one that does is an *intelligent proxy server*. For example, the CERN HTTP proxy server caches data, so that multiple requests for the same data don't go out across the Internet. Proxy servers (particularly application-level servers) can provide better logging and access controls than those achieved through other methods, although few existing proxy servers take full advantage of the opportunities. As proxy servers mature, their abilities are increasing rapidly. Now that there are multiple proxy suites that provide basic functionality, they're beginning to compete by adding features. It's easier for a dedicated, application-level proxy server to be intelligent; a circuit-level proxy has limited abilities.

Using Proxying with Internet Services

Because proxying interferes with communications between a client and a server, it has to be adapted separately to each service. Some things that are easy to do normally become much more difficult when a proxy is involved.

The ideal service for proxying makes a TCP connection in one direction; has only secure commands; has some piece of variable-length, user-specified data that's passed to the server; and is being used from an internal client to an external server. The following sections look at these ideal situations, and some that aren't so ideal.

TCP Versus Other Protocols

Because TCP is a connection-oriented protocol, you only go through the overhead of setting up the proxy once, and then you continue to use that connection. UDP has no concept of connections; every packet is a separate transaction requiring a separate decision from the proxy server. TCP is therefore easier to proxy (although the UDP Packet Relayer package is a generic UDP proxy server). ICMP is so low-level, it's almost impossible to proxy.

Unidirectional Versus Multidirectional Connections

It's easy for a proxy server to intercept the initial connection from a client to a server. It's harder for it to intercept a return connection. Either both ends of the conversation have to be aware of the existence of the proxy server, or the server needs to be able to interpret and modify the protocol to make certain the return connection is made correctly. For example, normal-mode FTP requires the proxy server to intercept the PORT command the client sends to the server, open a connection from the proxy to the client at that port, and send a different PORT command (for a port on the proxy) to the real server. It's not enough for the proxy server to simply read the PORT command on the way past, because that port may already be in use. Similar problems are going to arise in any protocol requiring a return connection.

Anything more complex than an outbound connection and a return is even worse. The *talk* service is an example; see the discussion in Chapter 8 for an example of a service with a tangled web of connections that's almost impossible to proxy. (It doesn't help any that *talk* is partly UDP-based, but even if it were all TCP, it would still be a proxy-writer's nightmare.)

Protocol Security

For some services, proxying may be technically easy, but pointless from a security point of view. If a protocol is inherently unsafe, proxying it without doing anything else will not make it any safer. For example, X11 is mildly tricky to proxy, for reasons discussed at length in Chapter 8, but the real reason it's not widely proxied through firewalls has nothing to do with technical issues (proxy X servers are not uncommon as ways to extend X capabilities). The real reason is that X provides a number of highly insecure abilities to a client, and a proxy system for a firewall needs to catch unsafe operations and at least offer the user the ability to prevent them. This is reasonably possible with X (and the TIS FWTK provides a proxy called *x-gw* that does this), but it requires more application knowledge than would be necessary for a safer protocol.

If it's difficult to distinguish between safe and unsafe operations in a protocol or impossible to use the service at all if unsafe operations are prevented, proxying may not be a viable solution. In that case, there may be no good solution, and you may be reduced to using a victim host, as discussed in Chapter 5. Some people consider HTTP to be such a protocol (because it may end up transferring programs that are executed transparently by the client).

User-Specified Data

If you're going to use modified-procedure proxying, you need a modifiable part of the procedure. Programs like FTP and HTTP clients in which the client passes a nice long user-specified string to the server, are perfect. (FTP clients pass a user name to the server; HTTP clients pass a URL.) A program like *ping* in which the client passes absolutely no data to the server is fundamentally impossible to proxy using an unmodified client.[*]

---

[*] People have been known to claim that forcing users to log into a bastion host to use *ping* is an extreme version of modified-procedure proxying. It's clearly a modified procedure, but the "proxy" part is hard to detect.

Internal Versus External Clients

Most proxy servers are designed for situations in which the client is on the inside and the server on the outside, of the firewall. This is because most proxy servers require some cooperation at the client's end, and the modifiable clients and the trainable users are probably both inside the firewall. Proxying for external clients works only in a few situations:

- Using modified procedures to provide inbound services for your own users. (See Chapter 10 for more information about this situation.)

- Using something like *plug-gw* to redirect connections from the proxy server to an internal machine. A program of this kind will support any number of clients, as long as they all want to connect to the same internal server.

- Providing a special service for which you distribute clients. If you write your own Internet service, you can easily design the clients to include proxy support.

Proxying Without a Proxy Server

Some services, particularly the so-called "store-and-forward" services such as SMTP, NNTP, and NTP, naturally support proxying. These services are all designed so that messages (email messages for SMTP, Usenet news postings for NNTP, and clock settings for NTP) are received by a server and then stored until they can be forwarded to another appropriate server or servers. For SMTP, the messages are forwarded towards an email message's destination. For NNTP and NTP, the messages are forwarded to all neighbor servers. With such a scheme, each intermediate server is effectively acting as a proxy for the original sender or server.

If you examine the "Received:" headers of incoming Internet email (these headers trace a message's path through the network from sender to recipient), you quickly discover that very few messages travel directly from the sender's machine to the recipient's machine. It's far more common these days for the message to pass through at least four machines:

- The sender's machine

- The outgoing mail gateway at the sender's site (or the sender's Internet service provider)

- The incoming mail gateway at the recipient's site

- Finally, the recipient's machine

Each of the intermediate servers (the mail gateways) is acting as a proxy server for the sender, even though the sender may not be dealing with them directly. Figure 7-2 illustrates this situation.

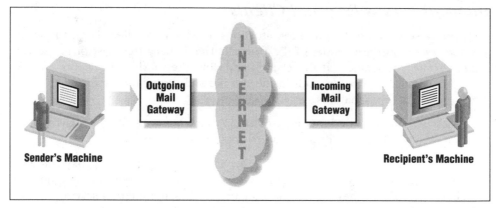

Figure 7–2: Store-and-forward services (like SMTP) naturally support proxying

Using SOCKS for Proxying

The SOCKS package, originally written by David Koblas and Michelle Koblas, and currently maintained by Ying-Da Lee, is an example of the type of proxy system that requires custom clients. SOCKS is freely available, and it has become the de facto standard proxying package on the Internet. The package is on track to become an official Internet standard: a Request For Comments (RFC) has been written and is currently undergoing the approval process. Appendix B tells you how to get SOCKS.

In order to make it easy to support new clients, SOCKS is extremely generic. This is part of what makes it so popular, but it has the disadvantage that SOCKS can't provide intelligent logging or access control. It provides logging, but most of the logging is done on the client, making it difficult to collect the information in a single place for examination. SOCKS does log connection requests on the server; provides access control by source, and destination host and protocol; and allows configurable responses to access denials. For example, it can be configured to notify an administrator of incoming access attempts and to let users know why their outgoing access attempts were denied.

One drawback of SOCKS is that it works only for TCP-based clients; it doesn't work for UDP-based clients (like Archie clients, for example). If you are using a UDP-based client, you may want to get another package, the UDP Packet Relayer. This program serves much the same function for UDP-based clients as SOCKS serves for TCP-based clients. Like SOCKS, the UDP Packet Relayer is freely available on the Internet.

The prime advantage of SOCKS is its popularity. Because SOCKS is widely used, server implementations and SOCKS-ified clients (i.e., versions of programs like FTP and Telnet that have already been converted to user SOCKS) are commonly available, and help is easy to find. This can be a double-edged sword; cases have been reported where intruders to firewalled sites have installed their own SOCKS-knowledgeable clients.

The SOCKS package includes the following components:

- The SOCKS server. This server must run on a UNIX system, although it has been ported to many different variants of UNIX.

- The SOCKS client library for UNIX machines.

- SOCKS-ified versions of several standard UNIX client programs such as FTP and Telnet.

In addition, client libraries for Macintosh and Windows systems are available as separate packages.

Figure 7-3 shows the use of SOCKS for proxying.

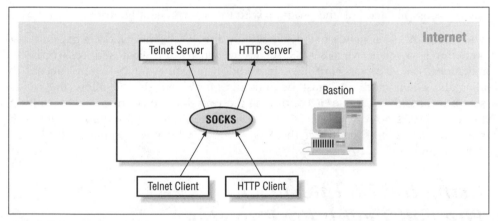

Figure 7–3: Using SOCKS for proxying

Many Internet client programs (both commercial and freely available) already have SOCKS support built in to them as a compile-time or a run-time option.

How do you convert a client program to use SOCKS? You need to modify the program so it talks to the SOCKS server, rather than trying to talk to the real world directly. You do this by recompiling the program with the SOCKS library.

Converting a client program to use SOCKS is usually pretty easy. The SOCKS package makes certain assumptions about how client programs work, and most client programs already follow these assumptions. For a complete summary of these assumptions, see the file in the SOCKS release called *What_SOCKS_expects*.

To convert a client program, you must replace all calls to standard network functions with calls to the SOCKS versions of those functions. Here are the calls:

Standard Network Function	SOCKS Version
connect()	Rconnect()
getsockname()	Rgetsockname()
bind()	Rbind()
accept()	Raccept()
listen()	Rlisten()
select()	Rselect()

You can usually do this simply by adding the following to the "CFLAGS=" line of the program's Makefile.

```
-Dconnect=Rconnect
        -Dgetsockname=Rgetsockname
        -Dbind=Rbind
        -Daccept=Raccept
        -Dlisten=Rlisten
        -Dselect=Rselect
```

Then, recompile and link the program with the SOCKS client library.

The client machine needs to have not only the SOCKS-modified clients, but also something to tell it what SOCKS server to contact for what services (on UNIX machines, the */etc/socks.conf* file). In addition, if you want to control access by user, the client machines must be running *identd*, which will allow the SOCKS server to identify what user is controlling the port that the connection comes from. Because there's no way for the SOCKS server to verify that the *identd* server is reliable, *identd* can't be trusted if there is anybody who might intentionally be circumventing it.

Using the TIS Internet Firewall Toolkit for Proxying

The free TIS FWTK, from Trusted Information Systems, includes a number of proxy servers of various types. The TIS FWTK also provides a number of other tools for authentication and other purposes, which are discussed where appropriate in other chapters of this book. Appendix B provides information on how to get the TIS FWTK.

Whereas SOCKS attempts to provide a single, general proxy, the TIS FWTK provides individual proxies for the most common Internet services (as shown in Figure 7-4). The idea is that by using small separate programs with a common configuration file, it can provide intelligent proxies that are provably safe, while still allowing central control. The result is an extremely flexible toolkit and a rather large configuration file.

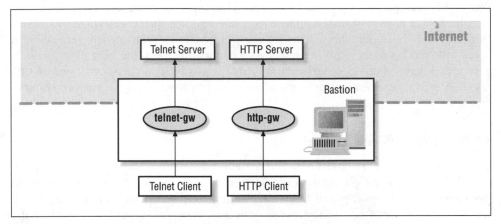

Figure 7–4: Using the TIS FWTK for proxying

FTP Proxying with TIS FWTK

The TIS FWTK provides FTP proxying either with modified client programs (*ftp-gw*) or modified user procedures. If you wish to use the same machine to support proxied FTP and straight FTP (for example, allowing people on the Internet to pick up files from the same machine that does outbound proxying for your users), the toolkit will support that but you will have to use modified user procedures.

Using modified user procedures is the most common configuration for the TIS FWTK. The support for modified client programs is somewhat half-hearted (for example, no modified clients or libraries are provided). Because it's a dedicated FTP proxy, it provides logging, denial, and extra user authentication of particular FTP commands.

Telnet and rlogin Proxying with TIS FWTK

The TIS FWTK Telnet (*telnet-gw*) and *rlogin* (*rlogin-gw*) proxies support modified user procedures only. Users connect via Telnet or *rlogin* to the proxy host, and instead of getting a "login" prompt for the proxy host, they are presented with a prompt from the proxy program, allowing them to specify what host to connect to (and whether to make an X connection if the *x-gw* software is installed, as we describe in "Other TIS FWTK Proxies" below).

Generic Proxying with TIS FWTK

The TIS FWTK provides a purely generic proxy, *plug-gw*, which requires no modifications to clients, but supports a limited range of protocols and uses. It examines the address it received a connection from and the port it the connection came in on, and it creates a connection to another host on an appropriate port. You can't specify which host it should connect to while making that connection; it's determined by the incoming host. This makes *plug-gw* inappropriate for services that are employed by users, who rarely want to connect to the same host every time. It provides logging but no other security enhancements, and therefore needs to be used with caution even in situations where it's appropriate (e.g., for NNTP connections).

Other TIS FWTK Proxies

TIS FWTK proxies HTTP and Gopher via the *http-gw* program. This program supports either modified clients or modified procedures. Most HTTP clients support proxying; you just need to tell them where the proxy server is. To use *http-gw*with an HTTP client that's not proxy-aware, you add `http://firewall/` in front of the URL. Using it with a Gopher client that is not proxy-aware is slightly more complex, since all the host and port information has to be moved into the path specification.

x-gw is an X gateway. It provides some minimal security by requiring confirmation from the user before allowing a remote X client to connect. The X gateway is started up by connecting to the Telnet or *rlogin* proxy and typing "x", which puts up a control window.

What If You Can't Proxy?

You might find yourself unable to proxy a service for one of three reasons:

- There's no proxy server available.

- Proxying doesn't secure the service sufficiently.

- You can't modify the client, and the protocol doesn't allow you to use modified procedures.

We describe each of these situations in the following sections.

No Proxy Server Is Available

If the service is proxyable, but you can't find a modified-procedure server or modified clients for your platform, you can always do the work yourself. Modifying a normal TCP client program to use SOCKS is relatively trivial. As long as the SOCKS libraries are available for the platform you're interested in, it's usually a matter of changing a few library calls and recompiling. You do have to have the source for the client.

Writing your own modified-procedure server is considerably more difficult, because it means writing the server from scratch.

Proxying Won't Secure the Service

If you need to use a service that's inherently insecure, proxying can't do much for you. You're going to need to set up a victim machine, as described in Chapter 5, and let people run the service there. This may be difficult if you're using a dual-homed nonrouting host to make a firewall where all connections must be proxied; the victim machine is going to need to be on the Internet side of the dual-homed host.

Using an intelligent application-level server that filters out insecure commands may help, but requires extreme caution in implementing the server and may make important parts of the service nonfunctional.

Can't Modify Client or Procedures

There are some services that just don't have room for modifying user procedures (for example *ping* and *traceroute)*. Fortunately, services that don't allow the user to pass any data to the server tend to be small, stupid, and safe. You may be able to safely provide them on the bastion host, letting users log in to the bastion host but giving them a shell that only allows them to run the un-proxyable services you want to support.

In This Chapter:
- *Electronic Mail*
- *File Transfer*
- *Telnet*
- *Remote Command Execution*
- *NNTP*
- *WWW and HTTP*
- *Other Information Services*
- *Information Lookup Services*
- *Real-Time Conferencing Services*
- *DNS*
- *syslog*
- *Network Management Services*
- *NTP*
- *NFS*
- *NIS/YP*
- *X11 Window System*
- *lpr and lp*
- *Analyzing Other Protocols*

8

Configuring Internet Services

This chapter describes the major Internet services: how they work, what their packet filtering and proxying characteristics are, what their security implications are with respect to firewalls, and how to make them work with a firewall. The purpose of this chapter is to give you the information that will help you decide which services to offer at your site and to help you configure these services so they are as safe and as functional as possible in your firewall environment.

This chapter is intended primarily as a reference; it's not necessarily intended to be read in depth from start to finish, though you might learn a lot of interesting stuff by skimming the whole thing.

This chapter assumes that you are familiar with what the various Internet services are used for, and concentrates on explaining how to provide those services through a firewall. For introductory information about what particular services are used for, see Chapter 2.

Where we discuss the packet filtering characteristics of particular services, we use the same abstract tabular form we used to show filtering rules in Chapter 6. You'll need to translate various abstractions like "internal," "external," and so on to appropriate values for your own configuration. See Chapter 6 for an explanation of how you can translate abstract rules to rules for particular products and packages, as well as more information on packet filtering in general.

Where we discuss the proxy characteristics of particular services, we rely on concepts and terminology discussed in Chapter 7.

Throughout this chapter, for each service, we'll show how its packets flow through a firewall. The following figures show the basic packet flow: when a service runs directly (Figure 8-1) and when a proxy service is used (Figure 8-2). The other figures in this chapter show variations of these figures for individual services. If there are no specific figures for a particular service, you can assume that these generic figures are appropriate for that service.

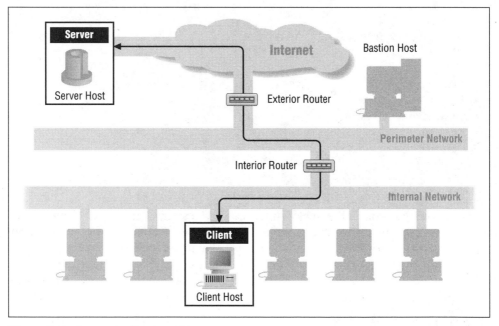

Figure 8–1: A generic direct service

You can find information on particular resources and tools (including where to get them) in Appendix A and Appendix B.

NOTE

We frequently characterize client port numbers as "a random port number above 1023." Some protocols specify this as a requirement, and on others it is merely a convention (spread to other platforms from UNIX,

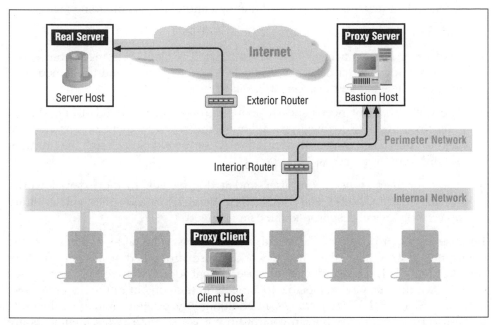

Figure 8–2: A generic proxy service

where ports below 1024 cannot be opened by regular users). Although
it is theoretically allowable for clients to use ports below 1024 on non-
UNIX platforms, it is extraordinarily rare: rare enough that many firewalls, including ones on major public sites that handle clients of all
types, rely on this distinction and report never having rejected a connection because of it.

Electronic Mail

From a user's point of view, electronic mail is perhaps the most fundamental Internet service. Unfortunately, it's also one of the most vulnerable. Mail servers make
extremely tempting targets, because they accept arbitrary data from arbitrary external hosts.

A mail system has three parts, which may be implemented by different programs
or may be implemented by the same program, in any combination.

- A server accepts mail from external hosts or sends it to external hosts

- A delivery agent puts the mail in the correct mailbox on the local host

- A user agent lets the recipient read the mail and compose outgoing mail

Each of these parts is vulnerable for a different reason:

- The server directly accepts commands (related to delivering mail) from external hosts; for this reason, if the server isn't secure, it may end up immediately giving an attacker all the access it has itself.

- The delivery agent needs special permissions because it needs to be able to write into every user's mailbox. Although the delivery agent doesn't need to talk to the external world, if it can be subverted somehow, the intruder obtains very broad access.

- The user agent runs as one user, and it doesn't talk to the external world, which limits its power and accessibility; however, it can often run arbitrary other programs in response to the data received.

Because it talks to the external world, the server is vulnerable to attacks in the commands it gets from the outside world; these are called *command channel attacks*. The delivery agent and the user agent don't receive the commands directly, but they may be vulnerable to dangers in the content of the mail message; these are called *data-driven attacks*. In addition, any program may be vulnerable to misuse by somebody who can control how it is executed (what arguments are used, what user is running it, what its data files are), through *command-line bugs*.

The Morris worm used a command channel attack against Sendmail; it issued a special Sendmail debugging command that allowed it to tell Sendmail to execute anything the intruder liked.

Data-driven attacks can exploit the delivery agent, the user agent, or the user. (The server generally pays no attention to the data.) For example, on UNIX machines, most versions of Sendmail use */bin/mail* as a local delivery agent. */bin/mail* is also a user agent and therefore has extensions to allow it to execute arbitrary commands. (If you have only one terminal, you're typing a mail message, and you want to see the output of some other command, it's very useful to be able to get your user agent to run the command for you.) Unfortunately, these extensions are not always disabled when */bin/mail* is running as a delivery agent, and the data in the mail message is sometimes capable of triggering them, allowing an outsider to run arbitrary commands on your system merely by sending appropriately formatted mail to you.

User agents may also be subverted even when they're acting as designed, as user agents. Today's multimedia mail readers are particularly subject to attacks of this kind, because they need to execute other programs to "display" a message for you (for example, a graphics program to display a picture or an audio program to play an audio attachment), but older mail readers were vulnerable as well. One Christmas, most of IBM's corporate network was put out of commission by a data-driven attack. Users received a message, usually from someone they knew and trusted, that said simply "run me". Because it appeared to be coming from a friend, most people did run it; when they did, it displayed a Christmas tree, and then resent itself to all of the entries in the reader's address book (personal alias file). It propagated very fast, and the network melted down under the force of trying to send millions of copies.

Finally, even if the server, the delivery agent, and the user agent are bug-free, some data-driven attacks work by subverting the user, and getting the user to perform some action the attacker wants. Sometimes that action involves running the program the attacker sent in the mail. Sometimes it's something more direct; for example, it's common for attackers to send mail to users that appears to come from their system's managers and that directs them to change their password to something specific. If the users do so, the attacker can now access their account.

How well does a firewall protect against these different types of attacks?

Command channel attacks

A firewall can protect against command channel attacks by restricting the number of machines to which attackers can open command channels and by providing a secured server on those machines.

Data-driven attacks

There isn't much a firewall can do about data-driven attacks; the data has to be allowed through, or you won't actually be able to receive mail. In some cases it's possible to filter out "dangerous" characters in the mail addresses if you can somehow recognize them. Your best bet, though, is to run up-to-date delivery and user agents and to educate your users. Doing so will protect against most data-driven attacks. In any case, because data-driven attacks tend to be complicated and difficult to get information back from, they are relatively rare.

Command-line bugs

Command-line bugs are outside the scope of a firewall, because they can be exploited only by someone who is already able to execute commands on your system. One purpose of a firewall is to keep attackers from getting that ability.

The following sections describe the two protocols commonly used for electronic mail: SMTP and POP, as well as the MIME extension.

Simple Mail Transfer Protocol (SMTP)

On the Internet, electronic mail exchange between mail servers is handled with SMTP. A host's SMTP server accepts mail and examines the destination address to decide whether to deliver the mail locally or to forward it on to some other machine. If it decides to deliver the mail locally, it recodes the mail headers and delivery address into the proper form for the local delivery program, and it then hands the mail to that program. If it decides to forward the mail to another machine, it modifies the headers, and contacts that machine (usually via SMTP, but sometimes via UUCP or another protocol), and forwards the mail.

SMTP is a store-and-forward system, and such systems are well-suited to firewall applications, particularly those using proxy services. In Chapter 7, Figure 7-2 shows how mail sent from an individual user's workstation is directed initially to a gateway system before leaving the user's own network. Mail entering a network goes to a gateway system on that network before being distributed to individual users on other hosts.

SMTP for UNIX: Sendmail

The mailer most commonly used on UNIX systems is Sendmail. Sendmail is very powerful, but it also has a long and troubling history of major and minor security problems. Other mailers are available, including smail 3, MMDF, and Z-Mail, but none of them appears to be particularly more secure than a modern version of Sendmail.

Sendmail's security problems have been widely discussed, while the problems of these other mailers have not. However, the lack of public discussion about other mailers should not lead you to assume these mailers are any more secure than Sendmail. While some of them are intended to be more secure than Sendmail, there is nothing to guarantee they are. Most of these alternative mailers are apparently intended to address Sendmail's incredibly baroque configuration files and its occasional failure to comply with standards, or to provide features Sendmail doesn't have. Additional security is often an afterthought, not a design feature. These mailers are simply not as widely used as Sendmail, and therefore, they have fewer people—with both good intentions and bad—who are examining them for security problems. This fact, more than any inherent superiority, is probably the reason for the apparently greater security of these alternative mailers; it's not that the problems aren't there, it's just that not as many people know what they are.

Sendmail is the devil that everybody knows; this is both an advantage and a disadvantage. On the one hand, problems are going to be found in Sendmail because that's where lots of people are looking for them (because lots of people use Sendmail). On the other hand, what problems are found are likely to be fixed very quickly (again, because lots of people use Sendmail). Sendmail is very actively supported on security issues.

Why does Sendmail have security problems?

One of the reasons Sendmail has security problems is that it's a very complex program. It performs several different functions, and it requires the collection of permissions necessary to perform *all* of those functions. Sendmail needs root privileges for a number of reasons; for example, these privileges allow Sendmail to:

- Listen on port 25 (a privileged port) for incoming SMTP connections.

- Operate as a particular user to read *.forward* files and *:include:* alias files owned by that user, and to run programs specified by those files.

- Execute certain kernel system calls that (in some versions of UNIX) are restricted to programs running as root, for example, to determine the amount of free disk space available to accept incoming messages.

- Protect files in the mail queue (i.e., messages in transit) from snooping by unprivileged users

These root permissions can be a liability, though, when Sendmail acts as an SMTP server; an attacker who manages to exploit a bug over an SMTP connection is now talking to a process that is running as root. The process can do essentially anything on the target machine at the attacker's bidding. Sendmail tries to be careful to give up its privileges whenever it doesn't really need them, but there have still been quite a number of privilege-related bugs over the years.

On a bastion host, it should be possible to make Sendmail run *setuid* to something other than root. You can use an alternative SMTP server (the *smap* package, discussed below) for incoming SMTP connections, so that Sendmail doesn't need to listen on port 25. You shouldn't have any users on the bastion host, so you shouldn't need the ability to operate as particular users to read protected *.forward* and *:include:* files. There probably aren't any privileged system calls on your system that are critical to Sendmail's operation (though you may need to recompile Sendmail from source to prevent it from attempting to use those calls). All you're left with is the need to keep ownership of files in the mail queue consistent, and to keep nonprivileged users (which the bastion host shouldn't have anyway) from snooping on messages in transit. Creating a *uid* just for Sendmail, and making that *uid* the owner of the queue directory should solve that problem.

Each of these tasks could probably be done in more secure ways, but this would require a major redesign and reimplementation of Sendmail, and nobody has yet stepped up to accept this challenge: among other reasons, out of fear that doing so would probably introduce new problems. Instead, we keep getting patch after patch for problem after problem, so that "the current Sendmail patch" has become something of a running joke in the network security community.

Sendmail has exhibited all of the types of general mailer vulnerabilities we discussed above. Patching has eliminated or reduced most of them; for example, it used to be easy to exploit command-line bugs in Sendmail as an unprivileged user, but modern versions strictly limit the options available to unprivileged users. Given the program's past history, however, there are sure to be more problems yet to be discovered. Also, patches for old problems have sometimes introduced new problems.

Improving SMTP security with smap and smapd

An important step a firewall can take to improve security is to prevent attackers from speaking SMTP directly to Sendmail and, instead, to use a substitute server. Fortunately, this is feasible. SMTP stands for "Simple Mail Transport Protocol," and it really is simple. There are only about a half-dozen or so commands in the protocol that an SMTP server needs to implement in order to accept incoming mail.

You should consider adopting the *smap* package that is part of the TIS FWTK as a "wrapper" for your SMTP server (whether it is Sendmail or something else). The package includes a pair of programs called *smap* and *smapd*.

smap is a very short, simple program intended solely to handle incoming SMTP connections; unlike Sendmail, which contains about 30,000 lines of code, *smap* contains only about 700 lines. The relative simplicity of *smap* means that, unlike Sendmail, it can be easily be examined and considered in its entirety for security problems. Furthermore, it's designed with least privilege and compartmentalization in mind. The *smap* program runs without root privileges. It is started by *inetd*, which takes care of binding it to port 25 before starting it, so that *smap* doesn't need to run as root to do that. It runs *chroot*'d to a particular queue directory, and thus can't access anything outside that directory. All it does is accept incoming messages from the Internet via SMTP. It speaks the very minimum necessary set of SMTP commands, and it stores each message it receives in a separate file in the queue directory.

The second program, *smapd*, comes along regularly (typically once a minute) to process the files queued in this directory, normally by handing them to Sendmail for delivery.

The result of using this substitute SMTP server is that an attacker never has a direct SMTP connection to Sendmail or any other complex SMTP server. Such a system does not protect against data-driven security holes, but such holes would be extremely hard for any firewall system to guard against. Fortunately, data-driven holes in Sendmail seem to be very rare anyway; there has only been one instance to date.[*]

You do give up certain capabilities by using the *smap* package, because *smap* quite intentionally handles only the minimum possible set of SMTP commands. In particular, you give up the ability to do Extended SMTP (ESMTP). ESMTP supports a number of enhancements to basic SMTP, such as better handling of MIME messages (discussed below) and messages containing eight-bit data. The basic SMTP service supports only seven-bit data, and requires that eight-bit data be converted using something like *uuencode* before being transmitted, which leaves the recipient with the problem of unconverting the data. This isn't a big problem right now, because only a few clients and servers currently support ESMTP and those that do have compatibility modes that let them talk regular SMTP. ESMTP is becoming more and

---

[*] This is covered in CERT Advisory 93:16. For information on obtaining CERT Advisories, see Appendix A.

more common, however, and this will become more of a problem as time goes by. Of course, it's always possible that the *smap* package will be updated to support ESMTP at some point, if it becomes a critical issue. Like many other situations involving security, by using *smap* you're trading off functionality for security.

Packet filtering characteristics of SMTP

SMTP is a TCP-based service. SMTP receivers use port 25. SMTP senders use a randomly selected port above 1023.

Direction	Source Addr.	Dest. Addr.	Protocol	Source Port	Dest. Port	ACK Set	Notes
In	Ext	Int	TCP	>1023	25	a	Incoming mail, sender to recipient
Out	Int	Ext	TCP	25	>1023	Yes	Incoming mail, recipient to sender
Out	Int	Ext	TCP	>1023	25	a	Outgoing mail, sender to recipient
In	Ext	Int	TCP	25	>1023	Yes	Outgoing mail, recipient to sender

[a] ACK is not set on the first packet of this type (establishing connection) but will be set on the rest.

Normally, you want to configure your packet filters to allow incoming and outgoing SMTP only between external hosts and the bastion host, and between the bastion host and your internal mail servers.

Do not allow external hosts to contact random internal hosts via SMTP. As we've discussed above, only specially configured hosts can safely accept SMTP connections.

If you cannot filter on the ACK bit, you cannot safely allow outgoing SMTP connections directly from random internal hosts, as we demonstrate in the final example in Chapter 6. If you can filter on the ACK bit, you allow internal hosts to send mail to external hosts, but there isn't much advantage in doing so. Although it shouldn't increase your vulnerability, it increases the likelihood that you're going to send misformatted mail, because the mail (mis)configurations of all your machines would be visible to the external world, and the chances that all your internal machines do all the right things with mail headers (particularly in adding fully qualified domain names to addresses and "Message-ID:" lines) are low. Sending outgoing mail via the bastion host allows the bastion host the opportunity to clean up the headers before the mail is loosed upon the world.

Figure 8-3 (outbound SMTP) and Figure 8-4 (inbound SMTP) show how packet filtering works with SMTP.

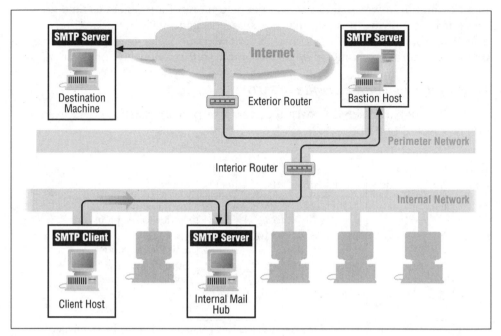

Figure 8–3: Outbound SMTP

Proxying characteristics of SMTP

Because SMTP is a store-and-forward protocol, it's inherently suited to proxying. Because any SMTP server can be a proxy, it's rare to set up separate proxying for it. Instead, most sites direct SMTP connections to a bastion host running a secure SMTP server that is the proxy.

Dedicated firewall products that provide proxying may proxy SMTP (they can't reasonably be expected to run a full SMTP server). This is straightforward to configure, because SMTP uses a single connection. In this configuration, it's not unreasonable to continue to direct the proxied SMTP connections to a single secured SMTP server on a bastion host that acts as a second proxy. Proxying protects you from unwanted connections, but not from misuses of connections; you don't want to let external hosts talk to a standard unsecured SMTP server, even through a proxy.

Configuring SMTP to work with a firewall

Because you want to send all your mail through your bastion host, you need to configure your mail system in a special way. Here are the important steps to follow:

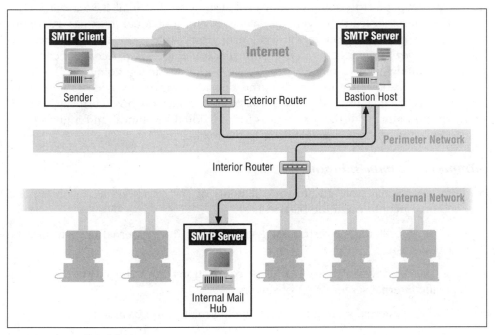

Figure 8–4: Inbound SMTP

1. Use DNS Mail Exchange (MX) records to specify that all your incoming mail should be directed to your bastion host(s).[*]

2. Configure the mailer on the bastion host to check the destination address on mail it receives. If the mail is being sent to an external host, the bastion host should process the mail as usual; if the mail is to an internal host, the bastion host should simply pass the mail to an internal mail server for processing, rather than attempt to deliver the mail itself. By passing the incoming mail to a single internal server for processing, the bastion host is relieved of having to keep track of internal aliases and internal mail configuration; this means you don't have to update the mailer configuration on the bastion host nearly as often. If the bastion host passes the incoming mail to a single internal server or small list of internal servers, the filtering system can restrict SMTP connections from the bastion host to just that host or hosts, reducing the number of internal systems that can be attacked via SMTP from the bastion host if the bastion host itself is compromised.

3. Configure your internal systems to send all outgoing mail to the bastion host.

---

* For a detailed discussion of MX records, how they work, and how to use them, see the books *TCP/IP Network Administration* by Craig Hunt (O'Reilly & Associates, 1992) and *DNS and BIND* by Paul Albitz and Cricket Liu (O'Reilly & Associates, 1992).

You may also want to configure your mail system so that mail is sent out with a central address, instead of with the name of an individual host, as its return address. For example, you might want mail from your users to appear as *person@bigcompany.com* not as *person@littlemachine.bigcompany.com*. Because all of the incoming mail (replies to the above addresses in outgoing mail) will be going to the bastion host in any case, this doesn't remove any necessary information. It helps to guarantee that mail will go to the bastion host correctly, even if there are problems with the MX records for individual machines, and it gives more consistent information to the recipients of the mail.

Summary recommendations for SMTP

- Use the normal store-and-forward features of SMTP to send all incoming and outgoing mail through the bastion host.

- Use packet filtering to restrict SMTP connections from external hosts to just the bastion host.

- Use packet filtering to restrict SMTP connections from the bastion host to a specific internal server or set of servers.

- Allow any internal system to send outgoing mail to the bastion host.

- Use *smap* instead of Sendmail as the SMTP server on your bastion host and probably on your internal mail server as well.

- Keep up to date with patches on delivery agents and user agents.

- Educate your users concerning mail-based scams, such as instructions to run particular programs or to change their passwords to some specified string.

Post Office Protocol (POP)

SMTP is used to exchange mail between servers. Normally, users access their mail as a file (directly, or using NFS or something similar) on the machine where it is delivered; however, there are sometimes reasons to use a separate protocol to distribute mail from a server to an individual user.

POP is a client-server protocol for handling user electronic mailboxes. With POP, a user's mailbox (the actual file where that user's incoming email is held for his later access) is kept on a server, rather than on the user's personal machine. The server is probably available to accept incoming mail more consistently than the user's personal machine is (particularly if the user's "personal machine" is a portable that he carries with him and that is only sometimes connected to the network). When the user wants his email, he accesses his mailbox using a client program (such as Eudora or Z-Mail) on his own machine using the POP protocol.

There are two major security issues involved in using POP across the Internet. First, be aware that standard POP clients and servers send the user's POP password over the Internet in the clear, so that anyone snooping on the connection can capture and reuse it later. In most cases, the POP password is the same as the user's login password, so that someone who snoops on it can get all of the user's privileges—not just the user's electronic mail. There are more secure variants of POP that support Kerberos (often called KPOP) and nonreusable passwords for authentication (often called APOP), but these secure variants are not widely available or widely supported. You may have trouble finding a combination of clients and servers that support these variants and that works for your site.

Second, regardless of the authentication issues, be sure to also consider the sensitivity of the email your users will be accessing over the Internet via POP. Whatever email your users access will be visible to anyone snooping on their POP sessions; you need to think about how sensitive email might be in your own environment. Many sites decide that, regardless of the authentication issues, their users' internal email is often too sensitive to risk being snooped on by someone monitoring their POP sessions. These sites decide to provide alternative access methods, such as dial-ups, that aren't as susceptible to snooping. If you provide your users with the ability to reach your network on the inside of the firewall (for example, with modems and PPP or SLIP), you can give them POP access while they're traveling without allowing it across the Internet.

Packet filtering characteristics of POP

POP is a TCP-based service. POP servers for the current version of the POP protocol (which is known as POP3 and is by far the most common version in use) use port 110. Servers for the older POP2 protocol use port 109. (POP1 was never in widespread use.) POP clients use ports above 1023.

Direction	Source Addr.	Dest. Addr.	Protocol	Source Port	Dest. Port	ACK Set	Notes
In	Ext	Int	TCP	>1023	110 109[a]	[b]	Incoming POP connection, client to server
Out	Int	Ext	TCP	110 109[a]	>1023	Yes	Incoming POP connection, server to client
Out	Int	Ext	TCP	>1023	110 109[a]	[b]	Outgoing POP connection, client to server
In	Ext	Int	TCP	110 109[a]	>1023	Yes	Outgoing POP connection, server to client

[a] Modern POP (POP3) servers use port 110; older POP2 servers use port 109.
[b] ACK is not set on the first packet of this type (establishing connection) but will be set on the rest.

An outgoing POP connection would allow your users to download their mail from other sites. This is no more dangerous than allowing outgoing Telnet, and you will probably want to allow such a POP connection if there is any demand. On the other hand, POP over the Internet is rare enough that there is unlikely to be anyone interested in outgoing POP at your site, and there is no point in its use.

Incoming POP connections are those that allow people at other sites to read mail delivered for them at your site. As discussed in the previous section, you probably don't want to allow incoming POP. If you do, you should certainly limit POP connections to a POP server running on a single host. That will limit the number of vulnerable accounts and the amount of information that's being passed across the Internet. Although there are no known vulnerabilities in POP servers, if any are found, you should patch them on just one host, without worrying about all your internal hosts. Because POP requires user accounts, you don't want to run it on your normal bastion host. Although you can prevent users from logging in on POP accounts, they represent a maintenance hassle.

Figure 8-5 shows how POP works with a firewall.

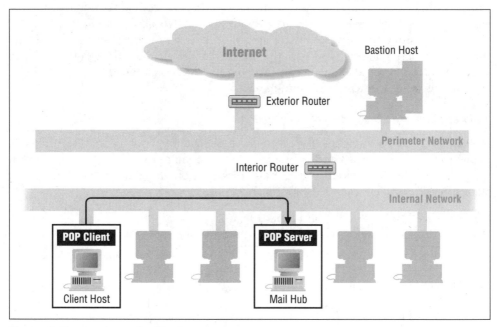

Figure 8-5: POP via packet filtering

Proxying characteristics of POP

POP is straightforward to proxy, because it uses a single connection. Precompiled proxy-enabled POP clients (those that work with SOCKS, for example) are not widely available. This is mostly because, although POP is used extensively within LANs, POP across the Internet is rare. UNIX POP clients are available in source form and trivial to adapt for modified-client proxying systems. It is generally more difficult to locate the source for personal-computer implementations but no more difficult to modify them.

There is no simple way to do modified-procedure proxying for connections between internal clients and external servers, or external clients and internal servers, unless all your clients are connecting to the same server. If that's the case, then you could run a generic TCP proxy program (such as the *plug-gw* program from the TIS FWTK) on the POP3 port on your bastion host, configured to relay all connections to the single POP server; you would then configure your clients to access the "POP server" (really the proxy program) on the bastion host.

If you do need to provide access to multiple POP servers and can ensure that all client connections from a given IP address or domain should be directed to a particular server, you could set up a more complex configuration with the *plug-gw* program to direct connections to the appropriate server based on where the connection request is coming from. If multiple users on the same client machine or machines need to access different POP servers across the firewall, however, there's no simple way to do it with the code that's currently available. It is possible to write a custom POP proxy server to run on the bastion host that authenticated the user, decided which server that user needed to talk to, opened a connection and authenticated the user to that server, and then sat back and played the traditional proxy server "pass-through" role; it would be difficult to make this work with non-reusable passwords, though.

Summary recommendations for POP

- Do not allow your users to transfer your site's mail over the Internet via POP, unless you can do so without revealing reusable passwords, and unless either you aren't concerned about the sensitivity of the mail itself or you have an encrypted channel to transfer it over.

- If you have users who wish to transfer mail from other sites via POP, allow it via packet filtering, perhaps restricted to connections from specific sites or to specific hosts on your end.

- Proxying would be an effective solution for some POP problems, but you might need to do at least minor code modifications.

Multimedia Internet Mail Extensions (MIME)

MIME is a set of extensions to the basic Internet electdronic mail message format supporting things like:

- Non-ASCII character sets

- Nontext data such as pictures and audio segments

- So-called "rich text" messages (messages containing formatted text, with different fonts and so on, rather than simple single-font unformatted text)

- Multipart messages (messages containing multiple pieces, each piece in its own format).

MIME support is mostly a client issue; to mail servers and transport systems, MIME messages are generally just another message. The question is whether or not a given client can generate outgoing MIME messages, and whether or not it can recognize and cope with incoming MIME messages.

The MIME standards define certain basic data types, such as plain text, formatted text, standard audio, and so on. MIME is designed to be extensible, so that new data types can be added as necessary. MIME-capable mail clients generally understand certain data types (often only multipart messages and plain text), and rely on other programs to handle other data types (for example, graphics programs to display images, and sound programs to play audio clips). The clients generally have a list of external programs to run for particular types of data; this list can be extended or modified by the user.

Ironically, the biggest use of MIME hasn't been in mail systems, but in World Wide Web browsers. Most mail systems have little or no MIME support, but MIME is a key service upon which the World Wide Web is built. Every WWW server uses MIME to describe the format of every WWW page it hands to a client; every WWW client uses MIME to determine how to display or otherwise process the data it receives.

Because MIME is used more extensively for WWW support than for electronic mail, we discuss it below in the section on WWW, even though it is theoretically email-related. If you do have email clients that support MIME, they will be subject to the same vulnerabilities discussed in "What can a malicious server do to your clients?" in the section on the World Wide Web later in this chapter.

One difference between MIME support in email clients and WWW clients is how data is obtained. With a WWW client, the user chooses what data to access; with email, the user accesses whatever anybody sends them. In theory, email clients are more vulnerable, because you can't control what other people send you by email. In practice, however, the difference isn't that important, because it's fairly easy to lure a WWW user into accessing whatever you want them to access. Either way, you need to carefully control what data types your clients understand and how they process that data. See the full discussion of this issue in the WWW section.

File Transfer

FTP is the de facto standard for file transfer on the Internet. In addition, there are some specialized protocols used for applications where FTP is not suitable. TFTP is used by dedicated devices to transfer configuration files. FSP is a UDP-based proto-col used when TCP-based connections won't work or aren't allowed. UUCP is used for batch transfers, particularly across phone lines.

File Transfer Protocol (FTP)

FTP is used to transfer files from one machine to another. You can use FTP to transfer any type of file, including executable binaries, graphics images, ASCII text, PostScript, sound and video files, and more. There are two types of FTP access: user FTP and anonymous FTP. User FTP requires an account on the server and lets users access any files they could access if they were logged in. Anonymous FTP is for people who don't have an account and is used to provide access to specific files to the world at large.

Anonymous FTP is by far the most common use of FTP on the Internet. Anony-mous FTP servers are the standard mechanism for distributing programs, informa-tion, and other files that sites wish to make available to the Internet at large. If a site provides an anonymous FTP server, anyone on the Internet can initiate an FTP connection to the site, tell the FTP server that their login name is "anonymous", and access whatever files the server's owners have chosen to make available in a restricted area.

Packet filtering characteristics of FTP

FTP uses two separate TCP connections: one to carry commands and results between the client and the server (commonly called the *command channel*), and the other to carry any actual files and directory listings transferred (the *data channel*). On the server end, the command channel uses well-known port 21, and the data channel normally uses well-known port 20. The client uses ports above 1023 for both the command and data channels.

To start an FTP session, a client first allocates two TCP ports for itself, each of them with a port number above 1024. It uses the first to open the command channel connection to the server and then issues FTP's PORT command to tell the server the number of the second port, which the client wants to use for the data channel. The server then opens the data channel connection. This data channel connection is backwards from most protocols, which open connections from the client to the server. This backwards open complicates things for sites that are attempting to do "start-of-connection" packet filtering to ensure that all TCP connections are initiated from the inside, because external FTP servers will attempt to initiate data connec-tions to internal clients, in response to command connections opened from those internal clients. Furthermore, these connections will be going to ports known to be in an unsafe range. Figure 8-6 shows this kind of FTP connection.

Most FTP servers (particularly those used at major anonymous FTP sites on the Internet) and many FTP clients support an alternative mode that allows the client to open both the command and the data channels to the server. This mode is

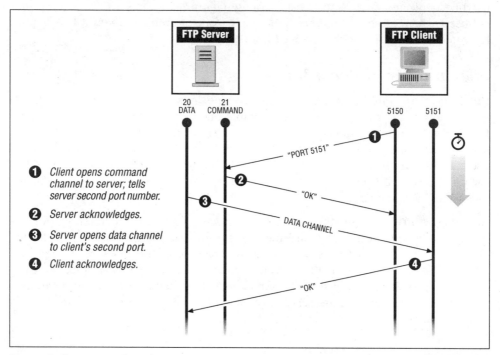

Figure 8–6: A normal-mode FTP connection

called "passive mode" or "PASV mode" (after the FTP command the client sends to the server to initiate this mode). If both your FTP client and the FTP server you're trying to connect to support passive mode, you can use it instead of the regular mode. This way, you can avoid start-of-connection filtering problems, because all connections will be opened from the inside, by the client.

To use passive mode, an FTP client allocates two TCP ports for its own use, and uses the first port to contact the FTP server, just as when using normal mode. However, instead of issuing the PORT command to tell the server the client's second port, the client issues the PASV command. This causes the server to allocate a second port of its own for the data channel (for architectural reasons, servers use random ports above 1023 for this, not port 20 as in normal mode; you couldn't have two servers on the same machine simultaneously listening for incoming PASV-mode data connections on port 20), and tell the client the number of that port. The client then opens the data connection from its port to the data port the server has just told it about. Figure 8-7 shows a passive-mode FTP connection.

Not all FTP clients support passive mode. If a given client does support passive mode, it will usually mention this as a feature in the documentation or description. Some clients support both normal and passive modes and provide the user some way to specify which mode to use. If you're having trouble finding passive-mode clients, it's useful to know that the built-in FTP clients in many WWW browsers

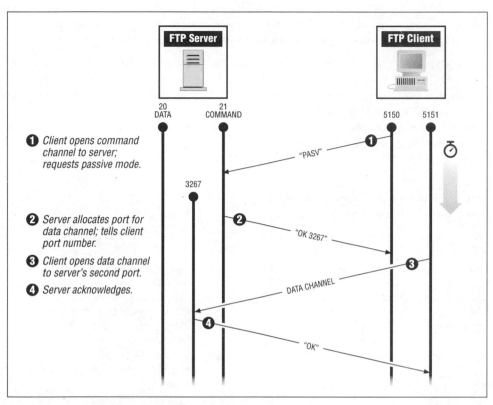

Figure 8–7: A passive-mode FTP connection

(Netscape Navigator, for example) use passive mode. Chances are, your users will want to have these browsers anyway for WWW access, and you can show them how to use the browsers as FTP clients as well.

Because passive mode has only recently become popular, many times even servers that support passive mode have problems with it. You may find that combinations of servers and clients that work well with normal-mode transfers hang periodically when you do passive-mode transfers.

If your FTP client (or one of the FTP servers you wish to communicate with) does not support passive mode, and you still want to allow FTP via packet filtering (rather than via proxy), you'll have to put a special-case exception in your packet filtering rules to allow the server to open the data channel back in to the client. If you do so, you will still be vulnerable to attackers launching a connection from port 20 on the attacker's end (nominally the FTP data channel, but you have no way to guarantee that on a machine you don't control) to a port above 1023 on your end (such as an X server, for example). Therefore, you should restrict this special-case exception as much as possible, e.g., by tying it to the address of the particular client or server that doesn't support passive mode. (Even an exception for a single server makes you vulnerable to forged connections from that server).

Some dynamic packet filtering implementations (such as FireWall-1 from Check-Point Software) monitor the commands sent over the FTP command channel and notice the PORT command the client sends to the server; This command tells the server on which port the client is listening for the server to open the data channel. These implementations also put in place a temporary (time-limited) exception in the packet filtering rules to allow the server to open the data channel back to the client.

Direction	Source Addr.	Dest. Addr.	Protocol	Source Port	Dest. Port	ACK Set	Notes
In	Ext	Int	TCP	>1023	21	a	Incoming FTP request
Out	Int	Ext	TCP	21	>1023	Yes	Response to incoming request
Out	Int	Ext	TCP	20	>1023	a	Data channel creation for incoming FTP request, normal mode
In	Ext	Int	TCP	>1023	20	Yes	Data channel responses for incoming FTP request, normal mode
In	Ext	Int	TCP	>1023	>1023	a	Data channel creation for incoming FTP request, passive mode
Out	Int	Ext	TCP	>1023	>1023	Yes	Data channel responses for incoming FTP request, passive mode
Out	Int	Ext	TCP	>1023	21	a	Outgoing FTP request
In	Ext	Int	TCP	21	>1023	Yes	Response to outgoing request
In	Ext	int	TCP	20	>1023	a	Data channel creation for outgoing FTP request, normal mode
Out	Int	Ext	TCP	>1023	20	Yes	Data channel responses for outgoing FTP request, normal mode
Out	Int	Int	TCP	>1023	>1023	a	Data channel creation for outgoing FTP request, passive mode
In	Ext	Int	TCP	>1023	>1023	Yes	Data channel responses for outgoing FTP request, passive mode

[a] ACK is not set on the first packet of this type (establishing connection) but will be set on the rest.

Proxying characteristics of FTP

Because of the problems with passive mode, and because of complications introduced in name service (the "double-reverse lookups" discussed in the "Domain Name Service (DNS)" section below), proxying is a particularly attractive solution for outbound FTP. Using a normal-mode proxied client allows you to talk reliably to external servers without having to allow incoming TCP connections for the data channel to any host except the bastion host doing the proxying. For this reason, you may choose to proxy FTP even if you allow most other protocols directly through the firewall via packet filtering. Both modified-client and modified-procedure proxies are available for FTP.

The SOCKS package includes an FTP client for UNIX that has been modified to use SOCKS. Because of the multiple simultaneous TCP connections involved in FTP, modifying other FTP clients yourself requires some work (more than modifying clients for straightforward single-connection protocols like SMTP and POP).

The TIS FWTK provides a proxy FTP server that operates with modified clients or modified user procedures. It provides additional logging, operation denial, and user authentication features, giving you finer control than you can achieve with packet filters or SOCKS proxying.

If you want to use modified clients with the TIS FWTK FTP proxy server, you will need to do all of the modification yourself; they do not provide a modified client or even a client library. Using modified clients with the TIS FWTK FTP proxy server will also prevent you from running a standard FTP server on the machine you're using as the proxy server. Some versions of the FWTK have had an FTP server that could act as a proxy server and a regular FTP server, but there have been some problems with it, and it's not clear that it will continue to be included with newer releases of the toolkit.

Some FTP clients are not sufficiently flexible to be used with modified user procedures involving the TIS FWTK FTP proxy server. The custom procedure users have to follow involve opening an FTP connection to the machine where the proxy server is running, and then logging into the FTP proxy server as *anonymous@host.some.net*, specifying the name of the host they really want to connect to as part of the login. Some FTP clients have "anonymous" simply hardcoded in, or limit the length of the login field to something too short to contain "anonymous@" plus a reasonably long hostname.

Any commercial proxying packages will almost certainly support outbound FTP proxying, because FTP is such a commonly used protocol on the Internet.

Many sites use both proxy and packet filtering solutions for FTP. You can sometimes reduce the number of modified clients you need by using proxying to support normal-mode connections, and packet filtering to support passive-mode connections. You can also use a combined solution for added security by using a proxy FTP server that uses passive mode to make external connections, regardless of the mode it uses to talk to the internal hosts; this converts all connections that cross the firewall to passive mode and allows you to tighten the packet filters that protect the host doing the proxying. On the other hand, it keeps you from using servers that don't support passive mode.

Providing anonymous FTP service

With anonymous FTP, a user logs in to the FTP server as "anonymous". The user is then asked for a password and is expected to enter his or her full email address in response. At most sites, this request is not enforced, however, and users can enter whatever they want, as long as it looks like an email address; even if the information is entered, it's usually just logged, not verified in any way beyond a superficial plausibility check (i.e., does it contain an at (@) sign?). Many standard FTP servers, like the ones shipped with most versions of UNIX, don't even log the information.

If you are providing anonymous FTP service, the challenge is to ensure that the anonymous FTP server makes available only the information that you want made available and that it doesn't give an outsider access to other, supposedly private, information on the machine.

In setting up anonymous FTP, one precaution you can take is to limit what other information is available on the machine that's providing anonymous FTP service. In this way, even if attackers get "outside" the anonymous FTP area on the machine, there is nothing of interest to them elsewhere on the machine (or reachable from the machine via NFS or some other mechanism).

Many FTP servers perform a *chroot* to the anonymous FTP area before the FTP server starts processing commands from an anonymous user. To support both anonymous and user FTP, however, FTP servers need access to all files. This means that *chroot*, which is normally regarded as extremely safe, doesn't guarantee as much for an FTP server, because the server is not always running in the *chroot*'d environment.

To deal with this problem, you can modify *inetd*'s configuration so that instead of starting the FTP server directly, it *chroots* (using something like the *chrootuid* program described in Appendix B) and then starts the FTP server. Normally, FTP runs with limited access only for anonymous users, and nonanonymous users have their normal access permissions. Doing the *chroot* before starting up the FTP server means that the nonanonymous users will also be limited; if you don't have any nonanonymous users of your FTP server (and you probably shouldn't), this is irrelevant.

The details of setting up an anonymous FTP system vary depending on the operating system and the particular FTP daemon code in use. Start with the instructions (if any) in the manual pages for your FTP daemon; this should get you through most of the vendor-specific steps. Then, once you've performed all the steps there, obtain and follow CERT Advisory 93:10 (for information on obtaining CERT advisories, see Appendix A), which addresses setting up anonymous FTP servers to close the holes left by most of the vendor instructions.[*]

Unfortunately, one of the most common ways that anonymous users get access to files they shouldn't be able to see is that an internal user innocently puts the files up for anonymous FTP, on the assumption that this is somehow safe. Usually, the internal user is relying on security through obscurity; he assumes that nobody will notice the files. This does not work well. People do notice, especially if the names of the new files are meaningful. At popular FTP sites, curious people poke around

---

[*] Many vendors ship instructions containing critical problems, ranging from security holes to missing steps that disable parts of FTP's functionality.)

randomly, and they notice new files almost immediately and may transfer them out of pure curiosity. On less-visited FTP sites, files may remain unnoticed until an Archie server indexes them. Unless you have explicitly arranged to have your FTP site skipped, you should assume that it is being indexed; Archie is quite talented at finding sites.

It's best to avoid putting files up for anonymous FTP if you don't want the entire world to read them. Use other methods of file transfer if possible. If not, you may want to use a modified FTP server, like the *wuarchive* server, which allows semi-anonymous access that requires an anonymous user to provide an additional password to get access to certain directories. You can also put up files in directories that have execute permission but not read permission. Doing so will let people who know the names transfer the files, but won't let people look to see what files exist.

Whatever method you choose, be sure that everybody at your site who can put files in the anonymous FTP directories knows not to put confidential files where they're world-readable. An easy way to do this is to prevent your internal users from writing to the anonymous FTP directories and to require them to ask a system administrator to make a file available.

Using the wuarchive FTP daemon

Many Internet sites—both major and minor—that provide anonymous FTP run the *wuarchive* version of the UNIX FTP server, developed at Washington University (the "wu" in the name) in St. Louis. This server provides a number of features that are especially useful for anonymous FTP servers. These include the following features and many others:

- Better and more complete logging. It can log uploads, downloads, or every command sent to it; it can also keep track of the number of accesses by user classes (e.g., by anonymous users).

- Per-directory message files; these are shown to a user when he visits that directory to provide relevant information about the directory's contents (for example,"This version is now obsolete").

- The ability to define classes of users; based on the account they log in to the server with, and/or the host from which they access, you can determine what files they have access to and when they can log in.

- Restrictions on certain classes of users. For example, *wuarchive* can limit the number of simultaneous anonymous users who are accessing the server; the limit can vary by time of day and day of the week. By using these restrictions, you control the load generated by the FTP server.

- The ability to compress, tar, and otherwise manipulate files automatically as they are transferred.

- Nonanonymous *chroot*ed access, for users who need only limited access to your machines. This allows you to give a specific account access to files that are not accessible to "anonymous" without giving them the ability to look around at everything on your disks.

For information about obtaining the *wuarchive* FTP daemon, see Appendix B. Be sure that you are installing the genuine, most recent version. This program has in the past been distributed by attackers with added trap doors, and older versions may have security problems that have since been fixed.

Be aware that one cost of the additional power and complexity offered by *wuarchive* is a bigger potential for security problems. The bigger and more complex a program is, the more likely it is to contain bugs. If the program is security-critical (as the FTP server is), many of those bugs are likely to have security impacts. Some features of the *wuarchive* server may also interact badly with some clients (in particular, some clients do not deal well with the displayed messages and hang). There are workarounds available, but if a significant percentage of your users have these clients, you may want to avoid *wuarchive*.

Using the TIS FWTK FTP daemon

Instead of using the *wuarchive* version of the FTP server, you might consider using the FTP server from the TIS Internet Firewall Toolkit. The TIS FWTK FTP daemon has an emphasis different from that of the *wuarchive* daemon. The *wuarchive* version adds code in order to add features that support anonymous FTP. The TIS FWTK version, by contrast, concentrates on simplifying the server and making it more secure, stripping it down to the bare minimum capabilities necessary to provide anonymous FTP service. However, the maintainers of the FWTK have been considering removing it from the FWTK release, because despite all the work they've done on it, they're still not convinced that it's as secure as they'd like it to be (though it is almost certainly more secure than any alternative). It's possible that it will have been removed from the release by the time you read this.

You'll have to decide for yourself whether you really need the enhanced features provided by the *wuarchive* server (and are willing to accept the potential security implications of those features), or whether you'd rather have the enhanced security provided by the TIS FWTK server (assuming it's still available), at a cost of fewer features. Many users are accustomed to using *wuarchive* FTP and have come to depend on its features; it is probably not reasonable to attempt to run a major anonymous FTP site with the TIS FWTK server. For a site that provides only occasional anonymous FTP, however, the FWTK server is probably a more secure and reliable option.

Be careful of writable directories in the anonymous FTP area

Regardless of which FTP daemon you use, you'll have to confront a particularly troublesome issue raised by anonymous FTP servers: writable directories in the anonymous FTP area. Sites frequently provide writable space in this area, so that outsiders can upload files to them as well as download files from them; for example, a software company's customers might be asked to upload crash dump files (which are too big to conveniently send through email) so the company can do a crash analysis on them.

Writable areas can be very useful, but they have a dark side. Such writable directories *will* (notice that we didn't say *may*) be found and used by "the underground" on the Internet as storage space and distribution areas for illicit material; generally this means pirated software packages and pornographic image files.

The folks who do this are amazingly well organized and hard to track down. They have their own communication mechanisms for telling each other about new sites—places they've found to store their stuff—without revealing who they are. When they find a new site, they typically create a hidden subdirectory in which to store their files and images. They give the subdirectory an innocuous name such as ".. " (that's "dot dot space space"). When casually looking around an anonymous FTP area, you probably won't notice a name like this. It's particularly easy to miss because file and directory names beginning with "." are ignored by the UNIX *ls* command, unless you give the command a special argument or run it as root.

On some sites in which intruders play this game, you can see a barter economy in operation. Someone leaves a note saying they're seeking a certain package or file, and listing what they have to offer in exchange. A short time later, someone else comes along, uploads the requested files, and leaves another note telling the original poster what they want in return.

What's wrong with this misuse of your anonymous FTP areas? There are several problems:

- It consumes your resources, such as disk space and network bandwidth (particularly on your Internet connection), and it interferes with the legitimate use of those resources: it's a denial of service attack.

- It potentially exposes your site to legal action for assisting (even unwittingly) in software piracy, or perhaps sexual harassment, or even sexual exploitation of minors. Even if such actions are unlikely to succeed, your attorneys will probably tell you that they'd rather avoid the issue and not have to fight the battle in the first place.

- Even if no legal actions are undertaken, such an incident could generate significant negative publicity and embarrassment for your site or organization. Once your name has been linked to software piracy or child pornography in any way, you are in bad trouble regardless of how innocent your involvement was.

How can you protect your anonymous FTP areas from such misuse? The first question to ask yourself is this: do you really need to provide writable space in your anonymous FTP area? Often there other acceptable ways (electronic mail, for example) for folks to send files to you. If you decide that you must provide writable space in your anonymous FTP area, there are a number of ways to limit your vulnerability, as we describe below.

Making your incoming directory write-only   The most obvious approach, if you're using a UNIX machine as your bastion host, is to make your "incoming" directory write-only (directory permissions 773 or 733—that is, "rwxrwx-wx" or "rwx-wx-wx"). Make sure that the directory is owned by some user other than "ftp" (or whatever your anonymous FTP server runs as when doing anonymous FTP). If the mode is 773 instead of 733, then also make sure that the group of the directory is something other than the default group of the "ftp" login.

The problem with this approach is that all you're doing is keeping people from being able to see what's in the top-level directory. They can still see what's in subdirectories, and they can still access files and directories they create in the top-level directory if they communicate exact filenames among themselves. (Unfortunately, they can, via their mailing lists and other communications channels.) So, this really isn't a very effective approach.

Disabling the creation of directories and certain files   Another approach you can take is to disable the creation of directories and files with funny names (for example, files that begin with ".") in your anonymous FTP server. Depending on your server, you may be able to do this with a configuration file (for example, the *wuarchive* server lets you restrict anonymous users from deleting, overwriting, or creating certain types of files), or you may have to modify the server source code. (This is a nontrivial modification, which requires a reasonably competent C programmer.)

This approach doesn't keep people from uploading stuff to the writable directory you provide; it simply makes it more difficult for them to hide that stuff so that it escapes your notice. If you do this, you will still need to look at the writable area every day (and look at the content of files, not just the names) to be sure everything is something that belongs there.

Uploading by prearrangement   Another approach is used frequently by sites that want people to be able to upload files, but only by prearrangement. These sites basically take a page from the underground's own book by creating hidden writable subdirectories that you can only access if you know they're there. The attackers can't see them; they're unaware that there's a "there" there for their wares.

Here's what you do, assuming you're using a UNIX system for your FTP server:

1. Make an "incoming" directory.

2. Make a subdirectory there with a "secret" name, chosen in much the same way you'd choose a password—that is, something unguessable.

3. Make the subdirectory with the secret name be writable.

4. Make the parent directory (the incoming directory) mode execute-only (mode 111—that is, --x--x--x).

For example:

```
unix# cd ~ftp/pub
unix# mkdir incoming
unix# cd incoming
unix# mkdir b2b_Free
unix# chmod a+w b2b_Free # or "chmod 0777 b2b_Free"
unix# cd ..
unix# chmod a=x incoming # or "chmod 0111 incoming"
```

Users can now upload files to the writable directory only if they know (presumably because you've told them) its secret, password-like name. You can create as many of these secret subdirectories as necessary, and you can change or delete them as often as necessary, to meet your needs.

Beware that some FTP clients with graphical user interfaces will only let a user access a directory that the FTP client can see; they don't provide a way for the user to jump blindly to a directory that doesn't appear in a directory listing. Such clients won't work with this scheme because, by design, the client can't see the names of the subdirectories containing the actual data. This is not usually a problem for people coming in from UNIX machines, and there are publicly available clients for most platforms that do not have this problem, so you may be able to work around this limitation.

Removing the files There is one other approach you might take, particularly if you find that your anonymous FTP area is already being abused and you're curious to see what people are uploading there. Basically, you run a short shell script once a minute as a *cron* job that moves files from the writable incoming directory to another directory outside the anonymous FTP area. This will ensure that the intruders won't be able to see what's been uploaded. You may need to rename files when you move them to avoid overwriting files with the same name. Because the files aren't there to look at, it's easy for people to unintentionally create name conflicts (particularly if they're sending you crash dumps, which probably all start out having the same name).

Make sure that the new directory is on the same filesystem, so the operating system doesn't have to copy the data. Because of the way that the UNIX filesystem works, this approach works even if the file is still being written when the "move" takes place, as long as the directory you're moving it to is on the same filesystem as the original directory ("moving" a file in such a case doesn't actually move the data; it merely renames the file).

This doesn't avoid denial of service attacks; people can still fill up your disk space. In fact, they may retry downloads multiple times (because the files keep mysteriously disappearing) and unintentionally fill up your disks.

Summary of recommendations for FTP

- If you have FTP clients that properly support passive mode, then allow internal hosts to contact external FTP servers via packet filtering. This is only safe if you can filter on the TCP ACK bit, so that you can allow only outgoing TCP connections from ports above 1023 to ports above 1023.

- If you have FTP clients that don't support passive mode, then use an FTP proxy server such as the one in the TIS Internet Firewall Toolkit.

- Consider providing FTP access via both packet filtering and proxies, supporting passive mode via packet filtering and normal mode via proxies.

- If you want to allow incoming FTP, use packet filters to allow incoming FTP only to your bastion host.

- If you allow incoming FTP (anonymous or user), use an up-to-date FTP server.

- If you allow anonymous FTP users to write files, protect the writable area so it can't be used to transfer files between third parties.

- Be careful about who within your organization can put up files for anonymous FTP, and make sure they understand what they're doing.

- If you want to allow nonanonymous FTP, see Chapter 10 for a discussion of the password and authentication issues involved.

Trivial File Transfer Protocol (TFTP)

TFTP is a simplified file transfer protocol; it is simpler than FTP, and is designed to be implemented in ROM for booting diskless systems like X terminals, diskless workstations, and routers. There is no authentication with TFTP; a TFTP client simply connects to the server and asks for a file, without saying who the file is for. If the file is one that the server can access, the server gives the client the file. For this reason, you need to be very careful about what your TFTP server (if you have one) can access, and what clients can access the server.

Generally, there's no reason at all to allow TFTP across your firewall, even if you use it internally. You do not want to boot diskless systems across the Internet, and people do not transfer files with TFTP.

Packet filtering characteristics of TFTP

TFTP is a UDP-based protocol. Servers use port 69. Clients use ports above 1023.

Direc-tion	Source Addr.	Dest. Addr.	Pro-tocol	Source Port	Dest. Port	ACK Set	Notes
In	Ext	Int	UDP	>1023	69	a	Incoming TFTP request
Out	Int	Ext	UDP	69	>1023	a	Response to incoming request
Out	Int	Ext	UDP	>1023	69	a	Outgoing TFTP request
In	Ext	Int	UDP	69	>1023	a	Response to outgoing request

[a] UDP packets do not have ACK bits.

Proxying characteristics of TFTP

TFTP does not lend itself well to proxying. Because TFTP clients are often implemented in hardware, with no users involved, neither modified clients nor modified user procedures are generally implementable. A transparent proxy could easily support TFTP, providing the same extremely minimal amount of security achievable if you allow TFTP through packet filters.

Summary of TFTP recommendations

- Do not allow TFTP across your firewall.

File Service Protocol (FSP)

FSP is a file transfer protocol that was designed to circumvent FTP restrictions. Very few sites provide supported FSP service; most FSP servers are set up by users or attackers, without the knowledge or consent of a machine's managers. In fact, FSP activity is often a clue that attackers have compromised a site; attackers often use FSP to move their files from site to site. FSP activity can be difficult to detect, however, because, as we discuss below, there are no standard port numbers that FSP clients and servers use.

Packet filtering characteristics of FSP

FSP is intentionally difficult to suppress with packet filtering. Filtering out all UDP services except those you need, and restricting those to specific hosts, will pretty well get rid of it except on the hosts you're allowing other UDP services to. If you want to allow FSP, that's extremely simple; allowing UDP packets to and from a host, at any port number, will allow it to be an FSP server and/or client.

FSP is a UDP-based protocol. There is no "standard" port number that the server runs on; anyone running a server chooses the port that server will use. If they have root access, they often choose port 21, the UDP equivalent of the TCP port used by FTP; if they don't have root access, they have to use a port above 1023, and there's no predicting what it will be. Clients generally use ports above 1023.

Direc-tion	Source Addr.	Dest. Addr.	Pro-tocol	Source Port	Dest. Port	ACK Set	Notes
In	Ext	Int	UDP	>1023[a]	[a]	[b]	Incoming FSP request
Out	Int	Ext	UDP	[a]	>1023[a]	[b]	Response to incoming request
Out	Int	Ext	UDP	>1023[a]	[a]	[b]	Outgoing FSP request
In	Ext	Int	UDP	[a]	>1023[a]	[b]	Response to outgoing request

[a] FSP does not have standard port numbers, although people running FSP servers often put them on port 21 if they have root access (paralleling FTP servers, which use TCP port 21). Clients usually use ports above 1023, but not always.
[b] UDP packets do not have ACK bits.

Proxying characteristics of FSP

Using generic proxies to proxy a UDP-based application with no standard port number is as difficult as trying to suppress it with packet filters. No standard proxy package supports FSP. A dedicated FSP proxy would be possible to write.

Summary of FSP recommendations

* Do not allow FSP across your firewall. Block all UDP except for specific services you wish to intentionally allow, such as DNS.

UNIX-to-UNIX Copy Protocol (UUCP)

UUCP was designed for transferring files, including electronic mail and news, between UNIX machines; it is the original UNIX networking system. UUCP is primarily used as a dial-up protocol (as the sole protocol over a modem connection), but some sites, particularly those with intermittent dial-up Internet service, use UUCP over TCP to transfer mail and news from their service provider. UUCP allows the service provider to collect and hold all of the site's mail and news; when the site brings up its Internet connection and contacts the service provider using UUCP, the service provider transfers all of the accumulated mail and news at once.

UUCP over TCP is also used by some sites that have much faster permanent Internet connections (56 Kb/s lines, for example) to transfer Usenet news, because UUCP over TCP is more bandwidth-efficient than NNTP for this purpose. (It has recently become difficult or impossible to keep up with the news in every group over a 56 Kb/s line using NNTP, for example; there just isn't enough bandwidth. As the volume of Usenet news continues to grow, this problem is only going to get worse.)

One of the nice features of UUCP is that, once a connection between two sites is established, that connection is used to transfer all the pending data between the two sites, regardless of which site initiated the connection. This means that you could allow only outgoing UUCP connections, and poll your service provider on a regular basis (hourly, for example) to both send your outgoing messages and collect your incoming messages.

Most sites do not use UUCP in any form any more. If you don't have any special needs, you can simply not allow it across your firewall.

Because UUCP uses reusable passwords, someone who snoops on one of your UUCP sessions will later be able to connect to your service provider and impersonate you, or connect to you and impersonate your service provider. The passwords are also generally stored unencrypted in the configuration files on the calling machine, so it may be possible to do this without even snooping on a connection first. You may be able to defend against this with various mechanisms that depend on what version of UUCP you and your service provider are using.[*]

Packet filtering characteristics of UUCP

UUCP over TCP is obviously a TCP-based service. Servers use port 540. Clients use ports above 1023.

Direction	Source Addr.	Dest. Addr.	Protocol	Source Port	Dest. Port	ACK Set	Notes
In	Ext	Int	TCP	>1023	540	[a]	Incoming UUCP connection, client to server
Out	Int	Ext	TCP	540	>1023	Yes	Incoming UUCP connection, server to client
Out	Int	Ext	TCP	>1023	540	[a]	Outgoing UUCP connection, client to server
In	Ext	Int	TCP	540	>1023	Yes	Outgoing UUCP connection, server to client

[a] ACK is not set on the first packet of this type (establishing connection) but will be set on the rest.

Proxying characteristics of UUCP

UUCP is a store-and-forward protocol, and as such is not used with general-purpose proxies; instead, it's configured to effectively do its own proxying. It is a straightforward single-connection protocol used with a small number of clients, and thus is well-suited to both modified-client and modified-procedure proxying. On the other hand, it is rare for people to want to proxy it, so there are no widely available proxies specifically written for it. Generic proxy servers, such as the *plug-gw* program in the TIS FWTK, should work if you can decide which real server to connect to based on which client the connection request is coming from (in other words, if all connections are to the same server, or if a given client host always connects to the same server).

---

[*] For a more detailed discussion, see the book *Managing UUCP and Usenet* by Tim O'Reilly and Grace Todino (O'Reilly & Associates, 1992).

Summary of UUCP recommendations

- You probably do not need to allow UUCP over TCP at your site. If you do wish to use it, use packet filters to limit access to a bastion host.

Terminal Access (Telnet)

Telnet allows a user to remotely access a command shell on another computer. Telnet is supported by most platforms on the Internet, even some MS-DOS and Microsoft Windows systems (which provide access to a DOS shell via a Telnet server). The major exception is the Macintosh operating system, which doesn't have a command-line-oriented shell to give users access to, regardless of whether they're local or not; if MacOS did have a shell, however, somebody would probably create a Telnet server to give remote access to it. (And, having written this, we're sure someone will tell us that there *is* a Telnet server for MacOS which we simply didn't know about.)

Although remote terminal access is the most common use of Telnet, most Telnet clients support the specification of arbitrary port numbers to access text-based TCP services at other ports. This is useful if you have a service for which you don't want to distribute a dedicated client, for example, it's often used to give access to MUDs (Multi-User Domains) and MOOs (Multi-user domains, Object Oriented), which are multiuser environments for games, collaborative work environments, or chat areas. Telnet clients are also used fairly often for debugging protocols that are normally accessed by dedicated clients. For example, people will check SMTP servers or verify user names by using *telnet hostname 25* to connect to the SMTP server directly on port 25 and type SMTP commands at it. It's important to understand that, although you may be using the program named *telnet* for these purposes, all it's doing is opening a simple TCP connection to the specified port number. The *telnet* program doesn't use the Telnet protocol (which provides for things like option negotiation between client and server, line-at-a-time and character-at-a-time modes, and so on) unless it is talking to a server on the standard Telnet port (port 23). This section discusses only the use of Telnet clients to access Telnet servers.

Incoming and outgoing Telnet have very different security implications. Most sites want to allow their users access to outgoing Telnet service, so their users can get to command shells and information services provided via Telnet on remote systems on the Internet. (Figure 8-8 illustrates outbound Telnet.) On the other hand, most sites don't want to allow (or want to allow but very strictly control) incoming Telnet access to their site. Chapter 10 describes reasons for, and ways of, controlling incoming access, so we won't discuss these in any detail here.

Regardless of whether the access is incoming or outgoing, Telnet is a cleartext protocol (just like most others). Whatever information your users access or provide over a Telnet session (for example, accessing sensitive data, or providing their passwords for other systems) is going to be visible to someone snooping on the

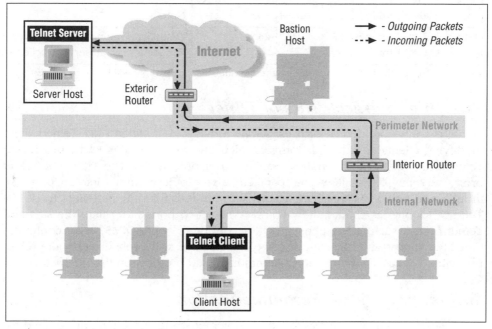

Figure 8–8: Outbound Telnet

Telnet connection. Encrypting versions of Telnet are starting to become available, but none are widely used yet. As these tools become more capable and more widely supported, they should become more useful. The best place to see what's currently available would be one of the general Internet security Web pages (such as the COAST Web page) discussed in Appendix A.

Users should be warned to use different passwords on external hosts from those they use on your hosts. When they make outgoing Telnet connections, their passwords may be sniffed.

Packet Filtering Characteristics of Telnet

Telnet is a TCP-based service. Telnet servers normally use port 23 (they can be set to use any port number, but very rarely use any port but 23). Telnet clients use ports above 1023. (Telnet is used as an example in Chapter 6 so its filtering characteristics are discussed in more detail there.)

Direction	Source Addr.	Dest. Addr.	Protocol	Source Port	Dest. Port	ACK Set	Notes
In	Ext	Int	TCP	>1023	23	a	Incoming session, client to server
Out	Int	Ext	TCP	23	>1023	Yes	Incoming session, server to client

Direc-tion	Source Addr.	Dest. Addr.	Pro-tocol	Source Port	Dest. Port	ACK Set	Notes
Out	Int	Ext	TCP	>1023	23	a	Outgoing session, client to server
In	Ext	Int	TCP	23	>1023	Yes	Outgoing session, server to client

a ACK is not set on the first packet of this type (establishing connection) but will be set on the rest.

Proxying Characteristics of Telnet

Telnet is well-supported by proxies. SOCKS provides a modified UNIX Telnet client; modifying clients on other platforms is relatively trivial. The TIS FWTK provides a Telnet proxy server that requires modified user procedures. The TIS FWTK Telnet proxy server will not allow you to reach servers other than Telnet (on port 23), though you could use their *plug-gw* proxy with a standard Telnet client to do so. The SOCKS proxies should allow you to connect to ports other than the standard Telnet port, if such connections are OK according to your SOCKS server configuration file. Almost any commercial proxying package will probably provide Telnet proxying, because Telnet is such a commonly used protocol on the Internet.

Summary of Telnet Recommendations

- Restrict incoming Telnet as far as possible; most sites have little or no need for it. Whatever you're going to allow, follow the authentication guidelines in Chapter 10.

- Outgoing Telnet can safely be allowed via packet filtering or proxying.

- If you're concerned about the sensitivity of the data accessed over Telnet sessions, consider using an encrypting version of Telnet; check one of the general Internet security Web pages (such as the COAST page) to see what tools are currently available.

Remote Command Execution

A variety of protocols exist primarily to allow users to execute commands on remote systems. This section describes the BSD "r" commands, *rexec* and *rex*.

BSD 'r' Commands

The BSD "r" commands (*rsh*, *rlogin*, *rcp*, *rdump*, *rrestore*, and *rdist*) are designed to provide convenient remote access (access without passwords) to services such as remote command execution (*rsh*), remote login (*rlogin*), and remote file copying (*rcp* and *rdist*).

These programs are extremely useful, but as we discuss below, they are safe to use only in an environment in which all of the machines are more or less trusted to play by the rules. While it may be appropriate to use these services within a LAN, it's almost never appropriate to use them across the Internet. It's just too easy for someone to convince these services that they're OK and that the service should perform what's requested.

Proxying can be used to allow some of these commands safely, particularly outbound.

The difficulty with these commands is that they use address-based authentication. The server looks at the source address of the request and decides whether or not it trusts the remote host to tell it who the user is (this is controlled by the */etc/hosts.equiv* file on UNIX systems).

If the host is not in */etc/hosts.equiv,* it can still be granted access if it is in the *.rhosts* file in the home directory of the user who is asking for the service. (In fact, if the requester is running as root, only */.rhosts* is consulted; */etc/hosts.equiv* applies only to normal users.) The security can be further weakened by users adding to their *.rhosts* files; these files specify which additional remote machines and users should be trusted. In some implementations, it is possible to disable checking of *.rhosts* files with command-line arguments to the servers.

If either of the following is true:

- The account the user is coming from, on the host he is coming from, is listed in the *.rhosts* file for the account he is trying to access on the server.

- The account name is the same on both ends and the hostname is listed in *.rhosts* or */etc/hosts.equiv.*

then the authorization for the account he is trying to access is applied. That is, if the account is verified on the server, the user is authorized.

An attacker who convinces one of these servers that he is coming from a "trusted" machine can essentially get complete and unrestricted access to your system. He can convince the server by impersonating a trusted machine and using its IP address, by confusing DNS so that DNS thinks that the attacker's IP address maps to a trusted machine's name, or by any of a number of other methods.

If the trusted host check described above fails (that is, if the user is not coming from a trusted host), most of these services simply deny the client's request and disconnect. The *rlogind* server, however, will prompt the client for a password if the trusted host check fails. The password entered is sent in the clear over the net, just as with Telnet, so you have to worry about attackers capturing passwords from *rlogin* sessions, as they can from Telnet sessions. See Chapter 10 for a discussion of ways to address password sniffing attacks.

On some systems, it is possible to disable the trusted host checks with a command line argument to the servers; even if your server doesn't provide a convenient switch to disable the checks, if you have (or can get) source code for the servers, it's usually a relatively simple fix. However, without the trusted host mechanism, the *rshd* server is completely pointless, because it provides no way to prompt for a password or anything like that if the trusted host check fails. The *rlogind* server is still somewhat useful without the trusted host check, because it can ask for a password, but it's not much more useful than Telnet.

Packet filtering characteristics of the BSD 'r' commands

The "r" commands are TCP-based services. For the server, they use well-known port 513 (*rlogin*) or 514 (*rsh, rcp, rdump, rrestore,* and *rdist*; these are just different clients for the same server). They are somewhat unusual in that they use random ports *below* 1023 for the client end.

Using ports below 1023 for the client end is an attempt at a security scheme that allows password-less access to these services as long as the requests come from a trusted host and user, as discussed above. The idea is that, if the request comes from a port below 1023 on the client end, then the request must be OK with root on the client machine; if it were not, the client never could have gotten the port below 1023 to use for the request.

Further, some of the clients of the server on port 514 (*rsh*, for example) use a second TCP connection for error reporting. This second TCP connection is opened from a random port below 1023 on the server to a random port below 1023 on the client; that is, an outgoing *rsh* command involves an incoming TCP connection for the error channel.

Direction	Source Addr.	Dest. Addr.	Protocol	Source Port	Dest. Port	ACK Set	Notes
In	Ext	Int	TCP	<1023	513	[a]	Incoming *rlogin*, client to server
Out	Int	Ext	TCP	513	<1023	Yes	Incoming *rlogin*, server to client
Out	Int	Ext	TCP	<1023	513	[a]	Outgoing *rlogin*, client to server
In	Ext	Int	TCP	513	<1023	Yes	Outgoing *rlogin*, server to client
In	Ext	Int	TCP	<1023	514	[a]	Incoming *rsh/rcp/rdump/rrestore/rdist*, client to server
Out	Int	Ext	TCP	514	<1023	Yes	Incoming *rsh/rcp/rdump/rrestore/rdist*, server to client
In	Ext	Int	TCP	<1023	<1023	Yes	Incoming *rsh*, error channel, client to server
Out	Int	Ext	TCP	<1023	<1023	[a]	Incoming *rsh*, error channel, server to client
Out	Int	Ext	TCP	<1023	514	[a]	Outgoing *rsh/rcp/rdump/rrestore/rdist*, client to server

Direction	Source Addr.	Dest. Addr.	Protocol	Source Port	Dest. Port	ACK Set	Notes
In	Ext	Int	TCP	514	<1023	Yes	Outgoing *rsh/rcp/rdump/rrestore/rdist*, server to client
Out	Int	Ext	TCP	<1023	<1023	Yes	Outgoing *rsh*, error channel, client to server
In	Ext	Int	TCP	<1023	<1023	a	Outgoing *rsh*, error channel, server to client

[a] ACK is not set on the first packet of this type (establishing connection) but will be set on the rest.

Proxying characteristics of the BSD 'r' commands

The only one of these commands that's widely used across the Internet is *rlogin*. The TIS FWTK provides a proxy *rlogin* server that uses modified user procedures to provide outbound *rlogin*.

The other commands rely completely on address-based authentication, and don't allow the user to specify a password at all. They're used so seldom across the Internet that proxies for them are not widely available. All of them allow the user to specify enough data that's passed to the server that it would be possible to write modified-procedures proxies for them. Modifying the *rcmd()* and related functions in the standard UNIX library allow you to create clients that use a generic proxy server.

Summary of the BSD 'r' command recommendations

- Don't allow any of the "r" commands across your firewall except outbound by proxy; they're unsafe. Use alternative protocols such as Telnet, FTP, and so on that can be made more secure.

- There is no way to safely provide outgoing *rsh* service, because to do so you would have to allow incoming TCP connections to random ports below 1023 for the error channels.

- If you absolutely have to allow them, make sure that the trusted host mechanisms are strictly controlled (preferably by disabling that code in the server, which may require modifying the source code).

- Beware disclosure of reusable passwords when using *rlogin*, just as when using Telnet.

rexec

rexec is a widely run but rarely used server. It's rarely used because it has no standard clients; it does not appear to be used by any utility commonly shipped with

UNIX systems. It is unclear to us why it is widely run, but almost every UNIX system ships with *rexecd* enabled in */etc/inetd.conf*, apparently just in case somebody should be moved to write a local client for it.

rexec is usually lumped in with the BSD "r" commands, but is actually slightly more secure than the others. Rather than providing source-address authentication, it always requires the user to provide a user name and password. Unfortunately, it passes these across the network in the clear, so it has no security advantage over Telnet, for example.

Packet filtering characteristics of rexec

rexec is a TCP-based service. The server uses port 512. The client uses a random port below 1023 (see the previous explanation for the BSD "r" commands).

Direction	Source Addr.	Dest. Addr.	Protocol	Source Port	Dest. Port	ACK Set	Notes
In	Ext	Int	TCP	<1023	512	a	Incoming *rexec*, client to server
Out	Int	Ext	TCP	512	<1023	Yes	Incoming *rexec*, server to client
Out	Int	Ext	TCP	<1023	512	a	Outgoing *rexec*, client to server
In	Ext	Int	TCP	512	<1023	Yes	Outgoing *rexec*, server to client

[a] ACK is not set on the first packet of this type (establishing connection) but will be set on the rest.

Proxying characteristics of rexec

Because there are no widely available clients of *rexec*, there are no widely available proxies for it. If you had a client that did use *rexec*, it would not be terribly difficult to modify it to use a generic proxy like SOCKS. If the *rexec* clients on a given machine were always accessing the same server, you could also use a generic proxy server like the *plug-gw* program in the TIS FWTK. It would be somewhat trickier, but by no means impossible, to write a dedicated proxy server that would use modified user procedures.

Summary of rexec recommendations

*   *rexec* is pointless; disable it.

rex

rex is an RPC-based service for remote command execution. For an understanding of the problems RCP-based services pose for firewalls, see the discussion of RPC-based services in Chapter 6. There are worse problems with *rex*, however; in particular, it places all of its security checks in the client (which is a program named *on*), and anyone can use a modified client that bypasses these checks.

Packet filtering characteristics of rex

rex is an RPC-based service. As described in the section on RPC in Chapter 6, it's very difficult to handle RPC-based services with a packet filtering system, because the servers usually don't use predictable port numbers. While the port numbers to be used are too unpredictable for a packet filtering system to cope with, they're not so unpredictable that an attacker can't find them. (If nothing else, the attacker could try sending *rex* requests to all ports, to see which respond as they would expect a *rex* server to.)

rex is provided over TCP. Like other RPC-based services, however, there's no predicting what port number the server is going to use. Clients generally use port numbers above 1023.

Proxying characteristics of rex

RPC-based protocols are almost as unpleasant to proxy as they are to allow with packet filtering; they cannot be adequately handled with generic proxies. A dedicated *rex* proxy server would be possible, but we do not know of one.

Summary of rex recommendations

- Don't allow *rex* across your firewall; better yet, don't allow it at all, because it's completely insecure even within a LAN environment.

Network News Transfer Protocol (NNTP)

NNTP is the service generally used to transfer Usenet news across the Internet (as we mentioned above, UUCP over TCP is sometimes used for this purpose). A news server is the place where Usenet news flows into and out of your organization, and which your users access (via news clients) to read and post news. There are a number of news servers available, including B-News, C-News, and INN, and they generally speak NNTP among themselves so they can transfer news between sites. In addition, many news clients use NNTP to access news servers for users reading news.

Packet Filtering Characteristics of NNTP

NNTP is a TCP-based service. NNTP servers use port 119. NNTP clients (including servers transferring news to other servers) use ports above 1023.

Figure 8-9 shows NNTP via packet filtering.

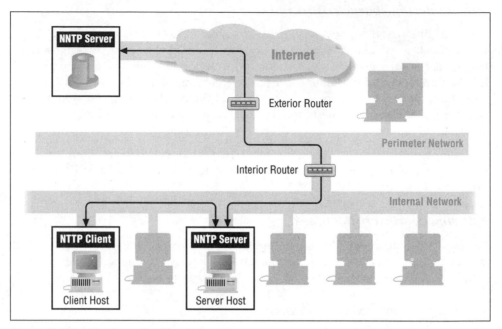

Figure 8–9: NNTP via packet filtering

Direction	Source Addr.	Dest. Addr.	Protocol	Source Port	Dest. Port	ACK Set	Notes
In	Ext	Int	TCP	>1023	119	a	Incoming news
Out	Int	Ext	TCP	119	>1023	Yes	Incoming news responses
Out	Int	Ext	TCP	>1023	119	a	Outgoing news
In	Ext	Int	TCP	119	>1023	Yes	Outgoing news responses
b	Int	News Server	TCP	>1023	119	a	Newsreader client reading news
b	News Server	Int	TCP	119	>1023	Yes	Server sending articles to news-reader client

[a] ACK is not set on the first packet of this type (establishing connection) but will be set on the rest.
[b] Both ends are internal in most cases.

Proxying Characteristics of NNTP

NNTP is a store-and-forward protocol, capable of doing its own proxying. It is also easy to proxy as a straightforward single-connection protocol. The TIS FWTK provides a generic proxy, *plug-gw*, which is frequently used with NNTP as well as modified user procedures (the NNTP connection is directed to the proxy server, which redirects the connection based on the client address). It would be easy to modify clients to use a generic modified-client proxy like SOCKS.

Figure 8-10 shows NNTP via proxy services.

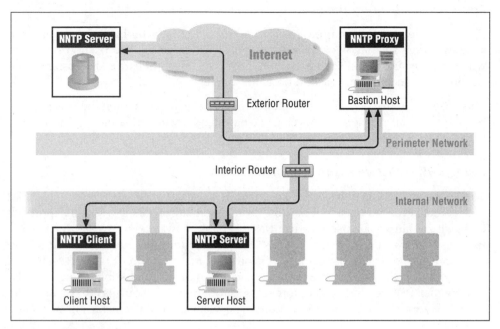

Figure 8–10: NNTP via proxy services

Dangerous Ways to Set up NNTP in a Firewall Environment

It may seem obvious that the bastion host should be your site's Usenet news server. However, there are some subtle problems that can be caused by such a configuration.

First, it is advisable to dedicate a machine to news service; news has a tendency to absorb all available disk space and processing time, and does not coexist well with critical services. If you use a bastion host for news, you will probably need to have multiple bastion hosts, which is not in itself a bad thing, but does raise maintenance overhead. It may not be worth it to you to have multiple bastion hosts just so you can provide news service on one of them.

Second, if your news server is your bastion host, you can't have any private or proprietary newsgroups for internal discussions. You wouldn't want those newsgroups to be exposed if the bastion host gets broken into, or if some outsider manages to connect to your NNTP server and convinces it to show him your newsgroups.

Third, if your bastion host is your news server, you will have to choose one of four approaches to letting your users read news; each of these approaches, described in the sections below, has its own problems.

Letting users log into the bastion host to read news

The most straightforward approach is to let users log into the bastion host and run a newsreader. This involves giving many users accounts on the bastion host, and will seriously compromise the bastion host's security. (See the discussions concerning user accounts on bastion hosts in Chapter 5.)

This approach may not be very popular with the users, either, because it will require them all to use whichever UNIX newsreaders are available on the bastion host.

Using only NNTP clients to read news

The second and somewhat safer approach is to make your users use only NNTP clients to read news from the bastion host. The main problem with this approach is that it requires your users to use NNTP-capable newsreaders. While many, perhaps even most, newsreaders are NNTP-capable, there are some that are still in common usage (such as certain versions of *nn*) that are not NNTP-capable. Depending on the NNTP server you are using, it may be impossible to get popular newsreader features like article threading through NNTP. You may have difficulty finding a server that has all the features you want for both transferring news and serving newsreaders.

Exporting news to clients via NFS

The third approach you could take to making your bastion host be your news server is to export the news to clients via NFS. This approach solves one of the problems we've identified: it allows you to use non-NNTP-capable newsreaders. However, it doesn't solve the other major problem, that of not being able to support any private or proprietary newsgroups for fear of exposure. If your users can use NFS to access your news server, chances are that an attacker can too, because the security of NFS is so weak. You're much better off disabling NFS altogether on your bastion host (see the section on NFS later in this chapter and Chapter 5 for further discussion of this point).

Relaying news through your bastion host to an internal news server

The fourth approach is to simply relay news through your bastion host, and make some internal system your "real" news server. The most obvious way to do this is to set up a news server on the bastion host that simply relays news to and from the internal news server.

The problem with this approach is that it requires a lot of maintenance. It takes a fair amount of ongoing attention to keep a news system functioning; ideally, you'd like to be able to set your bastion host up and leave it alone, maintenance free. Also, tightly coupled news systems like these are very susceptible to cascading problems. A problem on one causes news to stop flowing, stopping things up on the other system and causing problems there; when you fix the first problem, the other system floods the first, and the whole process starts over. However, if you have experienced news administrators and a large amount of disk space, you may find this approach acceptable, and it can be set up to allow for private news-groups.

Good Ways to Set up NNTP in a Firewall Environment

One of the key differences between NNTP and other protocols, such as SMTP, is in how they are used. You might get SMTP connections from all over the world, as folks from everywhere send electronic mail to your site. On the other hand, you'll only get legitimate NNTP connections from your news feed site (or sites).

The most convenient and reliable way to deal with news on a firewall is usually to arrange for the news to flow directly between your feed site(s) and your internal news server. This can be arranged either through packet filtering, or through a proxy system on the bastion host, as we describe in the following sections.

If you set up NNTP using either packet filtering or a proxy server, you'll greatly reduce your vulnerability to attacks via NNTP. With NNTP configured as we describe here, both of the following conditions would have to hold true in order for you to be attacked via NNTP:

- Your NNTP server would have to have some bug or configuration error that could be exploited.

- The attack would have to come from (or appear to come from) one of your feed sites, because the feed sites are the only sites that are allowed to open NNTP connections to your server.

NNTP is a relatively simple protocol. There have been no known attacks that use NNTP itself. There has been one known data-driven attack on UNIX news systems, which relied on the willingness of some news server software to create news-groups automatically. It was possible to specify newsgroup names with semicolons (;) in them, so that when the news server went to create the group it also exe-cuted commands contained after the semicolon in the malformed group name. Because the control messages were malformed, they weren't recognized and prop-agated by all servers, and many sites were immune anyway because they didn't automatically create newsgroups. This bug is fixed in current releases of various news server software packages, but it highlights the importance of staying up to date, as we describe in Chapter 12.

You may want to disable automated group creation in any case; it's a maintenance hassle to keep up with valid requests, but users can find it seriously annoying to deal with the side effects of automated group creation when somebody decides that it's amusing to send a few thousand creation requests overnight, most of them obscene.

Using Packet Filtering with NNTP

If you've set up a packet filtering system between the internal news server and your news feed site, you can arrange to pass NNTP between them. Set up the packet filtering system to allow the following, as shown in the table below:

- Incoming NNTP connections, so that you can receive news: that is, TCP packets from ports above 1023 on the remote system to port 119 on your news server, and TCP packets with the ACK . set from port 119 on your news server to ports above 1023 on the remote system. (Rules A and B)

- Outgoing NNTP connections, so that you can send news: that is, TCP packets from ports above 1023 on your news server to port 119 on the remote system, and TCP packets with the ACK bit set from port 119 on the remote system to ports above 1023 on your news server (Rules C and D).

Rule	Direction	Source Addr.	Dest. Addr.	Protocol	Source Port	Dest. Port	ACK Set	Action
A	In	Service Provider	Your Server	TCP	>1023	119	Any	Permit
B	Out	Your Server	Service Provider	TCP	119	>1023	Yes	Permit
C	Out	Your Server	Service Provider	TCP	>1023	119	Any	Permit
D	In	Service Provider	Your Server	TCP	119	>1023	Yes	Permit

Summary of NNTP Recommendations

- Don't use a bastion host as a news server.

- Don't allow automated group creation.

- Allow external NNTP connections only from the sites you exchange news with.

- Use packet filtering or proxying to connect trusted external NNTP servers to an internal news server, and vice versa.

World Wide Web (WWW) and HTTP

The existence of the World Wide Web (WWW) is a major factor behind the recent explosive growth of the Internet. Since the introduction of the NCSA Mosaic package (the first graphical user interface to the WWW to gain widespread acceptance) in 1993, WWW traffic on the Internet has been growing at an explosive rate, far faster than any other kind of traffic (e.g., SMTP email, FTP file transfers, Telnet remote terminal sessions, etc.). You will certainly want to let your users use a browser to access WWW sites, and you will very likely to want to run a site your-self, if you do anything that might benefit from publicity.

Most WWW browsers are capable of using protocols other than HTTP, which is the basic protocol of the Web. For example, these browsers are usually also Gopher and FTP clients, or are capable of using your existing Telnet and FTP clients trans-parently (without its being visible to the user that he is starting an external pro-gram). Many of them are also NNTP, SMTP, and Archie clients. They use a single, consistent notation called a Uniform Resource Locator (URL) (see sidebar) to spec-ify connections of various types.

Uniform Resource Locator (URL) Syntax

The general form of URLs is `service://host/path/to/file/or/page`.

There are several possible values for the *service* field, including "ftp", "http", "gopher", and "telnet".

The *host* part generally specifies the hostname or IP address of the host to connect to. If the service to be accessed is on a nonstandard port on that host (for example, if it's an HTTP server on something other than port 80), the host field can be optionally specified as "host:port" (e.g., `http://www.somewhere.com:8080` would refer to an HTTP server on port 8080 on machine `www.somewhere.com`.

The *path* field (what comes after the "/" following the host part) varies by type of URL, but generally that field specifies the particular file or document to access on that server using that service. For example, the URL `ftp://ftp.greatcircle.com/pub/firewalls/FAQ` refers to the file `/pub/firewalls/FAQ` to be obtained via anonymous FTP from host `ftp.greatcircle.com`.

For more information about URLs, see any good book on the World Wide Web.

Packet Filtering Characteristics of HTTP

HTTP is a TCP-based service. Clients use random ports above 1023. Most servers use port 80, but some don't. To understand why, you need some history.

Many of the modern information access services (notably HTTP, WAIS, and Gopher) were designed so that the servers don't *have* to run on a fixed well-known port on all machines. A standard well-known port was established for each of these services, but the clients and servers are all capable of using alternate ports as well. When you reference one of these servers, you can include the port number it's running on (assuming that it's not the standard port for that service) in addition to the name of the machine it's running on. For example, an HTTP URL of the form `http://host.domain.net/file.html` is assumed to refer to a server on the standard HTTP port (port 80); if the server were on an alternate port (port 8000, for example), the URL would be written `http://host.domain.net:8000/file.html`.

The protocol designers had two good and valid reasons for designing these services this way:

- Doing so allows a single machine to run multiple servers for multiple data sets. You could, for example, run one HTTP server that's accessible to the world with data that you wish to make available to the public, and another that has other, nonpublic data on a different port that's restricted (via packet filtering or the authentication available in the HTTP server, for example).

- Doing so allows users to run their own servers (which may be a blessing or a curse, depending on your particular security policy). Because the standard well-known ports are all in the "below 1024" range that's reserved for use only by root on UNIX machines, unprivileged users can't run their servers on the standard port numbers.

The ability to provide these services on nonstandard ports has its uses, but it complicates things considerably from a packet filtering point of view. If your users wish to access a server running on a nonstandard port, you have several choices:

- You can tell the users they can't do it; this may or may not be acceptable, depending on your environment.

- You can add a special exception for that service to your packet filtering setup. This is bad for your users because it means that they first have to recognize the problem and then wait until you've fixed it, and it's bad for you because you'll constantly have to be adding exceptions to the filter list.

- You can try to convince the server's owner to move the server to the standard port. While encouraging folks to use the standard ports as much as possible is a good long-term solution, it's not likely to yield immediate results.

- You can use some kind of proxied version of the client. This requires setup on your end, and may restrict your choice of clients. On the other hand, both Mosaic and Netscape Navigator support proxying, and they are by far the most popular clients.

- If you can filter on the ACK bit, you can allow all outbound connections, regardless of destination port. This opens up a wide variety of services, including passive-mode FTP. It also is a noticeable increase in your vulnerability.

The good news is that the vast majority of these servers (probably much greater than 90%) use the standard port, and that the more widely used and important the server is, the more likely it is to use the standard port. Many servers that use nonstandard ports use one of a few easily recognizable substitutes (81, 800, 8000, and 8080).

Your firewall will probably prevent people on your internal network from setting up their own servers at nonstandard ports (you're not going to want to allow inbound connection to arbitrary ports above 1023). You could set up such servers on a bastion host, but wherever possible, it's kinder to other sites to leave your servers on the standard port.

Direc-tion	Source Addr.	Dest. Addr.	Pro-tocol	Source Port	Dest. Port	ACK Set	Notes
In	Ext	Int	TCP	>1023	80[a]	[b]	Incoming session, client to server
Out	Int	Ext	TCP	80[a]	>1023	Yes	Incoming session, server to client
Out	Int	Ext	TCP	>1023	80[a]	[b]	Outgoing session, client to server
In	Ext	Int	TCP	80[a]	>1023	Yes	Outgoing session, server to client

[a] 80 is the standard port number for HTTP servers, but some servers run on different port numbers.
[b] ACK is not set on the first packet of this type (establishing connection) but will be set on the rest.

Proxying Characteristics of HTTP

Various HTTP clients (such as Mosaic and Netscape Navigator) transparently support various proxying schemes. Some clients support SOCKS; others support user-transparent proxying via special HTTP servers, and some support both. (See the discussion of SOCKS and proxying in general in Chapter 7.)

The CERN HTTP server, developed at the European Particle Physics Laboratory in Geneva, Switzerland, has a proxy mode in which the server handles all requests for remote documents from browsers inside the firewall. The server makes the remote connection, passing the information back to the clients transparently. See Appendix B for information about getting the CERN HTTP server.

Using the CERN HTTP server as a proxy server can provide an additional benefit, because the server can locally cache WWW pages obtained from the Internet. This caching can significantly improve client performance and reduce network bandwidth requirements. It does this by ensuring that popular WWW pages are retrieved only once at your site. The second and subsequent requests get the locally cached copy of the page, rather than a new copy each time from the original server out on the Internet.

The TIS FWTK also includes an HTTP proxy server, called *http-gw*, that can be used with any client program. Clients that support HTTP proxying can use the FWTK HTTP proxy server transparently (all you have to do is configure the client to tell it where the server is), but you must enforce custom user procedures for clients that don't support HTTP proxying. Basically, URLs have to be modified to direct the clients to the proxy server rather than the real server. URLs embedded in HTML documents that pass through the server are modified automatically, but users must know how to do it by hand for URLs they type in from scratch or obtain through other channels. Chapter 7 describes the TIS FWTK in more detail.

HTTP Security Concerns

There are two basic sets of security concerns regarding HTTP:

- What can a malicious client do to your HTTP server?

- What can a malicious HTTP server do to your clients?

The following sections describe these concerns:

What can a malicious client do to your HTTP server?

In most ways, the security concerns we have for an HTTP server are very similar to the security concerns we have for any other server that handles connections from the Internet, e.g., an anonymous FTP server. You want to make sure that the users of those connections can access only what you want them to access, and that they can't trick your server so they get to something they shouldn't.

There are a variety of methods to accomplish these goals, including:

- Carefully configure the security and access control features of your server to restrict its capabilities and what users can access with it.[*]

- Run the server as an unprivileged user.

- Use the *chroot* mechanism to restrict the server's operation to a particular section of your filesystem hierarchy. You can use chroot either within the server or through an external wrapper program.

- Don't put anything sensitive on the server machine in the first place. In this way, even if somebody does "break out" somehow, there's nothing else of interest on the machine; at least, nothing that they couldn't already get to anyway via the normal access procedures.

- Configure the rest of your network security so that even if an attacker manages to totally, compromise the server host, they're going to have a hard time getting any further into your network. To start with, don't put the server on an internal net.

HTTP servers themselves are providing a limited service and don't pose major security concerns. However, there is one unique feature of HTTP servers that you need to worry about: their use of external programs, particularly ones that interact with the user via the Common Gateway Interface (CGI) which is the piece of HTTP that specifies how user information is communicated to the server and from it to

---

[*] For a more complete discussion of these features and their use, see the chapters on HTTP servers in *Managing Internet Information Services*.

external programs. Many HTTP servers are configured to run other programs to generate HTML pages on the fly. These programs are generically called CGI scripts, even if they don't use CGI and aren't scripts. For example, if someone issues a database query to an HTTP server, the HTTP server runs an external program to perform the query and generate an HTML page with the answers.

There are two things you need to worry about with these external programs:

- Can an attacker trick the external programs into doing something they shouldn't?

- Can an attacker upload his own external programs and cause them to be executed?

You may want to run your HTTP server on a Macintosh, DOS, or Windows machine. These machines have good HTTP server implementations available, but don't generally have the other capabilities that would make those servers insecure. For example, they are unlikely to be running other servers, they don't have a powerful and easily available scripting facility, and they're less likely to have other data or trusted access to other machines. The downside of this is that it's hard to do interesting things on them; the easier it gets, the less secure they'll be.

Tricking external programs   The external programs run by HTTP servers are often shell scripts written by folks who have information they want to provide access to, but who know little or nothing about writing secure shell scripts (which is by no means trivial, even for an expert).

Because it's difficult to ensure the security of the scripts themselves, about the best you can do is try to provide a secure environment (using *chroot* and other mechanisms) that the scripts can run in (one which, you hope, they can't get out of). There should be nothing in the environment you'd worry about being revealed to the world. Nothing should trust the machine the server is running on. If you set up the environment in this way, then even if attackers somehow manage to break out of the restricted environment and gain full access to the machine, they're not much further along towards breaking into the really interesting stuff on your internal network.

Alternatively, or in addition, if you have people who you feel sure are capable of writing secure scripts, you can have all the scripts written, or at least reviewed, by these people. Most sites don't have people like this readily available, but if you are going to be seriously involved in providing WWW service, you may want to hire one. It's still a good idea to run the scripts in a restricted environment; nobody's perfect.

Uploading external programs   The second concern is that attackers might be able to upload their own external programs and cause your server to run them. How could attackers do this? Suppose the following:

- Your HTTP server and your anonymous FTP server both run on the same machine.

- They can both access the same areas of the filesystem.

- There is a writable directory somewhere in those areas, so that customers can upload core dumps from your product via FTP for analysis by your programmers, for example.

In this case, the attacker might be able to upload his own script or binary to that writable directory using anonymous FTP, and then cause the HTTP server to run it.

What is your defense against things like this? Once again, your best bet is to restrict what filesystem areas each server can access (generally using *chroot*), and to provide a restricted environment in which each server can run.

What can a malicious server do to your HTTP clients?

The security problems of HTTP clients are far more complex that those of HTTP servers. The basis of these client problems is that HTTP clients (like Mosaic and Netscape Navigator) are generally designed to be extensible and to run particular external programs to deal with particular data types. This extensibility can be abused by an attacker.

HTTP servers can provide data in any number of formats: plain text files, HTML files, PostScript documents, still video files (GIF and JPEG), movie files (MPEG), audio files, and so on. The servers use MIME, discussed briefly above in the section on electronic mail, to format the data and specify its type. HTTP clients generally don't attempt to understand and process all of these different data formats. They understand a few (such as HTML, plain text, and GIF), and they rely on external programs to deal with the rest. These external programs will display, play, preview, print, or do whatever is appropriate for the format.

For example, UNIX Web browsers confronted with a PostScript file will ordinarily invoke the GhostScript program, and UNIX Web browsers confronted with a JPEG file will ordinarily invoke the *xv* program. The user controls (generally via a configuration file) what data types the HTTP client knows about, which programs to invoke for which data types, and what arguments to pass to those programs. If the user hasn't provided his own configuration file, the HTTP client generally uses a built-in default or a systemwide default.

All of these external programs present two security concerns:

- What are the inherent capabilities of the external programs an attacker might take advantage of?

- What new programs (or new arguments for existing programs) might an attacker be able to convince the user to add to his configuration?

An example   Let's consider, for example, what an HTTP client is going to do with a PostScript file. PostScript is a language for controlling printers. While primarily intended for that purpose, it is a full programming language, complete with data structures, flow of control operators, and file input/output operators. These operators ("read file", "write file", "create file", "delete file", etc.) are seldom used, except on printers with local disks for font storage, but they're there as part of the language. PostScript previewers (such as GhostScript) generally implement these operators for completeness.

Suppose that a user uses Mosaic to pull down a PostScript document. Mosaic invokes GhostScript, and it turns out that the document has PostScript commands in it that say "delete all files in the current directory." If GhostScript executes the commands, who's to blame? You can't really expect Mosaic to scan the PostScript on the way through to see if it's dangerous; that's an impossible problem. You can't really expect GhostScript not to do what it's told in valid PostScript code. You can't really expect your users not to download PostScript code, or to scan it themselves.

Current versions of GhostScript have a safer mode they run in by default. This mode disables "dangerous" operators such as those for file input/output. But what about all the other PostScript interpreters or previewers? And what about the applications to handle all the other data types? How safe are they? Who knows?

Even if you have safe versions of these auxiliary applications, how do you keep your users from changing their configuration files to add new applications, run different applications, or pass different arguments (for example, to disable the safer mode of GhostScript) to the existing applications?

Why would a user do this? Suppose that the user found something in the WWW that claimed to be something he really wanted—a game demo, a graphics file, a copy of Madonna's new song, whatever. And, suppose that this desirable something came with a note that said "Hey, before you can access this Really Cool Thing, you need to modify your Mosaic configuration, because the standard configuration doesn't know how to deal with this thing; here's what you do . . . " And, suppose that the instructions were something like "remove the '-dSAFER' flag from the 'ghostscript' line of your *.mosaicrc* file," or "add this line to your *.mosaicrc* file."

Would your users recognize that they were being instructed to disable the safer mode in GhostScript, or to add some new data type with */bin/sh* as its auxiliary program, so that whatever data of that type came down was passed as commands straight to the shell? Even if they recognized it, would they do it anyway (nice, trusting people that they are)?

Some people believe that Macintosh and PC-based versions of WWW browsers are less susceptible to some of these security problems than UNIX-based browsers. On Mac and PC machines, there is usually no shell (or only a shell of limited power, like the MS-DOS command interpreter) that an attacker can break out to, and a limited and highly unpredictable set of programs to access once they're there. Also, if any damage occurs, it can often be more easily isolated to a single machine. On the other hand, "highly unpredictable" does not mean "completely unpredictable". (For example, a very large percentage of Macs and PCs have copies of standard Microsoft applications, like Word and Excel.) Further, if your Macs and PCs are networked with AppleShare, Novell, PC-NFS, or something similar, you can't make any assumptions about damage being limited to a single machine.

What can you do? There is no simple, foolproof defense against the type of problem we've described. At this point in time, you have to rely on a combination of carefully installed and configured client and auxiliary programs, and a healthy dose of user education and awareness training. This is an area of active research and development, and both the safeguards and the attacks will probably develop significantly over the next couple of years.

Because Mac and PC clients seem less susceptible to some of the client-side problems, some sites take the approach of allowing WWW access only from Macs or PCs. Some go even further and limit access to particular machines (often placed in easily accessible locations like libraries or cafeterias) that have been carefully configured so they have no sensitive information on them, and no access to such information. The idea is this: If anything bad happens, it will affect only this one easily rebuilt machine. The machine can't be used to access company data on other machines.

Some people have experimented, at least in UNIX environments, with running Mosaic and its auxiliary programs under the X Window System in a restricted environment—or on a "sacrificial goat" machine that has nothing else on it—with the displays directed to their workstation. This provides a certain measure of protection, but it also imposes a certain amount of inconvenience. Consider the following problems with this approach:

- This approach works only for the UNIX/X version of Mosaic. If you have Mac and PC users, they're going to have to run X on their system, log in to the goat system, set up the restricted environment, and start Mosaic. All in all, this may be more interaction with UNIX than they're willing to put up with.

- Any files legitimately retrieved during the session are going to wind up in the restricted environment or on the goat machine. Then, they're going to have to be transferred separately to the machine where they are really wanted.

- This approach generally doesn't work for audio files, which will end up being played on the audio system of the goat machine (or wherever the restricted environment is), not on the user's machine.

As discussed above in the section called "Packet Filtering Characteristics of HTTP," there is another complication of WWW clients in environments in which packet filtering is part of the firewall solution: not all HTTP servers run on port 80. To address this, you might consider using proxy servers for HTTP access. If you do this, the internal clients talk on standard ports through the packet filtering system to the proxy server, and the proxy server talks on arbitrary ports (because it's outside the packet filtering system) to the real server.

Secure HTTP

You may hear discussions of Secure HTTP and wonder how it relates to firewalls and the configuring of services. Secure HTTP is not designed to solve the kinds of problems we've been discussing in this section. It's designed to deal with privacy issues by encrypting the information that is being passed around via HTTP. A mechanism like Secure HTTP is necessary to be able to do business using HTTP so that things like credit card numbers can be passed over the Internet without fear of capture by packet sniffers. In order to distinguish between privacy issues, on the one hand, and vulnerability to malicious servers, on the other hand, people working on HTTP and similar extensible protocols usually use the word "safe" to refer to protocols that protect you from hostile servers, and the word "secure" to refer to protocols that protect you from data snooping.

Because it provides authentication as well as encryption, Secure HTTP could eventually provide some assistance with safety. If you are willing to connect only to sites that you know, that run Secure HTTP, and that authenticate themselves, you can be sure that you're not talking to a hostile site. However, even when Secure HTTP is released and in wide usage, this approach (limited connections) is unlikely to be a popular and practical one; part of the glory of the Web is being able to go to new and unexpected places.

Although people are working on HTTP-like protocols that are safe, safe HTTP is probably not a viable concept. It's not HTTP that's unsafe; it's the fact that HTTP is transferring programs in other languages. This is a major design feature of HTTP and one of the things responsible for its rapid spread.

Summary of WWW Recommendations

- If you're going to run an HTTP server, use a dedicated bastion host if possible.

- If you're going to run an HTTP server, carefully configure the HTTP server to control what it has access to; in particular, watch out for ways that someone could upload a program to the system somehow (via mail or FTP, for example), and then execute it via the HTTP server.

- Carefully control the external programs your HTTP server can access.

- You can't allow internal hosts to access all HTTP servers without allowing them to access all TCP ports, because some HTTP servers use nonstandard port numbers. If you don't mind allowing your users access to all TCP ports, you can use packet filtering to examine the ACK bit to allow outgoing connections to those ports (but not incoming connections from those ports). If you do mind, then either restrict your users to servers on the standard port (80), or use proxying.

- Proxying HTTP is easy, and a caching proxy server offers network bandwidth benefits as well as security benefits.

- Configure your HTTP clients carefully and warn your users not to reconfigure them based on external advice.

Other Information Services

In addition to the World Wide Web services described in the previous section, there are a number of other popular information services as well, including Gopher, WAIS, and Archie.

Gopher

Gopher is a menu-driven text-based tool for browsing through files and directories across the Internet. When a user selects a Gopher menu item, Gopher retrieves the specified file and displays it appropriately. This means that if a file is compressed, Gopher automatically uncompresses it; if it's a GIF image, Gopher automatically runs a GIF viewer.

The security concerns for Gopher are essentially the same—from both a server and a client point of view—as those described in the preceding section for HTTP servers and clients.

For servers, you have to worry about what a malicious client can trick you into running. Like HTTP servers, some Gopher servers use auxiliary programs to generate Gopher pages on the fly. Gopher servers are therefore susceptible to the same kinds of problems as HTTP servers:

- Can an attacker trick the auxiliary program?

- Can the attacker upload his own auxiliary program and cause it to be run?

For clients, you have to worry about what a malicious server can trick you into doing. Gopher uses the same kinds of extensible data type and auxiliary program mechanisms as HTTP, so the concerns are similar to those described for HTTP.

Like HTTP servers, Gopher servers also sometimes live on nonstandard ports, so those concerns are similar to HTTP as well. Some Gopher clients support transparent proxying (via SOCKS or other mechanisms), but many don't.

Most of the common WWW browsers such as Mosaic and Netscape Navigator are Gopher clients as well as being HTTP clients. These browsers generally support the proxying of Gopher via SOCKS or via transparent HTTP proxy servers such as the CERN HTTP server described in the preceding section. Even if you can't find a dedicated Gopher client that does proxying, you can probably use one of these WWW browsers (and an appropriate proxy server) instead. Your users may even prefer this approach to using a separate Gopher client, because it means they only have one application—a client for HTTP, Gopher, and several other protocols—to learn and configure, rather than a separate application for each protocol.

Packet filtering characteristics of Gopher

Gopher is a TCP-based service. Gopher clients use ports above 1023. Most Gopher servers use port 70, but some don't; see the discussion of nonstandard server ports above, in the section called "Packet Filtering Characteristics of HTTP."

Direction	Source Addr.	Dest. Addr.	Protocol	Source Port	Dest. Port	ACK Set	Notes
In	Ext	Int	TCP	>1023	70[a]	[b]	Incoming session, client to server
Out	Int	Ext	TCP	70[a]	>1023	Yes	Incoming session, server to client
Out	Int	Ext	TCP	>1023	70[a]	[b]	Outgoing session, client to server
In	Ext	Int	TCP	70[a]	>1023	Yes	Outgoing session, server to client

[a] 70 is the standard port number for Gopher servers, but some servers run on different port numbers.
[b] ACK is not set on the first packet of this type (establishing connection) but will be set on the rest.

Proxying characteristics of Gopher

The TIS FWTK *http-gw* proxy server can serve Gopher as well as HTTP. SOCKS does not include a modified Gopher client, but Gopher clients are, in general, not difficult to modify to use SOCKS; many of the Gopher clients freely available on the Internet support SOCKS as either a compile-time or run-time option. Using a Web browser that supports proxying, like Netscape Navigator or Mosaic, will give you proxy support for Gopher automatically.

Summary of Gopher recommendations

These recommendations are basically the same as for HTTP:

*   If you're going to run a Gopher server, use a dedicated bastion host if possible.

*   If you're going to run a Gopher server, carefully configure the Gopher server to control what it has access to; in particular, watch out for ways that someone could upload a program to Gopher system somehow (via mail or FTP, for example), and then execute it via the Gopher server.

*   Carefully control the external programs your Gopher server can access.

*   You can't allow internal hosts to access all Gopher servers without allowing them to access all TCP ports, because some Gopher servers use nonstandard port numbers. If you don't mind allowing your users access to all TCP ports, you can use packet filtering to examine the ACK bit to allow outgoing connections to those ports (but not incoming connections from those ports). If you do mind, then either restrict your users to servers on the standard port (70), or use proxying.

*   Configure your Gopher clients carefully, and warn your users not to reconfigure them based on external advice.

*   If possible, use a Web browser such as Mosaic or Netscape Navigator for your Gopher client, rather than a dedicated client. Your users are probably going to demand WWW access before Gopher access anyway, so you might as well only have to figure out and secure one application.

Wide Area Information Servers (WAIS)

WAIS indexes large text databases so that they can be searched efficiently by simple keyword or more complicated Boolean expressions. For example, you can ask for all the documents that mention "firewalls" or all the documents that mention "firewalls" but don't mention "fire marshals". (You might do this to make sure you don't get documents about literal firewalls.) WAIS was originally developed at Thinking Machines as a prototype information service, and is now widely used on the Internet for things like mailing-list archives and catalogs of various text-based information (library card catalogs, for example).

WAIS servers present the same basic security concerns as the servers for all of the other common Internet services, such as FTP and HTTP: Can an attacker use this server to access something he shouldn't?

You address this problem just as you do with other servers: Secure and restrict the environment the server runs in. In this way, you ensure that even if the attacker gets out of the server, there's nothing else of interest to be found on the machine. Further, nothing else should trust the machine enough to significantly facilitate further break-ins.

Generally, WAIS servers do not run auxiliary programs the way HTTP and Gopher servers do, so with WAIS, you don't need to worry that attackers will trick your servers or upload auxiliary programs as they can with the HTTP and Gopher servers. Because WAIS clients are not generally extensible with new data types and auxiliary programs, as HTTP and Gopher clients are, you also don't have that can of worms to worry about.

WAIS servers do share one characteristic of HTTP and Gopher servers, however: while there is a standard port number for WAIS servers (TCP port 210), not all of them use it. See the discussion of this in the section on HTTP above for an understanding of the problems this can cause.

WAIS clients are generally standalone programs. They help you find WAIS servers, submit queries to those servers, display the results, submit follow-on queries based on previous results, and so on. WAIS information is generally text-based, so WAIS clients generally don't have the problems that HTTP and Gopher clients do regarding the safety of the data they retrieve.

Some WWW browsers include limited WAIS client support.

Packet filtering characteristics of WAIS

WAIS is a TCP-based service. WAIS clients use random ports above 1023. WAIS servers usually use port 210, but sometimes don't; see the discussion of nonstandard server ports above, in the section about HTTP.

Direc-tion	Source Addr.	Dest. Addr.	Pro-tocol	Source Port	Dest. Port	ACK Set	Notes
In	Ext	Int	TCP	>1023	210[a]	[b]	Incoming session, client to server
Out	Int	Ext	TCP	210[a]	>1023	Yes	Incoming session, server to client
Out	Int	Ext	TCP	>1023	210[a]	[b]	Outgoing session, client to server
In	Ext	Int	TCP	210[a]	>1023	Yes	Outgoing session, server to client

[a] 210 is the standard port number for WAIS servers, but some servers run on different port numbers.
[b] ACK is not set on the first packet of this type (establishing connection) but will be set on the rest.

Proxying characteristics of WAIS

If you use a proxying Web browser like Netscape Navigator or Mosaic to access WAIS, you automatically get client support. As a straightforward single-connection protocol with plenty of user-specified information, WAIS lends itself to both modified-client and modified-procedure proxying. SOCKS support is commonly available in standalone WAIS clients.

Gateways to WAIS

A number of sites on the Internet provide WAIS gateways for HTTP clients, allowing people using WWW browsers to access WAIS servers indirectly. Gateways include:

```
http://www.ai.mit.edu/the-net/wais.html
http://www.wais.com/
```

Summary of WAIS recommendations

- If you want to run a WAIS server, run it on a bastion host and on the standard port for WAIS (TCP port 210). Carefully configure the server to control what information it has access to.

- You can't allow internal hosts to access all WAIS servers without allowing them to access all TCP ports, because some WAIS servers use nonstandard port numbers. If you don't mind allowing your users access to all TCP ports, you can use packet filtering to examine the ACK bit to allow outgoing connections to those ports (but not incoming connections from those ports). If you do mind, then either restrict your users to servers on the standard port (TCP port 210) or use proxying.

- If possible, use a Web browser such as Mosaic or Netscape Navigator for your WAIS client, rather than a dedicated client. Your users are probably going to demand WWW access before WAIS access anyway, so you might as well figure out and secure just one application.

Archie

Archie is an Internet service that lets users search through indexes of anonymous FTP servers for strings or regular expressions that match file and directory names in the FTP archives. Archie continually polls public anonymous FTP servers to keep up to date with what's available at the sites.

Packet filtering characteristics of Archie

Archie is a UDP-based service. Dedicated Archie clients use ports above 1023; Archie servers use port 1525. As we discuss in Chapter 6, UDP-based services in general are a problem for packet filtering firewalls. Alternative ways to access Archie (other than directly via the Archie protocol) are discussed in the sections below.

Direction	Source Addr.	Dest. Addr.	Protocol	Source Port	Dest. Port	ACK Set	Notes
Out	Int	Ext[a]	UDP	>1023	1525	[b]	Outgoing query, client to server
In	Ext[a]	Int	UDP	1525	>1023	[b]	Incoming response, server to client

[a] The external address should be one of the well-known Archie servers.
[b] UDP packets do not have ACK bits.

Most sites with packet filtering systems typically filter out all UDP traffic, and then open specific, restricted peepholes between their internal hosts and their bastion host (*not* the whole outside world) for key UDP-based services.

Proxying characteristics of Archie

Because Archie is a UDP-based service, it is not supported by SOCKS; however, it can be proxied by the UDP Packet Relayer. TIS FWTK does not provide an Archie proxy server and does not provide a generic proxy server for UDP (*plug-gw* supports only TCP). Using one of the HTTP-Archie gateways (discussed below) gives you the proxying of your Web browser, and provides a better user interface than many dedicated Archie clients.

Providing Archie service to your users

There are several ways to let your users access Archie servers, including Telnet, email, and WWW gateways, and the dedicated Archie protocol. Sites running Archie servers generally prefer people to access them via the dedicated Archie protocol (or via WWW gateways, which in turn access the Archie servers via the dedicated Archie protocol) because this is more efficient for them and allows them to serve a greater number of users.

Archie access via Telnet If you allow outgoing Telnet, Archie servers can be accessed by opening a Telnet session to the machine and logging in as "archie" (no password required). This will give you access to a command-line-oriented Archie query program. Now you can either capture a log of the Telnet session to save your results or tell the server to email you the results after you're done. Issue the command "help" to get started with a description of the server's command language.

Archie access via email Generally, Archie servers can also be accessed by email. If you send an email message to "archie" at one of the Archie sites (e.g., *archie@archie.ans.net*), it will treat the mail as a query to be processed and will email back the results. Send the query "help" to find out how to use the service.

Archie access via WWW gateways Like many services, Archie servers can also be accessed via a variety of WWW gateways; simply point your Web browser at one of the following:

```
http://www.lerc.nasa.gov/Doc/archieplex-httpd.html
http://hoohoo.ncsa.uiuc.edu/archie.html
http://www.nexor.co.uk/archie.html
```

Archie access via packet filtering and the dedicated Archie protocol Archie servers can be accessed directly with dedicated Archie clients. The problem is, as we've discussed above, Archie is UDP-based, and most sites block all but a very restricted set of UDP packets through their firewall in order to avoid security problems with RPC-based services like NFS and NIS/YP.

What makes it possible to provide direct Archie access via packet filtering is that there are so few Archie servers. Many sites consider it safe enough to open a peephole in the packet filtering for Archie to the well-known Archie servers their users are likely to use. There are several reasons for this:

- The list of servers is small and fairly stable.

- In order to be attacked through this peephole, the attack would have to come (or at least convincingly appear to come) from one of these sites. Given that these are all well-known and very heavily used sites, any break-in to them is probably going to be noticed very quickly, particularly if it takes down the Archie server in order to use its port to attack some other site. Even forging packets is likely to result in widespread service outages and quick detection.

- Even if someone did break into one of the Archie servers, what are the chances that the attacker would then go after your site in particular?

You may also decide that you are willing to take a chance and open your packet filtering sufficiently to allow your users to access the handful of major Archie servers in the world, or at least the default servers you've configured into the client you're distributing.

Running an Archie server

Providing an Archie server is a major undertaking, requiring the dedication of a fairly substantial amount of computing power, disk space, and network bandwidth. Because of this, there are only about 20 Archie servers in the world; telling you how to become the 21st is beyond the scope of this book. In any case, it's unlikely to be beneficial to the world for you to do it. If there are too many servers, they are more likely to be incomplete or out of date and to consume bandwidth people need to access the FTP servers.

Summary of Archie recommendations

- Don't run an Archie server.

- Teach your users to access Archie via WWW gateways.

Information Lookup Services

The *finger* and *whois* services look up information about users and sites on the Internet. They are the closest thing we have to real services for finding out information about people on the Internet at large.

finger

The *finger* service looks up information about users. This information may include the person's real name, username, and information about when they most recently logged in and where they logged in from. *finger* can also be used to show the list of all users currently logged into a host. *finger* is designed to allow people to find each other, but it gives out more information than you probably want to make available. Intruders find it invaluable; it will tell them what the valid usernames on the host are, which of them are not in use, and when people are logged in who are likely to notice their activity.

We recommend that you limit incoming *finger* requests to a bastion host, and that you run a replacement *finger* server on that host. Chapter 5 discusses how to construct and install a replacement *finger* server.

Outgoing *finger* requests are also mildly problematic. The *finger* protocol has no command channel to the client, so command channel attacks are nonexistent, but data-driven attacks are possible. Most common *finger* clients do no filtering on the data they receive from the server. The attacks possible through this data channel are mostly annoyances; the nasty *finger* server sends back immense amounts of data or makes your terminal beep 400 times and start displaying black letters on a black background. Some of them are more serious. There are terminals that are programmable with control characters, so that a *finger* server can send back data that reprograms the "e" key so that it executes the command "rm -rf/*" or a command that mails your password file off. Such terminals are not particularly widespread these days (the most popular terminal emulators don't support this kind of thing), but they still exist, and so do terminal emulators that are overly faithful and reproduce these behaviors. If you are using intelligent terminals, or terminal emulators set up to emulate mainframe terminals with programmable function keys, you may be vulnerable.

In general, data-driven attacks on *finger* are not a major concern, but if your users frequently use *finger* to external sites—particularly universities, which have lots of people who still think making your terminal beep 400 times is amusing—you may want to run a replacement *finger* client that filters out control characters and limits the amount of returned data it will accept. [*]

A modified *finger* with an extended protocol is available from the GNU Project. This version of *finger* supports some useful features for large sites (for example, it lets one machine keep track of the most recent login times for an entire network, so that users are not constantly complaining that they're incorrect), but it does not include any security enhancements on either the server or the client ends. Several pieces of information it makes available are clearly undesirable to provide to attackers (for example, it will provide a list of machines that are idle and/or have

---

[*] This will prevent you from appreciating the cleverness of people who have managed to put animations in their *.plan* files using only VT100 control sequences, but that's not a major loss.

no users logged in). The security implications of the extended protocol it uses are unclear.

Packet filtering characteristics of finger

finger is a TCP-based service. Servers use port 79. Clients use ports above 1023.

Direction	Source Addr.	Dest. Addr.	Protocol	Source Port	Dest. Port	ACK Set	Notes
In	Ext	Int	TCP	>1023	79	a	Incoming query, client to server
Out	Int	Ext	TCP	79	>1023	Yes	Outgoing response, server to client
Out	Int	Ext	TCP	>1023	79	a	Outgoing query, client to server
In	Ext	Int	TCP	79	>1023	Yes	Incoming response, server to client

[a] ACK is not set on the first packet of this type (establishing connection) but will be set on the rest.

Proxying characteristics of finger

SOCKS provides a modified *finger* client for UNIX, and *finger* clients on other platforms should be easy to modify to use SOCKS. Some *finger* servers support the notation *finger user@host@proxying-host*, which sends the request to the proxying host and from there to the destination host. If this form of proxying is available, however, it will work equally for external and internal users. External users will be able to use it to reach your internal hosts, which you may find undesirable.

Summary of finger recommendations

* Limit incoming *finger* requests to a bastion host.

* Run a replacement *finger* service on the bastion host.

* Permit outgoing *finger* requests, but consider running a replacement *finger* client.

whois

whois is another information-lookup protocol, much like *finger*. It is commonly used to obtain public information about hosts, networks, domains, and the people who manage them from various Network Information Centers (NICs, such as *rs.internic.net*). Sites generally don't provide their own *whois* server; they merely access the *whois* servers at the NICs. People don't expect other sites to run *whois* servers (in fact, the user doesn't ordinarily specify a server when he runs *whois*; instead, the program uses a server that was specified when it was compiled).

The data that is available via *whois* is not necessarily of much interest to normal users. Although long-time Internet users may believe otherwise, *whois* provides data about only a fraction of the people on the Internet. Unless you're looking for information about somebody who runs a site, *whois* probably isn't going to tell you anything useful, and what it does tell you may not be up to date. At most sites, the only people who have any use for it are system and network administrators. Many NICs also make much of this data available via other methods, such as the World Wide Web.

On the other hand, there have been no known security problems with *whois* clients and any that occurred would have to be data-driven. (All that a *whois* server can do to a client is to return data.) Because *whois* is almost never used with arbitrary servers, in order to do any real damage somebody who manages to find a data-driven bug in a *whois* client would have to compromise, subvert, or forge packets from the most frequently used and most secure machines on the Internet. Furthermore, while *finger* shows data that was entered by random users, *whois* pulls its information from a central database. Therefore, if your users want to use *whois* clients, there's no reason to prevent them. If they don't have any particular desire to use *whois*, there's no reason to make it available.

Packet filtering characteristics of whois

whois is TCP-based. Servers use port 43. Clients use random ports above 1023.

Direction	Source Addr.	Dest. Addr.	Protocol	Source Port	Dest. Port	ACK Set	Notes
Out	Int	Ext	TCP	>1023	43	[a]	Outgoing query, client to server
In	Ext	Int	TCP	43	>1023	Yes	Incoming response, server to client

[a] ACK is not set on the first packet of this type (establishing connection) but will be set on the rest.

Proxying characteristics of whois

SOCKS does not provide a modified *whois* client, and TIS FWTK does not provide a *whois* proxy server. Because *whois* is a straightforward single-connection protocol with plenty of user-specified data, it would be trivial to modify *whois* clients for SOCKS, and relatively simple to write a modified-procedure proxy server for it. Because most *whois* connections are to a single host (*rs.internic.net*), you could use the TIS FWTK *plug-gw* program on your bastion host to relay all connections to the *whois* port on the bastion host on to *rs.internic.net*.

Summary of whois recommendations

- You don't need to run an externally visible *whois* server.

- Don't allow incoming *whois* queries unless you put a server up.

- Allow outgoing *whois* queries, at least from the machines your system and network administrators are likely to use.

Real-Time Conferencing Services

There are several services available on the Internet that allow people to interact in real time on the Internet, including *talk*, IRC, and various services provided over the MBONE.

talk

talk is a text-based real-time two-person conferencing system; it allows two people to establish a "chat" session with each other. Each of their screens gets split into two sections; what one person types appears in one section; what the other person types appears in the other section.

talk is very convoluted in that it uses UDP to negotiate the connections between the two sites and then uses TCP to actually move the data back and forth between the participants. UDP is used between the calling client and the answering server, and again between the answering client and the calling server; TCP is then used between the two clients.

To further complicate matters, there are two incompatible versions of the *talk* protocol, commonly referred to as either *talk* and *ntalk* (for "new talk") or *otalk* (for "old talk") and *talk*, depending on who you ask. The earlier version depended on bytes being in a certain order in memory, and basically worked only between machines of the same CPU type. The later version fixes this problem, but is incompatible with the earlier version.

The calling client contacts the answering server via UDP to announce the call. The answering server tells the user being called that someone is requesting a *talk* session and how he should respond if he wishes to accept the call. While waiting for the user to respond, the calling client also contacts the calling server to say that it's expecting an incoming call and to specify what TCP port it wishes to use for that call (somewhat like calling your secretary to say that you're expecting a call back from someone, and that it should be put through to the extension you're currently at). When the answering user accepts, that user's client (the answering client) contacts the calling server via UDP to find out what port the calling client is waiting on; the answering client then contacts the calling client on that TCP port. Figure 8-11 shows how *talk* works.

Because of the incompatible *talk* protocols, *talk* fails relatively often even between sites that do no packet filtering, or between machines of different types within the same site. *talk* clients and servers are generally provided only on UNIX machines.

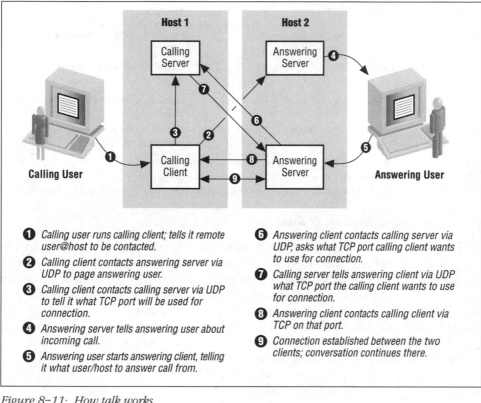

Figure 8–11: How talk works

Packet filtering characteristics of talk

talk servers (which broker connections between *talk* clients, and then get out of the way) use either UDP port 517 (for old versions of *talk*) or UDP port 518 (for newer versions). *talk* clients use UDP ports above 1023 to interact with *talk* servers. *talk* clients also use TCP ports above 1023 to interact with each other. This means that, in order to allow *talk* across your firewall, you'd have to allow TCP connections where both ends are using arbitrary ports above 1023; this isn't safe because of vulnerabilities like X11 servers that use ports above 1023.

Direction	Source Addr.	Dest. Addr.	Protocol	Source Port	Dest. Port	ACK Set	Notes
In	Ext	Int	UDP	>1023	517 518[a]	[b]	External client contacting internal server
Out	Int	Ext	UDP	517 518[a]	>1023	[b]	Internal server answering external client

Direction	Source Addr.	Dest. Addr.	Protocol	Source Port	Dest. Port	ACK Set	Notes
Out	Int	Ext	UDP	>1023	517 518 [a]	[b]	Internal client contacting external server
In	Ext	Int	UDP	517 518 [a]	>1023	[b]	External server answering internal client
Out	Int	Ext	TCP	>1023	>1023	[c]	Internal client communicating with external client
In	Ext	Int	TCP	>1023	>1023	[c]	External client communicating with internal client

[a] Old versions of *talk* use port 517; newer versions use port 518.
[b] UDP packets do not have ACK bits.
[c] ACK is not set on the first packet of this type (establishing connection) but will be set on the rest.

Proxying characteristics of talk

There are no available proxies for *talk*. It would theoretically be possible to write one. Because *talk* involves internal and external clients simultaneously, it would almost have to be a modified-procedure proxy server. (No generic server would handle it, in any case, because it involves both TCP and UDP.) Given the considerable difficulty of writing a *talk* proxy, and the extreme fragility of the process, it's unlikely that one will become available any time soon. It's more likely that *talk* will be abandoned altogether for cross-Internet conversations, in favor of something like IRC, which we describe in the next section.

Summary of talk recommendations

- It is impossible to safely allow *talk* through filters, or to proxy it, so you can't allow *talk* between the Internet and your internal machines. If, for some reason, you absolutely must allow *talk*, you will need to put a victim machine on your perimeter net that is untrusted and has no confidential data, and allow users to log into it and run *talk* from there.

Internet Relay Chat (IRC)

IRC is a multiuser text-based real-time conferencing system. Users run IRC client programs to connect to IRC servers. IRC servers are arranged in a spanning tree, and talk to each other to pass messages to all of the clients. Figure 8-10 shows how the IRC servers are connected. Clients might connect to any of these servers.

Most of the security problems with IRC are related to who uses it and how, not to the protocol per se. As we mentioned in Chapter 2, many clients allow servers far more access to local resources (files, processes, programs, etc.) than they should, and a malicious server can wreak havoc with a weak or poorly configured client. Further, some of the frequent users of IRC have a nasty habit of persuading new users to naively run commands which those systems think will do neat things on their systems, but which instead trash these systems.

Many well-intentioned IRC users are simply naive about security. For example, they think it's really neat to distribute software by putting up a little server on their machine, and advising people to "telnet myhost myport | sh" to have the software installed for them, which allows external users to install the software without interaction from the user, but would also let them run any command whatsoever on the internal user's host as that user. It's close to impossible to distinguish hostile people from naive ones, and users should be advised to never issue any command, in or out of their IRC client, just because somebody advised them to over IRC.

Although these problems are widespread on IRC, IRC is also a useful and popular way for people to talk to each other. Text-based, multiuser, real-time communication can be handy; it has many of the advantages of teleconferencing for a much lower price tag.

You should be able to safely run an IRC server in a restricted (*chroot*ed) environment on a bastion host, but it would be somewhat bizarre to run a server without having any local clients that could access it, and a server that could access the Internet would probably not be safe for clients to talk to. You may want to run one inside your firewall for private IRC conferencing.

Many IRC clients support something called Direct Client Connections (DCC). DCC allows two IRC clients to negotiate and establish a direct TCP connection between themselves, bypassing all the servers except for the initial negotiation. Figure 8-12 depicts the IRC server tree.

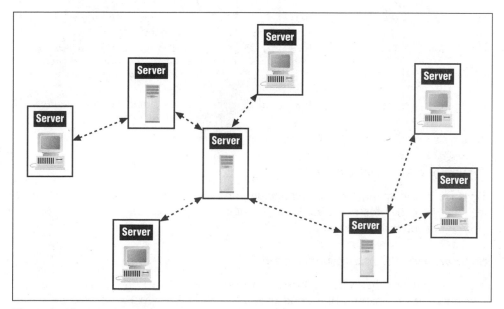

Figure 8–12: IRC server tree

Packet filtering characteristics of IRC

IRC is a TCP-based service. Servers generally listen for incoming connections (from both clients and other servers) on port 6667, although some servers use other port numbers. Clients (and servers contacting other servers) use ports above 1023.

Clients use ports above 1023 to talk to other clients using DCC. To start, the calling client passes an invitation to the called client through the normal IRC server channels. The invitation includes a TCP port number where the calling client is listening for an incoming connection. The called client, if it chooses to accept the invitation, opens a TCP connection to that port.

Direction	Source Addr.	Dest. Addr.	Protocol	Source Port	Dest. Port	ACK Set	Notes
In	Ext	Int	TCP	>1023	6667	[a]	External client or server contacting internal server
Out	Int	Ext	TCP	6667	>1023	Yes	Internal server answering external client or server
Out	Int	Ext	TCP	>1023	6667	[a]	Internal client or server contacting external server
In	Ext	Int	TCP	6667	>1023	Yes	External server answering internal client or server
In	Ext	Int	TCP	>1023	>1023	[a]	DCC connection requested by internal client; external client answering invitation from internal client
Out	Int	Ext	TCP	>1023	>1023	Yes	DCC connection requested by internal client
Out	Int	Ext	TCP	>1023	>1023	[a]	DCC connection requested by external client; internal client answering invitation from external client
In	Ext	Int	TCP	>1023	>1023	Yes	DCC connection requested by external client

[a] ACK is not set on the first packet of this type (establishing connection) but will be set on the rest.

Proxying characteristics of IRC

Because of the spanning tree architecture, any IRC server serves as a proxy server. To configure IRC for proxying, simply put an IRC server on the proxy host and point your internal clients at it.

Summary of IRC recommendations

- Although it's theoretically possible to proxy IRC, or to allow just IRC through filters, it's probably not a good idea, because of the weaknesses of the clients. The best way to allow IRC is to put an untrusted victim machine with no confidential data on a perimeter network and let users log into that machine to run IRC.

- If you run an internal IRC server, be sure it can't contact or be contacted by external IRC servers; otherwise it will effectively proxy for your IRC clients and for attacks against them from the outside.

- If you do allow IRC across your firewall, you can't allow DCC connections to be requested by internal clients, because that would involve accepting incoming TCP connections from external clients to any port above 1023 on the internal machines. You could allow internal clients to establish DCC connections requested by external clients, however, if you're willing to let internal machines talk to any TCP port above 1023 on any external machine.

The Multicast Backbone (MBONE)

Most network technologies provide a way for a sending station to address a message to a particular receiving station: this is called *unicasting*. Many network technologies also provide a way for a sending station to address a message to all possible receiving stations: this is called *broadcasting*. Some network technologies also provide something in the middle, a way for a sending station to address a message to a particular set of receiving stations, without broadcasting the message to all stations: this is called *multicasting*.

Multicasting is particularly useful when you're dealing with high-bandwidth applications like audio and video conferencing. With such applications, you may have a number of stations all receiving the same stream of packets, and the stream may consume a significant fraction of the available network bandwidth. If a given stream consumes 10% of your available network bandwidth (which is not uncommon), you wouldn't want to unicast it to each interested host, because each of these unicasts would consume another 10% of your bandwidth, limiting you to 10 participating hosts, and that assumes that you did nothing else with the network. You also wouldn't want to broadcast it to all hosts unless all (or almost all) of your hosts were actually interested in the stream, because it places a significant load on each host to process a broadcast packet and then decide to ignore it.

IP multicasting provides a way to send packets to groups of IP hosts. With IP multicasting, groups of hosts that wish to receive a particular type of packet (e.g., a particular video stream) are assigned an IP multicast address they all share. An IP multicast address looks like a normal IP address in the range 224.0.0.0 through 239.255.255.255. IP multicast addresses are only used as destination addresses; they are never valid as source addresses (multicast packets use the regular IP address of the sending host as their source address).

Multicast groups are somewhat like cable television channels. There are a variety of channels (multicast groups) available, such as HBO, CNN, ESPN, and MTV, but most homes (hosts) subscribe to only a few of the available channels. Some multi-cast groups are permanent; that is, certain addresses are reserved for certain uses, such as Internet Engineering Task Force (IETF) meetings, NASA select video feeds (whenever the space shuttle is in orbit), and so on. Other multicast groups are transient: set up for a particular purpose or event and then shut down when they are no longer needed, to be reused for something else later on.

Multicasting is being used on the Internet today primarily for real-time conferencing services, including video, audio, and electronic whiteboard services. It's starting to be used for other services as well, such as transmitting Usenet news efficiently to a wide body of recipients.

Commercial products, such as routers and hosts, are just starting to support multicasting. Some networking technologies such as Ethernet support multicast directly. You can send an Ethernet packet of information to a magic Ethernet address on a given Ethernet segment, and all hosts on that segment that are listening for that Ethernet address will receive that packet. Other networking technologies, e.g., point-to-point leased lines, don't support multicast, so the effect has to be faked by turning a multicast packet into a series of duplicate unicast packets, each addressed to one of the multicast participants.

Obviously, you want to limit the number of duplicate unicast packets on these point-to-point leased lines, so a common approach to linking two multicast-capable networks (such as Ethernets) over a unicast-only network (such as a T1 leased line) is to create a *tunnel* over the unicast network, with multicast routers (often called *mrouters*) at either end of the tunnel. These *mrouters* take multicast IP packets, encapsulate them into unicast IP packets, and send them (via regular IP unicast) through the tunnel to the *mrouter* on the other end, which unencapsulates them to turn them back into multicast IP packets. By creating a web of *mrouters* and tunnels, you can create a virtual multicast network on top of a unicast backbone.

The MBONE is the ad hoc Multicast Backbone on the Internet, and is just such a web of *mrouters* and tunnels. Its participants are sites that are interested in using IP multicasting for a variety of services on the Internet.

IP multicasting brings up several firewall issues. If a site uses tunneling to take part in the MBONE, what do the packets for the tunnels look like? What could be sent through the tunnels? If a site doesn't use tunnels, but uses IP multicasting directly, how will the site's packet filtering system deal with it? Can nonmulticast services (such as SMTP, NFS, NIS/YP, and so on) be accessed by attackers via multicast, whether tunneled or not?

IP multicast tunneling is currently done with IP-in-IP encapsulation. That is, a multicast IP packet is encapsulated into a regular IP packet, in much the same way that a TCP or UDP packet normally is. Instead of the usual IP packet containing a

UDP packet, for example, you have an IP unicast packet that contains an IP multicast packet that, in turn, contains a UDP packet. Thus, if tunneled multicast packets need to cross a packet filtering system, the system needs to recognize IP-in-IP packets, in much the same way that it recognizes TCP, UDP, and ICMP packets. If your packet filtering system doesn't recognize IP-in-IP by name, but will allow you to specify protocol numbers instead, you need to know that IP-in-IP is protocol number 4 (for comparison, ICMP is 1, TCP is 6, and UDP is 17).

IP multicast tunnels used to be done with source-routed IP packets, but this practice caused a number of problems (not the least of which was upsetting folks who had firewalls), and it is no longer recommended.

To prevent a multicast tunnel from being used as a back door into or out of a network, the current publicly available *mrouter* code will only accept multicast packets through the tunnel; it won't accept unicast packets shoved through the tunnel in an attempt to bypass your firewall. If you're using a commercial multicast router, rather than the publicly available code off the Internet, you should verify that it will behave in a similar way.

If you have routers and a network topology that support multicast directly, without tunnels, you still have to worry about how any packet filtering system you use is going to cope with it. It shouldn't be too difficult, though, because from a packet filtering point of view, multicast packets just look like regular packets with somewhat unusual destination addresses (in the range 224.0.0.0 through 239.255.255.255). Treat them just as you would anything else: block them all by default and allow the ones you understand and want to support. Keep in mind that each of these multicast addresses is going to apply to multiple internal machines, and that if you're accepting multicast packets from the outside world, then all of the internal machines that are accepting those packets will have to be protected against attack from the outside world—just as if you were accepting any other packets directly from the outside world.

Even if your tunnel is restricted to only multicast packets, or if you're using multicast directly without tunneling, there is still the question of how your hosts will respond to multicast packets addressed to regular ports, such as your NIS/YP and NFS ports. Unfortunately, behavior varies from operating system to operating system, and even from release to release within the same operating system. If your operating system's code is based on Release 3.3 or later of the "IP Multicast Extensions for BSD-Derived UNIX Systems" from Xerox PARC and the University of Delaware, then your system should be safe against these kinds of attacks. Unless you installed the multicast extensions yourself, however, you could have a very difficult time determining what your operating system's multicast code is based on. (Your best bet is to ask your vendor, but don't be surprised if it's difficult to find anybody who knows.)

Domain Name System (DNS)

DNS is a distributed database system that translates hostnames to IP addresses and IP addresses to hostnames (e.g., it translates hostname *miles.somewhere.net* to IP address 192.168.244.34). DNS is also the standard Internet mechanism for storing and accessing several other kinds of information about hosts; it provides information about a particular host to the world at large. For example, if a host cannot receive mail directly, but another machine will receive mail for it and pass it on, that information is communicated with an MX record in DNS.

DNS clients include any program that needs to do any of the following:

- Translate a hostname to an IP address
- Translate an IP address to a hostname
- Obtain other published information about a host (such as its MX record)

Fundamentally, any program that uses hostnames can be a DNS client. This includes essentially every program that has anything to do with networking, including both client and server programs for Telnet, SMTP, FTP, and almost any other network service. DNS is thus a fundamental networking service, upon which other network services rely.

Other protocols may be used to provide this kind of information. For example, NIS/YP is used to provide host information within a network. However, DNS is the service used for this purpose across the Internet, and clients that need to access Internet hosts will have to use DNS, directly or indirectly. On networks that use NIS/YP or other methods internally, the server for the other protocol usually acts as a DNS proxy for the client. Many clients can also be configured to use multiple services, so that if a host lookup fails, it will retry using another method. Thus, it might start by looking in NIS/YP, which will show only local hosts, but try DNS if that fails, or it might start by looking in DNS, and then try a file on its own disk if that fails (so that you can put in personal favorite names, for example).

In UNIX, DNS is implemented by the Berkeley Internet Name Domain (BIND). On the client side is the resolver, a library of routines called by network processes. On the server side is a daemon called *named* (also known as *in.named* on some systems).

DNS is designed to forward queries and responses between clients and servers, so that servers may act on behalf of clients or other servers. This capability is very important to your ability to build a firewall that handles DNS services securely.

How does DNS work? Essentially, when a client needs a particular piece of information (e.g., the IP address of host *ftp.somewhere.net*), it asks its local DNS server for that information. The local DNS server first examines its own cache to see if it already knows the answer to the client's query. If not, the local DNS server asks other DNS servers, in turn, to discover the answer to the client's query. When the local DNS server gets the answer (or decides that it can't for some reason), it caches any information it got[*] and answers the client. For example, to find the IP address for *ftp.somewhere.net*, the local DNS server first asks one of the public root nameservers which machines are nameservers for the *com* domain. It then asks one of those *com* nameservers which machines are nameservers for the *somewhere.net* domain, and then it asks one of those nameservers for the IP address of *ftp.somewhere.net*.

This asking and answering is all transparent to the client. As far as the client is concerned, it has communicated only with the local server. It doesn't know or care that the local server may have contacted several other servers in the process of answering the original question.

Packet Filtering Characteristics of DNS

There are two types of DNS network activities: lookups and zone transfers. *Lookups* occur when a DNS client (or a DNS server acting on behalf of a client) queries a DNS server for information, e.g., the IP address for a given hostname, the hostname for a given IP address, the name server for a given domain, or the mail exchanger for a given host. *Zone transfers* occur when a DNS server (the secondary server) requests from another DNS server (the primary server) everything the primary server knows about a given piece of the DNS naming tree (the zone). Zone transfers happen only among servers that are supposed to be providing the same information; a server won't try to do a zone transfer from a random other server under normal circumstances. People occasionally do zone transfers in order to gather information (this is OK when they're calculating what the most popular hostname on the Internet is, but bad when they're trying to find out what hosts to attack at your site).

For performance reasons, DNS lookups are usually executed using UDP. If some of the data is lost in transit by UDP (remember that UDP doesn't guarantee delivery), the lookup will be redone using TCP. There may be other exceptions; for example, machines running IBM's AIX operating system always use TCP, even for the initial query. Figure 8-13 shows a DNS name lookup.

A DNS server uses well-known port 53 for all its UDP activities and as its server port for TCP. It uses a random port above 1023 for TCP requests. A DNS client uses a random port above 1023 for both UDP and TCP. You can thus differentiate between the following:

• A client-to-server query—source port is above 1023, destination port is 53.

---

[*] Some servers will cache the fact that the query failed, on some types of failures; others cache only information retrieved on a successful query.

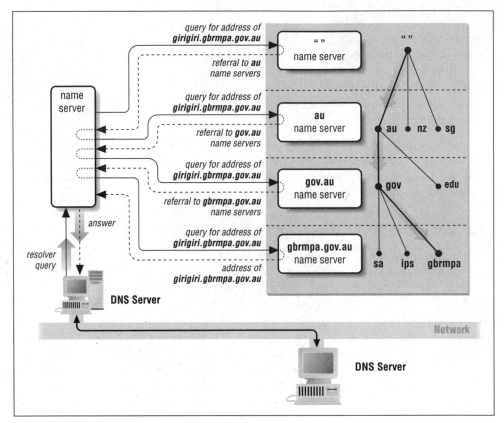

Figure 8–13: DNS name lookup

- A server-to-client response—source port is 53, destination port is above 1023.

- A server-to-server query or response—at least with UDP, where both source and destination port are 53; with TCP, the requesting server will use a port above 1023.

DNS zone transfers are performed using TCP. The connection is initiated from a random port above 1023 on the secondary server (which requests the data) to port 53 on the primary server (which sends the data requested by the secondary). A secondary server must also do a regular DNS query of a primary server to decide when to do a zone transfer. Figure 8-14 shows a DNS zone transfer.

Direction	Source Addr.	Dest. Addr.	Protocol	Source Port	Dest. Port	ACK Set	Notes
In	Ext	Int	UDP	>1023	53	[a]	Incoming query via UDP, client to server
Out	Int	Ext	UDP	53	>1023	[a]	Answer to incoming UDP query, server to client
In	Ext	Int	TCP	>1023	53	[b]	Incoming query via TCP, client to server
Out	Int	Ext	TCP	53	>1023	Yes	Answer to incoming TCP query, server to client
Out	Int	Ext	UDP	>1023	53	[a]	Outgoing query via UDP, client to server
In	Ext	Int	UDP	53	>1023	[a]	Answer to outgoing UDP query, server to client
Out	Int	Ext	TCP	>1023	53	[a]	Outgoing query via TCP, client to server
In	Ext	Int	TCP	53	>1023	Yes	Answer to outgoing TCP query, server to client
In	Ext	Int	UDP	53	53	[a]	Query or response between two servers via UDP
Out	Int	Ext	UDP	53	53	[a]	Query or response between two servers via UDP
In	Ext	Int	TCP	>1023	53	[b]	Query from external server to internal server via TCP; also zone transfer request from external secondary server via TCP
Out	Int	Ext	TCP	53	>1023	Yes	Answer from internal server to external server via TCP; also zone transfer response to external secondary server via TCP
Out	Int	Ext	TCP	>1023	53	[b]	Query from internal server to external server via TCP
In	Ext	Int	TCP	53	>1023	Yes	Answer from external server to internal server via TCP

[a] UDP packets do not have ACK bits.
[b] ACK is not set on the first packet of this type (establishing connection) but will be set on the rest.

Proxying Characteristics of DNS

DNS is structured so that servers always act as proxies for clients. It's also possible to use a DNS feature called *forwarding* so that a DNS server is effectively a proxy for another server. The remainder of this DNS discussion describes the use of these built-in proxying features of DNS.

In most implementations, it would be possible to modify the DNS libraries to use a modified-client proxy. On machines that do not support dynamic linking, using a modified-client proxy for DNS would require recompiling every network-aware program. Because users don't directly specify server information for DNS, modified-procedure proxies seem nearly impossible.

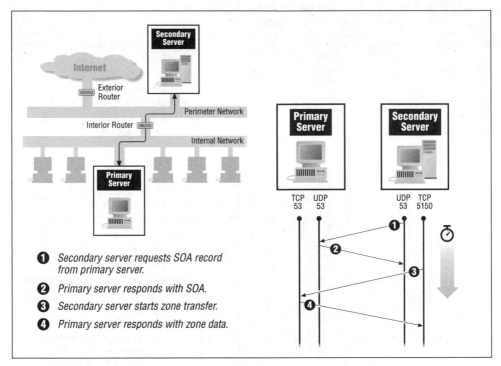

Figure 8–14: DNS zone transfer

DNS Data

The DNS is a tree-structured database, with servers for various subtrees scattered throughout the Internet. There are a number of defined record types in the tree, including:[*]

Record Type	Usage
A	Translates hostname to IP address
PTR	Translates IP address to hostname
CNAME	Translates host alias to hostname ("canonical" name)
HINFO	Gives hardware/software information about a host
NS	Delegates a zone of the DNS tree to some other server
SOA	Denotes start of authority for a zone of the DNS tree
TXT	Unstructured text records

In fact, there are two separate DNS data trees: one for obtaining information by hostname (such as the IP address, CNAME record, HINFO record, or TXT record that

---

* For detailed information about DNS record types, what they mean, and how to use them, see *DNS and BIND*, referenced earlier in this chapter.

corresponds to a given hostname), and one for obtaining information by IP address (the hostname for a given address).

For example, here is a sample of the DNS data for a fake domain *somebody.net*:

```
somebody.net. IN SOA tiger.somebody.net.root.tiger.somebody.net. (
                        1001        ; serial number
                        36000       ; refresh (10 hr)
                        3600        ; retry (1 hr)
                        3600000     ; expire (1000 hr)
                        36000       ; default ttl (10 hr)
                        )
                IN  NS      tiger.somebody.net.
                IN  NS      lion.somebody.net.
    tiger       IN  A       192.168.2.34
                IN  MX      5 tiger.somebody.net.
                IN  MX      10 lion.somebody.net.
                IN  HINFO   INTEL-486 BSDI
    ftp         IN  CNAME   tiger.somebody.net.
    lion        IN  A       192.168.2.35
                IN  MX      5 lion.somebody.net.
                IN  MX      10 tiger.somebody.net.
                IN  HINFO   SUN-3 SUNOS
    www         IN  CNAME   lion.somebody.net.
    wais        IN  CNAME   lion.somebody.net.
    alaska      IN  NS      bear.alaska.somebody.net.
    bear.alaska IN  A       192.168.2.81
```

This domain would also need a corresponding set of PTR records to map IP addresses back to hostnames. To translate an IP address to a hostname, you reverse the components of the IP address, append *.IN-ADDR.ARPA*, and look up the DNS PTR record for that name. For example, to translate IP address 1.2.3.4, you would look up the PTR record for *4.3.2.1.IN-ADDR.ARPA*.

```
2.168.192.IN-ADDR.ARPA. IN  SOA tiger.somebody.net.root.tiger.somebody.net. (
                        1001        ; serial number
                        36000       ; refresh (10 hr)
                        3600        ; retry (1 hr)
                        3600000     ; expire (1000 hr)
                        36000       ; default ttl (10 hr)
                        )
                IN  NS  tiger.somebody.net.
                IN  NS  lion.somebody.net.
    34          IN  PTR tiger.somebody.net.
    35          IN  PTR lion.somebody.net.
    81          IN  PTR bear.alaska.somebody.net.
```

DNS Security Problems

There are some security problems with DNS that are described below.

Bogus answers to DNS queries

The first security problem with DNS is that many DNS servers and clients can be tricked by an attacker into believing bogus information. Many clients and servers don't check to see whether all the answers they get relate to questions they actually asked, or whether the answers they get are coming from the server they asked. Servers, in particular, may cache these "extra" answers without really thinking about it, and answer later queries with this bogus cached data. This lack of checking can allow an attacker to give false data to your clients and servers. For example, an attacker could use this capability to load your server's cache with information that says that his IP address maps to the hostname of a host you trust for password-less access via *rlogin*. (This is only one of several reasons you shouldn't allow the BSD "r" commands across your firewall; see the full discussion of these commands earlier in this chapter.)

NOTE

Later versions of DNS for UNIX (BIND 4.9 and later) check for bogus answers and are less susceptible to these problems. Earlier versions, and DNS clients and servers for other platforms, may still be susceptible.

Mismatched data between the hostname and IP address DNS trees

The attack described in the previous section points out the problem of mismatched data between the hostname and IP address trees in the DNS. In a case like the one we've described, if you look up the hostname corresponding to the attacker's IP address (this is called a *reverse lookup*), you get back the name of a host you trust. If you then look up the IP address of this hostname (which is called a *double-reverse lookup*), you should see that the IP address doesn't match the one the attacker is using. This should alert you that something suspicious is going on. Reverse and double-reverse lookups are described in more detail in the section called "Set up a 'fake' DNS server on the bastion host for the outside world to use" later in this DNS discussion.

Any program that makes authentication or authorization decisions based on the hostname information it gets from DNS should be very careful to validate the data with this reverse lookup/double-reverse lookup method. In some operating systems (for example, SunOS 4.x and later), this check is automatically done for you by the *gethostbyaddr()* library function. In most other operating systems, you have to do the check yourself. Make sure that you know which approach your own operating system takes and make sure that the daemons that are making such decisions in your system do the appropriate validation. (And be sure you're pre-serving this functionality if you modify or replace the vendor's *libc*.) Better yet, don't do any authentication or authorization based solely on hostname or even on IP address; there is no way to be sure that a packet comes from the IP address it claims to come from, unless there is some kind of cryptographic authentication within the packet that only the true source could have generated.

Some implementations of double-reverse lookup fail on hosts with multiple addresses, e.g., dual-homed hosts used for proxying. If both addresses are regis-tered at the same name, a DNS lookup by name will return both of them, but many programs will read only the first. If the connection happened to come from the second address, the double-reverse will incorrectly fail even though the host is correctly registered. Although you should avoid using double-reverse implementa-tions that have this flaw, you may also want to ensure that on your externally visi-ble multi-homed hosts, lookup by address returns a different name for each address, and that those names have only one address returned when it is looked up. For example, for a host named "foo" with two interfaces named "e0" and "e1", have lookups of "foo" return both addresses, lookups of "foo-e0" and "foo-e1" return only the address of that interface, and lookups by IP address return "foo-e0" or "foo-e1" (but not simply "foo") as appropriate.

NOTE

> For internal multi-homed hosts, you probably don't want to set things up in the way we've described; if you do, you may end up needing to list them by multiple names anywhere you want to give them permis-sions, such as in */etc/exports* files.

Revealing too much information to attackers

Another problem you may encounter when supporting DNS with a firewall is that it may reveal information that you don't want revealed. Some organizations view internal hostnames (as well as other information about internal hosts) as confiden-tial information. They want to protect these host names much as they do their internal telephone directories. They're nervous because internal hostnames may reveal project names or other product intelligence, or because these names may reveal the type of the hosts (which may make an attack easier). For example, it's easy to guess what kind of system something is if its name is "lab-sun" or "cisco-gw".

Even the simplest hostname information can be helpful to an attacker who wants to bluff his way into your site, physically or electronically. Using information in this way is an example of what is commonly called a *social engineering* attack. The attacker first examines the DNS data to determine the name of a key host or hosts at your site. Such hosts will often be listed as DNS servers for the domain, or as MX gateways for lots of other hosts. Next, the attacker calls or visits your site, posing as a service technician, and says he needs to work on these hosts. He'll either ask for the passwords for the hosts (if he calls on the telephone), or ask to be shown to the machine room (if he visits the site). Because the attacker seems legitimate, and seems to have inside information about the site—after all, he knows the names of your key hosts—he'll often gain access. Social engineering attacks like this takes a lot of brazenness on the part of the attacker, particularly if he actually visits your site, but you'd be amazed at how often such attacks succeed.

Besides internal hostnames, other information is often placed within the DNS; information which is useful locally, but which you'd really rather an attacker not have access to. DNS HINFO and TXT resource records are particularly revealing:

HINFO: Host information records
> These name the hardware and operating system release that a machine is running. Such information is very useful for system and network administrators, but it also tells an attacker exactly which list of bugs to try when attacking that machine.

TXT: Textual information records
> These are essentially short unformatted text records used by a variety of different services to provide various information. For example, some versions of Kerberos and related tools use these records to store information that, at another site, might be handled by NIS/YP.

Attackers will often obtain DNS information about your site wholesale by contacting your DNS server and asking for a zone transfer, as if they were a secondary server for your site. You can either prevent this with packet filtering (by blocking TCP-based DNS queries, which will unfortunately block more than just zone transfers) or through the *xfernets* directive of current implementations of BIND (see the BIND documentation for more information).

The question to keep in mind when considering what DNS data to reveal is, "Why give attackers any more information than necessary?" The following sections provide some suggestions to help you ensure you reveal only the data you want people to have.

Setting Up DNS to Hide Information

We've mentioned that DNS has a query-forwarding capability. By taking advantage of this capability, you can give internal hosts an unrestricted view of both internal and external DNS data, while restricting external hosts to a very limited ("sanitized") view of internal DNS data. You might want to do this for such reasons as:

- Because you feel that your internal DNS data is too sensitive to show to everybody.

- Because you know that your internal DNS servers don't all work perfectly and you want a better-maintained view for the outside world.

- Because you want to give certain information to external hosts and different information to internal hosts (for example, you want internal hosts to send mail directly to internal machines, but external hosts to see an MX record directing the mail to a bastion host).

Figure 8-15 shows how to set up DNS to hide information; the following sections describe all the details.

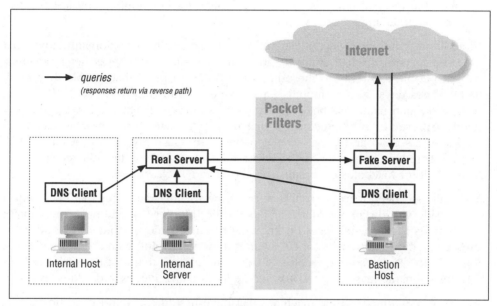

Figure 8–15: A firewall can be used to hide DNS information

Set up a 'fake' DNS server on the bastion host for the outside world to use

The first step in hiding DNS information from the external world is to set up a fake DNS server on a bastion host. This server claims to be authoritative for your domain. Make it the server for your domain that is named by the Name Server records maintained by your parent domain. If you have multiple such servers for the outside world to talk to (which you should—some or all of the rest may belong to your service provider), make your fake server the primary server of the set of authoritative servers; make the others secondaries of this primary server.

As far as this fake server on the bastion host is aware, it knows everything about your domain. In fact, though, all it knows about is whatever information you want revealed to the outside world. This information typically includes only basic host-name and IP address information about the following hosts:

- The machines on your perimeter network (i.e., the machines that make up your firewall).

- Any machines that somebody in the outside world needs to be able to contact directly. One example of such a machine is an internal Usenet news (NNTP) server that is reachable from your service provider. (See the section on NNTP elsewhere in this chapter for an example of why you might want to allow this.) Another example is any host reachable over the Internet from trusted affiliates. External machines need an externally visible name for such an internal machine; it need not be the internal machine's real name, however, if you feel that the real name is somehow sensitive information, or you just want to be able to change it on a whim.

In addition, you'll need to publish MX records for any host or domain names that are used as part of email addresses in email messages and Usenet news postings, so that people can reply to these messages. Keep in mind that people may reply to messages days, weeks, months, or even years after they were sent. If a given host or domain name has been widely used as part of an email address, you may need to preserve an MX record for that host or domain forever, or at least until well after it's dead and gone, so that people can still reply to old messages. If it has appeared in print, "forever" may be all too accurate; sites still receive electronic mail for machines decommissioned five and 10 years ago.

You will also need to publish fake information for any machines that can contact the outside world directly. Many servers on the Internet (for example, most major anonymous FTP servers) insist on knowing the hostname (not just the IP address) of any machines that contact them, even if they do nothing with the hostname but log it. In the DNS resource records, A (name-to-address mapping) records and PTR (address-to-name mapping) records handle lookups for names and addresses.

As we've mentioned earlier, machines that have IP addresses and need hostnames do reverse lookups. With a reverse lookup, the server starts with the remote IP address of the incoming connection, and looks up the hostname that the connection is coming from. It takes the IP address (for example, 172.16.19.67), permutes it in a particular way (reverses the parts and adds *.IN-ADDR.ARPA* to get *67.19.16.172.IN-ADDR.ARPA*, and looks up a PTR record for that name. The PTR record should return the hostname for the host with that address (e.g., *mycroft.somewhere.net*), which the server then uses for its logs or whatever.

How can you deal with these reverse lookups? If all these servers wanted was a name to log, you could simply create a wildcard PTR record. That record would indicate that a whole range of addresses belongs to an unknown host in a particular domain. For example, you might have a lookup for **.19.16.172.IN-ADDR.ARPA* return *unknown.somewhere.net*). Returning this information would be fairly helpful; it would at least tell the server administrator whose machine it was (*somewhere.net*'s). Anyone who had a problem with the machine could pursue it through the published contacts for the *somewhere.net* domain.

There is a problem with doing only this, however. In an effort to validate the data returned by the DNS, more and more servers (particularly anonymous FTP servers) are now doing a double-reverse lookup, and won't talk to you unless the double-reverse lookup succeeds. This is the same kind of lookup we mentioned above; it's certainly necessary for people who provide a service where they need any degree of authentication of the requesting host. Whether or not anonymous FTP is such a service is another question. Some people believe that once you put a file up for anonymous FTP, you no longer have reason to try to authenticate hosts; after all, you're trying to give information away. People running anonymous FTP servers that do double-reverse lookup argue that people who want services have a responsibility to be members of the network community and that requires being identifiable. Whichever side of the argument you're on, it is certainly true that the maintainers of several of the largest and best-known anonymous FTP servers are on the side that favors double-reverse lookup, and will not provide service to you unless double-reverse lookup succeeds.

In a double-reverse lookup, a DNS client:

- Performs a reverse lookup to translate an IP address to a hostname.

- Does a regular lookup on that hostname to determine its nominal IP address.

- Compares this nominal IP address to the original IP address.

Your fake server needs to provide consistent fake data for all hosts in your domain whose IP addresses are going to be seen by the outside world. For every IP address you own, the fake server must publish a PTR record with a fake hostname, as well as a corresponding A record that maps the fake hostname back to the IP address. For example, for address 172.16.1.2, you might publish a PTR record with the name *host-172-16-1-2.somewhere.net* and a corresponding A record which maps *host-172-16-1-2.somewhere.net* back to the corresponding IP address (172.16.1.2). When you connect to some remote system that attempts to do a reverse lookup of your IP address (e.g., 172.16.1.2) to determine your hostname, that system will get back the fake hostname (e.g., *host-172-16-1-2*). If the system then attempts to do a double-reverse lookup to translate that hostname to an IP address, it will get back 172.16.1.2, which matches the original IP address and satisfies the consistency check.

If you are strictly using proxying to connect internal hosts to the external world, you don't need to set up the fake information for your internal hosts; you simply need to put up information for the host or hosts running the proxy server. The external world will see only the proxy server's address. For a large network, this by itself may make using proxy service for FTP worthwhile.

Set up a real DNS server on an internal system for internal hosts to use

Your internal machines need to use the real DNS information about your hosts, not the fake information presented to the outside world. You do this through a standard DNS server setup on some internal system. Your internal machines may also want to find out about external machines, though, e.g., to translate the hostname of a remote anonymous FTP site to an IP address.

One way to accomplish this is to provide access to external DNS information by configuring your internal DNS server to query remote DNS servers directly, as appropriate, to resolve queries from internal clients about external hosts. Such a configuration, however, would require opening your packet filtering to allow your internal DNS server to talk to these remote DNS servers (which might be on any host on the Internet). This is a problem because DNS is UDP-based, and as we discuss in Chapter 6, you need to block UDP altogether in order to block outside access to vulnerable RPC-based services like NFS and NIS/YP.

Fortunately, the most common DNS server (the UNIX *named* program) provides a solution to this dilemma: the *forwarders* directive in the */etc/named.boot* server configuration file. The *forwarders* directive tells the server that, if it doesn't know the information itself already (either from its own zone information or from its cache), it should forward the query to a specific server and let this other server figure out the answer, rather than try to contact servers all over the Internet in an attempt to determine the answer itself. In the */etc/named.boot* configuration file, you set up the *forwarders* line to point to the fake server on the bastion host; the file also needs to contain a "slave" line, to tell it to only use the servers on the *forwarders* line, even if the *forwarders* are slow in answering.

The use of the *forwarders* mechanism doesn't really have anything to do with hiding the information in the internal DNS server; it has everything to do with making the packet filtering as strict as possible (i.e., applying the principle of least privilege), by making it so that the internal DNS server need only be able to talk to the bastion host DNS server, not to DNS servers throughout the whole Internet.

If internal hosts can't contact external hosts, you may not want to bother setting things up so that they can resolve external host names. SOCKS proxy clients can be set up to use the external name server directly. This simplifies your name service configuration somewhat, but it complicates your proxying configuration, and some users may want to resolve hostnames even though they can't reach them (for example, they may be interested in knowing whether the hostname in an email address is valid).

Figure 8-16 shows how DNS works with forwarding; Figure 8-17 shows how it works without forwarding.

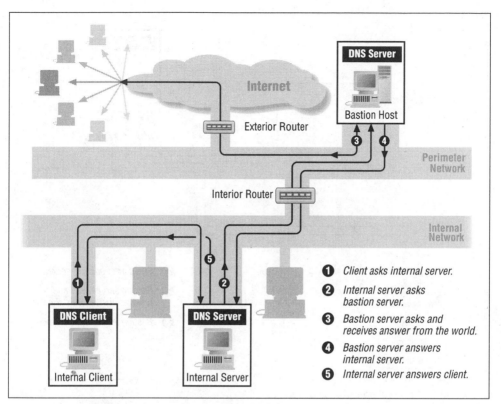

Figure 8–16: DNS with forwarding

Internal DNS clients query the internal server

The next step is to configure your internal DNS clients to ask all their queries of the internal server. On UNIX systems, you do this through the */etc/resolv.conf* file. There are two cases:

- When the internal server receives a query about an internal system, or about an external system which is in its cache, it answers directly and immediately because it already knows the answers to such queries.

- When the internal server receives a query about an external system that isn't in its cache, the internal server forwards this query to the bastion host server (because of the *forwarders* line described above). The bastion host server obtains the answer from the appropriate DNS servers on the Internet and relays the answer back to the internal server. The internal server then answers the original client and caches the answer.

In either case, as far as the client is concerned, it asked a question of the internal server and got an answer from the internal server. The client doesn't know whether the internal server already knew the answer or had to obtain the answer

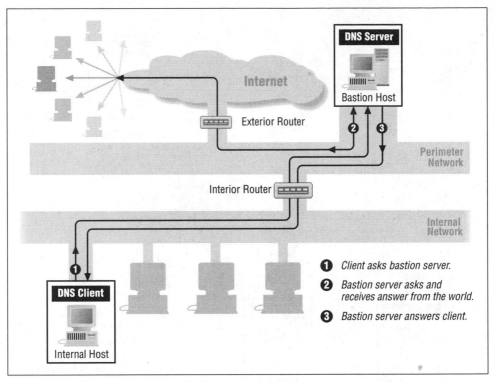

Figure 8–17: DNS without forwarding

from other servers (indirectly, via the bastion server). Therefore, the */etc/resolv.conf* file will look perfectly standard on internal clients.

Bastion DNS clients also query the internal server

The key to this whole information-hiding configuration is that DNS clients on the bastion host must query the internal server for information, not the server on the bastion host. This way, DNS clients on the bastion host (such as Sendmail, for example) can use the real hostnames and so on for internal hosts, but clients in the outside world can't access the internal data.

DNS server and client configurations are completely separate. Many people assume that they must have configuration files in common, that the clients will automatically know about the local server, and that pointing them elsewhere will also point the server elsewhere. In fact, there is no overlap. Clients never read */etc/named.boot*, which tells the server what to do, and the server never reads */etc/resolv.conf*, which tells the clients what to do.

Again, there are two cases:

- When a DNS client on the bastion host asks about an internal system, it gets the real answer directly from the internal server.

- When a DNS client on the bastion host asks about an external system, the internal DNS server forwards the query to the bastion DNS server. The bastion server obtains the answer from the appropriate DNS servers on the Internet, and then relays the answer back to the internal server. The internal server, in turn, answers the original client on the bastion host.

DNS clients on the bastion host could obtain information about external hosts more directly by asking the DNS server on the bastion host instead of the one on the internal host. However, if they did that, they'd be unable to get the "real" internal information, which only the server on the internal host has. They're going to need that information, because they're talking to the internal hosts as well as the external hosts.

What your packet filtering system needs to allow

In order for this DNS forwarding scheme to work, any packet filtering system between the bastion host and the internal systems has to allow all of the following (see the table below for details):

- DNS queries from the internal server to the bastion host server: UDP packets from port 53 on the internal server to port 53 on the bastion host (rule A), and TCP packets from ports above 1023 on the internal server to port 53 on the bastion host (rule B).

- Responses to those queries from the bastion host to the internal server: UDP packets from port 53 on the bastion host to port 53 on the internal server (rule C), and TCP packets with the ACK bit set from port 53 on the bastion host to ports above 1023 on the internal server (rule D).

- DNS queries from the bastion host DNS clients to the internal server: UDP and TCP packets from ports above 1023 on the bastion host to port 53 on the internal server (rules E and F).

- Responses from the internal server to those bastion host DNS clients: UDP packets and TCP packets with the ACK bit set from port 53 on the internal server to ports above 1023 on the bastion host (Rules G and H).

Rule	Direction	Source Addr.	Dest. Addr.	Protocol	Source Port	Dest. Port	ACK Set	Action
A	Out	Internal Server	Bastion Host	UDP	53	53	[a]	Permit
B	Out	Internal Server	Bastion Host	TCP	>1023	53	Any	Permit
C	In	Bastion Host	Internal Server	UDP	53	53	[a]	Permit

Rule	Direction	Source Addr.	Dest. Addr.	Protocol	Source Port	Dest. Port	ACK Set	Action
D	In	Bastion Host	Internal Server	TCP	53	>1023	Yes	Permit
E	In	Bastion Host	Internal Server	UDP	>1023	53	a	Permit
F	In	Bastion Host	Internal Server	TCP	>1023	53	Any	Permit
G	Out	Internal Server	Bastion Host	UDP	53	>1023	a	Permit
H	Out	Internal Server	Bastion Host	TCP	53	>1023	Yes	Permit

a UDP packets do not have ACK bits.

Setting up DNS Without Hiding Information

The approach we've described above is not the only option. Suppose that you don't feel it's necessary to hide your internal DNS data from the world. In this case, your DNS configuration is similar to the one we've described above, but it's somewhat simpler. Figure 8-18 shows how DNS works without information hiding.

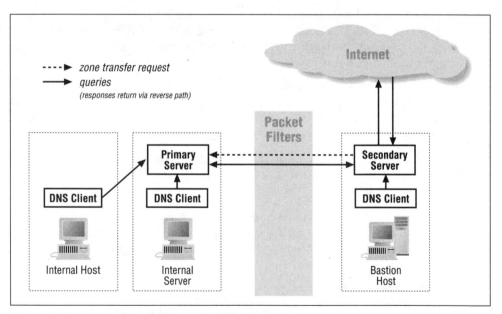

Figure 8–18: DNS without information hiding

With this alternate approach, you should still have a bastion host DNS server and an internal DNS server; however, one of these can be a secondary server of the other. Generally, it's easier to make the bastion DNS server a secondary of the internal DNS server, and to maintain your DNS data on the internal server. You should still configure the internal DNS server to forward queries to the bastion host DNS server, but the bastion host DNS clients can be configured to query the bastion host server instead of the internal server.

You need to configure any packet filtering system between the bastion host and the internal server to allow the following (see the table below for details):

- DNS queries from the internal DNS server to the bastion DNS server: UDP packets from port 53 on the internal server to port 53 on the bastion host (rule A) and TCP packets from ports above 1023 on the internal server to port 53 on the bastion host (rule B).

- Responses from the bastion DNS server to the internal DNS server: UDP packets from port 53 on the bastion host to port 53 on the internal server (rule C) and TCP packets with the ACK bit set from port 53 on the bastion host to ports above 1023 on the internal server (rule D).

If the bastion host is also a DNS secondary server and the internal host is the corresponding DNS primary server, you also have to allow the following:

- DNS queries from the bastion host DNS server to the internal DNS server: UDP packets from port 53 on the bastion host to port 53 on the internal server (note that this is the same as rule C), and TCP packets from ports above 1023 on the bastion host to port 53 on the internal server (rule E).

- Responses from the internal DNS server back to the bastion DNS server: UDP packets from port 53 on the internal server to port 53 on the bastion host (note that this is the same as rule A), and TCP packets with the ACK bit set from port 53 on the internal server to ports above 1023 on the bastion host (rule F).

- DNS zone transfer requests from the bastion host to the internal server: TCP packets from ports above 1023 on the bastion host to port 53 on the internal server (note that this is the same as rule E).

- DNS zone transfer responses from the internal server to the bastion host: TCP packets with the ACK bit set from port 53 on the internal server to ports above 1023 on the bastion host (note that this is the same as rule F).

Rule	Direction	Source Addr.	Dest. Addr.	Protocol	Source Port	Dest. Port	ACK Set	Action
A	Out	Internal Server	Bastion Host	UDP	53	53	[a]	Permit
B	Out	Internal Server	Bastion Host	TCP	>1023	53	Any	Permit

Rule	Direc- tion	Source Addr.	Dest. Addr.	Pro- tocol	Source Port	Dest. Port	ACK Set	Action
C	In	Bastion Host	Internal Server	UDP	53	53	a	Permit
D	In	Bastion Host	Internal Server	TCP	53	>1023	Yes	Permit
E	In	Bastion Host	Internal Server	TCP	>1023	53	Any	Permit
F	Out	Internal Server	Bastion Host	TCP	53	>1023	Yes	Permit

[a] UDP packets do not have ACK bits.

Summary of DNS Recommendations

- Set up an external DNS server on a bastion host for the outside world to access.

- Do not make HINFO records visible to the outside world; either don't use them, or configure DNS for information hiding as described above.

- Use an up-to-date BIND implementation and double-reverse lookups to avoid spoofing.

- Consider hiding all internal DNS data and using forwarding and fake records; this doesn't make sense for all sites, but it might for yours.

- Disable zone transfers to anyone but your secondaries, using packet filtering or the *xfernets* directive. Even if you've chosen not to hide your DNS informa- tion, there's probably no valid reason for anyone but your secondaries to do a zone transfer, and disallowing zone transfers makes life a bit harder for attack- ers.

syslog

syslog is used to manage log messages in a centralized way. *syslog* got its start as a way of centrally recording messages for a set of UNIX machines, but many net- work devices (routers, hubs, etc.) now use *syslog* to report status and usage infor- mation. Such devices often don't even have a way to record this information locally, because they don't have any writable storage media; if you want to know what they're reporting, something has to be listening to their *syslog* messages.

Attackers will often attempt to flood a site's *syslog* server in order to cover their tracks, so that the server runs out of disk space and stops logging new messages, or so that the evidence of their activities is lost in the noise.

Packet Filtering Characteristics of syslog

syslog is a UDP-based service. *syslog* servers (which record messages logged by other systems) listen on UDP port 514. *syslog* clients generally (but not always) use ports above 1023 to talk to servers. *syslog* servers never send messages back to clients. *syslog* servers can be configured to pass messages along to other *syslog* servers; in such cases, the sending server generally uses port 514 as the client port.

Direc-tion	Source Addr.	Dest. Addr.	Pro-tocol	Source Port	Dest. Port	ACK Set	Notes
In	Ext	Int	UDP	>1023[a]	514	[b]	External client contacting internal *syslog* server
Out	Int	Ext	UDP	>1023[a]	514	[b]	Internal client contacting external *syslog* server
In	Ext	Int	UDP	514	514	[b]	External *syslog* server passing message to internal *syslog* server
Out	Int	Ext	UDP	514	514	[b]	Internal *syslog* server passing message to external *syslog* server

[a] Some *syslog* clients sometimes use ports below 1023.
[b] UDP packets do not have ACK bits.

Proxying Characteristics of syslog

syslog is a self-proxying protocol; that is, *syslog* servers can generally be configured to simply pass messages they receive on to other *syslog* servers.

Summary of syslog Recommendations

- Do not allow *syslog* in from the outside world. In this way, you'll prevent attackers from attempting to flood your *syslog* servers.

Network Management Services

This section describes a number of protocols that are used by people and programs to manage and maintain networks: SNMP, RIP, and ICMP—and, where appropriate, the tools, such as *ping* and *traceroute*, that use them.

Simple Network Management Protocol (SNMP)

SNMP is a standardized remote monitoring and management mechanism for network devices like hubs, routers, and bridges, as well as servers and workstations. The theory is that any SNMP-capable management station should be able to monitor and control any SNMP-capable network device.

Normally, SNMP management stations act as clients, contacting SNMP servers in the various network devices to request information or to issue commands. Sometimes, network devices act as SNMP clients to contact special SNMP servers (known as *trap* servers) on management stations to report critical information that can't wait until the next time the management station polls the device. SNMP trap servers are separate from regular SNMP servers so that a given machine can run both—that is, both an SNMP server (and thus be manageable via SNMP) and an SNMP trap server (and thus be a management station and receive traps from other devices).

In general, you don't want someone from the outside to be able to manage your network via SNMP. Therefore, you shouldn't allow SNMP to cross your firewall, and you should carefully configure (or disable) SNMP on your systems that are outside your firewall so that attackers can't use it to change that configuration.

SNMP does support some rudimentary security; when information is requested, the requester needs to specify a "community" that it's in. Different communities can be shown different information, and a reusable password can be required for certain communities. At its best, this is quite primitive security; anybody who's doing packet sniffing can easily discover a community name and password.

Not all SNMP devices support even this much. Fortunately, the most insecure SNMP features (for example, allowing SNMP clients to set parameters) are also the most complex to implement, and therefore the least often implemented. SNMP servers that don't implement passwords probably implement only straightforward queries. That may still give away information that you'd prefer not be made public, e.g., the addresses you're communicating with and presumably trust, or the precise amount of extra traffic you'd have to generate to bring down a gateway.

Packet filtering characteristics of SNMP

SNMP is a UDP-based service. SNMP servers (in network devices) listen on both TCP and UDP port 161. SNMP trap servers (in management stations) listen on both TCP and UDP port 162. SNMP clients generally use ports above 1023 to talk to both regular and trap servers.

Direction	Source Addr.	Dest. Addr.	Protocol	Source Port	Dest. Port	ACK Set	Notes
In	Ext	Int	UDP	>1023	161	[a]	External management station (client) contacting internal SNMP network device (server)
Out	Int	Ext	UDP	161	>1023	[a]	Internal SNMP network device (server) replying to external management station (client)
In	Ext	Int	TCP	>1023	161	[b]	External management station (client) contacting internal SNMP network device (server)

Direction	Source Addr.	Dest. Addr.	Protocol	Source Port	Dest. Port	ACK Set	Notes
Out	Int	Ext	TCP	161	>1023	Yes	Internal SNMP network device (server) replying to external management station (client)
Out	Int	Ext	UDP	>1023	161	[a]	Internal management station (client) contacting external SNMP network device (server)
In	Ext	Int	UDP	161	>1023	[a]	External SNMP network device (server) responding to internal management station (client)
Out	Int	Ext	TCP	>1023	161	[b]	Internal management station (client) contacting external SNMP network device (server)
In	Ext	Int	TCP	161	>1023	Yes	External SNMP network device (server) responding to internal management station (client)
In	Ext	Int	UDP	>1023	162	[a]	External network device (client) contacting internal SNMP management station (trap server)
Out	Int	Ext	UDP	162	>1023	[a]	Internal SNMP management station (trap server) replying to external network device (client)
In	Ext	Int	TCP	>1023	162	[b]	External network device (client) contacting internal SNMP management station (trap server)
Out	Int	Ext	TCP	162	>1023	Yes	Internal SNMP management station (trap server) replying to external network device (client)
Out	Int	Ext	UDP	>1023	162	[a]	Internal network device (client) contacting external SNMP management station (trap server)
In	Ext	Int	UDP	162	>1023	[a]	External SNMP management station (trap server) responding to internal network device (client)
Out	Int	Ext	TCP	>1023	162	[b]	Internal network device (client) contacting external SNMP management station (trap server)
In	Ext	Int	TCP	162	>1023	Yes	External SNMP management station (trap server) responding to internal network device (client)

[a] UDP packets do not have ACK bits.

[b] ACK will not be set on the first packet of this type (establishing connection) but will be set on the rest.

Proxying characteristics of SNMP

SNMP is not commonly used across the Internet, so proxies for it are not widely available. Although it is a straightforward single-connection protocol, it's often implemented in devices (like dedicated routers) for which source code and compilers are not readily available, making it almost impossible to use with a modified-client proxy system like SOCKS. It shouldn't be too difficult to make it work with modified-procedure proxy systems.

Routing Information Protocol (RIP)

RIP is the oldest routing protocol on the Internet. In fact, it predates IP; it was taken almost verbatim from the older Xerox Network Services (XNS) system. It is also still the most commonly used routing protocol on local area IP networks. Routers (including general-purpose machines with multiple interfaces, that can act as routers) use RIP to periodically broadcast which networks they know how to reach, and how far away those networks are. By listening to these broadcasts, a router or host can determine what networks are reachable and choose the best (shortest) path to each. RIP servers generally just broadcast this information every 30 seconds or so for anyone interested to hear, but a RIP client can request a special update from a RIP server, which will cause the server to reply directly to the client with the information requested.

Packet filtering characteristics of RIP

RIP is a UDP-based service. RIP servers listen on port 520 for broadcasts from other servers and requests from clients. RIP servers generally send their broadcasts from port 520. RIP clients generally use ports above 1023.

Direc-tion	Source Addr.	Dest. Addr.	Pro-tocol	Source Port	Dest. Port	ACK Set	Notes
In	Ext	Int	UDP	>1023	520	[a]	External client request to internal server
Out	Int	Ext	UDP	520	>1023	[a]	Internal server response to external client
Out	Int	Ext	UDP	>1023	520	[a]	Internal client request to external server
In	Int	Ext	UDP	520	>1023	[a]	External server response to internal client
In	Ext	Broad-cast	UDP	520	520	[a]	External server broadcasting to internal servers
Out	Int	Broad-cast	UDP	520	520	[a]	Internal server broadcasting to external servers

[a] UDP packets do not have ACK bits.

Proxying characteristics of RIP

Because RIP allows a host to develop routing tables that are specific to where that host is in the network, it doesn't make any sense to proxy RIP to another host elsewhere in the network.

ping

The *ping* program checks network connectivity. The *ping* application generates an ICMP "echo request" packet. The destination system responds with an ICMP "echo response" packet. ICMP is typically implemented in the kernel, so it's the kernel that generates the "echo response" packet; there is no separate server for ICMP on most systems. (On some machines, the echo response is actually generated in the network interface itself, not in the operating system, and the machine need not even be fully running to respond to *ping*.) *ping* is not the only program that uses ICMP echo; others include *spray* and almost any dedicated network management tool.

ping is a useful network trouble-shooting tool, and it is reasonably safe. You'll probably want to allow *ping* outbound from at least the machines your network operations staff uses and inbound from at least the network operations center machines of your network service provider.

Because of where it is implemented, it is almost impossible to disable replies to *ping* on individual hosts; packet filtering is the only way to control it.

There are two dangers in allowing ICMP echo:

* It can be used for a denial of service attack: that is, to flood your network. Although any protocol you accept can be used in this way, ICMP echo is particularly tempting, because there are commonly available programs designed for network testing (including some versions of *ping*) that let you flood networks with simple command line options.

* Anybody who can send ICMP echo requests to and receive ICMP echo responses from your network can discover how many machines you have, and what network addresses they're at; this increases the efficiency of any further attacks. That's why you want to limit requests to machines that have a legitimate reason to be probing your network.

Packet filtering characteristics of ping

Many packet filtering systems let you filter ICMP packets in much the same way as TCP or UDP packets: by specifying the ICMP message type code instead of the TCP or UDP source or destination port number. If your packet filtering system has this capability, its documentation should include a list of the ICMP numeric codes or keywords that the packet filtering system understands.

To allow the *ping* program to operate outbound (i.e., *ping*'ing remote hosts), you'll have to allow ICMP echo request packets outbound and ICMP echo response packets inbound. To allow inbound *ping* (i.e., a remote host *ping*'ing a local host), you'll have to allow ICMP echo request packets inbound and ICMP echo response packets outbound.

Direction	Source Addr.	Dest. Addr.	Protocol	Message Type[a]	Notes
In	Ext	Int	ICMP	8	Incoming *ping*
Out	Int	Ext	ICMP	0	Response to incoming *ping*
Out	Int	Ext	ICMP	8	Outgoing *ping*
In	Ext	Int	ICMP	0	Response to outgoing *ping*

[a] ICMP messages do not have source or destination port numbers; they have a single ICMP message type field instead. ICMP packets also do not have ACK bits.

Proxying characteristics of ping

Because *ping* is neither TCP nor UDP-based, it won't work with any widely available generic proxy server for modified-client proxying. Because *ping* transmits no user-supplied data to the destination host, modified-procedure proxying for *ping* is not possible. Modified-procedure proxying also relies on the ability of the proxy server to intercept the request before the machine it's running on generates a reply, which is difficult with *ping*. In a pure proxying environment, *ping* will have to be provided by letting users connect to the proxying host and run *ping* from there, as discussed in Chapter 7.

traceroute

traceroute is an application that shows you the route that packets take to a particular IP destination. Because no system typically knows the full path to the destination (merely the next step towards the destination), this is a neat trick.[*] *traceroute* works by carefully constructing special UDP packets. The destination address of the packets is the remote host; the destination port is an unused (or so we hope, as we'll discuss below) UDP port on the remote host. The really special thing about the packets, though, is that the "time to live" (TTL) fields are set very low (starting at 1), so that the packets will be rejected by intermediate routers as if they were looping in the network. By looking at where the rejections (ICMP "time to live exceeded" messages) come from, *traceroute* can determine who the intermediate routers are.

TTL is an IP header that normally isn't of interest from a firewall point of view. The name is somewhat misleading; it might be more intuitively called "hops to live." When a packet is first created, its TTL field is set to some value (typically 16, 30, or 255). Every router that handles the packet along its journey decrements the TTL field by 1. If the TTL field ever reaches 0, the packet is assumed to be in some sort of a loop; it is encapsulated within an ICMP "time to live exceeded" message, and is returned to the source address.

Thus, the first router that handles the first of *traceroute*'s specially constructed packets (which has a TTL of 1) will decrement the TTL field, see that it's 0, and

---

* *traceroute* is, fundamentally, a "cool hack."

return an ICMP "time to live exceeded" message, telling *traceroute* the IP address of the first router (the source of the ICMP message).

traceroute then constructs another UDP packet, this time with a TTL of 2, and sends it out. This packet gets to the second router before TTL gets decremented to 0, and *traceroute* knows that the router that returns the ICMP "time to live exceeded" for that packet is the second router along the path to the destination. *traceroute* then constructs a UDP packet with a TTL of 3, then 4, and so on, to determine the path to the destination.

traceroute knows it's finished when it gets back an ICMP "service unavailable" message, rather than an ICMP "time to live exceeded" message from some intermediate router.

Most versions of *traceroute* will also note and display relevant ICMP "host unreachable", "network unreachable", and other ICMP messages received.

If *traceroute* can't reach the destination host (or can't get anything back from it), it eventually times out.

Packet filtering characteristics of traceroute

To allow *traceroute* outbound through your packet filters (i.e., someone running *traceroute* from the inside, to an external destination), you have to allow the constructed UDP packets outbound, and the relevant ICMP packets (particularly "time to live exceeded" and "service unavailable" back inbound.

To allow *traceroute* inbound, you have to allow the constructed UDP packets inbound, and the relevant ICMP messages back outbound. You may wish to limit this capability to the machines used by the network operations center of your network service provider, in order to keep a tight reign on the UDP packets allowed through your firewall. Doing so protects RPC-based services like NFS and NIS/YP) and keeps attackers from using *traceroute* to discover which addresses at your site are actually assigned to hosts.

Some versions of *traceroute* can be told (via a command line or a compile-time option) which range of UDP ports to use for the destination. You may need to establish a convention for your site of what port(s) will be allowed through the packet filters for use by *traceroute*. You don't want to allow any more latitude in your packet filters for *traceroute* than absolutely necessary (particularly for incoming *traceroute*). Because *traceroute* is UDP-based, an attacker could potentially take advantage of the UDP-based rules in your packet filtering that are there to allow *traceroute* in order to attack other UDP-based services like NFS and NIS/YP.

Direc-tion	Source Addr.	Dest. Addr.	Pro-tocol	Source Port[a]	Dest. Port[a]	Message Type[a]	Notes
Out	Int	Ext	UDP	b	b	a	Outgoing *traceroute* probe
In	Ext	Int	ICMP	a	a	11	Incoming "TTL exceeded"
In	Ext	Int	ICMP	a	a	3	Incoming "service unavailable"
In	Ext	Int	UDP	b	b	a	Incoming *traceroute* probe
Out	Int	Ext	ICMP	a	a	11	Outgoing "TTL exceeded"
Out	Int	Ext	ICMP	a	a	3	Outgoing "service unavailable"

[a] UDP packets have source and destination ports; ICMP packets have only message type fields. Neither UDP nor ICMP packets have ACK bits.

[b] *traceroute* probe packet UDP source/destination ports vary by implementation, invocation, and/or command-line arguments. They are generally >32768, but that's about the only generalization you can make about them. Specific implementations (particularly in routers and on non-UNIX platforms) may vary. Destination ports, in particular, are usually in the range 33434 through 33523. (Why this is the case is somewhat complicated, and you should read the comments in the UNIX *traceroute* source code if you're perversely curious.)

Proxying characteristics of traceroute

Like *ping, traceroute* could easily be supported by an ICMP-knowledgeable modi-fied-client proxy server. Unfortunately, no such proxy server is widely available. Modified-procedure proxying is not possible with *traceroute*.

Other ICMP Packets

There are a number of ICMP message types that are used for network management that don't have programs associated with them. These are automatically generated and interpreted by various programs and network devices.

What to do with ICMP messages depends on the message, and the direction it's going in. We've already talked about "echo request", "echo reply", "destination unreachable", "service unavailable" (actually a special type of "destination unreachable"), and "time to live exceeded" messages. The other ICMP message types you probably want to allow, both inbound and outbound, are "source quench" (used by a receiver to tell a sender to "slow down," because it's sending data too fast) and "parameter problem" (which is sort of a catch-all code to return when there is a problem with packet headers that can't be reported any other way).

Many other ICMP message types have the potential to change local information on your hosts (for example, "redirect" causes changes to a host's routing tables), so you probably don't want to allow such messages inbound through your packet fil-ters.

In general, you only want to allow ICMP outbound when it has the chance of doing you some good. Both "source quench" and "parameter problem" are used to get the sending host to be nicer to you, and are worth allowing outbound. Any of the ICMP types that indicates that the connection can't be made ("destination unavailable", "network unavailable", "service unavailable", "destination adminstratively unavailable", or "network administratively unavailable", for example) will help an attacker probe your network without giving you much benefit, and you may want to block these outbound.

Packet filtering characteristics of ICMP

As we've said earlier, ICMP packets do not have source or destination port numbers, but have a single ICMP message type field instead. Many packet filtering systems will let you filter ICMP packets based on that field in the same way they allow you to filter TCP or UDP packets based on the source and destination port number fields. Here are some common ICMP message types, and how you should handle them (whether you should allow them through your firewall, or block them).

Message Type[a]	Description
0	Echo reply (reply to *ping*; see *ping* section above).
3	Destination unreachable (see *traceroute* section above). May indicate host unreachable, network unreachable, port unreachable, or other.
4	Source quench (somebody telling destination "slow down; you're talking too fast"); should probably be allowed.
5	Redirect (somebody telling destination to change a route); is supposed to be ignored by your systems unless it comes from a directly connected router, but should probably be blocked anyway. In particular, make sure the routers that are part of your firewall ignore it.
8	Echo request (generated by *ping*; see *ping* section above); should probably be allowed.
11	Time exceeded (packet appears to be looping); should probably be allowed.
12	Parameter problem (problem with a packet header); should probably be allowed.

[a] ICMP messages do not have source or destination port numbers; they have a single ICMP message type field instead. ICMP packets also do not have ACK bits.

Summary of Network Management Recommendations

- Do not allow SNMP across your firewall from the Internet. (This may require special SNMP configurations on your packet filtering routers, which are probably themselves SNMP-capable devices.)

- Do not allow routing protocols (RIP or otherwise) across your firewall to or from the Internet. Routing on the firewall is generally very simple and accomplished best with static routes. Simply configure the firewall to direct packets bound for internal source addresses to an internal router and to direct all other packets to your Internet connection.

- Allow ICMP echo requests outbound, but limit incoming ICMP echo requests to those coming from machines with a legitimate need to probe your network (such as your network service provider's network operations center). Allow ICMP echo responses either way.

- Allow *traceroute* outbound, but limit incoming *traceroute* requests to those coming from machines with a legitimate need to probe your network, and limit the port range used.

- Allow only safe ICMP message types, as described above.

Network Time Protocol (NTP)

NTP allows you to set the clocks on your systems very accurately, to within 100ms and sometimes even 10ms. Knowing the exact time is extremely important for certain types of applications and protocols:

- It's much easier to correlate information from multiple machines (log files, for example, when analyzing a break-in attempt) when the clocks on those machines are all synchronized. It's helpful to know exactly who was attacked, and in what order, if you're going to understand what the attacker was after—and what he might do next.

- Some security protocols depend on an accurate source of time information in order to prevent "playback" attacks. Such protocols tag their communications with the current time, so that those same communications, e.g., a login/password interaction or even an entire communication, can't be replayed at a later date as part of an attack. This tagging can be circumvented if the clock can be set back to the time the communication was recorded.

NTP servers communicate with other NTP servers in a hierarchy to distribute clock information. The closer a system is to a reference clock (an atomic clock, radio clock, or some other definitive clock), the higher it is in the hierarchy. Servers communicate with each other frequently to estimate and track network delay between themselves, so that this delay can be compensated for. NTP clients simply ask servers for the current time without worrying about compensating for communications delays.

Packet Filtering Characteristics of NTP

NTP is a UDP-based service. NTP servers use well-known port 123 to talk to each other and to NTP clients. NTP clients use random ports above 1023. As with DNS, you can tell the difference between:

- An NTP client-to-server query—source port above 1023, destination port 123.

- An NTP server-to-client response—source port 123, destination port above 1023.

- An NTP server-to-server query or response—source and destination ports both 123.

Unlike DNS, NTP never uses TCP, and NTP has no analog to the DNS zone transfer operation.

Direction	Source Addr.	Dest. Addr.	Protocol	Source Port	Dest. Port	ACK Set	Notes
In	Ext	Int	UDP	>1023	123	[a]	Incoming query, client to server
Out	Int	Ext	UDP	123	>1023	[a]	Answer to incoming UDP query, server to client
Out	Int	Ext	UDP	>1023	123	[a]	Outgoing query, client to server
In	Ext	Int	UDP	123	>1023	[a]	Answer to outgoing UDP query, server to client
In	Ext	Int	UDP	123	123	[a]	Query or response between two servers
Out	Int	Ext	UDP	123	123	[a]	Query or response between two servers

[a] UDP packets do not have ACK bits.

Figure 8-19 shows how packet filtering works with NTP.

Proxying Characteristics of NTP

As a UDP-based application, NTP can't be proxied by SOCKS, but can be used with the UDP Packet Relayer. Because NTP employs a hierarchy of servers, it can be configured to run on a bastion host without using explicit proxying, as shown below.

Configuring NTP to Work with a Firewall

Do you really need to configure NTP to work with a firewall? That's your first decision. You may not need to if either of the following cases is true at your site:

- If you have an accurate source of time within your internal network—for example, a radio clock receiving time signals from the National Bureau of Standards atomic clocks on one of their radio stations (or the equivalent from non-U.S. standards organizations), or a satellite clock receiving data from the Global Positioning System (GPS) satellites.

- If you're more worried about having time be consistent *within* your network than *between* your network and the outside world.

In either of these cases, you don't need to run NTP across your firewall; you can simply run it internally.

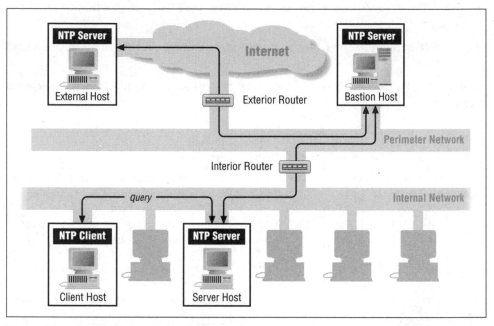

Figure 8-19: NTP with packet filtering

If you do want to run NTP across your firewall, the best way is to set up an NTP server on a bastion host that talks to multiple external NTP servers and another NTP server on some internal host that talks to the bastion host. (You want the bastion host to talk to multiple external NTP servers because it increases accuracy and makes it harder to fool.) Next, configure internal NTP clients and other internal NTP servers to talk to the internal server that talks to the bastion server. You need to configure any packet filtering system between the internal server and the bastion host to allow the following:

- Queries from the internal NTP server to the bastion host NTP server: UDP packets from port 123 on the internal server to port 123 on the bastion host.

- Answers from the bastion host NTP server to the internal NTP server: UDP packets from port 123 on the bastion host to port 123 on the internal host.

Summary of NTP Recommendations

- Consider running NTP purely internally.

- If you run NTP to the Internet, use an NTP server on a bastion host as a proxy for an internal server.

Network File System (NFS)

The NFS protocol is designed to allow systems to access files across the network on a remote system, as conveniently as if the files were on directly attached disks. Machines may be NFS servers (exporting their disks for access by other machines), NFS clients (accessing disks exported by NFS servers), or both. NFS is heavily used within LANs, but it is unsafe to allow across a firewall for a variety of reasons.

The primary problem with NFS is its weak authentication of requests. Access to a given NFS-exported filesystem is all or nothing; a given client machine is either trusted to access the filesystem, or it isn't. If the server trusts a given client machine, the server believes whatever the client tells it about who is trying to access which files. It then uses that information for authorization according to the standard UNIX file protection mechanisms (i.e., user, group, and other permissions). There are a few extra protections some NFS servers can optionally apply.

The server's trust in the client is established when the client mounts the filesystem from the server. The client contacts the server and tells the server what filesystem it wants to access. The server checks whether or not the client (based on IP address) is allowed to access that filesystem. If it is, the server gives the client a "file handle" (basically a magic set of credentials for the client), which the client uses for all further access to the filesystem.

Once the client has mounted the filesystem (and received a file handle from the server) the client sends a request to the server each time it wants to act on a file on that filesystem. The request describes the action the client wants to take and includes the file handle obtained from the server, so the server assumes that the client is authorized to request that action.

NFS's main security problems are:

- The NFS server relies on IP address to authenticate client hosts, making it vulnerable to address forgery.

- The NFS server relies on the client to authenticate the user, making it vulnerable to any user who has compromised a client machine.

- The NFS server doesn't recheck the client authentication on every request. The server assumes that if the client uses a valid file handle, the client is authorized to access that filesystem. An attacker with a forged or captured file handle can access the filesystem just as easily as a legitimate client can.

The file handle for a given filesystem is established when the filesystem is created on the server or when it is mounted for the first time on a new server mount point or from a new disk/controller pair. Unfortunately, the method for generating file handles is fairly predictable, and an attacker can probably guess the file handle if he can guess when the filesystem was created. Most NFS servers will allow any number of bad guesses without complaining or shutting down. If the attacker can somehow guess at least the day the filesystem was created—which is especially easy if the attack is against a newly installed machine—he can probably guess the file handle without too much difficulty, by trying the range of file handles that would have been assigned to filesystems created that day.

NFS servers have no mechanism for canceling file handles; once a file handle has been issued, it's good until the server filesystem is reinitialized or mounted elsewhere (even if only temporarily; when it is remounted in its original location again, it will have a new file handle). A client which had access at one time can keep using the file handle it obtained, even if the access controls (the */etc/exports* file on most UNIX NFS servers) are later changed to deny access to that client.

Under NFS, root may be treated differently from normal users. Some UNIX NFS servers always treat root the same way they treat normal users: the client's root user gets the same access that the server's root user would have. Some of them always translate the client's root user to a UID known as "nobody" that is never used as a regular user; thus, this user will only have the permissions granted to the world. This "nobody" UID may be either the highest possible UID, or a UID which translates to -1 (which might be written as -1, or as the highest possible UID plus 1). On some UNIX machines, all three of these numbers (-1, 65535, and 65536) are listed in the password file as "nobody." Most UNIX NFS servers allow you to choose whether you wish to allow root access or translate it to "nobody" via an option in the */etc/exports* file. Non-UNIX servers normally treat root as if it were any other user, but because that user is unlikely to have special privileges on the server, this isn't a problem.

Translating root to "nobody" is an extremely minor security improvement. Anybody who is capable of being root on the client is capable of pretending to be any user whatsoever on the client, and can therefore see and do anything any user can do. The translation hides only those files on the server restricted to access by root itself. You will still probably want to use translation wherever you can for the minimal protection it does give you, but you should not feel that it makes it safe to export filesystems to possibly hostile clients.

Better protection for the server is available by exporting the filesystem read-only. If the filesystem is exported purely read-only (no host is allowed to write it) you can be reasonably certain the data cannot be modified via NFS. If you allow any host to write it, you're vulnerable to forgery.

NFS clients may also be in danger from NFS servers. For example, an NFS-mounted filesystem may contain *setuid* programs; users on the client would be able to use those programs to become root. Device entries on an NFS-mounted partition are considered to apply to the client's devices, not the server's devices. Somebody with an account on an NFS client and root permission on an NFS server, can use this to get unlimited, if inconvenient, read-write access to all data on the client.

Some NFS clients provide options to *mount* that can be used to disable devices and *setuid/setgid* on mounted filesystems. If *mount* is not available to users other than root, or if it always uses these options for users other than root, this will protect the client from the server. If these options are not available, even if only root can mount filesystems, you should consider mounting a filesystem to be equivalent to granting root access to the server machine.

Some vendors also support a version of NFS based on Secure RPC. Secure RPC has several problems that also apply to NFS implemented on top of it:

- It is not widely supported; it is available almost exclusively on Suns.

- The process of exchanging keys between machines is difficult.

- It doesn't perform as well as standard RPC. (NFS is particularly performance-sensitive.)

If you have an immutable requirement to run NFS across your firewall to some other site, you should investigate either a private connection to that site or network-level encryption (described in Chapter 10). Be aware that NFS generally doesn't perform well over networks running at anything less than Ethernet speed anyway. You might want to investigate alternatives such as FTP for your particular situation or alternate network filesystems such as the Andrew File System (AFS) (see Appendix B for more information).

Packet Filtering Characteristics of NFS

NFS is an RPC-based service. As mentioned in Chapter 6, it's very difficult to handle RPC-based services with a packet filtering system, because the servers normally don't use predictable port numbers. While the port numbers to be used are too unpredictable for a packet filtering system to cope with, they're not so unpredictable an attacker can't find them. (If nothing else, the attacker could try sending NFS requests to all ports to see which respond as he would expect an NFS server to respond.)

NFS is generally provided over UDP; there are TCP-based NFS servers and clients available, but they are rare and seldom used. NFS is somewhat unusual for an RPC-based service in that it normally uses a predictable port number (port 2049)—apparently for obscure reasons related to how NFS servers interact with the kernel on most UNIX systems. We wouldn't recommend depending on NFS servers to always wind up on port 2049, however. RFC 1094, the NFS protocol specification, says "The NFS protocol currently uses the UDP port number 2049. This is not an officially assigned port, so later versions of the protocol use the 'Portmapping' facility of RPC."

Proxying Characteristics of NFS

RPC-based protocols are almost as unpleasant to proxy as they are to allow with packet filtering; they cannot be adequately handled with generic proxies. A dedicated NFS proxy server would be possible, but we do not know of one. NFS is particularly problematic for proxying, because it is data-intense, exchanging large volumes of data in situations where delay is very noticeable to the user. A host doing NFS proxying is going to need to deal with multiple connections transferring large packets at high speeds.

Summary of NFS Recommendations

*   Don't allow NFS across your firewall.

Network Information Service/Yellow Pages (NIS/YP)

NIS/YP is designed to provide distributed access to centralized administrative information (such as host tables, password files, site-wide email aliases, and so on) shared by machines at a site.

The main problem with NIS/YP is that its security isn't good enough to adequately protect some of the data it contains. In particular, a site's NIS/YP servers generally contain the shared password file (equivalent to the */etc/passwd* file on a single system) for the site, complete with encrypted passwords. All you need to get data from an NIS/YP server is the NIS/YP domain name with which the data is associated. An attacker who can talk to a site's NIS/YP server, and who can guess what the site has chosen as its NIS/YP domain name (often the same as, or a derivative of, their regular Internet domain name), can request any information the server has. If the attacker gets their shared password file, these passwords can be cracked at the attacker's leisure.

NOTE

> NIS/YP transfers include the encrypted passwords even if the machines
> are configured to use shadow passwords and the encrypted passwords
> are not readable on the NIS/YP server.

There is a revised version of NIS/YP, called NIS+, available from some vendors. NIS+ has not achieved wide acceptance, partly because of licensing and compatibility issues, but mostly because the majority of sites have managed to work around the deficiencies of NIS/YP already, and therefore aren't motivated to switch to something new. NIS+ improves security only if it is configured so that it will not support NIS/YP. If you configure NIS+ to support NIS/YP clients (and because few NIS+ clients are available, most NIS+ sites do use it in this mode), it is no more secure than original NIS/YP.

A few NIS/YP servers (notably Sun's) support a configuration file called *securenets*. This allows you to use IP address authentication to control which hosts your NIS/YP server will release data to. This is an order of magnitude improvement in NIS/YP security. It changes NIS/YP attacks from guessing games (guess the domain name and the NIS/YP server and you get a free prize) to requiring you to do all the same guessing and then go to serious effort to determine what addresses the NIS/YP server will respond to and forge packets from them. Unfortunately, an order of magnitude is probably not enough of an improvement for data as crucial as your encrypted passwords. While *securenets* (if you have it available) will protect you from casual attackers who want to get into any site they can, it will not protect you from an attacker who knows your site and wants to attack it in particular.

The trick, then, is to keep an attacker from being able to talk to your NIS/YP servers.

Packet Filtering Characteristics of NIS/YP

NIS/YP is an RPC-based service, generally provided over UDP. As mentioned in Chapter 6, it's very difficult to handle RPC-based services with a packet filtering system, because the servers normally don't use predictable port numbers. While the port numbers to be used are too unpredictable for a packet filtering system to cope with, they're not so unpredictable that an attacker can't find them. (If nothing else, the attacker could try sending NIS/YP requests to all ports, to see which respond as they would expect an NIS/YP server to.)

Proxying Characteristics of NIS/YP

RPC-based protocols are almost as unpleasant to proxy as they are to allow with packet filtering; they cannot be adequately handled with generic proxies. A dedicated NIS/YP proxy server would be possible, but we do not know of one, except for the proxying capabilities available with NIS+. In any case, proxying alone does not adequately deal with the vulnerabilities of NIS/YP.

Summary of NIS/YP Recommendations

* Don't allow NIS/YP across your firewall.

X11 Window System

The X11 window system poses a number of problems for a firewall system. (Note that most window systems supplied by UNIX vendors are either based on or very similar to X11—from a firewalls point of view, most of the considerations are the same—so this discussion of X11 applies to other window systems as well.)

The first problem with X11 is that the client/server relationship is backwards from most other protocols. The X11 "server" is the display/mouse/keyboard unit, and the "clients" are the application programs driving windows or interacting with the mouse and keyboard on that server. Thus, the server is typically inside the firewall (sitting on the user's desk), and the clients are outside (running on whatever remote computers the user has accessed).

X11 servers have certain capabilities that make them a very tempting target for attackers. There are a number of things an attacker can do with access to an X11 server, including:

- Getting screen dumps—obtaining a copy of whatever information is being displayed on the screen at any given time.

- Reading keystrokes—for example, reading a user's password as he or she types it at the keyboard.

- Injecting keystrokes as if they were typed by the user; this potentially allows the attacker to do all kinds of mean and nasty things, especially in a window where the user happens to be running a root shell.

X11 has certain security mechanisms, but to date they've proven either too weak or too cumbersome to be truly useful against determined attack. One, commonly referred to as the "magic cookie" mechanism, relies on a secret shared between the server and legitimate clients; clients are allowed to access the server only if they can prove they know the secret. The problem is, even though the secret is never passed directly between the X11 client and server, most ways that users make the secret available to both the server and the client (via an NFS-accessible file in their home directory that's accessible to both server and client, for example) compromise the secret to anybody who is snooping on the network. While the magic cookie mechanism is theoretically secure, in practice it is undermined by the way that it is commonly and incorrectly used; unfortunately, there's no easy way to use it correctly.

Another of X11's security mechanisms, called the *xhost* mechanism, allows the user to tell the server which remote IP addresses the server should accept connections from. Users are supposed to authorize only specific hosts where they intend to run X11 clients. The problem is, users forget to preauthorize the hosts before starting the clients, and the clients are refused access; after this happens a few times, many users disable the controls altogether. For example, they issue an *xhost* + command to allow connections from any and all hosts in the name of convenience (so they can easily run programs on remote systems), without giving any thought to the security implications of their actions. Even if users don't disable *xhost* altogether, they're still vulnerable to any connections from the machines they've approved; there's no way for the *xhost* mechanism to determine whether or not any given connection from one of those machines is legitimate.

Few sites need to run X11 across their firewalls from the Internet. There are occasional WWW sites that provide X clients as a way to provide real-time displays, but they are few and far between. If you need to allow X11 from the Internet, consider using one of the X11 proxies discussed in Chapter 7, for example, *x-gw* in the TIS Firewall Toolkit.

Packet Filtering Characteristics of X11

X11 uses TCP. X11 uses port 6000 for the first server on a machine. This choice of ports presents another problem for packet filtering systems: the X11 ports are in the middle of the "above 1023" range of ports that most applications use for random client-side ports. Thus, any packet filtering scheme that allows packets in to ports above 1023 (in order to allow packets from remote servers to local clients) needs to be very careful not to allow connections in to X11 servers. It can do this either by totally blocking access to the range of ports used by these servers (which can be a tricky proposition because of the possibility of multiple servers per machine, per the discussion below) or by using "start-of-connection" filtering (looking at the TCP ACK bit) to disallow inbound TCP connections to any ports.

Some machines run multiple X11 servers. The first server is at port 6000, the second at 6001, and so on. On a UNIX system, the DISPLAY environment variable tells clients what X11 server to contact. This variable is of the form *hostname:n*; this tells clients to contact the server on port 6000+*n* on machine *hostname*.

Sometimes such machines actually have multiple display/keyboard/mouse setups, but more often the multiple servers are *virtual* servers for some remote X terminal. X11 is a very verbose, high-bandwidth protocol; it doesn't run well over dial-up links. One of the solutions that's been adopted (for example, by NCD's *XRemote* package) is to run a virtual X11 server on a well-connected machine (for example, linked by Ethernet to the machines the client programs are running on), and then to speak some other, more frugal protocol over the slow link between this virtual server and the real X terminal. Every machine running X11 will have a server at port 6000. A few will have servers at 6000 and 6001. Only a very few machines will have more than that.

Thus, to block access to all these servers, assuming that you can't do start-of-connection filtering, you need to block access to ports 6000 through 6000+*n*, where *n* is some undetermined number. You don't want to make *n* too small, because that might expose some of the virtual X11 servers to attack. On the other hand, you don't want to make it too big, either, because you're blocking ports in the range of random ports that could be used by other application clients. You don't want to keep another protocol's client (e.g., Telnet or FTP) from working simply because it happened to pick as its random client port a port blocked to prevent X11 access.

You do have one thing going for you: the way most operating systems allocate such random ports. Generally, when a client application asks the operating system to allocate a random port for its use, the kernel allocates the next available port after the last one allocated (wrapping around to the beginning of the port number space when necessary). If a client happens to grab a port blocked because of X11, the client will fail. If the user tries to run the client again a few times, the client will get a new port each time, and will eventually succeed when the port allocated moves beyond the blocked range.

A common approach (again, assuming that you can't do start-of-connection filtering to block external connections to internal servers) is to block, say, four ports (ports 6000 through 6003) on all hosts, and more ports on hosts where you know or suspect people will run lots of virtual X11 servers, e.g., the hosts people dial in to from their X terminals at home. A more straightforward approach is to use proxying to direct connections to a bastion host that is not running a window system. It can make outbound connections on any port without worrying about hitting the blocked range, because it doesn't need a blocked range.

What should you do on a machine where you've blocked a large range of ports (because of the potential for many X11 servers on that machine)? If you have problems with clients of other protocols because of the blocked ports, you could run a simple program to keep the kernel's "next port" assignment out of the blocked range. The program would simply need to ask the kernel for a random port, and if the port it was assigned was in the blocked range, keep asking for more random ports until the ports being assigned were no longer in the blocked range. The program would then need to perform this check every minute or so. Most sites will choose to either avoid the problem altogether with proxying, or ignore the problem, rather than going to this length to deal with it, but if you have a server that must provide heavily used Internet client access and multiple X servers, it may be worth it to you.

Some vendors provide modified or enhanced X11 servers with somewhat different characteristics; for example, Sun's OpenWindows server listens at both port 6000 (for X11) and port 2000 (for Sun's older NeWS window system protocol), with second servers at ports 6001 and 2001, and so on.

Direction	Source Addr.	Dest. Addr.	Protocol	Source Port	Dest. Port	ACK Set	Notes
In	Ext	Int	TCP	>1023	$6000+n$	[a]	Incoming X11 connection to nth server, client to server
Out	Int	Ext	TCP	$6000+n$	>1023	Yes	Incoming X11 connection to nth server, server to client
Out	Int	Ext	TCP	>1023	$6000+n$	[a]	Outgoing X11 connection to nth server, client to server

Direction	Source Addr.	Dest. Addr.	Protocol	Source Port	Dest. Port	ACK Set	Notes
In	Ext	Int	TCP	6000+n	>1023	Yes	Outgoing X11 connection to nth server, server to client

[a] ACK is not set on the first packet of this type (establishing connection) but will be set on the rest.

Summary of X11 Recommendations

- Do not allow clients on the Internet to connect to X11 servers on your internal network. If you have to, use an X11 proxy server (such as the one in the TIS FWTK) running on a bastion host.

- If you cannot use start-of-connection filters, blocking X11 may block other connections. You will need to use proxying or special programs if you have large numbers of X11 servers on the same machine.

Printing Protocols (lpr and lp)

The BSD *lpr* printing system is very similar to the BSD "r" commands discussed earlier in this chapter (*rsh, rlogin, rcp, rdump, rdist*). Unlike the "r" commands, *lpr* authorizes hosts, not individual users, and it will accept jobs from hosts in */etc/printers.equiv* as well as */etc/hosts.equiv.*

The System V *lp* printing system doesn't really have a remote printing component. When it does remote printing, it usually does it by handing the job off to a BSD *lpr* printing system, or by using the BSD *rsh* command (which is often called *remsh* on System V systems, because such systems have another program called *rsh* that does something else entirely).

Given the deficiencies of both *lp* and *lpr*, many UNIX vendors implement their own solutions to remote printing. Other platforms may support *lp*, *lpr*, a separate protocol, or some combination. Because it has its own protocol, which is somewhat easier to implement than *rsh*, *lpr* is more popular than *lp* on non-UNIX systems, but many of them have their own protocols. Some printers are network devices in their own right, sometimes speaking *lp* or *lpr* directly, and sometimes (particularly older printers) speaking a protocol developed by the printer manufacturer.

For the most part, the wide variety of other network printing protocols that are out there share a common feature; they're no more secure than *lpr*. Most of them are not even as secure as *lpr* (if you can reach the system with a print request in the right protocol, it will print it). Because modern PostScript printers can be intelligent Ethernet devices with their own disks, it is theoretically possible for a rogue print job to turn one into a network sniffing device. In practice, this is a baroquely complex approach; attackers aren't very likely to succeed at it. However, more mundane denial of service attacks on printers are eminently possible, and in fact have been known to happen.

Some are merely annoying, such as simply printing page after page of garbage (or, better yet, something offensive to the victim or their coworkers) until the printer runs out of paper. Unfortunately, the nastiest of them are enabled by a security feature in PostScript. PostScript was designed to protect certain dangerous commands by requiring a password before they were executed. This password is stored in an EEPROM chip on the printer, and is factory-set to "0" on every brand of PostScript printer. It's always the same because it *must* always be the same. Some of the commands that the PostScript designers considered dangerous are routinely used by standard PostScript drivers, and if you change the password, those drivers will no longer work. Because, in order to reset it, you need either the old password or a ROM burner, a program that uses the well-known "0" password to reset the password to something unknown can make printers effectively unusable until new EEPROMs are sent from the factory. (Some printers will run without the EEPROM, with an effective password of 0.) Removing or replacing the EEPROM resets not only the password, but also the printer ID and the page count; if you have fonts licensed to the printer, they will have to be relicensed. Since the last wave of such attacks, licensing of fonts to individual printers has become uncommon.

The intelligence and vulnerability of PostScript devices makes it important to protect your printers from Internet access. Make sure you have blocked any remote printing protocols your machines and printers use. You will need to check every printer type and every machine type separately.

Packet Filtering Characteristics of lpr

lpr is TCP-based. Servers use port 515. Clients use random ports below 1023, just like the BSD "r" commands, as discussed above.

Direction	Source Addr.	Dest. Addr.	Protocol	Source Port	Dest. Port	ACK Set	Notes
In	Ext	Int	TCP	<1023	515	[a]	Incoming *lpr*, client to server
Out	Int	Ext	TCP	515	<1023	Yes	Incoming *lpr*, server to client
Out	Int	Ext	TCP	<1023	515	[a]	Outgoing *lpr*, client to server
In	Ext	int	TCP	515	<1023	Yes	Outgoing *lpr*, server to client

[a] ACK is not set on the first packet of this type (establishing connection) but will be set on the rest.

Proxying Characteristics of lpr

lpr is a store-and-forward protocol, capable of being configured to do its own proxying. You can simply run a standard *lpr* configuration on your proxy server and configure it to drive whatever printers you like or pass jobs to another server. This does not provide security improvements over direct *lpr*, but it will let it cross a nonrouting host.

Packet Filtering and Proxying Characteristics of lp

lp itself provides no remote printing support. It handles printing across the network by using either *rsh*, which is covered above with the other BSD "r" commands, or *lpr*. To determine what your printer configuration is using, configure a remote printer and read its interface file (which is usually stored in */usr/spool/lp/interfaces/printername*). Some vendors may also provide novel remote printing systems for use with *lp*; you will need to consult your vendor documentation.

Summary Recommendations for Printing Protocols

* Do not permit printing protocols across your firewall.

Analyzing Other Protocols

How do you go about analyzing protocols that we haven't discussed here? The first question to ask is: Do you really need to run the protocol across your firewall, or is there some other satisfactory way to provide or access the service desired using a protocol already supported by your firewall?

If you really need to provide a protocol across your firewall, and it's not discussed above, how do you determine what ports it uses and so on? While it's sometimes possible to determine this information from program or protocol documentation, the easiest way to figure it out is usually to ask somebody else, such as the members of the Firewalls mailing list.[*] (See Appendix A).

If you have to determine the answer yourself, the easiest way to do it is usually empirically. Here's what you should do:

1. Set up a test system that's running as little as possible other than the application you want to test.

2. Next, set up another system to monitor the packets to and from the test system (using *etherfind* or *tcpdump* or some other package that lets you watch traffic on the local network).

3. Run the application on the test system and see what the monitoring system records.

You may need to repeat this procedure for every client implementation and every server implementation you intend to use. There are occasionally unpredictable differences between implementations (e.g., the AIX DNS clients always use TCP, even though most DNS clients use UDP by default).

---

[*] But make sure you check the archives first, to see if the question has already been asked and answered.

In This Chapter:
• *Screened Subnet
  Architecture*
• *Screened Host
  Architecture*

9

Two Sample Firewalls

In this chapter, we describe two sample configurations for basic firewalls. Almost any real firewall is going to be more complex than those described in this chapter, but this presentation should give you some idea of the tasks involved in building a firewall and how the various pieces fit together.

NOTE

We want to emphasize that these examples are just that: examples. You shouldn't blindly implement one of these examples, without first taking the time to understand your own needs, your environment, and the implications and complications of the services you want your firewall to provide.

The services that we're going to provide through these sample firewalls are just the basics: terminal access, file transfer, electronic mail, Usenet news, the World Wide Web, and DNS. See Chapter 8 for a full discussion of these and other services.

Screened Subnet Architecture

The screened subnet architecture, described in Chapter 4 and shown in Figure 9-1, is probably the most common do-it-yourself firewall architecture. This architecture provides good security (including multiple layers of redundancy) at what most sites feel is a reasonable cost.

There are two-router and single-router variations of the screened subnet architecture. Basically, you can use either a pair of two-interface routers or a single three-interface router. The single-router screened subnet architecture works about as well as the two-router screened subnet architecture, and is often somewhat cheaper. However, you need to use a router that can handle both inbound and outbound packet filtering on each interface. (See the discussion of this point in

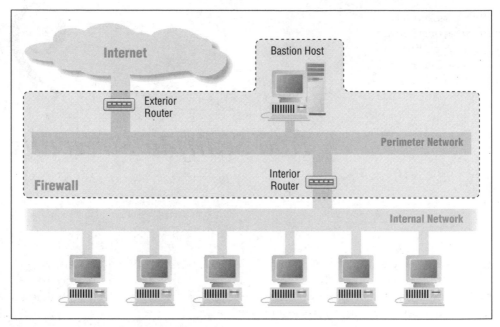

Figure 9–1: Screened subnet architecture

Chapter 6.) We're going to use a two-router architecture as our example in this section because it is conceptually simpler.

The components of this type of firewall include the following:

- Perimeter network
- Exterior router
- Interior router
- Bastion host

Let's review briefly the purposes of these various components, presented originally in Chapter 4.

Perimeter network
   Isolates your bastion host from your internal network, so a security breach on the bastion host won't immediately affect your internal network.

Exterior router
   Connects your site to the outside world. If possible, the exterior router also provides at least some protection for the bastion host, interior router, and internal network. (This isn't always possible, because some sites use exterior routers that are managed by their network service providers and are therefore beyond the site's control.)

Interior router

Protects the internal network from the world and from the site's own bastion host.

Bastion host

Serves as the site's main point of contact with the outside world. (It should be set up according to the guidelines in Chapter 5.)

In addition to the machines that make up the firewall itself, assume there are machines on the internal network (internal hosts) that fulfill the following roles. (Note that any given internal machine might fill any, or even all, of these roles.)

- Mail server

- Usenet news server

- DNS server

- Client for various Internet services

Each of these internal services is provided directly (via packet filtering) or indirectly (via proxy servers running on the bastion host).

We're going to assume (at least for the purposes of this example) that internal users in our system are trusted not to actively try to circumvent the firewall, and that there is no particular need to monitor or log their Internet activities.

We're also going to assume that you are using properly assigned and routed IP addresses (that is, addresses assigned to your site, and properly routed and advertised to the rest of the Internet by your service provider) for your internal and perimeter networks. If you aren't, you have no choice but to use proxies, because you can't allow packets with those unassigned IP addresses out onto the Internet; even if you did, replies would have no way to come back to you.

Finally, we're going to assume you're using separate network numbers for your perimeter net and internal net, so that you can detect forged packets easily. (See the discussion in "Risks of Filtering by Source Address" in Chapter 6.)

Service Configuration

Given the architecture we've just described, how do we provide the basic Internet services?

Telnet

Outgoing Telnet could be provided through packet filtering or through proxies. Which approach should we use?

Proxying will require either modified clients or modified user procedures; either one will be tedious to implement for somebody. Proxying would allow us to restrict or monitor Telnet usage by user by forcing our users to authenticate to a proxy server before completing their requests. However, remember that we have decided to assume internal users are trustworthy, so there is no need for authentication. Proxying would be necessary if we were using unassigned or unadvertised IP addresses internally, but that's not the case here, either. Because we have trustworthy users and proper IP addresses, proxying for Telnet doesn't provide any advantage over packet filtering, and it's more difficult to set up and maintain. Therefore, for this example we're going to provide outgoing Telnet via packet filtering.

Incoming Telnet is considerably more difficult to provide safely and conveniently. If it were necessary, incoming Telnet could be provided on the bastion host using extra authentication. However, for a site that is looking for a simple configuration, the reasonable thing to do is to disallow incoming Telnet altogether. That's what we'll do for this example.

FTP   .

Unlike Telnet, FTP doesn't lend itself to a pure packet filtering solution. Because normal mode FTP requires an incoming connection to an arbitrary port over 1023, trying to allow it without doing anything else gives attackers access to all kinds of services running on our internal systems. That leaves us two choices:

- Support passive mode via packet filtering

- Support normal mode via proxies

In either case, the standard FTP clients shipped with UNIX operating systems, and most of the popular, publicly available clients for personal computers, won't work the normal way. If we use the TIS FWTK *ftp-gw* proxy gateway (described in Chapter 7), we can use unmodified clients, but at the cost of teaching the users to follow special procedures. Some popular FTP clients—the ones built in to Web browsers like Netscape Navigator or Mosaic—do use passive mode without being modified, but then again, not all servers support it well.

A reasonable compromise would be to use packet filtering and proxies, using a proxying gateway like *ftp-gw* from the TIS FWTK that doesn't require modification of the clients. Clients that support passive mode will work via the packet filters. On platforms where we can easily replace the provided clients, we can provide passive mode clients; on platforms where we can't easily replace the clients, we can modify user procedures.

As we've said, if we wanted to monitor FTP usage, or if we were using an unassigned or unrouted network number, we'd have to do exclusively proxying, but that's not the case here. We also might want to use proxying exclusively if we decided to hide DNS data—it would save us the trouble of faking data for double-reverse lookups—but hiding DNS data is more trouble than it's worth. In a situation where proxying is used exclusively, we'd have to reconsider which proxy server to use. Requiring users to modify their procedures makes sense here, because there are no other options. The balance might come out differently if everybody were proxying.

Be aware that in order to use the TIS FWTK *ftp-gw* proxy server on your bastion host, your packet filtering will have to allow TCP connections from ports above 1023 on your bastion host to ports above 1023 on internal hosts, and from port 20 on external hosts to ports above 1023 on your bastion host, for FTP data channels. (See the discussion of FTP in Chapter 8.) This means that someone who breaks in to the bastion host could easily connect to any server on any internal host that uses a TCP port above 1023 (for example, an X11 server on port 6000). Further, any servers that are using such ports (that is, TCP ports above 1023) on the bastion host itself are also vulnerable. For this reason, if you allow these FTP data connections at all for proxying, you probably want to explicitly block access to internal systems to TCP ports above 1023 where you know, or have good cause to suspect, that servers might be listening. At the very least, such ports probably include 6000 through around 6003 (assuming four or fewer real or virtual X11 servers per machine; see the discussion of X11 in Chapter 8).

Keep in mind, however, that blocking specific ports, rather than blocking all ports by default and then allowing specific ports, is generally a dangerous strategy. It's hard to develop and maintain a complete list of ports that need to be blocked at your site. It would be better to block everything by default and then allow only specific ports, but you can't do that with standard (nonpassive) FTP, because of the way it works.

Allowing passive-mode FTP with packet filtering is a fairly liberal approach, because it allows pretty much any connection to go through as long as it is initiated by the inside. The number of servers above port 1023 is very large. This has some advantages (it lets users access nonstandard HTTP servers, for example), but it may also allow users to access all kinds of services that are unsafe. In allowing it, we're assuming that our users are not only well-intentioned, they're also capable of telling the difference between a safe and an unsafe connection, or at least avoiding the temptation to do unexpected things.

Because we've denied incoming Telnet, it makes sense to deny incoming user FTP as well. Both services require approximately the same security measures, and making one of them available would make configuring the other trivial.

Incoming anonymous FTP is a different matter, and we'll provide it. Because we're not a major Internet service provider, and because we're using the TIS FWTK already anyway, we can go for security over features and use the TIS FWTK anonymous FTP server. If we were going to provide major anonymous FTP, we'd probably want to use the more feature-filled *wuarchive* FTP server (see Chapter 8 for a description of its capabilities), and run it on a machine that was not the main bastion host but that was still a bastion host on the perimeter network.

SMTP

There aren't many options for SMTP in any configuration. We want all external SMTP connections to go to a single machine with a secured SMTP server, and we don't trust random internal machines to have safe SMTP servers. That means we'll put a secured SMTP server on the bastion host and use DNS MX records to direct all incoming mail to the bastion host, which will then pass all the incoming mail to a single internal secured SMTP server.

What other options do we have? We could put a secure SMTP server on the internal mail server and direct incoming mail to it, but if that SMTP server were compromised, the entire internal net would then be at risk. Alternatively, we could have the bastion host send mail directly to machines on the internal network, but once again, we'd be increasing our vulnerability if the SMTP server on the bastion host were compromised. The compromised bastion host would be speaking to untrustworthy internal SMTP servers, and compromise of the internal net would quickly follow. If the bastion host can speak only to the internal mail server, that narrows the possible attacks it can make; the internal mail server can run a secured SMTP server. Furthermore, by making this choice, messy maintenance tasks are transferred from the security-critical bastion host to the less vulnerable internal mail server.

How about outgoing mail? It would probably be safe to allow internal machines to send mail directly to the outside world, but doing so creates a maintenance headache. (You have to watch the mail configuration on all the internal machines.) Besides, doing this opens another direct connection between the internal and external networks. There aren't any known ways for an SMTP server to attack an SMTP client, but stranger things have happened.

Allowing internal machines to send mail directly to the outside world doesn't seem to bring much advantage either. The only difference it makes is that we'd be able to send mail (but not receive it) when the bastion host is down.

No matter what decision we make, we'll have to configure our mail clients. (Unlike FTP and Telnet, SMTP does not work as installed without modifying configuration files.) In addition, the work to direct the mail to a server is less than the work to correctly send it to the external universe.

The only real question is whether to direct the outgoing mail from the internal machines to the internal mail server or to the bastion host. Directing it to the internal mail server has the same advantages for incoming mail, but the advantages are much smaller. Sending outgoing mail presents little risk to start with, so reducing the risk isn't worth much. Sending outgoing mail also doesn't involve configurations that change often enough to make it worrisome to maintain the bastion host. On the other hand, the cost of going through the internal mail server—in complexity, possible points of failure, and delay—is just as high for outgoing mail as for incoming mail. It no longer looks like an attractive bargain, so we'll direct the outgoing mail to the bastion host without using the internal mail server as an intermediary.

We'll set up SMTP, as outlined in Chapter 8, with the bastion host acting as a middleman for incoming and outgoing mail. Here's what to do:

- Publish DNS MX records that direct incoming mail for the site to the bastion host.

- Configure internal machines to send all outgoing mail to the bastion host.

- Configure the bastion host to send all incoming mail to a single internal mail server and to send outgoing mail directly to destination machines.

For this example, we're going to assume there is a single internal mail server for incoming mail, and that internal machines send their outgoing mail directly to the bastion host (rather than indirectly via the mail server).

NNTP

As we've discussed in Chapter 8, the most practical way to set up NNTP across a firewall is to allow your NNTP service provider(s) to talk directly to your internal Usenet news host, and vice versa. We'd need an overwhelming reason to do something else, and it's hard to imagine one. Even if we didn't have an existing internal news host, building one isn't any harder than building a news server on the bastion host, and it's safer by a vast margin. News servers fail with dreary regularity; while the problems usually aren't security-related, you still don't want to install anything high-maintenance on a bastion host.

For this example, we're going to assume a single external NNTP newsfeed.

HTTP

As with the other services, for HTTP we can use either packet filtering or proxy servers to provide service to internal clients. Packet filtering will allow our users to access HTTP servers only on standard ports; proxying will allow them to reach all HTTP servers. Which approach should we take?

For Telnet and FTP, the major drawback of proxying was that it required special clients; for HTTP, though, standard browsers support HTTP proxying. Proxying will increase configuration overhead, but that price seems fair for the increased abilities it offers. On the other hand, we've already decided to allow internal hosts to create outgoing connections to any port at or above 1024 in order to allow passive-mode FTP directly from internal hosts to external hosts. That will allow access to almost any HTTP server (any one using a port at or above 1024, anyway). Using pure packet filtering would lose us only HTTP servers at nonstandard ports below 1024, and those ports are all supposed to be reserved anyway.

If we use the CERN HTTP server as our proxy server, the server can also cache Web pages. Doing so can significantly improve performance for all of the following:

HTTP clients
> They obtain pages from the cache over the internal network, rather than from the original server over our Internet connection, which is probably much slower.

Non-HTTP clients
> The HTTP clients won't be using so much of the bandwidth of our Internet connection.

HTTP servers at other sites
> They will only get one request from our site for a given page, rather than multiple requests.

The CERN server will also allow us to provide HTTP service to external sites, so we'll take advantage of that to publish our site's own public WWW pages.

HTTP proxying is also trivial to add once you have other things proxied via SOCKS or TIS FWTK. If we had SOCKS running, it would be very tempting to simply proxy through it, because SOCKS is one of the systems that many of the browsers support. All of the proxy servers we've already decided to run are part of the TIS FWTK, however, and we'd have to install SOCKS just for HTTP if we wanted to use it. If we used the TIS FWTK HTTP proxy, we'd have to get the users to modify URLs they use. In this case, the proxy servers wouldn't be able to cut and paste out of their electronic mail when people tell them about cool new things. Neither SOCKS nor TIS FWTK makes an attractive option in this situation.

However, both proxying (through the CERN server) and packet filtering appear to be attractive and reasonable choices. Proxying would definitely be preferable if we weren't already providing passive-mode FTP directly (which gives our users the ability to talk to servers on any TCP port above 1023). On the other hand, packet filtering would definitely be preferable if we wanted to use clients that didn't come with built-in support for proxying, or if we wanted not to provide an HTTP server and had no other services being proxied.

For this example, we're going to assume that we're providing HTTP service to internal clients via a CERN proxy server running on the bastion host, and that we're using the same server to publish our public WWW pages to the world.

DNS

As discussed in Chapter 8, DNS across a firewall is best provided with a pair of servers: one on the bastion host, the other on an internal host. Like NNTP, DNS presents a situation in which the number of rational solutions is clearly limited. We need to decide whether to use separate internal and external servers to do information hiding, or whether we should allow the external world to see all of our host data. By deciding to allow direct passive-mode FTP, we've already made that decision indirectly. Direct passive-mode FTP would require intricate DNS setup to support information hiding and still provide valid data for the internal hosts that are FTP clients.

For this example, we're going to assume the DNS server on the bastion host is a secondary server for our domain, and the primary server is on an internal host. We're not going to do any DNS information hiding.

Packet Filtering Rules

Based on the configuration decisions we've made in the previous sections, let's look at the packet filtering rules necessary to support this configuration. We assume an "ideal" router (as discussed in "Choosing a Packet Filtering Router" in Chapter 6). If our router were less than ideal in terms of capabilities, we'd need to modify these rules accordingly, probably at the cost of security. We might have to rethink several crucial decisions entirely. For example, if we couldn't filter on the ACK bit, direct outbound passive-mode FTP would no longer be acceptably safe, and a lot of our other decisions have used that as a major factor. (See Chapter 6 for a full discussion of packet filtering capabilities, and the implications of not having particular capabilities.)

In the packet filtering rules presented below, we assume that the filtering system:

- Can distinguish between incoming and outgoing packets

- Can filter on source address, destination address, packet type (TCP or UDP), source port, and destination port

- Can filter on whether or not the ACK bit is set (for TCP packets)

- Applies rules in the order listed

Interior Router

The purpose of the interior router is to protect the internal network from the Internet and from your own bastion host. The interior router needs the following rules to support the outlined configuration. Explanations of each rule follow the table.

Rule	Direc-tion	Source Address	Dest. Address	Pro-tocol	Source Port	Dest. Port	ACK Set	Action
Spoof	In	Internal	Any	Any	Any	Any	Any	Deny
Telnet-1	Out	Internal	Any	TCP	>1023	23	Any	Permit
Telnet-2	In	Any	Internal	TCP	23	>1023	Yes	Permit
FTP-1	Out	Internal	Any	TCP	>1023	21	Any	Permit
FTP-2	In	Any	Internal	TCP	21	>1023	Yes	Permit
FTP-3	Out	Internal	Any	TCP	>1023	>1023	Any	Permit
FTP-4	In	Any	Internal	TCP	>1023	>1023	Yes	Permit
FTP-5	Out	Internal	Bastion	TCP	>1023	21	Any	Permit
FTP-6	In	Bastion	Internal	TCP	21	>1023	Yes	Permit
FTP-7	In	Bastion	Internal	TCP	Any	6000-6003	Any	Deny
FTP-8	In	Bastion	Internal	TCP	>1023	>1023	Any	Permit
FTP-9	Out	Internal	Bastion	TCP	>1023	>1023	Yes	Permit
SMTP-1	Out	Internal	Bastion	TCP	>1023	25	Any	Permit
SMTP-2	In	Bastion	Internal	TCP	25	>1023	Yes	Permit
SMTP-3	In	Bastion	Internal SMTP server	TCP	>1023	25	Any	Permit
SMTP-4	Out	Internal SMTP server	Bastion	TCP	25	>1023	Yes	Permit
NNTP-1	Out	Internal NNTP server	NNTP feed server	TCP	>1023	119	Any	Permit
NNTP-2	In	NNTP feed server	Internal NNTP server	TCP	119	>1023	Yes	Permit
NNTP-3	In	NNTP feed server	Internal NNTP server	TCP	>1023	119	Any	Permit
NNTP-4	Out	Internal NNTP server	NNTP feed server	TCP	119	>1023	Yes	Permit
HTTP-1	Out	Internal	Bastion	TCP	>1023	80	Any	Permit
HTTP-2	In	Bastion	Internal	TCP	80	>1023	Yes	Permit
DNS-1	Out	Internal DNS server	Bastion	UDP	53	53	[a]	Permit
DNS-2	In	Bastion	Internal DNS server	UDP	53	53	[a]	Permit
DNS-3	Out	Internal DNS server	Bastion	TCP	>1023	53	Any	Permit

Rule	Direction	Source Address	Dest. Address	Protocol	Source Port	Dest. Port	ACK Set	Action
DNS-4	In	Bastion	Internal DNS server	TCP	53	>1023	Yes	Permit
DNS-5	In	Bastion	Internal DNS server	TCP	>1023	53	Any	Permit
DNS-6	Out	Internal DNS server	Bastion	TCP	53	>1023	Yes	Permit
Default-1	Out	Any	Any	Any	Any	Any	Any	Deny
Default-2	In	Any	Any	Any	Any	Any	Any	Deny

[a] UDP packets do not have ACK bits.

Here is some additional information about each set of rules in this table:

Spoof

Blocks incoming packets that claim to have internal IP addresses (that is, forged packets presumably sent by an attacker).

Telnet-1 and Telnet-2

Allow outgoing Telnet connections.

FTP-1 and FTP-2

Allow outgoing connections to FTP servers, for use by passive-mode internal clients that are interacting with those servers directly.

FTP-3 and FTP-4

Allow the FTP data channel connections from passive-mode internal clients to external FTP servers. Note that these rules actually allow all connections from internal TCP ports above 1023 to external TCP ports above 1023. That may be more than you want to allow, but there's no way to cover passive-mode FTP with anything less broad, and connections are at least restricted to those opened from the inside.

FTP-5 and FTP-6

Allow normal (nonpassive-mode) internal FTP clients to open an FTP command channel to the proxy FTP server on the bastion host. Note that these rules are actually redundant if you have rules FTP-1 and FTP-2 in place earlier in the list, because "Bastion" as a source or destination (covered by rules FTP-5 and FTP-6) is a subset of "All" (covered by rules FTP-1 and FTP-2). Having these redundant rules is going to impose a slight performance cost, but makes the rule set easier to understand. It also makes it possible to change rules FTP-1 and FTP-2 (e.g., if you decide you don't want to support passive-mode clients) without accidentally breaking normal-mode client access to the proxy server.

FTP-7 through FTP-9

Allow FTP data connections from the proxy server on the bastion host to non-passive internal clients. The FTP-7 rule prevents an attacker who has gained access to the bastion host from attacking internal X11 servers via the hole created by rules FTP-8 and FTP-9. If you have other servers internally listening for connections on TCP ports above 1023, you should add similar rules for them. Note that trying to list things that should be denied (as in rule FTP-7) is generally a losing proposition, because your list will almost always be incomplete somehow (e.g., because you overlooked or didn't know about some internal service, or because the service was added after the filters were established). However, it's the best you can do in this situation to support normal-mode FTP clients.

SMTP-1 and SMTP-2

Allow outgoing mail from internal hosts to the bastion host.

SMTP-3 and SMTP-4

Allow incoming mail from the bastion host to your internal mail server.

NNTP-1 and NNTP-2

Allow outgoing Usenet news from your news server to your service provider's news server.

NNTP-3 and NNTP-4

Allow incoming Usenet news from your service provider's news server to your news server.

HTTP-1 and HTTP-2

Allow internal HTTP clients to connect to the HTTP proxy server on your bastion host.

DNS-1

Allows UDP-based DNS queries and answers from the internal DNS server to the bastion host DNS server.

DNS-2

Allows UDP-based DNS queries and answers from the bastion host DNS server to the internal DNS server.

DNS-3 and DNS-4

Allow TCP-based DNS queries from the bastion host DNS server to the internal DNS server, as well as answers to those queries. Also allow zone transfers in which the bastion host DNS server is the secondary server and the internal DNS server is the primary server.

DNS-5 and DNS-6

Allow TCP-based DNS queries from the internal DNS server to the bastion host DNS servers, as well as answers to those queries. Also allow zone transfers in which the bastion host DNS server is the primary server and the internal DNS server is the secondary server.

Default-1 and Default-2

Block all packets not specifically allowed by one of the preceding rules.

How you translate these abstract rules into specific rules for your particular filtering system depends on the syntax used by your system. Some systems allow you to enter the rules as a single table, much as we show here in this table. Other systems require you to specify rules for incoming and outgoing packets in separate rule sets. Splitting these rules between incoming and outgoing packets is not a problem, as long as you preserve the order for rules of each type; that is, as long as all the incoming rules stay in the same order relative to each other, and all the outgoing rules stay in the same order relative to each other.

Exterior Router

The purpose of the exterior router is twofold:

- To connect the perimeter net (and thus your site) to the outside world

- To protect the perimeter net and the internal net against the outside world

In many circumstances, only the former purpose is possible, because the exterior router is often provided and managed by your network service provider. That provider may be unable or unwilling to set up and maintain packet filtering rules on the exterior router (and unable or unwilling to let you do it yourself).

If you can set up filtering on the exterior router, it's a good idea to do so. If nothing else, this can serve as a backup to some of the filtering on the interior router. For this example, you would need to establish the following rules:

Rule	Direction	Source Address	Dest. Address	Protocol	Source Port	Dest. Port	ACK Set	Action
Spoof-1	In	Internal	Any	Any	Any	Any	Any	Deny
Spoof-2	In	Perim.	Any	Any	Any	Any	Any	Deny
Telnet-1	Out	Internal	Any	TCP	>1023	23	Any	Permit
Telnet-2	In	Any	Internal	TCP	23	>1023	Yes	Permit
FTP-1	Out	Internal	Any	TCP	>1023	21	Any	Permit
FTP-2	In	Any	Internal	TCP	21	>1023	Yes	Permit
FTP-3	Out	Internal	Any	TCP	>1023	>1023	Any	Permit
FTP-4	In	Any	Internal	TCP	>1023	>1023	Yes	Permit
FTP-5	Out	Bastion	Any	TCP	>1023	21	Any	Permit
FTP-6	In	Any	Bastion	TCP	21	>1023	Yes	Permit

Rule	Direction	Source Address	Dest. Address	Protocol	Source Port	Dest. Port	ACK Set	Action
FTP-7	In	Any	Bastion	TCP	20	6000-6003	Any	Deny
FTP-8	In	Any	Bastion	TCP	20	>1023	Any	Permit
FTP-9	Out	Bastion	Any	TCP	>1023	20	Yes	Permit
FTP-10	In	Any	Bastion	TCP	>1023	21	Any	Permit
FTP-11	Out	Bastion	Any	TCP	21	>1023	Yes	Permit
FTP-12	Out	Bastion	Any	TCP	20	>1023	Any	Permit
FTP-13	In	Any	Bastion	TCP	>1023	20	Yes	Permit
FTP-14	In	Any	Bastion	TCP	>1023	>1023	Any	Permit
FTP-15	Out	Bastion	Any	TCP	>1023	>1023	Any	Permit
SMTP-1	Out	Bastion	Any	TCP	>1023	25	Any	Permit
SMTP-2	In	Any	Bastion	TCP	25	>1023	Yes	Permit
SMTP-3	In	Any	Bastion	TCP	>1023	25	Any	Permit
SMTP-4	Out	Bastion	Any	TCP	25	>1023	Yes	Permit
NNTP-1	Out	Internal NNTP server	NNTP feed server	TCP	>1023	119	Any	Permit
NNTP-2	In	NNTP feed server	Internal NNTP server	TCP	119	>1023	Yes	Permit
NNTP-3	In	NNTP feed server	Internal NNTP server	TCP	>1023	119	Any	Permit
NNTP-4	Out	Internal NNTP server	NNTP feed server	TCP	119	>1023	Yes	Permit
HTTP-1	Out	Bastion	Any	TCP	>1023	Any	Any	Permit
HTTP-2	In	Any	Bastion	TCP	Any	>1023	Yes	Permit
HTTP-3	In	Any	Bastion	TCP	>1023	80	Any	Permit
HTTP-4	Out	Bastion	Any	TCP	80	>1023	Yes	Permit
DNS-1	Out	Bastion	Any	UDP	53	53	[a]	Permit
DNS-2	In	Any	Bastion	UDP	53	53	[a]	Permit
DNS-3	In	Any	Bastion	UDP	Any	53	[a]	Permit
DNS-4	Out	Bastion	Any	UDP	53	Any	[a]	Permit
DNS-5	Out	Bastion	Any	TCP	>1023	53	Any	Permit
DNS-6	In	Any	Bastion	TCP	53	>1023	Yes	Permit
DNS-7	In	Any	Bastion	TCP	>1023	53	Any	Permit
DNS-8	Out	Bastion	Any	TCP	53	>1023	Yes	Permit
Default-1	Out	Any	Any	Any	Any	Any	Any	Deny
Default-2	In	Any	Any	Any	Any	Any	Any	Deny

[a] UDP packets do not have ACK bits.

Here is some additional information about each set of rules in this table.

Spoof-1 and Spoof-2

Block incoming packets that claim to have internal or perimeter net IP addresses—that is, forged packets presumably sent by an attacker. Rule Spoof-1 is the same as the Spoof rule on the interior router; rule Spoof-2 is unique to the exterior router.

Telnet-1 and Telnet-2

Allow outgoing Telnet connections. These are identical to the corresponding rules on the interior router (as are all rules on the exterior router that involve internal and external hosts, but nothing on the perimeter net).

FTP-1 through FTP-4

Allow outgoing passive-mode FTP connections and are identical to the corresponding rules on the interior router.

FTP-5 and FTP-6

Allow the FTP proxy server on the bastion host to open an FTP command channel to FTP servers on the Internet. Note that, unlike the corresponding rules on the interior router, these rules are *not* redundant if you have rules FTP-1 and FTP-2 in place earlier in the list. Why? Because "Bastion" as a source or destination (covered by rules FTP-5 and FTP-6) is not a subset of "Internal" (covered by rules FTP-1 and FTP-2).

FTP-7 through FTP-9

Allow FTP data connections from external FTP servers to the proxy server on the bastion host. The FTP-7 rule prevents an attacker from attacking X11 servers on the bastion host via the hole created by rules FTP-8 and FTP-9. If you have other servers on the bastion host listening for connections on TCP ports above 1023, you should add similar rules for them. Note that trying to list things that should be denied (as in rule FTP-7) is a losing proposition, because your list will almost always be incomplete, e.g., because you overlooked or didn't know about some service, or because the service was added after the filters were established. However, it's the best you can do in this situation, if you must support normal-mode FTP.

FTP-10 through FTP-15

Allow passive- and normal-mode FTP from external clients to the anonymous FTP server on the bastion host. There are no equivalent rules on the internal router because there are no FTP servers on the internal network that external clients can access.

SMTP-1 and SMTP-2

Allow outgoing mail from the bastion host to the outside world.

SMTP-3 and SMTP-4

Allow incoming mail from the outside world to the bastion host.

NNTP-1 to NNTP-4

Allow Usenet news both ways between your Usenet news server and your service provider's news server. These rules are identical to the corresponding rules on the interior router.

HTTP-1 and HTTP-2

Allow the bastion host HTTP proxy server to connect to the HTTP servers on any machine on the Internet. Actually, these rules allow any TCP client program on the bastion host using a port above 1023 to contact any server program on any host on the Internet using any port. This is done so that the HTTP proxy server can contact HTTP servers on nonstandard port numbers (i.e., other than port 80). As broad as these rules are, it's important that they allow only outgoing connections, by examining the ACK bit.

HTTP-3 and HTTP-4

Allow external clients to contact the bastion host HTTP server. There are no equivalent rules on the internal router because there are no HTTP servers on the internal network that external clients can access.

DNS-1

Allows UDP-based DNS queries and answers from the bastion host DNS server to DNS servers in the outside world.

DNS-2

Allows UDP-based DNS queries and answers from Internet DNS servers to the bastion host DNS server.

DNS-3 and DNS-4

Allow external UDP-based DNS clients to query the DNS server on the bastion host and it to answer them.

DNS-5 and DNS-6

Allow TCP-based DNS queries from the bastion host to DNS servers on the Internet, as well as answers to those queries. Also allow zone transfers in which the bastion host DNS server is the secondary server and an external DNS server is the primary server.

DNS-7 and DNS-8

Allow TCP-based DNS queries from the outside world to the bastion host DNS server, as well as answers to those queries. Also allow zone transfers in which the bastion host DNS server is the primary server and an external DNS server is the secondary server.

Default-1 and Default-2

> Block all packets not specifically allowed by one of the preceding rules, just as the corresponding rules do on the interior router.

Other Configuration Work

In addition to setting up the packet filtering rules, we need to do various other kinds of configuration work, as described below.

On all of the internal machines

> Configure electronic mail so that it gets sent to the bastion host. We're also going to need to install passive mode FTP clients if they're available.

On the internal mail server

> Install the *smap* and *smapd* programs from the TIS FWTK and an up-to-date mailer release so that we have a trusted SMTP server.

On the internal (primary) name server

> Put in an MX record for every A record, pointing incoming mail to the bastion host; further MX records may be necessary for the internal mail server to direct the traffic internally. We also need to configure the bastion host as a recognized secondary name server, and remove any TXT or HINFO records we don't want the external world to see (i.e., pretty much any records the external world could possibly make any sense of).

On the bastion host

> Do all the standard bastion host configuration (removing unused servers, adding logging, and so on), as discussed in Chapter 5. We need to install TIS FWTK and configure FTP proxying, *smap* and *smapd,* and anonymous FTP service from it. We also need to install the CERN HTTP server and configure it to do proxying, as well as to serve the HTTP pages we want to show the outside world.

Analysis

Just how good a firewall is this one we've configured? Let's consider it in relation to the strategies and principles discussed in Chapter 3.

Least privilege

The principle of least privilege is that an object (a program, a person, a router, or whatever) should have the minimum privileges necessary to perform its assigned task and no more. A corollary of this principle is that systems should be configured so they require as little privilege as possible. You can see this principle in action in several places in this setup. For example, configuring SMTP so that outgoing mail goes out via the bastion host (rather than directly to remote systems) is an application of least privilege, because it lets you control more tightly how internal systems connect to external systems. (In this case, it makes it unnecessary for internal systems to talk directly to external systems in order to provide this service.)

Defense in depth

The principle of defense in depth is something else that you can see in the setup we've described. For example, internal hosts are protected from the outside world by the exterior and interior routers. Similarly, the bastion host is protected against attack both by its own careful configuration and by the exterior router.

Several times, we've explicitly made decisions to increase the depth of defense. For example, that's one of the main purposes of using an internal mail server between the bastion host and the internal clients. The interior and exterior routers often deny the same packets. Defense in depth is almost the only reason for having the interior router deny packets that it supposedly can't receive (because they've already been denied by the exterior router).

Choke point

The principle of a choke point is clearly applied in our setup, because everything between internal clients and the Internet comes through the perimeter net. Further, much of it comes through the bastion host, via proxies. Only Telnet and FTP are provided in ways that leave them relatively open. These services could have been better choked by using proxies everywhere.

Weakest link

There is no single obvious weak link to attack in this configuration. Probably the weakest link is the bastion host, but even a completely compromised bastion host isn't going to help an attacker when it comes to attacking the internal systems; there just aren't that many connections allowed from the bastion host to internal systems. Some of the weakest links you can see remaining in this setup include proxy FTP and SMTP from the bastion host to the internal mail server.

The proxy FTP setup we've described would allow an attacker who has compromised the bastion host to attack servers on ports above 1023 (if there are any) on internal hosts. How can you address this vulnerability? Obtain and use only passive-mode FTP clients internally, don't run proxy FTP, and remove the rules allowing proxy FTP from the filters.

Similarly, the SMTP setup we've described would allow an attacker who has compromised the bastion host to attack your mail server via SMTP. How can you address this vulnerability? Improve the security of the SMTP server on your mail server, e.g., by using an up-to-date version of Sendmail, and by using the TIS FWTK *smap* package.

You can keep playing this game of thinking "If I were an attacker, what would I do?", and then addressing the problems you discover ad nauseam, or until you run out of time or money. At some point, though, you (or your management) will probably decide you've done enough (based on your own site's definition of "enough").

Fail-safe stance

You can see the principle of a fail-safe stance applied through the packet filtering rules. In general, the rules specify what you're going to allow, and deny everything else by default. This is a fail-safe approach, because if something unanticipated comes along (a new service, for example), it won't be allowed through your firewall; unless, of course, it mimics or is tunneled through some other service you do allow. The redundant router rules also provide a fail-safe against failure of one router or the other. If filtering accidentally or temporarily gets turned off on one router (causing it to pass all packets), the other still does most of the same filtering, at least as far as the outside world is concerned.

Universal participation

If this is our site's only connection to the Internet, we have involuntary universal participation; everybody has to go through the firewall to get to the Internet. Of course, we'd be much better off with voluntary universal participation, but that may require some user education about the goals of and the need for the security measures we're adopting.

To some extent, we're relying on voluntary universal participation. We've granted free Telnet and FTP access, and in the process we've allowed any outbound connection to ports at or above 1024 (which is plenty of rope for the users to hang us with). FTP is by no means the only service above 1024, and Telnet is a perfectly good client to use to get to many of them.

In particular, we've assumed that this is your sole connection to the Internet and that internal users aren't just going to bypass the firewall entirely by setting up their own Internet connections. All it takes is one joker with a modem, a PPP software package, and an outside phone line, and you too could have an unprotected back door into your network.

Diversity of defense

There are opportunities in this configuration to apply the principle of diversity of defense, e.g., using routers from different vendors for the interior and exterior packet filtering systems. Most sites will probably conclude that such an approach is not worth the hassle. However, even if you use similar or identical hardware, you still might get some diversity by having different people do at least the initial configuration of the different filtering systems, and then having them cross-check each other's work.

Using different SMTP servers on the internal mail server and the bastion host would be a fairly major advance in this configuration, because that's one of the main weak points of your setup. Even a less secure SMTP server on the internal mail server is arguably better than one that's going to yield to the exact same attack that just succeeded on the bastion host. The more vulnerable the SMTP server you're using, the more important an issue this is.

Conclusions

There are a lot of advantages offered by a scheme such as the one we've described in the sections above. The main potential disadvantages we can see are cost and complexity; but we don't think that the configuration we've presented is too expensive for most sites, and we think that it presents the minimum necessary level of complexity.

What if you really need to save some money? It would be feasible to construct a screened subnet architecture using a single three-interface router, instead of the pair of two-interface routers we've described above. The solution would be a little more complex, because you'd have to merge the two separate filtering sets described above, but doing so shouldn't be too difficult.

It would also be relatively easy to construct a more secure configuration with the same basic architecture. A less trusting site would force all Telnet and all FTP through proxies, which would allow much better logging and remove the nagging holes created by allowing every outbound connection to ports above 1024. Once you'd forced Telnet and FTP through proxies, you'd also find that DNS information hiding would be both more practical and more reasonable. However, the price of this increased security would be a more complex and fragile configuration, and one that presents more annoyance to the users.

It would also be possible to increase the services offered without major architecture changes. For example, incoming Telnet and incoming user FTP could be supported relatively easily for a few users on the bastion host or on a dedicated host on the screened network. Serious anonymous FTP service or HTTP service could be provided by configuring extra machines on the screened network. Similarly, you could scale up the firewall to support a second Internet connection or redundant bastion hosts to provide more reliable service or service for a much larger internal network.

Screened Host Architecture

The screened host architecture, described in Chapter 4 and shown in Figure 9-2, is a lower-security, lower-cost alternative to the screened subnet architecture discussed in the previous sections. The screened host architecture is often used by very small sites that are facing significant cost constraints.

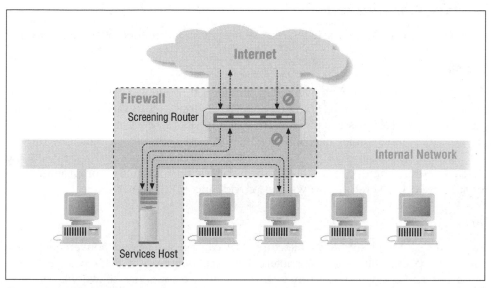

Figure 9–2: Screened host architecture

In a screened host architecture, there is no perimeter net, no interior router, and often no bastion host per se. (Obviously, there is a host that the outside world talks to, but this host is often not dedicated solely to that task.) What you have instead is a single router (most analogous to the exterior router in the dual-router screened subnet architecture) and a services host that provides Internet services to internal and external clients (and is often used for other tasks as well).

The router is there to protect and control access to the internal net, and the services host is there to interact with the outside world, much like a bastion host. We call it a *services host,* rather than a bastion host, because it's often fulfilling many other roles. For example, it's probably the mail server, Usenet news server, and DNS server for the site; it might possibly be a file server, print server, and so on, as well; it might even be the only machine the site has.

In this example, we're going to assume:

- That the services host is the site's mail server, news server, and DNS server, but that it's not the only machine at the site.

- As in the previous example, that internal users are trusted not to actively try to circumvent the firewall, and that we have no particular need to monitor or log their Internet activities.

- Also as in the previous example, that you're using proper IP addresses: addresses that have been properly assigned to your site and that are being properly routed and advertised to the rest of the Internet by your service provider.

Service Configuration

How do we provide the basic Internet services with a screened host architecture?

Telnet

Telnet can be safely and conveniently provided through packet filtering. For this example, that's what we're going to do. We've discussed in the previous sections how proxying Telnet is usually too expensive for its benefits in a larger configuration; it's that much sillier here in the screened host architecture. Similarly, providing incoming Telnet is difficult in the larger configuration, and verges on the suicidal here, where compromising the services host instantly compromises the entire network. Therefore, we will not provide incoming Telnet service.

FTP

As in the screened subnet architecture, FTP can be safely and conveniently provided via packet filtering if our internal FTP clients support FTP's passive mode. We'll need to set up an FTP proxy server on the services host if we wish to support clients that can't use passive mode. We can support both passive- and normal-mode FTP clients, if needed, but doing so is not as likely at a smaller site. At smaller sites, it's better to do one or the other, rather than try to keep track of both. In this example, we'll do only passive mode.

Be aware that in order to use an FTP proxy server on your services host, your filtering router would have to allow TCP connections from port 20 on external systems to ports above 1023 on your services host. For a regular bastion host, this wouldn't be a problem, because nothing should be using such ports. For a services host that's also serving other purposes, however, that may not be true.

Incoming user FTP goes the same way as incoming Telnet in any configuration. Because we've already decided to deny incoming Telnet, we'll deny incoming user FTP as well.

As we've seen with the screened subnet architecture, incoming anonymous FTP is an acceptable risk when it's going to a bastion host. However, it's not an acceptable risk going to the services host, with confidential data and full access to the internal network right there. We will therefore deny it.

SMTP

In this architecture, there is probably only one good way to set up SMTP. Incoming mail should be directed (via DNS MX records) to the services host, and outgoing mail should go out via the services host. There really is no feasible alternative. As we've discussed above, it's never advisable to let incoming mail go directly to all of your internal machines. Also, once you're directing incoming mail through a single point, it's actually easier—not to mention safer—to route outgoing mail through there than to send it direct.

NNTP

As with SMTP, there is probably only one good way to set up NNTP in the screened host architecture, and that is to make another internal machine a Usenet news server and allow NNTP directly to it. We could, if forced to do so, make the services host a news server. However, it might be better to forgo news altogether, given how much of a load news places on a machine and how critical the services host is.

HTTP

As we've discussed in the previous example, HTTP can be provided directly via packet filtering or indirectly via a proxy server. However, it makes the most sense to provide HTTP indirectly via a caching proxy server such as the CERN HTTP server. There is one good reasons for this: better performance due to caching.

For this example, we're going to assume we're providing HTTP service via a CERN proxy server running on the services host. Once again, we decide to deny service to external clients due to the risks (which are further compounded by the sensitive position of the services host).

DNS

As with most of the other services, there is really only one good place to put the DNS server in the screened host architecture: on the services host. For this example, we're going to assume that:

- The services host is your primary DNS server.

- You have an external DNS secondary server for your domain, e.g., one of your service provider's machines.

- You're not going to do any DNS information hiding: you can't if the services host is your internal and external primary server.

Packet Filtering Rules

Let's look at the packet filtering rules necessary to support the screened host configuration we've described in the previous sections. As in the earlier example of the screened subnet architecture, we're going to assume an "ideal" router. The router needs the following rules to support the configuration we've outlined.

Rule	Direction	Source Address	Dest. Address	Protocol	Source Port	Dest. Port	ACK Set	Action
Spoof	In	Internal	Any	Any	Any	Any	Any	Deny
Telnet-1	Out	Internal	Any	TCP	>1023	23	Any	Permit
Telnet-2	In	Any	Internal	TCP	23	>1023	Yes	Permit

Rule	Direction	Source Address	Dest. Address	Protocol	Source Port	Dest. Port	ACK Set	Action
FTP-1	Out	Internal	Any	TCP	>1023	21	Any	Permit
FTP-2	In	Any	Internal	TCP	21	>1023	Yes	Permit
FTP-3	Out	Internal	Any	TCP	>1023	>1023	Any	Permit
FTP-4	In	Any	Internal	TCP	>1023	>1023	Yes	Permit
SMTP-1	Out	Services	Any	TCP	>1023	25	Any	Permit
SMTP-2	In	Any	Services	TCP	25	>1023	Yes	Permit
SMTP-3	In	Any	Services	TCP	>1023	25	Any	Permit
SMTP-4	Out	Services	Any	TCP	25	>1023	Yes	Permit
NNTP-1	Out	News server	NNTP feed server	TCP	>1023	119	Any	Permit
NNTP-2	In	NNTP feed server	News server	TCP	119	>1023	Yes	Permit
NNTP-3	In	NNTP feed server	News server	TCP	>1023	119	Any	Permit
NNTP-4	Out	News server	NNTP feed server	TCP	119	>1023	Yes	Permit
HTTP-1	Out	Services	Any	TCP	>1023	Any	Any	Permit
HTTP-2	In	Any	Services	TCP	Any	>1023	Yes	Permit
DNS-1	Out	Services	Any	UDP	53	53	[a]	Permit
DNS-2	In	Any	Services	UDP	53	53	[a]	Permit
DNS-3	In	Any	Services	UDP	Any	53	[a]	Permit
DNS-4	Out	Services	Any	UDP	53	Any	[a]	Permit
DNS-5	Out	Services	Any	TCP	>1023	53	Any	Permit
DNS-6	In	Any	Services	TCP	53	>1023	Yes	Permit
DNS-7	In	Any	Services	TCP	>1023	53	Any	Permit
DNS-8	Out	Services	Any	TCP	53	>1023	Yes	Permit
Default-1	Out	Any	Any	Any	Any	Any	Any	Deny

Rule	Direc-tion	Source Address	Dest. Address	Pro-tocol	Source Port	Dest. Port	ACK Set	Action
Default-2	In	Any	Any	Any	Any	Any	Any	Deny

[a] UDP packets do not have ACK bits.

Here is some additional information about each set of rules in this table:

Spoof

Blocks incoming packets that claim to have internal IP addresses, that is, forged packets, presumably sent by an attacker.

Telnet-1 and Telnet-2

Allow outgoing Telnet connections.

FTP-1 through FTP-4

Allow outgoing passive-mode FTP connections. The FTP-1 and FTP-2 rules allow the command channel, and the FTP-3 and FTP-4 rules allow the data channel. In fact, FTP-3 and FTP-4 allow any TCP connection to be opened from the services host to any host on the Internet, as long as the port numbers used on both ends are above 1023.

SMTP-1 and SMTP-2

Allow outgoing mail from the services host to the outside world.

SMTP-3 and SMTP-4

Allow incoming mail from the outside world to the services host.

NNTP-1 to NNTP-4

Allow Usenet news both ways between your news server and your service provider's news server.

HTTP-1 and HTTP-2

Allow the services host HTTP proxy server to connect to the HTTP servers on any machine on the Internet. Actually, these rules allow any TCP client program on the services host using a port above 1023 to contact any server program on any host on the Internet using any port. This is done so that the HTTP proxy server can contact HTTP servers on nonstandard port numbers (i.e., other than port 80). As broad as these rules are, it's important that these rules allow only outgoing connections; they can do this by examining the ACK bit. Note the overlap between these rules and rules FTP-3 and FTP-4; removing either set would still allow both FTP and HTTP clients access to most servers.

DNS-1

Allows UDP-based DNS queries and answers from the services host DNS server to DNS servers in the outside world.

DNS-2

Allows UDP-based DNS queries and answers from Internet DNS servers to the services host DNS server.

DNS-3 and DNS-4

Allow external UDP-based DNS clients to query the DNS server on the services host, and it to answer them.

DNS-5 and DNS-6

Allow TCP-based DNS queries from the services host to DNS servers on the Internet, as well as answers to those queries. Also allow zone transfers in which the services host DNS server is the secondary server and an external DNS server is the primary server.

DNS-7 and DNS-8

Allow TCP-based DNS queries from the outside world to the services host DNS server, as well as answers to those queries. Also allow zone transfers in which the services host DNS server is the primary server and an external DNS server is the secondary server.

Default-1 and Default-2

Block all packets not specifically allowed by one of the preceding rules.

Analysis

Just how good a firewall is this? The short answer is, "not very." Let's consider it in relation to the strategies and principles discussed in Chapter 3, and in comparison to the screened subnet architecture we configured in the first example.

Least privilege

You can see the principle of least privilege in action in some places in this setup. For example, configuring SMTP so that outgoing mail goes out via the services host rather than directly to remote systems is an application of least privilege. Why? Because it lets you control more tightly how internal systems connect to external systems. (In this case, it makes it unnecessary for internal systems to talk directly to external systems in order to provide this service.)

On the other hand, having the services host fulfill so many roles (and thus requiring it to have the aggregate set of privileges required for all those roles) is definitely not in accord with the principle of least privilege. The services host has far too much privilege for most of the services it needs to provide.

The screened subnet architecture we described earlier in this chapter does a somewhat better job of applying the principle of least privilege than the screened host architecture described in this section.

Defense in depth

The principle of defense in depth is almost completely missing from this setup. Internal hosts are protected from the outside world by the filtering router and the services host, but nothing protects them from the services host if it is compromised. The filtering router and the services host are providing separate protection, not backing each other up. If either one is compromised, the entire site is compromised.

The screened subnet architecture we described earlier in this chapter does a much better job of applying the principle of defense in depth.

Choke point

The principle of a choke point is clearly applied in this example of a screened host architecture, because everything between internal clients and the Internet comes through at least the filtering router. Further, much of it comes through the services host, via proxies.

The screened subnet architecture described earlier in the chapter does a slightly better job of applying the principle of a choke point, but not by much.

Weakest link

The obvious weak link to attack in the screened host architecture is the services host. A compromised services host is going to severely affect the security of the rest of the internal hosts, because it's on the same network as these internal hosts and because there is nothing to protect them from it. With the screened subnet architecture, on the other hand, the interior router protects the internal hosts from the bastion host.

Further, because of the multitude of services being provided by the services host, it's more likely an attacker will be able to find a way to break in than with the bastion host in the screened subnet example.

All in all, the screened subnet architecture presents a much stronger "weakest link" to an attacker.

Fail-safe stance

You can see the principle of a fail-safe stance applied through the packet filtering rules specified for the screened host architecture. In general, the rules specify what you're going to allow, and deny everything else by default. This is a fail-safe approach, because if something unanticipated comes along (for example, a new service), it won't be allowed through your firewall, unless, of course, it mimics or is tunneled through some other service that you do allow.

However, the design of the screened host architecture itself is not fail-safe. If the services host is compromised, your whole site's security is severely compromised. The screened subnet architecture is much better about this.

Universal participation

If this is your site's only connection to the Internet, you've got involuntary universal participation: everybody has to go through the firewall to get to the Internet. Voluntary universal participation would be better, but that would require some user education concerning the goals of and the need for your security measures.

In terms of the universal participation principle, there really isn't much difference between the screened subnet and screened host architectures.

Diversity of defense

There are few opportunities here to apply the principle of diversity of defense, because you pretty much have only one of everything: there is only one router on which to set up filtering and only one services host.

This is another area in which the screened subnet architecture is superior to the screened host architecture.

Conclusions

The screened host architecture may be cheaper to implement than the screened subnet architecture, but it's much less secure. There is little or no redundancy in the design, and it's not really fail-safe. Even so, it is providing fewer services than the screened subnet architecture, and it can't increase either the security or the services.

To do a screened host architecture right, you pretty much need to dedicate a machine to being the services host and nothing else; you essentially need a bastion host. At that point, if you compare the equipment between a screened subnet architecture and a screened host architecture, you see that the only difference in equipment is either:

- For a two-router screened subnet architecture—a second router.

- For a one-router screened subnet architecture—a third interface on your single router.

The cost of a suitable second router really isn't that much: a couple of thousand dollars. The cost of an additional interface for a router is often much less: a few hundred dollars difference in price between a two-interface and a three-interface model of the same router. The incremental cost might actually be nothing if you already have a suitable spare PC lying around, and if you can use one of the PC-based filtering packages freely available off the Internet (such as Drawbridge or KarlBridge, described in Appendix B).

The difference between the screened subnet architecture and the screened host architecture is gigantic in terms of security, scalability, and services. You can't reasonably offer inbound services of even the most limited type in a screened host architecture. You can't increase anything, even the number of supportable machines, without making an architecture change.

In This Chapter:
- *Risks of Using
  Inbound Services*
- *What Is
  Authentication?*
- *Authentication
  Mechanisms*
- *Complete
  Authentication
  Systems*
- *Network-Level
  Encryption*
- *Terminal Servers and
  Modem Pools*

10

Authentication and Inbound Services

This book concentrates primarily on how to safely let your users go *out to* the Internet, but there's also another side to Internet security: how do you safely allow users to come *in from* the Internet?

For anonymous services, such as accessing an anonymous FTP server, HTTP server, or Gopher server that you provide, the solution is clear: you protect the servers as best you can to allow outsiders to access the information you want to provide and to prevent them from accessing anything else. In these anonymous services, all the information you release is intended to be readable by anybody. (See the discussion of these services in Chapter 8.)

For nonanonymous services, however, the situation is much more complex. For nonanonymous services (or "authenticated" services, as they're commonly called), the user who is attempting to access the service first needs to prove his identity to your server so that your server can decide whether the user is authorized to do what he is requesting. Examples of authenticated services you might want to provide include:

- Allowing your users to log in (via Telnet) from the Internet, e.g., while they're away at conferences or visiting other sites.

- Allowing researchers and collaborators from affiliated sites to log in to your systems.

- Allowing selected customers or clients to log in to your systems.

Authentication is basically verified, proven identification. How do users prove to a system that they're really who they say they are? Don't confuse authentication (figuring out who somebody is) and authorization (figuring out what they're allowed to do). Authentication is a prerequisite for authorization (unless everybody is authorized to do something, such as anonymous FTP), but they are separate and distinct concepts.

This chapter focuses on inbound services and how authentication can reduce the risks associated with using these services. It also touches on a few additional encryption and authentication issues that apply to both inbound and outbound services, such as network-level encryption and where to place modem pools.

NOTE

> Although this chapter mentions aspects of cryptography—cryptography is the basis for many of the authentication mechanisms described in this book—we do not attempt to discuss cryptography itself here in any depth. There are many excellent books on this broad and complex topic, and we can't hope to do justice to the topic in a few pages here, where our focus is practical, rather than theoretical. You will be better served by referring to a book such as Bruce Schneier's *Applied Cryptography* for a definitive treatment. (See Appendix A for information.)

Risks of Using Inbound Services

Inbound services pose a number of security risks. In this section, we focus on Telnet as an example, but the same problems, principles, and solutions apply to other authenticated services (such as nonanonymous FTP) as well.

There are three principal risks associated with allowing inbound services:

Hijacking
: Having someone steal a connection after the user has authenticated himself or herself to your system.

Packet sniffing
: Having someone read confidential data as it passes across the network, without interfering with the connection itself.

False authentication
: Having someone who is not a valid user convince your system he or she *is* a valid user.

Hijacking

Hijacking attacks allow an attacker to take over an open terminal or login session from a user who has been authenticated by the system. Hijacking attacks generally take place on a remote computer, although it is sometimes possible to hijack a connection from a computer on the route between the remote computer and your local computer.

Cryptography

What are the basic differences between private and public key cryptography?

Private key algorithms include the Data Encryption Standard (DES) (used by Kerberos), IDEA, and the Skipjack algorithm that underlies the Clipper Chip. With private key, a single key is shared by two parties and must be kept secret by both of them (this is the private key). The sender of a communication encrypts the message with this secret key; the recipient must decrypt it with the same key. To communicate with someone securely, you must tell that person the cryptographic key you are using; you must also keep anyone else from discovering or overhearing the key. This process, called key distribution, is difficult and cumbersome to do securely.

Public key algorithms include RSA, and Diffie-Hellman. With public key systems, a mathematical process generates two mathematically related keys for each individual. A message encrypted with one key (the public key) can be decrypted only with the other key (secret or private key). Public keys can be known to anyone, but secret keys must be kept so. To transmit a secret message, the sender encrypts his message with the public key of the intended recipient. The recipient decrypts that message with his own secret key; the only key that will decrypt the message is the secret key associated with the public key used to encrypt it. Public key cryptography also gives you the ability to "sign" messages. If the sender signs a message with his secret key, the recipient can validate the signature by applying the sender's public key to the message; if the public key successfully decrypts the message, it must have been signed with the corresponding secret key.

Public key algorithms are slow, often thousands of times slower than equivalently secure private key algorithms. For this reason, public and private key algorithms are often used in conjunction with each other. For example, the Pretty Good Privacy (PGP) encryption package works this way. To send an encrypted message to a recipient, the sending PGP program generates a random "session key." This session key is used with a private key algorithm to encrypt the message to be sent (this is fast). The session key itself is encrypted with a public key algorithm (this is slow, but the session key is small, especially compared to the whole message), using the recipient's public key, and is sent along with the encrypted message. The recipient first uses the public key algorithm and his secret key to decrypt the session key (this is slow, but the session key is small), and then uses the session key and private key algorithm to decrypt the whole message (this is fast). For a detailed discussion of PGP, see Simson Garfinkel's book, *PGP: Pretty Good Privacy* (referenced in Appendix A).

How can you protect yourself from hijacking attacks on the remote computer? The only way is to allow connections only from remote computers whose security you trust; ideally, these computers should be at least as secure as your own. You can apply this kind of restriction by using either packet filters or modified servers. Packet filters are easier to apply to a collection of systems, but modified servers on individual systems allow you more flexibility. For example, a modified FTP server might allow anonymous FTP from any host, but authenticated FTP only from specified hosts. You can't get this kind of control from packet filtering. Connection control at the host level is available from wrappers in the TIS FWTK (the *netacl* program) or Wietse Venema's TCP Wrapper; these may be easier to configure than packet filters, but provide the same level of discrimination—by host only.

Hijacking by intermediate sites can be avoided using end-to-end encryption. (See the discussion of network-level encryption later in this chapter.) If you use end-to-end encryption, intermediate sites won't be able to encrypt the data stream properly (because they don't know the appropriate key), and therefore won't be able to hijack sessions traversing them.

Hijacking is a fairly technical attack. The overall risk to an organization from hijacking attacks is probably pretty small. Most sites choose to accept this small risk and allow some accounts to access systems from anywhere on the Internet. You may decide that hijacking is an acceptable risk for your own organization, particularly if you are able to minimize the number of accounts that have full access and the time they spend logged in remotely. However, you probably do not want to allow hundreds of people to log in from anywhere on the Internet. Similarly, you do not want to allow users to log in consistently from particular remote sites without taking special precautions.

Packet Sniffing

Attackers may not need to hijack a connection in order to get the information you want to keep secret. By simply watching packets pass—anywhere between the remote site and your site—they can see any information that is being transferred. *Packet sniffing* programs automate this watching of packets.

Sniffers may go after passwords or data. There are different risks associated with each type of attack. Protecting your passwords against sniffing is easy: use one of the several mechanisms described later in this chapter to use nonreusable passwords. With nonreusable passwords, it doesn't matter if the password is captured by a sniffer; it's of no use to them, because it cannot be reused.

Protecting your data against sniffers is more difficult. You could encrypt the data at your site if you always knew in advance which data to encrypt, and if you could rely on the remote site to have the appropriate decryption programs. It isn't safe for a user to ask for data to be encrypted while the user is logged in across the network; the sniffer will see the commands issued by the user (perhaps even the key used for encryption), and may be able to use that information to decrypt the data. If the user doesn't provide a key directly, the system has to somehow use a stored key, which might be compromised in other ways (such as a break-in to the system doing the encryption).

Unfortunately, encryption in advance is not practical. It may serve if you need to transfer files occasionally, but it isn't going to provide any kind of meaningful connection. In order to preserve data confidentiality for real interactive access, you'll need end-to-end encryption. Most end-to-end encryption systems require advance coordination between the two ends in order to set the system up. If you have ongoing sensitive interactions with particular sites, however, it may be worth the effort.

As we've described for hijacking, if only a small number of people from a site are doing occasional work from random hosts over the Internet, most organizations are willing to accept the relatively small risk associated with the sniffing of data. However, you need to make sure that nobody at your site purposefully accesses confidential information across the Internet without taking precautions. Moreover, you certainly do not want to set up situations in which confidential information consistently crosses the Internet unencrypted. For example, you would not want a human resources person to work from home on your unencrypted personnel files across the Internet.

False Authentication

The third main risk to inbound services is *false authentication*: the subversion of the authentication that you require of your users, so that an attacker can successfully masquerade as one of your users.

In most cases, if you have a secret you want to pass across the network, you can encrypt the secret and pass it that way. There is one case in which the encryption solution does not work, and that is the case in which information does not have to be understood to be used. For instance, encrypting passwords will not work, because an attacker who is using packet sniffing can simply intercept and resend the encrypted password without having to decrypt it. (This is called a *playback attack*, because the attacker records an interaction and plays it back later.) Therefore, dealing with authentication across the Internet requires something more complex than encrypting passwords. What you need is an authentication method where the data that passes across the network is nonreusable, so an attacker can't capture it and play it back.

The next section describes authentication and how it works. As we explain there, there are many types of authentication methods, some more secure than others.

What Is Authentication?

Usually, people think of authentication in terms of passwords. Although passwords are frequently used for authentication, there are actually a variety of authentication mechanisms. These mechanisms can generally be categorized as verifying one or more of the following:

Something you are
> This is the field of biometrics, including techniques such as fingerprint scans, retina scans, voiceprint analysis, and so on.

Something you know
> This is a traditional password system.

Something you have
> This includes mechanisms such as challenge-response lists, one-time pads, smart cards, and so on.

Some systems combine these approaches. For example, a smart card that requires the user to enter a personal identification number (PIN) to unlock it is a combination of something you have (the card) and something you know (the PIN). In theory, it is considered a good idea to combine at least two mechanisms, because people can steal either one: the thing you have is susceptible to ordinary theft, and the thing you know is compromised by sniffing if it passes over the Internet; but it's rare for somebody to be able to get both at once. Automatic teller machines use this combination; however, ATMs also demonstrate the flaw in the theory: when you are authenticating (standing at the ATM), you reveal what you have (your card) and what you know (your PIN) simultaneously, making yourself vulnerable to a thief who watches you use the machine to capture your PIN, then steals your card as you leave.

Something You Are

There are many types of biometric systems in use or under development today; they test such diverse personal characteristics as your voice, your fingerprint or handprint, your retina, your signature, and your typing patterns. Biometric systems are extremely attractive, because they get around the problems associated with using things that can be stolen or revealed. (Even the horror movie scenario of hacking off somebody's thumb to use in the fingerprint scanner is taken into account; most scanners insist that a pulse be present.) Unfortunately, biometric systems are not practical for normal Internet applications.

Commonly available computer hardware is not capable of reading fingerprints, much less retinas. Voiceprint technology is more tempting; it's not unusual for machines these days to have microphones. But it's not universal, either, and you can't guarantee that every machine you'll want to log in from has a microphone, much less the client application to digitize and transmit your voice. Moreover, every machine may not have the disk space and network bandwidth needed for this approach. Finally, if the biometric information has to be communicated from where you are to where it can be checked, you run the risk of an attacker's capturing it and replaying it later, unless you have some way of encrypting or otherwise protecting it.

Even if every machine had all the capabilities it needed, reliable voiceprint identification is surprisingly hard to accomplish. Many people wish to use their computers even when they have head colds, which throw off many voice-recognition systems. You can't use a fixed phrase as a password, or you would be vulnerable to a literal playback attack involving a tape recorder. (These problems have been addressed in dedicated systems, but there are no widely available authentication systems for general-purpose computers that can deal with them, and it's not at all trivial to develop one.) You can't use a different phrase every time, because voiceprint comparison on arbitrary text is not a real-time operation—unless you have a spare supercomputer lying around to do it with. Almost everybody wants to log in with a delay measured in seconds, at worst; getting back to the user with an answer in a few hours is not going to work.

Keystroke timing, used to characterize someone's typing pattern, is a surprisingly reliable biometric identification system and requires no special hardware. The computer provides a phrase to type, and then times the gaps between characters as you type it. On a phrase of reasonable length, people type in an identifiable pattern, and imitating it is much harder than it looks. Like voiceprints, keystroke timings may change for environmental reasons; in the case of keystroke timings, colds aren't a problem, but people have great difficulty authenticating while drunk. (This is not necessarily a disadvantage, of course.) The genuine disadvantage is that keystroke timings can be gathered only at the machine to which the keyboard is attached. That means that use of this method across the Internet requires modified clients. In addition, there are some people, mostly poor typists, who have trouble ever authenticating because their typing patterns are inconsistent.

Something You Know

If the long-lost heir to a fortune turns up in a novel, you can bet that fingerprints aren't going to be available to do biometric authentication. Instead, the claimant is probably going to try to prove that she is who she says she is because she knows the name of the stuffed animal she slept with at age three. This is authentication by knowledge, just like the traditional UNIX password system. (And, just like traditional UNIX passwords, the claimant's answers can be faked if she's a good guesser and gets enough tries.)

Authentication that depends on something you know relies on that something's being both hard to guess and secret. In order for you to authenticate reliably, you have to know the secret reliably, too. This isn't as easy as it sounds. Most people are bad at making up and remembering unguessable things, and they're worse at keeping secrets. If you use short keys, it's easy to guess them; if you use long keys, it's hard to remember them. If you write them down, you're basically converting to a different type of authentication; now, it's something you have.

System administrators who unblushingly tell their users never to write down passwords probably have a few stashed in their wallets anyway; this is a combination of "what you know" and "what you have." "What you know" is how to read your own handwriting, and which slip of paper contains the passwords, rather than last week's lunch order. "What you have" is the slip of paper itself.

Despite all of the risks of "what you know" systems, it is still practical to use such systems, as long as you aren't revealing the secret to everybody in the near vicinity every time you authenticate. There is a reason why passwords are so popular: they're fast, they're cheap, and, in practice, people don't forget them or lose the pieces of paper all that often. However, it is absolutely impractical to pass them across the Internet in any form that can be used safely.

Is there any way to use a "what you know" system safely on the Internet? Yes. Use passwords, but make sure that they are nonreusable (one-time) passwords.

There are two ways to make traditional, memorized passwords nonreusable. One is to include an *encrypted time-stamp*—this is the method that Kerberos uses. As long as you can't modify the time-stamp without knowing the password, this prevents playback. Unfortunately, it requires two things:

*   Special client software that knows how to time-stamp the password.

*   Synchronized time between the client and the server. If the server and the client have different times, the password will be either invalid already or not yet valid when it arrives.

The other way to make traditional, memorized passwords nonreusable is to use a *challenge-response system*. With such a system, the password you give depends on a prompt that the server gives you. Challenge-response is the traditional method for identifying yourself at a speakeasy, entering a military camp, or meeting fellow spies in art museums. It may seem to be an impractical approach, because in order to be reasonably safe from playback attacks you need a wide variety of challenges, each with a separate response. If you have trouble remembering one password, you certainly aren't going to remember 47 of them.

In fact, however, challenge-response systems for computers are designed so that instead of memorizing the response to each challenge, you memorize a rule for converting the challenge into a response. This concept has yet to become popular as a pure "what you know" option, because it's difficult to apply to a large number of people. A rule like "reverse the first three letters, capitalize the fourth, delete the fifth, and uppercase the rest of them" is easy to program, but it's not necessarily easy to represent so that you can have a different rule for each user. Even if you can remember your own rule, you're apt to follow along the challenge with a finger, muttering the rule to yourself while you try to implement it; someone watching over your shoulder can pretty easily determine the rule.

Something You Have

In practice, the most successful authentication systems for Internet use today are based on the third type of authentication: "something you have." What you have may be a printed list of single-use passwords or an electronic card; it's usually, but not always, combined with "something you know."

The use of electronic cards makes it practical to use challenge-response or time-based encryption. For challenge-response, you encode in the card itself the rule that converts the challenge to the response. For time-based encryption, you encode in the card both the time source and the encryption smarts. Either way, you can do authentication without needing modified clients or users with trick memories.

Using printed lists of passwords is generally referred to as using *one-time passwords*. This confuses people because all nonreusable passwords are good only one time, by definition. Printed password lists are called that because they resemble a spy device called a *one-time pad* that consists of a pad of paper with different instructions on each page. You encrypt one message with each page, so that the opposite side doesn't get multiple chances to break the code.[*]

Authentication Mechanisms

In order to use any of the methods of authentication we've outlined above, you need hardware or software to implement them. This section discusses some of the commonly available hardware and software authentication mechanisms that are at the heart of authentication systems (in particular, it discusses those supported by the TIS FWTK, which is the most widely available system). The most popular of the full-blown systems are discussed in "Complete Authentication Systems" later in this chapter.

---

[*] In fact, printed one-time password lists resemble one-time pads so closely that it's inadvisable to bring one to the attention of a customs agent when travelling internationally.

One-Time Passwords

There are two ways a one-time password system may work:

- The list can be generated randomly, and a copy kept by the user and the system.

- The list (or, more likely, a specific entry from the list) can be generated on demand by the user and validated by the system.

The problem with keeping a list on the system is that if the system is compromised, so is the list, and the list could then be used for future access. This is as bad as having someone snoop on a reusable password while you use it.

The TIS FWTK supports an elegant, one-time password solution called S/Key, originally designed by Leslie Lamport and developed by Bellcore, which addresses this problem. While it allows a system to reliably authenticate a user, there is nothing on the system that compromises the user's password if the system itself is compromised. The system has the ability to validate a user's current response, but does not have the ability to predict what that user's *next* response will be.

S/Key works by iteratively applying a cryptographically secure hash algorithm, starting with some initial seed value. A cryptographically secure hash algorithm is one that takes an arbitrary-sized input and produces a much smaller output (something like a checksum) that has two special properties:

- The input cannot be regenerated from the output; thus, it's not simply a compression or encryption algorithm.

- The probability of two different inputs (particularly two different inputs of the same size) producing the same output is vanishingly small.

S/Key uses such an algorithm, known as MD4.[*] S/Key works by starting with a seed (which is either provided by the user or generated randomly), and applying MD4 iteratively to get a sequence of keys. It applies MD4 to the seed to get the first key, applies MD4 to the first key to get the second key, applies MD4 to the second key to get the third key, and so on. In order to validate a user, the system has to know some key (call it key number n) in the sequence. The system prompts the user for the previous key (key n-1), applies MD4 to the user's answer (supposedly key n-1), and checks to see if the result is the key n that it knows. If the result is the key n, the user must have supplied the correct key n-1.

S/Key encodes each key into a series of short words, so they are easier for a user to read and type, rather than simply generating a random-looking jumble of characters. Figure 10-1 shows how S/Key works.

Because MD4 is nonreversible (you can't determine the input given the output), the system can't easily figure out what key n-1 is, even though it knows key n. All

---

[*] MD4 stands for Message Digest function #4 and was developed by Ron Rivest, the codeveloper of the RSA algorithm.

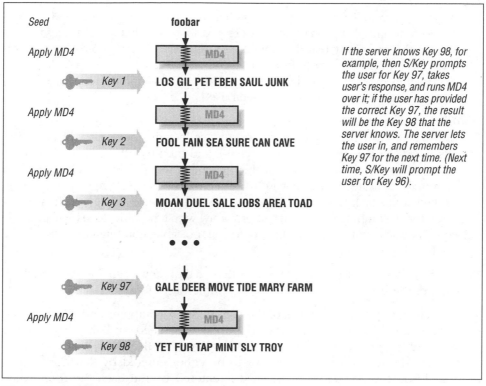

Figure 10–1: How S/Key works

the server can do is to verify that key *n*-1 (when presented by the user) is the key that generates key *n*. This means that even if an attacker can somehow obtain key *n* (for example, by snooping on a user's login session), he won't be able to easily figure out the next key (key *n*-1).

S/Key isn't absolutely invulnerable to attack. Several attacks are possible:

Brute force attacks

Attackers could try a whole series of possibilities for key *n*-1 until they found one that MD4 translated to key *n*. However, this type of attack is very unlikely to succeed. Because of the size of the key space (the number of possible keys) and the computation requirements of the MD4 algorithm, a brute force approach of this kind is considered to be computationally infeasible for all but the most serious and well-financed attackers. (It would probably take a significant amount of supercomputer time before they found the right key.)

Dictionary attacks

If the user provides the initial seed (rather than having the initial seed be generated randomly), dictionary attacks are possible. Attackers could guess at the seed in the same way that they might guess at reusable passwords; they'd typically try things like words from the dictionary, names, places, etc. To these words, they would apply the MD4 algorithm an appropriate number of times to see if it generates a key they've seen used.

Modified sniffing attacks

An attacker can run a packet sniffer and collect the beginning of an S/Key password (all but the last few characters), and then try all the possible combinations for the last characters, before the user finishes. This relies on extremely delicate timing, but in Telnet connections, user input is frequently set keystroke by keystroke as it is generated. This creates a lag which is significant for a computer. An attacker probably won't be able to try all possible combinations, but may be able to try all possible combinations that make English words.

There are two ways for users to use S/Key: either keys can be generated on demand, or the user can be supplied with a printed list of keys.

To generate S/Key keys on demand, the user needs a computer and a program to generate them. That user will have to provide the seed and the key number desired, and the program will iterate the MD4 algorithm that many times to generate the key desired. The seed will have to be either entered by the user or read from a file on the computer. If the seed is entered by the user, the user would probably pick a seed the same way he'd pick a password. Because users are notoriously poor at picking passwords, this makes the system subject to dictionary attacks, as we've described above. If the seed is read from a file, it can be more random (and therefore less guessable) than something the user would provide, but you have to worry about the risks—probably low—of the computer or file being stolen.

The alternative way to use S/Key is to have the system generate and print a list of keys, enough keys to last the user for a reasonable period of time. In this case, the system randomly generates the initial seed, thus protecting itself against dictionary attacks. The printout should simply be a numbered list of keys, with no further identification or explanation. It is possible that the list could be stolen from a user, but you have to decide which you think is more likely: that the list will be stolen (and that the thief will know what it is and what to do with it), or that the user's session will be snooped on. If your users are generating keys on demand, they're probably using a seed that's subject to dictionary attack (otherwise, they would find it too hard to remember the seed); if one of their sessions is snooped on, their keys can be attacked.

We think that using a seed that's subject to dictionary attack is a bigger risk than having a list of keys stolen, so we prefer using printed lists of keys to using keys generated on demand.

Time-based Passwords

Time-based password systems, such as those implemented by Security Dynamics products, are a special type of one-time password. In such a system, the password varies every minute or so, by an algorithm known to the system and the user's authentication device. This device is typically a small card, which Security Dynamics calls SecurID, with a liquid crystal display readout for the current password. One possible algorithm would be to encrypt the current time with a key known by the system and programmed into the card. With such an algorithm, the system would have to make allowances for clock drift (i.e., the clock in the card running at a slightly different rate from that of the system clock).

The Security Dynamics cards are supported by a wide variety of commercial products. The TIS FWTK doesn't support the cards directly, but it includes hooks to libraries that you can license separately (at a significant cost) from Security Dynamics.

The Security Dynamics cards are not without their critics. Various security professionals have expressed concern over Security Dynamics' decision to use a secret, proprietary encryption algorithm, rather than an algorithm, such as DES or IDEA, that has been subjected to public scrutiny and analysis. Other people don't like the fact that some versions of the Security Dynamics cards combine "something you have" with "something you know" by having the user send a traditional password over the Internet along with the key displayed by the card; if an attacker monitors a connection made using the card, and then steals the card itself, he now has everything he needs to break in. Finally, since the cards don't have replaceable batteries, the entire card has to be replaced when the batteries die (typically after about three years).

On the plus side, the keypad-less Security Dynamics cards are user-friendly; it's hard to use something incorrectly when it has exactly one button to press. If the button is accidentally pressed, nothing horrible happens; it will wear the battery down faster, but it won't make it impossible for you to authenticate. Also, because the cards turn themselves off as soon as the displayed key times out, pressing the button accidentally doesn't wear the battery down that fast.

By contrast, cards that require PINs are more complex to use and usually disable themselves if the wrong buttons are pressed too often. This means they can't be kept loose in a purse or backpack without extra protection. Keypad-less Security Dynamics cards are perfectly happy rattling around in a purse or backpack. The three-year battery life is also arguably about the expected lifetime of an authentication mechanism anyway; at the end of three years, you may want to change the entire system, not just the batteries.

Programming a Security Dynamics card, e.g., to set it for the system with which it needs to synchronize, generally requires special hardware.

Challenge-Response Schemes

Challenge-response systems are another way to support nonreusable passwords.

The TIS FWTK supports the SNK-004 card from Digital Pathways for challenge-response. When the user attempts to log in, the system generates a random challenge. The user unlocks the SNK-004 card with a 4-digit PIN, and then keys in the challenge. The card encrypts the challenge, using the DES algorithm and a key programmed into the memory of the card, and displays the encrypted result. The user sends the result back to the system as his response to the challenge.

In the meantime, the system has encrypted the same challenge with the key that is supposed to be in this user's card. If the system's result is the same as the user's response, then the user has successfully authenticated himself. All that has passed over the wire (and thus all that could be snooped on) is the random challenge and the encrypted result: not the user's PIN (used to unlock the SNK-004 card) or the key (programmed into the memory of the SNK-004 card, and known by the system).

Figure 10-2 shows how this challenge-response works.

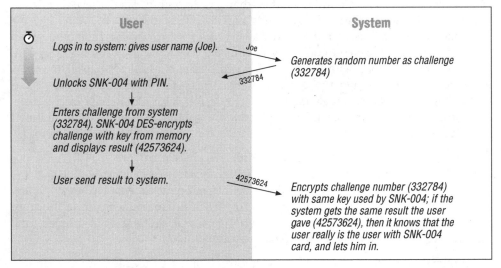

Figure 10-2: How the SNK-004 card works

The TIS FWTK includes, for free, almost everything you need to support the SNK-004 cards; the only exception is a DES library, several of which are available for free on the Internet.

Digital Pathways also sells programs for Macintosh, MS-DOS, and Microsoft Windows that emulate the SNK-004 card in software. Users who carry portable computers they log in from (or who always connect from the same desktop computer) will probably find it more convenient to use that software than to carry the separate SNK-004 card.

SNK-004 cards can be configured to disable themselves if the wrong PIN is entered more than five consecutive times. Unfortunately, accidentally turning on the card counts as a "wrong PIN" attempt, so the card can end up disabling itself if it's floating around loose in your luggage and something keeps pressing the "On" button; many people carry them in hard cases to prevent accidental activations. (Digital Pathways doesn't provide a hard case, but an 8mm tape case makes a good improvised one.) Digital Pathways reportedly has a new card to replace the SNK-004 that addresses this problem and may have other new features.

The SNK-004 can be programmed from its own keyboard with no special hardware, but anybody who doesn't do it every day will need to step through the procedure from the manual. (Warning: The SNK-004 programming procedure makes VCR programming look intuitive by contrast!) Programming hardware is available, and is probably a useful investment if you need to initialize more than a handful of the units.

Complete Authentication Systems

There are two common freely available systems that allow you to avoid sending reusable passwords over the Internet. These are Kerberos and the authentication server portion of the TIS FWTK. The number of commercial authentication solutions is growing as well.

Kerberos

Kerberos was developed at MIT by Project Athena (the same folks who developed the X Window System). It is designed to provide authentication and encryption services through modified versions of standard clients and servers, e.g., Telnet clients and servers.

Kerberos provides strong authentication in a distributed environment, and it is widely available. Some vendors provide Kerberos support with their operating systems; MIT has freely available implementations for many versions of UNIX; and the code is freely available if you wish it to port it to an operating system that does not yet have an implementation.

Kerberos isn't an ideal solution, though. There are three major problems with it:

- Kerberos requires custom client and server software. As with proxy systems, this limits your choice of client and server software. If the software you want to use doesn't support Kerberos, and if you can't modify it to support Kerberos (because the source code isn't available, or because you simply don't have the time or expertise required), you're out of luck, and you won't be able to use it. Unlike proxy systems, Kerberos does not let you use custom user procedures to make Kerberos work with arbitrary client/server software.

- Kerberos tends to be difficult to set up and manage. Unless your operating-system vendor supports Kerberos (or you can find a third-party vendor who supports it for your platform), you'll have to obtain the Kerberos software and integrate it into your environment yourself. This is a nontrivial task, typically much more difficult than the integration work required for most other solutions outlined in this book. Once Kerberos is set up, management of it provides another ongoing challenge. Kerberos requires a dedicated, carefully secured server, which is accessible to all clients.

- Kerberos doesn't scale up well beyond a single administrative domain (a single set of machines managed in common, which share user names and passwords). Each Kerberos realm (the Kerberos term for a single administrative domain) is independent. To do inter-realm authentication, the Kerberos servers in the two realms essentially have to trust each other, and have to share a key known only to each other. A separate key is required for each pair of realms that are going to do inter-realm authentication; as the number of realms involved increases, the number of keys required increases geometrically, to the point where it quickly becomes unmanageable.

Kerberos shows great promise for the future, particularly if more sites adopt the Distributed Computing Environment (DCE), which uses Kerberos as the basis of its security. It could very well become the de facto standard mechanism for authentication on the Internet sometime in the next decade or so. In order for that to happen, though, it will need wider support from developers and vendors, and easier setup and maintenance. Meanwhile, it will probably only be used within individual sites.

Right now, most sites don't have Kerberos clients available, so even if you install Kerberos versions of your servers, your users will not be able to log in from arbitrary other sites, because it requires modified software on both ends.

TIS FWTK Authentication Server

The authentication server in the TIS FWTK is another commonly used solution for authenticating users coming in from the Internet. The server implements a variety of authentication mechanisms, such as standard reusable passwords (not recommended), S/Key, Security Dynamics SecurID cards, and Digital Pathways SNK-004 cards. In addition, the server is modular and extensible, and is designed so that new authentication mechanisms can easily be integrated.

Traditionally, programs wishing to authenticate a user (such as the *login* program, or the *ftpd* daemon) have had to know *how* to authenticate a user; they have had to understand and implement whatever authentication method or methods were to be used. In a UNIX system, this means that these programs have to do all of the following to authenticate a user:

1. Prompt the user for a login name.

2. Look up that login name and obtain its encrypted password.

3. Prompt the user for a password.

4. Use the user-provided password and the first two characters from the encrypted password to encrypt a known string (eight bytes of nulls).

5. Check to see if the result of this encryption matches the encrypted password for the user.

If you want to add a second authentication mechanism (for example, the S/Key mechanism, which we discussed earlier), you have to modify all of these programs to understand this second mechanism as well as, or instead of, the standard UNIX password mechanism. And if you later want to add a third authentication mechanism (for example, support for the SecurID cards), you have to modify the programs yet again; and so it would go for each additional authentication mechanism. Each time you modify these programs, you're making them bigger and more complex, and increasing the chances that you've introduced some kind of bug that's going to result in a security problem. (This is a serious risk because these are very security-critical programs—they control access to your system.)

The TIS FWTK authentication server takes a different approach. With it, you modify all the authenticating programs (e.g., *login*, *ftpd*) once, to make them talk to the authentication server instead of doing the authentication themselves. All of the details of the authentication mechanism—e.g., what to prompt the user with, how to validate the user's response, etc.—are then handled by the authentication server. When you want to add or modify authentication methods, you do so by changing the authentication server (which is modular and designed to accommodate such changes), not by changing the individual authenticating programs.

A single authentication server can handle any number of client machines and programs, and any number of different authentication methods; different users within the same server can use different authentication methods. For example, some might use S/Key while some might use the Digital Pathways SNK-004 cards.

When a client program (such as *login*, or *ftpd*) wishes to authenticate someone using the TIS FWTK authentication server, it has to go through the following steps:

1. Prompt the user for a login name.

2. Contact the authentication server and tell it who is trying to log in.

3. Receive a response from the authentication server that tells it what to prompt the user with.

4. Display the prompt specified by the authentication server.

5. Collect the user's response and send it to the authentication server.

6. Receive either an OK or an error message from the authentication server.

7. Allow the user access (if OK) or display the error message.

This whole process is carried out with a single TCP connection between the client and the authentication server, so that the server knows it's talking to the same client and the client knows it's talking to the same server throughout the authentication process.

The authentication server consults its databases to determine how to authenticate that user and determines the appropriate prompt for the authentication mechanism for that user. For example:

- If traditional passwords are being used as the authentication method, the prompt will be a simple "Password:" prompt.

- If the authentication method is S/Key, the prompt will be the number of the key the user is to respond with.

- If the authentication method is the Digital Pathways SKN-004 card, the prompt will be a randomly generated challenge number.

Figure 10-3 shows how the TIS FWTK authentication server works.

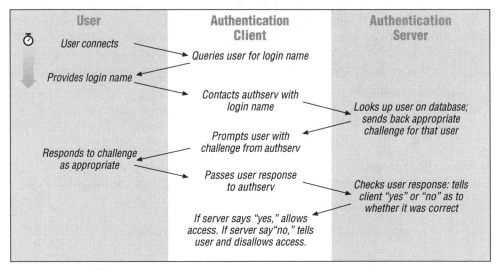

Figure 10–3: How the TIS FWTK authentication server works

The TIS FWTK includes a number of programs (such as *ftpd*) that, in addition to other modifications and enhancements for security, have already been modified to use the authentication server. Converting an existing program to use the authentication server, rather than traditional UNIX passwords, is pretty straightforward. It typically involves only 20 or so lines of C code, examples of which are given in the toolkit.

The toolkit also includes some programs to support binary-only systems where you don't have the source to modify. For example, for systems in which you don't have the source code to the *login* program available for modification, the toolkit includes a program you can use as the user's shell (which is specified for each user in the */etc/passwd* file) instead of one of the normal shells (e.g., */bin/csh* or */bin/sh*) This replacement shell authenticates the user with the authentication server, and, if the user passes, starts his real shell.

Problems with the authentication server

The major problem in running an authentication server is getting secure communication between the client and the server. An attacker who can convincingly pretend to be the authentication server can authenticate as anybody.

Some configurations may have additional problems; for example, using shell replacement can produce problems, because not all programs deal well with situations in which a user's shell environment variable and the entry for that user in the */etc/passwd* file do not match.

Commercial Solutions

Many commercial systems offering to do authentication are now on the market. In particular, "single sign-on" systems are a hot topic right now. These are systems that supposedly let a user log in once (presumably once each day), and then automatically log the user in to whatever other systems that user needs to access, without the user having to log in to each system individually.

There are a variety of issues you need to think about when you are considering a commercial solution; the primary considerations are availability, security, and cost.

Availability
> This is a simple consideration. Is the system available for all the platforms and programs you need to use it for? Many systems address only certain types of machines (e.g., PCs or UNIX systems), and many handle only certain types of access (e.g., login but not FTP access).

Security

This consideration is tougher to get a handle on. There are several things you need to think about. First, how hard is the system going to be to compromise? Second, if it *is* compromised, what implications does that have for the rest of your security?

Many of these commercial systems use proprietary algorithms that are not available for client or academic scrutiny. Unfortunately, there are a lot more ways to do these algorithms wrong than to do them right. Without an independent analysis of the system, you have to rely on the vendor's word that they got it right.

Other systems build their single sign-on capability on top of the standard UNIX *.rhosts* mechanisms used by the so-called Berkeley "r" commands (*rsh, rlogin rcp, rdist,* etc.). These commands are notoriously easy for an attacker to exploit because they create a web of trust among machines. (The weaknesses and vulnerabilities of these commands are discussed in Chapter 8.)

Cost

This consideration is almost always an issue. What will it cost to deploy this system in your environment to meet your needs? Some costs are one-time capital expenses; e.g., some systems require a dedicated piece of hardware, essentially a single-purpose PC, to generate the challenges and check the responses. Others are per-user expenses; for example, some systems require smart cards for all your users. Still others are licensing or support expenses. The systems are often priced depending on the number of users you'll support; systems to support more users obviously cost more.

The only commercial authentication system that is used extensively on the Internet is the SecurID system from Security Dynamics discussed earlier. A variety of commercial products, particularly terminal servers, support the system.[*]

Network-Level Encryption

Encryption allows you to create secure connections over insecure channels. Encrypting your network traffic provides two useful guarantees: privacy and authentication. Privacy is obvious; if your data is encrypted by the sending end, sent over an unsecured network, and then decrypted by the receiving end, your data is kept private from someone snooping on the unsecured network. Authentication is less obvious, but very useful. Basically, if the receiving end is successfully able to decrypt the data, it knows the data must have really come from the sending end (not from somebody in the middle pretending to be the sending end). Why? Because the data was properly encrypted, and only the sending end could do that. This all assumes, of course, that the keys that need to be kept secret *have*

---

[*] Apparently because of aggressive marketing and partnering by Security Dynamics, and not because of any inherent advantage of the product.

been kept secret; someone who knows your keys can violate both your privacy and your authentication.

At What Level Do You Encrypt?

Encryption over the Internet can take place at various levels; the most common are the application, link, and network levels.

Application-level encryption requires support in all the applications (both clients and servers) you want to use. This might be an effective approach if you have one or two applications that you use heavily (or are particularly concerned about) across the Internet among a small number of machines, because you can install custom, encrypting versions of those clients and servers on those machines. For general use, however, it doesn't scale up well; you may not even have source code available for all the applications you wish to operate encrypted. Some applications use PGP to provide application-level encryption. Senders use PGP to encrypt their outgoing mail before sending it across the Internet, and recipients use PGP to decrypt it. (PGP is also frequently used independently of applications, which is less convenient for the user, but extremely flexible.)

Application-level encryption is done at too high a level to be useful as a blanket protection for a network link; you have to spend too much time and effort integrating support for it into too many different clients, servers, and procedures. However, application-level encryption may be useful if you only need a single application to work securely.

Link-level encryption protects only a single network link. For example, encryption in modems at either end of a leased line will protect your data as it traverses that leased line, but not elsewhere, as it traverses other lines, or passes through routers or other intermediate hosts. Link-level encryption is done at too low a level to be widely useful. Usually, you don't control all the links in the untrusted network between the source and the destination, so you can't really ensure that the link-level encryption is being done properly (or at all) at each of those points.

Network-level encryption seems to be a workable middle ground between application-level encryption and link-level encryption. With network-level encryption, all network traffic between two trusted sites is encrypted at one end, sent across the untrusted intermediate network, and then decrypted at the other end. The encryption and decryption is done by routers or other network devices at the perimeter of each trusted site. A firewall, which all traffic must pass through anyway, is thus a natural place to do network-level encryption. To machines within either trusted site, the traffic is unencrypted; this means that those machines don't require any custom applications or configuration to use or benefit from the encryption. To machines outside the trusted sites, the packets are encrypted, and thus are private (unintelligible to those without the keys) and authenticated (could only have been sent by a key-holder).

What Do You Encrypt?

When you are performing network-level encryption, how much of the packet do you want to encrypt?

- Only the TCP, UDP, or ICMP data segments (leaving the TCP, UDP, or ICMP headers, as well as the IP headers, unencrypted)?

- The IP data segment (including the whole TCP, UDP, or ICMP packet)?

- The whole IP packet?

If you encrypt only the TCP, UDP, or ICMP data segments, you're protecting the data itself from compromise by an attacker, and you're making life easy for your packet filtering system (it can still see all the headers it needs to for normal packet filtering). However, a snooper can still see which machines are using which protocols to communicate with which other machines.

If you encrypt the IP data segment (which means that the whole UDP, TCP, or ICMP packet, headers and all, is encrypted), you prevent a snooper from seeing what protocols you're using (they can still see what hosts are talking to what other hosts), but you may make life harder for your own packet filtering system. Unless the packet filtering system is between the encryption unit and the internal network, it can no longer see the TCP, UDP, or ICMP headers, because they're encrypted as part of the IP data segment. If your packet filtering system is outside the encryption unit (between the encryption unit and the untrusted network), it would have to make all of its decisions strictly on the basis of IP source and destination addresses, which is very rarely enough.

If you encrypt the whole IP packet, you prevent an attacker from seeing anything, but you may also prevent your packet filtering system from seeing anything either, depending on where it's located relative to the encryption unit. To fully encrypt an IP packet between two sites, you have to provide some sort of encapsulation "tunnel"—e.g., a simple TCP connection—between the encryption units at the two sites to send the encrypted packets through. The reason the tunnel is necessary is because the IP headers are no longer there for the intermediate routers to look at. All an attacker can see is that the two encryption units are talking to each other. Some commercial routers, such as Morning Star Express routers (as well as UNIX machines running Morning Star PPP software) are capable of creating such "virtual private networks." Morning Star does it by running encrypted PPP over a TCP connection between two of their boxes; so you have your original packet encapsulated in an encrypted PPP packet, which is itself encapsulated in a TCP packet from one Morning Star box to the other.

Most sites using network-level encryption don't mind if attackers can determine which machines are talking to each other, or even what protocols they're using (this attack is commonly called *traffic analysis*). Such sites generally encrypt only the TCP, UDP, or ICMP data segments of packets, for their own convenience in processing the packets. Sites that encrypt the whole TCP, UDP, or ICMP packet (the IP data segment) generally do it for performance reasons, rather than for security reasons: it's faster for a router to find the start of the IP data segment than for it to find the start of the IP data segment and, within that, the start of the TCP, UDP, or ICMP data segment.

Where Do You Encrypt?

If you're going to set up network-level encryption, the question of where you do the encryption and decryption relative to your packet filtering is an important one. If you do the encryption and decryption inside the packet filtering perimeter (i.e., on your internal net), then the filters just have to allow the encrypted packets in and out. This is especially easy if you're doing tunneling, because all the tunneled packets will be addressed to the same remote address and port number at the other end of the tunnel (the decryption unit). On the other hand, doing the encryption and decryption inside your filtering perimeter means that packets arriving encrypted are not subject to the scrutiny of the packet filters. This leaves you vulnerable to attack from the other site if that site has been compromised.

If you do the encryption and decryption outside the packet filtering perimeter (i.e., on your perimeter net or in your exterior router), then the packets coming in from the other site can be subjected to the full scrutiny of your packet filtering system. On the other hand, they can also be subjected to the full scrutiny of anyone who has broken into a machine on your perimeter net, such as your bastion host.

Encryption is starting to appear as a feature in some commercial router products, and several vendors have announced their intentions to add encryption. This trend will probably continue over the next few years. As yet, though, there are few or no standards for IP network-level encryption, so few of the products interoperate with each other. They all assume that you have another one of their products at the other end. We hope that his will change, and that standards will emerge as encryption becomes more common.

Figure 10-4 shows a simplified view of network-level encryption scheme.

Key Distribution

As with any encryption system, key distribution for network-level encryption can be a very sticky problem. All of the discussion above assumes that the two ends share a key so that each knows how to encrypt and decrypt data sent to and from the other. Most of the systems in use today rely on "out of band" key distribution: their manufacturers say "key distribution is your problem, not ours." Customers have to manually establish keys (by transferring them by voice over the phone, or on floppy disk, or through some other secure, private mechanism) on each participating system. This means that this network-level encryption can work well for sites you exchange information with frequently (e.g., partners, key clients, or other

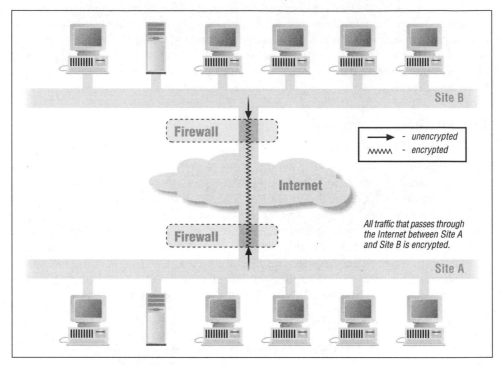

All traffic that passes through
the Internet between Site A
and Site B is encrypted.

Figure 10–4: Network-level encryption

branches of your own organization). But it doesn't work well for ad hoc or transient connections, because of the setup time and effort involved. Some systems use public key technology or key distribution systems, and can deal more quickly and effectively with ad hoc or transient connections.

Terminal Servers and Modem Pools

Another issue that is only somewhat related to firewalls (but that the security folks putting up firewalls are often asked to address) is where to locate the terminal servers and modem pools within a site's network. You definitely need to pay as much attention to the security of your dial-up access ports as you do to the security of your Internet connection. However, dial-up security (authentication systems, callback systems, etc.) is a whole topic of its own, separate from firewalls. We'll therefore restrict our comments to those related to firewalls.

The big firewall question concerning terminal servers and modem pools is where to put them: do you put them inside your security perimeter, or outside? Our advice is to put them on the inside and to protect them carefully. You'll not only be doing yourself a favor, you'll also be a good neighbor. Putting open terminal servers on the Internet is a risk to other people's sites as well as your own.

If the modem ports are going to be used primarily to access internal systems and data (that is, employees working from home or on the road), then it makes sense to put them on the inside. If you put them on the outside, you'd have to open holes in your perimeter to allow them access to the internal systems and data—holes that an attacker might be able to take advantage of. Also, if you put them on the outside, then an attacker who has compromised your perimeter (broken into your bastion host, for example) could potentially monitor the work your users do, essentially looking over their shoulders as they access private, sensitive data. If you do put the modems on the inside, you'll have to protect them very carefully, so they don't become an easier break-in target than your firewall. It doesn't do any good to build a first-class firewall if someone can bypass it by dialing into an unprotected modem connected to the internal network.

On the other hand, if the modem ports are going to be used primarily to access external systems (that is, by employees or guests who mainly use your site as an access point for the Internet), then it makes more sense to put them on the outside. There's no sense in giving someone access to your internal systems if they don't need it. This external modem pool should be treated just as suspiciously as the bastion host and the other components of your firewall.

If you find that you need both types of access, then you might want to consider two modem pools: one on the inside, carefully protected, to access internal systems and another on the outside to access the Internet.

If your terminal servers and modem pools are being used to support dial-up network connections from homes or other sites, you should make sure you enforce any implicit assumptions you have about that usage. For instance, people setting up PPP accounts on terminal servers generally assume that the PPP account is going to be used by a single remote machine running standalone. More and more machines, however, are part of LANs, even at home (Dad's PC is in the den, Mom's in the living room). That PPP connection could be used not just by the machine you set it up for, but by anything that machine is connected to, and anything those machines are connected to, and so forth. The machine that uses the PPP account might be connected to a LAN, with any number of other machines on it; any of them might be connected (via other PPP connections, for example) to another site or an Internet service provider. If you don't do anything to prevent it, traffic could flow from the Internet, to the second PC, to the "legitimate" PC, and finally into your own net, completely bypassing your firewall.

You can prevent this problem by simply enabling packet filtering on the PPP connection that limits what it *can* do to what you *expect* it to do (i.e., that limits packets on the connection to only packets to or from the machine you expect to be at the other end of the connection).

Some sites with significant dial-up networking activity take the approach of building a separate firewall just for that activity. See the discussion of multiple perimeter networks in Chapter 4.

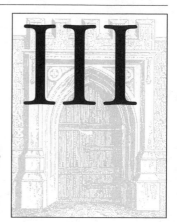

Keeping Your Site Secure

Part III describes how to establish a security policy for your site, maintain your firewall, and handle the security problems that may occur with even the most effective firewalls.

Chapter 11, *Security Policies*, discusses the importance of having a clear and well-understood security policy for your site, and what that policy should and should not contain. It also discusses ways of getting management and users to accept the policy.

Chapter 12, *Maintaining Firewalls*, describes how to maintain security at your firewall over time and how to keep yourself aware of new Internet security threats and technologies.

Chapter 13, *Responding to Security Incidents*, describes what to do when a break-in occurs, or when you suspect that your security is being breached.

In This Chapter:
- *Your Security Policy*
- *Putting Together a Security Policy*
- *Getting Strategic and Policy Decisions Made*
- *What If You Can't Get a Security Policy?*

11

Security Policies

The word "policy" makes many people flinch, because it suggests impenetrable documents put together by unknowledgeable committees, which are then promptly ignored by everyone involved (except when they make a good excuse or weapon). That's not the kind of policy we're discussing in this chapter.

The policy we're talking about here is like a nation's foreign policy. It might be discussed in documents—of varying amounts of legibility—but its primary purpose is to lay out a direction, a theory of what you're trying to achieve. People sometimes confuse the words "policy," "strategy," and "tactics." A *policy* is what determines what wars you're going to fight and why. A *strategy* is the plan for carrying out the war. A *tactic* is a method for carrying out a strategy. Presidents determine policy; generals determine strategies; and anybody down to a foot soldier might determine a tactic.

Most of this book is about tactics. The tactics involved in building a firewall, the nitty-gritty details of what needs to be done here, are complex and intricate. However, no matter how good your tactics are, if your strategy and policy are bad, you can't succeed. In the 1800s, an American named William Walker set out to conquer Nicaragua for the United States. His strategy and tactics were, if not impeccable, certainly successful: he conquered Nicaragua. Unfortunately, there was a literal fatal flaw in his plan. The United States did not at the time want Nicaragua, and when he announced that he had conquered it, the U.S. government was completely uninterested in doing anything about it. Walker ended up ruling Nicaragua very briefly, before he was killed in a popular uprising. This was the result of getting the strategy and the tactics right, but completely botching the policy.

Your Security Policy

Most technical computer people consider a single, unified, published security policy to be desirable in the abstract, but believe—with a strong basis in personal experience—that attempting to come up with one is going to be extremely painful. For example, walk up to any system administrator and ask about users and passwords, and you are almost guaranteed to be rewarded with a rant. Everybody has a story about the apparent insanity of people faced with passwords, one of the simplest and most comprehensible security issues: the professor who explained that he was too important to need a good password; the mathematician who was told that he couldn't use a password because it was in an English dictionary (and who replied that he wasn't using the *English* word that was spelled that way, he was using the *Russian* word that was spelled that way, and nobody had told him not to use Russian words). This kind of experience is apt to convince system administrators that their user community is incapable of dealing intelligently with security issues.

There is no doubt that putting together a security policy is going to be a long, involved process, and that it's the exact opposite of the types of tasks most technical people enjoy. If you like to program, you are extremely unlikely to enjoy either the meetings or the bureaucracy involved in policy making. On the other hand, putting together a security policy is a great deal more amusing than dealing with the side effects of not having a policy. In the long run, you'll spend less time in meetings arguing about security if you get it out of the way ahead of time.

Developing a security policy also doesn't need to be as bad as you may be expecting. Many of the problems with security policies are caused by people who are trying to write a security policy that sounds like a security policy, which is to say that it's written in big legal and technical words and says threatening things about how users had better behave themselves. This doesn't work. It's also the most unpleasant way to do things, because it involves hostility and incomprehension all around. It's true that your organization may at some point need a security policy that's written in big legal words (to satisfy some big legal requirements). In that case, the security policy you write shouldn't contradict the legalistic document, but the policy you write doesn't need to be that legalistic one.

Another problem people have in trying to write security policies is that they have a strong feeling about what the policy ought to be, and they're uncomfortable that the actual policy they enforce does not meet that standard. There is a great deal of lip service paid to the notion that security should be absolute: you should have a site that nobody could ever break in to; where every user has exactly one account, and every account has exactly one user; and where all the passwords are excellent, and nobody ever uses anybody else's password for anything.

In the real world, nobody's site is like that, a fact that is well-known and well-accepted. That doesn't keep people from claiming that they want to make their site like that, sometimes in big words on many pieces of paper that they call a security policy. Invariably, every time, without exception, these policies are not followed by anybody.

It's unlikely that your policy is one that emphasizes security at all costs. Such a policy would be irrational. It is reasonable to value other things highly enough to be willing to compromise security.

Most houses would be more secure with bars over all the windows. Few people are willing to put bars over their windows, despite a desire to protect themselves. People have a number of reasons for compromising their security in this way. To start with, bars are expensive and they interfere with using the windows for many of their normal purposes (e.g., seeing out of, climbing out of in an emergency). But people are willing to go to equal expense and inconvenience to apply other security solutions, and they may avoid barring windows even when it's the cheapest and most convenient solution, because it looks bad and makes them feel oppressed.

This is entirely reasonable, and it's entirely reasonable to make the same type of decision about your computer security. You may not want the best security money can buy, or even the best security you can afford.

What do you want? You want the best security that meets your requirements for:

Affordability
How much money does the security cost?

Functionality
Can you still use your computers?

Cultural compatibility
Does it conflict with the way people at your site normally interact with each other and the outside world?

Legality
Does it meet the your site's legal requirements?

Don't pretend that you want to be absolutely secure, if only you could afford it. You don't live your life with the most perfect security money could buy. For the same reasons, it's extremely unlikely that your institution can maintain the characteristics that are important to it if it also installs the most perfect security money could buy. People don't like learning or working in a hostile environment; because they won't do it, you'll either lose the security or lose the organization.

Sometimes a small concession to insecurity can buy a large payoff in morale. For example, rulemakers reel at the idea of guest accounts, but a guest account for a spouse can make a big difference in how people feel about work. And there are sometimes unexpected results. One university computer center was asked why its student employees were allowed to hang around at all hours, even after the labs were closed, doing random activities of dubious value to the computer center; it seemed insecure at best. The answer was that several years before, an operator who was typing his girlfriend's term paper in a lab after hours had discovered and responded to a critical emergency. Because he had saved the facility from what seemed likely to be a million dollars worth of uninsured damage (insurance companies have a nasty tendency to consider floods in windowless third-floor computer rooms to be acts of God, and thus uninsurable), the computer facility management figured that all the computer time the operators wanted had already been paid for.

On the other hand, if you have too little security, you can lose the organization to lawyers or attackers, and what matters there is what you do, not what you write down. Writing down marvelous policies that don't get enforced certainly won't save you from people who are trying to break into your computer, and it generally won't save you from lawsuits, either. The law counts only policies that you make some attempt to enforce. Writing it down and brazenly not doing it proves that you aren't simply too stupid to know what to do: it demonstrates that you actually knew what you had to do, and didn't do it!

What Should a Security Policy Contain?

First and foremost, a security policy is a way of communicating with users and managers. It should tell them what they need to know to make the decisions they need to make about security.

Explanations

It's important that the policy be explicit and understandable about why certain decisions have been made. Most people will not follow rules unless they understand why they're important. A policy that specifies what's supposed to be done, but not why, is doomed. As soon as the people who wrote it leave, or forget why they made those decisions, it's going to stop having any effect.

Everybody's responsibilities

A policy sets explicit expectations and responsibilities among you, your users, and your management; it lets all of you know what to expect from each other. It's a mistake to distribute a policy that concentrates entirely on what users need to do to make the site secure (it seems hostile and unfair), or entirely on what system administrators need to do (it encourages the users to believe that somebody else will handle it, and they don't have to worry about it).

Regular language

Most people are not lawyers, and they're not security experts. They're comfortable with casual descriptions. You may be afraid to write a policy that way because it may seem uncomfortably casual and too personal. But it's more important to make your security policy friendly and understandable than to make it precise and official-looking. Write it as if you were explaining it to a reasonably bright but nontechnical friend. Keep it a communication between peers, not a memo from Mount Olympus. If that's not acceptable in your corporate culture, write two separate policy descriptions.

You will not get people to comply unless they understand the document and want to comply with it, and that means they have to at least be willing to read it. If they shut their brains off in paragraph two because the document sounds legal and threatening, you lose. You also lose if they decide that you think they're stupid, or if they decide that you don't care. Don't get so informal that you seem condescending or sloppy. If necessary, get a technical writer to clean up the punctuation and spelling.

Enforcement authority

Writing down the policy is not the point; living by it is. That means that when the policy isn't followed, something should happen to fix it. Somebody needs to be responsible for making those corrections happen, and the policy needs to specify who that's going to be and the general range of corrections. Here are some examples of what a security policy might specify:

- Managers of certain services have the authority to revoke access.

- Managers will be asked to take care of some kinds of transgressions.

- Facilities that don't meet certain standards may be cut off from the corporate network and external access by the people who run the corporate network.

The policy should specify who is going to decide and give some indication of what kinds of penalties are available to them. It should not specify exactly what will happen when; it's a policy, not a mandatory sentencing law.

Provision for reviews

You can't expect to set a policy up once and forget it. The needs of your site will change over time, and policies that were perfectly sensible may become either too restrictive or too lax. Sometimes change is obvious: if you work for a startup company that goes from six people to 6,000 people, it will probably occur to you that things are different in important ways (but you still may not get around to redoing the security policy if you didn't set up a mechanism for that in advance). If you work for a 200-year old university, however, you may not expect much change.

However, even if the organization appears to be doing its best to fossilize, the computers change, the external networks change, and new people come in to replace ones who leave. You still need to review and change your policies on a regular basis.

Discussion of specific security issues

Because of the differences between organizations, it's hard to be specific about issues without writing an entire book just about security policies. However, here are some common issues to consider when you are writing a policy:

- Who is allowed to have an account at your site? Do you have guest accounts? What do you do about contractors, vendors, and clients?

- Can accounts be shared between multiple people? What about a secretary who uses an executive's account to process that person's electronic mail? What about joint projects? What about family members? Is it sharing an account if you let somebody else borrow a window on your machine really quickly?

- When do people lose the privilege of having an account, and what do you do about it? What happens if people leave or are denied access?

- Who can set up dial-in modems? Is it OK for other people to set up dial-out modems? Is there anything special about PPP, SLIP, or ISDN lines?

- What do people need to do before they connect a computer to the main network?

- How secure do computers need to be before they get services from centrally maintained machines?

- How secure do computers need to be in order to connect to a network with unprotected access to the Internet?

- How is financial data going to be protected?

- How is confidential information about people going to be protected?

- What do individual users need to do to protect themselves and the site? What kinds of passwords should they have, and when should they change them?

- What can people do on the Internet? Should they be transferring random executables in and running them?

- What precautions do you need to take against viruses on personal computers?

- Who can connect your site to external networks, and what's an external network? Is it OK for a project manager to connect your site to another specific site? How about putting in a second Internet connection?

- How are home computers going to be secured? How are they going to get secure access to your network?

- How are people who are traveling going to get access to the network?

- What information is considered company confidential? How is it going to be protected? Can it be sent outside the site via electronic mail?

- If you have remote sites, how are they going to get secure access to your main network?

What Should a Security Policy Not Contain?

Some pieces of information don't belong in your site's security policy, as we discuss in this section.

Technical details

The security policy needs to describe what you're trying to protect and why; it doesn't necessarily need to describe the details of how. It's much more useful to have a one-page document that describes "what" and "why" in terms that everyone in your organization can understand, than a 100-page document that describes "how," but that nobody except your most senior technical staff can understand.

For example, consider a policy that includes a requirement that says:

> Nonreusable passwords shall be used to authenticate all incoming connections from the outside world, in order to prevent potential attackers from being able to capture reusable passwords by monitoring such connections.

This requirement is much more useful than a policy that says:

> S/Key will be used for all incoming connections.

Why? Because the first policy describes *what* is to be protected and *why*, and it leaves *how* open so the technical staff can select the best implementation.

A policy that says the following is better yet:

> Regular passwords are often stolen and reused when they pass across networks. We won't use passwords that can be reused across networks our company doesn't control.

This policy communicates the same information without the legal-style language. It also clarifies some other points. For example, in the original language does the "outside world" include companies that have special relationships with yours? It may seem obvious to you that it does, but it probably doesn't seem obvious to the managers who are arranging to work with those companies. The reworded language makes it clear what the criterion is (although you may still end up arguing about what networks meet it).

Policy can guide you in selecting and implementing technology, but it shouldn't be used to specify it. It's often much easier to get management to buy into, and sign off on, an overall policy than on a specific technology.

Somebody else's problems

Every site's security policy is different. Different sites have different concerns, different constraints, different users, and different capabilities; all of these lead to different policies. Further, a site's policy may change over time, as the site grows and changes. Don't assume that you need to do things the way they've always been done, or that you can borrow somebody else's policy and simply change the names in it.

Putting Together a Security Policy

Once you know what you want in a security policy, how do you put one together?

What Is Your Security Policy?

The first step towards putting together a working security policy for your site is to decide what your personal opinion is. If you've been administering a site or making any decisions about security, you've been enforcing an internal theory about securiy, even if you've never articulated it. You're going to need to come to a clear and explicit understanding of what that internal policy is before you can discuss policy issues with other people in order to produce a written policy for your site.

With that in mind, look at the decisions you've made about security and decide what you think your site's security goals should be. That may not be the policy that your site ends up with, but it's an important first step.

What Is Your Site's Security Policy?

The second step towards putting together a working security policy for your site is to determine what everybody else's security policy is. What do the users and managers expect security to do for them? What do they think of the way security is handled currently? What are other computer facilities doing and why?

Every site has at least one security policy. The problem is that most sites have more than one; perhaps as many as there are people involved with the site's computers. Sometimes this proliferation of policies is purely unconscious; different computer facilities within the same site may be doing radically different things without even realizing it. Sometimes it's an open secret; administrators may be trying to maintain a security policy that they believe is necessary, even though the user population does not agree with them. Sometimes it's out-and-out war. Generally, people think of universities as the main place where computer users and computer administrators are engaged in open security warfare, but in fact many companies spend large amounts of time fighting about security issues (for example, administration and the engineers are often at odds).

Some of the security policies for a site may be written down already, but most are likely to be implicit and unpublicized. The only way to find out about them is to go and ask. Be sure to ask managers, system administrators, and users. Then look at the actual computers and see what's really going on. It's unlikely that anybody will actually lie to you. However, they may be telling you what they think is going on, or what they wish was going on, or what they know is supposed to be going on, instead of reporting the actual state of affairs.

Managers who are used to dealing with computers that have been secured may believe that computers are automatically secure; the shipped configuration will be reasonably safe if it is connected to a network. This is not true. In fact, the truth is almost the exact opposite. The default configuration that machines are shipped with is usually laughably insecure, and it requires considerable expertise to arrive at a secure configuration. Therefore, a manager who says that all of the computers are perfectly secure may be completely incorrect, without having the least intention of deceiving you.

If you ask questions that have clear "right" answers, most people will tend to try to give you those answers. Other people will become defensive. Try to ask neutral questions that don't have a clear bias. For example, don't ask people if they think security is important; instead, ask which is more important to them, security or a cooperative work environment, and then get them to expand on that answer.

When you talk to people, make it extremely clear why you're asking. Asking about security policies tends to give people the impression that you're trying to check up on them. Some people will try to get a good grade, rather than discussing reality. Others will become hostile (after all, why should you be checking up on them?). If you get either of these reactions, stop asking questions about security policies (there's no point in it if they're not going to give useful answers), and go back to trying to explain what you're doing and why. If they never believe you, ask somebody else.

External Factors That Influence Security Policies

Your site isn't completely independent. There are issues outside of a computer facility that influence security policy. These include legal requirements, contractual obligations, and existing organizational policies.

Let's look first at legal issues. In the United States, a publicly traded company has a legal responsibility to its shareholders to protect its assets. This means that if you work for such a company, even if everybody at the company agrees that you ought to remove all of the passwords and let the Internet in, you can't choose that as a security policy. Your security policy must show evidence that you are safe-guarding the company's computers and information. What's required is "due diligence," an attempt in good faith to take normal precautions. "Normal precautions" limit what you need to do; you don't have a legal responsibility to require retinal scans before people can touch the computers!

Regardless of the type of institution you work for, in most places in the United States there is also a legal responsibility to safeguard certain types of information about employees. Employee reviews are generally legally protected; so are straightforward personnel records of information like home addresses. Universities have legal responsibilities regarding the safeguarding of student records, right down to the information about which students attend the university. Data about individuals has even more legal protection in some European countries. If you do not work for Human Resources or Student Records, you may think you don't have to worry about protecting this kind of information, but you're probably wrong. Usually, every manager or supervisor has confidential employee data to deal with; similarly, the information used to maintain accounts at universities contains confidential student data (e.g., whether or not the student is enrolled, and what classes they're taking).

Your organization may also have contractual obligations to protect data. If you have customer or client data on your systems, your contracts probably require you to protect it. (This may apply to research contracts at universities as well.) If you have source code or prerelease software, you almost certainly have a license that requires you to protect it.

Your organization may also have existing policies that influence security policies. Often, these are policies about the protection of data (usually written to meet the many and varied legal obligations discussed above), but there may be policies requiring that people have access to data, especially at universities and public institutions.

If your organization has a legal department, consult them. (Don't invite them to write up a policy; just ask them to explain the institution's legal obligations.) If your organization does not have a legal department, consult a senior manager. In any case, find any existing written policies and wade through them to see what they say that's relevant to security. Going through these written policies will also give you a good idea for what works and doesn't work in a written policy. If you like the existing policies, base your new ones on them. If you hate the existing policies, resist the temptation to make your new ones like them just because it's the way it's always been done before.

Getting Strategic and Policy Decisions Made

Strategic decisions need to be understood and made by top-level management or they will never be successfully implemented. If you don't have top-level management support for security, you aren't going to have security; it's that simple. Why wouldn't you have support from top-level managers? Probably because you haven't addressed their concerns in ways they understand. Here are some things to consider in making your case.

Involve Everybody Who's Affected

You may be the person with the best understanding of the technical issues, but you aren't necessarily the person with the best understanding of the institution's needs as a whole. Strategic and policy decisions must be made by people working together. You can't just come up with a policy you like, take it around to a lot of people, and have them rubber stamp it. Even if you manage to get them to do it—which may well be more difficult than getting them to help make intelligent decisions—they won't actually follow it.

One major computer manufacturer had a policy forbidding dial-in modems. Unfortunately, the company's centralized dial-in access didn't satisfy all of their programmers. Some of these programmers figured out that, although they couldn't request modem lines, they could redirect existing fax lines to modems, go home at night, and dial up their work computers. Even more unfortunately, a programmer in one of the groups with this habit was fired and proceeded to break into the site. He systematically tried all the phone numbers in the range the company had assigned to fax machines until he connected to one of the redirected ones and got a login prompt from an unsecured machine inside the corporate firewall. The former employee did significant damage before he was detected and shut out. He was able to gain a lot of time because the people trying to shut him out didn't know the modems existed. When they did figure out that modems were involved, the process of getting rid of them all proved to be tedious and prolonged, because lines were diverted only when people planned to use them.

That whole incident was the result of the fact that management and system administrators had a policy that ignored some genuine needs of the people using the computer facility. The official policy required dial-in access to be so secure it was almost completely unusable, and the unofficial policy required dial-in access to be so usable that it was almost completely insecure. If there had been a policy that allowed moderately insecure dial-in access, the break-in might have been avoided, and it certainly would have been easier to detect and stop. It would also have been avoided if the programmers had agreed that security was more important than dial-in access, but that kind of agreement is much harder to achieve than a compromise.

In fact, in this case there wasn't much actual disagreement between the parties involved. If the managers had been asked, they would have said that letting people work from home was important to them; they didn't understand that the existing dial-in system was not providing acceptable service. If the programmers had been asked, they would have said that preventing people from maliciously deleting their work was important to them; they didn't understand the risks of what they were doing. But nobody thought about security and usability at the same time, and the result was pure disaster.

Accept 'Wrong' Decisions

You may find that the security policy you come up with is one you don't particularly like. If this happens because the people who made it don't understand what they've done, then you should fight strongly to get it fixed. If, on the other hand, people understand the risks, but they don't share your priorities, put your objections down in writing and go ahead with the policies. Yes, this will sometimes lead to disasters. Nonetheless, if you ask a group to make a decision, you can't insist that it be your decision. You also can't be sure that your way is the only right way.

Sometimes managers have a genuine willingness to accept risks that seem overwhelming to system administrators. For example, one computer manufacturer chose to put one of their large and powerful machines on an unprotected net, and to give out accounts on the machine to customers and prospective customers upon request. The system administrator thought this was a terrible idea and pointed out that the machine was fundamentally impossible to secure; there were a large number of accounts, changing rapidly, with no pattern, and they belonged to people the company couldn't control. Furthermore, the reason the company was giving out test accounts was that the machine was a fast parallel processor, which also meant that it might as well have been designed as the ultimate password-cracking machine. To the system administrator, it seemed extremely likely that once this machine was broken into (which was probably inevitable), it was going to be used as a tool to break into other machines.

A battle ensued, and eventually, a compromise was reached. The machine was made available, but extra security was employed to protect internal networks from it. (This was a compromise because it interfered with employees' abilities to use the machine, which they needed to do to assist the outsiders who were using it.) Management chose to accept the remaining risk that the machine would be used as a platform to attack other sites, knowing that there was a potential for extremely bad publicity as a result.

What happened? Sure enough, the machine *was* compromised, and was used to attack at least the internal networks. The attacks on the internal networks were extremely annoying, and cost the company money in system administrators' time, but they didn't produce significant damage, and there was little or no bad publicity. Management considered this expense to be acceptable, however, given the sales generated by letting people test-drive the machine. In this case, conflicting security policies were resolved explicitly—by discussion and compromise—and the result was a policy that seemed less strong than the original, but that provided sufficient protection. By openly and intentionally choosing to accept a risk, the company brought it within acceptable limits.

Present Risks and Benefits in Different Ways for Different People

You need to recognize that different people have different concerns. Mostly, these concerns are predictable from their positions, but some are personal. For example, suppose that:

- Your chief financial officer is concerned about the cost of security, or the cost of not having enough security.

- Your chief executive officer is concerned about the negative publicity a security incident involving your site could bring, or about potential loss or theft of intellectual property via the Internet.

- A department chair is concerned that tenure reviews will be revealed.

- A mid-level manager is concerned his employees are squandering all their time reading Usenet news or surfing the Web.

- Another mid-level manager is concerned her employees are importing virus-infected PC software from the Internet.

- Still another mid-level manager is concerned how best to provide technical support to customers over the Internet.

- A professor is concerned her data won't be accessible from other institutions while she's on sabbatical.

- An instructor is concerned that students are stealing answers from each other or tests from instructors.

- Users are concerned about the availability of Internet services they feel are vital for their jobs.

- Users are concerned they won't be able to work together if there are too many security issues.

- Students are concerned they won't be able to play with the computers, which is a part of how they learn.

- Graduate students and project managers are concerned that security measures are going to slow down projects with strict timelines.

You need to take the time to discover all of these different, legitimate concerns and address them. You may also decide there are things that these various people *should* be worried about, but aren't, because they don't know any better; you have to educate them about those issues. This means you need to take the time to understand their jobs, what they want to accomplish with the network, and how well they appreciate the security issues.

Talk to each of these people in terms they care about. This requires a lot of listening before you ever start talking. To managers, talk about things like probable costs and potential losses; to executives, talk about risk versus benefit; and to technical staff, talk about capabilities. Before you go in with a proposal, be prepared with an explanation that suits your audience's point of view and technical level. If you have trouble understanding or communicating with a particular group, you may find it helps to build a relationship with someone who understands that group and can translate for you.

You're not trying to deceive anybody. The basic information is the same, no matter who you're talking to. On the other hand, if a particular decision saves money and makes for a more enjoyable working environment, you don't go to the chief financial officer and say "We want to do it this way because it's more fun," and then go the programmers and say "We want to do it this way because it's cheaper."

Avoid Surprises

When it comes to security, nobody likes surprises. That's why you need to make sure that the relevant people understand the relevant issues and are aware of, and agree with (or at least agree to abide by), the decisions made concerning those issues.

In particular, people need to know about the consequences of their decisions, including best, worst, and probable outcomes. Consequences that are obvious to you may not be obvious to other people. For example, people who are not extremely UNIX-knowledgeable may be quite willing to give out root passwords. They don't realize what the implications are, and they may be very upset when they find out.

People who have been surprised often overreact. They may go from completely unconcerned to demanding the impossible. One good break-in, or even a prank, can convert people from not understanding all the fuss about passwords to inquiring about the availability of voiceprint identification and machine gun turrets. (It's preferable to get them to make decisions while they are mildly worried, instead of blindly panicked!)

Condense to Important Decisions, with Implications

When you're asking a top manager to decide issues of policy, present only the decision to be made and the pros, cons, and implications of the various options: not a lot of extraneous decisions. For example, you shouldn't waste your CEO's time by asking him or her to decide whether you should run Sendmail or SMAIL as your mailer; that's primarily a technical issue, and one that should be resolved by the relevant technical staff and managers. On the other hand, you may need to call upon your CEO to decide strategic issues regarding mail, such as whether or not everyone in the organization is to have email access, or only certain people (and if it's to be limited, to whom).

Don't offer people decisions unless they have both the authority and the information with which to make those decisions. Always make it clear why they're being asked to decide (instead of having the decision made somewhere else). In most cases, you want to avoid open-ended questions. It's better to ask "Should we invest money in a single place to be a defense, or should we try to protect all the machines?" than "What do you think we should do about Internet security?" (The open question gives the replier the option of saying "nothing," which is probably not an answer you're going to be happy with.)

Justify Everything Else in Terms of Those Decisions

All of the technical and implementation decisions you make should follow from the high-level guidance you've obtained from your top managers and executives. If you don't see which way you should go with a technical issue because it depends on nontechnical issues, you may need to request more guidance on that issue. Again, explain clearly the problem; the options; and the pros, cons, and implications of each option.

When you explain policies or procedures, explain them in terms of the original decisions. Show people the reasoning process.

Emphasize that Many Issues Are Management and Personnel Issues, not Technical Issues

Certain problems, which some people try to characterize or solve as technical problems, are really management or personnel problems. For example, some managers worry that their employees will spend all their time at work reading Usenet news or surfing the Web. However, this is not a technical problem, but a personnel problem: the online equivalent of employees spending the day at their desks reading the newspaper or doing crossword puzzles.

Another common example of misdirected concern involves managers worrying that employees will distribute confidential information over the Internet. Again, this usually isn't a technical problem; it's a management problem. The same employee who could email your source code to a competitor could also carry it out the door in his pocket on an 8mm tape (generally far more conveniently and with less chance of being caught). It is irrational to place technological restrictions on information that can be sent out by email unless you also check everybody's bags and pockets as they leave the premises.

Don't Assume That Anything Is Obvious

Certain things that seem obvious to a technical person who is interested in security may not be at all obvious to nontechnical managers and executives. As we've mentioned, it's obvious to anyone who understands IP that packet filtering will allow you to restrict access to services by IP addresses, but not by user (unless you can tie specific users to specific IP addresses). Why? Because "user" is not a concept in IP, and there's nothing in the IP packet that reflects what "user" is responsible for that packet. Conversely, certain things that seem obvious to managers and executives are not at all obvious to technical staff, e.g., that the public's perception (which is often incomplete or simply incorrect) of a problem at your company is often more important than the technical "truth" of the matter.

What If You Can't Get a Security Policy?

What do you do if, despite your best efforts, you can't get a security policy written down? The safest answer is this: document, document, document. Write down what you're doing, and why, and what the existing policies are, and what you tried, and why you think the situation is bad. Print it out on paper, sign it, and deliver it—at least to your manager, if not to several managers above your manager. File a paper copy, with your signature and the dates you gave it to people.

Every year, or every time there is a significant change in the situation, try to get the policy created again. If it doesn't work, repeat the entire documentation process. Be sure to edit the document; it's tempting to just change the date and resend it, but it probably won't be quite right any more, and it weakens your position.

Doing what we recommend is fairly confrontational behavior, and it can look as if you're more interested in making certain that you're safe than in making certain your site is safe.* It's worth working a long time on getting your document to say exactly what you want it to say. Don't fall into the trap of feeling that you have to use formal language. If what you want to say is "I understand that we're an informal company and we don't do written policies, but I think this issue is so important that we still need to have something written down," just say exactly that.

---

* This may be true, but it's not going to get anybody to fix anything.

In This Chapter:
- *Housekeeping*
- *Monitoring Your System*
- *Keeping Up to Date*
- *How Long Does It Take?*
- *When Should You Start Over?*

12

Maintaining Firewalls

If you've done a good job of designing a firewall that fits the needs of your organization, maintaining that firewall should be fairly straightforward. What does it mean to maintain a firewall? Maintenance tasks fall into three major categories:

- Housekeeping

- Monitoring your system

- Keeping up to date

Once you've designed and built your firewall, it really shouldn't take a great deal of effort to keep it going, especially because much of the maintenance work can be automated.

Housekeeping

Housekeeping is the eternal round of small tasks that need to be done to keep your firewall clean and safe. There are three main tasks you'll need to deal with again and again:

- Backing up your firewall

- Managing your accounts

- Managing your disk space

Backing Up Your Firewall

Make sure to back up all parts of your firewall. That means not only the general-purpose computers you may be using as bastion hosts or internal servers, but also the routers or other special-purpose devices. Rebuilding router configurations usually isn't easy, and your security depends on having your routers configured correctly.

Put your general-purpose machines on a regular, automated backup system. Preferably, that system should produce confirmation mail when it is running normally and distinctly different messages when it sees errors.

Why not produce mail only when errors occur? If the system produces mail only on errors, you won't notice the system if it fails to run at all. (Silence is not necessarily golden, as any parent of small children knows. If they aren't making noise, they're probably making mischief.)

Why distinctly different messages? If the system produces even vaguely similar messages when it is running normally and when it fails, people who are accustomed to ignoring the success messages will also ignore the failure messages. Ideally, a separate program should check to make sure that the backups have run, and to produce messages when they haven't.

Special-purpose machines like routers change much less often, and probably don't need an automated backup system. (This is fortunate, because they rarely support them.) When you do make changes, take advantage of any means available to record the configuration. Most systems write their configuration to a local floppy disk; some of them also support FTP. Write two floppy disks, clearly label and date them, and store one of them separate from the machine. Make these backups even if you have downloaded the configuration with FTP; you don't want the router to be completely dependent on another machine. If you have written the configuration on the router, rather than FTP'ing it, make an FTP copy as well as the floppy disks. Why? Sometimes it's easier to find files than to find small physical objects like floppy disks, and sometimes the floppy drive dies when the rest of the router still works.

NOTE

> The design of backup systems is outside the scope of this book. This description, along with the section in Chapter 13 called "Backing Up Your Filesystems" provide only a summary. If you're uncertain about your backup system, you'll want to look at a general system administration reference. See Appendix A for complete information on additional resources.

Managing Your Accounts

Account management—adding new accounts, removing old ones, aging passwords, etc.—is one of the most often neglected housekeeping tasks. On firewall systems, it's absolutely crucial that new accounts be added correctly, old accounts removed promptly, and passwords changed appropriately. (See your own system's documentation for how to do all this.)

Establish a procedure for adding accounts; wherever you can, use a program to add them. Even though there shouldn't be many users on your firewall systems, every one of them is a possible danger, and it's worth the effort to ensure they're set up correctly every time. People have an unfortunate tendency to leave out steps, or to pause for a few days in the middle of a process. If that gap leaves an account that has no password, you're creating open invitations to intruders.

Make sure your account creation procedure includes dating the account, and that accounts are automatically reviewed every few months. You don't need to automatically turn them off, but you do need to automatically inform somebody that they've timed out. This is relatively easy to do on a UNIX system; it may be harder on other systems, particularly dedicated systems like routers. If possible, set things up so that the accounts can be watched by an automated system. This can be done by generating account files on the UNIX side and then transferring them to the other machine, or by generating the accounts on the machine itself, but automatically copying the account files to the UNIX side and examining them.

You should also arrange to get termination notices from the appropriate authorities whenever someone leaves your organization. Most companies are able to send around notices for full-time employees, and most universities can provide graduation notification for students. It may be much harder to keep track of contractors and students who drop out, so you shouldn't rely on official notifications to tell you about everybody who has left. You may also need to confirm notifications: for example, you may get termination notices for people who are actually converting to contract status, or graduation notices for people who are continuing as graduate students or junior faculty. These people are going to be annoyed if you get rid of all their files (although it's probably acceptable to temporarily disable their accounts if their status is in doubt).

If your operating system supports password aging, you may want to turn it on. Use a relatively long time period—perhaps three to six months. If you time out passwords more frequently (e.g., every month), users will be willing to go to great lengths to circumvent the timeout, and you probably won't see any real gain in security. Similarly, if your password aging doesn't guarantee that the user will see a notification before the account becomes unusable, don't turn it on. Otherwise, you will annoy your users, and you will run the risk of accidentally locking out administrators who have a critical need to use the machine.

If password aging on your system is going to require a user to change his password as he is logging in, you need a password program that strictly enforces good passwords. If you don't do this, people will choose simple passwords in the heat of the moment, honestly intending to change them to better ones later. All in all, you may find it more effective to simply send people notices on a regular basis, even though you'll get less compliance that way.

Managing Your Disk Space

Data always expands to fill all available space, even on machines that have almost no users. People dump things in odd corners of the filesystem, "just for now," and they build up there. This causes more problems than you may realize. Aside from the fact that you may want that disk space, this random junk complicates incident response. You'll end up asking yourself:

> Is that a program that you left lying around last time you needed to install a new version, or did an intruder put it in?

> Is that truly a random data file, or does it have some deep meaning to an intruder?

Unfortunately, there is no automatic way to find junk; human beings, particularly system administrators who can write anywhere on the disk, are too unpredictable. Another person needs to look around on a regular basis. It's particularly effective to send every new system administrator on a tour of the disks; they'll notice things the old hands have become accustomed to.

Auditing programs like Tripwire, discussed in Chapter 5, will tell you about new files that appear in supposedly static areas, and this information will help you keep things straight. You will still need to check all the areas where you intentionally allow changes, and you should periodically go back and re-check the static areas. You will probably get the alert while you still know why you put that file in that place, and that knowledge may wear off over time.

On most firewall machines, your main disk space problem will be logs. These can and should be rotated automatically, and you may want to compress them as well; a program like *trimlog* (see Appendix B) helps automate the process. It's important to stop programs or cause them to suspend logging while you are trying to truncate or move logs. If a program is trying to write to a log file while you're trying to move or truncate it, you're obviously going to have problems. In fact, though, you may run into difficulties even if a program is simply holding the file open in preparation for writing to it later, e.g., you may discover the program is still logging to the file you renamed.

Monitoring Your System

Another important aspect of firewall maintenance involves monitoring your system. Monitoring is intended to tell you several things:

- Has your firewall been compromised?

- What kinds of attacks are being tried against your firewall?

- Is your firewall in working order?

- Is your firewall able to provide the service your users need?

In order to answer these questions, you'll need to know what the normal pattern of usage is.

Special-Purpose Monitoring Devices

You'll do most of your monitoring using the tools and the logging provided by the existing parts of your firewall, but you may find it convenient to have some dedicated monitoring devices as well. For example, you may want to put a monitoring station on your perimeter net so you can be sure only the packets you expect are going across it. You can use a general-purpose computer with network snooping software on it, or you can use a special-purpose network sniffer.

How can you make certain that this monitoring machine can't be used by an intruder? In fact, you'd prefer that an intruder not even detect its existence. On some network hardware, you can disable transmission in the network interface (with sufficient expertise and a pair of wire cutters), which will make the machine impossible to detect and extremely difficult for an intruder to use (because it can't reply). If you have source for your operating system, you can always disable transmission there; however, in this case, it's much harder to be certain you've been successful. In most cases, you'll have to settle for extremely cautious configuration of the machine. Treat it like a bastion host that needs to do less and be more secure.

What Should You Watch For?

In a perfect world, you'd like to know absolutely everything that goes through your firewall—every packet dropped or accepted, every connection requested. In the real world, neither the firewall nor your brain can cope with that much information. To come up with a practical compromise, you'll want to turn on the most verbose logging that doesn't slow down your machines too much and that doesn't fill up your disks too fast; then, you'll want to summarize the logs that are produced.

You can improve the disk space problem by writing verbose logs to high-capacity tapes. DAT and 8mm tapes are cheap, and they hold a lot of data, but they have some drawbacks. They're not particularly fast; they rarely can write at more than 800K a second, under the best circumstances, and log entries are generally too short to achieve maximum performance. They're also annoying to read data from. If you're interested in using them, write summary logs to disk, and write everything to tape. If you find a situation where you need more data, you can go back to the tape for it. A tape drive can probably keep up with the packets on an average Internet connection, but it won't keep up with an internal connection at full LAN speeds or even with a T-1 connection to the Internet that's at close to its maximum performance.

In particular, you want to log the following cases:

- All dropped packets, denied connections, and rejected attempts

- At least the time, protocol, and user name for every successful connection to or through your bastion host

- All error messages from your routers, your bastion host, and any proxying programs

NOTE

For security reasons, some information should never be logged where an intruder could possibly be able to read it. For example, although you should log failed login attempts, you should not log the password that was used in the failed attempt. Users frequently mistype their own passwords, and logging these mistyped passwords would make it easier for a computer cracker to break into a user's account.

Some system administrators believe that the account name should also not be logged on failed login attempts, especially when the account typed by the user is nonexistent. The reason is that users occasionally type their passwords when they are prompted for their user names. If invalid accounts are logged, it might be possible for an attacker to use those logs to infer people's passwords.

What are you watching for? You want to know what your usual pattern is (and what trends there are in it), and you want to be alerted to any exceptions to that pattern. To recognize when things are going wrong, you have to understand what happens when things are going right. It's important to know what messages you get when everything is working. Most systems produce error messages that sound peculiar and threatening even when they're working perfectly well. For example, in the sample *syslog* output in Example 12-1, messages 10, 14, and 17 all look vaguely threatening, but are in fact perfectly OK.[*] (See the section in Chapter 5 called "Setting Up System Logs.") If you see those messages for the first time when you're trying to debug a problem, you're likely to leap to the conclusion that the messages have something to do with your problem and get thoroughly side-tracked. Even if you never do figure out what the messages are and why they're appearing, just knowing that certain messages appear even when things are working fine will save you time.

---

[*] Message 10 is a common network failure that will result in a retry, and how good do you expect your connection to Cameroon to be? 14 is *traceroute* running. 17 says there are no synonyms defined, which you presumably already know.

Example 12–1: A Sample syslog File (Line Numbers Added)

```
1:  May 29 00:00:58 localhost wn[27194]: noc.nca.or.bv - - [] "GET
    /long/consulting.html HTTP/1.0" 200 1074  &lt;Sent file: >
2:  May 29 00:00:58 localhost wn[27194]: &lt;User_Agent: Mozilla/1.0N
    (X11; SunOS 4.1.3-KL sun4m)> &lt;Referrer: http://www.longitude.com/>
3:  May 29 00:02:38 localhost ftpd[26086]: 26086: 05/29/95 0:02:38
    spoke.cst.cnes.vg(gupta@) retrieved
    /pub/firewalls/digest/v04.n278.Z(15788 bytes)
4:  May 29 00:15:57 localhost ftpd[27195]: 27195: 05/29/95 0:01:52
    client42.sct.io connected, duration 845 seconds
5:  May 29 00:18:04 localhost ftpd[26086]: 26086: 05/29/95 23:26:32
    spoke.cst.cnes.vg connected, duration 3092 seconds
6:  May 27 01:13:38 mv-gw.longitude.com user: host
    naismith.longitude.com admin login failed
7:  May 27 01:13:47 mv-gw.longitude.com last message repeated 2 times
8:  May 27 01:15:17 mv-gw.longitude.com user: host
    naismith.longitude.com admin login succeeded
9:  May 27 01:19:18 mv-gw.longitude.com 16 permit: TCP from
    192.168.20.35.2591 to 172.16.1.3.53 seq 324EE800, ack 0x0, win
    4096, SYN
10: May 29 02:20:09 naismith sendmail[27366]: CAA27366: SYSERR(root):
    collect: I/O error on connection from atx.eb.cm, from=&lt;Mailer-
    Daemon@eb.cm>: Connection reset by peer during collect
    with atx.eb.cm
11: May 29 02:30:28 naismith named[79]: sysquery: server name mismatch
    for [172.16.8.25]: (sun.nhs-relay.ac.cv != nhs-relay.ac.cv) (server
    for cus.ox.ac.cv)
12: May 29 02:31:00 naismith named[79]: sysquery: server name mismatch
    for [172.16.8.25]: (nhs-relay.ac.cv != sun.nhs-relay.ac.cv) (server
    for PANSY.CSV.WARWICK.AC.CV)
13: May 29 02:47:04 naismith named[79]: sysquery: server name mismatch
    for [172.16.8.25]: (nhs-relay.ac.cv != sun.nhs-relay.ac.cv) (server
    for LUPUS.CNS.UMIST.AC.CV)
14: May 29 07:50:59 mv-gw.longitude.com  8 deny: UDP from
    192.168.69.250.33072 to 192.168.20.34.33467
15: May 29 08:06:16 naismith popper: (v1.831beta) Servicing request
    from "penta.longitude.com" at 192.168.20.36
16: May 29 08:06:56 naismith popper: (v1.831beta) Ending request from
    "penta.longitude.com" at 192.168.20.36
17: May 29 10:04:02 localhost waisserver1[28430]: -2: Warning: couldn't open
    wais-sources/firewalls-digest.syn - synonym translation
    disabled
18: May 29 16:26:46 mv-gw.longitude.com  8 deny: UDP from
    192.168.186.11.20 to 192.168.20.34.1937
```

Most of your logging will probably be done via the UNIX *syslog* facility or some other similar file-based log mechanism. You'll need to develop log-scanning scripts to analyze each of these log files on a regular basis. Some firewall packages, such as the TIS FWTK, come with scripts to analyze and summarize their own logs. You could use these scripts as templates for your own logging, or you could write your own scripts from scratch in *awk, perl,* or some other suitable language. Chapter 5 discusses a package named SWATCH, often used for log monitoring and analysis.

As you can see, the log file is verbose and not particularly readable (even with better linebreaks inserted!). An unimportant error condition on a distant host (the server name mismatch on *nbs-relay.ac.cv*) is producing multiple error messages (11, 12, and 13, in this highly condensed version). The log file is also in chronological order, which is not particularly the order of importance. Example 12-2 shows a report based on a log file, with messages arranged in a more useful order, and somewhat summarized.

Example 12-2: A Report Based on a syslog File

```
May 27 06:42:07 localhost ftpd[10159]: securityalert: refused passwd
    file to chen@calm.com from chen.dialup.zarf.net
May 27 06:42:10 localhost ftpd[10159]: securityalert: refused passwd
    file to chen@calm.com from chen.dialup.zarf.net
------------------------------------------------------------------
May 26 12:33:39 localhost su: nxn to root on /dev/ttyp1
May 27 01:23:17 naismith su: bart to root on /dev/ttyp3
------------------------------------------------------------------
May 26 12:29:44 naismith kernel: uid 31 on /naismith_b: file system full
May 26 12:31:33 naismith kernel: uid 31 on /naismith_b: file system full
------------------------------------------------------------------
May 26 02:49:03 naismith named[79]: Malformed response from
    [192.168.192.2].53 (ran out of data in answer)
------------------------------------------------------------------
May 26 12:14:36 mv-gw.longitude.com 16 deny: UDP from 192.168.69.1.58899
    to 192.168.20.35.33459
May 26 12:15:15 mv-gw.longitude.com 16 deny: UDP from 192.168.69.1.58962
    to 192.168.20.35.33459
May 27 01:24:05 mv-gw.longitude.com 16 permit: TCP from
    192.168.20.34.2637 to 192.168.54.72.23 seq BE793A01, ack 0x0, win
    4096, SYN
May 27 01:24:11 mv-gw.longitude.com 16 permit: TCP from
    192.168.20.34.2637 to 192.168.54.72.23 seq BE793A01, ack 0x0, win
    4096, SYN
------------------------------------------------------------------
FTP:    Connections: 240
        Files: 733
        Bytes: 32,747,429 (31.23  M)
        Seconds: 92,787 (25.77  hours)
```

In general, it's safer to write scripts to filter out messages to be ignored (leaving unusual stuff), rather than writing scripts to identify the unusual stuff directly. The reason for this is that you seldom know all of the different messages your firewall might produce. It's easier to ignore the benign messages than to recognize the dangerous ones.

Log messages fall into three categories:

*   *Known to be OK* (e.g., "login succeeded for user smith"): You would like to ignore these. Message 3 is clearly in this category.

- *Known to be dangerous* (e.g., "bad disk block at location 0x47c7a8"): You would like these to cause some action to happen; this may be anything from sending someone email, to submitting a trouble ticket, to paging you.

- *Unknown*: You would like these to be sent off for a human to examine. Message 18 is one of these; why is someone sending UDP packets from port 20 to an arbitrary port above 1024? That doesn't match any common protocol.

Setting up the criteria is an iterative process; once a human has examined a mystery message, future examples of that message can probably be classified as either OK or dangerous without being examined again. You'll change the rules as time goes on.

Often, log entries must be considered in context. A message that's mildly mysterious if it occurs once is cause for serious worry if it occurs every minute. For example, "login succeeded for user smith" is good, unless it's preceded by three "login failed" messages for every user above "smith" in your password file; in that case, it's very bad indeed. In the *syslog* example, message 9 shows an unexceptional outbound TCP connection, logged just on general principles. It wouldn't be at all worrying if it weren't preceded by messages 6 through 8. In context, you know that someone made three failed tries at logging in as "admin," finally succeeded, and then immediately started up an outbound connection. This looks extremely suspicious. Message 7 doesn't mean anything at all without context.

The Good, the Bad, and the Ugly

Once you go beyond the obvious (for example, it's OK for users to log in; it's not OK for the disk to be bad) how can you tell when you're in trouble? Some rules of thumb:

Once is an accident; twice is coincidence; three times is enemy action
> One user who tries to log in at 2 A.M. and fails is up too late and can't type. Two users who try to log in at 2 A.M. may have been at the same party, but you're certainly going to be curious about the incident. Three or more attempts to log in at 2 A.M., and someone is trying to break in. This rule of thumb applies mostly to attempts on separate accounts; stubborn repeated attempts by the same user to do the same thing that doesn't work probably merely indicates that the user is single-minded—and wrong.

Accidents don't try to cover themselves up
> If your log files are missing, if entries have been deleted, or if there is any other evidence that somebody has been covering his tracks, you probably have a break-in. If not, you have some other serious problem. (Either something is broken, or somebody administering the machine is deleting things inappropriately.)

Most mysteries don't mean anything

For everybody who sets out to track down a mysterious problem or a strange log entry, and finds an intruder, there are 99 people who set out to track down a mysterious problem or a strange log entry, and find an annoying but trivial bug. You should still try to track these things down, but there's no need to panic.

Straightforward explanations are usually correct

It's possible that you were broken into at the same time you had another known problem, but it's not likely. If you know that you had a hardware failure, or a person wandering around doing misguided things, you'll want to spend some time ruling out side effects of the known problem before you decide that you also have an intruder. On the other hand, if your files are mysteriously disappearing and there's nothing apparently wrong with your disk, somebody is probably deleting them, and you'll want to spend a very long time ruling out an intruder before you decide that your filesystem code is buggy.

You're going to end up classifying suspicious events into several categories:

- You know what caused it, and it's not a security problem.

- You don't know what caused it, you're probably never going to know what caused it, but whatever it was, it's not happening anymore.

- Somebody was trying to break in, but not very hard; this is a probe.

- Somebody made a serious attempt to get in; this is an attack.

- Somebody actually broke in.

The boundaries between these categories are vague. Unless you're dealing with messages from the first category (i.e., a known nonproblem), it's going to come down to a judgment call most of the time. It's impossible to provide an exhaustive list of the symptoms of any of these situations, but here are some generalizations that may help.

You should suspect that someone's been probing your site if you see:

- A few attempts to access services at insecure ports (e.g., attempts to contact *portmapper* or an X server).

- Attempts to log in with common account names (e.g., *guest* or *lp*; most attempts to log in as "anonymous" are mistakes).

- Requests to *tftp* files or to transfer NIS maps.

- Somebody feeding the *debug* command to your SMTP server.

You should be more concerned if you see any of the following; an attack may be going on:

- Multiple failed attempts to log in to valid accounts on your machines, particularly accounts that are used across the Internet, or attempts on accounts in the order in which they appear in your password file.

- Unusual accepted packets or commands whose purpose you don't understand.

- Packets sent to every port in a range.

- Successful logins from an unexpected site.

You should suspect a successful break-in if you see:

- Deleted or modified log files.

- Programs that suddenly omit expected information (this suggests that they have been replaced with versions that ignore the intruder's files and programs). On UNIX machines, the most frequent victims are *ls*, *ps*, and *ifconfig*.

- New log files containing password information or packet traces that you can't explain.

- Directories that contain more administrative entries than they should. For example, on UNIX machines, a directory that contains more than two files with names made out of periods ("." and "..") should exist, but should not be duplicated. If it looks as if there is more than one entry for each, the extra entry probably has spaces in it and is being used to conceal the file or directory from casual observation.

- Unexpected logins as privileged users (for example, root) or unexpected users who are suddenly able to become privileged users.

- Apparent probes or attacks coming from your own machines.

- Extra processes with names that are variants of common system processes (e.g., both *sendmail* and *Sendmail* are running, or *init* and *initd*; this is another trick for sneaking things in where you won't notice them).

- An unexpected change in the login prompt for your machine, or for other machines you reach from yours. This indicates the program that displays the prompt has been modified.

Responding to Probes

Inevitably, you're going to detect apparent probes of your firewall—packets sent to services you don't offer to the Internet, attempts to log in to nonexistent accounts, and so on. Probes are the Internet equivalent of someone walking down a line of doors and checking every door knob to see if it's locked. Probers generally try one or two things, and, if they don't get an interesting response, they move on. If you're inclined to do so, you can spend a lot of time chasing down incidents like this, attempting to figure out where the probes are coming from and who is behind them. However, in most situations, it probably isn't worth the effort. The novelty of chasing down probes of this kind fades quickly. If you're getting persistent probes from some site, you might contact the management of that site to let them know what's going on, but that's usually about as far as folks need to go in responding to these probes.

It's unfortunate that on the Internet today, probes are so frequent that the laissez faire attitude we've described is often an appropriate one. In good neighborhoods, people don't get away with trying doorknobs. You have a right to be unhappy with people who behave this way, and trying to get them to stop is perfectly reasonable. However, you do need to decide where you're going to spend your energy. Save extreme responses for extreme situations. Treating probers with maximum harshness is just going to convince people that you are unreasonable.

Some people amuse themselves by setting up firewall machines to lead on people who try common probes. For example, they put a password file in the anonymous FTP area that appears to contain user account data. However, if the prober breaks the encrypted passwords, he sees a snide message. This is a harmless way to spend your spare time, and it provides a satisfactory feeling of revenge, but it doesn't actually improve your security much. It simply annoys attackers, and doing so may cause them to take a personal interest in breaking into your site.

Different sites have different opinions about what constitutes a probe, and what constitutes a full-fledged attack. Most people call something a probe as long as they know it's not going to work, even if it is determined and drawn out. For example, somebody who determinedly tries every possible combination of lower-case alphabetic characters as your root password is not going to succeed, and can probably be ignored as a probe until you get tired of reading the log messages. (That kind of attack isn't going to succeed, no matter how many combinations are tried.) However, if you have the time and the energy, it's probably worth pursuing people who are making determined attempts, even when you know they're going to fail.

There are several freely available packages that probe for known vulnerabilities in a system. The most famous one these days is SATAN, developed by Dan Farmer and Wietse Venema. SATAN, as distributed, does nothing but probe; it does not take advantage of the vulnerabilities it looks for.[*] On the other hand, there is no benign reason for anybody but you to be running SATAN against your site. The program is highly configurable, and, therefore, it might have been configured to probe for more obscure vulnerabilities. SATAN's probes will be detected by normal firewall logging, either by packet filters rejecting the packets or by the servers on the bastion host doing the same. Specialized SATAN detectors are now available, but most of them rely on the ability to start up promiscuous mode on an Ethernet interface (which you should have disabled on your bastion hosts). These detectors

---

[*] These are well-known vulnerabilities that you will be protected against if you follow this book's advice and keep up with CERT-CC advisories.

also distinguish SATAN from random attempts by timing, which is easily modified. If you already have reasonable logging turned on, running a SATAN detector will not increase your security.

Because SATAN is widely available and does not pose a threat to a firewalled site, it is reasonable to regard people who run it as merely probing your system, rather than mounting a determined attack. They have expended little effort and have little chance of success. Probes based on the use of SATAN will appear in your logs like any other probe—as a cluster of rejected packets from the same source.

Responding to Attacks

If your logs show that someone is making a determined attack against your system (see the rules of thumb we presented in "The Good, the Bad, and the Ugly," earlier in this chapter), you probably want to do a little more than sit back and watch. Chapter 13 describes in detail how you should respond to a real security incident.

Keeping Up to Date

The final important aspect of firewall maintenance involves keeping up to date. You obviously need to keep your system up to date, but before you can do that, you need to keep yourself up to date.

Keeping Yourself Up to Date

The hardest part of firewall maintenance is staying abreast of the continuous developments in the field. New things are happening every day; new bugs are being discovered and exploited; new attacks are being carried out; new patches and fixes for your existing systems and tools are being made available; and new tools are becoming available. Staying up to date with all these changes can easily be the most time-consuming part of a firewall maintainer's job.

How do you stay up to date? Well, primarily by staying involved. Find a set of mailing lists, newsgroups, magazines, and professional forums you feel comfortable with and follow them carefully. This section describes the most important ways you can keep involved. Appendix A provides a more complete list, along with contact information.

Mailing lists

There are several mailing lists that might be of interest to anyone who maintains a firewall; instructions for subscribing to these are included in Appendix A. The most important list for folks interested in firewalls is the Firewalls mailing list at *greatcircle.com*. This list hosts discussions of the design, installation, configuration, maintenance, and philosophy of Internet firewalls of all types. The main drawback of the list is that it can be very busy; there are sometimes more than 100 messages per day posted to the list. To address the problem of volume, a Firewalls-Digest version of the list is also available; Firewalls-Digest subscribers receive all of the same messages that subscribers to the main Firewalls list receive, but the messages are bundled into "digest" format (there are usually 10 to 20 messages per digest).

Another list you should almost certainly subscribe to is the CERT-Advisory mailing list. This is the list to which CERT-CC posts its new security advisories. If you are served by a response team other than CERT-CC (e.g., one of the other teams in the FIRST, described in Appendix A), check to see if that team has its own advisory list and subscribe to that one as well as to the CERT-CC list. Your team will probably mirror most of CERT-CC's advisories, and may produce advisories of its own that are relevant to its constituency (you) that aren't mirrored by CERT-CC.

Beyond the Firewalls and CERT-Advisory mailing lists, the choices are less clear. There are several geographic or industry-specific firewalls lists, e.g., the Academic-Firewalls and Firewalls-UK lists. There is also a mailing list called Bugtraq, where detailed discussions of network security holes take place; if you can wade through the seemingly perpetual flame wars, you can occasionally find some gems there.

There are also product- and package-specific lists for many firewalls products and packages; for example, there are lists for Livingston, Telebit, and Cisco routers, Morning Star software, and the TIS FWTK. If you are using (or contemplating using) a particular product or package, you should probably subscribe to the list for that product or package, if there is one. Lists of this kind are often an invaluable source of technical support, particularly during widespread security incidents.

Newsgroups

In addition to the various mailing lists you might subscribe to, there are a variety of newsgroups that are directly or indirectly relevant to firewalls. Many of these parallel the mailing lists mentioned in the previous section. For example, CERT-CC advisories are posted to the *comp.security.announce* group, and there are newsgroups for a variety of commercial and noncommercial network products. There has been talk of creating a firewalls newsgroup (probably *comp.security.firewalls*, or perhaps a pair of related newsgroups: *comp.security.firewalls.misc* and *comp.security.firewalls.announce*), which would be completely independent of the Firewalls mailing list discussed above.[*]

Magazines

Many trade magazines are beginning to include occasional or regular features on firewalls, although there isn't yet an entire magazine devoted to Internet security. (However, it's probably just a matter of time before one appears.) At this point, none of the magazines stand head and shoulders above the rest in terms of their coverage of firewalls. One thing to keep in mind about magazines (even tabloid

---

[*] This may or may not have happened by the time you read this.

weeklies like *Network World* and *MacWeek*) is their lead time; you often hear about something on the Net—on the various mailing lists and newsgroups discussed above—weeks before it appears in the trade press.

Professional forums

There are many professional forums available for your participation. These include conferences, vendor user groups, local user groups, professional societies (such as IEEE and ACM special interest groups), and so on. Many people find attending these events invaluable, not so much for the formal programs presented, but for the contacts they make with other people who have solved problems similar to those they are currently facing.

At this point, one of the best conferences for Internet firewall builders and maintainers is the USENIX Security Symposium (generally held annually). If you are a UNIX system administrator, then one of the best possible ways you can spend a week each year is at the USENIX LISA conference.[*] You can find more information about both of these conferences and about USENIX in general in Appendix A.

Local user and special interest groups are also a great way to keep in touch between conferences; most meet monthly or bimonthly.

Keeping Your Systems Up To Date

If you take care to keep yourself up to date, then keeping your system up to date is a fairly straightforward job. You just need to deal with whatever new problems you hear about, as you hear about them.

You should be able to collect enough information from the sources described in the previous section to decide whether or not a new problem is a problem for your site in particular. Beware that you may not be able to determine instantaneously whether a problem applies to your site; it may take a few hours or days for the information you need to become available to you. You may need to make a judgment call about what to do about a particular problem in the absence of solid information, with only vague reports about the problem and its consequences to go on. Which way you err—towards caution or convenience—is going to be dictated by your particular circumstances. These circumstances include the potential problem involved, what you can realistically do about it, how much your site cares about security versus availability and convenience, and so on. Caution would dictate blocking the problem if it's at all possible that it applies to you. Convenience, on the other hand, would dictate waiting to take action until you're fairly sure that the problem does apply to you.

---

[*] LISA used to mean "Large Installation System Administration," back in the days when a large installation meant having more than a dozen machines; today, most sites would qualify under that definition, and the focus of the conference has widened to include all types of UNIX system administration, but the name lives on.

There are a couple of principles to keep in mind when you are deciding what fixes to apply and when.

Don't be in a hurry to upgrade

Don't be in too big a hurry to install a patch or a fix unless you have reason to believe that the problem is being, or could be, exploited against you. It's always better to let somebody else go first, to discover what new problems the patch or fix creates. We're not suggesting you should delay very long in installing a relevant patch, but it's often wise to wait at least a few hours or a couple of days to see if the patch blows up on anybody else.

Don't patch problems you don't have

You don't want to apply patches for problems you don't have. If you do apply patches in this way, you run a great risk of introducing new problems. If a patch applies only to a particular piece of software or a particular release, and you don't use that software or that release, don't install the patch. If it applies to features that you don't use in programs that you do use, apply it anyway; you may start using the features in the future, and at that point you won't remember whether or not you patched it.

Beware of interdependent patches

While you generally shouldn't apply patches for problems you don't have, be aware that patches for problems you do have may depend on previous patches for problems you don't have. With any luck, the documentation for the patch you want to apply says what other patches (if any) are prerequisites, but this isn't always the case. Sometimes you just have to make your best guess. Situations like this are where it really helps to be tied in to the support mailing lists and newsgroups concerning your platform; you can ask there and see if anybody else has already figured this out.

How Long Does It Take?

As we've said, the hardest part of maintaining your firewall is keeping yourself up to date. How long does it take to keep up to date? If you're a novice at this, just getting started and at the steepest part of the learning curve, keeping up to date can easily occupy you full time. After you've been at it for a few weeks or months, and you've learned the fundamentals of what you need to know, your time requirement can drop off to just an hour or so a day to follow the various mailing lists, newsgroups, magazines, and other sources that you've decided to track.

Most of this time will be devoted to maintaining your own knowledge, not maintaining the firewall itself. Monitoring the firewall itself should only take minutes a day: long enough to scan the daily log summaries and make sure that nothing unusual or noteworthy has happened.

Obviously, you're occasionally going to have to devote more time to the firewall when it's time to fix something, upgrade something, or add new functionality. How long this takes depends on how complex the fix, upgrade, or addition is. The better job you've done anticipating your site's needs and designing and building the firewall in the first place, the less time you're going to spend adapting your firewall to changes. Many sites find that they need to update their firewall only about once every few months. The rest of the time, it sits in the corner just humming along.

When Should You Start Over?

One of the most important things to recognize about maintaining a firewall is that the older it is, the more maintenance it's going to require. At some point, you simply need to say "enough," and start over with a new firewall. At the rate the firewall arena is changing today, we generally tell people that if they build the best firewall they can today, they should probably plan on replacing it in 18 to 36 months. Lots of things that affect firewalls are changing very fast, including the attacks they're subjected to, the tools for building them, and the services their users demand.

Here are a few examples of how quickly things can change on the Internet:

- In 1993, password sniffing was not a major problem. Today, just two years later, it's a major problem.

- In 1993, there were only a handful of tools available for building firewalls, mostly in the form of limited packet filtering implementations in routers. Today there are dozens of tools of many different types (both commercial and noncommercial) to choose from.

- In 1993, the World Wide Web was a nonissue, and few Internet users had even heard of it. Today, it is the major factor behind the current growth of the Internet.

In another two years, we're going to be facing a whole new series of attacks, have a whole new set of tools at our disposal, and be dealing with a whole new set of services demanded by our users. Nobody knows for sure what these attacks, tools, and services will be, but you can safely predict that the Internet will be significantly different from what it is today. Of course, that's true for just about any two-year period in the history of the Internet that you care to examine. The one constant about the Internet is constant change—constant growth, a constant stream of new services and new tools, and so on.

In This Chapter:
- *Responding to an Incident*
- *What To Do After an Incident*
- *Pursuing and Capturing the Intruder*
- *Planning Your Response*
- *Being Prepared*

13

Responding to Security Incidents

The CERT Coordination Center (CERT-CC) reports that, despite increased awareness, the first time many organizations start thinking about how to handle a computer security incident is *after* an intrusion has occurred. Obviously, this isn't a great approach. You need a plan for how you're going to respond to a computer security incident at your site, and you need to develop that plan well before an incident occurs.

There isn't room here to detail everything you need to know to deal with a security incident: attacks are many and varied; they change constantly; and responding to them can involve a Byzantine assortment of legal and technical issues. This chapter is intended to give you an outline of the issues involved, and the practical steps you can take ahead of time to smooth the process. Appendix A provides a list of resources that may provide additional help.

Responding to an Incident

This section discusses a number of steps you'll need to take when you respond to a security incident. You won't necessarily need to follow these steps in the order they're given, and not all of these steps are appropriate for all incidents. But, we recommend that you at least contemplate each of them when you find yourself dealing with an incident.

In the section called "Planning Your Response," later in this chapter, we'll look again at each of these rules and help you figure out how to work them into the overall response plan that you should develop before an incident actually occurs.

Rules for Incident Response

In their book *Practical UNIX Security*, Simson Garfinkel and Gene Spafford provide two excellent, overriding rules for incident response. Keep these rules in mind as you read this chapter and during any real-life incident response.

- Rule 1: Don't Panic!

- Rule 2: Document!

Evaluate the Situation

The first step in responding to a security incident is to decide what response, if any, needs to be made immediately. Ask these questions:

- Has an attacker succeeded in getting into your systems? If so, you have a genuine emergency on your hands, whether or not the attacker is currently active.

- Is the attack currently in progress? If so, you need to decide how you're going to react right now. If the attack isn't currently in progress, you may not be in such a hurry.

If the incident looks like an aggressive attack on your system, you probably want to take strong steps quickly. These steps might include shutting down the system or your Internet connection until you figure out how to deal with the situation.

On the other hand, if the incident is a less aggressive one—perhaps someone has just opened a Telnet connection to your machine and is trying various login/password pairs—then you may want to move more slowly. If you're reasonably confident that the attack won't succeed (e.g., you can see that the attacker is trying passwords that consist of all lower-case letters, and you know for certain that no account on the system has such a password), you might want to leave things alone and just watch for a while to see what the attacker does. This may give you an opportunity to trace the attack. (However, see the section below called "Pursuing and Capturing the Intruder" for a discussion of the issues involved in tracing an attack.)

Whatever you do, remember Rule 1: Don't Panic!

Disconnect or Shut Down, as Appropriate

Once you've evaluated the situation, your next priority is to give yourself the time to respond without risking your systems further. The least disruptive alternative is usually to disconnect the affected machine from all networks; this will shut down any active connections. Shutting down active connections may make it harder to trace the intruder, but it will allow the rest of the people at your site to continue to do their work, and it will leave the intruder's programs running. This may help you to identify who the intruder might be.

If you're afraid that other machines have been compromised or are vulnerable to the same attack, you'll probably want to disconnect as many machines as you can as a unit. This may mean taking down your connection to the Internet, if possible. If your Internet connection is managed elsewhere in your organization, you may need to detach just your portion of the network, but you'll also need to talk to other parts of your organization as soon as possible to let them know what's happening.

In some situations, you may want to shut down the compromised system. However, this should be a last resort for a number of reasons:

- It destroys information you may need.

- You won't be able to analyze or fix the machine while it's down; you'll have to disconnect it from the network eventually anyway to bring it back up again.

- It's even more disruptive to legitimate users than removing the network connection.

- It protects only one machine at a time. (It's much easier to cleanly disconnect a set of systems than to cleanly shut them down.)

Even if you're responding to an incident that has already ended, you still might want to disconnect or shut down the system, or at least close it to users, while you analyze what happened and make any changes necessary to keep it from happening again. This will keep you from being confused by things users are doing, and it will prevent the intruder from returning before you're done.

Analyze and Respond

Your next priority is to start to fix what's gone wrong. The first step in actually correcting the problem is to relax, think for a while, and make sure you really understand what's happening and what you're dealing with. The last thing you want to do is make the situation worse by doing something rash and ill-considered. Whatever corrective actions you're contemplating, think them through carefully. Will they really solve the problem? Will they, in turn, cause other problems?

When you're working in an unusual, high-stress situation like this, the chances of making a major error go way up. Because you're probably going to be working with system privileges (for example, working as root on a UNIX system), the consequences of an error could be serious.

There are several ways you can reduce the chances of making an error. One good way is to work with a partner; each of you can check the other's commands after they're typed but before they're executed. Even if you're working alone, many people find that reading commands aloud and checking the arguments in reverse order before executing them helps avoid mistakes. Resist the temptation to try to work fast. You will go home sooner if you work slowly and carefully.

Try not to let your users get in the way of your response. You may want to give someone the specific job of dealing with user inquiries so the rest of your response team can concentrate on responding to the incident.

Also, try to keep your responders from tripping over each other. Make it clear which system managers and investigators are working on which task, so they won't step on each other's toes (or wind up unintentionally chasing each other as part of the investigation!).

Make 'Incident in Progress' Notifications

You're not the only person who needs to know what's going on. A number of other people—in a number of different places—have to be kept informed.

Your own organization

Within your own organization, there are people who need to know that something is happening: management, users, and staff. At the very least, let them know that you are busy responding to an incident, and that you may not be available to them for other matters. Usually, they need to know why they're being inconvenienced and what they should do to speed recovery (even if the only thing they can do is to go away and leave you alone).

Depending on the nature of your site and the incident in question, you may also need to inform your legal, audit, public relations, and security departments.

If there are multiple computer facilities at your site, you'll need to inform the other facilities as soon as possible; they are likely sources and future targets for similar attacks.

CERT-CC or other incident response teams

If your organization is served by an incident response team such as CERT-CC, or has its own such team, let them know what's going on and try to enlist their aid. (For instructions on how to contact CERT-CC or another response team, see

Appendix A.) What steps response teams can take to help you will depend on the charter and resources of the response team. Even if they can't help you directly, they can tell you whether the attack on your site looks as if it is part of a larger pattern of incidents. In that case, they may be able to coordinate your response with the responses of other sites.

Vendors and service providers

You might want to get in touch with your vendor support contacts or your Internet service provider(s), if you think they might be able to help or should be aware of the situation. For example, if the attackers appear to be exploiting an operating system bug, you should probably contact the vendor to see if they know about it and have a fix for it. At the very least, they'll be able to warn other sites about the bug. Similarly, your Internet provider is unlikely to be able to do much about your immediate problem, but they may be able to warn other customers. There is also a possibility that your Internet provider has itself been compromised, in which case they need to know immediately. Your vendors and service provider may have special contacts or procedures for security incidents that will yield much faster results than going through normal support channels.

Other sites

Finally, if the incident appears to involve other sites—that is, if the attack appears to be coming from a particular site, or if it looks as if the attackers have gone after that site after breaking into yours—you should inform those other sites. These sites are usually easy to identify as the sources or destinations of connections. It's often much harder to figure out how to find an actual human being with some responsibility for the computer in question, who is awake and reachable, and has a common language with you.

If you don't know who to inform, talk to your response team (or CERT-CC). They will probably either know or know how to find out, and they have experience in calling strangers to tell them they have security problems.

Snapshot the System

Another early step to take is to make a "snapshot" of each compromised system. You might do this by doing a full backup to tape, or by copying the whole system to another disk. In the latter case, if your site maintains its own spare parts inventory, you might consider using one of the spares for this purpose, instead of a disk that is already in use and might itself turn out to have been compromised.

The snapshot is important for several reasons:

- If you misdiagnose the problem or blow the recovery, you can always get back to the time of the snapshot.

- The snapshot may be vital for investigative and legal proceedings. It lets you get on with the work of recovering the system without fear of destroying evidence.

- You can examine the snapshot later, after you're back in operation, to determine what happened and why.

Because the snapshot may become important for legal proceedings, you need to secure the evidence trail. Here are some guidelines:[*]

- Uniquely identify (label) the snapshot media, and put the date, time, your name, and your signature on it.

- Write-protect the media—permanently, if possible.

- Safeguard the media against tampering (for example, put it in a locked container) so that if and when you hand it over to law-enforcement or other authorities, you can tell them whose custody the media has been in, and why you're certain it hasn't been tampered with since it was first created.

It's a good idea to set aside an adequate supply of fresh media just for snapshots, because you never know when you're going to need to produce one. It's very frustrating to respond to an incident, and be ready to do the snapshot, only to discover that the last blank tape got used for backups the day before, and the new order hasn't come in yet.

Restore and Recover

Finally, you're at the point of actually dealing with the incident. What do you do? It depends on the circumstances. Here are some possibilities:

- If the attacker didn't succeed in compromising your system, you may not need to do much. You may decide not to bother reacting to casual attempts. You may also find that your incident was actually something perfectly innocent, and you don't need to do anything at all.

- If the attack was a particularly determined one, you may want to increase your monitoring (at least temporarily), and you'll probably want to inform other people to watch out for future attempts.

- If the attacker became an intruder, that is, he actually managed to get into your computers, you're going to need to at least plug the hole the intruder used, and check to make certain he hasn't damaged anything, or left anything behind.

At worst, you may need to rebuild your system from scratch. Sometimes you end up doing this because the intruder damaged things, purposefully or accidentally.

---

[*] See *Computer Crime: A Crimefighter's Handbook*, by David Icove, Karl Seger, and William VonStorch (O'Reilly & Associates, 1995), for a detailed discussion of labeling and protecting evidence.

More often, you'll rebuild things because it's the only way to ensure you have a clean system that hasn't been booby-trapped. Most intruders start by making sure they'll be able to get back into your system, even if you close their initial entry point. As a result, your systems may be compromised even if the intruder was present only for a short time.

NOTE

Always assume that an intruder has created back doors into your system so that he can get back in again easily. This is one of the first things many intruders do when they break in to a system.

If you need to rebuild your system, first ensure that your hardware is working properly. You want to make sure it passes all relevant self-tests and diagnostics; you don't want to restore onto a flaky system. A reinstall may reveal previously unnoticed hardware problems. For instance, a disk may have bad spots that are in unused files. When you reinstall the operating system, you will attempt to write over the bad parts and the problem will suddenly become apparent.

Next, make sure you are using trusted media and programs, not necessarily your last backup, to restore the system. Unless you are absolutely sure that you can accurately date the first time the intruder accessed your system, you don't know whether or not programs had already been modified at the time the backups happened. It's often best to rebuild your system from vendor distribution media (that is, the tapes or CD-ROM your operating system release came on), and then reload only user data (not programs that multiple users share) from your backup tapes.

If you need programs you didn't get from your vendor (for instance, packages from the Internet), then do one of the following:

- Rebuild and reinstall these programs from a trusted backup (one you're absolutely positive contains a clean copy).

- Obtain and install fresh copies from the site you got the packages from in the first place.

Do not recompile software until you've reinstalled the operating system, including the compiler; you don't know whether the compiler itself, and the libraries it depends on, have been compromised.

This implies that if you're heavily customizing your system or installing a lot of extra software beyond what your vendor gives you, you need to work out a way of archiving those customizations and packages that you're sure can't be tampered with by an attacker. This way, you can easily restore those customizations and packages if you need to. One good way is to make a special backup tape of new software immediately after it's installed and configured, before an attacker has a chance to modify it.

You may have programs that were locally written, and in these cases you may not be able to find even source code that's guaranteed to be uncontaminated. In this situation, someone—preferably the original author—will need to look through the source code. People rarely bother to modify source code, and when they do they aren't particularly subtle most of the time. That's because they don't need to be; almost nobody actually bothers to look at the source before recompiling it.

In one case, a programmer installed a back door into code he expected would run on only one machine, as a personal convenience. The program turned out to be fairly popular and was adopted in a number of different sites within his university. Years after he wrote it, and long after the original machine was running a version without the back door, he discovered that the back door was still present on all the other sites, despite the fact that it was clearly marked and commented and within the first page of code. You can't make a comprehensive search of a large program, but you can at least avoid humiliation by looking for obvious changes.

Document the Incident

Life gets very confusing when you're discovering, investigating, and recovering from a security incident. A good chain of communication is important in keeping people informed and preventing them from tripping over each other. Keeping a written (either hardcopy or electronic) record of your activities during the incident is also important. Such a record serves several purposes:

- It can help keep people informed (and thereby help them to resolve the incident more quickly).

- It tells you what you did, and when, in responding, so that you can analyze your response later on (and maybe do better next time).

- It will be vital if you intend to pursue any legal action.

From a legal standpoint, the best records are hardcopy records generated and identified at the time of occurrence. Just about anything else (particularly anything kept online) could be tampered with or falsified fairly easily—or at least a judge and jury could be convinced of that. You need to produce records on pieces of paper, label and date them, and sign them. Furthermore, unless the pages are actually bound together, so that pages can't be inserted or removed without indication, you'll need to date and sign every page. (And you thought continuous tractor-feed paper was useless these days!)

You need to have legal documentation even if you aren't completely certain you're going to need it. An incident that looks fairly simple to start with may turn out to be serious. Don't assume it isn't going to be worth bringing in the police.

Here are several useful documentation methods you might want to consider:

- Notebooks—Carbon copy lab notebooks are especially useful, because you can write a note, tear it out and give it to someone, and still have a copy of the note. Another benefit is that the pages are usually numbered, so you can determine later on whether any pages have been removed or added.

- Terminals running with attached printers or old-fashioned printing terminals.

- A shell running under the UNIX *script* command, with the resulting typescript immediately printed and identified.

- A personal-computer terminal program running in "capture" mode, with the resulting typescript immediately printed and identified.

- A microcassette recorder for verbal notes.

You will probably want to use multiple methods, one to record what's happening online and one to record what's happening outside of the computer. For example, you might have a typescript of the commands you were typing, but a handwritten log for phone calls.

It's easy to decide what to record online; you simply record everything you do. Remember to use the terminal or session that's being recorded. (With some methods, like *script*, you can record every session you've got going; just make sure you record each session in a separate file.) It's harder to decide what to record of the events that don't just get automatically captured. You certainly want to record at least this much:

- Who you called, when, and why.

- A summary of what you told them.

- A summary of what they told you. (That summary may end up being "see above" some of the time, but you still want to be able to figure out who you were talking to, and when, and why.)

- Meetings and important decisions and actions that aren't captured online (e.g., the time at which you disconnected the network).

What To Do After an Incident

There are a variety of things you'll need to take care of after you finish responding to an incident. Don't relax just yet.

First and foremost, you want to figure out what happened and how to keep it from happening again. Now is the time to examine the snapshot you made of your system before you started the recovery process. When you've figured out what happened, you obviously want to take steps to keep it from happening again. You also need to think about anything you or others did during the response (for example, enabling or disabling certain software) that now need to be undone, fixed, or documented and made permanent.

In addition to analyzing the incident, this is the time to analyze your response to the incident. In this phase, it's important to concentrate on critiquing the response, not on assigning blame for the original incident. Don't be confrontational, but talk to any folks involved with, or affected by, the response. With them, try to determine what you did right, what you did wrong, what worked and didn't work, what other tools or resources would have helped, how to respond better next time, and what you've all learned from the experience.

If you made "incident in progress" notifications to various people and organizations, now is probably the time to tell them that the incident is over. Be sure to follow up with appropriate information about what happened, how you responded, and how you plan to keep it from happening again.

Pursuing and Capturing the Intruder

If you discover a security incident—particularly one in progress—you're going to be tempted to go gunning for the bad guys who are invading your system.

Going after the bad guys has a certain emotional appeal, but it's generally not very practical. There are a variety of approaches you can take, but there are also a variety of technical and legal hurdles.

For an appreciation of the problems involved in hunting down an intruder, see Cliff Stoll's book, *The Cuckoo's Egg*. In the late 1980s, Cliff was a system manager at Lawrence Berkeley Labs. While tracking down a minor inconsistency in the accounting system LBL used for computer time billing, he discovered evidence that an intruder had broken in over the Internet. He spent the next many months on an odyssey trying to chase down the attackers. Although Cliff succeeded admirably (and wrote an entertaining and useful book to boot), few of us are going to be able to emulate his feats. Most sites just don't have the time and resources to track their attackers the way Cliff did; most are going to have to be satisfied with simply getting them off their systems.

There are two main problems in tracking down intruders; one is technical and the other is legal.

The first problem is that tracking an attack back to its ultimate source is usually technically difficult. It's usually easy to tell what site an attack came from (simply by looking at the IP addresses the attacker's packets are coming from), but once you find the apparent source of the attack, you usually find out that the attack isn't really being carried out by a user from that site. Instead, it's very likely that the site has itself been broken into, and it's being used as a base by the person who attacked you.

If that site traces its own break-in, it will usually discover the same thing: the attacker isn't wherever the attacks appear to be coming from. Moreover, where the attacks appear to be coming from is simply another site in the chain that's been broken into. Each link in the chain between the attacker and you involves more sites and more people. There is a practical limit to how far back you can trace someone in a reasonable period of time. Eventually, you're probably going to run into a site in the chain that you can't get in touch with, or that doesn't have the time or expertise to pursue the matter, or that simply doesn't care about the attack or about you. As Figure 13-1 illustrates, these are many links in any network connection.

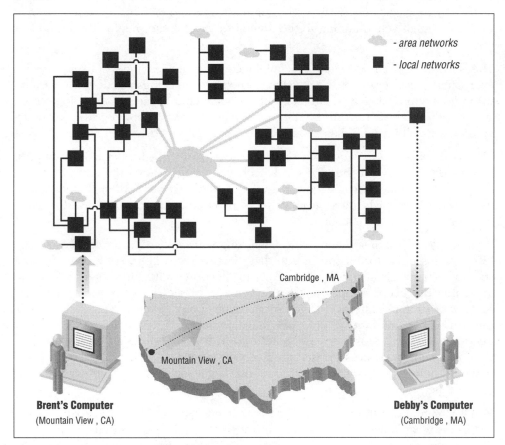

Figure 13–1: A network connection has many links

Furthermore, at some link in the chain, you are likely to discover that the attacker is coming in over a telephone line, and tracing telephone calls involves whole new realms of technical and legal problems.

You may well find the same attacker coming in from multiple sites. In one incident, responders kept correcting each other, until they realized that nobody was confused; one set of people was referring to SFU (Simon Fraser University, in Canada) and the other to FSU (Florida State University). The similarity of the abbreviations had momentarily concealed the fact that there were two separate sites, physically distant from each other, being concurrently used by the same attacker. The attacker had not started from either of them, and when SFU and FSU closed down access, identical attacks starting occurring from other sites.

Be wary when using email or voicemail to contact administrators at other sites when tracking down an intruder. How do you know it's really the administrator that's receiving and responding to your messages and not the intruder? Even if you're sure that you're talking to the administrator of a site, maybe the intruder *is* the administrator.

The second problem is legal. You might contemplate leaving your site "open," even after you're aware of the attacker, in hopes of tracking him down while he's using your site. This may seem like a clever idea; after all, if you shut down your system or disconnect it from the Internet, the attacker will know he's been discovered, and it will be much harder for you to track him down.

The problem is this: leaving your site open doesn't just risk further loss or damage at your own site. What the attacker is probably doing at your site is using it as a base to attack other sites. If you're aware of this, and do nothing to prevent it, those other sites might have grounds to sue you and your organization for negligence or for aiding the attacker.

If you're dealing with someone who's attacking your system unsuccessfully, there's less risk. It's polite to inform the site that the attacker is apparently coming from, so the system administrators there can do their own checking. It also lets you straighten out people who aren't really trying to break in, but are just very confused. For example, attempts to log in as "anonymous", even extremely persistent ones, usually come from people who have confused FTP with Telnet and simply need better advice. Most sites are grateful to be told that there are attacks coming from them, but don't be surprised if universities seem somewhat bored to hear the news. Although they will usually follow up, large universities see these incidents all the time.

You'll also find that the occasional site is uninterested, hostile, or incapable of figuring out what you're talking about, and it's not worth your time to worry about them unless the attacks from them are persistent, determined, and technically competent enough to have a chance of succeeding. In this case, you should enlist the assistance of a response team.

Planning Your Response

All of the actions we've outlined in the previous sections sound fine in theory, but you can't actually do any of them reliably without an incident response plan. You may personally be able to mount a sensible response to an attack, but you aren't necessarily going to be the person who discovers one. You may not even be available at the time. How will your organization react if someone attacks your system? Unless you have an incident response plan in place, the people involved will waste valuable time trying to figure out what to do first.

If you already have a plan in place for disaster or emergency response of any kind (e.g., fire, earthquake, electrical problems), you're probably not going to have to change it significantly to meet your security needs. If you don't have such a plan already, you can probably use your security incident response plan with only minor modifications for most emergencies.

Your incident response plan need not be an elaborate document, but you need to have *something*, even if it's only an email message that records and confirms the details you've all worked out over lunch at the local sushi bar. You'll be better off than many sites even if you do nothing more than think about the issues and discuss them with the relevant people.

What's in your plan?

The response plan is primarily concerned with two issues: authority and communication. For each part of the incident response, the plan should say who's in charge, and who they're supposed to talk to. Although you'll specify a few steps people will take, incidents vary so much that the response plan mostly details who's going to make decisions, and who they're going to contact after they've decided—not what they're going to decide. This section summarizes the different parts of a response plan.

Planning for Detection

An incident starts when somebody detects an intruder or attacker. That person might be a system administrator, but more often it's someone with no official responsibility. If you've properly educated the people who use your computers, they know they're supposed to report weird events. Somebody then needs to sort run-of-the-mill peculiarities from a security incident in progress. Who are the users going to report to? Who are those people going to report to if they're still not sure? What are they authorized to do if they are sure?

The two cases you really want to plan for are these:

* Somebody notices a real security incident in progress at 3 A.M.

- Somebody notices one of your perfectly legitimate users who happens to be doing vital work from halfway across the globe at 3 A.M. local time. (In Australia, where he's consulting at the moment, it's a reasonable 5 P.M.)

In the first case, you need a procedure which is going to reliably start up a full incident response immediately. Don't waste any time. It's going to be embarrassing and expensive if you don't actually get around to doing anything until your senior security person arrives in the next morning, takes in enough caffeine to become able to think, and gets around to looking at some report. (And that's if there is a report in the first place; without a response plan, it may be weeks before anyone actually tells someone who can begin to do something about the situation.)

In the second case, it's going to be embarrassing and expensive if you disconnect the network and get five people out of bed, all to prevent somebody from doing the work they're paid to do.

Either way, it's not a decision you probably want made by a night operator, or by a user acting alone because he can't figure out how to call somebody who knows how to tell a real incident from a false alarm.

At a small site, you might want to simply post a number that users can call to get help outside of office hours (for instance, a pager number). Users might be encouraged to shut down personal machines if they suspect an attack and know how to shut the machine down gracefully. You want to be very cautious about this, however, because an ungraceful shutdown, particularly of a multiuser machine, may be more damaging than an intruder.

At a larger site, one that has on-site support after hours, you should instruct the on-site support people to call a senior person if they see a possible security incident. They should be told explicitly not to do anything more than that unless circumstances are extreme, but to keep trying to contact senior personnel until they get somebody who can take a look at what's going on.

Planning for Evaluation of the Incident

Who's going to decide that you don't just have a suspicious situation—you actually have a security problem? You need to designate one specific person who will have responsibility for making the important decisions. It's tempting to pick one specific person in advance and put his or her name in your plan. But, what if that person isn't available in the event of an actual incident? Who, then, will have the responsibility?

Teamwork is great, but emergencies call for leadership. You don't want to have everybody doing their own thing and nobody in charge, and you certainly can't afford to stand around arguing about it. If your senior technical person is absent, do you want someone less senior but more technical to do the evaluation, or do you want someone more senior but less technical? How much time are you going to spend searching for the senior technical person when you have an emergency to deal with, before proceeding to your next candidate for the hot seat?

At a small site, you may not have a lot of options; if there's only one person who has the skills necessary to do something about an attack, your policy will simply list that person as the one in charge in case of a security incident. If that person is unavailable, authority should go to somebody levelheaded and calm who can take stopgap actions and arrange for assistance (for example, from a relevant response team). In this situation, technical skills would be nice, but resourcefulness and calm are more important.

At a larger site, there is probably more than one person who could be in charge. Your plan may want to say that the most senior of them will be in charge by default, or that whoever is specified as being on call will be in charge. Either way, the plan should state that if the default person in charge is unavailable, the first of the other possible people to respond is in charge. Specifying what order they're going to be contacted in is probably overkill; let whoever is trying to reach these people use his or her knowledge of the situation. If none of those people are available, you'll usually want to work up the organizational hierarchy rather than down. (A manager, particularly a technical one, is probably better equipped to cope than an operator.)

In a small organization, you will pick your fallback candidates by name. In a large one, you will usually specify fallbacks by job title. If job title is your criterion, it's important to base your decision on the characteristics of the job, not of the person who's currently in it. Don't write into your plan that the janitor should decide, on the theory that the current janitor also is the most sensible and technical of the nonsystem administrators. Tomorrow's janitor might be an airhead with a mop.

Planning for Disconnecting or Shutting Down Machines

Your response plan needs to specify what kind of situation warrants disconnecting or shutting down, and who can make the decision to do that. Most importantly, as we've discussed in "Pursuing and Capturing the Intruder," are you ever willing to allow a known intruder to remain connected to your systems? If you're not, are you going to take down the system, or are you going to disconnect from the network altogether?

If you are at a site with multiple computer facilities, do you want to take the entire site off the Internet if one facility has been compromised, or is it better (or even possible) to take just that facility off the Internet?

At most sites, the reasonable plan is to disconnect the site as a whole from the network as soon as you know for sure that you have an intruder connected to your systems. You may have a myriad of internal connections, with a triply redundant, diversely cabled, UPS-protected routing mesh, which can make "disconnecting" a daunting prospect (the system keeps "fixing" itself). On the other hand, you probably only have one (or a small handful) of connections to the outside world, which can be more easily severed.

Your plan needs to say how to disconnect the network, and how the machines should be shut down. Be very careful about this. You do not want to tell people to respond to a mildly suspicious act by hitting the circuit breakers and powering off every machine in the machine room. On the other hand, if an intruder is currently removing all the files on the machine, you don't want them to give that intruder a 15-minute warning for a graceful shutdown.

This is one case in which you need clear, security-specific instructions in your plan. Here's what we recommend you do:

- In most security emergencies, the correct way to shut down the machine is to do an immediate but graceful shutdown, with no explanations or warnings sent. Your plan should state that and specify the appropriate commands to issue.

- If the intruder is actively destroying things, you want people to shut the machine down by the fastest method possible. If they are physically near the machine, cutting off the power to the machine or the disk drive is completely appropriate, despite the damage it may cause. This implies that the relevant power switches must be easy to locate; a master switch for each machine is a good idea.

Whoever is going to disconnect the network needs to know how to do that. Often, the safest and easiest way is to unplug cables and clean up the side effects afterwards. With networks, this tends to result in voluminous error messages but to cause no actual damage. You do have to unplug the *relevant* cables, however, and the voluminous error messages may make it difficult to determine whether or not the cables that were unplugged were actually the correct ones. Your plan needs to tell people what to unplug, and how to make things functional afterwards.

Planning for Notification of People Who Need to Know

Your incident response plan needs to specify who you're going to notify, who's going to do the notification, when they're going to do it, and what method they're going to use. As we described earlier in this chapter, you may need to notify:

- People within your own organization

- CERT-CC or other incident response teams

- Vendors and service providers

- People at other sites

Your own organization

To start with, you need to notify the people who are going to be involved in the response. You'll have an urgent need to get hold of them, so you need telephone and pager numbers. Be sure you have all the relevant phone numbers; in addition to home and work numbers, check to see if people have car phones or portable phones at which they might be reached. This list includes anybody who manages computers within your site and anybody who manages those people, plus anybody else who might be needed to provide resources (to sign off on emergency purchases or to unlock doors, for example). Ideally, the list—or at least the key portions of it—should be reduced down so it's small enough to carry easily (for example, it might be laser-printed onto business card-sized stock). Obviously, the list isn't much use unless it's kept up to date.

If there are many people to be notified, you may wish to use a phone tree or an alert tree. In such a tree, shown in Figure 13-2, each person notifies two or three other people; this is a geometric progression, so a large number of people can be rapidly notified with relatively little work to any one person. Everybody should have a copy of the entire tree, so that if people are unavailable their calls can be taken over by someone else (usually the person above them on the tree). It's best to set it up so as many calls as possible are toll-free, and so that people are notifying other people they know relatively well (which increases their chances of knowing how to get through). There's no need for an alert tree to reflect an organizational chart or a chain of command.

Next, you're going to notify other people within your organization who need to know, starting with the users of your computer facility. For that, you'll use whatever your organization normally uses for relatively urgent notifications to everybody, whether that's memos or electronic mail. Your plan should specify how to do that (system administrators rarely send memos to all personnel and may not know how).

Your plan should also show a sample notification message for the users of your systems. This can sometimes be tricky. Your message needs to contain enough information so that legitimate users understand what's happening. They need to know:

- What has been taken out of service

- Why you're making their lives miserable

- Exactly which things that they normally do aren't going to work

- When service will be restored.

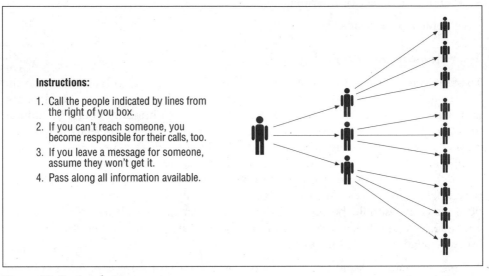

Instructions:

1. Call the people indicated by lines from the right of you box.
2. If you can't reach someone, you become responsible for their calls, too.
3. If you leave a message for someone, assume they won't get it.
4. Pass along all information available.

Figure 13–2: An alert tree

- What they're supposed to do (including leave you alone so that you can concentrate on the response)

- That you realize you're making life unpleasant for them

- That you're doing everything possible to improve matters

- That you're going to tell them the details later

Things that are obvious to you may not be obvious to your users (e.g., they might not even understand why it's so bad to have an intruder). Writing an appropriate message (see Figure 13-3) is not easy, particularly if you're busy and tired.

For the remaining people within your organization—people from other computer facilities, legal, audit, public relations, or security—the plan needs to specify who gets notified. Do you need to call the legal department? If so, who should you talk to? Who are the administrators for other sites within your organization? During the Morris worm incident in 1988, at least one large government lab was reduced to having the guards hand out flyers at the gate to everyone as they came to work, asking "Are you a system administrator?" because they had no idea who all the system administrators were, much less how to contact them.

Think about *how* you are going to send your message. If you send it via electronic mail, remember that the intruder may see it. Even if you know that your own systems are clean, don't assume that other people's are. Don't say anything in your message that you don't want the attacker to know. Better yet, use a telephone.

Some sites use a simple code phrase to announce a system attack that they can include in electronic mail. This can rapidly degenerate into bad spy fiction, but if you have an agreed-upon phrase that isn't going to alert an intruder (and isn't

---

From: Anastasia Administrator

To: All Users of the Big and Cool Computer Facility

Because of a security incident in progress, The Big and Cool computer facility is not currently connected to the Internet, and the machines big and cool are not available for use. This means that you will not be able to send mail offsite, FTP files, use Netscape to external hosts, or read news, until the situation has been resolved. In addition, the following services are provided from big and cool, and won't work:

database access (including the coolness forecasting reports)

Mail service for personal computers

We appreciate that this represents a major inconvenience, and will prevent people from getting work done. We took these steps because we had reason to believe that there was imminent risk that confidential data would be destroyed or released to the outside world. We are working to restore service as fast as possible. Big and cool should be available by 10 A.M.; we expect to restore Internet connectivity by noon.

You can assist us by reporting any anomalies, but otherwise contacting system staff for emergencies only until service has been restored. At that time we'll be glad to discuss the incident with everybody. Right now, the entire staff is occupied in working on restoring service as fast as is safe.

Figure 13–3: A notification message

going to cause people who don't know it or don't remember it to give the game away by asking what on earth you're talking about), it can be effective. Something like "We're having a pizza party; call 3-4357 to RSVP" should serve the purpose.

Should you contact your organization's security department? At some organizations, the security department is responsible only for physical security. You'll want to have a contact number for them in case you need doors unlocked, for example, but they are unlikely to be trained in helping with an emergency of this kind, so you probably won't need to notify them routinely of every computer security incident. However, if there is a group responsible for computer security within your organization, you are probably required to notify them. Find out ahead of time when they want to be notified and how, and put that information in the plan. Even if that group cannot help you respond to your particular type of incident (e.g., they may be personal-computer specialists, or government-security specialists), it's advisable to at least brief them on the incident after you have finished responding to it.

CERT-CC and other incident response teams

Your plan should also specify what emergency response team, if any, you're served by and how to contact them. CERT-CC and many teams in the FIRST have 24-hour numbers, and they prefer to be called immediately if a security incident occurs.

Vendors and service providers

Your plan should also contain the contact numbers for your vendors and Internet service providers. These people probably do not need to be called immediately, unless you need their help. However, if you have any reason to suspect that your Internet provider itself has been compromised, you should contact them immediately.

Many vendors and service providers have special contact procedures for security incidents. Using these procedures will yield much faster results than going through normal support channels. Be sure to research these procedures ahead of time, and include the necessary information in your response plan.

Other sites

You will not ordinarily need to talk to other sites as part of the immediate incident response. Instead, you'll call them after the immediate emergency is over, when you have time to work without needing everything written down in the plan. In addition, no plan could cover all the information needed to find out what other sites were involved and to contact them. Therefore, your plan doesn't need to say much about informing other sites.

If you are providing Internet service for other sites, however, or have special network connections to other sites, you should have contact information in the plan and should contact them promptly. They need to know what happened to their service and to check that the attacker didn't reach them through your site.

Planning for Snapshots

Your incident response plan should specify how you're going to do snapshots of the compromised system. Make sure that your plan contains the answers to these questions:

- Where are the necessary supplies and what program are you going to use?

- How should the snapshot be labeled and where should it be stored?

- How should they be preserved against tampering, for possible later use in legal proceedings?

Planning for Restoration and Recovery

Different incidents are going to require different amounts of recovery. Your response plan should provide some general guidelines.

Reinstalling an operating system from scratch is time-consuming, unpleasant, and often exposes underlying problems. For example, you may discover that you no longer know where some of your programs came from. For this reason, people are extremely reluctant to do it. Unless your incident response plan says explicitly that they need to reinstall the operating system, they probably won't. The problem is, this leads to situations where you have to get rid of the same intruder over and over again, because the system hasn't been properly cleaned up. Your response plan should specify what's acceptable proof that the operating system hasn't been tampered with (for instance, a comparison against cryptographic checksums of an operating system known to be uncompromised). If you don't have those tools, which are discussed in Chapter 5, or if you can't pass the inspection, then you must install a clean operating system, and the plan should say so.

The plan should also provide the information needed to reinstall the operating system; for example:

- Where are the distribution media kept?

- How do you find out how to install the operating system?

- Where are the backups, and how do you restore from them?

- Where are the records that will let you reconstruct third-party or locally written programs?

Planning for Documentation

Your plan should include the basic instructions on what documentation methods you intend to use and where to find the supplies. If you might pursue legal action, your plan should also include the instructions on dating, labeling, signing, and protecting the documentation. Remember that you aren't likely to know when you start out whether or not there will be legal action, so you will always need to document if you ever want to be able to take legal steps; this is not something you can go back and "fix" later on.

Periodic Review of Plans

However solid your security incident response plans may seem to be, make sure to go back and review them periodically. Changes—in requirements, priorities, personnel, systems, data, and other resources—are inevitable, and you need to be sure that your response plans keep up with these changes. The right question to ask about each item isn't "Has it changed?," but "*How* has it changed?"

A good time to review your incident response plan is after a live drill, which may have exposed weaknesses or problems in the plan. (See the section called "Do Drills" at the end of this chapter.) For example, a live drill may uncover any of the following:

- That you've changed all your storage since the plan was written.

- That you can't actually restore your operating system from scratch.

- That your plan relies on the ability to use the network to reach external sites, but at the same time instructs you to disconnect the network.

Being Prepared

The incident response plan is not the only thing that you need to have ready in advance. There are a number of practices and procedures that you need to set up so that you'll be able to respond quickly and effectively when an incident occurs. Most of these procedures are general good practice; some of them are aimed at letting you recover from any kind of disaster; and a few are specific to security incidents.

Backing Up Your Filesystems

Your filesystem backups are probably the single most important part of your recovery plan. Before you do anything else (including writing your response plan), make sure that your site's backup plan is a solid one and that it works. Don't assume that it's OK just because you haven't had a problem yet. It is entirely possible to go for months without noticing that you have no backups at all, and it may take you years to notice that they're only partially broken. Unfortunately, when you do notice, it's often when you need the backups most, and the outcome is likely to be disastrous.

Backups are vital for two reasons:

- If your site suffers serious damage and you have to restore your systems from scratch, you will need these backups.

- If you aren't sure of the extent of the damage, backups will help you to determine what changes were made to a system and when.

Every organization needs a backup plan and not just for security reasons. If you don't have one, that's probably a sign that your current backup system is *not* OK. When you are doing incident-response planning, however, pay special attention to your backup plan.

For your security-critical systems (e.g., bastion hosts and servers), you might want to consider keeping your monthly or weekly backups indefinitely, rather than recycling them as you would your regular systems. If an incident does occur, you can use this archive of backup tapes to recover a "snapshot" of the system as of any of the dates of the backups. Snapshots of this kind can be helpful in investigating security incidents. For example, if you find that a program has been modified, going back through the snapshots will tell you approximately when the modification took place. That may tell you when the break-in occurred; if the modification happened before the break-in, it may tell you that it was an accident and not part of the incident at all.

If you're not sure whether or not you should be worried, try testing your backup system. Play around and see what you can restore. Ask these questions:

- Can you restore files from all of your tapes?

- Can you do a restore of an entire filesystem?

- If you pick a specific file, can you figure out how to restore it?

- If you have a corrupt file and want a version from before it was corrupted, can you do that?

- If all of your disks died (or were trashed by an attacker) simultaneously, would you be able to rebuild your computer facility?

Even the best backup system won't work if the backup images aren't safeguarded. Don't rely on online backups and keep your media in a secure place separate from the data they're backing up.

NOTE

The design of backup systems is outside the scope of this book. This description, along with the description in Chapter 12, provides only a summary. If you're uncertain about your backup system, you'll want to look at a general system-administration reference. See Appendix A for complete information on additional resources.

Labeling and Diagraming Your System

As organizations grow, they acquire hardware; they configure networking in different ways; and they add or change equipment of various kinds. Usually only one or two people really know what a site's systems look like in any detail.

Information about system configuration may be crucial to investigating and controlling a security incident. While you may know exactly how everything works and fits together at your site, you may not be the person who has to respond to the incident. What if you're on vacation? Think about what your managers or coworkers would need to know about each system in order to respond effectively to an incident involving that system.

Labels and diagrams are crucial in an emergency. System labels should indicate what a system is, what it does, what its physical configuration is (how much disk space, how much memory, etc.), and who is responsible for it. They should be attached firmly to the correct systems and easily legible. Use large type sizes, and put at least minimal labels on the back as well as the front (the front of a machine may have more flat space, but you're probably going to be looking at it from behind when you're trying to work on it). Network diagrams should show how the various systems are connected, both physically and logically, as well as things like what kind of packet filtering is done where.

Be sure that labels are kept up to date as you move systems around; wrong labels are worse than no labels at all. It's particularly important to label racked equipment and equipment with widely scattered pieces. There's nothing more frustrating than turning off all the equipment in a rack, only to discover that some of it was actually part of the computer in the next rack over, which you meant to leave running.

Information that's easily available when machines are working normally may be impossible to find if machines are not working. For example, you'll need disk partition tables written down in order to reformat and reinstall disks, and you may need a printed copy of the host table in order to configure machines as they're brought back up.

Keeping Secured Checksums

Once you've had a break-in, you need to know what's been changed on your systems. The standard tools that come with your operating system won't tell you; intruders can fake modification dates and match the trivial checksums most operating systems provide. You will need to install a cryptographic checksumming program (such as Tripwire, which is discussed in Chapter 5), make checksums of important files, and store them where an intruder can't modify them (which generally means somewhere off-line). You may not need to checksum every system separately if they're all running the same release of the same operating system, although you should make sure that the checksum program is available on all your systems.

Keeping Activity Logs

An activity log is a record of any changes that have been made to a system, both before an incident and during the response to an incident. Normally, you'll use an activity log to list programs you've installed, configuration files you've modified, or peripherals you've added. During an incident, you'll be doing a lot more logging.

What is the purpose of an activity log? A log allows you to redo the changes if you have to rebuild the system. It also lets you determine whether any of the changes affect the incident or the response. Without a log, you may find mystery programs; you don't know where they came from and what they were supposed to do, so you can't tell if the intruder installed them or not, if they still work the way they're supposed to, or how to rebuild them. Figure 13-4 shows a sampling of routine log entries and incident log entries.

There are a variety of easy ways to keep activity logs, both electronic and manual; email, notebooks, and tape recorders can also be used. Some are better for routine logs (those that record your activities *before* an incident occurs). Others may be more appropriate for incident logs (those that keep track of your activities *during* an incident).

Routine entries

Date 1/12/95
From: Bartholomew

Installed gnutar in /usr/local/bin; source is in /usr/source/local.

Date 4/8/95
From: Clementine

Modified /etc/fstab to mount /dev/dsk/c0d1s3 on /scratch.

Incident Entries

Date: 4/15/95 10:37 pm
From: Desmond

Noticed unusual login activity from a machine at Whatsamatta University.

Initiated planned incident response; attempted to contact Bartholomew to evaluate situation, but he was unavailable, so contacted Clementine instead.

Clementine said she'd log in from home and check things out, and would take responsibility for any further response.

Date: 4/15/95 10:41 pm
From: Clementine

Logged in from home to investigate report from Desmond. Crackers working from Whatsamatta University seem to have broken into machine "big"; not sure how yet, or how far they ve gotten.

Called Desmond to tell him to shut down network connection per response plan, and to start contacting other members of response team, also per plan, while I drive in to work.

Date: 4/15/95 10:52 pm
From: Desmond

Disconnected from external net per response plan, on instructions from Clementine.

Date: 4/15/95 11:33 pm
From: Clementine

Arrived on site. Verified network disconnection and that other response team members had been notified and were on their way. Made incident in progress modifications to VP of Engineering and CERT, per plan.

Beginning to analyze how attackers got in and what they've done.

Figure 13–4: Activity logs

Email to an appropriate staff alias that also keeps a record of all messages is probably the simplest approach to keeping an activity log. Not only will email keep a permanent record of system changes, but it has the side benefit of letting everybody else know what's going on as the changes are made. The email approach is good for routine logs, whereas manual methods are likely to work more reliably during an incident. During an actual security incident, your email system may be down, so any messages generated during the response may be lost. You may also be unable to reach existing on-line logs during an incident, so keep a printed copy of these email messages up to date in a binder somewhere.

Notebooks make a good incident log, but people must be disciplined enough to use them. For routine logs, notebooks may not be convenient, because they may not be physically accessible when people actually make changes to the system. Some sites use a combination of electronic and paper logs for routine logs, with a paper logbook kept in the machine room for notes. This works as long as it's clear which things should be logged where; having two sets of logs to keep track of can be confusing.

Pocket tape recorders make good incident logs, although they require that somebody transcribe them later on. They're not reasonable for routine logging.

Keeping a Cache of Tools and Supplies

Well before a security incident, collect the tools and supplies that you are likely to need during that incident. You don't want to be running around, begging and borrowing, when the clock is ticking.

Here are some of the things you'll need to have in order to respond well to an incident. (Actually, these are things you ought to have around at all times; they come in handy in all sorts of disasters.)

- Blank backup tapes and possibly spare disks as well.

- Basic tools; you'll need them if you disconnect your system from the external network, or if you need to rewire the internal network to disconnect compromised hosts. Make sure you have a ladder if your site uses in-ceiling cabling or tall equipment racks.

- Spare networking equipment—at least transceivers and cables.

Set aside basic supplies (e.g., a backup's worth of media, a few transceivers and cables, the most critical tools, notebooks or tape recorders for incident logs) in a cache to be used only in case of disaster. This should be separate from your normal stock of spare parts and tools.

Testing the Reload of the Operating System

If a serious security incident occurs, you may need to restore your system from backups. In this case, you will need to load a minimal operating system before you can load the backups. Are you equipped to do this?

Make sure that you:

- Understand your system's operating system installation procedures

- Understand the procedures for restoring from backups

- Have all the materials (distribution media, manuals, etc.) available to restore the system

- Test your reload plans and procedures before you really need them

Testing your ability to reload the operating system is a good idea, and too few organizations ever do it. You can learn a lot by doing this. While you're trying to reload a dead system is not a good time to discover that you've got a bad copy of the distribution media. It's also not a good time to discover that the people who have to do the reload can't figure out how to do it. The best way to test is to designate the least experienced people who might have to do the work, and let them try out the reload well ahead of time.

Most organizations find that the first time they try to reinstall the operating system and restore on a completely blank disk, the operation fails. This can happen for a number of reasons, although the usual reason is a failure in the design of the backup system. One site found that they were doing their backups with a program that wasn't distributed with the operating system, so they couldn't restore from a fresh operating system installation. (After that, they made a tape of the restore program using the standard operating system tools; they could then load the standard operating system, recover their custom restore program, and reload their data from backups.)

Doing Drills

Don't assume that responding to a security incident will come naturally. Like everything else, such a response benefits from practice. Test your own organization's ability to respond to an incident by running occasional drills.

There are two basic types of drills:

- In a paper (or "tabletop") drill, you gather all the relevant people in a conference room (or over pizza at your local hangout), outline a hypothetical problem, and work through the consequences and recovery procedures. It's important to go through all the details, step by step, to expose any missing pieces or misunderstandings.

- In a live drill, you actually carry out a response and recovery procedure. A live drill can be performed, with appropriate notice to users, during scheduled system downtimes.

You might also test only parts of your response. For example, before configuring a new machine, use it to test your recovery procedures by recovering an existing machine onto it. If you have down time scheduled for your facility, you may be able to use it to test what happens when you disconnect from the network. Run your checksum comparison program before and after you install changes to the operating system to see what changes it catches when you think everything's the same, and what it does about the things you know have changed. Coordinate with another site to see what messages are logged when various types of attacks occur (pick someone you know and trust and who'll reliably tell you exactly what they did, or do it yourself). Try taking all of your central machines down at the same time and see whether they'll all come back up in this situation. (Do this when you have a few hours to spare; if it doesn't work, it often takes a while to figure out how to coax the machines past their interdependencies.)

This is all a lot of trouble, but there is a certain amount of perverse amusement to be had by playing around with fictitious disasters, and it's much less stressful than having to improvise in a real disaster.

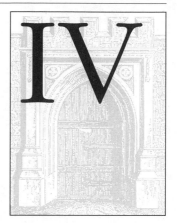

Appendixes

Part IV consists of the following summary appendixes:

Appendix A, *Resources*, contains a list of places you can go for further information and help with Internet security—World Wide Web pages, FTP sites, mailing lists, newsgroups, response teams, books, papers, and conferences.

Appendix B, *Tools*, summarizes the best freely available Internet security tools and how you can get them.

Appendix C, *TCP/IP*, contains background information on TCP/IP that is essential for anyone building or managing a firewall.

In This Appendix:
- *WWW Pages*
- *FTP Sites*
- *Mailing Lists*
- *Newsgroups*
- *Response Teams and Other Organizations*
- *Conferences*
- *Papers*
- *Books*

Resources

This book can't hope to tell you everything you need to know about firewalls and the broader issues of network and Internet security. In this appendix we have pulled together references to what we think are the most useful additional resources. These include both electronic and offline resources: World Wide Web pages, FTP sites, mailing lists, newsgroups, emergency response teams, other types of organizations, papers, conferences, and books. This is not an exhaustive list. Because there are so many resources, and because technologies and publications change so rapidly, there is no way we can keep completely up to date. However, this list should point you in some useful directions.

WWW Pages

You'll find these two WWW pages particularly informative.

Telstra

        http://www.telstra.com.au/info/security.html

This outstanding WWW page is maintained by Telstra Corporation (formerly maintained by Telecom Australia). It is very useful as a jumping-off point to other WWW pages and Internet resources related to network security.

COAST

        http://www.cs.purdue.edu/coast/coast.html

COAST has an excellent WWW page, which describes COAST's mission as follows:

> COAST—Computer Operations, Audit, and Security Technology—is a multiple project, multiple investigator effort in computer security research in the Computer Science Department at Purdue University. It is intended to function with close ties to researchers and engineers in major companies and government agencies. We focus our research on real-world needs and limitations.

FTP Sites

These two sites are an excellent source of tools, papers, security patches, and other Internet security resources.

coast.cs.purdue.edu

```
ftp://coast.cs.purdue.edu/
```

This archive is maintained by the COAST computer and network security project at Purdue University (see the description under the COAST WWW page above) under the direction of Gene Spafford. It contains a large collection of software and papers related to UNIX and network security, collected from all over the world.

Collected abstracts for the many tools and papers on the server are in the */pub/aux* directory:

```
ftp://coast.cs.purdue.edu/pub/aux/tools.abstract
ftp://coast.cs.purdue.edu/pub/aux/documents.abstract
```

info.cert.org

```
ftp://info.cert.org/
```

This site contains all of the Computer Emergency Response Team Coordination Center (CERT-CC) past advisories (see the discussion of CERT-CC under "Organizations" below), as well as a small collection of tools and papers.

Mailing Lists

It's hard to stay up to date, because technologies and approaches for firewalls and other Internet security mechanisms change so rapidly. You'll find these mailing lists helpful in keeping informed.

Firewalls

The Firewalls mailing list, which is hosted by Great Circle Associates, is the primary forum for folks on the Internet who want to discuss the design, construction, operation, maintenance, and philosophy of Internet firewall security systems. Send a message to *majordomo@greatcircle.com* with "subscribe firewalls" in the body of the message to subscribe to the list.

The Firewalls mailing list is fairly high-volume (sometimes as many as 100 messages per day, though usually more like 10 to 20 per day). To accommodate subscribers who don't want their mailboxes flooded with lots of separate messages from Firewalls, there is also a Firewalls-Digest mailing list available. Subscribers to Firewalls-Digest receive daily (more frequent on busy days) digests of messages sent to Firewalls, rather than each message individually. Firewalls-Digest subscribers get all the same messages as Firewalls subscribers; that is, Firewalls-Digest is not moderated, just distributed in digest form.

Mail to *ftp.greatcircle.com* for archives of the Firewalls mailing list.

```
ftp://ftp.greatcircle.com/pub/firewalls/
```

There is also a WWW-browsable for Firewalls currently under construction; it should be available by the time this book hits the shelves:

```
http://www.greatcircle.com/firewalls
```

Finally, there is also a WAIS server available for searching past messages. The server is on host *wais.greatcircle.com*; the database name is "firewalls-digest".

FWALL-Users

The FWALL-Users mailing list is for discussions of problems, solutions, and so on among users of the TIS Internet Firewall Toolkit (FWTK). Send email to *fwall-users-request@tis.com* to subscribe to this list.

Academic-Firewalls

The Academic-Firewalls mailing list is for people interested in discussing firewalls in the academic environment. This mailing list is sponsored by Texas A&M University. To subscribe, send "subscribe academic-firewalls" in the body of a message to *majordomo@net.tamu.edu*. Mail to *net.tamu.edu* for archives.

```
ftp://net.tamu.edu/pub/security/lists/academic-firewalls/
```

BugTraq

This list is for *detailed* discussion of UNIX security holes: what they are, how to exploit them, and what to do to fix them. This list is not intended to be about cracking systems or exploiting their vunerabilities. It is about defining, recognizing, and preventing use of security holes and risks.

Send "subscribe bugtraq" in the body of a message to *bugtraq-request@fc.net* to subscribe to this list.

CERT-Advisory

New CERT-CC advisories of security fixes for Internet systems are posted to this list. Send to *cert-advisory-request@cert.org* for subscription requests.

Archived past advisories are available from *info.cert.org* via anonymous FTP.

```
ftp://info.cert.org/
```

RISKS

RISKS is officially known as the ACM Forum on Risks to the Public in the Use of Computers and Related Systems. It's a moderated forum for discussion of risks to society from computers and computerization. Send email subscription requests to *RISKS-Request@csl.sri.com*. Back issues are available from *crvax.sri.com* via anonymous FTP.

```
ftp://crvax.sri.com/risks/
```

RISKS is also distributed as the *comp.risks* Usenet newsgroup.

WWW-Security

The WWW-Security mailing list is for the discussion of the security aspects of WWW servers and clients. Send "subscribe www-security" in the body of a message to *majordomo@nsmx.rutgers.edu* to subscribe to this list.

Newsgroups

There are a variety of Usenet newsgroups that you might find an interesting source of information on network security and related topics:

- *comp.security.announce*—computer security announcements, including new CERT-CC advisories

- *comp.security.unix*—UNIX security

- *comp.security.misc*—miscellaneous computer and network security

- *comp.security.firewalls*—proposed newsgroup on firewalls; might never be created

- *alt.security*—alternative discussions of computer and network security

- *comp.admin.policy*—computer administrative policy issues, including security

- *comp.protocols.tcp-ip*—TCP/IP internals, including security

- *comp.unix.admin*—UNIX system administration, including security

- *comp.unix.wizards*—UNIX kernel internals, including security

Response Teams and Other Organizations

These organizations are particularly helpful if you experience a break-in or any kind of security incident at your site. They are also sources of useful general information about Internet security and incident response.

CERT-CC

```
ftp://info.cert.org/pub/cert_faq
```

From the Computer Emergency Response Team Coordination Center's (CERT-CC) Frequently Asked Questions (FAQ) document:

> The CERT Coordination Center is the organization that grew from the computer emergency response team formed by the Defense Advanced Research Projects Agency (DARPA) in November 1988 in response to the needs exhibited during the Internet worm incident. The CERT-CC charter is to work with the Internet community to facilitate its response to computer security events involving Internet hosts; to take proactive steps to raise the community's awareness of computer security issues; and to conduct research targeted at improving the security of existing systems.

> CERT-CC products and services include 24-hour technical assistance for responding to computer security incidents, product vulnerability assistance, technical documents, and seminars. In addition, the team maintains a number of mailing lists (including one for CERT-CC advisories) and provides an anonymous FTP server: *info.cert.org*, where security-related documents, past CERT-CC advisories, and tools are archived.

The CERT-CC FAQ, and other information about CERT-CC are available from *info.cert.org* via anonymous FTP.

You can contact CERT-CC:

- By telephone: +1 412 268-7090 (24 hours a day, seven days a week)

- By email: *cert@cert.org*

FIRST

```
http://www.first.org/first/
```

From the FIRST WWW page:

> This coalition, the Forum of Incident Response and Security Teams (FIRST), brings together a variety of computer security incident response teams from government,

commercial, and academic organizations. FIRST aims to foster cooperation and coordination in incident prevention, to prompt rapid reaction to incidents, and to promote information sharing among members and the community at large. Currently FIRST has more than 40 members.

If you're not sure if you are served by an incident response team, contact FIRST; they can probably tell you. You can contact FIRST:

- By telephone: +1 301-975-3359

- By fax: +1 301 948-0279

- By email: *first-sec@first.org*

NIST CSRC

http://csrc.ncsl.nist.gov/

From the U.S. National Institute of Standards and Technology CSRC WWW page:

You are currently accessing the NIST Computer Security Resource Clearinghouse. The Clearinghouse is a National Performance Review (NPR) action. The Clearinghouse project at NIST is on-going; its goals are to

- Unify computer security-related information

- Ensure the information is complete and accurate

- Make the information easily searchable and convenient to obtain

- Keep the information current

- Make the Clearinghouse self-documenting; a model for how to do it

The main focus is on crisis response information; information on computer security-related threats, vulnerabilities, and solutions. At the same time, the Clearinghouse strives to be a general index to computer security information on a broad variety of subjects, including general risks, privacy, legal issues, viruses, assurance, policy, and training.

USENIX Association

http://www.usenix.org/

From the USENIX WWW page:

Since 1975 the USENIX Association has brought together the community of engineers, scientists, and technicians working on the cutting edge of the computing world. The USENIX Conferences and Technical Workshops have become the essential meeting grounds for the presentation and discussion of the most advanced information on the developments of all aspects of computing systems.

USENIX and its members are dedicated to:

- problem-solving with a practical bias

- Fostering innovation and research that works

- Communicating rapidly the results of both research and innovation

- Providing a neutral forum for the exercise of critical thought and the airing of technical issues

USENIX serves its members and supports professional and technical development through a variety of on-going activities, including:

- Annual technical conference.

- Frequent specific-topic conferences and symposia.

- A highly regarded tutorial program covering a wide range of topics, introductory through advanced.

- Numerous publications, including a book series, in cooperation with The MIT Press, on advanced computing systems; proceedings from USENIX symposia and conferences; the quarterly journal *Computing Systems*; and the biweekly newsletter.

- Participation in various ANSI, IEEE and ISO standards efforts.

- Sponsorship of local and special technical groups relevant to the UNIX environment. The chartering of the System Administrators Guild as a Special Technical Group within USENIX is the most recent.

- *comp.org.usenix*, the association's newsgroup.

USENIX sponsors a variety of conferences and symposia, many of which are related to or touch on network and system security. The proceedings of past events are also available. You can contact USENIX:

- By telephone: +1 510 528 8649

- By email: *office@usenix.org*

System Administrators Guild (SAGE)

```
http://www.sage.usenix.org/
```

From the SAGE WWW page:

> SAGE stands for the Systems Administrators Guild (don't ask what happened to the E). It is a subgroup of the USENIX Association. SAGE is devoted to the Advancement of System Administration as a distinct profession, within the realm of computer science but with similarities to facilities management and other service industries.

> SAGE answers the widely felt need for an organization dedicated to advancing the profession of systems administration. SAGE brings together system administrators to:

- Recruit talented individuals to the profession

- Share technical problems and solutions

- Establish standards of professional excellence while providing recognition for those who attain them

- Promote work that advances the state-of-the-art or propagates knowledge of good practice in the profession

SAGE cosponsors the annual LISA and SANS conferences. For more information about SAGE, contact the USENIX office:

- By telephone: +1 510 528 8649

- By email: *office@usenix.org*

Conferences

Although there are many other conferences, these are the ones you will probably find the most interesting from a firewalls and Internet security point of view.

USENIX Association Conferences

http://www.usenix.org/events/

The USENIX Association and SAGE sponsor a number of good conferences every year, including the USENIX Security Symposium, the USENIX System Administration (LISA) Conference, and the USENIX Technical Conferences. For information about any of them, contact USENIX:

- By telephone: +1 510 528-8649

- By email: *office@usenix.org*

USENIX UNIX Security Symposium

The USENIX UNIX Security Symposium is one of the best venues for learning about practical solutions to UNIX and network security issues. From the announcement for the 1995 symposium:

> The goal of this symposium is to bring together security practitioners, researchers, system administrators, systems programmers, and others with an interest in computer security as it relates to networks and the UNIX operating system.

USENIX System Administration (LISA) Conference

Jointly sponsored by SAGE and USENIX, the USENIX System Administration (LISA) Conference is the premier conference for UNIX system and network administrators. It covers a wide range of topics, including host and network security. If you are a UNIX system or network administrator, and you only get to go to one conference a year, this should be it. From the announcement for the 1995 conference:

The USENIX Systems Administration (LISA) Conference is widely recognized as the leading technical conference for system administrators. Historically, LISA stood for "Large Installation Systems Administration," back in the days when having a large installation meant having over 100 users, over 100 systems, or over one gigabyte of disk storage. Today, the scope of the LISA conference includes topics of interest to system administrators from sites of all sizes and kinds. What the conference attendees have in common is an interest in solving problems that cannot be dealt with simply by scaling up well-understood solutions appropriate to a single machine or a small number of workstations on a LAN.

USENIX Technical Conferences

The main USENIX Technical Conferences are less focused on practical security issues than the Security or LISA conferences, but you can still learn a lot and make many valuable contacts there. If you have an opportunity to attend one, you should certainly consider it.

UNIX System Administration, Networking, and Security (SANS) Conference

This conference is sponsored by the Open Systems Conference Board, with the cooperation of SAGE and USENIX, and is usually held in Washington, DC. According to the conference documentation, this annual event:

> ... is a technical conference offering system administrators, security administrators, and network managers a unique forum in which to gain up-to-date information about immediately useful tools and techniques, in addition to sharing ideas and experiences and network with peers.

For information, contact the conference office:

- By telephone: +1 719/599-4303

- By email: *sans@fedunix.org*

Internet Society Symposium on Network and Distributed System Security (SNDSS)

```
http://www.isoc.org/
```

The Internet Society sponsors an annual symposium on network security. From the 1995 symposium announcement:

> The symposium will bring together people who are building software and/or hardware to provide network and distributed system security services. The symposium is intended for those interested in the more practical aspects of network and distributed system security, focusing on actual system design and implementation, rather than on theory. We hope to foster the exchange of technical information that will encourage and enable the Internet community to apply, deploy, and advance the state of the available security technology.

For more information, contact the Internet Society:

- By telephone: +1 703/648- 9888

- By email: *membership@isoc.org*

Papers

This section contains a list of papers about firewalls, security attacks, and related topics. It is by no means an exhaustive list, but it does contain references to some of the papers that we find the most interesting. To get most of these, as well as many other papers, consult the extensive collections available from the Telstra and COAST WWW pages described earlier in this appendix.

The list below does not include papers that describe topics that are adequately described in this book, nor does it include papers that simply describe software (such as Tripwire, TCP Wrapper, etc.) that are mentioned in this book and cited in Appendix B; up-to-date papers about tools are ordinarily included with the tools themselves. The published versions of the papers are out of date, so you will do better to get the papers or documentation distributed with the software.

Bellovin, Steve, *smb@research.att.com*. "Packets Found on an Internet." *Computer Communications Review.* 23(3): 26-31. July 1993. Describes some of the stranger and more malevolent packets seen by one of AT&T's gateways.

> `ftp://ftp.research.att.com/dist/smb/packets.ps`

Bellovin, Steve, *smb@research.att.com*. "There Be Dragons." *Proceedings of the Third USENIX UNIX Security Symposium.* USENIX Association. Baltimore. September 14-16, 1992. This paper describes some of the probes and attacks against one of AT&T's gateways.

> `ftp://research.att.com/dist/internet_security/dragon.ps.Z`

Cheswick, Bill, *ches@research.att.com*. "An Evening With Berferd in Which a Cracker Is Lured, Endured, and Studied." *Proceedings of the Winter 1992 USENIX Technical Conference.* USENIX Association. San Francisco. January 20-24, 1992. Describes AT&T's experiences with one particular cracker who walked right into a trap and never knew he was the mouse being toyed with by the cat. The best part of the story isn't in the paper, however: how they got him to finally go away. The cracker was in the Netherlands, and they were sure they knew who it was, but there were no diplomatic channels through which they could get the Dutch police to do anything about it (what the cracker was doing wasn't illegal in the Netherlands, at least not at the time). Finally, one of the Dutch system administrators they'd been working with throughout the investigation got frustrated, called the cracker's mother, and the problem went away.

```
ftp://research.att.com/dist/internet_security/berferd.ps.Z
```

Eichlin, Mark W., and Jon A. Rochlis, "With Microscope and Tweezers: An Analysis of the Internet Virus of November 1988." *Proceedings, IEEE Symposium on Research in Security and Privacy.* Pages 326-345. Oakland, CA. May 1989. A detailed dissection of the Morris Internet worm (this paper's authors prefer "Internet virus") of 1988: what it was, how it worked, what it did, and so on, as well as a discussion of the response.

```
ftp://athena-dist.mit.edu/pub/virus/mit.PS
```

Farmer, Dan, and Wietse Venema. "Improving the Security of Your Site by Breaking Into It." A guide from the authors of COPS and SATAN (Dan) and TCP Wrapper, *portmap*, and *chrootuid* (Wietse) to testing your own security before attackers do it for you.

```
ftp://ftp.win.tue.nl/pub/security/admin-guide-to-cracking.101.Z
```

Hess, David K., David R. Safford, and Udo W. Pooch, *David-Hess@net.tamu.edu.* "A UNIX Network Protocol Security Study: Network Information Service." Texas A&M University. An interesting analysis of the security weaknesses in the NIS/YP protocol, which is one of the fundamental RPC-based services.

```
ftp://net.tamu.edu/pub/security/TAMU/NIS_Paper.ps.gz
```

Holbrook, P, and J. Reynolds. RFC1244: *Site Security Handbook.* July 1991. This RFC is a guide to establishing a security policy for your site. From the introduction:

This handbook is a guide to setting computer security policies and procedures for sites that have systems on the Internet. This guide lists issues and factors that a site must consider when setting their own policies. It makes some recommendations and gives discussions of relevant areas.

```
ftp://ftp.internic.net/rfc/rfc1244.txt.Zhttp://ds.internic.net/rfc/rfc1244.txt
```

Note that the Internet RFCs ("Requests for Comments") are the defining documents for almost all Internet protocols and services. Start with file *rfc-index.txt*; this is the index to the rest of the documents.

```
ftp://ftp.internic.net/rfc/http://ds.internic.net/
```

Ranum, Marcus (maintainer), *mjr@tis.com.* "Internet Firewalls Frequently Asked Questions (FAQ)." It is updated and posted to the Firewalls mailing list (*firewalls@greatcircle.com*) on a regular basis.

```
http://www.tis.com/Home/NetworkSecurity/Firewalls/FAQ.html
http://www.greatcircle.com/firewalls/FAQ
ftp://ftp.greatcircle.com/pub/firewalls/FAQ
```

Safford, David R., Douglas Lee Shales, and David K. Hess, *David-Hess@net.tamu.edu.* "The TAMU Security Package: An Ongoing Response to Internet Intruders in an Academic Environment." Texas A&M, University Supercomputer Center. A fascinating account of how fast things can go to hell in a handbasket when dealing with an attack. Due to rapid escalation of coordinated attacks against Texas A&M, the university was forced to go from no firewall at all (and never really having thought about one) to having to design, build from scratch, and install a rather significant firewall over the course of less than two weeks. This paper describes the situation and genesis of the TAMU security package, which includes the Tiger security analysis and Drawbridge packet-filtering systems discussed elsewhere in this book.

> ftp://net.tamu.edu/pub/security/TAMU/tamu-security-overview.ps.gz

Books

This section describes a number of books that are useful as references or for further understanding of particular topics.

Cheswick, Bill and Steve Bellovin. *Firewalls and Internet Security.* Reading, MA: Addison-Wesley, 1994. ISBN 0-201-63357-4. This was the first book published on firewalls, describing the authors' experiences building a series of firewalls for AT&T Bell Labs. The book tends to be good on theory and background, but weak on implementation details; it tells you how they build firewalls, but you probably can't duplicate their tools and methods without the same kind of backing they have (AT&T Bell Labs). Even so, it's a classic in the field.

Comer, Douglas E. *Internetworking with TCP/IP.* Second Edition. Englewood Cliffs, NJ: Prentice Hall, 1991. ISBN 0-13-468505-9. This book provides a good introduction to the nuts and bolts of TCP/IP networking. It discusses the basics about what packets look like and how routing works, etc. It also includes an introduction to some of the higher-level protocols such as SMTP and FTP.

Garfinkel, Simson. *PGP: Pretty Good Privacy,* Sebastopol, CA: O'Reilly & Associates, 1995, ISBN 1-56592-098-8. This is an excellent guide to the very popular program, PGP, which lets you encrypt and apply digital signatures to your messages. In addition to technical details, it contains the fascinating, behind-the-scenes stories of Phil Zimmermann's development of PGP, electronic privacy, and cryptography export and patents in the United States.

Garfinkel, Simson and Gene Spafford. *Practical UNIX Security.* Sebastopol, CA: O'Reilly & Associates, 1991. ISBN 0-937175-72-2. This is a very good guide to UNIX host security. Simson Garfinkel is also the author of *PGP: Pretty Good Privacy.* Gene Spafford is now one of the principals of the COAST project at Purdue University (see references to COAST above).

Hunt, Craig. *TCP/IP Network Administration.* Sebastopol, CA: O'Reilly & Associates, 1992. ISBN 0-937175-82-X. This book is an excellent system administrator's overview of TCP/IP networking (with a focus on UNIX systems), and a very useful reference to major UNIX networking services and tools such as BIND (the standard UNIX DNS server) and Sendmail (the standard UNIX SMTP server). Our Appendix C, which talks about the underlying TCP/IP protocols, is adapted from the first couple of chapters of this book.

Liu, Cricket, Jerry Peek, Russ Jones, Bryan Buus, and Adrian Nye. *Managing Internet Information Services,* Sebastopol, MA: O'Reilly & Associates, 1994. ISBN 1-56592-062-7. This is an excellent guide to setting up and managing Internet services such as the World Wide Web, FTP, Gopher, and more, including discussions of the security implications of these services.

Nemeth, Evi, Garth Snyder, Scott Seebass, and Trent R. Hein. *UNIX System Administration Handbook.* Second Edition. Englewood Cliffs, NJ: Prentice Hall , 1995. ISBN 0-13-151051-7. This is the standard reference guide to practical UNIX system administration issues. It includes good, real-world coverage of thorny issues like backups. It also includes a CD-ROM full of tools for UNIX system administrators.

Schneier, Bruce. *Applied Cryptography.* New York: John Wiley & Sons, 1994. ISBN 0-471-59756-2. This is an extremely comprehensive book about cryptography algorithms and techniques. It covers the Data Encryption Standard, the RSA algorithm, and all of the other private and public key algorithms, with mathematical details for all of them. Source code is available.

Stallings, William. *Network and Internetwork Security.* Englewood Cliffs, NJ: Prentice Hall, 1995. ISBN 0-02-415483-0. This is a good academic text on network and internetwork protocols, standards, and security features. It covers a variety of encryption products and standards, as well as the underpinnings of network architectures.

Stevens, Richard W. *TCP/IP Illustrated, Volume 1: The Protocols.* Reading, MA: Addison-Wesley, 1994. ISBN 0-201-63346-9. This is a good guide to the nuts and bolts of TCP/IP networking. Its main strength is that it provides traces of the packets going back and forth as the protocols are actually in use, and uses this to illustrate the discussions of the protocols.

Stoll, Cliff. *The Cuckoo's Egg.* Garden City, NJ: Doubleday, 1989. ISBN 0-671726889. This is a fascinating true story about a hunt for crackers on the Internet. It gives you an appreciation of the time and effort it takes to track an attack against your site, and it also includes a good chocolate chip cookie recipe.

In This Appendix:
- *Authentication Tools*
- *Analysis Tools*
- *Packet Filtering Tools*
- *Proxy Systems Tools*
- *Daemons*
- *Utilities*

Tools

This appendix describes some of the tools and packages available on the Internet that you might find useful in building and maintaining your firewall. Many of these tools are mentioned in this book. Although this software is freely available, some of it is restricted in various ways by the authors (e.g., it may not be permitted to be used for commercial purposes or be included on a CD-ROM, etc.) or by the U.S. government (e.g., if it contains cryptography, it can't ordinarily be exported outside the United States). Carefully read the documentation files that are distributed with the packages.

Although we have used most of the software listed here, we can't take responsibility for ensuring that the copy you get will work properly and won't cause any damage to your system. As with any software, test it before you use it.

As we've mentioned, the Computer Operations, Audit, and Security Technology (COAST) project at Purdue University provides a valuable service to the Internet community by maintaining a current and well-organized repository of the most important security tools and documents on the Internet. The repository is available on host coast.cs.purdue.edu via anonymous FTP; start in the*/pub/aux* directory for listings of the documents and tools available. Many of the descriptions of tools in the list below are drawn from COAST's *tools.abstracts* file, and we gratefully acknowledge their permission to use this information. To find out more about COAST, point a WWW viewer at their Web page:

    http://www.cs.purdue.edu/coast/coast.html

Authentication Tools

The tools in this category provide support for various types of authentication. See Chapter 10 for information about different authentication approaches.

TIS Internet Firewall Toolkit (FWTK)

```
ftp://ftp.tis.com/pub/firewalls/toolkit/
```

The TIS Internet Firewall Toolkit (FWTK), from Trusted Information Systems, Inc., is a very useful, well-designed, and well-written set of programs you might find useful for authentication and other purposes. It includes:

- An authentication server that provides several mechanisms for supporting non-reusable passwords (described in Chapter 10).

- An access control program, *netacl* (described in Chapter 5).

- Proxy servers for a variety of protocols (FTP, HTTP, Gopher, *rlogin*, Telnet, and X11) (described in Chapter 7).

- A generic proxy server for simple TCP-based protocols using one-to-one or many-to-one connections, such as NNTP (described in Chapter 7).

- A wrapper (the *smap* package) for SMTP servers such as Sendmail to protect them from SMTP-based attacks (described in Chapter 8).

- A wrapper for *inetd*-started servers such as *telnetd* and *ftpd* to control where they can be contacted from (much like the TCP Wrapper package described later in this appendix)

The toolkit is designed so that you can pick and choose only the pieces you need; you don't have to install the whole thing. The pieces you do install share a common configuration file, however, which makes managing configuration changes somewhat easier.

Some parts of the toolkit (the server for the non-reusable password system, for example) require a Data Encryption Standard (DES) library in some configurations. If your system doesn't already have one (look for a file named *libdes.a* in whatever directories code libraries are kept on your system), you can get one from:

```
ftp://ftp.psy.uq.oz.au/pub/DES/
```

TIS maintains a mailing list for discussions of improvements, bugs, fixes, and so on among people using the toolkit; Send email to *fwall-users-request@tis.com* to subscribe to this list.

Kerberos

```
ftp://athena-dist.mit.edu/pub/kerberos/
ftp://coast.cs.purdue.edu/pub/tools/unix/kerberos/
```

Kerberos was developed by Project Athena at the Massachusetts Institute of Technology. From the Kerberos Frequently Asked Questions (FAQ) file:

> Kerberos is a network authentication system for use on physically insecure networks, based on the key distribution model presented by Needham and Schroeder. It allows entities communicating over networks to prove their identity to each other while preventing eavesdropping or replay attacks. It also provides for datastream integrity (detection of modification) and secrecy (preventing unauthorized reading) using cryptography systems such as DES.

Analysis Tools

The tools in this category let you audit your system. Some perform audits and check for well-known security holes; others establish databases of checksums of all of the files in a system (to allow you to watch for changes to those files); some do both.

COPS

```
ftp://coast.cs.purdue.edu/pub/tools/unix/cops
```

COPS, by Dan Farmer, is the Computer Oracle and Password System, a system that checks UNIX systems for common security problems (such as unsafe permissions on key files and directories).

Tiger

```
ftp://net.tamu.edu/pub/security/TAMU/
ftp://coast.cs.purdue.edu/pub/tools/unix/tiger
```

Tiger, by Doug Schales of Texas A&M University (TAMU), is a set of scripts that scan a UNIX system looking for security problems, in the same fashion as Dan Farmer's COPS. Tiger was originally developed to provide a check of UNIX systems on the A&M campus that users wanted to be accessible from off campus. Before the packet filtering in the firewall would be modified to allow off-campus access to the system, the system had to pass the Tiger checks.

Tripwire

```
ftp://coast.cs.purdue.edu/pub/COAST/Tripwire
```

Tripwire, by Gene H. Kim and Gene Spafford of the COAST project at Purdue University, is a file integrity checker: a utility that compares a designated set of files and directories against information stored in a previously generated database. Added or deleted files are flagged and reported, as are any files that have changed from their previously recorded state in the database. Run Tripwire against system files on a regular basis. If you do, the program will spot any file changes when it next runs, giving system administrators information to enact damage control measures immediately.

SATAN

        ftp://ftp.win.tue.nl/pub/security/satan.tar.Z

SATAN, by Wietse Venema and Dan Farmer, is the Security Administrator Tool for Analyzing Networks. (If you don't like the name, it comes with a script named *repent* that changes all references from SATAN to SANTA: Security Administrator Network Tool for Analysis.) Despite the authors' strong credentials in the network security community (Wietse is from Eindhoven University in the Netherlands and is the author of the TCP Wrapper package and several other network security tools; Dan is the author of COPS), SATAN is a somewhat controversial tool. Why? Because, unlike COPS, Tiger, and other tools that work from within a system, SATAN probes the system from the outside, just as an attacker would. The unfortunate consequence of this is that someone (such as an attacker) can run SATAN against any system, not just those he already has access to. According to the authors:

> SATAN was written because we realized that computer systems are becoming more and more dependent on the network, and at the same becoming more and more vulnerable to attack via that same network.

> SATAN is a tool to help systems administrators. It recognizes several common networking-related security problems, and reports the problems without actually exploiting them.

> For each type or problem found, SATAN offers a tutorial that explains the problem and what its impact could be. The tutorial also explains what can be done about the problem: correct an error in a configuration file, install a bugfix from the vendor, use other means to restrict access, or simply disable service.

> SATAN collects information that is available to everyone on with access to the network. With a properly-configured firewall in place, that should be near-zero information for outsiders.

ISS

```
ftp://coast.cs.purdue.edu/pub/tools/unix/iss.shar.Z
```

ISS, by Christopher William Klaus, is the Internet Security Scanner. When ISS is run from another system and directed at your system, it probes your system for software bugs and configuration errors commonly exploited by crackers. Like SATAN, it is a controversial tool; less so, however, in that it is older and less capable than SATAN, and it was written by someone who (at the time it was released) was relatively unknown in the network-security community. (Much of the controversy about SATAN concerns whether or not the authors "sold out," as opposed to any technical or philosophical point.)

Packet Filtering Tools

These tools allow you to add packet filtering to a PC or UNIX system.

screend

```
ftp://ftp.vix.com/pub/vixie/
ftp://coast.cs.purdue.edu/pub/tools/unix/screend
```

screend, which was originally written by Jeff Mogul at Digital Equipment Corporation and is now maintained by Paul Vixie, is a package that lets you add packet filtering capabilities to the kernel of BSD-based UNIX systems.

Drawbridge

```
ftp://net.tamu.edu/pub/security/TAMU/
ftp://coast.cs.purdue.edu/pub/tools/unix/TAMU/
```

Drawbridge, by Texas A&M University, is a package that lets you turn a PC (one that is running MS-DOS and has two Ethernet or two FDDI boards) into an IP packet filter. There are three programs: Filter, Filter Compiler, and Filter Manager. Filter is the program that runs on the PC itself. Filter Compiler and Filter Manager are support programs that run on a UNIX box, and allow you to compile the filter lists into the form needed by the PC, and then download them over the Internet to the PC. (Alternatively, you can transfer them to the PC on floppy, if you can write an MS-DOS floppy disk from your UNIX box.)

KarlBridge

```
ftp://coast.cs.purdue.edu/pub/tools/dos/kbridge.zip
```

The KarlBridge package, by Doug Karl, is a program that runs on a PC with two Ethernet boards. It turns the PC into a packet-filtering bridge.

Proxy Systems Tools

The tools in this category let you add proxy capabilities to your system. See the discussion in Chapter 7.

TIS Internet Firewall Toolkit (FWTK)

See the discussion of the TIS FWTK in the "Authentication Tools" section of this appendix.

SOCKS

        ftp://ftp.nec.com/pub/security/socks.cstc/
        ftp://coast.cs.purdue.edu/pub/tools/unix/socks/

SOCKS, originally written by David Koblas and Michelle Koblas and now maintained by Ying-Da Lee, is a proxy-building toolkit that allows you to convert standard TCP client programs to proxied versions of those same programs. There are two parts to SOCKS: client libraries and a generic server. Client libraries are available for most UNIX platforms, as well as for Macintosh and Windows systems. The generic server runs on most UNIX platforms and can be used by any of the client libraries, regardless of their platform.

UDP Packet Relayer

        ftp://coast.cs.purdue.edu/pub/tools/unix/udprelay-0.2.tar.gz

This package, by Tom Fitzgerald, is a proxy system that provides much the same functionality for UDP-based clients that SOCKS provides for TCP-based clients.

Daemons

When you are building your firewall, you may wish to replace your standard daemons with the daemons described below.

wuarchive ftpd

        ftp://ftp.wustl.edu/packages/wuarchive-ftpd/
        ftp://ftp.uu.net/networking/archival/ftp/wuarchive-ftpd/

The *wuarchive* FTP daemon offers many features and security enhancements, such as per-directory message files shown to any user who enters the directory, limits on number of simultaneous users, and improved logging and access control. These enhancements are specifically designed to support anonymous FTP.

CERN httpd

```
ftp://www.w3.org/pub/src/WWWDaemon.tar.Z
```

CERN is the European Laboratory for Particle Physics, in Switzerland, and is "the birthplace of the World-Wide Web." The CERN HTTP daemon is one of several common HTTP servers on the Internet. What makes it particularly interesting from a firewalls point of view are its proxying and caching capabilities. (We describe these in Chapter 7.)

portmap

```
ftp://coast.cs.purdue.edu/pub/tools/unix/portmap.shar
```

portmap, from Wietse Venema, is a *portmapper* replacement which offers access control in the style of the TCP Wrapper program, described in the next section.

gated

```
ftp://gated.cornell.edu/pub/gated/
```

gated is a routing daemon that allows you to specify the hosts from which you'll accept routing information.

Andrew File System (AFS)

```
http://www.transarc.com/
http://www.cis.ohio-state.edu/hypertext/faq/usenet/afs-faq/faq.html
```

AFS is a network filesystem that is more suitable for use across wide area networks such as the Internet than traditional LAN-oriented network filesystem protocols such as NFS. From the AFS document:

> AFS is a distributed filesystem that enables cooperating hosts (clients and servers) to efficiently share filesystem resources across both local area and wide area networks.

> AFS is marketed, maintained, and extended by Transarc Corporation.

> AFS is based on a distributed file system originally developed at the Information Technology Center at Carnegie-Mellon University.

Utilities

A number of additional utilities provide services you'll find useful when you build and maintain your firewall.

TIS Internet Firewall Toolkit (FWTK)

See the discussion of the TIS FWTK in the "Authentication Tools" section of this appendix.

TCP Wrapper

```
ftp://ftp.win.tue.nl/pub/security/
ftp://coast.cs.purdue.edu/pub/tools/unix/tcp_wrappers/
```

With this package, from Wietse Venema, you can monitor and filter incoming requests for servers started by *inetd*. These servers include FTP, Telnet, *finger*, *rlogin*, *rsh*, SMTP, HTTP, and others.

chrootuid

```
ftp://ftp.win.tue.nl/pub/security/
ftp://coast.cs.purdue.edu/pub/tools/unix/chrootuid
```

chrootuid, from Wietse Venema, makes it easy to run a network service at a low privilege level and with restricted filesystem access. The program can be used to run Gopher, HTTP, WAIS, and other network daemons in a minimal environment: the daemons have access only to their own directory tree and run under a low-privileged *userid*. The arrangement greatly reduces the impact of possible security problems in daemon software.

SWATCH

```
ftp://sierra.stanford.edu/pub/sources/swatch.tar.gz
ftp://coast.cs.purdue.edu/pub/tools/unix/swatch/
```

SWATCH, by Todd Atkins of Stanford University, is the Simple Watcher. It monitors log files created by *syslog*, and allows an administrator to take specific actions (such as sending an email warning, paging someone, etc.) in response to logged events and patterns of events.

trimlog

```
ftp://coast.cs.purdue.edu/pub/tools/unix/trimlog
```

trimlog, by David A. Curry, is a program that helps you manage log files. It reads a configuration file to determine which files to trim, how to trim them, how much they should be trimmed, and so on. The program helps keep your logs from growing until they consume all available disk space.

In This Appendix:
- *Introduction to TCP/IP*
- *A Data Communications Model*
- *TCP/IP Protocol Architecture*
- *Network Access Layer*
- *Internet Layer*
- *Transport Layer*
- *Application Layer*
- *Addressing, Routing, and Multiplexing*
- *The IP Address*
- *Internet Routing Architecture*
- *The Routing Table*
- *Protocols, Ports, and Sockets*

C

TCP/IP Fundamentals

You need a good understanding of TCP/IP to be able to follow the details of the discussions of packet filtering in this book. If you are not already familiar with TCP/IP, we strongly recommend that you read at least this appendix. This appendix is adapted from Chapters 1 and 2 of *TCP/IP Network Administration* by Craig Hunt (O'Reilly & Associates, 1992). See that book for complete information about administering TCP/IP-based services.

Introduction to TCP/IP

The name TCP/IP refers to an entire suite of data communications protocols. The suite gets its name from two of the protocols that belong to it: the Transmission Control Protocol and the Internet Protocol. Although there are many other protocols in the suite, TCP and IP are certainly two of the most important.

TCP/IP Features

The popularity of the TCP/IP protocols on the Internet did not grow rapidly just because the protocols were there, or because military agencies mandated their use. They met an important need (worldwide data communication) at the right time, and they had several important features that allowed them to meet this need. These are:

- Open protocol standards, freely available and developed independently from any specific computer hardware or operating system. Because it is so widely supported, TCP/IP is ideal for uniting different hardware and software, even if you don't communicate over the Internet.

- Independence from specific physical network hardware. This allows TCP/IP to integrate many different kinds of networks. TCP/IP can be run over an Ethernet, a token ring, a dial-up line, an X.25 net, and virtually any other kind of physical transmission media.

- A common addressing scheme that allows any TCP/IP device to uniquely address any other device in the entire network, even if the network is as large as the worldwide Internet.

- Standardized high-level protocols for consistent, widely available user services.

Protocol Standards

The open nature of TCP/IP protocols requires publicly available standards documents. All protocols in the TCP/IP protocol suite are defined in one of three Internet standards publications. A number of the protocols have been adopted as Military Standards (MIL STD). Others were published as Internet Engineering Notes (IEN)—though the IEN form of publication has now been abandoned. But most information about TCP/IP protocols is published as Requests for Comments (RFC). RFCs contain the latest versions of the specifications of all standard TCP/IP protocols.[*] As the name "Request for Comments" implies, the style and content of these documents is much less rigid then most standards documents. RFCs contain a wide range of interesting and useful information, and are not limited to the formal specification of data communications protocols.

As a network system administrator, you will no doubt read many of the RFCs yourself. Some contain practical advice and guidance that is simple to understand. Other RFCs contain protocol implementation specifications defined in terminology that is unique to data communications.

A Data Communications Model

To discuss computer networking, it is necessary to use terms that have special meaning in data communications. Even other computer professionals may not be familiar with all the terms in the networking alphabet soup. As is always the case, English and computer-speak are not equivalent (or even necessarily compatible) languages. Although descriptions and examples should make the meaning of the networking jargon more apparent, sometimes terms are ambiguous. A common frame of reference is necessary for understanding data communications terminology.

---

* Interested in finding out how Internet standards are created? Read *The Internet Standards Process*, RFC 1310.

OSI Reference Model

An architectural model developed by the International Standards Organization (ISO) is frequently used to describe the structure and function of data communications protocols. This architectural model, called the Open Systems Interconnect (OSI) Reference Model, provides a common reference for discussing communications. The terms defined by this model are well understood and widely used in the data communications community—so widely used, in fact, that it is difficult to discuss data communications without using OSI's terminology.

The OSI Reference Model contains seven *layers* that define the functions of data communications protocols. Each layer of the OSI model represents a function performed when data is transferred between cooperating applications across an intervening network. Figure C-1 identifies each layer by name and provides a short functional description for it. Looking at this figure, you can see that the protocols are like a pile of building blocks stacked one upon another. Because of this appearance, the structure is often called a *stack* or *protocol stack*.

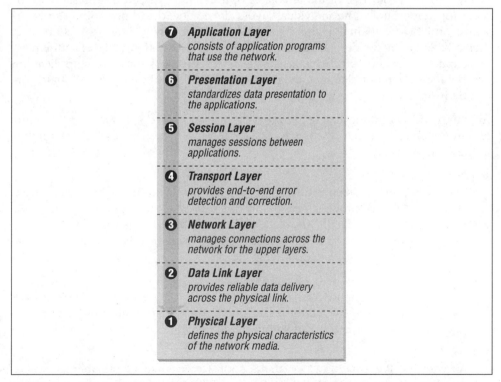

Figure C–1: The OSI Reference Model

A layer does not define a single protocol; it defines a data communications function that may be performed by any number of protocols. Therefore, each layer may contain multiple protocols, each providing a service suitable to the function of that layer. For example, a file transfer protocol and an electronic mail protocol both provide user services and both are part of the Application Layer. Every protocol communicates with its peer. A *peer* is an implementation of the same protocol in the equivalent layer on a remote system (i.e., the local file transfer protocol is the peer of a remote file transfer protocol). Peer level communications must be standardized for successful communications to take place. In the abstract, each protocol is only concerned with communicating to its peer; it does not care about the layer above or below it.

However, there must also be agreement on how to pass data between the layers on a single computer, because every layer is involved in sending data from a local application to an equivalent remote application. The upper layers rely on the lower layers to transfer the data over the underlying network. Data is passed down the stack from one layer to the next, until it is transmitted over the network by the Physical Layer protocols. At the remote end, the data is passed up the stack to the receiving application. The individual layers do not need to know how the layers above and below them function; they only need to know how to pass data to them. Isolating network communications functions in different layers minimizes the impact of technological change on the entire protocol suite. New applications can be added without changing the physical network, and new network hardware can be installed without rewriting the application software.

Although the OSI model is useful, the TCP/IP protocols don't match its structure exactly. Therefore, in our discussions of TCP/IP we use the layers of the OSI model in the following way:

Application Layer

> The Application Layer is the level of the protocol hierarchy where user-accessed network processes reside. In this text a TCP/IP application is any network process that occurs above the Transport Layer. This includes all of the processes that users directly interact with, as well as other processes at this level that users are not necessarily aware of.

Presentation Layer

> For cooperating applications to exchange data, they must agree about how data is represented. In OSI, this layer provides standard data presentation routines. This function is handled within the applications in TCP/IP.

Session Layer

> As with the Presentation Layer, the Session Layer is not identifiable as a separate layer in the TCP/IP protocol hierarchy. The OSI Session Layer manages the sessions (connection) between cooperating applications. In TCP/IP, this function largely occurs in the Transport Layer, and the term "session" is not used. For TCP/IP, the terms "socket" and "port" are used to describe the path over which cooperating applications communicate.

Transport Layer

Much of our discussion of TCP/IP is directed to the protocols that occur in the Transport Layer. The Transport Layer in the OSI reference model guarantees that the receiver gets the data exactly as it was sent. In TCP/IP this function is performed by the Transmission Control Protocol (TCP). However, TCP/IP offers a second Transport Layer service, User Datagram Protocol (UDP) that does not perform the end-to-end reliability checks.

Network Layer

The Network Layer manages connections across the network and isolates the upper layer protocols from the details of the underlying network. The Internet Protocol (IP), which isolates the upper layers from the underlying network and handles the addressing and delivery of data, is usually described as TCP/IP's Network Layer.

Data Link Layer

The reliable delivery of data across the underlying physical network is handled by the Data Link Layer. TCP/IP rarely creates protocols in the Data Link Layer. Most RFCs that relate to the Data Link Layer talk about how IP can make use of existing data link protocols, such as Ethernet, FDDI, ATM, and so on.

Physical Layer

The physical layer defines the characteristics of the hardware needed to carry the data transmission signal. Things such as voltage levels, and the number and location of interface pins, are defined in this layer. Examples of standards at the Physical Layer are interface connectors such as RS232C and V.35, and standards for local area network wiring such as IEEE 802.3. TCP/IP does not define physical standards; it makes use of existing standards.

The terminology of the OSI reference model helps us describe TCP/IP, but to fully understand it, we must use an architectural model that more closely matches the structure of TCP/IP. The next section introduces the protocol model we'll use to describe TCP/IP.

TCP/IP Protocol Architecture

While there is no universal agreement about how to describe TCP/IP with a layered model, it is generally viewed as being composed of fewer layers than the seven used in the OSI model. Most descriptions of TCP/IP define three to five functional levels in the protocol architecture. The four-level model illustrated in Figure C-2 is based on the three layers (Application, Host-to-Host, and Network Access) shown in the DOD Protocol Model in the *DDN Protocol Handbook, Volume 1*, with the addition of a separate Internet layer. This model provides a reasonable pictorial representation of the layers in the TCP/IP protocol hierarchy.

As in the OSI model, data is passed down the stack when it is being sent to the net, and up the stack when it is being received from the network. The four-layered structure of TCP/IP is seen in the way data is handled as it passes down the

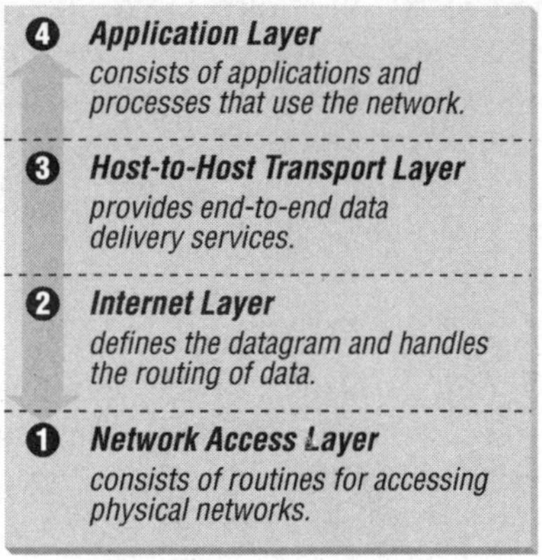

Figure C-2: Layers in the TCP/IP protocol architecture

protocol stack from the Application Layer to the underlying physical network. Each layer in the stack adds control information to ensure proper delivery. This control information is called a *header* because it is placed in front of the data to be transmitted. Each layer treats all of the information it receives from the layer above as data and places its own header in front of that information. The addition of delivery information at every layer is called *encapsulation*. (Figure C-3 illustrates this.) When data is received, the opposite happens. Each layer strips off its header before passing the data on to the layer above. As information flows back up the stack, information received from a lower layer is interpreted as both a header and data.

Each layer has its own independent data structures. Conceptually a layer is unaware of the data structures used by the layers above and below it. In reality, the data structures of a layer are designed to be compatible with the structures used by the surrounding layers for the sake of more efficient data transmission. Still, each layer has its own data structure and its own terminology to describe that structure.

Let's look more closely at the function of each layer, working our way up from the Network Access Layer to the Application Layer.

Network Access Layer

The Network Access Layer is the lowest layer of the TCP/IP protocol hierarchy. The protocols in this layer provide the means for the system to deliver data to the other devices on a directly attached network. It defines how to use the network to transmit an IP datagram.

Unlike higher-level protocols, Network Access Layer protocols must know the details of the underlying network (its packet structure, addressing, etc.) to

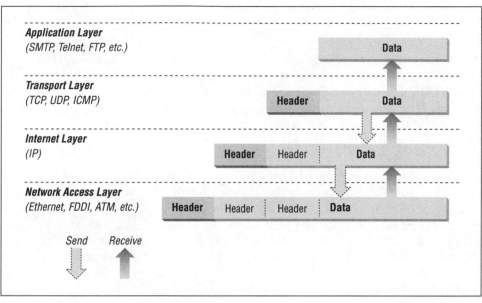

Figure C-3: Data encapsulation

correctly format the data being transmitted to comply with the network constraints. The TCP/IP Network Access Layer can encompass the functions of all three lower layers of the OSI Reference Model (Network, Data Link, and Physical).

The Network Access Layer is often ignored by users. The design of TCP/IP hides the function of the lower layers, and the better known protocols (IP, TCP, UDP, etc.) are all higher-level protocols. As new hardware technologies appear, new Network Access protocols must be developed so that TCP/IP networks can use the new hardware. Consequently, there are many access protocols—one for each physical network standard.

Functions performed at this level include encapsulation of IP datagrams into the frames transmitted by the network, and mapping of IP addresses to the physical addresses used by the network. One of TCP/IP's strengths is its addressing scheme that uniquely identifies every host on the Internet. This IP address must be converted into whatever address is appropriate for the physical network over which the datagram is transmitted.

Two examples of RFCs that define network access layer protocols are:

- RFC 826, *Address Resolution Protocol (ARP)*, which maps IP addresses to Ethernet addresses

- RFC 894, *A Standard for the Transmission of IP Datagrams over Ethernet Networks,* which specifies how IP datagrams are encapsulated for transmission over Ethernet networks

As implemented in UNIX, protocols in this layer often appear as a combination of device drivers and related programs. The modules that are identified with network device names usually encapsulate and deliver the data to the network, while separate programs perform related functions such as address mapping.

Internet Layer

The layer above the Network Access Layer in the protocol hierarchy is the Internet Layer. The Internet Protocol, RFC 791, is the heart of TCP/IP and the most important protocol in the Internet Layer. IP provides the basic packet delivery service on which TCP/IP networks are built. All protocols, in the layers above IP (TCP, UPD) and below it (Ethernet, FDDI, ATM, etc.) use IP to deliver data. All TCP/IP data flows through IP, incoming and outgoing, regardless of its final destination.

Internet Protocol

IP is the building block of the Internet. Its functions include:

- Defining the datagram, which is the basic unit of transmission in the Internet

- Defining the Internet addressing scheme

- Moving data between the Network Access Layer and the Host-to-Host Transport Layer

- Routing datagrams to remote hosts

- Performing fragmentation and reassembly of datagrams

But before describing these functions in more detail, let's look at some of IP's characteristics. First, IP is a *connectionless protocol.* This means that IP does not exchange control information (called a *handshake*) to establish an end-to-end connection before transmitting data. In contrast, a *connection-oriented protocol* exchanges control information with the remote system to verify that it is ready to receive data before sending it. When the handshaking is successful, the systems are said to have established a *connection.* IP relies on protocols in other layers to establish the connection if they require connection-oriented service.

IP also relies on protocols in the other layers to provide error detection and error recovery. The Internet Protocol is sometimes called an *unreliable protocol* because it contains no error detection and recovery code. This is not to say that the IP protocol cannot be relied on—quite the contrary. IP can be relied upon to accurately deliver your data to the connected network, but it doesn't check whether the data was correctly received. Protocols in other layers of the TCP/IP architecture provide this checking when it is required.

The datagram

The TCP/IP protocols were built to transmit data over the ARPANET, which was a *packet switching network*. A *packet* is a block of data that carries with it the information necessary to deliver it—in a manner similar to a postal letter, which has an address written on its envelope. A packet switching network uses the addressing information in the packets to switch packets from one physical network to another, moving them toward their final destination. Each packet travels the network independently of any other packet.

The *datagram* is the packet format defined by IP. Figure C-4 is a pictorial representation of an IP datagram. The first five or six 32-bit words of the datagram are control information called the *header*. By default, the header is five words long; the sixth word is optional. Because the header's length is variable, it includes a field called Internet Header Length (IHL) that indicates the header's length in words. The header contains all the information necessary to deliver the packet.

A Note About Terminology

This adapted appendix is very precise in its definitions and usage of terms such as *packet* and *datagram*. Throughout the rest of this book, we tend to be more relaxed about the terminology, and simply use the term "packet" regardless of what layer of the protocol stack we're discussing.

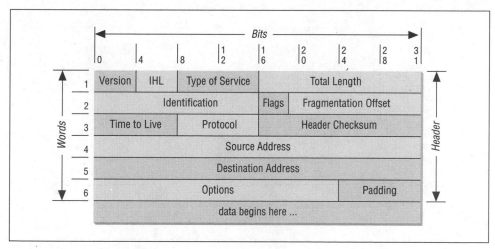

Figure C-4: IP datagram format

IP delivers the datagram by checking the *Destination Address* in word 5 of the header. The Destination Address is a standard 32-bit IP address that identifies the destination network and the specific host on that network. (The format of IP addresses is explained later in this appendix.) If the Destination Address is the address of a host on the directly attached network, the packet is delivered directly to the destination. If the Destination Address is not on the local network, the packet is passed to a gateway for delivery. *Gateways* are devices that switch packets between the different physical networks. Deciding which gateway to use is called *routing*. IP makes the routing decision for each individual packet.

Routing datagrams

Internet gateways are commonly (and perhaps more accurately) referred to as *IP routers* because they use IP to route packets between networks. In traditional TCP/IP jargon, there are only two types of network devices: *gateways* and *hosts*. Gateways forward packets between networks and hosts don't. However, if a host is connected to more than one network (called a *multi-homed host*), it can forward packets between the networks. When a multi-homed host forwards packets, it acts like any other gateway and is considered to be a gateway. Current data communications terminology sometimes makes a distinction between gateways and routers,[*] but we'll use the terms gateway and IP router interchangeably.

Figure C-5 shows the use of gateways to forward packets. The hosts (or *end systems*) process packets through all four protocol layers, while the gateways (or *intermediate systems*) process the packets only up to the Internet Layer where the routing decisions are made.

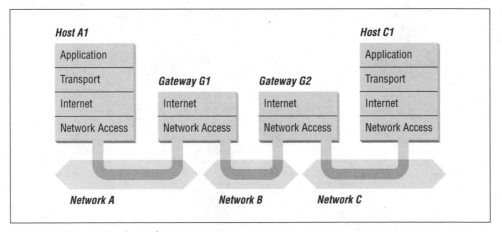

Figure C-5: Routing through gateways

---

* In current terminology, a gateway moves data between different protocols and a router moves data between different networks. So a system that moves mail between TCP/IP and OSI is a gateway, but a traditional IP gateway is a router.

Systems can only deliver packets to other devices attached to the same physical network. Packets from A1, destined for host C1, are forwarded through gateways G1 and G2. Host A1 first delivers the packet to gateway G1, with which it shares network A. Gateway G1 delivers the packet to G2, over network B. Gateway G2 then delivers the packet directly to host C1, because they are both attached to network C. Host A1 has no knowledge of any gateways beyond gateway G1. It sends packets destined for both networks C and B to that local gateway, and then relies on that gateway to properly forward the packets along the path to their destinations. Likewise, host C1 would send its packets to G2, in order to reach a host on network A, as well as any host on network B.

Figure C-6 shows another view of routing. This figure emphasizes that the underlying physical networks a datagram travels through may be different and even incompatible. Host A1 on the token ring network routes the datagram through gateway G1, to reach host C1 on the Ethernet. Gateway G1 forwards the data through the X.25 network to gateway G2, for delivery to C1. The datagram traverses three physically different networks, but eventually arrives intact at C1.

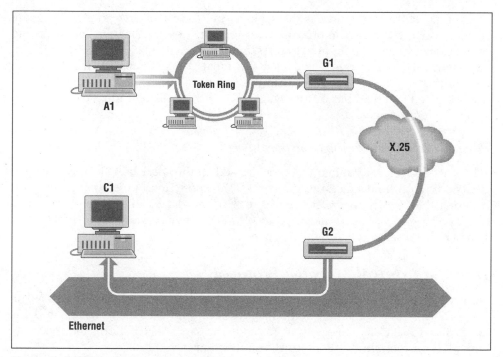

Figure C-6: Networks, gateways, and hosts

Fragmenting datagrams

As a datagram is routed through different networks, it may be necessary for the IP module in a gateway to divide the datagram into smaller pieces. A datagram received from one network may be too large to be transmitted in a single packet on a different network. This condition only occurs when a gateway interconnects dissimilar physical networks.

Each type of network has a *maximum transmission unit (MTU)*, which is the largest packet it can transfer. If the datagram received from one network is longer than the other network's MTU, it is necessary to divide the datagram into smaller fragments for transmission. This process is called *fragmentation*. Think of a train delivering a load of steel. Each railway car can carry more steel than the trucks that will take it along the highway; so each railway car is unloaded onto many different trucks. In the same way that a railroad is physically different from a highway, an Ethernet is physically different from an X.25 network; IP must break an Ethernet's relatively large packets into smaller packets before it can transmit them over an X.25 network.

The format of each fragment is the same as the format of any normal datagram. Header word 2 contains information that identifies each datagram fragment and provides information about how to reassemble the fragments back into the original datagram. The Identification field identifies what datagram the fragment belongs to, and the Fragmentation Offset field tells what piece of the datagram this fragment is. The Flags field has a More Fragments bit that tells IP if it has assembled all of the datagram fragments.

Passing datagrams to the transport layer

When IP receives a datagram that is addressed to the local host, it must pass the data portion of the datagram to the correct Transport Layer protocol. This is done by using the *Protocol Number* from word 3 of the datagram header. Each Transport Layer protocol has a unique protocol number that identifies it to IP. Protocol numbers are discussed later in this appendix.

Internet Control Message Protocol

An integral part of IP is the Internet Control Message Protocol (ICMP) defined in RFC 792. This protocol is part of the Internet Layer and uses the IP datagram delivery facility to send its messages. ICMP sends messages that perform the following control, error reporting, and informational functions for TCP/IP:

Flow control
> When datagrams arrive too fast for processing, the destination host or an intermediate gateway sends an ICMP Source Quench Message back to the sender. This tells the source to temporarily stop sending datagrams.

Detecting unreachable destinations

When a destination is unreachable, the system detecting the problem sends a Destination Unreachable Message to the datagram's source. If the unreachable destination is a network or host, the message is sent by an intermediate gateway. But if the destination is an unreachable port, the destination host sends the message. (We discuss ports later in this appendix.)

Redirecting routes

A gateway sends the ICMP Redirect Message to tell a host to use another gateway, presumably because the other gateway is a better choice. This message can only be used when the source host is on the same network as both gateways. To better understand this, refer to Figure C-6. If a host on the X.25 network sent a datagram to G1, it would be possible for G1 to redirect that host to G2 because the host, G1, and G2 are all attached to the same network. On the other hand, if a host on the token ring network sent a datagram to G1, the host could not be redirected to use G2. This is because G2 is not attached to the token ring.

Checking remote hosts

A host can send the ICMP Echo Message to see if a remote system's IP is up and operational. When a system receives an echo message, it sends the same packet back to the source host. The UNIX *ping* command uses this message.

Transport Layer

The protocol layer just above the Internet Layer is the Host-to-Host Transport Layer. This name is usually shortened to Transport Layer. The two most important protocols in the Transport Layer are Transmission Control Protocol (TCP) and User Datagram Protocol (UDP). TCP provides reliable data delivery service with end-to-end error detection and correction. UDP provides low-overhead, connectionless datagram delivery service. Both protocols deliver data between the Application Layer and the Internet Layer. Applications programmers can choose whichever service is more appropriate for their specific applications.

User Datagram Protocol

The User Datagram Protocol gives application programs direct access to a datagram delivery service, like the delivery service that IP provides. This allows applications to exchange messages over the network with a minimum of protocol overhead.

UDP is an unreliable, connectionless datagram protocol. (As noted before, "unreliable" merely means that there are no techniques in the protocol for verifying that the data reached the other end of the network correctly.) Within your computer, UDP will deliver data correctly. UDP uses 16-bit *Source Port* and *Destination Port* numbers in word 1 of the message header, to deliver data to the correct applications process. Figure C-7 shows the UDP message format.

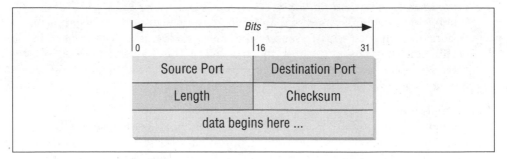

Figure C-7: UDP message format

Why do applications programmers choose UDP as a data transport service? There are a number of good reasons. If the amount of data being transmitted is small, the overhead of creating connections and ensuring reliable delivery may be greater than the work of retransmitting the entire data set. In this case, UDP is the most efficient choice for a Transport Layer protocol. Applications that fit a "query-response" model are also excellent candidates for using UDP. The response can be used as a positive acknowledgment to the query. If a response isn't received within a certain time period, the application just sends another query. Still other applications provide their own techniques for reliable data delivery, and don't require that service from the transport layer protocol. Imposing another layer of acknowledgment on any of these types of applications is inefficient.

Transmission Control Protocol

Applications that require the transport protocol to provide reliable data delivery use TCP because it verifies that data is delivered across the network accurately and in the proper sequence. TCP is a *reliable, connection-oriented, byte-stream* protocol. Let's look at each of the terms—reliable, connection-oriented, and byte-stream—in more detail.

TCP provides reliability with a mechanism called *Positive Acknowledgment with Retransmission (PAR)*. Simply stated, a system using PAR sends the data again, unless it hears from the remote system that the data arrived okay. The unit of data exchanged between cooperating TCP modules is called a segment (see Figure C-8). Each segment contains a checksum that the recipient uses to verify that the data is undamaged. If the data segment is received undamaged, the receiver sends a *positive acknowledgment* back to the sender. If the data segment is damaged, the receiver discards it. After an appropriate time-out period, the sending TCP module retransmits any segment for which no positive acknowledgment has been received.

TCP is connection-oriented. It establishes a logical end-to-end connection between the two communicating hosts. Control information, called a *handshake*, is exchanged between the two endpoints to establish a dialogue before data is

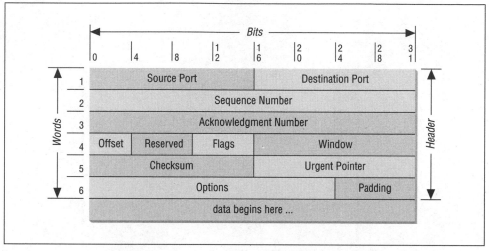

Figure C-8: TCP segment format

transmitted. TCP indicates the control function of a segment by setting the appropriate bit in the Flags field in word 4 of the *segment header*.

The type of handshake used by TCP is called a *three-way handshake* because three segments are exchanged. Figure C-9 shows the simplest form of the three-way handshake. Host A begins the connection by sending host B a segment with the "Synchronize sequence numbers" (SYN) bit set. This segment tells host B what sequence number host A will use as a starting number for its segments. (Sequence numbers are used to keep data in the proper order.) Host B responds to A with a segment that has the "Acknowledgment" (ACK) and SYN bits set. B's segment acknowledges the receipt of A's segment, and informs A which Sequence Number host B will start with. Finally, host A sends a segment that acknowledges receipt of B's segment, and transfers the first actual data.

In this figure, note that the first packet in each direction has the SYN bit set, and all subsequent packets have the ACK bit set.

After this exchange, host A's TCP has positive evidence that the remote TCP is alive and ready to receive data. As soon as the connection is established, data can be transferred. When the cooperating modules have concluded the data transfers, they will exchange a three-way handshake with segments containing the "No more data from sender" bit (called the *FIN bit*) to close the connection. It is the end-to-end exchange of data that provides the logical connection between the two systems.

TCP views the data it sends as a continuous stream of bytes, not as independent packets. Therefore, TCP takes care to maintain the sequence in which bytes are sent and received. The "Sequence Number" and "Acknowledgment Number" fields in the TCP segment header keep track of the bytes.

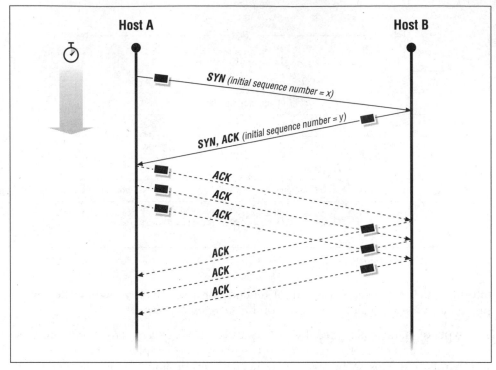

Figure C-9: Three-way handshake

The TCP standard does not require that each system start numbering bytes with any specific number; each system chooses the number it will use as a starting point. To keep track of the data stream correctly, each end of the connection must know the other end's initial number. The two ends of the connection synchronize byte-numbering systems by exchanging SYN segments during the handshake. The "Sequence Number" field in the SYN segment contains the Initial Sequence Number (ISN), which is the starting point for the byte-numbering system. The ISN is chosen at random.

Each byte of data is numbered sequentially from the ISN, so the first real byte of data sent has a sequence number of ISN+1. The Sequence Number in the header of a data segment identifies the sequential position in the data stream of the first data byte in the segment. For example, if the first byte in the data stream was sequence number 1 (ISN=0) and 4,000 bytes of data have already been transferred, then the first byte of data in the current segment is byte 4001, and the Sequence Number would be 4001.

The Acknowledgment Segment (ACK) performs two functions: *positive acknowledgment* and *flow control*. The acknowledgment tells the sender how much data has been received, and how much more the receiver can accept. The

Acknowledgment Number is the sequence number of the last byte received at the remote end. The standard does not require an individual acknowledgment for every packet. The acknowledgment number is a positive acknowledgment of all bytes up through that number. For example, if the first byte sent was numbered 1 and 2,000 bytes have been successfully received, the Acknowledgment Number would be 2000.

The Window field contains the number of bytes the remote end is able to accept. If the receiver is capable of accepting 6,000 more bytes, the Window would be 6000. The window indicates to the sender that it can continue sending segments as long as the total number of bytes that it sends is smaller than the window of bytes that the receiver can accept. The receiver controls the flow of bytes from the sender by changing the size of the window. A zero window tells the sender to cease transmission until it receives a non-zero window value.

Figure C-10 shows a TCP data stream that starts with an Initial Sequence Number of 0. The receiving system has received and acknowledged 2,000 bytes, so the current Acknowledgment Number is 2000. The receiver also has enough buffer space for another 6,000 bytes, so it has advertised a Window of 6000. The sender is currently sending a segment of 1,000 bytes starting with Sequence Number 4001. The sender has received no acknowledgment for the bytes from 2001 on, but continues sending data as long as it is within the window. If the sender fills the window and receives no acknowledgment of the data previously sent, it will, after an appropriate time-out, send the data again starting from the first unacknowledged byte. In Figure C-10, retransmission would start from byte 2001 if no further acknowledgments are received. This procedure ensures that data is reliably received at the far end of the network.

TCP is also responsible for delivering data received from IP to the correct application. The application that the data is bound for is identified by a 16-bit number called the *port number*. The *Source Port* and *Destination Port* are contained in the first word of the segment header. Correctly passing data to and from the Application Layer is an important part of what the Transport Layer services do.

Application Layer

At the top of the TCP/IP protocol architecture is the Application Layer. This layer includes all processes that use the Transport Layer protocols to deliver data. There are many applications protocols. Most provide user services, and new services are always being added to this layer. The most widely known and implemented applications protocols are:

- Telnet, the Network Terminal Protocol, provides remote login over the network

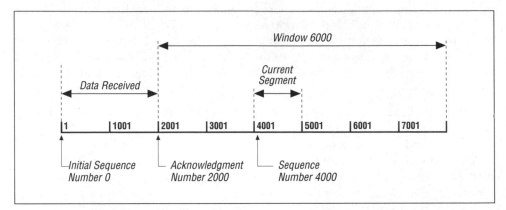

Figure C-10: TCP data stream

- FTP, the File Transfer Protocol, is used for interactive file transfer

- SMTP, the Simple Mail Transfer Protocol delivers electronic mail

While FTP, SMTP, and Telnet are the most widely implemented TCP/IP applications, you will work with many others as both a user and a system administrator. Some other commonly used TCP/IP applications are:

Domain Name Service (DNS)
   Also called *name service*, this application maps IP addresses to the names assigned to network devices.

Routing Information Protocol (RIP)
   Routing is central to the way TCP/IP works. RIP is used by network devices to exchange routing information.

Network File System (NFS)
   This protocol allows files to be shared by various hosts on the network.

Some protocols, such as Telnet and FTP, can only be used if the user has some knowledge of the network. Other protocols, like RIP, run without the user even knowing that they exist. As system administrator, you are aware of all these applications and all the protocols in the other TCP/IP layers.

Figure C-11 shows the hierarchy of protocols in an imaginary computer. As you look at this figure, please remember that reducing the complexity of a protocol stack to a block diagram is, by its very nature, an oversimplification. This illustration is only to help you visualize the relationship of the many protocols in a single host. Not all of the protocols shown in Figure C-11 have been discussed yet, but it should be helpful to get an idea of the overall structure.

At the top of the figure are the applications protocols, like FTP and Telnet. Lines run from each box to the lower layer service that the protocol uses. We see that FTP, Telnet, and SMTP rely primarily on TCP; while NFS, DNS, and RIP rely primarily

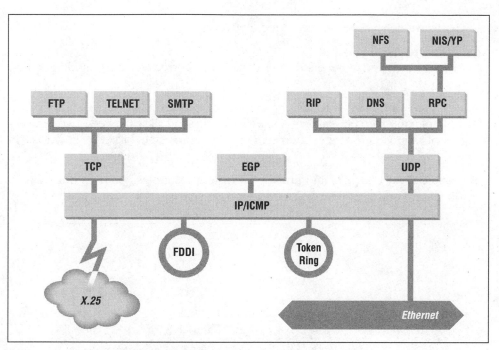

Figure C–11: TCP/IP protocols inside a sample gateway

on UDP. A few application-type protocols, like the Exterior Gateway Protocol (EGP), another routing protocol, do not use Transport Layer services; they use IP services directly.

Below the applications are the Transport Layer protocols: TCP and UDP. They interface directly with IP. All data, in and out of the system, flows through IP. IP delivers data from the upper layers to the correct network, and it delivers data from the network to the correct transport service. Likewise, the transport services deliver the data they receive from IP to the correct application.

Addressing, Routing, and Multiplexing

To deliver data between two Internet hosts, it is necessary to move the data across the network to the correct host, and within that host to the correct user or process. TCP/IP uses three schemes to accomplish these tasks:

Addressing
> IP addresses, which uniquely identify every host on the Internet, deliver data to the correct host.

Routing

Gateways deliver data to the correct network.

Multiplexing

Protocol and port numbers deliver data to the correct software module within the host.

Each of these functions—addressing between hosts, routing between networks, and multiplexing between layers—is necessary to send data between two cooperating applications across the Internet. Let's examine each of these functions in detail.

To illustrate these concepts and provide consistent examples, we use an imaginary corporate network. This network's structure, or *topology*, is shown in Figure C-12.

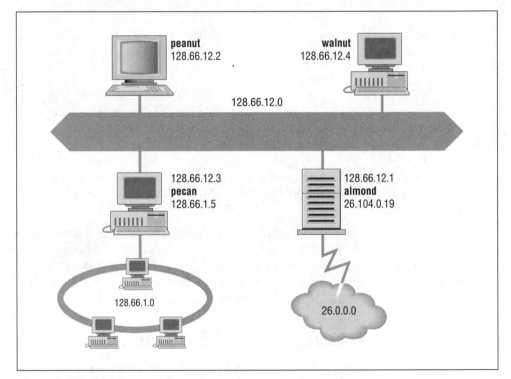

Figure C–12: Sample network

The icons in the figure represent computer systems. There are, of course, several other imaginary systems on our imaginary network. You'll just have to use your imagination! But we'll use the hosts *peanut* (a workstation) and *almond* (a system that serves as a gateway) for most of our examples. The thick line is our computer center Ethernet, and the circle is the local network that connects our various corporate networks. The cloud is Milnet, one of the major segments of the Internet. What the numbers are, how they're used, and how datagrams are delivered are the topics of this appendix.

The IP Address

IP moves data between hosts in the form of datagrams. Each datagram is delivered to the address contained in the Destination Address (word 5) of the datagram's header. The Destination Address is a standard 32-bit IP address that contains sufficient information to uniquely identify a network and a specific host on that network.

An IP address contains a *network part* and a *host part,* but the format of these parts is not the same in every IP address. The number of address bits used to identify the network, and the number used to identify the host, vary according to the *class* of the address. The three main address classes are *class A, class B,* and *class C.* The following table summarizes the characteristics of each address class.

Class	Bits in First Byte	Range of Network Addresses	Network Portion	Host Portion
A	0xxxxxxx	0.0.0.0 - 127.0.0.0	1 byte	3 bytes
B	10xxxxxx	128.0.0.0 - 191.255.0.0	2 bytes	2 bytes
C	110xxxxx	192.0.0.0 - 223.255.255.0	3 bytes	1 byte
D & E	111xxxxx	224.0.0.0 - 255.255.255.0	Special/ reserved Multicast	—

By examining the first few bits of an address, IP software can quickly determine the address' class, and therefore its structure. IP follows these rules to determine the address class; the table below summarizes them:

You can compute the number of nets as follows (not relevant for Class D and E networks):

- Class A: 128

- Class B: 64 * 256 = 16,128

- Class C: 32 * 256^2 = 2,097,152

You can compute the number of hosts per net as follows (not relevant for Class D and E networks):

- Class A: 256^3 = 16,777,216

- Class B: 256^2 = 65,536

- Class C: 256

The following further explains the characteristics of the address classes:

- If the first bit of an IP address is 0, it is the address of a class A network. The first bit of a class A address identifies the address class. The next seven bits identify the network, and the last 24 bits identify the host. There are fewer than 128 class A network numbers, but each class A network can be composed of millions of hosts.

- If the first two bits of the address are 1 0, it is a class B network address. The first two bits identify class; the next fourteen bits identify the network; and the last sixteen bits identify the host. There are thousands of class B network numbers, and each class B network can contain thousands of hosts.

- If the first three bits of the address are 1 1 0, it is a class C network address. In a class C address, the first three bits are class identifiers; the next 21 bits are the network address; and the last eight bits identify the host. There are millions of class C network numbers, but each class C network is composed of fewer than 254 hosts.

- If the first three bits of the address are 1 1 1, it is a special reserved address. These addresses are sometimes called class D addresses, but they don't really refer to specific networks. The Multicast addresses are used to address groups of computers all at one time. Multicast addresses identify a group of computers that share a common protocol, as opposed to a group of computers that share a common network.

Luckily, this is not as complicated as it sounds. IP addresses are usually written as four decimal numbers separated by dots (periods).[*]

Each of the four numbers is in the range 0-255 (the decimal values possible for a single byte). Because the bits that identify class are contiguous with the network bits of the address, we can lump them together and look at the address as composed of full bytes of network address and full bytes of host address. A first byte value:

- Less than 128 indicates a class A address; the first byte is the network number, and the next three bytes are the host address.

- From 128 to 191 is a class B address; the first two bytes identify the network, and the last two bytes identify the host.

---

[*] Addresses are occasionally written in other formats (e.g., as hexadecimal numbers). However, the "dot" notation form is the most widely used. Whatever the notation, the structure of the address is the same.

- From 192 to 223 is a class C address; the first three bytes are the network address, and the last byte is the host number.

- Greater than 223, indicates the address is reserved. We can ignore reserved addresses.

Figure C-13 illustrates how the address structure varies with address class. The class A address is 26.104.0.19. The first bit of this address is 0, so the address is interpreted as host 104.0.19 on network 26. One byte specifies the network, and three bytes specify the host. In the address 128.66.12.1, the two high-order bits are 1 0 so the address refers to host 12.1 on network 128.66. Two bytes identify the network, and two identify the host. Finally, in the class C example, 192.178.16.1, the three high-order bits are 1 1 0, so this is the address of host 1 on network 192.178.16: three network bytes and one host byte.

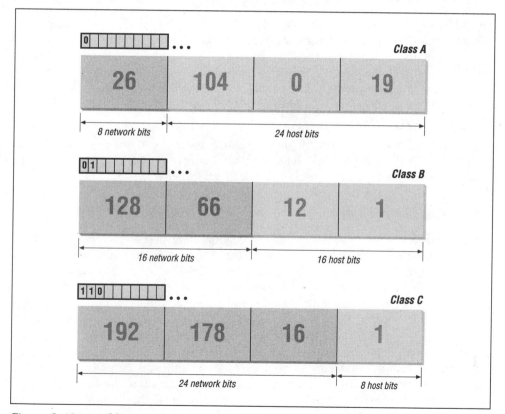

Figure C-13: IP address structure

Not all network or host addresses are available for use. We have already said that addresses with a first byte greater than 223 are reserved. There are also two class

A addresses, 0 and 127, that are reserved for special uses. Network 0 designates the *default route* and network 127 is the *loopback address*. The default route is used to simplify the routing information IP must handle. The loopback address simplifies network applications by allowing the local host to be addressed in the same manner as a remote host. We use these special network addresses when configuring a host.

There are also some host addresses reserved for special uses. In all network classes, host numbers 0 and 255 are reserved. An IP address with all host bits set to zero identifies the network itself. For example, 26.0.0.0 refers to network 26, and 128.66.0.0 refers to network 128.66. Addresses in this form are used in routing table listings to refer to entire networks.

An IP address with all bits set to one is a *broadcast address*.[*] A broadcast address is used to simultaneously address every host on a network. The broadcast address for network 128.66 is 128.66.255.255. A datagram sent to this address is delivered to every individual host on network 128.66.

IP addresses are often called host addresses. While this is common usage, it is slightly misleading. IP addresses are assigned to network interfaces, not to computer systems. A gateway, such as *almond* (see Figure C-12), has a different address for each network it is connected to. The gateway is known to other devices by the address associated with the network that it shares with those devices. For example, *peanut* addresses *almond* as 128.66.12.1, while Milnet hosts address it as 26.104.0.19.

IP uses the network portion of the address to route the datagram between networks. The full address, including the host information, is used to make final delivery when the datagram reaches the destination network.

Address Depletion

The IP address, which provides universal addressing across all networks of the Internet, is one of the great strengths of the TCP/IP protocol suite. However, the structure of the IP address does have some problems. The TCP/IP designers did not envision the enormous scale of today's network. When TCP/IP was being designed, networking was limited to large organizations that could afford substantial computer systems. The idea of a powerful UNIX system on every desktop did not exist. At that time, a 32-bit address seemed so large that it was divided into classes to reduce the processing load on routers, even though dividing the address into classes sharply reduced the number of host addresses actually available for use. For example, assigning a large network a single class B address, instead of six class C addresses, reduces the load on the router because the router only needs to keep one route for that entire organization. However, the organization that was given the class B address probably does not have 64,000 computers, so most of the host addresses available to the organization will never be assigned.

---

[*] Unfortunately there are implementation-specific variations in broadcast addresses.

The current address design, which favors routers over growth, is under critical strain from the rapid growth of the Internet. This is a major factor in the move from the current IP version 4 towards IP version 6 (IPv6).

Subnets

The standard structure of an IP address can be locally modified by using host address bits as additional network address bits. Essentially, the "dividing line" between network address bits and host address bits is moved, creating additional networks, but reducing the maximum number of hosts that can belong to each network. These newly designated network bits define a network within the larger network, called a subnet.

Organizations usually decide to subnet in order to overcome topological or organizational problems. Subnetting allows decentralized management of host addressing. With the standard addressing scheme, a single administrator is responsible for managing host addresses for the entire network. By subnetting, the administrator can delegate address assignment to smaller organizations within the overall organization, which may be a political expedient, if not a technical requirement. If you don't want to deal with the data processing department, assign them their own subnet and let them manage it themselves.

Subnetting can also be used to overcome hardware differences and distance limitations. IP routers can link dissimilar physical networks together, but only if each physical network has its own unique network address. Subnetting divides a single network address into many unique subnet addresses, so that each physical network can have its own unique address.

A subnet is defined by applying a bit mask, the *subnet mask*, to the IP address. If a bit is on in the mask, that equivalent bit in the address is interpreted as a network bit. If a bit in the mask is off, the bit belongs to the host part of the address. The subnet is only known locally. To the rest of the Internet, the address is still interpreted as a standard IP address.

For example, the subnet mask that would be associated with standard class B addresses is 255.255.0.0. The most commonly used subnet mask extends the network portion of a class B address by an additional byte. The subnet mask that does this is 255.255.255.0; all bits on in the first three bytes, and all bits off in the last byte. The first two bytes define the class B network; the third byte defines the the subnet address; the fourth byte defines the host on that subnet.

Many network administrators prefer to use byte-oriented masks because they are easier to read and understand. However, defining subnet masks on byte boundaries is not a requirement. The subnet mask is bit-oriented and can be applied to any address class. For example, a small organization could subdivide a class C address into four subnets with the mask 255.255.255.192.* Applying this mask to a class C address defines the two high-order bits of the fourth byte as the subnet part of the address. This same mask, applied to a class B address, creates more than a thousand subnets because ten bits (the full third byte, and two bits of the fourth byte) are used to define the subnets (2^10=1024).

As subnets become more and more common, an alternative way of writing subnet masks is becoming popular: as "/bits" instead of as the four-octet netmask. For instance, "/24" specifies a 24-bit netmask, equivalent to 255.255.255.0, but much faster to write. The new nomenclature makes the assumption that your netmasks are made up of contiguous bits (i.e., that you never use a netmask of something like 255.0.255.0), but that's standard practice anyway.

You will also sometimes hear people talk about wildcard masks, particular with respect to Cisco routers and packet filtering specifications. Wildcard masks are essentially the inverse of subnet masks; where subnet masks use 1 bit to specify the significant bits (the bits to be looked at), wildcard masks use 1 bit to specify the insignificant bits (the bits to be ignored). Thus, a subnet mask of 255.255.0.0 is equivalent to a wildcard mask of 0.0.255.255, and a subnet mask of 255.255.240.0 is equivalent to a wildcard mask of 0.0.15.255. The table below shows the effect of various subnet masks on different network addresses.

IP Address	UNIX Subnet Mask	Equiv. Cisco Wildcard	Equiv. /bits Mask	Interpretation
128.66.12.1	255.255.255.0	0.0.0.255	/24	host 1 on subnet 128.66.12.0
130.97.16.132	255.255.255.192	0.0.0.63	/26	host 4 on subnet 130.97.16.128
192.178.16.66	255.255.255.192	0.0.0.63	/26	host 2 on subnet 192.178.16.64
132.90.132.5	255.255.240.0	0.0.15.255	/20	host 4.5 on subnet 132.90.128.0
18.20.16.91	255.255.0.0	0.0.255.255	/16	host 16.91 on subnet 18.20.0.0

---

* This is just an illustration. A mask that creates four subnets is not a good idea because a subnet address of all ones and an address of all zeros are reserved addresses. Therefore two of the four subnets could not be used.

Internet Routing Architecture

In the traditional Internet structure, there was a hierarchy of gateways. This hierarchy reflected the history of the Internet, which was built upon the existing ARPANET. When the Internet was created, the ARPANET was the backbone of the network: a central delivery medium to carry long-distance traffic. This central system was called the *core*, and the centrally managed gateways that interconnected it were called the *core gateways*.

When a hierarchical structure is used, routing information about all of the networks in the Internet is passed into the core gateways. The core gateways process this information, and then exchange it among themselves using the Gateway to Gateway Protocol (GGP). The processed routing information is then passed back out to the external gateways. You won't run GGP on your local gateway; it is only used by core gateways.

Outside of the Internet core are groups of independent networks called *autonomous systems* (AS). The term "autonomous system" has a formal meaning in TCP/IP routing. An autonomous system is not merely an independent network. It is a collection of networks and gateways with its own internal mechanism for collecting routing information and passing it to other independent network systems. The routing information passed to the other network systems is called *reachability information*. Reachability information simply says which networks can be reached through that autonomous system. The Exterior Gateway Protocol (EGP) is currently the protocol most frequently used to pass reachability between autonomous systems (see Figure C-14).

The Defense Data Network (DDN) portion of the Internet still uses the core model to distribute routing information. But this hierarchical model has a major weakness: every route must be processed by the core. This places a tremendous processing burden on the core, and as the Internet grows larger, the burden increases. In network-speak, we say that this routing model does not scale well and for this reason, a new model is emerging.

The new routing model is based on coequal collections of autonomous systems, called *routing domains*. Routing domains exchange routing information with other domains using Border Gateway Protocol (BGP) or EGP. Each routing domain processes the information it receives from other domains. Unlike the hierarchical model, this model does not depend on a single core system to choose the "best" routes. Each routing domain does this processing for itself; therefore, this model is more expandable. Figure C-15 represents this model with three intersecting circles. Each circle is a routing domain. The overlapping areas are border areas, where routing information is shared. The domains share information, but do not rely on any one system to provide all routing information.

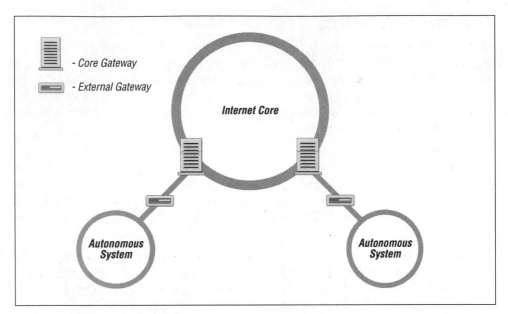

Figure C-14: Gateway hierarchy

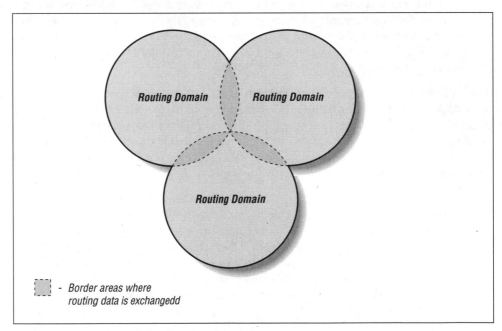

Figure C-15: Routing domains

No matter how it is derived, eventually the routing information winds up in your local gateway, where it is used by IP to make routing decisions.

The Routing Table

Gateways route data between networks but all network devices, hosts as well as gateways, must make routing decisions. For most hosts, the routing decisions are simple:

- If the destination host is on the local network, the data is delivered to the destination host.

- If the destination host is on a remote network, the data is forwarded to a local gateway.

Because routing is network oriented, IP makes routing decisions based on the network portion of the address. The IP module determines the network part of the destination's IP address by checking the high-order bits of the address to determine the address class. The address class determines the portion of the address IP uses to identify the network. If the destination network is the local network, the local subnet mask is applied to the destination address.

After determining the destination network, the IP module looks up the network in the local *routing table*.* Packets are routed toward their destination as directed by the routing table. The routing table may be built by the system administrator or by routing protocols, but the end result is the same; IP routing decisions are simple table look-ups.

On a UNIX system, you can display the routing table's contents with the *netstat -nr* command. The *-r* option tells *netstat* to display the routing table, and the *-n* option tells *netstat* to display the table in numeric form. It's useful to display the routing table in numeric form because the destination of most routes is a network, and networks are usually referred to by network numbers.

The *netstat* command displays a routing table containing the following fields:

Destination
> The destination network (or host)

Gateway
> The gateway to use to reach the specified destination.

Flags
> The flags describe certain characteristics of this route. The possible flag values are:
>
>> *U:* Indicates that the route is up and operational.
>>
>> *H:* Indicates this is a route to a specific host (most routes are to networks).

---

* This table is also called the *forwarding table*.

G: Means the route uses a gateway. The system's network interfaces provide routes to directly connected networks. All other routes use remote gateways. Directly connected networks do not have the G flag set; all other routes do.

D: Means that this route was added because of an ICMP redirect. When a system learns of a route via an ICMP redirect, it adds the route to its routing table, so that additional packets bound for that destination will not need to be redirected. The system uses the D flag to mark these routes.

Refcnt

Shows the number of times the route has been referenced to establish a connection.

Use

Shows the number of packets transmitted via this route.

Interface

The name of the network interface.[*]

The two fields important for our current discussion are the destination and gateway fields. The following is a sample routing table:

```
peanut% netstat -nr
Routing tables
Destination Gateway      Flags Refcnt      Use  Interface
127.0.0.1   127.0.0.1      UH       1       298       lo0
default     128.66.12.1    UG       2     50360       le0
128.66.12.0 128.66.12.2     U      40    111379       le0
128.66.2.0  128.66.12.3    UG       4      1179       le0
128.66.1.0  128.66.12.3    UG      10      1113       le0
128.66.3.0  128.66.12.3    UG       2      1379       le0
128.66.4.0  128.66.12.3    UG       4      1119       le0
```

The first table entry is the *loopback route* for the local host. This is the loopback address mentioned earlier as a reserved network number. Because every system uses the loopback route to send datagrams to itself, this entry is in every host's routing table. The H flag is set because it is a route to a specific host (127.0.0.1), not a route to an entire network (127.0.0.0).

Another unique entry in the routing table is the entry with the word "default" in the destination field. This entry is for the *default route*, and the gateway specified in this entry is the *default gateway*. The default gateway is used whenever there is no specific route in the table for a destination network address. For example, this routing table has no entry for network 192.178.16.0. If IP receives any datagrams addressed to this network, it will send the datagram via the default gateway 128.66.12.1.

---

* The network interface is the network access hardware and software that IP uses to communicate with the physical network.

You can tell from the sample routing table display that this host (*peanut*) is directly connected to network 128.66.12.0. The routing table entry for that network does not specify an external gateway; i.e., the routing table entry for 128.66.12.0 does not have the G flag set. Therefore, *peanut* must be directly connected to that network.

All of the gateways that appear in a routing table are on networks directly connected to the local system. In the sample shown above this means that, regardless of the destination address, the gateway addresses all begin with 128.66.12. This is the only network to which *peanut* is directly attached, and therefore it is the only network to which *peanut* can directly deliver data. The gateways that *peanut* uses to reach the rest of the Internet must be on *peanut*'s subnet.

Figure C-16 shows how routing works on our imaginary network. The IP layer of each host and gateway is replaced by a small piece of a routing table, showing destination networks and the gateways used to reach those destinations. When the source host (128.66.12.2) sends data to the destination host (128.66.1.2), it first determines that 128.66.1.2 is the local network's class B address and applies the subnet mask. (Network 128.66.0.0 is subnetted using the mask 255.255.255.0; this could also be written as 128.66.0.0/24.) After applying the subnet mask, IP knows that the destination's network address is 128.66.1.0. The routing table in the source host shows that data bound for 128.66.1.0 should be sent to gateway 128.66.12.3. Gateway 128.66.12.3 makes direct delivery thorough its 128.66.1.5 interface. Examining the routing tables shows that all systems list only gateways on networks they are directly connected to. Note that 128.66.12.1 is the default gateway for both 128.66.12.2 and 128.66.12.3. But because 128.66.1.2 cannot reach network 128.66.12.0 directly, it has a different default route.

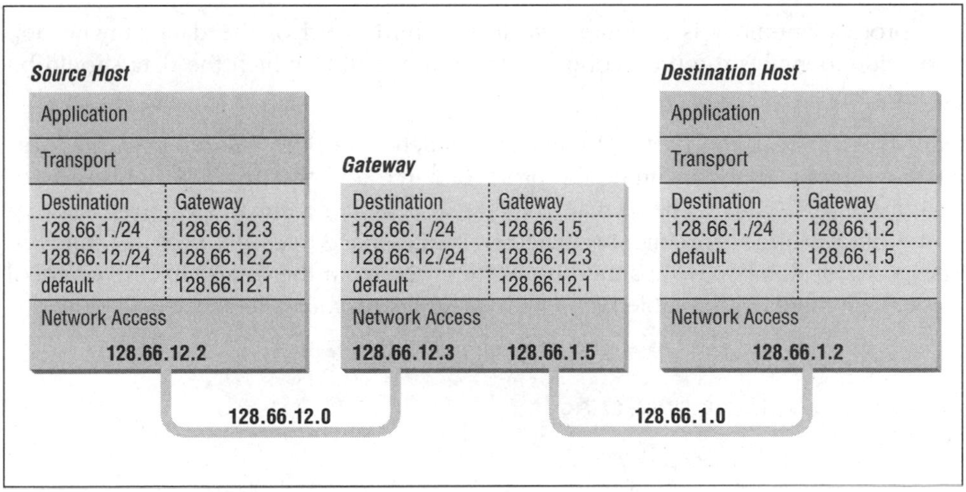

Figure C-16: Table-based routing

A routing table does not contain end-to-end routes. A route only points to the next gateway, called the *next hop,* along the path to the destination network. The host relies on the local gateway to deliver the data, and the gateway relies on other gateways. As a datagram moves from one gateway to another, it should eventually reach one that is directly connected to its destination network. It is this last gateway that finally delivers the data to the destination host.

Protocols, Ports, and Sockets

Once data is routed through the network and delivered to a specific host, it must be delivered to the correct user or process. As the data moves up or down the layers of TCP/IP, a mechanism is needed to deliver data to the correct protocols in each layer. The system must be able to combine data from many applications into a few transport protocols, and from the transport protocols into IP. Combining many sources of data into a single data stream is called *multiplexing.* Data arriving from the network must be *demultiplexed*—divided for delivery to multiple processes. To accomplish this, IP uses *protocol numbers* to identify transport protocols, and the transport protocols use *port numbers* to identify applications.

Some protocol and port numbers are reserved to identify *well-known services.* Well-known services are standard network protocols, such as FTP and Telnet that are commonly used throughout the network. The protocol numbers and port numbers allocated to well-known services are documented in the *Assigned Numbers* RFC. UNIX systems define protocol and port numbers in two simple text files, */etc/protocols* and */etc/services.*

Protocol Numbers

The protocol number is a single byte in the third word of the datagram header. The value identifies the protocol in the layer above IP to which the data should be passed.

On a UNIX system, the protocol numbers are defined in the */etc/protocols* file. This file is a simple table containing the protocol name and the protocol number associated with that name. The format of the table is a single entry per line, consisting of the official protocol name, separated by white space from the protocol number. The protocol number is separated by white space from the "alias" for the protocol name. Comments in the table begin with *#*. An */etc/protocol* file is shown below.

```
% cat /etc/protocols
#
# @(#)protocols 1.8 88/02/07 SMI
#
# Internet (IP) protocols #
ip      0       IP      # internet protocol, pseudo protocol number
icmp    1       ICMP    # internet control message protocol
igmp    2       IGMP    # internet group multicast protocol
ggp     3       GGP     # gateway-gateway protocol
```

```
tcp    6     TCP    # transmission control protocol
pup    12    PUP    # PARC universal packet protocol
udp    17    UDP    # user datagram protocol
```

The listing shown above is the contents of the */etc/protocols* file from an actual workstation. This list of numbers is by no means complete. If you refer to the Protocol Numbers section of the *Assigned Numbers* RFC (which itself gets a new RFC number every time it is updated; that's why we don't give you the RFC number for it here), you'll see many more protocol numbers. However, a system only needs to include the numbers of the protocols it actually uses. Even the list shown above is more than this specific workstation needed, but the additional entries do no harm.

What exactly does this table mean? When a datagram arrives and its destination address matches the local IP address, the IP layer knows the datagram has to be delivered to one of the transport protocols above it. To decide which protocol should receive the datagram, IP looks at the datagram's protocol number. Using this table you can see that, if the datagram's protocol number is 6, IP delivers the datagram to TCP. If the protocol number is 17, IP delivers the datagram to UDP. TCP and UDP are the two transport layer services we are concerned with, but all of the protocols listed in the table use IP datagram delivery service directly. Some, such as ICMP and GGP, have already been mentioned. You don't need to be concerned with these minor protocols, but IGMP is an extension to IP for multicasting explained in RFC 988, and PUP is a packet protocol similar to UDP.

Port Numbers

After IP passes incoming data to the transport protocol (TCP or UDP), the transport protocol passes the data to the correct application process. Application processes (also called network services are identified by port numbers, which are 16-bit values. The *source port number*, which identifies the process that sent the data, and the *destination port number*, which identifies the process that is to receive the data, are contained in the first header word of each TCP segment and UDP packet.

On UNIX systems, port numbers are defined in the */etc/services* file. There are many more network applications than there are transport layer protocols, as the size of the table shows. Port numbers below 256 are reserved for well-known services (like FTP and Telnet) and are defined in the *Assigned Numbers* RFC. Ports numbered from 256 to 1024 are used for UNIX-specific services, which are services like *rlogin*, that were originally developed for UNIX systems. However, most of them are no longer UNIX-specific.

Port numbers are not unique between transport layer protocols; the numbers are only unique within a specific transport protocol. In other words, TCP and UDP can, and do, both assign the same port numbers. It is the combination of protocol and port numbers that uniquely identifies the specific process the data should be delivered to.

A partial */etc/services* file is shown below. The format of this file is very similar to the */etc/protocols* file. Each single-line entry starts with the official name of the service, separated by white space from the port number/protocol pairing associated with that service. The port numbers are paired with transport protocol names, because different transport protocols may use the same port number. An optional list of aliases for the official service name may be provided after the port number/protocol pair.

```
peanut% cat /etc/services
#
# @(#)services 1.12 88/02/07 SMI
#
# Network services, Internet style
#
echo            7/udp
echo            7/tcp
ftp-data        20/tcp
ftp             21/tcp
Telnet          23/tcp
smtp            25/tcp          mail
time            37/tcp          timserver
time            37/udp          timserver
domain          53/udp
domain          53/tcp
#
# Host specific functions
#
finger          79/tcp
nntp            119/tcp         usenet    # Network News Transfer
ntp             123/tcp                   # Network Time Protocol
#
# UNIX specific services
#
exec            512/tcp
login           513/tcp
shell           514/tcp         cmd       # no passwords used
biff            512/udp         comsat
who             513/udp         whod
syslog          514/udp
talk            517/udp
route           520/udp         router routed
```

This table, combined with the */etc/protocols* table, provides all of the information necessary to deliver data to the correct application. A datagram arrives at its destination based on the destination address in the fifth word of the datagram header. IP uses the protocol number in the third word of the datagram header, to deliver the data from the datagram, to the proper transport layer protocol. The first word of the data delivered to the transport protocol contains the destination port number that tells the transport protocol to pass the data up to a specific application. Figure C-17 shows this delivery process.

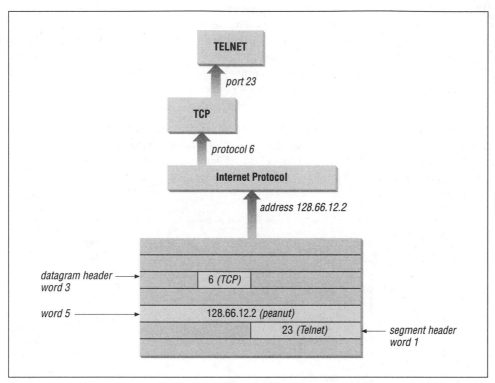

Figure C–17: Protocol and port numbers

Sockets

Well-known ports are standardized port numbers that enable remote computers to know which port to connect to for a particular network service. This simplifies the connection process because both the sender and receiver know in advance that data bound for a specific process will use a specific port. For example, all systems that offer Telnet, offer it on port 23.

There is a second type of port number called a *dynamically allocated port*. As the name implies, dynamically allocated ports are not preassigned. They are assigned to processes when needed. The system ensures that it does not assign the same port number to two processes, and that the numbers assigned are above the range of standard port numbers.

Dynamically assigned ports provide the flexibility needed to support multiple users. If a Telnet user is assigned port number 23 for both the source and destination ports, what port numbers are assigned to the second concurrent Telnet user? To uniquely identify every connection, the source port is assigned a dynamically allocated port number, and the well-known port number is used for the destination port.

In the Telnet example, the first user is given a random source port number and a destination port number of 23 (Telnet). The second user is given a different random source port number and the same destination port. It is the pair of port numbers, source and destination, that uniquely identifies each network connection. The destination host knows the source port, because it is provided in both the TCP segment header and the UDP packet header. Both hosts know the destination port because it is a well-known port.

Figure C-18 shows the exchange of port numbers during the TCP handshake. The source host randomly generates a source port, in this example 3044. It sends out a segment with a source port of 3044 and a destination port of 23. The destination host receives the segment, and responds back using 23 as its source port and 3044 as its destination port.

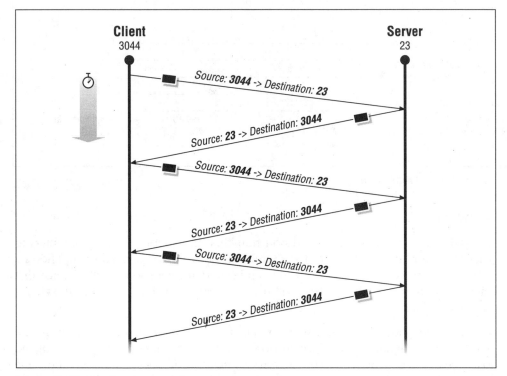

Figure C–18: Passing port numbers

The combination of an IP address and a port number is called a *socket*. A socket uniquely identifies a single network process within the entire Internet. Sometimes the terms "socket" and "port number" are used interchangeably. In fact, well-known services are frequently referred to as "well-known sockets." In the context of this discussion, a "socket" is the combination of an IP address and a port number. A pair of sockets, one socket for the receiving host and one for the sending host, define the connection for connection-oriented protocols such as TCP.

Let's build on the example of dynamically assigned ports and well-known ports. Assume a user on host 128.66.12.2 uses Telnet to connect to host 192.178.16.2. Host 128.66.12.2 is the source host. The user is dynamically assigned a unique port number—3382. The connection is made to the Telnet service on the remote host which is, according to the standard, assigned well-known port 23. The socket for the source side of the connection is 128.66.12.2.3382 (IP address 128.66.12.2 plus port number 3382). For the destination side of the connection, the socket is 192.178.16.2.23 (address 192.178.16.2 plus port 23). The port of the destination socket is known by both systems because it is a well-known port. The port of the source socket is known, because the source host informed the destination host of the source socket when the connection request was made. The socket pair is therefore known by both the source and destination computers. The combination of the two sockets uniquely identifies this connection; no other connection in the Internet has this socket pair.

Figure C-19 shows how clients on multiple machines can all connect to the same port on a single server. The server can tell the difference between the connections because they each involve different remote IP addresses. Even if the connections are all coming from a single remote machine, as shown in Figure C-20, the server can still tell them apart because each connection uses a different port number on the remote machine.

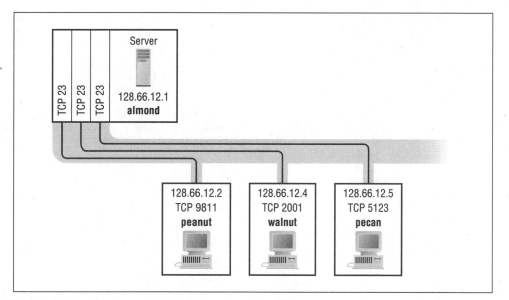

Figure C-19: Clients on multiple hosts connecting to the same port on a server

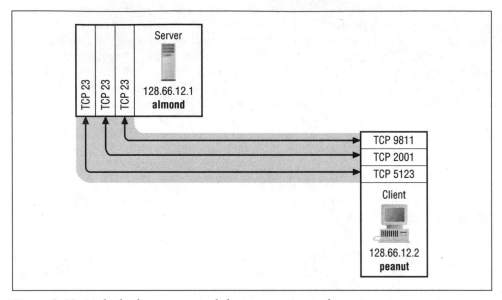

Figure C–20: Multiple clients on a single host connecting to the same port on a server

Index

Academic-Firewalls mailing list, 445
access
    and fail safety, 49-51
    least privilege, 45-47
    logging (see logging activity)
    monitoring at choke point, 48
    to networks, 15
    to unbuilt bastion host, 103
access router (see exterior routers)
accidents, 13
account management, 396-397
ACK (acknowledgment) bit, 141, 479
    with SMTP, 215
    and TCP connections, 145
activity logs (see logs)
address depletion, 488
address-based authentication, 42
addresses
    accepted by router, 158-161
    broadcast, 488
    email (see email)
    filtering by, 161-163
    IP (see IP addresses)
    loopback, 487
AFS (Andrew File System), 41, 463
anonymous FTP, 28, 115, 223
    Archie, 35
    providing, 227-229
    via proxy server, 194
    removing files from, 233
    writing directories in, 231-234

    wuarchive server, 229
    (see also FTP)
APOP (version of POP), 218
application-level
    encryption, 371
    gateways (see proxy systems)
    proxy servers, 195-196
Archie, 35, 171
    access via email, 265
    access via WWW, 265
    across Telnet, 265
    configuring, 264-266
    protocol, 265
    server, running, 266
AS (autonomous systems), 491
attackers (see intruders)
    revealing DNS information to, 285
    and slower machines, 97
attacks (see incidents)
audit, security, 123-126
    checksums, 125-126
    of packages, 123-125
    tools for, 459-461
authentication, 351-375
    address-based, 42
    client, network filesystems and, 41
    commercial systems for, 369
    complete systems for, 365-370
    false, 355
    NFS, 309
    of remote logins, 30
    TIS FWTK server, 366-369

authentication (cont'd)
    tools for, 458-459
    types of, 356-359
autonomous systems (AS), 491

backups, 46, 128-129, 434
    if firewalls, 395
    and logs, 129
    using to restore system, 419
bastion hosts, 58, 68, 91-129
    backups of, 128-129
    building, 103
    fake DNS server on, 287-289
    graphics on, 98
    internal, 93
    on internal firewalls, 88
    isolating, 66-71
    merging with exterior router, 74
    merging with interior router, 74
    multiple, 71-72
    network location of, 99
    as news server, 247
    nonrouting dual-homed, 93
    operating, 126-128
    physical location of, 98
    selecting services for, 100
    Sendmail on, 213, 217
    speed of, 95
    usage profile, 126
    user accounts on, 102
Berkeley Internet Name Domain (BIND),
    278
Berkeley Software Distribution (see BSD)
bidirectionality of protocol, 136
booting services, 113
broadcast address, 488
broadcasting, 275
browsers, WWW, 33
    as FTP clients, 224
    as Gopher clients (see Gopher)
    MIME in, 222
BSD (Berkeley Software Distribution), 42
    "r" commands, 113, 136
        configuring, 240-243
bugs, 136
    command-line, 210-211
    in packet filtering packages, 136
    (see also debugging)
BugTraq mailing list, 445

building bastion hosts, 103

capturing intruders, 422-424
catastrophe logs, 105-106
CD-ROM drive, 98
CERN HTTP daemon, 462
CERN HTTP server, 253
CERT-CC response teams, 431, 444, 446-447
    contacting regarding incident, 416
CGI (Common Gateway Interface), 254
challenge-response system, 358, 364
checksums, 125-126
    keeping secure, 436
    using Tripwire for, 124
choke points, 48, 338, 347
    using router as, 133
choke router (see interior router)
chroot mechanism, 95
chroot command, 228
chrootuid program, 464
circuit-level proxy servers, 195-196
Cisco routers, 158
client
    authentication, network filesystems and,
        41
    internal versus external, 199
    port numbers, 208
    software for proxying, 193
clocks
    configuring, 306-308
    setting, 40
COAST, 443-444
command channel attacks, 210-211
command execution, 30
command-line
    bugs, 211
command-line bugs, 210
commenting out lines, 110
commercial authentication systems, 369
Common Gateway Interface (CGI), 254
computer viruses, 21-22
conferencing services real-time, 37-38
    configuring, 270-277
configuration of labeling system, 435
configuring
    Archie, 264-266
    audit packages, 124
    clocks, 306-308

configuring (cont'd)
DNS (Domain Name Service), 278-296
in screened host architecture, 343
in screened subnet architecture, 329
email, 209-222
exterior routers, 333-337
FSP (File Service Protocol), 235-236
FTP (File Transfer Protocol), 223-234
in screened host architecture, 342
in screened subnet architecture, 324
Gopher, 260-262
hardware, 97
HTTP (Hypertext Transfer Protocol)
in screened host architecture, 343
in screened subnet architecture, 327
information lookup services, 266-270
interior router, 329-333
Internet services, 207-319
IRC (Internet Relay Chat), 272-275
kernel, 120-121
machine, 119-123
MBONE (Multicast Backbone), 275-277
network management services, 297-306
NFS (Network File System), 309-312
NIS/YP (Network Information Service),
312
NNTP (Network News Transfer Protocol), 245-250
in screened host architecture, 343
in screened subnet architecture, 327
NTP (Network Time Protocol), 306-308
packet filtering router, 136-138
ping program, 301-302
printing protocols, 317-319
"r" commands, 240-243
real-time conferencing services, 270-277
RIP (Routing Information Protocol), 300
SMTP (Simple Mail Transfer Protocol)
in screened host architecture, 342
in screened subnet architecture,
326-327
with firewalls, 216
SNMP (Simple Network Management
Protocol), 297-300
syslog, 296
Telnet, 238-240
in screened host architecture, 342
in screened subnet architecture, 323

TFTP (Trivial File Transport Protocol),
234-235
traceroute program, 302-304
UUCP (UNIX-to-UNIX Copy Protocol),
236-238
WAIS (Wide Area Information Servers),
262-264
WWW (World Wide Web) and HTTP,
250-260
X11 window system, 313-317
connections
between Internet and unbuilt bastion
host, 103
checking network (see ping)
disconnecting after incident, 415
disconnecting machine, 427
killed by TCP, 145
multiple Internet, 78-81
unidirectional versus multidirectional,
197
**COPS (Computer Oracle and Password Sys-
tem),**
459
auditing package, 124
crashes, system, 128
CRC (cyclic redundancy counter), 126
crypt program, 110
cryptographic checksum algorithms, 126
cryptography, 352
**CSRC (Computer Security Resource Clear-
inghouse),**
448
custom
client software for proxying, 193
user procedures for proxying, 194
customized system, 419
cyclic redundancy counter (CRC), 126

daemons, tools for, 462-463
data, 4
communications protocols (see TCP/IP)
DNS, 282
mismatched, 284
protecting from sniffers, 354
theft of (see information theft)

data (cont'd)
    transferring, 131-188
        allowing/disallowing, 132
        via TCP, 144-146
    user-specified, and proxying, 198
data-driven attacks, 210-211
datagrams, 473-476
    fragmenting, 476
DCC (Direct Client Connections), 273
DDN (Defense Data Network), 491
debugging, 136
    operating system, 104
    (see also bugs)
dedicated proxy servers, 196
default deny stance, 50, 137
default permit stance, 51, 137
Defense Data Network (DDN), 491
defense in depth, 47, 338, 347
delivery agent, email, 209
Demilitarized Zone (DMZ), 58
denial of service, 7-9
    accidental, 13
designing firewalls, 22-23
destination unreachable codes (see ICMP)
diagramming the system, 435
dictionary attacks, 362
Direct Client Connections (DCC), 273
disabling Internet services, 108-117
disabling routing (see routing, disabling)
disconnecting after incident, 415
disconnecting machine, 427
disk space (see memory; resources)
disks, needs for, 98
diversity of defense systems, 53
DMZ (Demilitarized Zone), 58
DNS (Domain Name Service), 38, 101
    configuring, 278-296
        in screened host architecture, 343
        in screened subnet architecture, 329
        without hiding information, 294
    data, 282
    fake server, 287-289
    hiding information with, 286-294
    revealing information to attackers, 285
    server for internal hosts, 290
documenting
    incidents, 420
    plan for, 433
    system after incident, 417, 432

Domain Name Service (see DNS)
dot (.) files, disabling creation of, 232
double-reverse lookup, 284
double-reverse lookups, 289
Drawbridge package, 461
dual-homed hosts, 189
    architecture of, 63-64
        with screen subnet architecture, 81
    as firewall, 116
    nonrouting, 93
    and proxy services (see proxy services)
    (see also proxy services)
dynamic packet filtering, 147
    and FTP, 226

electronic mail (see email)
electronic sabotage (see denial of service)
email, 26-27, 101
    addresses, searching for, 36
    Archie access via, 265
    configuring, 209-222
    flooding, 7-9
    mailing lists
        resources via, 444-446
    Sendmail, 27
    SMTP (Simple Mail Transfer Protocol),
        26
    to trace intruders, 424
encapsulation, 138, 470
encrypted time-stamp, 358
encrypting executables, 110
encryption
    application-level, 371
    key distribution, 373
    network-level, 370-374
    and packet filtering perimeter, 373
errors, ICMP codes for, 156-157
espionage, 12
/etc/hosts.deny file, 118
/etc/rc files, services started by, 108
Ethernet
    packet layer, 140
exporting news via NFS, 248
exterior routers, 70-71
    configuring, 333-337
    merging with bastion host, 74
    merging with interior router, 73
    multiple, 78-80

external
    clients, and proxying, 199
    programs on HTTP servers, 255-256

fail safety, 49-51
fail-safe stance, 339, 347
false authentication, 355
File Service Protocol (see FSP)
File Transfer Protocol (see FTP)
files
    removing from anonymous FTP area,
        233
    transferring, 28-30, 222-238, 309
        (see also NFS)
    uploading by prearrangement, 232
filesystems
    backing up, 434
    mounting as read-only, 122
    network, 41-42
filtering, packet (see packets, filtering)
filtering router (see screening router)
finger service, 36, 101, 114, 267-268
fingerd server, 114-115
fingerprint authentication, 356
firewalls, 17
    architecture of, 63-71
    backing up, 395
    buying versus building, 22-23
    configuring NTP with, 307
    configuring SMTP with, 216
    definition of, 17-19
    designing, 57-89
    dual-homed host as, 116
    FAQ for, 453
    internal, 82-88
        bastion hosts on, 88
    and IP multicasting, 276
    and IPv6, 152
    on joint networks, 86-88
    keeping current, 407-410
    layering, 47
    mailing lists on, 444-445
    maintaining, 395-411
    multiple bastion hosts, 71-72
    recreating entirely, 411
    resources for, 443-455
    responding to probes of, 405-407
    responding to security incidents,
        413-440
    samples of, 321-349
    security policies for, 379-394
    setting up NNTP in, 247
    testing, 179
    tools for, 457-464
    utilities for, 463-464
    and weakest link, 48
    what to protect, 4-6
    and X11 window system, 313-317
    (see also network security)
FIRST response teams, 447
flooding, 7-9
flow control, 480
flows, IPv6, 153
forged packets, 154
forgery
    man-in-the-middle, 163
    source address, 162
fragmentation, 476
fragments, packet, 140, 142
FSP (File Service Protocol), 29
    configuring, 235-236
FTP (File Transfer Protocol), 28-29, 115, 234
    Archie, 35
    configuring, 223-234
        in screened host architecture, 342
        in screened subnet architecture, 324
    passive (or PASV) mode, 223-226
    via proxy server, 194
    proxying with TIS FWTK, 203
    resources for, 444
    write-only incoming directory, 232
    wuarchive daemon, 462
    wuarchive server, 229
    (see also TFTP)
ftpd program, 115
ftp-gw proxy server, 325
functions
    SOCKS versus standard network, 201
FWALL-Users mailing list, 445

gated, 113
gated daemon, 463
gateways, 474
    application-level (see proxy systems)
    WAIS, 263
general-purpose routers, 169

generic proxy servers, 196
GGP (Gateway to Gateway Protocol), 491
Gopher, 34
  configuring, 260-262
  proxying with TIS FWTK, 204
graphics, 98

handshakes, 478
hardware
  configuration of, 97
  router (see router)
header packet, 138
headers
  nested IP, 152
  and packet filtering, 171-173
hiding information with DNS, 286-294
hijacking, 352-354
HINFO records, 286
host
  architecture, screened, 340-349
  security of, 14
host unreachable codes (see ICMP)
hosts
  architecture of
    dual-homed, 63-64
    screened, 65-66
  bastion (see bastion hosts)
  name service for, 38
  speed of, 95
  victim (see victim hosts)
housekeeping, 395-398
HTML (Hypertext Markup Language), 33
HTTP (Hypertext Transfer Protocol), 32
  CERN server, 253
  configuring, 250-260
    in screened host architecture, 343
    in screened subnet architecture, 327
  proxying with TIS FWTK, 204
  Secure, 259
  TIS FWTK proxy server, 253
http-gw proxy, 204
http-gw server, 253
Hypertext Markup Language (see HTML)
Hypertext Transfer Protocol (see HTTP)

ICMP (Internet Control Message Protocol),
    39, 147, 476
  echo, 301
    (see also ping)

packets, configuring, 304
  returning error codes, 156-157
immutable attribute (BSD 4.4-Lite), 123
inbound
  packets, 137
    filtering rules for, 177-180
    Telnet, 165
  services, 351-375
incident response teams, 416, 431, 447-450
  resources for, 444
incidents
  accidental, 13
  command channel, 211
  command channel attacks, 210
  contacting service providers about, 432
  data-driven attacks, 210-211
  detecting, plan for, 425
  documenting, 420
  documenting system after, 417
    planning for, 432
  evaluating, plan for, 426
  having tools and supplies for, 438
  hijacking, 352-354
  intrusions, 7
  multiple failed attacks, 405
  notifying people about, 416
  notifying people of, 428
  password attacks, 361
  practicing drills for, 439
  recovering from, 418-420
    planning to, 432
  responding to, 407, 413-440
  reviewing response strategies, 433
  types of, 7-10
incoming directories, FTP, 231-232
inetd, 109
  modifying for anonymous FTP, 228
information lookup services
  configuring, 266-270
information theft, 9-10
  espionage, 12
insecure networks, 83
installing
  filesystems as read-only, 122
  Internet services, 117-119
  kernel, 120-121
  operating system, 104
  software on machine, 119-123
intelligent proxy servers, 197

interior router, 69
    configuring, 329-333
    merging with bastion host, 74
    merging with exterior router, 73
    multiple, 75-78
internal
    bastion hosts, 93
    clients, and proxying, 199
    firewalls, 82-88
        bastion hosts on, 88
    news server, 248
Internet
    conferencing services, real-time, 37-38
    connections to unbuilt bastion host, 103
    Control Message Protocol (see ICMP)
    defense in depth, 47
    email over (see email)
    firewalls (see firewalls)
    future of IP addresses, 89
    layer, TCP/IP, 472-477
    logging activity on (see logging activity)
    multicasting, 275
    multiple connections to, 78-81
    Protocol (see IP)
    Relay Chat (see IRC)
    routing architecture, 491
    search programs for, 34-36
    security resource, 446
    services (see services, Internet)
    WWW (see World Wide Web)
intruders
    pursuing and capturing, 422-424
    recovering from, 418
    reviewing response strategies, 433
    types of, 10-13
intrusions (see incidents)
IP addresses, 38
    future of, 89
    private, 89
IP (Internet Protocol), 142-144, 472-476
    addresses, 152, 485-490
    encryption, 372
    fragmentation, 142
    multicasting, 275-277
    nested over IP, 151
    packet layer, 140
    packet routes to (see traceroute program)

    routers, 474
    source route option, 142
    status and control messages, 147
    Version 6 (IPv6), 152-153
IRC (Internet Relay Chat), 37
    configuring, 272-275
ISS (Internet Security Scanner), 460

joint networks, 86-88
joyriders, 11

KarlBridge package, 461
Kerberos authentication system, 42,
    365-366, 459
    supporting versions of POP, 218
kernel, reconfiguring, 120-121
key distribution, encryption, 373
keystroke timing authentication, 357
keyword search, 34
KPOP (Kerberos-supporting Post Office Protocol),
    218

labeling the system, 435
laboratory networks, 82
LAN-oriented service, 101
layering firewalls, 47
least privilege, 45-47, 337, 346
legal
    documentation of incidents, 420
    issues on pursuing intruders, 424
    security responsibilities, 387
link-level encryption, 371
Livingston routers, 158
local newsgroups, 32
logins
    remote, 30
    successful, from unexpected site, 405
logs, 105-107, 296, 436
    and backups, 129
    creating with SOCKS, 200
    documenting incidents, 420
    of dropped packets, 180
    memory required for, 398-399
    and proxy services, 191
    of router actions, 154
    trimlog program for, 464
    unexpectedly deleted or modified, 405

logs (cont'd)
  what to watch for, 399-403
  (see also syslog)
lookups, DNS, 279, 284
loopback address, 487
lp printing system, 42
  configuring, 317-319
lpr printing system, 42
  configuring, 317-319

machine
  auditing (see audit, security)
  backing up, 434
  choosing, 94-98
  configuring, 119-123
  connecting, 126
  disconnecting or shutting down, 427
  hardware (see hardware)
  hijacking, 352-354
  physical location of, 98
  securing, 103-107
  software (see software)
  speed of, 95
mail (see email)
mailing lists
  keeping current, 407
  resources via, 444-446
maintaining firewalls, 395-411
management tools, 39
managing accounts, 396-397
man-in-the-middle forgery, 163
maximum transmission unit (MTU), 476
MBONE (Multicase Backbone), 38
  configuring, 275-277
MD4 algorithm, 360
memory, 97
  for logs, 398-399
  managing, 398
merging interior and exterior routers, 73
meta-packets, and filtering, 171-173
MIME (Multimedia Internet Mail Exten-
    sions),
    221-222
modem pools, 374-375
modifying Internet services, 117-119
monitoring system automatically, 127
monitoring the system, 398-407
Morris worm, 210
Mosaic, 33

mountd, 112
mounting filesystems, 122
mrouter, 151
mrouters, 276
MTU (maximum transmission unit), 476
Multicase Backbone (see MBONE)
multicast IP, 151
multicasting, 275-277
multidirectional connections, 197
multi-homed hosts, 474
Multimedia Internet Mail Extensions
    (see MIME)
multimedia mail (see email)
MX records, 288

name service (see DNS)
named programs, DNS, 290
NCSA Mosaic, 33
nested IP over IP, 151
netacl program, 118
Netscape Navigator, 33
network
  access layer, TCP/IP, 470
  architecture (see firewalls, architecture
      of)
  checking connectivity of (see ping)
  disconnecting from, after incident, 415
  disconnecting, plan to, 428
  encryption, 370-374
  File System (see NFS)
  filesystems, 41-42
  functions, SOCKS version of, 201
  insecure, 83
  joint, 86-88
  lab/test, 82
  location of bastion host on, 99
  management services, 39
    configuring, 297-306
  monitoring automatically, 127
  perimeter, 58, 67
  protecting internally, 82-88
  security (see security)
  taps, 9
  Time Protocol (see NTP)
  transferring information across (see
      packets, filtering)
Network Information Service (see NIS/YP)
network news, 31

Network News Transfer Protocol (see NNTP)
network unreachable codes (see ICMP)
news (see NNTP)
newsgroups, 31
    keeping current, 408
    security resources via, 446
next hop, 496
NFS (Network File System), 41
    configuring, 309-312
    exporting news via, 248
    services of, 112
NIS+, 312
NIST CSRC (Computer Security Resource Clearinghouse), 448
NIS/YP (Network Information Service/Yellow Pages), 39, 112, 278
    configuring, 312
NNTP (Network News Transfer Protocol), 32, 199
    configuring, 245-250
        in screened host architecture, 343
        in screened subnet architecture, 327
nonrouting dual-homed hosts, 93, 116
notifying people of incident, 428
notifying people of problems, 416
NTP (Network Time Protocol), 40, 199
    configuring, 306-308
numbers, port, 497
numbers, protocol, 496

obscurity (see security through obsurity)
on program, 31
one-time passwords, 360-362
operating systems
    choosing, 94-95
    fixing bugs in, 104
    installation of, 104
    multiple, and proxying, 190
    testing reload of, 438
    UNIX (see UNIX)
OSI (Open Systems Interconnect) model, 467-469
outbound
    finger requests, 267
    packets, 137
        filtering rules for, 177-180
        Telnet, 164

packages, auditing, 123-125
packet filtering, 58-60, 131-188
    by address, 161-163
    advice for, 158
    bugs in packages, 136
    characteristics of
        Archie, 264
        DNS, 279, 293
        finger, 268
        FSP, 235
        FTP, 223-226
        Gopher, 261
        HTTP, 251-253
        ICMP, 305
        IRC, 274
        lp, 319
        lpr, 318
        NFS, 311
        NIS, 313
        NNTP, 245, 249-250
        NTP, 306
        ping, 301
        POP, 219
        "r" commands, 242
        rex, 245
        rexec, 244
        RIP, 300
        SMTP, 215
        SNMP, 298
        syslog, 297
        talk, 271
        Telnet, 239
        TFTP, 235
        traceroute, 303
        UUCP, 237
        WAIS, 263
        whois, 269
        X11, 315-317
    choosing a router, 168-180
    configuring router, 136-138
    conventions for, 170
    dynamic, 147
    example of, 182-188
    with exterior router, 70
    inbound versus outbound, 177-180
    with interior router, 69
    IP (see see IP)
    performance level of, 168
    perimeter, and encryption, 373

packet filtering (cont'd)
 rule sequence of, 173-176
 rules for, 158-188
 rules in screened host architecture,
  343-346
 rules in screened subnet architecture,
  329-337
 with screened host architecture, 65-66
 by service, 164-168
 by source port, 167
 testing, 179
 tools for, 461
 transparency of, 134
 where to do, 180-181
packets, 58, 131, 302
 encrypting (see encryption)
 forged, 154
 fragmenting, 142
 fragments, 140
 handling (by router), 154-157
 headers of, 138
 ICMP, 304
 inbound versus outbound, 137
 rates of, 168
 sniffing, programs for, 354
 source-routed, 116
 structure, 138-154
 TCP, 144-146
 UDP, 146
 (see also traceroute program)
PAR (Positive Acknowledgment with
 Retransmission), 478
passive (or PASV) mode, FTP, 223-226
password aging, 397
passwords, 356-370
 and false authentication, 355
 one-time, 360-362
 stealing with network taps, 9
 time-based, 363-364
 (see also authentication)
patches, 410
pcbind service, 113
performance
 with multiple interior routers, 76
 of packet filter, 168
perimeter nets
 multiple, 80-81
 shared, 87
perimeter network, 58, 67

ping service, 39, 191
 configuring, 301-302
platforms, xxiv
plug-gw proxy, 203
policy, security (see security, policies of)
POP (Post Office Protocol), 218-221
 multiple services, 221
port numbers, 497
portmap service, 113, 463
portmapper server, 149-150
ports, source, filtering by, 167
ports, well-known, 499-501
positive acknowledgment, 480
prearranging file transfer, 232
printing, 46
 configuring protocols, 317-319
 systems, 42
private
 IP addresses, 89
 key cryptography, 352
 newsgroups, 32
probes, responding to, 405-407
procedures for proxying, custom, 194
processing speed, 95
programs, removing nonessential, 121
promiscuous mode, 99
protocols
 analyzing, 319
 bidirectionality of, 136
 data (see TCP/IP)
 dedicated Archie, 265
 above IP, 144-151
 non-IP, 153
 numbers for, 496
 and packet filtering, 136
 routing (see RIP)
 security of, and proxying, 198
 time-dependence of, 306
 weaknesses of, and proxy services, 193
proxy services, 58, 61-63, 189-205
 application- versus circuit-level, 195-196
 characteristics of
  Archie, 265
  Berkeley "r" commands, 243
  DNS, 281
  finger, 268
  FSP, 236
  FTP, 226
  Gopher, 261

proxy services, characteristics of (cont'd)
HTTP, 253
IRC, 274
lp, 319
lpr, 318
NFS, 312
NIS, 313
NNTP, 246, 249-250
NTP, 307
ping, 302
POP, 220
Berkeley , 243
rex, 245
rexec, 244
RIP, 300
SMTP, 216
SNMP, 299
syslog, 297
talk, 272
Telnet, 240
TFTP, 235
traceroute, 304
UUCP, 237
WAIS, 263
whois, 269
generic versus dedicated, 196
intelligent servers, 197
internal versus external clients, 199
Internet services and, 197-199
and multiple operating systems, 190
protocol security, 198
SOCKS package for, 200-202
software for, 193-195
TIS FWTK for, 202-204
tools for, 461
versus packet filtering, 134
when unable to provide, 204
without proxy server, 199
public key cryptography, 352
pursuing intruders, 422-424

"r" commands, 113
configuring, 240-243
and packet filtering, 136
rcp transfer program, 30
read-only filesystems, 122
real-time conferencing (see conferencing
services, real-time)
rebooting, 128

recording activity (see logs)
recovering after incident, 418-420
plan for, 432
remote
command execution, 240-245
computers, hijacking, 352-354
terminal access, 30
Remote Procedure Call (see RPC)
remote terminal access (see Telnet)
reputation, 6
resources, 5
response teams (see incident response
teams)
retina authentication, 356
reverse lookups, 284, 288
reviewing security policies, 383
rex service, 244
rexec server, 243
RFC1597 and RFC1627, 89
.rhosts file, 241
RIP (Routing Information Protocol)
configuring, 300
RISKS mailing list, 446
rlogin program, 31
proxying with TIS FWTK, 203
routed server, 113
routers, 131
as choke point, 133
choosing, 168-180
disabling, 115-117
exterior (or access) (see exterior routers)
handling packets, 154-157
interior (see interior router)
logging actions of, 154
merging interior and exterior, 73
multicast, 151, 276
returning ICMP error codes, 156-157
screening (see screening router)
single-purpose versus general-purpose,
169
testing, 83
where to filter, 180-181
routing
domains, 491
protocol (see RIP)
source, 116
table, 493-496
RPC (Remote Procedure Call), 148-151
portmapper server, 149-150

RPC (Remote Procedure Call) (cont'd)
  service number, 149
  services of, 112
  (see also NFS; NIS)
rsh program, 31

sabotage (see denial of service)
SAGE (System Administrators Guild), 449
SATAN package, 406, 460
score keepers, 11
screend package, 158, 461
screened host architecture, 65-66, 340-349
screened subnet architecture, 66-71,
      321-340
  with dual-homed host architecture, 81
screening router, 59-60, 131
  acceptable addresses for, 158-161
  choosing, 168-180
  and proxy systems, 189
  rules for, 158-188
  (see also packets, filtering)
screening routers
  configuring, 136-138
  where to use, 180-181
search programs, 34-36
Secure HTTP, 259
security, 17
  against system failure, 49-51
  audit, 123-126
  of backups, 128-129
  and bastion host speed, 97
  choke points, 338, 347
  of commercial authentication systems,
      370
  cryptography, 352
  default deny stance, 137
  default permit stance, 137
  defense in depth, 338, 347
  designing for network, 22-23
  diversity of defense, 53, 339, 348
  of DNS, 284
  encryption, network-level, 370-374
  fail-safe stance, 339, 347
  host, 14
  important of simplicity of, 54
  incident response teams (see incident
      response teams)
  incidents (see incidents)
  insecure networks, 83

and IRC, 272-274
  keeping checksums secure, 436
  lack of, 13
  least privilege, 337, 346
  legal responsibilities, 387
  of machine, 103-107
  modem pools, 374-375
  netacl, 118
  network (see network)
  operating system bugs, 104
  policies for, 19, 379-394
      reviewing, 383
  of POP, 218
  practicing drills for, 439
  protecting the network internally, 82-88
  protocol, and proxying, 198
  regarding HTTP, 254-259
  resources for, 443-455
  responding to incidents, 413-440
  reviewing response strategies, 433
  of Sendmail, 212-213
  SNMP, 298
  strategies for, 45-54
  TCP Wrapper, 117
  terminal servers, 374-375
  through obscurity, 13
  and time information, 306
  universal participation, 52
  weakest link, 338, 347
  and weakest link, 48
  when proxying is ineffective, 205
  when system crashes, 128
  with whois service, 269
  X11 window system mechanisms, 314
  (see also firewalls)
Sendmail, 27, 46, 212-213
  Morris worm, 210
  (see also SMTP)
servers
  Archie, running, 266
  DNS
      for internal hosts, 290
      setting up fake, 287-289
  routed, 113
servers, proxy (see proxy services)
services host, 341
services, inbound (see inbound services)
services, Internet, 25-42
  booting, 113

services, Internet (cont'd)
    configuring, 207-319
    contacting providers about incidents,
        417, 432
    default deny stance, 50
    default permit stance, 51
    direct access to, 191
    disabling those not required, 108-117
    filtering by, 164-168
    information lookup services, 266-270
    installing and modifying, 117-119
    LAN-oriented, 101
    NFS (Network File System), 112
    protecting with TCP Wrapper, 117
    proxying with, 197-199
    "r" commands, 113
    real-time conferencing, 270-277
    RPC (Remote Procedure Call), 112
    selecting for bastion host, 100
    started by /etc/rc, 108
    Telnet (see Telnet)
services, network management (see net-
        work management services)
services, proxy (see proxy services)
services, store-and-forward, 199
setgid capability, 95
setuid capability, 95
shell scripts, 108
shutting down, 415, 427
Simple Mail Transfer Protocol (see SMTP)
Simple Network Management Protocol (see
        SNMP)
single-purpose routers, 169
S/Key password program, 360-362
smap package, 214-215
smapd program, 214
SMTP (Simple Mail Transfer Protocol), 26,
        199, 211-218
    configuring
        and firewalls, 216
        in screened host architecture, 342
        in screened subnet architecture,
            326-327
    for UNIX (see Sendmail)
SMTP (simple Mail Transfer Protocol), 101
snapshots, system, 417
    planning for, 432
sniffers, 354
sniffing for passwords, 362

SNK-004 card, TIS FWTK, 364
SNMP (Simple Network Management Proto-
        col),
    40
    configuring, 297-300
snuffle program, 110
sockets, 499-501
SOCKS package, 200-202, 462
    functions, 201
    HTTP proxying on
        in screened subnet architecture, 328
    modified finger service, 268
software
    to automatically monitor the system, 127
    installing on machine, 119-123
    proxy, 61
    proxying, 192-195
        (see also proxy services)
    router (see router)
    and viruses, 22
source address
    filtering by, 162-163
    forgery, 162
source port
    filtering by, 167
source routing, 116
source routing option, IP, 142
speed, processing, 95
spell command, UNIX, 125
spies, 12
startup scripts, 108
store-and-forward services, 199
subnet architecture, screened, 66-71,
        321-340
subnets, 489-490
Sun RPC (see RPC)
supporting Internet services (see Internet
        services)
SWATCH program, 127, 464
SYN (synchronize sequence numbers) bit,
        479
syslog
    configuring, 296
    example output from, 400-402
syslog daemons, 106-107
    SWATCH program with, 127
system
    autonomous, 491
    crashes, watching carefully, 128

system (cont'd)
    customized, 419
    defense, diversity of, 53
    documenting after incident, 417, 432
    failure of, 49-51
    keeping up-to-date, 409
    labeling and diagramming, 435
    monitoring, 127, 398-407
    operating, testing reload of, 438
    rebuilding, 419
    restoring after incident, 418-420
        planning for, 432
    shutting down, 415
System Dynamics cards, 363-364
system logs (see logs)

talk conferencing system, 37, 270-272
tapes, needs for, 98
taps (see network taps)
TCP (Transmission Control Protocol),
        144-146, 478-481
    packet layer, 141
    proxying with, 197
    UUCP over (see UUCP)
TCP Wrapper package, 117, 463
tcpd program, 118
TCP/IP, 465-501
    packet, 139-141
    protocol architecture, 469-477
Telebit NetBlazer, 158
Telnet, 30, 164-167
    Archie across, 265
    configuring, 238-240
        in screened host architecture, 342
        in screened subnet architecture, 323
    inbound, 165
    inbound versus outbound, 238
    outbound, 164
    proxying with TIS FWTK, 203
Telstra, 443
terminal servers, 374-375
test networks, 82
testing
    firewalls, 179
    reload of operating system, 438
    routers, 83
TFTP (Trivial File Transport Protocol), 29,
        234-235

theft of information (see information theft)
three-way handshake, 479
Tiger auditing package, 124, 459
time service, 40
time-based passwords, 363-364
time-stamp, encrypted, 358
TIS Internet Firewalls Toolkit (TIS FWTK),
        458
    authentication server, 366-369
    FTP daemon, 230
    FTP proxy server, 227
    ftp-gw-proxy server, 325
    HTTP proxy server, 253
    HTTP proxying on
        in screened subnet architecture, 328
    for proxying, 202-204
    S/Key password program, 360-362
    smap package, 214-215
    SNK-004 card, 364
tools and supplies, 438
traceroute program, 39, 101
    configuring, 302-304
transferring files, 28-30
transparency, 61
    of client changes for proxying, 194
    of packet filtering, 134
trees, DNS, 282
trimlog program, 464
Tripwire package, 124, 459
Trivial File Transport Protocol (see TFTP)
tunnels, multicast, 276-277
TXT records, 286

UDP (User Datagram Protocol), 146, 477
    Packet Relayer, 200, 462
unicasting, 275
unidirectional connections, 197
universal participation, 52
UNIX, 94-95
    checksum programs, 126
    security holes resource, 445
    window system, 42
uploading
    programs on HTTP server, 255
URL (Uniform Resource Locator), 251
usage profile, 126
Usenet news (see NNTP)
Usenet newsgroups (see newsgroups)
USENIX Association, 448, 450

user accounts
 on bastion host, 102
User Diagram Protocol (see UDP)
UUCP (UNIX-to-UNIX Copy Protocol), 29
 configuring, 236-238

validating firewalls, 179
vandals, 11
victim hosts, 101
victim machines, 93
viruses, 21-22
voice authentication, 356

WAIS (Wide Area Information Servers), 34
 configuring, 262-264
weakest link, 48, 338, 347
well-known ports, 499-501
whois service, 36, 268-270
Wide Area Information Servers (see WAIS)
window systems, 42
 X11 (see X11 window system)
writable directories in anonymous FTP,
 231-234
wuarchive daemon, 462
wuarchive server, 229
WWW (World Wide Web), 32-34
 Archie access via, 265
 browsers, 33
  as FTP clients, 224
  as Gopher clients (see Gopher)
 configuring, 250-260
 MIME in, 222
 resources for, 443
 resources on, 446

X11 window system, 42
 configuring, 313-317
x-gw proxy, 204
xhost mechanism, 314

Yellow Pages (YP), 39
 (see also NIS/YP)

zone transfers, DNS, 279

About the Authors

D. Brent Chapman is a consultant in the San Francisco Bay Area, specializing in Internet firewalls. He has designed and built Internet firewall systems for a wide range of clients, using a variety of techniques and technologies. He is also the manager of the Firewalls Internet mailing list. Before founding Great Circle Associates, he was operations manager for a financial services company, a world-renowned corporate research lab, a software engineering company, and a hardware engineering company. He holds a Bachelor of Science degree in Electrical Engineering and Computer Science from the University of California, Berkeley. In his spare time, Brent is a volunteer search and rescue pilot, disaster relief pilot, and mission coordinator for the California Wing of the Civil Air Patrol (the civilian auxiliary of the United States Air Force).

Elizabeth D. Zwicky is a senior system administrator at Silicon Graphics and the president of the System Administrators Guild (SAGE). She has been doing large-scale UNIX system administration for 10 years, and was a founding board member of both SAGE and BayLISA (the San Francisco Bay Area system administrators' group), as well as a non-voting member of the first board of the Australian system administration group, SAGE-AU. She has been involuntarily involved in Internet security since before the Internet worm. In her lighter moments, she is one of the few people who makes significant use of the "rand" function in PostScript, producing PostScript documents that are different every time they're printed.

Colophon

The illustration on the cover of *Building Internet Firewalls* is of a doorway of Gothic design, topped by a crenelated parapet. The period of Gothic architecture is often said to have begun in the mid-12th century, when the church of Saint-Denis was built, in Paris in 1144. The architect of that church is unknown. Although Gothic architecture was mainly used in the building of churches, by the late 13th century it was used for secular purposes also, including fortifications. The structure of the merlons (the raised portions of the parapet) in this illustration give information about the date and place of its construction. The oblique sides of the merlons suggest that the doorway was built in the 14th century, and the plain but sloping top suggests that it was built in England or France.

Merlons were designed to provide defense to those inside the fortification, while crenels (the recessed portions between the merlons) let them shoot projectiles at attacking enemies. Given the size of this door, and the relatively low merlons, this may have been a postern, a doorway used by foot travellers to avoid lowering the main gate.

Edie Freedman designed the cover of this book, using a 19th-century engraving from the Dover Pictorial Archive. The cover layout was produced with Quark XPress 3.3 using the ITC Garamond font.

The inside layout was designed by Edie Freedman, with modifications by Nancy Priest. Text was prepared in SGML using the DocBook 2.1 DTD. The print version of this book was created by translating the SGML source into a set of gtroff macros using a filter developed at ORA by Norman Walsh. Steve Talbott designed and wrote the underlying macro set on the basis of the GNU gtroff -gs macros; Lenny Muellner adapted them to SGML and implemented the book design. The GNU groff text formatter version 1.09 was used to generate PostScript output. The text and heading fonts are ITC Garamond Light and Garamond Book. The illustrations that appear in the book were created in Macromedia Freehand 5.0 by Chris Reilley. This colophon was written by Clairemarie Fisher O'Leary.

SYSTEM ADMINISTRATION

Books from O'Reilly & Associates, Inc.

Summer 1995

"Good reference books make a system administrator's job much easier. However, finding useful books about system administration is a challenge, and I'm constantly on the lookout. In general, I have found that almost anything published by O'Reilly & Associates is worth having if you are interested in the topic."

—Dinah McNutt, UNIX Review

TCP/IP Network Administration

By Craig Hunt
1st Edition August 1992
502 pages, ISBN 0-937175-82-X

TCP/IP Network Administration is a complete guide to setting up and running a TCP/IP network for administrators of networks of systems or lone home systems that access the Internet. It starts with the fundamentals: what the protocols do and how they work, how to request a network address and a name (the forms needed are included in an appendix), and how to set up your network. Beyond basic setup, the book discusses how to configure important network applications, including sendmail, the r* commands, and some simple setups for NIS and NFS. There are also chapters on troubleshooting and security. In addition, this book covers several important packages that are available from the Net (such as *gated*). Covers BSD and System V TCP/IP implementations.

"Whether you're putting a network together, trying to figure out why an existing one doesn't work, or wanting to understand the one you've got a little better, *TCP/IP Network Administration* is the definitive volume on the subject."
—Tom Yager, *Byte*

Networking Personal Computers with TCP/IP

By Craig Hunt
1st Edition July 1995
408 pages, ISBN 1-56592-123-2

If you're like most network administrators, you probably have several networking "islands": a TCP/IP-based network of UNIX systems (possibly connected to the Internet), plus a separate Netware or NetBIOS network for your PCs. Perhaps even separate Netware and NetBIOS networks in different departments, or at different sites. And you've probably dreaded the task of integrating those networks into one.

If that's your situation, you need this book! When done properly, integrating PCs onto a TCP/IP-based Internet is less threatening than it seems; long term, it gives you a much more flexible and extensible network. Craig Hunt, author of the classic *TCP/IP Network Administration*, tells you how to build a maintainable network that includes your PCs. Don't delay; as Craig points out, if you don't provide a network solution for your PC users, someone else will.

Covers: DOS, Windows, Windows for Workgroups, Windows NT, and Novell Netware; Chameleon (NetManage), PC/TCP (FTP Software), LAN WorkPlace (Novell), and Super TCP; and Basic Network setup and configuration, with special attention given to email, network printing, and file sharing.

Computer Crime

By David Icove, Karl Seger & William VonStorch
1st Edition August 1995
464 pages, ISBN 1-56592-086-4

Computer crime is a growing threat. Attacks on computers, networks, and data range from terrorist threats to financial crimes to pranks. *Computer Crime: A Crimefighters Handbook* is aimed at those who need to understand, investigate, and prosecute computer crimes of all kinds.

This book discusses computer crimes, criminals, and laws, and profiles the computer criminal (using techniques developed for the FBI and other law enforcement agencies). It outlines the the risks to computer systems and personnel, operational, physical, and communications measures that can be taken to prevent computer crimes. It also discusses how to plan for, investigate, and prosecute computer crimes, ranging from the supplies needed for criminal investigation, to the detection and audit tools used in investigation, to the presentation of evidence to a jury.

Contains a compendium of computer-related federal statutes, all statutes of individual states, a resource summary, and detailed papers on computer crime.

Computer Security Basics

By Deborah Russell & G.T. Gangemi Sr.
1st Edition July 1991
464 pages, ISBN 0-937175-71-4

There's a lot more consciousness of security today, but not a lot of understanding of what it means and how far it should go. This handbook describes complicated concepts, such as trusted systems, encryption, and mandatory access control, in simple terms. For example, most U.S. government equipment acquisitions now require "Orange Book" (Trusted Computer System Evaluation Criteria) certification. A lot of people have a vague feeling that they ought to know about the Orange Book, but few make the effort to track it down and read it. *Computer Security Basics* contains a more readable introduction to the Orange Book—why it exists, what it contains, and what the different security levels are all about—than any other book or government publication.

"A very well-rounded book, filled with concise, authoritative information…written with the user in mind, but still at a level to be an excellent professional reference."
—Mitch Wright, System Administrator, I-NET, Inc.

PGP: Pretty Good Privacy

By Simson Garfinkel
1st Edition December 1994
430 pages, ISBN 1-56592-098-8

PGP is a freely available encryption program that protects the privacy of files and electronic mail. It uses powerful public key cryptography and works on virtually every platform. This book is both a readable technical user's guide and a fascinating behind-the-scenes look at cryptography and privacy. It describes how to use PGP and provides background on cryptography, PGP's history, battles over public key cryptography patents and U.S. government export restrictions, and public debates about privacy and free speech.

"I even learned a few things about PGP from Simson's informative book."—Phil Zimmermann, Author of PGP

"Since the release of PGP 2.0 from Europe in the fall of 1992, PGP's popularity and usage has grown to make it the de-facto standard for email encyrption. Simson's book is an excellent overview of PGP and the history of cryptography in general. It should prove a useful addition to the resource library for any computer user, from the UNIX wizard to the PC novice."
—Derek Atkins, PGP Development Team, MIT

Practical UNIX Security

By Simson Garfinkel & Gene Spafford
1st Edition June 1991
512 pages, ISBN 0-937175-72-2

Tells system administrators how to make their UNIX system—either System V or BSD—as secure as it possibly can be without going to trusted system technology. The book describes UNIX concepts and how they enforce security, tells how to defend against and handle security breaches, and explains network security (including UUCP, NFS, Kerberos, and firewall machines) in detail. If you are a UNIX system administrator or user who deals with security, you need this book.

It contains an excellent checklist of security procedures and dangerous UNIX system files, a detailed resource summary, and chapters on detecting security attacks, legal options, and viruses and worms.

"The book could easily become a standard desktop reference for anyone involved in system administration. In general, its comprehensive treatment of UNIX security issues will enlighten anyone with an interest in the topic."
—Paul Clark, Trusted Information Systems

Building Internet Firewalls

By D. Brent Chapman and Elizabeth D. Zwicky
1st Edition September 1995
350 pages (est.), ISBN 1-56592-124-0

Everyone is jumping on the Internet bandwagon, despite that fact that the security risks associated with connecting to the Net have never been greater. This book is a practical guide to building firewalls on the Internet. It describes a variety of firewall approaches and architectures and discusses how you can build packet filtering and proxying solutions at your site. It also contains a full discussion of how to configure Internetservices (e.g., FTP, SMTP, Telnet) to work with a firewall, as well as a complete list of resources, including the location of many publicly available firewall construction tools.

SYSTEM ADMINISTRATOR TOOLS

Essential System Administration

By Æleen Frisch
2nd Edition September 1995 (est.)
784 pages (est.), ISBN 0-56592-127-5

Essential System Administration takes an in-depth look at the fundamentals of UNIX system administration in a real-world, heterogeneous environment. Whether you are a beginner or an experienced administrator, you'll quickly be able to apply its principles and advice to your everyday problems.

The book approaches UNIX systems administration from the perspective of your job—the routine tasks and troubleshooting that make up your day. Whether you're dealing with frustrated users, convincing an uncomprehending management that you need new hardware, rebuilding the kernel, or simply adding new users, you'll find help in this book. You'll also learn about back up and restore and how to set up printers, secure your system, and perform many other systems administration tasks. But the book is not for full-time systems administrators alone. Linux users and others who administer their own systems will benefit from its practical, hands-on approach.

This second edition has been updated for the latest versions of all major UNIX platforms, including Sun OS 4.1, Solaris 2.3, AIX 4.1, Linux 1.1, Digital UNIX OSF/1, SCO UNIX version 3, HP/UX versions 9 and 10, and IRIX version 6. The entire book has been thoroughly reviewed and tested on all of the platforms covered. In addition, networking, electronic mail, security, and kernel configuration topics have been expanded.

Managing Internet Information Services

By Cricket Liu, Jerry Peek, Russ Jones,
Bryan Buus & Adrian Nye
1st Edition December 1994
668 pages, ISBN 1-56592-062-7

This comprehensive guide describes how to set up information services and make them available over the Internet. It discusses why a company would want to offer Internet services, provides complete coverage of all popular services, and tells how to select which ones to provide. Most of the book describes how to set up Gopher, World Wide Web, FTP, and WAIS servers and email services.

"*Managing Internet Information Services* has long been needed in the Internet community, as well as in many organizations with IP-based networks. Although many on the Internet are quite savvy when it comes to administering these types of tools, *MIIS* will allow a much larger community to join in and perhaps provide more diverse information. This book will be a welcome addition to my Internet shelf."
—Robert H'obbes' Zakon, MITRE Corporation

sendmail

By Bryan Costales, with Eric Allman & Neil Rickert
1st Edition November 1993
830 pages, ISBN 1-56592-056-2

This Nutshell Handbook® is far and away the most comprehensive book ever written on sendmail, the program that acts like a traffic cop in routing and delivering mail on UNIX-based networks. Although sendmail is used on almost every UNIX system, it's one of the last great uncharted territories—and most difficult utilities to learn—in UNIX system administration. This book provides a complete sendmail tutorial, plus extensive reference material on every aspect of the program. It covers IDA sendmail, the latest version (V8) from Berkeley, and the standard versions available on most systems.

"The program and its rule description file, sendmail.cf, have long been regarded as the pit of coals that separated the mild UNIX system administrators from the real fire walkers. Now, sendmail syntax, testing, hidden rules, and other mysteries are revealed. Costales, Allman, and Rickert are the indisputable authorities to do the text."
—Ben Smith, *Byte Magazine*

DNS and BIND

By Paul Albitz & Cricket Liu
1st Edition October 1992
418 pages, ISBN 1-56592-010-4

 *DNS and BIND* contains all you need to know about the Internet's Domain Name System (DNS) and the Berkeley Internet Name Domain (BIND), its UNIX implementation. The Domain Name System is the Internet's "phone book"; it's a database that tracks important information (in particular, names and addresses) for every computer on the Internet. If you're a system administrator, this book will show you how to set up and maintain the DNS software on your network.

"*DNS and BIND* contains a lot of useful information that you'll never find written down anywhere else. And since it's written in a crisp style, you can pretty much use the book as your primary BIND reference." —Marshall Rose, *ConneXions*

Managing NFS and NIS

By Hal Stern
1st Edition June 1991
436 pages, ISBN 0-937175-75-7

 *Managing NFS and NIS* is for system administrators who need to set up or manage a network filesystem installation. NFS (Network Filesystem) is probably running at any site that has two or more UNIX systems. NIS (Network Information System) is a distributed database used to manage a network of computers. The only practical book devoted entirely to these subjects, this guide is a "must-have" for anyone interested in UNIX networking.

System Performance Tuning

By Mike Loukides
1st Edition November 1990
336 pages, ISBN 0-937175-60-9

 *System Performance Tuning* answers the fundamental question: How can I get my computer to do more work without buying more hardware? Some performance problems do require you to buy a bigger or faster computer, but many can be solved simply by making better use of the resources you already have.

Linux Network Administrator's Guide

By Olaf Kirch
1st Edition January 1995
370 pages, ISBN 1-56592-087-2

 A UNIX-compatible operating system that runs on personal computers, Linux is a pinnacle within the free software movement. It is based on a kernel developed by Finnish student Linus Torvalds and is distributed on the Net or on low-cost disks, along with a complete set of UNIX libraries, popular free software utilities, and traditional layered products like NFS and the X Window System.

Networking is a fundamental part of Linux. Whether you want a simple UUCP connection or a full LAN with NFS and NIS, you are going to have to build a network.

Linux Network Administrator's Guide by Olaf Kirch is one of the most successful books to come from the Linux Documentation Project. It touches on all the essential networking software included with Linux, plus some hardware considerations. Topics include serial connections, UUCP, routing and DNS, mail and News, SLIP and PPP, NFS, and NIS.

Managing UUCP and Usenet

By Grace Todino & Tim O'Reilly
10th Edition January 1992
368 pages, ISBN 0-937175-93-5

 For all its widespread use, UUCP is one of the most difficult UNIX utilities to master. This book is for system administrators who want to install and manage UUCP and Usenet software.

"Don't even TRY to install UUCP without it!"—Usenet message 456@nitrex.UUCP

termcap & terminfo

By John Strang, Linda Mui & Tim O'Reilly
3rd Edition April 1988
270 pages, ISBN 0-937175-22-6

 For UNIX system administrators and programmers. This handbook provides information on writing and debugging terminal descriptions, as well as terminal initialization, for the two UNIX terminal databases.

Volume 8: X Window System Administrator's Guide:

By Linda Mui & Eric Pearce
1st Edition October 1992
372, pages, ISBN 0-937175-83-8

As X moves out of the hacker's domain and into the "real world," users can't be expected to master all the ins and outs of setting up and administering their own X software. That will increasingly become the domain of system administrators. Even for experienced system administrators, X raises many issues, both because of subtle changes in the standard UNIX way of doing things and because X blurs the boundaries between different platforms. Under X, users can run applications across the network on systems with different resources (including fonts, colors, and screen size.) Many of these issues are poorly understood, and the technology for dealing with them is in rapid flux.

This book is the first and only book devoted to the issues of system administration for X and X-based networks, written not just for UNIX system administrators, but for anyone faced with the job of administering X (including those running X on stand-alone workstations).

Note: The CD that used to be offered with this book is now sold separately, allowing system administrators to purchase the book and the CD-ROM in quantities they choose.

The X Companion CD for R6

By O'Reilly & Associates
1st Edition January 1995
(Includes CD-ROM plus 80-page guide)
ISBN 1-56592-084-8

The X CD-ROM contains precompiled binaries for X11, Release 6 (X11 R6) for Sun4, Solaris, HP-UX on the HP700, DEC Alpha, DEC ULTRIX, and IBM RS6000. It includes X11 R6 source code from the "core" and "contrib" directories and X11 R5 source code from the "core" directory. The CD also provides examples from O'Reilly and Associates X Window System series books and *The X Resource* journal.

The package includes a 126-page book describing the contents of the CD-ROM, how to install the R6 binaries, and how to build X11 for other platforms. The book also contains the X Consortium release notes for Release 6.

O'Reilly on the Net—
ONLINE PROGRAM GUIDE

O'Reilly & Associates offers extensive information through various online resources. We invite you to come and explore our little neck-of-the-woods.

Online Resource Center

Most comprehensive among our online offerings is the O'Reilly Resource Center. Here, you'll find detailed information on all O'Reilly products: titles, prices, tables of contents, indexes, author bios, software contents, reviews...you can even view images of the products themselves. With GNN Direct you can now order our products directly off the Net (GNN Direct is available on the Web site only; Gopher users can still use **order@ora.com**). We supply contact information along with a list of distributors and bookstores available worldwide. In addition, we provide informative literature in the field: articles, interviews, excerpts, and bibliographies that help you stay informed and abreast.

To access ORA's Online Resource Center:

Point your Web browser (e.g., **mosaic** or **lynx**) to:

`http://www.ora.com/`

For the plaintext version, **telnet** or **gopher** to:

`gopher.ora.com`

(telnet login: **gopher**)

FTP

The example files and programs in many of our books are available electronically via FTP.

To obtain example files and programs from O'Reilly texts:

ftp to:

`ftp.ora.com`

or `ftp.uu.net`
`cd published/oreilly`

Ora-news

An easy way to stay informed of the latest projects and products from O'Reilly & Associates is to subscribe to "ora-news," our electronic news service. Subscribers receive email as soon as the information breaks.

To subscribe to "ora-news":

Send email to:
listproc@online.ora.com

and put the following information on the first line of your message (not in "Subject"):
subscribe ora-news "your name" **of** "your company"

For example enter:

`mail listproc@online.ora.com`

`subscribe ora-news Kris Webber of`
`    Mighty Fine Enterprises`

Email

Many customer services are provided via email. Here are a few of the most popular and useful.

nuts@ora.com
> For general questions and information.

bookquestions@ora.com
> For technical questions, or corrections, concerning book contents.

order@ora.com
> To order books online and for ordering questions.

catalog@ora.com
> To receive a free copy of our magazine/catalog, *ora.com*. Please include a postal address.

Snailmail and Phones

O'Reilly & Associates, Inc.
103A Morris Street, Sebastopol, CA 95472
Inquiries: **707-829-0515, 800-998-9938**
Credit card orders: **800-889-8969** (Weekdays 6 A.M.- 5 P.M. PST)
FAX: **707-829-0104**

O'Reilly & Associates—
LISTING OF TITLES

INTERNET

!%@:: A Directory of Electronic Mail
    Addressing & Networks
Connecting to the Internet:
    An O'Reilly Buyer's Guide
The Mosaic Handbook for
    Microsoft Windows
The Mosaic Handbook for
    the Macintosh
The Mosaic Handbook for
    the X Window System
Smileys
The Whole Internet User's
    Guide & Catalog

SOFTWARE

Internet In A Box™
WebSite™

WHAT YOU NEED TO KNOW SERIES

Using Email Effectively
Marketing on the Internet
    (Winter '95/96 est.)
When You Can't Find Your
    System Administrator

HEALTH, CAREER & BUSINESS

Building a Successful Software Business
The Computer User's Survival Guide
    (Fall '95 est.)
The Future Does Not Compute
Love Your Job!
TWI Day Calendar - 1996

AUDIOTAPES

INTERNET TALK RADIO'S "GEEK OF THE WEEK" INTERVIEWS

The Future of the Internet Protocol
Global Network Operations
Mobile IP Networking
Networked Information and
    Online Libraries
Security and Networks
European Networking

NOTABLE SPEECHES OF THE INFORMATION AGE

John Perry Barlow

USING UNIX

BASICS

Learning GNU Emacs
Learning the Korn Shell
Learning the UNIX Operating System
Learning the vi Editor
MH & xmh: Email for Users &
    Programmers
SCO UNIX in a Nutshell
The USENET Handbook
Using UUCP and Usenet
UNIX in a Nutshell: System V Edition

ADVANCED

Exploring Expect
The Frame Handbook
Learning Perl
Making TeX Work
Programming perl
Running LINUX
sed & awk
UNIX Power Tools (with CD-ROM)

SYSTEM ADMINISTRATION

Building Internet Firewalls
Computer Crime:
    A Crimefighter's Handbook
Computer Security Basics
DNS and BIND
Essential System Administration
Linux Network Administrator's Guide
Managing Internet Information Services
Managing NFS and NIS
Managing UUCP and Usenet
Networking Personal Computers
    with TCP/IP
Practical UNIX Security
PGP: Pretty Good Privacy
sendmail
System Performance Tuning
TCP/IP Network Administration
termcap & terminfo
Volume 8 : X Window System
    Administrator's Guide
The X Companion CD for R6

PROGRAMMING

Applying RCS and SCCS
Checking C Programs with lint
DCE Security Programming
Distributing Applications Across DCE
    and Windows NT
Encyclopedia of Graphics File Formats
Guide to Writing DCE Applications
High Performance Computing
Learning the Bash Shell (Fall '95 est.)
lex & yacc
Managing Projects with make
Microsoft RPC Programming Guide
Migrating to Fortran 90
Multi-Platform Code Management
ORACLE Performance Tuning
ORACLE PL/SQL Programming
    (Fall '95 est.)
Porting UNIX Software (Fall '95 est.)
POSIX Programmer's Guide
POSIX.4: Programming for
    the Real World
Power Programming with RPC
Practical C Programming
Practical C++ Programming
Programming with curses
Programming with GNU Software
    (Winter '95/96 est.)
Software Portability with imake
Understanding and Using COFF
Understanding DCE
Understanding Japanese Information
    Processing
UNIX for FORTRAN Programmers
Using C on the UNIX System
Using csh and tcsh

BERKELEY 4.4 SOFTWARE DISTRIBUTION

4.4BSD System Manager's Manual
4.4BSD User's Reference Manual
4.4BSD User's Supplementary
    Documents
4.4BSD Programmer's Reference
    Manual
4.4BSD Programmer's Supplementary
    Documents
4.4BSD-Lite CD Companion
4.4BSD-Lite CD Companion:
    International Version

X PROGRAMMING

THE X WINDOW SYSTEM

Volume 0: X Protocol Reference Manual
Volume 1: Xlib Programming Manual
Volume 2: Xlib Reference Manual:
Volume 3: X Window System
    User's Guide
Volume. 3M: X Window System
    User's Guide, Motif Ed.
Volume. 4: X Toolkit Intrinsics
    Programming Manual
Volume 4M: X Toolkit Intrinsics
    Programming Manual, Motif Ed.
Volume 5: X Toolkit Intrinsics
    Reference Manual
Volume 6A: Motif Programming
    Manual
Volume 6B: Motif Reference Manual
Volume 7A: XView Programming
    Manual
Volume 7B: XView Reference Manual
Volume 8 : X Window System
    Administrator's Guide
PEXlib Programming Manual
PEXlib Reference Manual
PHIGS Programming Manual
PHIGS Reference Manual
Programmer's Supplement for Release 6
    (Fall '95 est.)
Motif Tools (with CD-ROM)
The X Companion CD for R6
The X Window System in a Nutshell
X User Tools (with CD-ROM)

THE X RESOURCE

A QUARTERLY WORKING JOURNAL FOR X PROGRAMMERS

The X Resource: Issues 0 through 16
    (Issue 16 available 10/95 est.)

TRAVEL

Travelers' Tales France
Travelers' Tales Hong Kong (10/95 est.)
Travelers' Tales India
Travelers' Tales Mexico
Travelers' Tales Spain (11/95 est.)
Travelers' Tales Thailand
Travelers' Tales: A Woman's World

O'Reilly & Associates—
INTERNATIONAL DISTRIBUTORS

Customers outside North America can now order O'Reilly & Associates books through the following distributors. They offer our international customers faster order processing, more bookstores, increased representation at tradeshows worldwide, and the high-quality, responsive service our customers have come to expect.

EUROPE, MIDDLE EAST, AND AFRICA
(except Germany, Switzerland, and Austria)

INQUIRIES
International Thomson Publishing Europe
Berkshire House
168-173 High Holborn
London WC1V 7AA, United Kingdom
Telephone: 44-71-497-1422
Fax: 44-71-497-1426
Email: itpint@itps.co.uk

ORDERS
International Thomson Publishing Services, Ltd.
Cheriton House, North Way
Andover, Hampshire SP10 5BE, United Kingdom
Telephone: 44-264-342-832 (UK orders)
Telephone: 44-264-342-806 (outside UK)
Fax: 44-264-364418 (UK orders)
Fax: 44-264-342761 (outside UK)

GERMANY, SWITZERLAND, AND AUSTRIA
International Thomson Publishing GmbH
O'Reilly-International Thomson Verlag
Königswinterer Straße 418
53227 Bonn, Germany
Telephone: 49-228-97024 0
Fax: 49-228-441342
Email: anfragen@ora.de

ASIA *(except Japan)*
INQUIRIES
International Thomson Publishing Asia
221 Henderson Road
#08-03 Henderson Industrial Park
Singapore 0315
Telephone: 65-272-6496
Fax: 65-272-6498

ORDERS
Telephone: 65-268-7867
Fax: 65-268-6727

JAPAN
International Thomson Publishing Japan
Hirakawa-cho Kyowa Building 3F
2-2-1 Hirakawa-cho, Chiyoda-Ku
Tokyo, 102 Japan
Telephone: 81-3-3221-1428
Fax: 81-3-3237-1459

Toppan Publishing
Froebel Kan Bldg. 3-1, Kanda Ogawamachi Chiyoda-Ku
Tokyo 101 Japan
Telex: J 27317
Cable: Toppanbook, Tokyo
Telephone: 03-3295-3461
Fax: 03-3293-5963

AUSTRALIA
WoodsLane Pty. Ltd.
7/5 Vuko Place, Warriewood NSW 2102
P.O. Box 935, Mona Vale NSW 2103
Australia
Telephone: 02-970-5111
Fax: 02-970-5002
Email: woods@tmx.mhs.oz.au

NEW ZEALAND
WoodsLane New Zealand Ltd.
21 Cooks Street (P.O. Box 575)
Wanganui, New Zealand
Telephone: 64-6-347-6543
Fax: 64-6-345-4840
Email: woods@tmx.mhs.oz.au

THE AMERICAS
O'Reilly & Associates, Inc.
103A Morris Street
Sebastopol, CA 95472 U.S.A.
Telephone: 707-829-0515
Telephone: 800-998-9938 (U.S. & Canada)
Fax: 707-829-0104
Email: order@ora.com

TO ORDER: **800-889-8969** (CREDIT CARD ORDERS ONLY); **ORDER@ORA.COM**

Please send me more info about Brent Chapman's

Building Internet Firewalls Tutorial

& other Great Circle Associates tutorials.

NAME
_____

ORGANIZATION
_____

ADDRESS
_____

CITY, STATE, ZIP, COUNTRY
_____

TELEPHONE _____ FAX _____

EMAIL
_____

Please send me the info via: ❑ **Postal mail** ❑ **E-mail** ❑ **FAX**

Great Circle Associates

Phone: 800.270.2562 • **Int'l:** +1.415.962.0841 • **FAX:** +1.415.962.0842
E-mail: tutorial-info@greatcircle.com • **WWW:** http://greatcircle.com/

O'REILLY WOULD LIKE TO HEAR FROM YOU

Please send me the following:

❑ *ora.com*
O'Reilly's magazine/catalog,
containing behind-the-scenes
articles and interviews on the
technology we write about, and
a complete listing of O'Reilly
books and products.

❑ *Global Network Navigator*™
Information and subscription.

Please print legibly

Which book did this card come from?

_____

Where did you buy this book?
   ❑ Bookstore   ❑ Direct from O'Reilly
   ❑ Bundled with hardware/software   ❑ Class/seminar

Your job description: ❑ SysAdmin   ❑ Programmer
   ❑ Other_____

What computer system do you use? ❑ UNIX   ❑ Windows 95 NT
   ❑ MAC   ❑ DOS(PC)   ❑ Other _____

Name _____ Company/Organization Name _____

Address _____

City _____ State _____ Zip/Postal Code _____ Country _____

Telephone _____ Internet or other email address (specify network) _____

http://www.greatcircle.com/

BUSINESS REPLY MAIL
FIRST-CLASS MAIL   PERMIT NO. 750   MOUNTAIN VIEW, CA

POSTAGE WILL BE PAID BY ADDRESSEE

Great Circle Associates
PO BOX 390517
MOUNTAIN VIEW CA   94039-9721

BUSINESS REPLY MAIL
FIRST CLASS MAIL   PERMIT NO. 80   SEBASTOPOL, CA

Postage will be paid by addressee

O'Reilly & Associates, Inc.
103A Morris Street
Sebastopol, CA   95472-9902